S0-AIH-845

134171

GV
211
.Z454x

A HISTORY OF
PHYSICAL EDUCATION & SPORT
IN THE UNITED STATES
AND CANADA

(Selected Topics)

(Edited, with essays by)
EARLE F. ZEIGLER
Ph.D., LL.D.
Professor and Dean
Faculty of Physical Education
The University of Western Ontario
London, Canada

ISBN 0-87563-087-1

Copyright © 1975
STIPES PUBLISHING COMPANY

Published By
STIPES PUBLISHING COMPANY
10 - 12 Chester Street
Champaign, Illinois 61820

GOSHEN COLLEGE LIBRARY
GOSHEN, INDIANA

DEDICATION

To the late Fred E. Leonard, A.M., M.D.
Oberlin College
Ohio

and

To Seward C. Staley, M.A., Ph.D.
University of Illinois
Urbana

and to those who follow
in their tradition

WITHDRAWN

Fred Eugene Leonard   Seward Charle Staley

PREFACE

Some people really enjoy reading history, while others can take it or leave it. A very few can't stand it in any form--not even in a highly adventurous, romantic novel. But this latter group is very decidedly in the minority. Most people seem to respect history; perhaps it's a case of revering and not speaking evil of the dead. Whatever the reason, just about everybody pays lip service to history and believes that it belongs in the educational curriculum at various points along the way--all the way up the line, in fact, to the historical review of related literature in the usual Ph.D. thesis!

From what has been related to this point, a foreigner viewing our educational system for the first time might be apt to think that history, in one form or another, is the most important subject in the curriculum--and it may well be from the standpoint of the time spent on it throughout the years. The child has it forced upon him throughout his early school years; some facets of it are thrust upon him during the junior high school experience; and world history and American history are typically included in the high school years. At the college or university level, he doesn't usually escape without a variety of course experiences involving a greater or lesser amount of history as well.

This point was emphasized in an unpublished study made by Dean Emeritus Seward C. Staley, University of Illinois, some fifteen years ago. In an effort to make a case for the sponsorship for a history of sport conference, he called a meeting of interested people at the Hotel Sheraton Gibson in Cincinnati on December 28, 1959. He explained to the group assembled that an assessment of the history offerings on the Urbana Campus of the University of Illinois showed that 1,400 of the 2,200 courses offered in the fall semester of 1959 included some history in the course outline. More specifically, he found that 350 (15%) of the courses were directly or basically historical in nature; that 350 (15%) others included a considerable amount of historical material (25 to 50%); and that 700 (30%) includes some (5 to 25%) historical materials.

The student specializing in physical education and sport is fair game for the history ploy at a slightly later stage of his development --that is, the period of general education is just about over when he falls prey to an often traditionalistic teacher who would ply him with historical data often from secondary and uninteresting sources. In the professional physical education curriculum this is usually accomplished--and for a number of reasons--in a fairly routine, pedestrian fashion. Still further, every teacher of all of the different theory and practice courses in the major program seems to believe that he has a responsibility to offer the student a short history of that particular subject's background. (This is fine, of course, if time permits, and if the material presented is accurate and reasonably comprehensive.) In the curriculum of general professional education--designed to produce master teachers--it may be presented in a slightly progressivistic manner under the heading of "social foundations" of education.

With such an array of courses covering the history of this and that to a greater or lesser extent, one might expect the new graduate student in physical education to really understand history, both generally and specifically, as it might apply to the world, to the United States and Canada, to general professional education, and to specialized professional education as related to physical education and and sport. Would that such were the cast! As a matter of fact, however, the average graduate student registering for a course in the history of physical education and sport seems to possess but a hazy concept of the sweep of man's history on this earth. In addition to the lack of information about the chronology of events, he is completely inadequate if questioned about what might be designated as the persistent or perennial problems which man has faced down through the centuries. Specific or general questions about educational history, even in the Western world, cannot be answered either. Having made these observations, the somewhat disheartened, graduate history of physical education professor hardly dares to inquire about historical knowledge relative to sport and physical activity!

Just how matters got this way is difficult to explain. The lodging of deprecatory remarks about earlier teachers will in all probability solve nothing. In the final analysis the parents will probably be blamed for bringing such stupid offspring into the world. The only reasonable approach would seem to be a concerted effort by dedicated physical education and sport historians to remedy the situation insofar as this may be possible. And this does appear to be happening in a variety of ways.

In the spring of 1968 the First International Seminar on the History of Physical Education and Sport was held at the Wingate Institute near Tel Aviv, Israel. Subsequent seminars of this type have been held in Canada, France, Asia, the United States, Austria, etc. (at the time this is being written). Professor (Dr.) Frantisek Kratky, Charles University, Prague, as President of the ICSPE Committee on the History of Physical Education and Sport, has been laying plans for the eventual preparation of a truly representative world history of physical education and sport.

Within the framework of the American Association for Health, Physical Education, and Recreation (prior to its change in name), Dr. Bruce L. Bennett and Dr. Betty Spears have served as Historians (in that order). Similarly, Dr. Mabel Lee, Dr. E. Craig Davis, and Dr. Ruth Schellberg have served as Archivists, respectively. Then a completely separate section for the History of Physical Education was organized under the Physical Education Division of the Association. There have also been very helpful sessions on teaching methods and other pertinent aspects of the work of the history of physical education and sport teacher at each annual convention. Professor Bennett has coordinated a regular column on history in the JOHPER, and Dr. Betty McCue spearheaded the question of information retrieval in this sub-area of the discipline, as did the Editor with the assistance of Mr. Thomas Abernathy and Mr. Melvin Adelman.

Still further, the Big Ten's Body-of-Knowledge Project has included the history of physical education and sport as a part of one of the six areas for investigation in the ongoing effort to develop the disciplinary aspect of the entire field. The Editor of this volume was related to this development from the outset, and in 1964 he presented a paper on the status of research in physical education history. At a subsequent meeting he coordinated a program which included a presentation on the history of physical education by the above-mentioned Dr. Bennett. Another development which the Editor conceived and helped to inaugurate was the establishment of the first oral history research office in physical education and sport at the University of Illinois, Urbana. This project has been guided since the outset by Professor Marianna Trekell and is providing a considerable amount of "warm, live historical material" for better teaching and research (upon demand of the investigator concerned). In 1971 the Big Ten Symposium on the History of Physical Education and Sport was held at The Ohio State University (coordinated by Professors B. L. Bennett and Seymour Kleinman).

Three highly significant history of physical education and sport symposia were held in 1970, 1971, and 1972 at Edmonton, Alberta; Banff, Alberta; and Windsor, Ontario, respectively. These sessions were spearheaded by Professor M. L. Howell, then of the University of Alberta and his associates at that time (Professors R. G. Glassford, Ann Hall, and Peter Lindsay). The most recent Canadian symposium at the University of Windsor was coordinated by Dr. Alan Metcalfe and his associates (Prof. Gordon Olafson and Dean P. J. Galasso). At the time of this writing the third Canadian Symposium is scheduled for August of 1974 at Dalhousie University, Halifax with Dr. Sandy Young as Chairman.

Lastly, before moving on (with apologies to people and places who may have been missed in physical education and sport history's "success story" above), the formation of NASSH (the North American Society for Sport History) must be mentioned. Dr. Marvin Eyler is the first President; Dr. Guy Lewis is the President-elect; and the tireless efforts of Dr. Ron Smith and Dr. John Lucas should all be cited. The 1973 Meeting was at The Ohio State University in Columbus, and in 1974 the sessions will be held at The University of

Western Ontario (with Dr. Robert Barney as Convention Manager).
NASSH, in addition to annual proceedings, will also begin a journal in
1974 to supplement the already highly successful journal organized by
Dr. Alan Metcalfe at the University of Windsor (now with Dr. Mike
Salter as Co-Editor).

Justification for this Book. In addition to the general discussion
of the present status of physical education and sport history as a sub-
disciplinary area within the field, more specific justification should
be provided for the publication of a book of readings in this area at
present. One substantial reason is that the body of historical knowledge about physical education and sport needs to be supplemented.
Still further, much of the work already completed is not readily available in a suitable form (and at a reasonable price) for professional
students. Nowhere is any publication is there a sampling of the
historical endeavor of many of our better and established physical
education and sport historians on this topic. In addition, an effort has
been made to include some of the work of a number of our fine, but
somewhat younger, historical scholars. Altogether twenty-five different historians of physical education and sport have their work represented in this volume.

The various selections are preceded by an essay outlining the
social and educational foundations of United States history, although
no effort has been made to specifically relate this essay to individual
readings. There is also a brief "lead-in" to each of the essays (readings) which were included. The several appendices include an approach to the description, explanation, and evaluation of the historical
role of sport in selected societies prepared by the Editor, as well as
analyses of completed theses (more than 500 of them) and an excellent
annotated bibliography of athletics in the United States at the interscholastic and intercollegiate levels.

The particular selections included cover the sweep of U. S.
history, and they represent in many cases condensations of much
longer investigations. Thus, this book includes the results of literally thousands of pages of historical writing. Of course, this does not
mean that the reader would not learn more about the history of this
field by referring to the original works. But at least the particular
work is being called to the attention of the reader; he will obtain some
of the essence of the study; and he will be able to follow through with
a specific investigation in great detail through the Microcard Project
(to become Microfiche), Doctoral Dissertation Abstracts and/or
microfilm, the purchase of a xerographic copy from University
Microfilm, or perhaps even inter-library loan in certain instances.

These readings on selected historical topics may be used in a
number of different ways in the professional preparation of a student.
(This is not to say, of course, that they could not be useful in the

general education of any college student.) An instructor could use this volume either as a required or supplementary text in a history of United States history of physical education and sport course. A professor could also build a foundations or "principles" course around it --depending upon his teaching method or technique. Still further, it can be an addition to all types of libraries. Those involved in teacher education in this field ought to have this book on a "personal reserve book shelf." At the graduate level such a readings volume can be most useful either as a text, supplementary text, or reference volume.

A word of explanation may be needed to justify the contention that this book can be used in so many ways. Normally one would not expect a book to be equally useful at both the undergraduate and graduate levels of education. In fact, the field of physical education, as well as the field of general professional education, must continue current efforts to distinguish correctly between what is undergraduate study and what is _true_ graduate endeavor. Times are changing, and many physical educators (and educators) are beginning to truly comprehend (as they try desperately to catalogue and file materials) that their body of knowledge (in physical education, for example) is increasing at a geometric ratio. This means that the results of scholarly work _must_ be made known - and in a reasonably "palatable" fashion--to teachers and prospective teachers promptly and regularly. Thus, the practitioner, the teacher of teachers and coaches, and the scholar and researcher must be truly research oriented. This is why a volume such as this, based on a large number of historical investigations, can be employed in so many ways.

It is so difficult to acknowledge the past assistance received that an editor (and co-author) is tempted to extend a general "thank you" and leave it at that. I am indeed grateful to all of those colleagues who permitted the use of their writings in this book   (Each will receive two copies of the volume, and an annual contribution of a percentage of the royalties will be donated in their names to the American Academy of Physical Education.) Professor John S. Brubacher, selected as one of eleven who made the greatest contribution to professional education in the United States recently, offered friendship, encouragement, and intellectual stimulation to the editor at a time when it was really needed (at Yale University in the 1940's where it was the Editor's good fortune to study under him while pursuing the Ph.D. degree). For this assistance I will always be grateful. My wife (Bert) - my best and worst critic at one and the same time - has been helpful and very patient. Mrs. Sue Richardson, my secretary at Illinois, Urbana, was extremely helpful and most patient as well. It is a sincere wish of the Editor that this publication will be of some help to those of us who are endeavoring to promote the study of physical education and sport history.

The Editor is most grateful for the continuing and enthusiastic support that he has received from Mr. Robert Watts of the Stipes Publishing Company--and, of course, from Mr. Stipes himself--in regard to his various contributions to the Stipes Series on Physical Education and Sport. Ms. Marie Mayer, who assisted with the preparation of the manuscript prior to the actual printing process, should be recognized for her invaluable assistance as well.

Our profession and discipline most assuredly needs to know "where it has been, and how it got there." By continuous, careful assessment of "where and what we are at present," the guideposts for the future should be somewhat more readily apparent. We need all of the help - and then some - that we can get in this truly perplexing world situation. Writing now from a Canadian perspective (even though a U. S. citizen), it is not difficult to see that the future of the United States is being challenged as perhaps never before in its relatively short history. A careful study of history is a first prerequisite along the way to full understanding.

Lastly, a few words about the dedication of this volume seem appropriate at this point. Professor Leonard had dedicated his A Guide to the History of Physical Education "to the memory of Dr. Edward Mussey Hartwell who first in America blazed the trail which I have tried to follow." Be that as it well may be, we felt that this book should be dedicated to Dr. Leonard for his valuable pioneering effort. Secondly, Dean Emeritus Staley of the University of Illinois, Urbana, has been retired more than ten years at the time of this writing, and he is still working away on a mammoth bibliography of sport history (being published by the University of Illinois Press). This represents a culmination of continuing interest and effort toward the promotion of sport and physical education history over a long period of time. Lastly, the Editor is very grateful to the other contributors, and he is certain that through their continued efforts the history of physical education and sport will be placed on an increasingly sound basis.

Earle F. Zeigler
London, Ontario, Canada
July, 1974

A HISTORY OF SPORT AND PHYSICAL EDUCATION IN THE
UNITED STATES AND CANADA
(Selected Topics)

TABLE OF CONTENTS

Table of Contents (Continued)

Table of Contents (Continued)

Table of Contents (Continued)

Table of Contents (Continued)

INTRODUCTION TO PIONEERS OF MODERN PHYSICAL TRAINING

the late Fred E. Leonard, A.M., M.D.
Professor of Hygiene and Physical Education
Oberlin College
Ohio

Since all human institutions and agencies as they exist today represent only the latest stage in a long process of growth and development, each is best understood when we turn back to the past and retrace the significant steps in its evolution to present forms. Such a study of beginnings yields many a useful clue to what would otherwise defy analysis. It gives perspective in assigning values to new solutions brought forward for old problems, and it enables one to start where others left off, profiting by their successes and avoiding their mistakes.[1]*

In ancient Greece[2] there were two strongly contrasted types of education, unlike in aim and method. The earlier Doric or Spartan type had discipline for its key-note and aimed to produce a citizen-warrior. The other and much broader type was the Ionic or Athenian, which became more and more the dominant one throughout Greece and her colonies. It regarded the individual as valuable in and for himself, and sought to promote first of all his full and free development. It we commence our review with Athens, in the fifth century before Christ, we find that each free citizen was required to provide his sons with instruction in gymnastics and music. The former trained primarily the body and the will; the latter, including literary branches as well as music in the narrower sense now conveyed by the term, developed the intellect and the emotions. Thus mind and body were to be educated together, and the end was individual completeness and harmony of parts. The gymnastic exercises practiced in private schools (palestrae) and usually given out-of-doors were little more than orderly contests in wrestling, running, jumping, and throwing the spear and the discus. Grown men met for exercise and conversation in the various gymnasia, state institutions maintained at public expense and administered by public functionaries. Probably by the end of this century no important Greek town, in the parent land and in

---

* With this particular selection, this and the following figures refer to corresponding numerals in the General Bibliography for the paper. This material, now in the public domain, was published in the Second Edition by the Association Press, New York City, 1915.

the far-scattered colonies that dotted the borders of the Black Sea and the Mediterranean, was without one, at least, of these structures. At the great national festivals, which helped to bind together the politically distinct members of the Greek race, interest was centered chiefly on competitive exercises--running, jumping, throwing the spear and the discus, wrestling, and boxing--between free-born citizens, of pure Hellenic descent and untainted by crime. There were also horse- and chariot-races. These athletic contests were the only ones at Olympia, the foremost gathering of them all, and held the chief place at others where musical and literary competitions were added.

Among the Romans[3] military training and the life of the camp furnished the only systematic bodily discipline. They were practical men, strangers to the Greek passion for beauty, and valued exercise only as it led to robust health and made capable soldiers. The Greek gymnastics never gained a foothold among them, either as a factor in education or in the form of the national games. These had now lost their original character of sacred festivals, and the contestants were professional athletes, tempted by the rich prizes offered, usually of low birth and not averse to trickery and falsehood. The public baths, found in Rome and in every important provincial town in the days of the Empire, present at first glance a striking resemblance to the Greek gymnasia, but one much less real than apparent, and the effect of the institutions on Roman life was on the whole an enervating one. Between the Panhellenic festivals celebrated in the stadium and hippodrome at Olympia in the time of Pericles, and those public spectacles which crowded the amphitheatre and circus of the degenerate Roman world during the first centuries of the Christian era, the contrast is even greater. The chariot races of the Circus Maximus and the combats in the Colosseum reveal a changed type of civilization and mark the lowest stages of athletic professionalism.

It was inevitable that the early Christians, living for the most part in cities and brought into close and daily contact with all the abominations of the decadent pagan society of the Empire, should exhibit a violent reaction from the prevailing luxury and sensual self-indulgence. In protest against its excesses they sometimes carried their stern self-restraint so far as to deny themselves the common comforts of life and decline to gratify those cravings of the body which are innocent and natural. Through the Alexandrian schools of philosophy they also felt the influence of that fundamental tenet of the Oriental religions which holds that evil inheres in matter, while mind or spirit is essentially divine and pure, that the flesh and the spirit, therefore, wage perpetual warfare on each other and the body is an enemy to be resisted at every point. Then, too, the persecution to which many converts of the growing Church were subjected kindled an intense religious enthusiasm which welcomed martyrdom and caused pain and torment to be considered meritorious of themselves. After the persecutions ceased the self-torture of the hermit and the monk took their place as a means and measure of human excellence. Mortification of the body thus acquired the dignity of a religious exercise, while the idea of pleasure came to be closely associated with that of vice. In spite of its disastrous physical effects upon the individual and the pernicious consequences of the doctrine among the people at large, <u>asceticism</u>[4] soon became a part of the accepted teaching of the Church and the practice of a large proportion of her leaders and adherents.*

In the cities of northern Italy, and throughout southern Europe generally, the inroads of the Germanic barbarians in the fourth and fifth centuries were not followed by the complete extinction of the race of lay teachers; but in transalpine Europe, from the sixth till the twelfth century, the Benedictine <u>monasteries</u>[5] were the chief, if not the only seats of learning, and education was almost wholly in the hands of monks of that order. Theological doctrines and religious interests absorbed human thought. Men were trained for the world to come, and the present world was deemed unworthy of attention. The soul was the one object of solicitude, and the body was regarded with contempt, so that there could be no such thing as physical training in schools conducted by the Church. The monastic discipline in all its severity was an essential part of school life.

A succession of influences, and chief among them the Crusades, operating in the eleventh and twelfth centuries, had widened the scope of human interests and produced a vague longing after knowledge which was not to be satisfied by the traditional teaching. Along with the demand for a different type and more advanced grade of instruction there arose here and there famous lecturers, who gathered about themselves great number of disciples. Centers were thus created to which other teachers and their followers were attracted, and this, in turn, led to an informal association of masters and pupils, out of which the <u>medieval university</u>[6] developed. In Italy the long-neglected legal system of ancient Rome was studied afresh, the medical sciences were foremost in Moorish Spain, and in the regions of Europe farther north dialectic and philosophy were applied to the study of theology. Teachers were bound by superstitious reverence for authority, however, and as regards treatment of the body the influence of asceticism was still supreme. Provision for lawful amusements was rarely made in university statutes, which appear frequently to have regarded harmless attempts at pleasure with more hostility than they displayed toward actual vice and crime.

---

* The reader is referred to a study in the companion volume by Ralph Ballou which gives us some new insight into the position of the Church on the matter of physical activity (EFZ, Ed.).

But meanwhile the hermit of early Catholic legends had been displaced as a popular hero by the knight. Military Christianity, as typified in the three orders of soldier-monks which had their origin in the twelfth century, could not fail to weaken the hold of the ascetic ideal. Chivalry[8], or the body of law and custom relating to knighthood, prevailed almost universally throughout western Europe between the eleventh and sixteenth centuries, and in its ideals of war, religion, and gallantry was summed up the whole duty of the gentleman of that age. The system can be traced in part to various customs of the rude German tribes[7] which overran southern and western Europe in the fourth and fifth centuries, developed later under the influence of feudalism; but its final form was not received until the time of the Crusades (1096-1270), when the Church, in order to further her own designs, adopted and modified its practices. The decline of chivalry as a military system, although it began soon after the last Crusade, did not become complete until the fifteenth century. The early training of the knight stood in sharp contrast to the education imparted in the monastery schools. Running, jumping, wrestling, swimming, climbing ropes and poles and ladders, hurling stones, casting the spear, shooting with the bow and the crossbow, wielding the battle-axe, and fencing, at first with dull wooden swords, helped to harden his body and give mastery of its powers. The most essential exercise, however, was horsemanship, including the adroit use of shield and lance, and the ability to endure the weight and overcome the hindrance of full armor. Out of the rough trials of strength and skill that were a natural occurrence whenever knights met at leisure were gradually developed the tournaments common all over Christendom in the thirteenth and fourteenth centuries, a public spectacle no less brilliant, fascinating, and characteristic of the age than were the Panhellenic games or the gladiatorial shows of the Roman world.

The universities of the Middle Ages made an important contribution to the intellectual advancement of Europe, but it is not till we racch the fifteenth and sixteenth centuries, the period of the Renaissance and the Reformation[9], that we find men escaping from a conception of the world and the flesh which associated them with the devil, and from the authority of that theological dogma which centered thought and imagination for centuries upon the rewards and punishments of a future state and meanwhile paralyzed or thwarted every effort to master the resources or investigate the phenomena of the material universe. Among the chief factors in this process of transition from the medieval to the modern world was the Revival of Learning, --that appreciative study of the Greek and Latin classics and all the long-neglected records of ancient civilization which supplied the Western nations with a new ideal of life and culture. Writers on education, influenced by their classical studies and also by the customs of chivalry, which had not ceased to shape the early training of the gentleman, began to speak in commendation of bodily exercise and recognition of its rights to a place in the curriculum, referring repeatedly to ancient Greeks and Romans as authorities or by way of illustration. A famous Italian physician, Hieronymus Mercurialis, in the first part of his treatise on the Gymnastics of the Ancients, published in Venice in 1569, sought to reproduce for his readers the Greek gymnastic and gymnastic exercises.

While the best of the Renaissance writers on education had begun to break away from authority and tradition, and with reason as a guide were groping their way toward a training better suited to the nature and present needs of man than any the past could supply, the fact that their ideas gained currency throughout all Europe, and the way was thus prepared for practical reforms, is very largely due to the powerful influence exerted by John Locke and Jean Jacques Rousseau,[10] men who belong to the seventeenth and eighteenth centuries. The former published "Some Thoughts on Education" in 1693, and the latter his "Emile," an educational romance, in 1762. Both urge the necessity of some sort of physical training in the scheme of education.

But it was not until 1774, when Basedow,[11] filled with thoughts of reform in methods of teaching and determined to found a model school which should embody his ideas and force them upon the attention of educators, opened his "Philanthropinum" in Dessau, on the Elbe north of Leipsic, that we come to the actual beginnings of modern physical training. In this private institution, open to all classses of society, bodily exercise was given a place in the daily program from the start, incorporated into the plan of instruction as an essential factor and entrusted to one of the regular teachers. The first to be introduced were the "knightly exercises,"--dancing, fencing, riding, and vaulting; then followed "Greek gymnastics," apparently nothing more than orderly contests in running, wrestling, throwing, and jumping; and before the school was closed in 1793 most of the forms of exercise advocated since that day had been employed, i.e., simple games and athletic sports, gymnastics, military drill, manual labor and manual training, and school excursions.

A long list of pioneers of the new art now appeared in various parts of Europe.

GutsMuths[12] taught gymnastics for nearly fifty years (1786-1835) in Salzmann's Educational Institute at Schnepfenthal, and published important volumes on gymnastics, games, swimming, and manual training. Outside of Berlin, from 1810 through 1818, Jahn[13] met boys and young men for exercise, beginning with a few pupils and a little portable apparatus, but later preparing and equipping an out-door gymnasium and playground, and with the help of squad leaders handling a membership of more than a thousand. Out of this voluntary association of "turners" developed thirty years later the popular gymnastic societies (Turnvereine) of Germany, which now number over

11,000 and have a total enrollment of more than a million men. Nachtegall[14], in Copenhagen, started a private gymnasium in 1799, the first institution in modern times devoted exclusively to physical training, and under his leadership Denmark became the first European state to introduce physical training into its schools as an integral part of the course and to prepare teachers of that subject by offering instruction tn theory and methods of gymnastics. Under the patronage of the King of Sweden Pehr Henrik Ling[15] opened in 1814 the Royal Central Institute of Gymnastics in Stockholm, and before his death in 1839 had laid the foundation of Swedish military, medical, and school gymnastics. The last branch was developed into its present form under his son Hjalmar[16] in the third quarter of the century. The Spanish Colonel Amoros[17] devoted himself to teaching gymnastics in Paris from 1817 till 1848; and Clias[18], born in the United States, but of Swiss and French Huguenot descent, was active in three countries,--Switzerland (after 1815), England (1822-1825), and France (1841-1848). The chief work of Spiess[19], the father of school gymnastics in Germany, was accomplished in the years 1833-1855.

In the United States the different systems or sorts of physical training which have been brought forward for trial, and the agencies which have promoted its spread, fall into three groups, centered about 1830, 1860, and the decade from 1880 to 1890. The first includes Captain Alden Partridge and his military academies[20]; the introduction of the Jahn gymnastics and the opening of school, college and city or public outdoor gymnasia under the director of the German refugees Beck, Follen, and Lieber[21]; the attempt to provide manual labor as a system of exercise in educational institutions[22]; and the earliest use of "calisthenics" for girls and women[23], by Catharine✓ Beecher in her schools in Hartford and Cincinnati. To the second belong the gymnastic societies formed by native Americans on the model of the German Turnvereine[24]; the building of the first college gymnasia, at Amherst, Harvard, and Yale, and the establishment of a chair of hygiene and physical education at Amherst[25]; the lectures and exhibitions of Dr. Winship[26], the advocate of heavy lifting; the "new gymnastic" of Dio Lewis[27]; the incorporation of military drill and instruction in colleges and universities organized under the terms of the Morrill Land Bill of 1862[28]; and our earliest acquaintance with the exercises of the "Swedish Movement Cure" (medical gymnastics). In the third group we find the system introduced by Dr. Sargent at Hemenway Gymnasium of Harvard University[29]; the organization of the American Association for the Advancement of Physical Education tion[30]; the report on physical education in American colleges and universities prepared by Dr. Hartwell for the Bureau of Education in 1885; the systematic efforts of German-American gymnastic societies and the North American Turnerbund to make their work known among native Americans; Dr. Wey's use of physical training with criminals and dullards at the Elmira (New York) Reformatory[31]; the starting of training courses for physical directors in Young Men's Christian Associations, first at Springfield, Mass., and later in Chicago, and the appointment of a secretary for that phase of Association activity by the International Committee; the Boston Conference of 1889, and the introduction of Swedish school gymnastics into this country; the opening of a number of normal schools and summer courses for the training of teachers; and the rapid spread of interest in athletic sports and active games.

Bibliography

1. No complete manual of the history of physical training has yet been written in English. Dr. Hartwell's reports contain summaries, and detailed treatment of certain periods, dealing especially with the earlier history in the United States. Dr. Leonard, the author of this volume, has published at intervals in the <u>American Physical Education Review</u> and <u>Mind and Body</u>. "Chapters from the History of Physical Training" which now cover systematically the main periods from the time of the Greeks down to the present for Europe, and through the Dio Lewis period for the United States (references to individual chapters are given below). The first twelve biographical sketches in the present book contain some of the same material in condensed form, but the last eight are concerned with men whose work has been done since the Civil War or is still in progress.

   In German, as general works of reference, one should possess Dr. Carl Euler's "Encyklopädisches Handbuch des gesamten Turnwesens" (Three large volumes. Leipsic and Vienna, A. Pichlers Witwe & Sohn), and Hirth-Gasch's "Das gesamte Turnwesen: Ein Lesebuch für deutsche Turner" (Four volumes. Hof. i. B., Rud. Lion). There are two excellent small handbooks, Angerstein-Kurth's "Geschichte der Leibesübungen in den Grundzügen" (Leipsic and Vienna, A. Pichlers Witwe & Sohn). and Rühl's "Entwicklungsgeschichte des Turnens" (Leipsic, Ed. Strauch). The standard large work is the Euler-Rossow "Geschichte des Turnunterrichts" (Gotha, E. G. Thienemann).

   In the Scandinavian languages much the best treatment will be found in Viktor Heikel's "Gymnastikens Historia" (Issued in four parts, 1905-1909. Helsingfors, Waseniuska Bokhandeln). Briefer works are Illeris and Trap's "Grundtraek af Gymnastikkens Historie" (Copenhagen, C. A. Reitzel), and the "Gymnastiken Historiskt Framstäld" of T. J. Hartelius (Stockholm, Albert Bonnier).

2. Leonard, in <u>American Physical Education Review</u> XII:225 (1907 September). E. N. Gardiner's "Greek Athletic Sports and Festivals" (New York, The Macmillan Co.) is a complete, scholarly, and recent treatment of that particular phase.

3. Leonard, in <u>American Physical Education Review</u> XII:234 (1907 September). Chapter 55 in Sienkiewicz's "Quo Vadis," and chapters 12-14 in Book V of Wallace's "Ben Hur" contain graphic descriptions of the spectacles presented in amphitheater and the circus.

4. Leonard, in <u>American Physical Education Review</u> XII:289 (1907 December). Consult Lecky, "History of European Morals" II:107-132, for details of the ascetic life. Tennyson's poem, "Saint Simeon Stylites," reveals the spiritual selfishness resulting from such a life.

5. Leonard, in <u>American Physical Education Review</u> XII:292 (1907 December).

6. Leonard, in <u>American Physical Education Review</u> XII:298 (1907 December).

7. Leonard, in <u>American Physical Education Review</u> XII:294 (1907 December).

8. Leonard, in <u>American Physical Education Review</u> XII:296 (1907 December). Chapters 8-12 in Scott's "Ivanhoe," and the whole book, for that matter, will be found interesting reading in this connection.

9. Leonard, in <u>American Physical Education Review</u> X:189 (1905 September).

10. Leonard, in <u>American Physical Education Review</u> X:284 (1905 December).

11. Leonard, in <u>American Physical Education Review</u> IX:89 (1904 June).

12. Leonard, in <u>American Physical Education Review</u> IX:92, 105 (1904 June), and <u>Mind and Body</u> XVII:321 (1911 January).

13. Leonard, in <u>American Physical Education Review</u> V:18 (1900 March) and X:1 (1905 March).

14. Leonard, in <u>American Physical Education Review</u> IX:97, 107 (1904 June).

15. Leonard, in American Physical Education Review IX:227 (1904 December). Consult Carl A. Westerblad's "Pehr Henrik Ling" (Stockholm, P. A. Norstedt & Soner), and articles by the same writer in Tidskrift i Gymnastik VI:561 (1907), VI:999 (1909), a and VII:193 (1911). The second article in the Tidskrift, written in English, is issued separately in London by Sampson Low, Marston & Co., Ltd., under the title: "Ling, the Founder of Swedish Gymnastics: His Life, His Work, and His Importance."

16. Leonard, in American Physical Education Review IX:238, 242 (1904 December). For further particulars consult Tidskrift i Gymnastik VII:891 and 950 (1909).

17. Leonard, in American Physical Education Review IX:99, 108 (1904 June).

18. Leonard, in American Physical Education Review IX:102, 109 (1904 June).

19. Leonard, in Mind and Body XL:217 (1904 November). The centenary of the birth of Spiess called forth three small volumes in 1910: J. Bollinger-Auer's "Adolf Spiess, sein Leben und seine Wirksamkeit" (Basel, Helbing & Lichtenhann), Dr. Karl Roller's "Adolf Spiess, ein Gedenkblatt . . ." (Berlin, Weidmann), and H. Schmeel's "Adolf Spiess, der Begrunder des deutschen Schulturnens" (Giessen, Emil Roth).

20. Leonard, in Mind and Body XIII:257 (1906 November).

21. Leonard, in Mind and Body XII:193, 217, 249, 281, 313, 345 (1905 September-1906 February).

22. Leonard, in Mind and Body XIII:65, 97, 129 (1906 May-July).

23. Leonard, in Mind and Body XIII:289 (1906 December).

24. Leonard, in American Physical Education Review XV:617 (1910 December), and especially page 621.

25. Hartwell, "Physical Training in American Colleges and Universities" (Washington, Circular of Information of the Bureau of Education, 1885, No. 5).

26. His "Autobiographical Sketches of a Strength Seeker" were published in the Atlantic Monthly IX:102 (1862).

27. Leonard, in American Physical Education Review XI:83, 187 (1906 June and September).

28. Hartwell, 1. c. under No. 25, pp. 101-105. An article on the originator of the Bill will be found in The Outlook for 1901 May, page 81.

29. Hartwell, 1. c. under No. 25, page 41.

30. Mrs. McCurdy, in American Physical Education Review XIV:537, 624 (1909, November and December).

31. Proceedings of American Association for the Advancement of Physical Education IV:17 (1888) and VIII:34 (1893), and Report of Boston Conference (1889) page 99. Consult the Year Books of the Reformatory, especially the 16th, 17th, 18th, 20th, and 23rd.

INTRODUCTION

HISTORICAL FOUNDATIONS: SOCIAL AND EDUCATIONAL

Earle F. Zeigler, Editor

The Colonial Period - Seventeenth Century. Conditions in the
American colonies in the seventeenth century were difficult to say the
least, and the finer elements of so-called civilized life were possible
only for a relatively few wealthy individuals. The culture itself had
been transported from Europe with its built-in class distinctions.
Slavery was general practice, especially in the South, and the right to
vote was generally restricted to property owners. Religion was
established legally. The rules of primogeniture and entail served to
strengthen the social distinctions. Cultural contrasts were marked,
and it may be assumed that geography had a great deal to do with the
differences that were evident. There was considerable feeling against
democratic principles both from a social and political standpoint.
Any consideration of educational practice must, therefore, be viewed
in the light of these conditions described above.

Most of the American colonies established between 1607 and
1682 were guided in their educational outlook and activities by
England's contemporary practices; the influence of the other countries
was negligible at first. Thus, education was thought to be a function
of the Church and not the State. Judging by today' standards the provisions made for education were extremely inadequate. In a pioneer
country limited by a hazardous physical environment, the settlers
were engaged in a struggle for existence. The early colonists mi-
grated into different regions mostly by chance. These differing environments influenced largely the social orders of the North and the
South; yet, there were many points of similarity in the traditions and
experiences of the people as a whole. They all possessed a common
desire for freedom and security--hopes that were to be realized only
after a desperate struggle.

The church was the institution by which means the religious
heritage, and also much of the educational heritage, was preserved
and advanced. The first schools can actually be regarded as the
fruits of the Protestant revolts in Europe. The settlers wanted religious freedom, and the reformers among them insisted that a knowledge of the Gospel was required for personal salvation. The natural

---

[1] Space does not permit nor does reason support, any more material than is included as an introduction at this point. The review of
the social and educational foundations only did seem to be necessary.

outcome was to create schools so that the children might learn to read, and the dominant Protestant churches brought about the establishment of the elementary schools. It is true further that localism, before the advent of the district school, meant that they would be randomly located. This was accomplished just as soon as the homes, the churches, and some form of civil government were established. The everyday needs of the citizens, of course, soon made the provision of elementary education even more essential.

Three types of attitudes toward education developed. The first was the compulsory-maintenance attitude of the New England Puritans, who established schools by colonial legislation of 1642 and 1647. The second attitude was that of the parochial school, and this was best represented in Pennsylvania where private schools were made available for those who could afford it. The pauper-school, non-State-interference attitude was the third, and it was best exemplified by Virginia and the southern colonies. Many of these people had come to America for profit rather than religious freedom, and they tended to continue school practice as it had existed in England. In all of these schools, discipline was harsh and sometimes actually brutal. The curriculum consisted of the three R's and spelling, but the books were few, and the teachers were generally unprepared. Although the school hours were long, there was no place for play and recreation.

The pattern of secondary education had been inherited from England, too, and in most of the colonies Latin grammar schools appeared. This type of school was developed more significantly in New England. Higher education was not neglected. Nine colleges were founded mainly through the philanthropy of certain individuals and groups. In all of these institutions, except the Academy and College of Philadelphia (the interest in which was fostered by Benjamin Franklin), theology formed an important part of the curriculum.

Growth and Development - Eighteenth Century. With the advent of the eighteenth century the old religious interest slackened somewhat, and as the government developed a more civil character a tendency to create schools with a native vein or spirit grew. This was accompanied by a breakdown in some of the former aristocratic customs. The settled frontier expanded, new interests in trade and shipping grew, and the population increased. A trend toward individualism characterized this period. Several American industries date back to this time, and notable among these were the iron mills. Particularly disturbing were the restrictions placed by the English on the use of money by the colonists. There was sufficient prosperity, however, to bring about a change in the appearance of the established communities. Social status was very important to a number of these people, and colonials felt that they "had arrived" when they held office and land. Beginning in the third decade a revival of religious interest became evident. From 1733 on to 1763 the colonies were involved in a series of small wars with the Spanish and the French. These struggles were interspersed by periods of "cold war" maneuvering. The Seven Years' War (1755-1763) ended with the colonies as a fairly solid political and economic unit, but the British evidently failed in their method of governance of the society, and a separatist and nationalistic feeling began to develop after 1775.

Thus, from the middle of the eighteenth century onward, economic, political, and nationalistic forces were stirring, and these influences were felt increasingly in the promotion of elementary education. This change was probably due to a growing religious tolerance again, as well as a broader interest in national affairs. Both of these factors served to take the emphasis away from the earlier, strictly religious domination of elementary education.

Secondary education was still provided by the grammar schools. These schools, generally located in every large town, were supported by the local government and by private tuition. The curricula were non-utilitarian and were designed to prepare boys for college entrance. Insofar as higher education was concerned, the pattern had been established from the beginning (Harvard College - 1636) after the European university type of liberal arts education with a strong emphasis on mental discipline and theology.

It should be kept in mind that there were very few heavily populated centers, relatively speaking, even at this time. In the main, frontier life, and life in the small villages, was still very rigorous, and such conditions were simply not conducive to the so-called intellectual life with higher educational standards. Educational theorists had visions of a fine educational system, of course, but the states did not have many definite constitutional provisions regarding education, and the Federal Constitution didn't say anything about it at all. There was promise, however, in the many new social forces at work. Then came the period of unrest, and with the outbreak of the War of Independence education of the formal type came almost to a complete standstill.

The last twenty-five years of the eighteenth century saw a great many changes in the life of the United States. In the first place, the revolutionaries who started the war lived to tell about it and to help in the sound reconstruction of the nation--no small feat by any standards. Thus began the process of writing state and federal constitutions. Furthermore, it was very important to the early success of the country that commerce be revived, and this was accomplished sooner by the South because of the nature of the commodities they produced. New lines of business and trade were established with Russia, Sweden, and the Orient. The Federal Convention of 1787 managed to complete what has turned out to be the most successful document in all of history--the Constitution of the United States of America. Then

Washington's Administration began, and it can be called successful both at home and abroad. The French Revolution became an issue in American politics, but Washington then declared a position of neutrality and was hard pressed to keep it.

As soon as the war was over, considerable attention was turned to education, and in the remaining years of the eighteenth century development of secondary and higher education continued. In the North both Phillips Andover and Phillips Exeter Academies were established. The colleges of the North seemed to suffer more from the War than did those in the South, where an imposing list of both private, religiously-endowed and state institutions were founded.

Nationalism, Growth, The Civil War, and Reconstruction - Nineteenth Century. The stage had now been set, and the United States entered a most important period in her history. Thomas Jefferson was in office from 1801 to 1809. This was followed by a second war with Great Britain--the War of 1812. In the ensuing nationalist era, a number of adjustments in relations with Britain and other nations were necessary. The Monroe Doctrine declared to the world that countries in this hemisphere should be left alone to develop as they saw fit and were not to be used by outside powers for colonization. This was a period in which the United States was finding itself, and the pattern was being set for future developments. Unfortunately the North and the South were being divided--the North was being changed by virtue of the Industrial Revolution and many educational and humanitarian movements, while the South was nurturing a different type of society regulated by what has been called a slave and cotton economy.

In the realm of education, the first fifty years of the new national life was a period of transition from the control of the church to that of the State. State control and support gradually seemed more feasible, although the change was perhaps somewhat slow in coming. Political equality and religious freedom, along with changing economic conditions, finally made education for all seem a necessity. This period was characterized by the introduction of a number of semi-private philanthropic agencies such as the Sunday School Movement, the city school societies, the Lancasterian Movement, and the infant school societies. The Lancasterian Movement was highly regarded for a period, since it made the education of all seem financially possible by the use of student monitors as instructors. But people soon understood the inefficiency of this method, and discussion was provoked which eventually led to the bearing of the necessary cost for adequate teaching and facilities by all of the citizens.

By 1825 a tremendous struggle for the creation of the American State School was underway, and in the field of public education the years from 1830 to 1860 are quite often called "The Architectural

Period." Educational leaders and a number of leading citizens were calling for public schools which were tax-supported, publicly-controlled, and non-sectarian. The problems of getting tax support, of eliminating the pauper-school idea, and of doing away with pro-rated tuitions were all difficult in themselves to solve. The elimination of sectarianism as a controlling factor and the appointment of public officials to administer school affairs were major problems. Then came the establishment of the first public high school, and thereafter the establishment of state universities. The first compulsory school attendance law was passed in Massachusetts in 1852. The various types of schools had been gradually amalgamated into state systems, and by 1860 the American educational ladder was fairly complete. Federal support came with the Morrill Act of 1862, which granted public land to each state for the founding of a college of agriculture and mechanical arts.

With the development of the public school system, it was quite natural that attention turned to the quality and type of teacher hired for so important a task as the education of the coming generation. Educational journalism had its beginnings in America in the 1820's, and interest was shown in the recent European educational advancements. Before the establishment of the first normal schools, the status of common-school teachers was very poor. Secondary teachers in the Latin grammar schools and academies evidently fared somewhat better. Specific professional preparation of teachers was almost unknown. Today one can be quite critical of the teachers of this era, but they were probably living up to the demands of the times reasonably well.

Certification of teachers, after a fashion, began in the early century. Ministers and town authorities usually assured themselves that the candidates for teaching positions were "strong in the faith" and also had a minimum knowledge of the subject matter of the curriculum. In the Dutch schools of New Netherlands, license requirements were gradually taken out of ecclesiastical hands by the civil authorities, but the standards were still low everywhere in 1839-- low, that is, according to present-day standards. It is true that there were legal requirements; nevertheless, the examinations involved were evidently poorly administered. The agencies issuing certificates were completely local and had only local validity.

The advances made in the training of American teachers in teaching techniques took place first in elementary education. This effort began around the time of and after the War of 1812. Private academies, private normal schools, state-subsidized academies or teachers seminaries, and state-controlled and state-supported normal schools were the first institutions that prepared teachers in any specific fashion.

Those leaders in this country who recommended teacher preparation during the first two decades of the nineteenth century actually knew very little about foreign normal schools until around 1825. It was at this time that travelers abroad reported back about the German normal schools, and these accounts gave impetus to the movement getting under way in this country. The German pattern was adopted but with some original modifications. The Reverend Samuel R. Hall is generally accepted as the founder of the first private normal school in the United States at Concord, Vermont in 1823. The first state normal school was established by Massachusetts legislation in 1839 for a three-year experimental period. It was begun at Lexington with Cyrus Peirce as principal. The second such school, actually authorized in 1838, was not opened until 1840 at Bridgewater in Plymouth Colony.

During the next quarter century the growth of institutions preparing teachers was not very great in comparison with later periods. The advances were small and achieved only after a struggle. Usually these normal schools were undertaken on an experimental basis. But with the rise of the public school movement, it was obvious that teacher-training would of necessity assume a larger role. Between 1840 and 1870 the country's population doubled, and, although it remained largely rural, the city populations were increasing at a great rate. Teacher education remained largely a problem of preparing elementary school teachers, and this is explained when it is known that of the 6,871,522 students enrolled in public schools in 1870 that 6,791,295 of this number were in the elementary schools.

During this period State support and control of schools increased steadily, which was made possible by the fact that national wealth was increasing much more rapidly in proportion than the population. Four states established boards of education before 1850. This trend was important, because the magnitude of the overall development seemingly demanded a strong centralized department of education in each state. Practically speaking, of course, federal control of education would have brought about unification of the school systems much more readily and expediently, but this was not to be the pattern. Control of education from the beginning was to be left in the hands of the states. The development, therefore, can be characterized as haphazard, and public school officials at the state level are still subject to popular election in a number of states. Yet such development has been deemed necessary by many in a democratic, pluralistic system.

Difficult days were in store for the American people after the Civil War--a war that had wrought a tremendous change in the lives of the people. Interestingly enough, the South was able to return to its former national allegiance relatively quickly, although there does appear to be ample evidence that the South won the peace by its decision to keep their states a "white man's country." Their economic plight was extremely serious, but the people were aided greatly by being allowed to restore normal trading relations. The Reconstruction Period is generally regarded as an unfortunate part of our history. Lincoln had seemingly possessed the wisdom to meet the critical situation, but his life had been taken through assassination. Those who remained felt that strict justice should be employed to punish a seemingly ungrateful loser. All in all, however, despite the fact that Lincoln and Johnson were followed by a twenty-four year series of Republican presidents who had all been military men of varying importance, the South had been treated reasonably well.

The period from 1870 to 1890, therefore, was marked by steady expansion and development. "Big business" became a reality; the country continued its march westward; organized labor made definite progress; and significant social and cultural developments took place. The development of urban society brought about a greater interest in social affairs than heretofore. Polite society became interested in music and literature, although it can be said that the literature produced was not of extraordinary quality. Several fine art galleries and museums were founded, but the majority of the people had little understanding of the aesthetic in life. The architecture of the period was eclectic, and the simple beauty of Colonial homes was seemingly lost. Formal religion as expressed by its leaders was challenged strongly by evolutionary theories and pragmatism, and the church was hard pressed.

In the field of education the idea of equality of educational opportunity had made great strides, and the educational ladder was gradually extending upward. The number of high schools increased five-fold between 1870 and 1890. The state was assuming a position of prime importance in public education. State universities turned their attention to advancing the welfare of the individual states with resultant marked increases in revenue and attendance. The Southern states lagged behind the rest of the country due to the War, reconstruction, racial conflict, and a continuing fairly aristocratic theory of education. But even in the North, President Eliot of Harvard called for educational reform in 1888, and one of his main points was the need for better training of teachers.

The status of teachers insofar as general teacher training improvement had come along slowly in this period. New Pestalozzian procedures had been introduced by Edward Sheldon in Oswego, New York in the 1860's, and this movement had gradually rather completely reshaped elementary education. Many state normal schools started at this time and were well distributed over the country as a whole. Although the facilities and courses of these institutions were poor at first, there has been a gradual improvement down through the years.

Professional courses of the time were not too effectual, mainly because scientific method had not yet been applied to educational research. In addition to the state normal schools, there was quite a rapid growth of city normal schools and classes which paralleled the enlargement of the cities. The college and university normal departments of this period were not very good, even though interest in teaching as an art had been started by New York University in 1832, by Brown in 1850, and by Michigan in 1860. After 1879 departments of pedagogy began to develop with the aim of preparing secondary teachers. The growth of in-service teacher education agencies began in this period of educational history. By 1890 such activities as reading circles, professional teachers organizations and institutes, and summer schools and extension work were contributing to the gigantic task of raising the levels of preparation of teachers in service.

Criticism of the educational system in the 1870's and 1880's had been present, but it assumed large-scale proportions in the last decade of the nineteenth century. All sorts of innovations and reforms were being recommended from a variety of quarters. This social movement in education undoubtedly had a relationship to political progressivism. In the universities themselves the formalism present in psychology, philosophy, and the social sciences was coming under severe attack. Out in the public schools other conflicts were raging, as the citizens were demanding that the promise of American life should be realized through the broadening of the school's purposes. Although the seeds of this educational revolution were sown in the nineteenth century, the story of its accomplishment belongs to the present century. That much progress has been made along these lines is self-evident; yet, the promise of the future is ever so much greater still.

Changing Times, World War I, Depression, World War II, The Cold War, and The Great Society - Twentieth Century. Looking back on the history of the twentieth century in the United States is frightening; so much has happened and it has all happened so quickly. The very tempo of life was increasing, and one can't help but wonder where we are going. The phenomenon of change is apparent at every turn of the road--from Teddy Roosevelt and his "Big Stick" to Taft, Wilson, and World War I. Then the twenties with booming prosperity, only to be followed by the Stock Market Crash of 1929 and the Great Depression. The rebuilding process seemed slow, but it was actually very rapid. Franklin Roosevelt and the New Deal followed, and things looked brighter again. But the war in Europe was not to be confined, and the attack on Pearl Harbor placed the United States squarely in the middle of World War II. Victory came for the Allies, but this period of peace was shortlived. The Iron Curtain, the Korean War, the Cold War, and the War in Vietnam followed in swift succession-- quite a century by any standards!

In the political area, social legislation and political reform made truly significant changes in the lives of the people despite the ever-present struggle between conservative and liberal forces. Industry and business assumed gigantic proportions, as did the regulatory controls of the federal government. The greatest experiment in political democracy in the history of the world was grinding ahead slowly. The ideals behind such a plan were being challenged from all quarters, and wars and financial booms and depressions weren't the types of developments that made planning a simple matter. It seemed conceivable that democracy might be made to work at home, but what about the condition of the rest of the world?

Laissez-faire capitalism had produced the "highest standard of low and mediocre living" for most people that the world had ever seen, but what was the "good life?" Was unmodified capitalism and vast technological expansion and advancement the answer; some were beginning to wonder. Organized labor, through its leaders, set about to get what it felt was the common man's fair share of the wealth. The population growth seemed to decline, but then it spurted upward again. The status of the family was disturbed as women entered the labor market in greatly increasing numbers in World War II. There were so many different "racial groups" and religious denominations and sects that understanding among peoples became extremely difficult. The concept of the WASP (White, Anglo-Saxon, Protestant) as the typical American was shattered into bits and pieces, probably never again to return.

The conservatives fought the liberals, and they both fought the Socialists and the Communists. Then they all turned against the fascism of Hitler, Mussolini, and Hirohito. Now we still have the inscrutable Oriental, an unreasonable fear of any type of Socialism and Communism, the "doves" and the "hawks" and what have you. For a while the United Nations appeared to be the hope of the world, but now people are wondering whether it can fulfill its hope of world peace and the advancement of mankind.

All of these developments mentioned above have had their influence on the subject at hand--education. Educational opportunities have been equalized, but there is still much work to be done. The Federal Government has participated increasingly in education, but where should it stop? The struggle between the state and the church in education has been reasonably well resolved, but what does the future hold in this regard? The schools are quite democratically administered, but do we truly know what the word "democracy" means? Or is it an evolving concept and will it change as our country changes? The school has traditionally reflected the social and cultural heritage; will it ever lead the way in educational reconstruction?

But now let us briefly return to the beginning of this remarkable twentieth century and trace the educational development somewhat more specifically. The goals of American education were that it would be free, non-sectarian, universal, publicly supported, publicly controlled, and compulsory up to a specified age.

The First Decade (1900-1910). What was the educational situation like in 1900? In the first place, the United States had a population of about seventy million people (62,947,714 in 1890), and thirty-two states had compulsory school attendance. Approximately 16,000,000 pupils were enrolled in elementary schools. From 1890 to 1900, secondary school attendance had increased from 202,963 to 519,251--a really remarkable increase! The higher education enrollment was 250,000, and the predominant institution was the four-year college. Seventy percent of the public school teachers were women. The average annual salary of teachers was three hundred and twenty-five dollars.

The elementary program was typically eight years in length, and was centered about what has been called the traditional subject-matter curriculum including reading, writing, and arithmetic, as well as spelling, grammar, geography, history, and civics. There was great variation in emphasis on such subjects as drawing, music, nature study, and physical education. But times were changing, and there is evidence that the center of gravity had shifted somewhat from the subject-matter of instruction to the child to be taught. A new understanding of the nature of a child was developing through the strong influence of such authorities as William James, G. Stanley Hall, John Dewey, and Edward L. Thorndike. The scientific revolution and the growing complexity of American economic life was forcing education to be modified so that the needs of the day would be met.

At the secondary level of education, a rather thoroughgoing revision of the curriculum was taking place due to several significant factors. The very character of the population was changing, and the needs and interests of their offspring were becoming different from that of the former "college-bound" group in secondary education. There was consequently a continued multiplication of subjects and courses and a trend toward great freedom of election. This trend was coupled with the introduction of a variety of survey and problems courses. It can be said, however, that the need for a common background of experience was not neglected.

In higher education the influences mentioned above brought about similar changes as well. There were those who wished to preserve the traditional concept of a liberal education, but a broader general education was being considered seriously. The elective system seemed to be the answer to an American way of life characterized by individualism, capitalism, and industrialism. Course requirements were altered, subject-matter fields were grouped into larger bodies of knowledge, and the individual received greater attention generally.

The normal school was a well-established part of the American school system by this time. These schools admitted students of secondary rank and usually scaled their offerings to the ability of their student population. The program was designed to give the students a command of elementary subject-matter, academic secondary studies, and professional education work. The education courses included the history and science (so-called at that time) of education, as well as instruction in the area of teaching methodology. The normal school had become the main agency for the preparation of elementary school teachers and was beginning to enter the field of training teachers for secondary education as well. It was some time before they were accepted generally as being qualified for this latter work, since the length and quality of this preparation had to be increased. The transformation of the normal schools to collegiate status was absolutely necessary because of the vast growth of the number of public high schools.

Interestingly enough, teacher training in the area of professional education courses within the colleges and the universities in this early period was in most cases no better than the normal school training. Some twenty or thirty different courses in professional education were offered. Many people would now argue that this number of courses should have remained fairly constant, and that research should have been directed at improving the scientific base and quality of these efforts. Unfortunately, by 1934 the number of professional courses in professional education had increased to nearly 600, and few would argue that this trend was justified. From another standpoint, it is interesting to note that there was fear on the part of college and university educators at this time that the normal schools were encroaching on territory far beyond their scope.

These first years of the new century certainly held great import for the field of education. In 1902 the township high school at Joliet, Illinois became the first public junior college through the encouragement of William Rainey Harper, who was the first president of the University of Chicago. In that same year, the distinguished school administrator and U. S. Commissioner of Education, William T. Harris, died, ending a notable career of service to education. In 1904, John Dewey was selected as a professor of philosophy at Columbia University.

In 1907, Dean Alexis F. Lange, of the University of California, encouraged California to enact the first junior college law, and the establishment of public junior colleges began there in 1910. Just one year prior to this, California had taken the lead in another direction with the inauguration of the first junior high school at Berkeley. Another significant development at this time, but in New York State, was the organization of the first class for speech defectives. In addition, at this time Abraham Flexner was carrying out his sweeping criticisms of medical education in particular and college education in general. Somewhere between 1890 and 1910 a so-called "fourth period" in American higher education began. The need had arisen for greater specialization, and the free elective system had seemingly gone too far. Now an attempt was made to bring some order into the confusing group of subjects which frequently characterized the college education of the time. Thus began the concept of a major program system.

The Second Decade (1910-1919). By 1910, with public high school enrollment at a new high of 1,000,000 students, the beginning can be traced of a movement which was to result in a rather complete reorganization of the educational ladder resulting in a six-year elementary school, a three-year junior high school, a three-year senior high school, and a two-year junior college (6-3-3-2), as compared to the former 8-4 plan. By 1917, for example, there were forty-six junior colleges, and one year later it was estimated that there were 557 junior high schools. Other developments included the passage of the Smith-Lever Act in 1914 stimulating agricultural extension service in education; the publication of Dewey's Democracy in Education in 1916, generally recognized as the most thorough presentation of the implications for education from a democratic society; and the Smith-Hughes Act in 1917 providing secondary vocational instruction. By 1918 compulsory school attendance laws had been passed in all states of the Union.

The Third Decade (1920-1929). The rate of change did not slacken in the 1920's after a slight depression in 1921-1922. Public high school enrollment reached 2,000,000 pupils, and the junior high school movement continued on unabated. The years just prior to 1920 had been an incubatory period for the Progressive Education Association, and it wasn't long before members were speaking of the "child-centered school," aided undoubtedly by Dewey's philosophy of democratic education. The new science of education produced strong interest in individual development, primarily because of the growing power of the psychology of individual differences. Testing and measuring of students and their various capacities expanded sharply. One result of this movement was the idea of classifying students according to abilities in "homogeneous groups." One widely-heralded innovation at this time was the Dalton Plan involving a series of contracts or projects as developed in Massachusetts by Helen Parkhurst.

With the introduction of educational and intelligence testing, a need was revealed for various types of instruction for many different types of people. This represented the beginning of what was to become a vast lateral expansion of the public educational system. Various state and national curriculum committees were established; there was a movement to establish a federal department of education; adult education activities were increased; and a Carnegie Survey was conducted to assess the in-service education of teachers. The Vocational Rehabilitation Act of 1920 exerted strong influence as well.

Education benefitted greatly from the economic prosperity of the 1920's, and building programs were soon in evidence at almost innumerable points around the country. The development of the junior high school was rapid, and some sixteen thousand public high schools were established by the year 1925. From 1920 on, the Junior College Movement grew rapidly, especially in the West. There were, for example, forty-six teachers colleges in 1920, and the trend toward this "expanded" normal school was gaining momentum. For those who may or may not have had the benefits of a formal education, adult education activities were being sponsored increasingly, and interest grew to the point where the American Association for Adult Education was formed in 1926.

Thus, educational developmentalism and the increasing emphasis on social education brought about a great many changes and innovations during this decade of material prosperity. All types of "extra-curricular" activities were added to the program of the school, and within the school curriculum itself a variety of special classes were made available for the handicapped and atypical student. The trend toward equalization of educational opportunity was provided with a stimulus by restrictions against child labor as well as by more stringent compulsory school attendance laws. Although it was pointed out that federal aid of much greater magnitude was necessary for full realization of this social ideal, such backing did not come to any appreciable extent. The George-Reed Act of 1929, however, did allow secondary vocational education to be increased.

Dewey's influence aided greatly in bringing about what has been referred to as an "educational transformation" and a movement toward aiding children to realize greater social efficiency. Two extremely important educational developmentalists, G. Stanley Hall and Edward L. Thorndike, have made truly unique contributions as well. Hall stressed race perpetuation, the basic need for early sound emotional experience, and the well-balanced personality developed in accordance with the child's own nature. Thorndike has emphasized the uniqueness of each individual, which meant that his differences should be recognized and that opportunities for creative experiences should be provided. The breadth of the new school curriculum had actually been caught in the now-famous Commission Report of 1918, and these aims were stated as the Seven Cardinal Principles of Education (health and safety; mastery of tools, techniques, and spirit of learning; worthy home membership; vocational and economic effectiveness; citizenship; worthy use of leisure; and ethical character).

The Fourth Decade (1930-1939). The 1930's were very difficult years for the United States. When the stock market had collapsed in 1929, this event had signalled the beginning of a most severe financial depression. It was inevitable that education would suffer from budgetary curtailment. Such curtailment meant that the educational program itself would have to be assessed most carefully to determine at which points money could be saved. Educational conservatives demanded that the "essentials" be retained, and that the "frills" had to go. The teaching profession suffered greatly as well, as salaries were cut and it became overcrowded by the return of many to a field that offered security, albeit at a very low salary.

All of this resulted in a strong reaction against the aims of progressive education by both laymen and educators alike. Even some of the liberal spirits criticized it for too great stress on individualism and insufficient emphasis on a theory of social welfare. It was stated that the real basis for curriculum organization should be the experience of the learners. Still further it was argued that the educational process should become a social process. From the depression onward, therefore, education assumed a new social emphasis.

In the area of higher education, a variety of occurrences were taking place. Alexander Meiklejohn had started an Experimental College at the University of Wisconsin designed to help the student to focus his study on a particular cultural epoch and to bring integrated knowledge to bear on social needs. Along with this and other educational experiments at this level, there was a separation generally of junior and senior colleges. To the former was assigned a general educational function, while the latter was to emphasize specialization to a point. In retrospect, that point was a program in which there was a limited major in a subject-matter field and several minor subjects in related disciplines. A further trend was to place greater responsibility on the individual student in acquiring his own education. From another standpoint, however, colleges and universities were faced with severe financial problems during this decade. The depression tended to curtail and in many cases eliminate significant private contributions to higher education, which forced an increasing amount of public monies into this level of education. An interesting sidelight to this latter development was a resurgence of interest in the social sciences, especially economics, because of a desire to comprehend the reasons underlying the economic crisis. It was during this period, also, that a gradual development of the University of Chicago's "aristocratic wing" of higher education was taking place under Hutchins. Another "sign of the time" was a reassertion of the need for academic freedom because of a number of "red scares" on various campuses.

In addition, the 1930's was a time when there were more than 4,000,000 students enrolled in public high schools, and it was estimated in 1930 that there was a grand total of 24,000,000 pupils in the elementary schools. The percentage of women teachers had risen to eighty percent in the public schools. During this decade, at least in some systems, teachers began to gain a voice in policy-making. In elementary education there was increased emphasis on the experience of the learners providing the fundamental basis for organization. Kilpatrick of Columbia Teachers College was a foremost exponent of the "learning by doing" dictum. A significant eight-year study at the secondary level involving thirty public and private high schools preparing students for college, with significantly altered curricula prior to guaranteed admittance, indicated that the students in the experimental curriculum made slightly higher grade point averages during their period of higher education.

The effects of the depression were in many ways unfortunate, but there were some beneficial occurrences as well. The educational and certification requirements for teachers were strengthened. The problem of unemployed youth forced the Federal Government to devote considerable attention and money to the solution of their difficulties as best possible under the circumstances. This was accomplished through such agencies as the Civilian Conservation Corps, the National Youth Administration, and the Works Progress Administration. The George-Deen Act in 1936 provided federal assistance to instruction at the secondary level related to occupations concerned with selling and marketing. Careful scrutiny and assessment of the purposes of education in American democracy resulted in the 1938 Educational Policies Commission statement that (1) self-realization, (2) human relationships, (3) economic efficiency, and (4) civic responsibility were the desired educational objectives.

The Fifth Decade (1940-1949). The year 1940 found the United States returning to normalcy again, although it can probably be stated that the word "normal" doesn't have a very precise meaning in such a rapidly-changing world. There were approximately 650,000 children enrolled in kindergartens, but the elementary school enrollment had decreased to under 20,000,000 because of a declining birth rate and restrictive immigration laws during the 1930's. Public high school enrollment had climbed to 7,000,000, and there were approximately 1,500,000 students in higher education. The average teacher salary was $1,350, but New York's average was $2,600, and Mississippi's was $526. These figures, from the standpoint of comparison among states, do not mean too much unless the cost of living is included as well. The average expenditure per pupil for education was $80.00 annually, but this figure needs careful interpretation.

Then came World War II, and necessary war production exerted a great variety of influences on the educational structure. With the entire nation mobilized for war, so many needed changes and improvements simply could not be implemented. Federal funds were made available through the U. S. Office of Education to train defense workers in schools and colleges, and many colleges and universities were saved from financial ruin by governmental subsidization in one form or another. A great many teachers were asked to serve their country in the armed forces.

Mid-Century to the Present. It is difficult to achieve any historical perspective on the period after the cessation of hostilities in World War II. We are all part of these times, and there is a "blurring that takes place as we attempt to bring trends into focus." The population figures are again soaring. The Cold War and the "Hot Wars" have become part of the way of life. Basic science "marches on," and those engaged in the social sciences and the humanities are striving valiantly to keep apace. New terms like "urban sprawl" and "multiversity" are with us, and the old terms of juvenile delinquency and racial unrest are still here, but in increasing quantity. Living costs are going higher steadily, and school boards, as well as boards of trustees, are searching for funds to provide the teachers and the facilities to get the job of education done. The standard of living is high for many, and it is miserably low for so many others. The United States is literally conducting the greatest experiment in democratic living in the history of the world, while the threat of non-militant and militant communism moves alongside with its own aims and ideals.

None can deny that it has been an interesting period in education. There was a return to the aims of social efficiency after the Global War, as well as a renewed emphasis upon the inculcation of moral values through the school. But the Cold War proceeded to bring insecurity, and a demand has arisen to place major emphasis on the development of man's rational powers. Education for international understanding has increased, but the seemingly ever-present nationalistic influence on education continues at home and in other lands.

At the elementary level, these social and political influences tended to bring about a return to what may be called the more traditional pattern of education with renewed emphasis on drill in fundamentals. Reappraisal is usually quite helpful, and it is probably inevitable that public confidence in the educational enterprise is disturbed at such time, but it is probably unfortunate that the attacks brought to bear on "professional education" was quite so bitter. At the secondary level, they centered on what their proponents believed to be the anti-intellectualism of the high school. This minority group appeared to be telling all Americans that they knew what was best and that the ends of democracy (in a republic!) would be served best by a return to a really essential curriculum including "solid" subjects that had been time-tested. It now appears to be very fortunate that a respected educator like James Bryan Conant was available to survey the situation through the support of the Carnegie Corporation. His report gave substantial support to the American comprehensive high school that was serving as a medium where the needs and interests of all might be served. In addition, he recommended special emphasis on the needs of the academically-gifted individual.

Higher education has faced many similar problems. Enrollments went up sharply after the war and have been increasing ever since. Junior and community colleges are springing up practically overnight in many communities. State colleges have become state universities, and state universities have emerged as state multi-versities. Private colleges have grown also, but they have usually managed to keep this growth under control. Graduate education has swelled enormously as well, and federal support for research has exerted great influence on the programs involved. Great strain has been placed on the various professional schools, as they seek to maintain quality while meeting partially the increased enrollment demands. In all of this, there has been a note of urgency due to the world situation and the resultant "pursuit of excellence." Professors have been less available for teaching, and often less interested in that phase of their work. Demands on their time for service to state and nation have been great. The three goals of many universities have been teaching, research, and service, but the question is often raised as to the order of priority, if any, in the attainment of these goals.

CHAPTER 1

ORIGINS OF SELECTED CONTEMPORARY SPORTS

Marvin H. Eyler
University of Maryland, College Park

The central purpose of this study was to determine, as far as practical, the origins of contemporary sports practiced in English-speaking countries. More specifically, the study attempted to (1) cite the earliest reference to the sport in the literature, (2) establish, if possible, the place of origin, (3) name, if possible, the person or persons connected with the origin, and (4) present, if possible, the circumstances of origin.

Some dates of origins could be definitely fixed; some could not. In the attempt to specify a date of origin for the latter, it was only possible to fix a date "ante quem." The critical point which had to be determined in these cases was the establishment of a date before which time it was reasonably certain that the sport did not exist, and after which time it was certain to have been in existence. For the most part, only when a date could be established beyond reasonable doubt was it included. With this approach as a guide, the writer may have erred, in some instances, on the side of conservatism. Quite probably, some of the sports included have an older history than that indicated. However, reasonable proof thereof is lacking. The sport of archery is a case in point. It is probable that for many years the bow and arrow played a triple role: (1) one of warfare, (2) one of livelihood, and (3) one of recreation. The problem here was to determine a point after which time archery was definitely practiced as a recreational activity, that is as a sport.

Certain limitations were imposed on the scope of the study. Sports that are practiced largely or exclusively in non-English-speaking countries were eliminated except for cases in which mention of such a sport was necessary to a full understanding. For example,

---

Editor's Note: The opening two chapters blend unusually well. The first represents the results of a study of the origins of some ninety-five selected sports. It is used here with the kind permission of Professor Marvin H. Eyler of the University of Maryland. Many readers will no doubt be most anxious to read this study in its entirety. In many cases the entire study can be ordered on microcards (microfiche) from the University of Oregon, or from University Microfilms (either on microfilm or reproduced xerographically) in Ann Arbor.

a statement explaining the relationship of jeu de paume and the origin of tennis is relevant. Extinct sports such as bull, bear, and badger baiting; jousting; cudgeling; and tournament were not included. Children's play activities--that is, games or sports such as hopscotch, blindman's buff, and battledore and shuttlecock were excluded. The study did not include games or pastimes which require little or no gross muscular movements such as card games, chess, and checkers. Sport-work activities or contests such as woodchopping, plowing, axe-throwing, and tree climbing were not investigated. Excluded also were miscellaneous sporting activities such as dog and horse shows. Omitted were some sports currently practiced in English-speaking countries for which there was insufficient source material available to warrant a valid statement. Finally, no attempt was made to present techniques, rules, or the development of the sports included.

Conclusions

1. The evidence shows that there was a substantial increase in the number of sports introduced during the nineteenth century (see Figures one through five). A close relationship seems to exist between the increase of leisure time, in part induced by the Industrial Revolution, and this development. Of the ninety-five sports covered, forty-nine or 52% of the sports came into being during the nineteenth century. A combination of the figures for the nineteenth and the twentieth centuries reveals that sixty-five or 68% of the sports reported originated during this period.

2. England and the United States were the sites of origin for fifty-six or 59% of the sports covered (see Figure six). When considered from a worldwide sport's viewpoint, this may or may not be significant. One of the limitations imposed upon the study was to include only those sports principally practiced in English-speaking countries. If the study could have included the origins of all known sports, the percentage attributed to England and the United States might have been reduced.

3. Of those origins attributed to the United States, (24) seventeen or 71% occurred since the relative late date of 1890, and many of these are not particularly popular or universally practiced. Compared to older European cultures, this finding implies a rather late sports awakening. This may be due, in part, to the relative short life of the country. Again, the concomitant results of the Industrial Revolution may not have affected the sporting life of the people of this country until late in the nineteenth century. (It has been rather well established that the Industrial Revolution did not fully develop here until after the Civil War.)

4. In a general sense, it appears that, of the ninety-five sports covered, three emanated from children's play activities (examples,

LEGEND: Figures 1 - 5

• Date	The earliest documented evidence of origin in extant, organized form.
- - -	Documented evidence of previous existence in extant form, but unorganized and/or non-competitive. Left termini of dashes before year zero are indicated by date.
? - - -	Reputed evidence previous to this date may not actually refer to this specific sport.

                    B.C.   A.D.

Wrestling   2160 - 1788
Boxing   ? - 850
Field Events   776
Track Events   776
Hunting   2357 - 400
Kite Flying   1121 - 221
Coursing   .7
Cock Fighting   .77
Angling   .200
Falconry   .350
Horse Racing   648 - - - - - - - - - - .1174
Tennis   .1230
Lawn Bowls   .1366
Quoits   450 - - - - - - - - - - - .1409
Golf   ? - .1457
Target Rifle Shooting   .1498
Fencing   .1517
Hurling   .1527
Shuffleboard   .1532
Archery (target)   - - - .1585

        0   500   1000   1500   1600   1700   1800   1900

Figure 1. Chronological Distribution of the Dates of Origin.

Sport	Date of Origin
Billiards	? - - .1590
Fowling	2475 - - - -.1596
Polo	.1596
Curling	.1607
Ice Skating	.1659
Cricket	.1744
Fives	.1746
Yacht Racing	.1775
Pedestrianism	.1792
Racquets	.1799
Horseshoes	? - .1801
Coaching	.1807
Steeplechasing	.1810
Mountaineering	? - - .1811
Gymnastics	-.1816
Pigeon Racing	-.1818
Harness Racing	.1825
Sculling	.1889
Lacrosse	.1839
Rowing	.1839

Axis: 0   500   1000   1500   1600   1700   1800   1900

Figure 2. Chronological Distribution of the Dates of Origin.

Sport	Date of Origin
Bowling (Ten Pins)	.1840
Croquet	.1840
Handball	? .1840
Baseball	.1846
Rugby	.1846
Iceboating	.1850
Weight Lifting	.1854
Canoe Racing	.1857
Soccer	.1859
Squash Racquets	.1859
Swimming	.1859
Roller Skating	.1863
Trap Shooting	.1866
Field Trials	.1866
Bicycle Racing	.1868
Badminton	.1870
Skiing	.1870
Target Pistol Shooting	.1871
Model Sailboat Racing	.1872
Lawn Tennis	.1873

0   500   1000   1500   1600   1700   1800   1900

Figure 3. Chronological Distribution of the Dates of Origin.

B.C. A.D.

Sport	Date
Football (American)	.1874
Dog Racing	? - - - .1876
Roque	.1879
Ice Hockey	- - - .1880
Rodeo	- - .1880
Judo	.1882
Tobogganing	? - - - .1883
Water Polo	.1885
Field Hockey	? - - - - .1886
Birling	.1888
Table Tennis	.1889
Darts	? - - - - .1890
Rope Spinning	? - - - - .1890
Squash Tennis	.1890
Basketball	.1891
Automobile Racing	.1895
Volleyball	.1895
Jai Alai	.1896
Paddle Tennis	.1898
Motorcycle Racing	.1902

0 500 1000 1500 1600 1700 1800 1900

Figure 4. Chronological Distribution of the Dates of Origin.

- 34 -

B.C. A.D.

Corkball		.1904
Motorboat Racing		.1904
Model Airplane Flying		.1905
Airplane Flying		.1907
Soaring		.1909
Speedball		.1920
Softball		- - -.1921
Miniature Golf		- - -.1923
Soapbox Racing		.1927
Football (Six-Man)		.1933
Skin Diving		.1934
Miniature Auto Racing		.1936
Water Skiing		.1939
Skish		- - - -.1939
Flickerball		.1948

0   500   1000   1500   1600   1700   1800   1900

Figure 5. Chronological Distribution of the Dates of Origin.

- 35 -

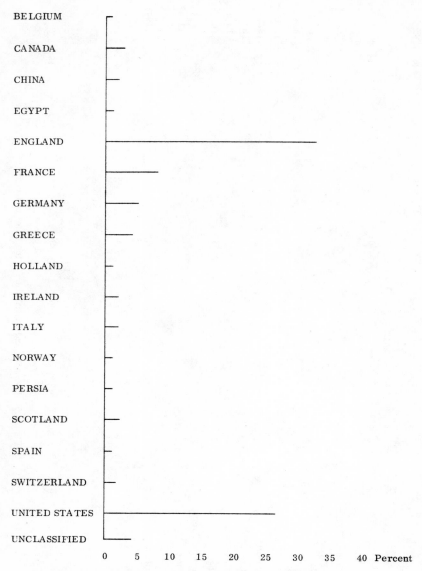

Figure 6. Percentage Distribution of Place of Origin of
the 95 Sports.

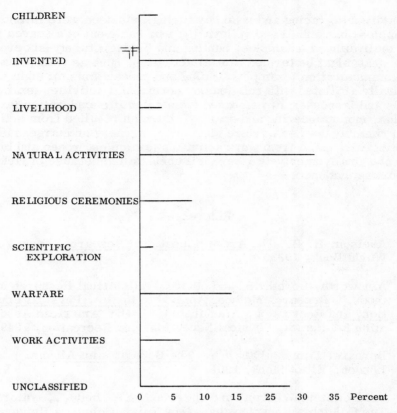

Figure 7. Percentage Distribution of Activities from Which the 95 Sports Evolved

miniature auto racing and soap box racing); nineteen were invented (examples, basketball and volleyball); four came out of a search for food or livelihood (examples, hunting and fishing); twenty-six evolved from what might be termed natural activities, such as transportation and communication (examples, skiing and pedestrianism); eight were originally affiliated with religious or ceremonial activities (examples, tennis and lacrosse); two emerged from scientific exploration (examples, mountaineering and soaring); thirteen resulted from activities primarily used in warfare (examples, archery and target rifle shooting); six came from work activities (examples, rodeo and birling); and finally twenty-two were left unclassified because of lack of supporting evidence.

References

1. Abelson, H. H. The Art of Educational Research. New York: World Book, 1933.

2. Ainsworth, Dorothy S. and others. "Historical Research Methods." Research Methods Applied to Health, Physical Education, and Recreation. Washington, D. C.: American Association for Health, Physical Education, and Recreation, 1949.

3. Berners, Dame Juliana (?). The Boke of Saint Albans. London: Elliot Stock, 1901.

4. Bridgewater, William, and Sherwood, Elizabeth J., editors. The Columbia Encyclopedia. New York: Columbia University Press, 1946.

5. Burton, Robert. Anatomy of Melancholy. Oxford: John Lichfield and James short for Henry Cripps, 1621.

6. Catlin, George. Letters and Notes on the Manners, Customs and Condition of the North American Indians. Volumes I and II. London: Henry G. Bohn, 1851.

7. Cleland, James. The Institution of A Young Nobleman. Oxford: Joseph Barnes, 1607.

8. A Collection in English of the Statutes Now in Force, Continued from the Beginning of Magna Charta. . . . Imprinted at London: by the Deputies of Christopher Baker, 1588.

9. Comenii, John Amos. Orbis Sensualium Pictus. Translated by Charles Hoole. London: Printed by S. Leacroft, 1777.

10.   Cotgrave, Randle, compiler. <u>A Dictionaire of the French and English Tongues</u>. London: Printed by Adam Islip, 1611.

11.   Culin, Stewart. "Games of the North American Indians." <u>Twenty-fourth Annual Report of the Bureau of American Ethnology</u>. Washington: Government Printing Office, 1907.

12.   Cummings, Parke, editor. <u>The Dictionary of Sports</u>. New York: A. S. Barnes and Company, 1949.

13.   Cummings, Parke. "Sports, Athletic." <u>Encyclopedia Americana</u> 25:434-43; 1955. pp. 434-443.

14.   Cureton, Thomas K. "Library Research Methods." <u>Research Methods Applied to Health, Physical Education, and Recreation</u>. Washington, D. C.: American Association for Health, Physical Education, and Recreation, 1949.

15.   Cushing, Frank H. "Outlines of Zuni Creation Myths." <u>Thirteenth Annual Report of the Bureau of Ethnology</u>. Washington: Government Printing Office, 1896.

16.   <u>Edward, Duke of York, The Master of Game</u>. Edited by William A. and T. Baillie-Grohman, London: Chatto & Windus, 1909.

17.   Fling, Fred M. <u>The Writing of History</u>. New Haven: Yale University Press, 1920.

18. e Frederick II. <u>De Arte Venandi Cum Avibus</u>. Translated by Casey A. Wood and F. Marjorie Fyfe. Stanford, California: Stanford University Press, 1943.

19.   Garraghan, G. J. <u>A Guide to Historical Method</u>. New York: Fordham University Press, 1946.

20.   Giles, Herbert A. <u>Adversaria Sinica</u>. Shanghai: Messrs. Kelly and Walsh, Ltd., 1914.

21.   Gini, Corrado. "Rural Ritual Games in Libya." <u>Rural Sociology</u> 4:283-99; 1939.

22.   Gottschalk, L. <u>Understanding History</u>. New York: Alfred Knopf, Inc., 1950.

23.   Hockett, Homer C. <u>Introduction to Research in American History</u>. New York: The Macmillan Company, 1949.

24. James I. <u>Basilikon Doran, or His Majesties Instructions to His Dearest Sonne, Henry the Prince</u>. Edinburgh: Printed by Robert Valdegrave, 1603.

25. Johnson, Leighton H. "Education Needs Historical Studies." <u>The Phi Beta Kappan</u>. 36:157-59; January 1955.

26. Keble, Joseph. <u>The Statutes at Large from Magna Charta Until This Time</u>. London: The assigns of John Bill, Thomas Newcomb and Henry Hills, the assigns of Richard Atkins and Edwards Atkins, 1681.

27. <u>Lavves and Acts of Parliament, Maid Be King James the First and His Successors Kinges of Scot</u>. Edinburgh: Imprinted by Robert, 1597.

28. Maigaard, J. "Battingball Games." <u>Genus</u> 1-2:57-72; December 1941.

29. Markham, Garvase. <u>Country Contentments, or the Husbandmans Recreations</u>. London: William Wilson for John Harison, 1649.

30. Massingham, H. J. <u>The Heritage of Man</u>. London: Jonathan Caps, 1929.

31. Mooney, James. "The Cherokee Ball Play." <u>The American Anthropologist</u> 3:105-32; April 1896.

32. Murray, James A., editor. <u>A New English Dictionary on Historical Principles</u>. Volumes I-X. New York: Macmillan and Company, 1888-1926. (Supp. 1933)

33. Nevins, Allan. <u>The Gateway to History</u>. New York: C. Appleton-Century Company, 1938.

34. Nichols, John. <u>The Progresses of Queen Elizabeth</u>. Volumes I-III. London: Printed by and for John Nichols and Sons, 1823.

35. <u>Rotuli Parliamentorum</u>; et petitiones, et placita, in Parliamento Tempore Edward R. I finem Henrichi VII, 6 vols. London: 1767-77.

36. Skeay, Walter W. <u>An Etymological Dictionary of the English Language</u>. Oxford: Clarendon Press, 1898.

37. Staley, S. C. <u>The World of Sport</u>. Champaign, Illinois: Stipes Publishing Company, 1955.

38. Stern, Theodore. "The Rubber-ball Games of the Americas."
     <u>Monographs of the American Ethnological Society</u> No. 18, 1948.

39. Stow, John. <u>A Survey of London</u>. Volumes I-II. Oxford:
     Clarendon Press, 1908.

40. Vincent, J. M. <u>Historical Research</u>. New York: Peter Smith,
     1929.

CHAPTER 2

ORIGINS OF THIRTY-THREE SPORTS

Asbury C. Moore, Jr.
University of Illinois, Urbana

Introduction

The purpose of the study was to search for the origins of as many sports as possible which were not included in a study of origins (Eyler, 1956). The need for a study of this kind was evident because in many cases the origins of sports are omitted from historical writings, especially in histories of sports, and because only 95 origins of the approximately 250 currently practiced sports listed by Staley, (1955, pp. 5-12) had been included in a documented study of origins. Incidentally, it may be noted that Staley did not attempt to list all of the known sports, but concluded many of the lists with "etc." For example, Staley listed under automobile racing, "big car, hot rods, midget, special, sport, stock, etc." To this list under "etc." Staley could have added quarter midgets, modified stock cars, drag racing, etc. In addition, since Staley's list was published in 1955, a number of new sports have been introduced. For example, the automobile racing group has been increased by go-karting and formula junior. The point is that if the list were completed, the number of sports would be greatly increased.

In order to try to determine the reason why origins are so frequently omitted from literature, an investigation was undertaken which resulted in the following findings: (1) the only available documented study of origins was made by Eyler (1956) covering 95 sports; (2) the origins of the remaining sports are scattered, undocumented, or unknown; (3) there is a lack of agreement among writers on the origin of some sports; and (4) sources of information concerning origins of many sports are either unknown or not readily available.

Editor's Note: A precis of the companion study to that of Professor Eyler was requested from Professor A. C. Moore of the University of Illinois, Urbana. It represents an interesting and direct follow-up to Dr. Eyler's slightly earlier investigation. Employing a somewhat different concept of a sport's origin, Professor Moore searched out the beginnings of thirty-three additional sports based on the date when the first set of rules appeared. In addition, he mentioned the earliest reference in the literature to a sport as he was able to uncover such data.

As a result of this preliminary investigation, it was decided to make a study of as many origins of sports as possible, covering insofar as possible the following specifics: (1) the earliest reference in the literature to a sport; and (2) the earliest reference in the literature to a sport indicating the date it was first performed as an organized sport with written rules, and denoting: (a) where it originated, (b) the person or persons involved in the origin, and (c) significant circumstances surrounding the origin.

The first specific is used to indicate that the sport was in existence in some form before it was organized with written rules. (Examples: (1) Quarter Horse racing has been in existence in some form since 1690; however, it was not until 1944 that the American Quarter Racing Association was organized to set up uniform standards of competitions; and (2) field archery had its beginning in 1934, but it was not until 1939 that the National Field Archery Association was formed to develop rules and regulations from competitive field-style shooting.)

Since many of the sports included in Eyler's study (1956) were established sports such as football, baseball, etc., it was decided to include in this work the origins of "splinter sports" and "combination sports." "Splinter sports" refer to sports derived from the basic components (equipment, playing area, rules, skills, etc.) of an established sport. (Examples: baseball--Little League baseball; basketball--Biddy basketball.) "Combination sports" refer to sports derived from the basic components (equipment, playing area, rules, skills, etc.) of two or more established sports. (Examples: archery and golf--archery golf; squash and handball--paddle rackets.)

The search for material and its analysis extended over a period of two years. It ended with the inclusion of 33 sports in the study. At least 50 additional sports were studied, but were not included because the evidence needed to meet the requirements of the study was insufficient.

In order to narrow the scope of the study the following were excluded: (1) children's play activities, such as marbles, parlor stunts, etc.: (2) extinct sports, such as bear baiting, gander pulling, coach driving, etc.: (3) work sports, such as horse pulling, wood chopping, axe throwing, etc.; (4) sports practiced largely by women, such as synchronized swimming, speedball, etc.; and (5) sports practiced principally in non-English-speaking countries, such as bullfighting, pato, etc. Also excluded were: (a) activities practiced exclusively for fitness, such as calisthenics, and (b) table games such as checkers, chess, card games, etc. No attempt was made to describe the techniques, rules, or development of the sports.

Sports used in the study were limited to those activities with recognizable rules or standards of performance, and which involved individual skill and physical ability. This definition varied in the degree of application with the individual activities covered. For example, the physical ability required for ballooning does not necessarily compare with the physical requirements necessary for canoe slalom. The individual skill required for drag boating is not necessarily equal to that of rebound tumbling. This definition also covers activities which are usually considered a part of another sport. For example, ski jumping is considered an event in skiing competition. However, ski jumping qualifies as a sport according to the criteria of the definition used in this study.

A brief summary of the information found on the origin of the sports included in the study follow in alphabetical order.

Archery Golf

From all available evidence, archery golf appears to have been played for at least a century, but the earliest rules found were those used in 1935 at the first annual Ohio championship tournament held at Ohio State University. In 1937 the only known official archery golf rules were those adopted by the Ohio Archery Golf and Hunting Association. (Metcalf, 1937, pp. 554-556).

Ballooning

Credit for the first experiments in ballooning must go to the Montgolfier brothers, who released a hot air balloon in 1783. (Alexander, 1902, p. 13; Valentine and Tomlinson, 1903, p. 17; Bacon, 1903, p. 13). Jean Pilatre de Rosier, in 1783, was the first to ascend in a balloon thus being the world's first aeronaut. The first successful trip with passengers was made on April 13, 1803. In 1881, Dr. Angerstein founded the German club in Berlin for the promotion of ballooning as a sport. (Hildebrandt, 1908, p. 197).

Biddy Basketball

The first biddy basketball game was played June 1, 1950 at the Catholic Youth Center, Scranton, Pennsylvania. Jay Archer, Executive Director of the Youth Center, conceived the game "as a 'phase' of a gym program, primarily to enable youngsters, both boys and girls, to play and enjoy the game of basketball, to its fullest capacity, without too much strain." (Archer, 1960).

GOSHEN COLLEGE LIBRARY
GOSHEN, INDIANA

- 45 -

Canoe Slalom

From the available sources it was impossible to fix a date marking the exact origin of canoe slalom. According to McNair (1960), "canoe slalom goes back to 1934 when the idea appeared in both Austria and Switzerland."

Dog Shows

Dog shows appear to have had their inception in England.

The first recorded dog show was Mr. Pepe's Show at Newcastle in 1859, followed by a Foxhound Show at Redcar. The first large show was 'The First Annual Grand National Exhibition of Sporting and Other Dogs,' held in 1863 at the Ashburnham Hall, Cremorne, Chelsea, from March 23 to 28. (Ash, 1927, p. 676).

In April, 1873, the Kennel Club was formed in England in order to regulate and guide future shows. (Randall, 1956, p. 520).

Drag Boating

Drag boating "began at the Long Beach Marine Stadium, in 1956, when a group of aquatic hot rodders decided that the acid test for the theory concerning hulls, props and engines, would be a standing-start acceleration trials over the standing one-quarter mile, timed by good electronic clocks." (Borgeson, 1960, p. 135).

Duck Pin Bowling

Falcaro and Goodman (1940, p. 39) believe that duck pins evolved as an offshoot of the game of lawn bowls in about 1910. In his New Encyclopedia of Sports published in 1944, Menke (1944, p. 164) states, "Back in 1906 or 1907 a group of gentlemen grew weary from lifting the heavy balls for regular 10 pin bowling, and thought up the duck pin idea."

Although there are differences of opinion in the origin of duck pin bowling, the National Duck Pin Bowling Congress was organized in 1927 to standardize rules, and to serve as a governing body for duck pin bowling. In 1928 the first National Tournament was held in Baltimore, Maryland. (Falcaro and Goodman, 1940, p. 39; Menke, 1944, p. 165).

Field Archery

Field archery had its beginning at a little club at Redlands, California, in the spring of 1934, when its members built the first field archery club. These members decided to build a course similar to the courses for "annual field shoots" which the target archers of Ohio, Michigan, Wisconsin, Oregon and other states were using for variety after a season of target shooting. (Yount, 1954, p. 1).

Go-Kart Racing

Murray (1959, p. 8) states that the name go-kart originated when Red and Custom Magazine decided to take pictures and write a story on the still-unnamed cars being driven in Pasadena's famed Rose Bowl. They elected to call the creation go-karts, a name originally given to a baby buggy manufactured in the early 1900's.

Karting as an organized sport began in 1957 when a group of individuals, who had been interested in karts since their inception, banded together and formed the Go-Kart Club of America. The chief functions of the club are the formation of rules governing races, kart construction, and safety practices, and to organize and promote races and other special events. ("The Go-Kart Club of America, 1959, p. 95; Murray, 1959, p. 88).

Hot Rod Racing

In a general sense, hot rod racing has existed in the United States since the late 1920's when second-hand Model-T Fords first became available at low cost. ("Hot Rod Racing," 1945, p. 86; "Hot Rodding Roared into Big Business," 1952, p. 46). However, it was not until the early 1930's that loosely-knit hot rod racing clubs were organized in California. It was soon evident that some governing organization was necessary to supervise and regulate the fast-growing sport; so, in 1938 several speed clubs organized the Southern California Timing Association, Inc., with Art Tilton as its Secretary. (Hamilton, 1947, pp. 183-191; Laurence, 1941, p. 56).

Little League Baseball

Little League baseball was inaugurated in 1939 by Carl E. Sotoz, an employee of a lumber company, in Williamsport, Pennsylvania, as a result of a promise made to two young nephews when they were pushed aside by the bigger ball players.

Midget Airplane Racing

The idea for midget airplane racing began in 1939 when the cost of building and maintaining "unlimited class" racers became too great for most race pilots. As a result, interested pilots, designers, and builders of racers met in Los Angeles (the center of interest in the sport), and drew up specifications for the 190 cubic inch class midget

racer. At this meeting were Art Chester, Ben O. Howard, Keith
Rider, Tony LaVier and others.

Midget Auto Racing

From the evidence available, midget auto racing appears to
have originated as a sport in 1932 in Los Angeles, California, when
Dominic Distarce organized the Midget Auto Racing Association.
("Sports," 1937, p. 28; Morgan, 1946, p. 30; "Doodlebug Derby,"
1937, p. 52; "Roaring Doodlebugs," 1936, p. 20).

Midget Football

"It all started in Philadelphia in 1930, when a group of Cham-
ber of Commerce men appointed Joe Tomlin, Swarthmore College
alumnus, to perk up community pride and spirit in run-down industrial areas." (LaBrum, 1952, p. 20). A few years later a national
organization was set up to encourage and supervise the sport and
interested Pop Warner, the famous coach, in giving his name and
support to the midget football movement. (Cloyd, 1952, p. 84).

Organized Camping

The idea for the first organized camp was conceived by Joseph
Trimble Rothrock, the unacknowledged father of camping. While Dr.
Rothrock was a practicing physician, he established the first boys'
camp in history on North Mountain, Luzerne County, Pennsylvania,
and called it "The North Mountain School of Physical Culture." Mr.
Keiser (1929, p. 4) quoting from a biographical sketch Dr. Rothrock
wrote:

"In 1876, I had the happy idea of taking weakly boys in summer
out into camp life in the woods and under competent instruction,
mingling exercises and study, so that pursuit of health could be
combined with acquisition of practical knowledge outside the
usual academic lines. I founded the school on North Mountain,
Luzerne County, Pennsylvania, and designated it a school of
Physical Culture. There had been, I think, but a single attempt
to do this work at an earlier period."

Mr. Keiser also said, "In private conversation, Dr. Rothrock often
stated that his 1876 camp was the first ever established. The other
attempt referred to probably did not pass the contemplation stage."

Paddle Rackets

Paddle rackets originated in 1954 at Greenwich, Connecticut.
The persons involved in the origin are Joseph Sobek, the originator,

assisted by Douglas P. Boyea, George Roberts, Frank S. Minnerly, Frank Sudell, A. U. Kutsay and Stephen Miser. (Boyea, 1960).

Pointing Dog Field Trials

Pointing dog trials appear to have commenced at the first recorded field trials at Cannock Chase, near Strafford, England, on May 1, 1866. (Brown, 1948, pp. 43-44).

Pushball

"The game of pushball originated in America. The first pushball was made in Newton, Massachusetts, in 1894." ("Pushball--The Biggest Plaything," 1916, pp. 80-81). Although St. Nicholas reported a pushball being made in 1894, the first documented evidence of the game being played is found in Every Boy's Book of Sport and Pastime, published in 1897. "Pushball--This is a new game in some respects resembling football, which has recently been introduced at Harvard University, America, and is said to yield capital sport." (Hoffman, 1897, p. 448).

Quarter Horse Racing

Although Quarter Horse races have been held since Colonial times, and records are available for outstanding Quarter Horse racers between 1880 and 1902, Quarter Horse racing for the purpose of this study is not considered as an organized sport before organizations were formed to govern standards and rules.

In 1939 a group of horsemen met in Fort Worth, Texas to discuss the formation of the American Quarter Horse Association to preserve and promote the Quarter Horse. This Association was formed in March, 1940. (Gorman, 1949, p. 293). The American Quarter Racing Association was formed to set up uniform standards of competition in 1944. (Crowell, 1951, p. 135). In 1945, due to differences of opinion among the breeders of the American Quarter Horse Association, the National Quarter Horse Breeders' Association was formed in Hockley, Texas. (Crowell, 1951, p. 131).

Rebound Tumbling

Rebound tumbling (trampolining, as we know it today) was first established through the efforts of Larry Griswold and George Nissen (Loken, 1948, p. 3), who made the first trampoline available for general use. In the 1930's Nissen manufactured the Nissen Trampoline, and has directed promotion and publicity toward developing rebound tumbling as a sport. In 1959 he was awarded the American Academy of Physical Education's creative award. He was cited for developing "The first new sport of this Century in large muscle activity." (McCormack, 1960).

Retriever Field Trials

The first retriever trial recorded by the English Kennel Club Calendar and Stud Book was held on the estate of B. J. Warwick near Havant, England on October 12-13, 1900. This trial was for all-age stake for retrievers. Earlier attempts had been made to stage competition for retrievers during the early 1870's, and a private trial was held in 1899, but these ventures did not establish the sport. (Brown, 1945, p. 80).

Roller Derby

Roller Derby, a copyrighted name, was introduced in Chicago by Leo ("Bromo") Seltzer in 1935. Although Seltzer toured in New York City; Miami, Florida; Louisville, Kentucky and Kansas City, Missouri, it was not until 1948 when players appeared on television from New York that Roller Derby gained national fame. ("Sport," 1936, p. 24; Menke, 1953, p. 730; Reynolds, 1936, p. 15).

Sand Yachting

The origin of sand yachting as a sport is not clearly established in available sources. (Dorsett, 1957, p. 119) states that:

Sand yachting originated sometime between 1895 and the turn of the century. . . . Primitive land yachts sped along Southport, England shores. Equally antique models were operated by François Dumont and eight brothers on Belgian beaches. Louis Bériot, the first aviator to fly across the English Channel, lured the Belgians to France for sand yacht races by offering a flight in his aircraft as a prize."

Scuba Diving

The sport of scuba diving as we know it today dates back to 1943 when Gagnan and Costeau developed the first completely automatic demand-type scuba, known as the Aqua-Lung. ("The Science of Skin and Scuba Diving," 1957, p. 169).

Skeet

"In 1910 a group of Massachusetts trapshooters grew tired of standing in one spot and firing at clay pigeons. They wanted something more like real hunting so they moved around the grounds and shot flying targets from different positions." ("Skeet: Shotgun Golf Holds Its First National Tournament," 1935, p. 25).

Sky Diving

Although parachuting dates back to the time in 1776 when Sebastian Leonormand, a Frenchman, used a 14-foot parachute to jump from a high tower, and Andrew Jacques Garnerin is credited with being the first parachutist in 1797 (Zim, 1942, p. 8), parachuting as a sport, according to (Zim, 1942, p. 129) and (Moshkovsky, 1939, p. 9) had its inception in 1930 when parachute clubs were organized in the Soviet Union. According to Moshkovsky, parachute jumping as a sport was introduced in the Soviet Union by women. The pioneers were Kuleshova, Grokhovskaya, Chirkova and Fyoderova.

Slalom

From available evidence slalom racing appears to have been originated in central Europe. Arnold Lunn, an Englishman, is credited with the development of slalom as we know it today. (Lunn, 1927, pp. 226-227).

Spaniel Field Trials

The Sporting Spaniel Club held the first field trial for Spaniels on the estate of William Arkwright, the President and Founder of the Club, in 1899, at Sutton Scarsdale, Derbyshire, England. (Phillips, 1932, p. 42; Camp, 1948, p. 799).

Star Class Yacht Racing

The Star Class yacht originated about 1835 with a boat called the "Sharpie," built for commercial purposes. However, the "Bug," which appeared in Long Island waters in 1907, designed by William Gardner, was a miniature Star boat. George A. Corry originated the idea for its design and he has since been called "The Father of the Stars." In 1910 it was decided by Corry and others to increase the size of the "Bug" from 17 feet to 22 feet and at the suggestion of Stuyvesant Wainwright the name was changed from the "Bug" to the "Star." (Menke, 1936, p. 442).

Tennessee Walking Horse Shows

Although the walking horse breed originated over one hundred years ago, it was not until after the Tennessee Walking Horse Breeders Association was formed in Lewisburg, Tennessee, in 1935, that it received much notice from the public. This Association was formed by prominent owners who wanted to protect the blood line of the horse. The United States Government officially recognized the Walking Horse as a separate and distinct breed of light horse in 1949. (Wells, 1955, p. 57; Kays, 1953, p. 226; Gorman, 1949, p. 226).

Touch Football

The exact origin of touch football appears to be unknown.
(Crombach, 1958, p. 3) states that "there is evidence that a kind of
touch football was played by the United States troops in the Spanish-
American War and in World War I," and that a type of touch football
was played in New Orleans grade schools and high schools before
World War I.

Stecher (1926, p. 216) included rules for tag football in a book
published in 1926; in 1930 Ortner (1930, p. 40) published a set of touch
touch football rules that were in use at Cornell University; and in 1932
Swain (1932, p. 34) published an article on the kick in touch football,
in which he states, "We have had the game in this form in play for
five years at Brown University in our intramural system with about
twenty-five groups participating."

Water Ski Jumping

In 1928 Dick Pope, Sr. was the first to jump on water skiis
from a wooden ramp at Miami Beach, Florida. (Pope, 1948, p. 52).
The first time jumping was included in a meet was in 1936 at a meet
held primarily for aquaplanists in Massapequa, New York, in which
Jack Anderson of Greenwood Lake, New York jumped from a ramp
about three and one-half feet high. (Prince, 1959, pp. 1-2; Anderson,
1950, pp. 163-164). However, the first jump made at a national
water ski tournament was in 1939 at Jones Beach, New York. This
was the first National Water Ski Tournament and was held under the
auspices of the American Water Ski Association. (Anderson, 1950,
p. 161).

Wheelchair Basketball

Level (1949, p. 626) gives credit for the conception of wheelchair basketball to the patients at Birmingham Veterans Administration Hospital, Van Nuys, California and to Bob Rynearson their
Assistant Athletic Director of Special Services.

Schweikert (1960, n.p.) states, "While the California Chapter
of the Paralyzed Veterans of America has been popularly credited
with the birth of wheelchair basketball, the New England Chapter of
the same organization offered documentary evidence antedating
California's claim to fame. However, both will agree that it started
sometime in 1946 and it started in the Veterans Administration Hospi-
tals."

Summary

    In most cases all of the specifics were ascertained for each
sport. However, in a few sports the location of the origin could not
be definitely established. For example, Austria and Switzerland
were both listed in available sources as the location of the origin of
canoe slalom. Also, there were a few sports for which there was no
available evidence of the person or persons involved. Examples are
pushball and sand yachting.

    In order to present a more comprehensive study of origins of
sport, the ninety-five origins of sports found by Eyler (1956) were included in a chronological distribution of the dates of origin in the
study. In some cases the dates of origins as found by Eyler have been
changed to conform with specifics used in this study. This was necessary because the primary purpose of Eyler's study was to ascertain
the date of origin or the earliest reference in the literature (when a
date could not be ascertained with any degree of accuracy), while the
primary purpose of the present study was to establish a date when the
sport was performed as an organized sport with written rules. For
example, Eyler (1956, p. 70) gives the origin of boxing as 850 B.C.
He states, "Probably the earliest account of what may be termed a
crude form of the sport was given in the Illiad (850 B.C.) concerning
the funeral games performed in honor of Patroklos." However, the
date of origin used in the chronological distribution in this study is
1743. This date is based on Eyler's (1956, p. 73) statement, "The
first set of modern rules were produced by Mr. Broughton on August
10, 1743, being seven in number." The 1743 date was used because
it is the first date mentioned by Eyler indicating the sport was performed at a specific time as an organized sport with written rules.
Therefore, when a date given by Eyler could be changed to conform to
the specifics of this study, it was done and placed in parentheses in
the chronological distribution.

    So that the reader might visualize origins of sports in terms of
several short periods rather than one continuous period, the chronological distribution was divided into thirty-year periods of time,
beginning in 1840. Prior to 1840, all origins are grouped together,
since they are infrequent and date back to B.C. The periods of time
are: prior to 1840; 1840-1869; 1870-1899; 1900-1929 and 1930-1959.

Conclusions

    1. The evidence shows that the thirty-three sports covered in
the study originated since 1862, with the greater percentage being
introduced during the period of 1930-1959 (twenty-one sports, or 64%).
The lack of origins in the study prior to 1862 appears to be due to the
thorough search of available sources by Eyler (1956), resulting in the
inclusion of origins during this period in his study. The probable

reason for the substantial increase of origins introduced in the study during the period 1930-1959 is due to a comprehensive search of current literature, sports periodicals, magazines, etc. The number and percent of origins for the thirty-three sports by time periods are: two (6%) during the period 1840-1869, three (9%) during the period 1870-1899, seven (21%) during the period 1900-1929 and twenty-one (64%) during the period 1930-1959.

2. Of the thirty-three sports covered in the study, the United States is the site of origin for twenty-three (70%). England is the site of origin for five (12%). Two (5%) originated in France and three (9%) are unclassified. The high percentage of origins of sports attributed to the United States is probably due to a more thorough search of American literature, and the limitations imposed on the study, that of the inclusion of only those sports principally practiced in English-speaking countries.

3. Of the one hundred and twenty-eight sports included in Eyler's (1956) study and this study, the number and per cent of origins of sports stated in terms of time periods are: thirty-two (25%) originated prior to 1840; nineteen (15%) during the period 1840-1869; twenty-eight (22%) during the period 1870-1899; twenty (15%) during the period 1900-1929 and twenty-nine (23%) during the period 1930-1959. The evidence shows that ninety-six (75%) of the one hundred and twenty-eight sports originated since 1840. This is apparently due to an increase in leisure time and the greater effort made toward the development and organization of sports (requirements imposed by the two studies).

4. In the distribution of place of origin of the one hundred and twenty-eight sports included in Eyler's (1956) study and this study, forty-seven (37%) had their origin in the United States, and thirty-seven (29%) originated in England. The high percentage of origins of sport attributed to the United States and England is probably due to the limitations imposed upon both studies--that of the inclusion of only those sports principally practiced in English-speaking countries.

Bibliography

Alexander, John. The Conquest of the Air. New York: A. Wessels Company, 1902. 160 p.

Anderson, Jack. Skiing on Water. New York: A. S. Barnes and Company, 1950. 182 p.

Ash, Edward C. Dogs: Their History and Development, Vol. II. London: Ernest Benn, Limited, 1927. 778 p.

Bacon, Rev. J. M. The Dominion of the Air. London: Cassell and
    Company, Limited, 1902. 348 p.

Borgeson, Griffith. "Drag Boating Roundup," Hot Rod Handbook,
    Fawcett 451:134-139, 1960.

Brown, William F. "Bird Dog Field Trials," American Sporting
    Dogs. New York: D. Van Nostrand Company, Incorporated,
    1948. 879 p.

Brown, William F. Retriever Gun Dogs. New York: A. S. Barnes
    and Company, 1945. 143 p.

Camp, Raymond R. (editor), "Spaniel Field Trials," The Hunter's
    Encyclopaedia, 1948.

Cloyd, Joseph. "Gangway for the Mighty Midgets," American, Vol.
    CLIV, pp. 28-29+, December, 1952.

Crowell, Pers. Cavalcade of American Horses. New York:
    McGraw-Hill Book Company, Incorporated, 1951. 311 p.

"Doodlebug Derby," Time, 30:52, September 27, 1937.

Dorsett, Robert E. "They Sail on Sand," Popular Mechanics,
    107:117-122, January, 1957.

Eyler, Marvin H. "Origins of Some Modern Sports." Unpublished
    Ph.D. Dissertation, University of Illinois, Urbana, Illinois,
    1956. 406 p.

Falcaro, Joe and Goodman, Murray. Bowling. New York:
    A. S. Barnes and Company, 1940. 72 p.

Gorman, John A. The Western Horse. Danville, Illinois: The
    Interstate Printers and Publishers, 1949. 396 p.

Grombach, John V. Touch Football. New York: The Ronald Press
    Company, 1958. 125 p.

Hamilton, Andrew. "Racing the Hot Rods," Popular Mechanics,
    87:138-139, January, 1947.

Hildebrandt, A. Airships Past and Present. New York:
    D. Van Nostrand Company, 1908. 361 p.

Hoffman, Professor (editor). Every Boy's Book of Sport and Pastime.
    London: George Rutledge and Sons, Limited, 1897. 900 p.

"Hot Rodding Roars into Big Business," Business Week, March 22, 1952.

"Hot Rod Racing," Life, 19:86-88, November, 1945.

Kays, D. J. The Horse. New York: A. S. Barnes and Company, 1953. 494 p.

Keiser, David S. "The First Cultural Camp," Camper and Hiker, 2:4, April, 1929.

LaBrum, Col. J. Harry. "Pop Warner Football," Industrial Sports, 13:20-21, October 15, 1952.

Lawrence, Edward. "Gow Jobs," Collier's, 108:14, July 26, 1941.

Level, Hildegard. "The Miracle of Ramp C," Hygeia, 27:626, September, 1949.

Loken, Newton C. Trampolining. Ann Arbor, Michigan: The Over-beck Company, 1948. 26 p.

Lunn, Arnold. History of Skiing. London: Oxford University Press, 1927. 492 p.

McCormack, Patricia. "Tumbling for Fun," New York World-Telegram and Sun, April 6, 1960.

Menke, Frank G. All Sports Record Book. New York: All Sports Record Book, Incorporated, 1936. 446 p.

_____. The Encyclopedia of Sports. New York: A. S. Barnes and Company, 1953. 1018 p.

_____. The Encyclopedia of Sports. Revised Edition. New York: A. S. Barnes and Company, 1960. 1106 p.

_____. The New Encyclopedia of Sports. New York: A. S. Barnes and Company, 1944. 1007 p.

Metcalf, Harlan G. "Archery Golf," Journal of Health and Physical Education, 8:554-556, November, 1937.

Morgan, Byron. "There Go the Thunderbugs!" Saturday Evening Post, 219:30-31, September 7, 1946.

Moshkovsky, Major V. Parachute-jumping and Gliding. Moscow: Foreign Languages Publishing House, 1939. 32 p.

Murray, Spence. "Background for Karting," Let's Go Karting, Trend, 185:4-10, 1959.

_____. "The Go-Kart Club of America," Let's Go Karting, Trend, 185:92-104, 1959.

Ortner, Howard B. "New Rules for Touch Football," Journal of Health and Physical Education, 1:40, September, 1930.

Phillips, C. A. "Spaniel Field Trials," Hounds and Dogs: Their Care and Working. London: Seeley, Service and Company, Limited, 1932. 320 p.

Pope, Dick, Sr. Water Skiing. Englewood Cliffs, New Jersey: Prentice-Hall, Incorporated, 1958. 242 p.

Prince, Walter N. Water Skiing for All. New York: Chilton Company, 1959. 181 p.

"Pushball--The Biggest Plaything," St. Nicholas, 44:80-81, November, 1916.

Randall, John. "Dog Shows," Collier's Encyclopedia, Volume VI. New York: Collier and Son Corporation, 1956. 668 p.

Reynolds, Quentin. "Round and Round," Collier's, 98:15, August 22, 1936.

"Roaring Doodlebugs," Sports Illustrated, 2:20-21, September, 1936.

Schweikert, Harry A., Jr. "The History of Wheelchair Basketball," Wheelchair Basketball Tournament, Official Program, 1960, n.p.

"The Science of Skin and Scuba Diving," A Project of the Conference for National Cooperation in Aquatics. New York: Association Press, 1957. 306 p.

"Skeet: Shotgun Golf Holds Its First National Tournament," Newsweek, 6:25, September 7, 1935.

"Sport," Time, 27:24, February 3, 1936.

"Sports," Literary Digest, 124:28, September 4, 1937.

Staley, S. C. The World of Sport. Champaign, Illinois: Stipes Publishing Company, 1955. 46 p. (Mimeographed).

Stecher, William A. <u>Games and Dances</u>. Philadelphia: John Joseph McVey, 1926. 405 p.

Swain, L. E. "Touch Football with the Kick," <u>Journal of Health and Physical Education</u>, 3:34, September, 1932.

Valentine, E. Seton and Tomlinson, F. L. <u>Travels in Space</u>. London: Hurst and Blackett, Limited, 1902. 328 p.

Wells, Reginald. "The World's Greatest Pleasure Horse," <u>Sports Illustrated</u>, 3:56-58, August 29, 1955.

"Why the National Clubs?" <u>Karting Handbook</u>, Trend, 195:88-91, 1960.

Zim, Herbert S. <u>Parachutes</u>. New York: Harcourt, Brace and Com-Company, 1942. 252 p.

CHAPTER 3

A CULTURAL HISTORY OF SPORT IN ILLINOIS, 1673-1820

Phyllis J. Hill
University of Illinois, Urbana

Introduction

The problem which motivated this particular piece of research
is actually a part of a larger problem: does the history of American
sport contain factors of change, adaptation, and expansion which parallel those of the culture as a whole? The basic premise of the study
is that the sporting habits and customs of any people are an index of
their national character. As the writer accepted this premise, it
seemed reasonable to conclude that a sports index must have evolved
in the same ways as other indices of national character.

In 1931, as an outcome of her doctoral dissertation at Columbia
University, Jennie Holliman published a book entitled American
Sports (1783-1835). The primary purpose of the work was "to show
. . . American people of this period, as revealed in their sports and
recreations." (Holliman, 1931, v). To accomplish a cultural approach to the history of sport, she attempted to trace the origins of
American sports which were practiced during the period and to show
the reactions of the people to them. Generally, she concluded that the
principal American sports were rooted in England, as can be witnessed by the following quotation:

> They (sports) were brought to America by the English. Here,
> the sports and recreations grew according to the environment
> found in the new country. Yet it is evident that sports in
> America during these years of history kept the color and form
> of European sports. (Holliman, 1931, p. 10).

Sports and physical education historians have largely agreed
with Miss Holliman that American sport is, indeed, a "gift" of our
English heritage, and while they have accepted the form of sport as
English, no very clear-cut answer has been given to the question:

Editor's Note: This third essay was obtained from Professor
Phyllis J. Hill of the University of Illinois, Urbana. It represents an
instance where a research technique was borrowed from cultural
anthropology and employed to strengthen an historical study. Dr.
Hill carried out a cultural history of frontier sport in Illinois from
1673 to 1820, and readers should find this article to be highly informative and exceptionally well done.

why are Americans unable or unwilling to apply the English philosophy of sport to English sporting forms? The ethics which largely control the practices and purposes of English sport have been deeply rooted in the philosophies of amateurism and of gentlemanly conduct, of sport for sport's sake, (McIntosh, 1958, pp. 13-24), while in America sport has been closely tied to personal achievement and success, which are largely controlled by the ethics of work and of professionalism. A historian might well ask: if the philosophies and ethics which govern the practices of English sport and of American sport are antithetical, can the forms of American and of English sport, in fact, be the same? Miss Holliman concluded, at least in the period from 1785-1835, that they were.

The conclusions of this study brought forth several concerns, which the writer believed had historical significance. In the first place, we were asked to believe that sport, possibly a fundamental form of human expression, was not altered appreciably by its contacts with a new environment even as late as 1835. This seemed strange in light of the changes in other forms of human expression, i.e., religious, political, economic, and educational philosophies as they were observed in the institutions of the time. One might conclude that either sport is not a fundamental form of human expression which is shaped and molded by its cultural environment and, therefore, would not parallel the development of other institutions, or that it is so fundamental that it transcends all nationalistic boundaries. Dixon Wecter, noted social historian, denied the latter premise in 1937 when he wrote (p. 428):

Some day sport will find its wide-visioned philosopher. He will show us how cricket, with its white clothes and leisured boredom, and sudden crises met with cool mastery to the ripple of applause among the teacups and cucumber sandwiches, is an epitome of the British Empire. Or the bullfight with its scarlet cape and gold braid, its fierce pride and cruelty, and the quixotism of its perils, is the essence of Spain. Or that football with its rugged individualism, and baseball with its equality of opportunity, are valid American symbols, while Soviet Russia favors mass games. . . . Most of these things have been felt or hinted before, but their synthesis has never been made.

In this quotation, Wecter implied that sports were an index of national character. If this is so, it seems reasonable to conclude that this index must have evolved historically in the same ways as other indices of national character. However, according to Holliman, no appreciable evolution had occurred by 1835, more than two hundred years after the founding of this country.

There are two conceivable answers to the questions raised by the Holliman study: (1) either the people studied were not representative enough and/or (2) the period in which she studied them was not long enough for her to detect the subtleties of cultural change. There is some evidence to support both of these possible criticisms, in that a study of her bibliography reveals that the major portion of the data was gathered from diaries, periodicals of the time, and newspapers of the Atlantic Seaboard. It is noted here that the lives of most literate people who continued to occupy East Coast cities (certainly not a representative group!) were closely tied to England at this time. This was particularly true of the Southern leisure class, by far the largest group studied by Holliman.

While the Holliman study had great merit, the generalizations based upon the data gathered have seemingly contributed some misinformation to the history of American sport. However, before any further conclusions could be drawn, additional research was necessary.

To study sport as an index to national character is the work of a lifetime, but it does appear that the question lends itself to numerous smaller studies whose collective answers would shed a great deal of light on the problem at hand. Additionally, if sport is a cultural phenomenon, its study must be approached through cultural analyses. The following study is an example of the research that is needed.

Statement of the Problem

In an attempt to answer the question: is sport an index to national character, a study was made of the habits and customs of three discrete cultures in ascendance in Illinois during the period of 1673 to 1820. The cultures subjects to analysis were the Indian tribes of Algonquin stock commonly referred to as the Illini or Illinouek; the French who settled the southwestern area of the territory after 1969 as a result of France's imperialistic ventures into the New World; and the English-speaking peoples who came out to the Illinois country during or shortly after the American War for Independence.

Method of Research

Following the assumption that all cultural institutions are but elaborations of the basic goals of each culture, the political structure, the community and family life, the economic system, and the forms of education, religion, and leisure of each cultural unit were probed for their commonalities. Throughout the above process, the researcher was testing the theory of cultural configuration--that is, that the basic values and drive states of a selected culture would show up in an analysis of each institution promulgated by that cultural unit. The next step was to identify and to analyze the basic sporting patterns and

ethics of that culture to determine what, if any, were the relationships between its sporting practices and its cultural institutions.
This process was based upon the premise that human behavior is invariably a total and patterned response. Thus, if sport had achieved
the status of a cultural institution, its forms and ethics would be
functionally related to those of the established cultural institutions.
If it could be determined further that a complete cultural configuration occurred, sport would qualify as a cultural institution and,
thereby, as an index to national character. The process described is
referred to by anthropologists as the cultural description approach;
its purpose is to seek out configurations of cultural values.
(Honigman, 1954, pp. 57-61) Although sport is not usually treated in
most studies using this approach, for reasons given in the above
discussion, the researcher felt justified in extending the use of
cultural description to another area of human behavior. In this study
all three cultures were treated by the same analysis, but no attempt
was made to seek relationships among the cultural units. Each culture was analyzed as a separate entity. When the research revealed
in some instances that there were common cultural features among
groups, these were accepted as tentative indications of universality.
The data were gathered by the historical-bibliographical method, subjected to analysis, and ordered chronologically by cultures.

As a sub-problem of the original problem, an attempt was made
to identify the dominant cultural practices in both the former and the
present environments of the American settlers. This was done to test
Webb's frontier thesis which suggests that the critical variable in the
alteration of cultural institutions is that of the environment. (Webb,
1952, p. 64) If all cultural institutions were adapted and changed
according to environmental conditions and if sport were altered
accordingly, much support would be gained for the original hypothesis.

For the purpose of this study, sports were defined as those activities which "required physical performance (movement), involved
some degree of skill and/or set of recognizable rules," (Eyler, 1961,
p. 8), and would be intended to amuse or to divert. However, soon
after the analysis was begun, it became apparent that this operational
definition would not discriminate clearly between certain work activities and certain sport activities. In the interest of the integrity and
original intent of the earlier definition, two questions were asked
which the writer believed would not substantially change the premise,
but would instead give it new dimensions and clarity: (1) did the analysis of each reference reveal that there were imposed limitations in
the forms of rules, codes, or techniques which heightened the difficulty of the task and, thereby, increased its challenge; and/or (2) did
the document contain references to the thrill and/or to the diversion-
ary nature of the activity, which added emotional peaks to everyday
life or changed a man's concept of his stature?

Discussion of Data

Indian Cultural Practices

The first culture studied was that of the Illinois Indian tribes.
The dominant institutions and beliefs were identified and probed for
their commonalities. A cultural configuration was present as it was
found that each institution was directly involded in pattern mainten-
ance--in the perpetuation of culturally-assigned roles. Among these
tribes, sport was found to serve a fundamental role in pattern maintenance and, therefore, qualified as a cultural institution.

The most popular activities among the male members of the
tribe was lacrosse (la crosse), a ball game somewhat like contemporary American football; a ball game resembling contemporary field
hockey; forms of hunting and fishing; running of foot races; and throwing games. The women played a game which greatly resembled
volleyball and one requiring extraordinary dexterity (the throwing and
catching of a two-inch ring with a long stick). Almost all of these activities had achieved ritualistic status. The movement patterns and
the goals of each game were symbolic of their mythical origins.
There was no evidence that any of the sports identified were imported
into America at any time before or after the coming of the European.
On the contrary, the Indian sporting practices appeared to be the direct and natural outgrowth of aboriginal institutions in America.

As to sporting ethics, Indian practices appeared to be more
closely related to what are usually regarded as work ethics. It is to
be noted that materialism was greatly apparent in this analysis. The
profit motive could be seen in sport as well as in work. The profit in
sport was also apparent in the gambling that took place. Among the
tribes, gambling was associated with even the most loosely organized
activities.

The analysis of the sporting activities revealed that there was
a positive relationship between such personality traits as dominance,
aggression, and individualism and the more popular sporting forms.
As these traits lend themselves readily to testing, it was natural in
the drive for power that competition was one of the distinguishing features of Indian sporting practices.

French Cultural Practices

The second culture to undergo cultural descriptive analysis was
that of the French who occupied the Mississippi lowlands between the
Illinois and the Kaskaskia Rivers. In the main, the cultural institutions and ideas of this group were merely imitations of those of former environments. Centuries of feudal, cleric, and monarchical
despotism had trained the French to tradition, to subjection, and to

dependence. The institutional structure of the Illinois French culture counteracted any innovation, and the Churcn and state had combined to check the development and expression of enterprise and individualism.

Of sporting practices, very little could be learned. The few existing records were concerned with accounts of team canoe races and of hunting and fishing. The lack of information led to the postulation that the French did not possess the characteristics necessary to the development of sporting patterns. They were seemingly a cooperative rather than a competitive society. Individualism, enterprise, and the need for adventure were simply not apparent from the analyses. If it could be agreed that these traits were necessary to sport, then some understanding of the failure of the French to develop sporting practices could be gained. Sport, or lack of it, was quite as much an index to the national character of the French as it was of the Tribes of Illini.

Cultural Practices of the American Settlers in Illinois before 1820

The third group studied were those English-speaking peoples who lived in the Illinois country between 1783 and 1820. These people were far from being a homogeneous group ethnically. Primarily, they were of German or Scotch-Irish descent, migrating most recently from the back-countries of Maryland, Virginia and the Carolinas or from Kentucky and Tennessee. Their first generation experiences in colonial America were in varying degrees patterned after their Old World heritages. However, their colonial experiences on the western slopes of the Appalachians had begun to modify their former cultural expressions, so that by the time they crossed the Ohio into Illinois certain generalizations as to character could be made. These people shared high energy levels, a love of speed, and a need for power or self-determination. An analysis of the existing institutions revealed that change and innovation were constantly in evidence to allow for the personal desires and characteristics of the people. The power factor was the significant variable in the determination of cultural practices. This factor so necessary to survival in the wilderness became the prominent value. A configuration occurred as all cultural practices reflected the major value: the power drive.

The most popular sporting practices were forms of hunting and shooting, fighting and wrestling, and horse racing. Whatever the form, all events were competitive. There was no evidence that ball games or games of European origin were among the practices of these people, nor was there any evidence that these people accepted any sporting ethic that did not develop out of environmental influence. The sporting practices in Illinois were distinctly American.

In regard to the relationship between sport and cultural institutions, once more a configuration occurred. Sport was only another arena for manifesting the same drives. On this basis, sport was accepted as a cultural institution and, therefore, as an index to national character.

Conclusions

In Illinois from 1673 to 1820, sport was definitely an index to national character. It not only reflected the goals and values of each of the three cultures, but was directly instrumental in the determination and maintenance of the goals and values of two of the three cultures. Moreover, in this period of study, sport qualified as a major cultural institution wherever the goal drives were positively related to self-determinism, materialism, and individualism.

The writer is well aware of the dangers inherent in universal prediction, of the risks of bringing the past too close to the present. It does seem, however, that these conclusions obligate some discussion of their implications.

The writer is forced to the position that American cultural practices, including sport, have been forged by environmental forces, rather than by Anglo-Saxon tradition unless one claims change and innovation as distinctly Anglo-Saxon traits. Following this line of thought, the English philosophy of sport, of amateurism, of gentlemanly conduct, and of sport for sport's sake is inoperable in a culture where sport is closely tied to personal achievement and success, and where work ethics and sport ethics are so close as to be virtually indistinguishable. Today, as we lament the professionalism and the conduct of American sport and seek to restore amateurism, let it be remembered that we have never recognized this as a value. Our cultural institutions stopped being English as the first settlers crossed the Appalachians. The solution to American sporting problems does not lie in English tradition. Rather, sport in America is a cultural phenomenon, and its problems must be studied and resolved in the American tradition. And, if all human behavior is, indeed, a total and patterned response, the understanding of sport can be furthered only when it is studied in reference to other human variables within the culture.

Selected Bibliography

Alvord, C. W. (editor). Cahokia Records, 1778-1790. Vol. II:
Collections of the Illinois State Historical Library. "Virginia
Series." Springfield: Illinois State Historical Library, 1907.

_____. The Illinois Country 1673-1818. Vol. I: The Centen-
nial History of Illinois. Springfield: Illinois Centennial Commission, 1920.

Babeau, Albert A. Le Village sous l'Ancien Regime. Paris: Didier,
1891.

Becker, Carl. Beginnings of the American People. Ithaca, New
York: Cornell University Press, 1963.

Belting, Natalie Marie. "Kaskaskia Under the French Regime 1703-
1763." Unpublished Ph.D. Dissertation, University of Illinois,
1940.

Birkbeck, Morris. Notes on a Journey in America, from the Coast
of Virginia to the Territory of Illinois, with Proposals for the
Establishment of a Colony of English. Philadelphia: Caleb
Richardson, 1817.

Blair, Emma (editor). Indian Tribes of the Upper Mississippi and
Great Lakes Regions Cleveland: The Arthur H. Clark Company, 1911.

Cadillac, Lemothe. Memoir of Cadillac. Reprinted in The Western
Country in the Seventeenth Century. Editor, Milo Quaife.
Chicago: Lakeside Press, 1947.

Clarkson, Matthew. Diary West of the Alleghenies, in 1766. Vol. IV
in Schoolcraft, Henry R. Information Respecting the History,
Conditions, and Prospects of the Indian Tribes of the United
States. Philadelphia: J. P. Lippincott, 1851-1857.

Collot, Victor. A Journey in North America. Paris: Printed for
Arthur Bertrand, 1796.

Continental Congress Papers, 1780-1788. Transcripts in Illinois
Historical Survey, Urbana.

Cullin, Stewart (editor). Twenty-fourth Annual Report of the American Bureau of Ethnology. Washington: Government Printing
Office, 1902-1903.

Eyler, Marvin H. "Origins of Contemporary Sports." Unpublished
Ph.D. Dissertation, University of Illinois, 1956.

Flagg, Gershom. Pioneer Letters of Gershom Flagg, 1817. Editor,
Solon Buck. Springfield: Illinois State Journal Company, 1912.

Flagg Manuscripts. Transcripts in Illinois Historical Survey,
Urbana.

Fox, Dixon (editor). Sources of Culture in the Middle West. New
York: D. Appleton-Century Company, Inc., 1934.

Gratz Papers. Transcripts of extracts from 1750 to 1850 in Illinois
Historical Survey, Urbana.

Holliman, Jennie. American Sports (1785-1835). Durham, North
Carolina: The Seeman Press, 1931.

Honigman, John J. Culture and Personality. New York: Harper and
Brothers, 1954.

Malinowski, Bronislaw. A Scientific Theory of Culture. Chapel Hill:
The University of North Carolina Press, 1944.

McIntosh, Peter. "The British Attitude Toward Sport." Sport and
Society, (editor) Alex Natan. London: Bowes and Bowes, 1958,
pp. 13-24.

Pease, Theodore C. The Frontier State, 1818-1848. Vol. II: The
Centennial History of Illinois. Springfield: Illinois Centennial
Commission, 1918.

_____ (editor). The Laws of the Northwest Territory,
1788-1800. Vol. XVII: Collections of the Illinois State Historical Library. "Law Series." Vol. I. Springfield: Illinois State
Historical Library, 1925.

_____, and Jenison, Ernestine. Illinois on the Eve of
the Seven Years' War, 1747-1755. Vol. XXIX: Collections of
the Illinois State Historical Library. "French Series."
Vol. III. Springfield: Illinois State Historical Library, 1940.

Pease, Theodore C., and Werner, Raymond. The French Founda-
tions, 1680-1693. Vol. XXXIII: Collections of the Illinois State
Historical Library. "French Series." Vol. I. Springfield:
Illinois State Historical Library, 1934.

Sparks, Edwin E. (editor). The English Settlement in the Illinois.
London: Museum Book Store, 1907.

Thwaites, Reuben (editor). Early Western Travels, 1748-1846: A Series of Annotated Reprints of Some of the Best and Rarest Contemporary Volumes of Travel . . . during the Period of Early American Settlement. 32 vols. Cleveland, Ohio: The Arthur H. Clark Company, 1904-7.

_____. Jesuit Relations and Allied Documents . . . . 73 vols. Cleveland, Ohio: The Burrows Brothers Company, 1896-1901.

U. S. Congress. House of Representatives Files, 1803-1820. Photostats in Illinois Historical Survey, Urbana.

Vaudreuil Manuscripts. Photostats in Library of the Illinois Historical Society, Springfield.

Webb, Walter. The Great Frontier. Boston: Houghton-Mifflin, 1952.

Wecter, Dixon. The Saga of American Society: A Record of Social Aspiration, 1607-1937. New York: Charles Scribner's Sons, 1937.

CHAPTER 4

MIND AND BODY IN AMERICAN THOUGHT DURING THE AGE OF JACKSON

the late John R. Betts
former Associate Professor of History
Boston College, Massachusetts

English works on health and the dictums of Benjamin Franklin, Thomas Jefferson, Benjamin Rush, and others had alerted Americans to the relationship of mind and body, but it was only in the Age of Jackson that the public began to recognize the dangers of sedentary life in a commercial, urban society. The twenties witnessed rowing races from New York to Charleston, pedestrian contests, and other athletic innovations such as German gymnastics. The writings of Gaspar Spurzheim and George Combes opened the doors to popular physiology, and the Journal of Health advocated "mens sana in corpore sano" as Andrew Jackson assumed the presidency in 1829.*

Physical strength of Americans in an urban society was inferior to that of their ancestors of the colonial era, and to that of frontiersmen, according to many reformers. The New York Mirror became concerned over health and physical degeneration, claimed "a healthy man in New York would be a curiosity," regretted the early fading of women's beauty, deplored the routine of schools, colleges, and seminaries, noted the total neglect of exercise in all social classes, and appealed for more writing on the subject of health. Businessmen foolishly excused their inactivity as the result of lacking time, and thousands were going to unnecessarily early graves.[1]

_____

Editor's Note: For Chapter 4 we are most grateful to the late Professor John R. Betts, an "outsider" to the field of physical education, who was warmly received because of his deep interest in the profession. He taught history at Boston College. His well-documented paper shows us that the gradual development of physical training in the schools did indeed receive support from the "outside world."

_____

* Permission was obtained from Martin Ridge, Managing Editor of The Journal of American History, as well as from the author himself, for this modification of an article by Professor Betts which was entitled "Mind and Body in Early American Thought," and which appeared in the March, 1968 issue of this professional journal (LIV, 797-805).

Health faddists were on the march. Sylvester Graham, a temperance lecturer, concerned himself with vegetarianism, over-indulgence, adequate sunlight, bathing, dress reform, sex hygiene, and exercise. The Graham Journal of Health and Longevity appeared in 1837 and related physical fitness to great achievement. Plato, Aristotle, Cicero, and Caesar had appreciated the dependence of a sound mind on a healthy body, it was argued, and so had Shakespeare, Gibbon, Byron, Scott, and Davy. The Boston Health Journal and Advocate of Physiological Reform carried Graham's appeal. He found exercise a tonic, thought horseback riding a preventive of pulmonary consumption, and warned, "Aged people, after they have retired from the active employments of life, must keep up their regular exercise, or they will soon become feeble and infirm."[2]

Medical men rivaled health cultists in discussing physical fitness. Dr. William A. Alcott edited the Moral Reformer and Teacher on the Human Constitution. His Library of Health encouraged swimming and gymnastics and praised exercise as a means of avoiding consumption.[3] The profession was especially concerned with the war on cholera, yellow fever, influenza, and other epidemics, but the well-being of individuals was thought to hinge in good part on exercise. Dr. John Collins Warren spoke to the American Institute of Instruction on the importance of physical education and lectured annually thereafter on the value of exercise in the development of the organic structure of the body. A study of muscular action was presented in Human Physiology by Dr. Robley Dunglison of the University of Virginia, while Dr. John Jeffries discussed "Physical Culture, The Result of Moral Obligations" in the American Quarterly Observer.

The plight of the American woman's physical development and health was emphasized in the medical and physiological writings of such physicians as William Alcott, E. W. Duffin, J. M. Keagy, Charles Caldwell, John Bell, Caleb Ticknor, and Abel L. Peirson. Alcott cited the English girl's vigor in his Young Woman's Guide to Excellence as a curative for deformity of the spine and noted Pestalozzi's influence. Caldwell, a student of Benjamin Rush, had toured Europe and held the chair of medical and clinical practice at Transylvania University when he published Lectures on Physical Education in 1834 and Thoughts on Physical Education in 1836. The doctor noted the increase of insanity and dyspepsia, which he blamed on political and religious agitation and the pursuit of wealth. Observing Dr. William Beaumont's discovery of the role of gastric juices in digestion, Caldwell recommended abandonment of excessive mental exercise exertion, regulation of passion, and the practice of muscular exercise. Physical education, he contended, was vital to the destiny of the republic: "Its aim should be loftier and more in accordance with the destiny and character of its subject--to raise man to the summit of his nature. And such will be its scope in future and more enlightened ages."[4] John Bell related exercise to feminity and grace in

Health and Beauty: An Explanation of the Laws of Growth and Exercise. Caleb Ticknor discussed walking and riding in his _Philosophy of Life_.

Abel Peirson, who had studied in Paris, edited the _Medical Magazine_. The prejudice against girls exercising in the open air, he declared, was aggravated by the passing of the spinning wheel with its muscular demands and by the imposition of a social code which permitted only sledding and battledore as feminine sport. Poor girls! "There is no amusement which could be contrived, better suited to improve the shape of females, by calling into action all the muscles of the back, than the game of billiards. But this game has unfortunately come into bad repute, from being the game resorted to by profligate men of pleasure, to destroy each other's health, and pick each other's pockets." According to the learned doctor, French women surpassed other Europeans in lightness of step, symmetry of form, and retention of agility and vivacity into old age. From duchess and leader of _ton_ to chambermaid and peasant girl, this vitality was due to the French love of dancing.[5] Feminist leaders also championed physical education for women. Catherine Beecher pioneered with _Suggestions Respecting Improvements in Education_ (1829) and _Course of Calisthenics for Young Ladies_ (1831); Mary Lyon at Mount Holyoke inaugurated a calisthenic quadrille; and Margaret Coxe features exercise in her _Young Lady's Companion_ as an antidote to the ravages inflicted by a half century of increasing luxury.

The wakening spirit caught hold of the educational movement. Professor Edward Hitchcock of Amherst cited the case of President Timothy Dwight of Yale as an example of the restorative powers of walking. He claimed that three or four hours daily were not too much to devote to moderate outdoor activity. Statistically, he found that 186 great men of ancient, medieval, and modern times had lived to the average age of seventy-eight, possibly due to physical culture as well as constitutional endowments. Andover seminarians heard Dr. Edward Reynolds of Boston deplore "the measured ministerial walk."

"Look at Germany," he advised, and imitate the ancients: "The same necessity which sent Plato and Aristotle to the gymnasium after severe mental labor, still exists with the hard students of our day."

Princeton's _Biblical Repertory_ lauded the intellectual benefits of rational gymnastics:

They not only minister present health, but look forward prospectively to firmness of constitution in subsequent life.

Most of the Gymnastic games, also, are of a social kind, and awakened an intense interest in the competitors; absorbing the attention, sharpening the perception, and communicating alertness to the motions of the mind as well as the body. Thus they become invaluable auxiliaries to the more direct methods of promoting intellectual culture.[6]

Theodore Weld's Society for Promoting Manual Labor in Literary Institutions encouraged active sports: "Their effects upon the economy are universal--are felt everywhere. A glow of pleasure, as indescribable as it is exquisite, diffuses itself over all the organs. . . The vigor of the intellect is revived, and study once more becomes easy and successful." Publisher Mathew Carey acknowledged the importance of Weld's work.

Other testimonials to exercise were given by numerous professors, ministers, and leading citizens. Thomas Grimke of Charleston declared the habit of exercise "creates a greater capacity for mental labor, a more enduring energy, a loftier enthusiasm, a more perfect harmony in the whole system of intellectual powers." Francis Wayland, president of Brown University, recommended three hours of exercise per day: "No man can have either high intellectual action, or definite control over his mental faculties, without regular physical exercise. The want of it produces also a feebleness of will, which is as fatal to moral attainment as it is to intellectual progress." In his inaugural address, Mark Hopkins of Williams claimed many students spent too much time in drinking, smoking, and eating rather than in exercises such as sawing wood, walking, or gardening. "It is now agreed," he observed, "that the health of the body is to be one great object of attention, not only for its own sake, but from its connection with a sound state and vigorous action of the mind."[7] The editor of the American Annals of Education and Instruction, William Channing Woodbridge, duly recorded the views of the Boston Medical and Surgical Journal and discussed the sports of children. Samuel R. Hall recognized play as the only source of pleasure for some school children, because "brilliancy and force of thought are the natural fruits of activity." And Orestes Brownson commented on the "Necessity and Means of Physical Education" at the American Institute of Instruction.[8]

Thought on exercise in the age of Jackson focused upon the common schools. The New York Mirror in 1833 warned:

The seeds of many diseases, which sweep hundreds and thousands of our most estimable men into premature graves, are planted at school by the injudicious ambition of teachers, who entirely overlook the body in their efforts to overcultivate the mind. Parents forget, in their zeal to clothe the brows of their children with the early laurel for the triumphs of learning, that learning itself is valueless without health. . . .

Pedagogues became aware of the refreshment of the mind provided b exercise. Victor Cousin's widely discussed Report on the State of Public Instruction in Prussia revealed that all Prussian primary schools supported gymnastic exercises, for graceful carriage strengthened "the good qualities of the soul." Jacob Abbott's The Teacher recommended battledore and softball at recess. The Essex County Teachers' Association in Massachusetts called for a quarter-acre area for play and exercise at each schoolhouse. Alexander Dallas Bache asserted, "A system of education, to be complete, must combine moral, intellectual, and physical education." Commissioned by Nicholas Biddle and the trustees of Girard College to study European schools, Bache noted the presence of commons or playgrounds for every school on the Rugby model. Central High School in Philadelphia and Houston Public School in New York featured the playground.[9] Entering upon his historic superintendency of Massachusetts schools and aware of the new conditions of urban life, Horace Mann read the Constitution of Man in 1837. Thus he commenced a long friendship and correspondence with George Combe, whom he considered the greatest living man. The first issue of Mann's Common School Journal appeared in 1838, asserting the involvement of mind and body and expressing dismay over the deterioration of the health of people:

> Mental power is so dependent for its manifestations on physical power, that we deem it not extravagant to say, that if, amongst those who lead sedentary lives, physical power could be doubled, their mental powers would be doubled also. The health and constitutional vigor of a people is a blessing not to be lost—certainly not to be regained—in a day. . . . Gradually and imperceptibly a race may physically deteriorate, until their bodies shall degenerate into places, which without being wholly untenantable, are still wholly unfit to keep a soul in.[10]

During the 1830s, sports gained a foothold in the press because of the rising interest in horse racing, prize fights, and walking matches. Popular publications were the American Turf Register, the Spirit of the Times, Horatio Smith's Festivals, Games and Amusements, Robin Carver's Book of Sports, and a few manuals on archery and games, treasured by lucky youngsters.

The rise of sports coincided with the social changes of the times—for example, with the growth of an affluent middle-class in the North and a leisured aristocracy in the South. It coincided with the emergence of a spirit of reform: interest in Utopian experiments, women's rights, penal legislation, capital punishment, a peace crusade, care of the insane, temperance, public education, and the abolition of slavery. Greater attention to outdoor recreation may also have been related to unemployment and the depression of the late

early forties. At any rate, labor editors concerned
with health and with the shorter work day. Men puzzled
flaws in an urbanizing society. Albert Brisbane, a popular-
of Fourierism, charged American schools with hostility to both
Nature and health; corporal dexterity and health, he thought, "were
sources of Internal riches."[11] Only a few reformers, however,
seriously advocated increased attention to public health and better
conditions for the working classes and the poor. Such was recommended by William Ellery Channing in 1840, by Dr. Lemuel Shattuck
in his study of the overcrowding and the tenement life of Boston, and
by the first report of the New York Association for the Improvement
of the Condition of the Poor (1845).

Sporting and athletic interest increased in the early forties as
reports of English activities became more common.[12] Pierce Egan's
Book of Sports and Donald Walker's British Manly Exercises capital-
ized on the acquaintance of many with Bell's Life in London, the
Sporting Magazine, and James Gordon Bennett's Herald, which pioneered in sports news. The transcendentalist Dial even published
Henry David Thoreau's translation of Pindar's Olympic Odes. Walt
Whitman used the columns of the Brooklyn Daily Eagle in the mid-
forties as a forum for discussing school playgrounds. In a pre-Freu-
dian speculation on a young boy's drive for power, Emerson observed:

> In playing with bat-balls, perhaps he is charmed with some
> recognition of the movement of the heavenly bodies, and a game
> of base or cricket is a course of experimental astonomy, and
> my young master tingles with a faint sense of being a tyrannical
> Jupiter driving spheres madly from their orbit.[13]

In the early forties, too, Caldwell's Thoughts on Physical Education
(1836) and Dr. J. Lee Comstock's Outlines of Physiology (1837) were
reissued and remained popular. Shortly before his historic surgical
experiment with Dr. William Morton's ether at Massachusetts
General Hospital, Dr. Warren published his lecture in expanded book
form and urged open-air exercise for factory workers.

Though specialization had begun to crowd discussion of personal
hygiene and exercise out of professional medical journals, popular interest seemed to persist and grow.[14] The water-cure system of
Vincent Priessnitz of Silesia, who came to the United States in 1831,
stressed walking, skipping, jumping, and running, "but what lady dare
do these things in these days of refinement?" The perils of urban
comfort brought a revival of the gymnasium. Sheridan's gymnasium
in New York catered to clergymen, lawyers, physicians, merchants,
artists, artisans, and schoolboys. Harvard scholars in 1842 worked
out under T. Belcher Kay, instructor in "the art of self-defense" to
Francis Parkman, who prided himself on "a rapid development of

frame and sinews."[15] In New Haven, however, activity
A student commented on the contrast with Cambridge in

> There is one great point in which the English have u_
> over us: they understand how to take care of their health. . .
> every Cantab takes his two hours' exercise per diem, by walk-
> ing, riding, rowing, fencing, gymnastics, etc. How many
> Yalensians take one hour's regular exercise? . . . The gym-
> nasium has vanished, wicket has been voted ungenteel, scarce
> even a freshman dares put on a pair of skates, and there have
> never been ridable horses in New Haven within the memory of
> "the oldest inhabitant."[16]

Taking note, men of Yale and Harvard formed sculling crews in 1843
and 1844.

Despite obstacles and even some religious objections, progress
in physical culture continued. Playgrounds were adopted in Cincinnati
and received the support of Henry Barnard. New York state schools
recognized the need of muscular exercise, and teachers "in almost
every school district" were said to have access to Andrew Combe's
Principles of Physiology. Illustrative of professional activity were
the work of the American Physiological Society by 1837 and the publication of Human Physiology for the Use of Elementary Schools by Dr.
Charles A. Lee. Charles Dickens, though noting the American deficiency in exercise and being shocked by the emaciated prisoners of
New York's Tombs, visited the Perkins Institute in Boston and found
blind boys engaged in active sports, games, and gymnastics.[17]
George B. Emerson lent the prestige of his name to the encouragement of walking, riding, gardening, sleighing, and general exercise
in the open air and sunlight.[18] In the Sixth Annual Report of the
Board of Education, Horace Mann expounded on the oxygenizing of the
blood through "the athletic exertions of manual labor or of gymnastic
sports," far superior to passive activities like sailing. Lack of space
in cities led to physical degeneration, Mann thought, but he was
pleased with recreational improvements in the schools during the decade up to 1845. Dr. David Thayer's gymnasium, he observed, was a
boon to Boston clerks, students, lawyers, and clergymen; and he
similarly praised Mrs. Hawley's gymnastic school for young misses.[19] The Michigan superintendent of education, O. C. Comstock,
declared exercise was "essential to physical health, mental vigor and
delightful study."[20]

Urban people, grappling with the need for schools and sound
pedagogy, also faced mounting sanitation, housing, and health problems in a society marked by its high mortality rate. The labor of
immigrant workers on canals and railroads and in factories and the
vigorous life of farmers and frontiersmen more than met their requirements of physical activity. But there were impediments for

.hers, such as old myths about night air and fashionable prejudices against athletic women. Early Victorian society in England, having reached a more advanced stage of industrialism, might hunt the fox, attend Ascot, encourage schoolboy games, introduce athletics and rifle shooting into the army and the military academies, and become disciples of Isaak Walton; but their contemporaries in America required an extra generation or two before the leisure provided by a maturing industrial system would become general enough to extend the health and sporting interests of the privileged classes to the populace at large. Religious hostility to amusement and recreation proved to be a continuing deterrent, and social acceptance of the machine raised doubts about the value of bodily strength and muscle. Still, the development of a nationwide system of education, the encouragement of child-centered educational programs, the immigrant's fondness for his active games, and the fear of physical degeneration made a breakthrough in attitudes toward recreation and sport by the late thirties and early forties. Rowing clubs in Boston, New York, Philadelphia, Savannah, and Detroit; throngs attending thoroughbred racing and trotting; matches between runners, pedestrians, and prize fighters; formation of numerous hunting and fishing clubs; sailing and yachting clubs in Atlantic coastal communities and on the Great Lakes; adoption of mass football, gymnastics, cricket, or crew at eastern colleges--all bore witness to the sporting fever.[21]

Mind and body were more intimately related to one another by the development of a native literature of pedagogues and physicians, by an awareness of English concern for exercise and German educational reforms, and by a mounting public recognition that the Puritan gospel of works lost some of its validity in a highly commercial, urban environment. Outdoor life took on greater appeal in the romantic call back to the solitude or to the primitive challenge of Nature; the woodland haunts of "Frank Forester" (Henry William Herbert) lured the angler and the hunter. Emulation of the frontiersman's vigor contributed to the mounting concern over the debility of college students, the fair sex, office workers, and children in the crowded tenement. Soon the voices of Edward Everett, Thoreau, Oliver Wendell Holmes, and others would aid the cause.

Events of the mid-forties were prophetic of things to come. As the nation looked to the threat of war with Mexico, the New York Yacht Club organized, and the Knickerbocker Club established the rules of baseball. In the near future German forty-eighters would establish Turner societies, Scottish Caledonians had introduced their native games, and Irish crewmen raced city regattas. Only in the generation after the Civil War would expectations be realized; but in the Age of Jackson, educators, physicians, and reformers had begun to develop a philosophical rationale concerning the relationship of physical to mental and spiritual benefits derived from exercise, games, and

sports. From the diffusion of ideas developed by the medical profession under the influence of the Enlightenment and by educators and
reformers affected by the romantic spirit, Americans were alerted to
the threat against their physical and mental powers that came with the
confinements of the home and school and the more sedentary habits of
the city.

General Bibliography
(as cited in the original article)

1. New York Mirror, X (April 6, 1833), 317-18, 343, 375, 392.

2. Richard H. Shryock, "Sylvester Graham and the Popular Health
   Movement, 1830-1870," Mississippi Valley Historical Review,
   XVIII (Sept. 1931), 172-83; Graham Journal of Health and
   Longevity, I (June 20, 1839), 298-99; Sylvester Graham, Lec-
   tures on the Science of Human Life (2 vols., Boston, 1839), II,
   658-59. Temperance advocates stressed the drinking of water,
   abstinence from or moderate use of liquor, wine, and tobacco,
   and the moral obligations of the pledge as keys to good health.
   Only a few linked exercise to temperance, although anatomy
   Professor Reuben Mussey of Dartmouth listed exercise as a
   substitute for "ardent spirits" in the cure of dyspepsia.
   Mussey noted J. B. Buckingham's story of Himalayan "athletae"
   in Calcutta who far surpassed British grenadiers and sailors in
   wrestling, boxing, and lifting of weights. Reuben J. Mussey,
   Prize Essay on Ardent Spirits (Washington, 1837), 44;
   G. J. Grosvenor, An Address on the Importance of Female Influence to the Temperance Reformation (Geneva, N. Y., 1842),
   20.

3. William A. Alcott, The Library of Health (5 vols., Boston,
   1837-1841), I, 250-53, II, 346; see also Health Tract No. 2
   (n.p., n.d.), 19 (American Antiquarian Society, Worcester).

4. Charles Caldwell, Thoughts on Physical Education and the True
   Mode of Improving the Condition of Man (Edinburgh, 1836), 77-
   91.

5. Abel L. Peirson, On Physical Education (Boston, 1840), 18-23.

6. Edward Hitchcock, Dyspepsy Forestalled and Resisted
   (Amherst, 1831), 203; American Annals of Education, II (Sept.
   1832), 449-59.

7. Promotion of Health in Literary Institutions (New Haven, 1833), 20-21; Mathew Carey, Societies for Promoting Manual Labor in Literary Institutions (Philadelphia, 1834); Mark Hopkins, An Inaugural Discourse (Troy, 1836), 13-19.

8. American Annals of Education and Instruction, III (Jan. 1833), 33-36, VI (Feb. 1836), 84-86, (Nov. 1836), 496; S. R. Hall, Lectures to Female Teachers on School-keeping (Boston, 1832), 110.

9. New York Mirror, X (May 25, 1833), 375; M. Victor Cousin, Report on the State of Public Institution in Prussia (New York, 1835), 194-98; Jacob Abbott, The Teacher (Boston, 1833), 205-06; supplement to the Report of the Board of Education on the Subject of School Houses (Boston, 1838), 35; J. Orville Taylor, The District School (New York, 1834), 213, 230; Common School Journal, I, (June 1836), 45, II (Feb. 1837), 16; Franklin Spencer Edmonds, History of the Central High School of Philadelphia (Philadelphia, 1839), 402; review of and extracts from George Combe, Notes on the United States of North America during a Phrenological Tour in 1838-39-40 (2 vols., Philadelphia, 1841) in Connecticut Common School Journal, III (June 1, 1841), 173.

10. Mary Peabody Mann, Life of Horace Mann (Boston, 1865), 59; Common School Journal for the Year 1839, I (Nov. 1838), 11.

11. Albert Brisbane, Social Destiny of Man, or Association and Reorganization of Industry (Philadelphia, 1840), 427-29.

12. The writings on sport for this period are extensive. Among the best general, yet critical, treatments are John Allen Krout, Annals of American Sport (New Haven, 1929); Jennie Holliman, American Sports, 1785-1835 (Durham, N. C., 1931); and Foster Rhea Dulles, America Learns to Play, A History of Popular Recreation, 1607-1940 (New York, 1940). See also John R. Betts, "Organized Sport in Industrial America" (doctoral dissertation, Columbia University, 1951).

13. Herman Melville, White-Jacket: The World in a Man-of-War (New York, 1860, 322-25; Dial, IV (Jan. 1844), 379-82; Edward Waldo Emerson and Waldo Emerson Forbes, eds., Journals of Ralph Waldo Emerson with Annotations (10 vols., Boston, 1909-1914), V, 410.

14. Among these were Guardian of Health; Health, a Home Maga-
     zine devoted to Physical Culture; Boston Health Journal and Ad-
     vocate of Physiological Reform; Monthly Miscellany and Journal
     of Health; Water-Cure Journal; and Journal of Health and Prac-
     tical Educator.

15. Mason Wade, Francis Parkman, Heroic Historian (New York,
     1942), 20.

16. Yale Literary Magazine, VII (Nov. 1841), 36-37.

17. Common School Journal of the State of Pennsylvania, I (Nov.
     15, 1844), 340; Eleventh Annual Report of the Condition of the
     Common Schools to the City Council of Cincinnati (Cincinnati,
     1840), 6; Henry Barnard, School-Houses (Providence, 1844),
     31, 45; District School Journal, II (Sept. 1, 1841), 21-22;
     Charles Dickens, American Notes for General Circulation
     (London, 1842), 15, 33-34.

18. George B. Emerson, The Schoolmaster (New York, 1842), 290.

19. Common School Journal, V (Nov. 1, 1843), 323, VII (June 16,
     1845), 177-80. Mann was said to appreciate "the great value
     of institutions for developing the muscular system in cities."
     Boston Medical and Surgical Journal, XXXII (June 25, 1845),
     844.

20. Comstock's 1845 report is quoted in Francis W. Shearman,
     (editor), System of Public Instruction and Primary School Law
     of Michigan (Lansing, 1852), 457.

21. The athletic movement was still in a formative stage. College
     men, in general, were not yet persuaded of the necessity of
     exercises and games; and many were guilty of "intense physical
     indolence." Francis Wayland, Thoughts on the Present Collegi-
     ate System in the United States (Boston, 1842), 118.

CHAPTER 5

A HISTORICAL STUDY OF THE CONCERN OF THE FEDERAL GOVERNMENT FOR THE PHYSICAL FITNESS OF NON-AGE YOUTH WITH REFERENCE TO THE SCHOOLS, 1790-1941

A. Gwendolyn Drew
Washington University, St. Louis

Introduction[1]

As the war threatened in 1939 the fitness of the youth of the United States became a subject of great importance. It had been known for some years that Germany had established a national program of vigorous physical training for all Aryan boys and girls. There was a note of warning for the world in the results of the rigid physical tests required of all German youth upon entering secondary school, and the order that every child be a member of a Hitler Youth group. Italy had adopted certain national methods in physical training and, as was revealed later, Japan had pursued a similar course.

Sports and activities of a recreational nature had been popular in the United States for some years; however, participation was far from universal. Three-fourths of the States had passed either mandatory or provisional laws in physical education, but the programs suffered, generally, from lack of facilities, personnel, and the legal provision for enforcing the laws.

Editor's Note: Professor Drew's willingness to allow the inclusion of this essay is greatly appreciated. It represents the "essence" of a doctoral study completed by her more than thirty years ago. The investigation traces the concern, or perhaps lack of concern, of the Federal Government for the physical fitness of non-age youth with reference to programs in public schools between the years of 1790 and 1941.

---

[1] An essay review of Drew, A. Gwendolyn. "A Historical Study of the Concern of the Federal Government for the Physical Fitness of Non-age Youth with Reference to the Schools, 1790-1941." Ph.D. dissertation, University of Pittsburgh, 1944. (Microcard, University of Oregon.)

Forewarned by the happenings in Europe and anticipating the role that physical fitness would again play in a world at war, educators appealed to the federal government for funds to promote a suitable program of physical education. Many professional persons believing that federal legislation and federal funds were solutions to this national problem supported this move for assistance to the States.

With the outbreak of war in December, 1941, the vigor and stamina of the youth of the United States became a focal interest. Though the war was obviously to be highly mechanized, the strength, endurance, and physical courage of men remained essential. The bodily condition which in peace time had been taken for granted became overnight the first major requirement for a nation at war.

The findings of the actual health status of men examined for the Army revealed that forty-five per cent of the registrants were found to have physical and mental defects. Immediately the government set up rigorous physical training programs for all of its military personnel. By Presidential order the Division of Physical Fitness as a federal agency was established in the Office of Civilian Defense for the purpose of developing a civilian program. The Division publicized the draft findings through public rallies and literature, and at the same time enlisted the support of schools, industrial organizations, clubs, and recreational groups to promote programs of physical fitness.

Recommendations for high schools made through the Division of Physical Fitness called for a physical training program of one hour each day, five days a week, with added hours of intramural and interscholastic competition in sports. No funds were available for the work, but it was hoped that local communities through their boards of education would make the program possible. The government, through the Office of Education, sponsored physical fitness clinics in each of the Army Corps areas to promote the program, inviting certain educational leaders to attend for the purpose of carrying the knowledge of the program and the desired results to their respective communities. The federal government, thus, because of the urgency of the problem, pressed the public schools to aid in the increment of physical fitness for all youth.

It was obvious through the years that the lack of funds had been one of the ills of physical education in the schools. It was obvious, also, that in the Second World War the government took a more active role in its relationship to the public school physical education program than it had previously assumed. It seemed logical to believe that some type of federal legislative action for physical education would be sought either in terms of mandatory laws or of financial asssitance. Using this information as a basis, it appears that the knowledge of the concern of the federal government for the physical fitness of youth

from a historical standpoint is valuable in order to underst[...]
quent government involvement.

Personal Views Expressed

Leaders in early American government recognized the practical attributes resulting from a program of muscular exercise. Their
writings evidence both personal and political concern for the dissemination of this point of view. Among these men, prominent and influential in national affairs, were the author of the Declaration of Independence, Thomas Jefferson; two of its signers, Benjamin Franklin
and Benjamin Rush; and the author of the dictionary, Noah Webster.

The projection of a concept of physical activity in national and
social affairs had advanced to a concrete educational provision suggested by Noah Webster. His recommendation appears to be one of
the first of this nature to be made by a man of national importance.
He pointed out that it was desirable for the growth of the young to
participate in athletic exercise, and specifically advised that a fencing school was as necessary a part of a college as a professorship of
mathematics.

Men of these times differed little in their view about the health
purposes they tried to serve; they differed more on the means by
which these purposes might be achieved. Manual labor attained the
focus among certain classes; military training appeared to army leaders the most adequate program for building physical efficiency; and to
others active exercise in gymnastics and sports appeared to warrant
major emphasis. Literature of this period contributed subject matter
in varying fields of thought. A number of writings were translations
from the German; others were of English derivation, while a number
were original American work. Terms used in the translations, such
as physical education and softness, were identical to those in use today. Dr. Edward Mussey Hartwell referred to this early era as the
"prehistoric period" of physical education.

Early Congressional Discussions

The need for the conditioning of youth was brought out as early
as 1790, when President Washington directed Henry Knox, Secretary
for the Department of War, to present his plan for a national system
of defense. The prospectus, known as the Knox Plan, invested the
legislatures of the States with the jurisdiction of seasonal camps, but
seemed to retain certain governmental rights of recommendation.
This was evidenced in the suggestion that no amusements should be
admitted in camp but those which correspond with war--the swimming
of men and horses, running, wrestling, and such other exercises as
shall render the body flexible and vigorous. The anticipated outcome

of the plan, so said General Knox, was to implant in youth a robustness of body which would be conducive to their personal happiness as well as to the defense of their country.

Although Congress took no action on the Knox Plan, it represents the initial consideration by the Congress of the United States for the physical conditioning of non-age youth. (Non-age is used in early Congressional records to signify non-voting age.) Furthermore, it served as the basic reference for the more advanced plan of William Henry Harrison in 1817. That it was initiated by General Knox may be of no significance, for in the diary of William Maclay, a senator from Pennsylvania, a notation under the date of April 20, 1790, divulges that a sentence from the Secretary (Knox) meant more than all the Constitutions in the United States to many people.

That the members of Congress were alert to the necessity of the good physical condition of the troops of the United States is brought out in an act approved during the presidency of John Adams and the vice-presidency of Thomas Jefferson. This set up the provision for specific stipulations concerning physical requirements.

The Congressional Report of the Board of Visitors to West Point in 1826 specifically pointed out the connection between preparation for war and emphasis on physical development. Military drills were held before 1826, but reference to gymnastic exercises was contained in the Report that year. The Board recommended that a gymnastical building be erected in order to provide accommodations for riding, fencing and military drill, and that, in order to provide for careful physical education, a teacher should be employed to superintend instruction in gymnastics. Nothing came of this recommendation nor of the next, for that matter. In the 1828 Report of the Board of Visitors to Congress, they reiterated their proposals of 1826 and added that the sedentary habits acquired at the Academy were particularly disastrous to the physical condition of the cadets, and that severe mental labor without corresponding exercise would undermine the strongest constitution. Even though there was a reiteration of the same subject the next year, no action was taken by Congress on any of the recommendations of the Board. The command at West Point changed in 1833. Evidently the new Colonel did not hold the view of the preceding one who was credited with influencing the Board in their reports, for the cause of gymnastics at the Academy slumbered peacefully for some years after that time.

No record is given during the period from 1790 to 1860 of any formal attempts to make legislative provision for the better conditioning of the militia except in 1817 and 1818. However, the difficulties encountered in training the militia were reviewed by Mr. Aaron Ward of New York in a speech before the House on May 31, 1843. Mr.

Ward's disclosure referred to the ineffective execution of the provision for specific exercise days in the program of the militia.

It would appear that legislative efforts to improve youth physically were initiated in this period but not sustained. Nevertheless, a growing concern for building youth toward physical fitness for service was developing.

Proposals for the Physical Fitness of Youth

The War of 1812 provoked reverberations in Congress concerning the efficiency of the militia, and President James Madison in his annual message to Congress in 1816 directed attention to this matter. In order to take some action in carrying out President Madison's suggestions, the House of Representatives passed a resolution which referred the question to a committee. With William Henry Harrison of Ohio as chairman, this report, made but six weeks later, was in the form of a prospectus for improving the physical condition of youth in order that they might be classified as able-bodied citizens.

Mr. Harrison, as spokesman for the committee, referred to the the inefficient physical showing of the men in the War of 1812. He derided the prevalent training plan of the period as incorporating an error common to all the military systems in use in the United States --the error of too short a training period. It would appear that Mr. Harrison was referring to physical conditioning, for he terminated this critical view with a reference to the physical decadence of the Romans. He said that it was not until the amusements of the theatre, the baths, and the public gardens had superseded the exercise of the Campus Martius that this degradation began to take place. The Committee made specific recommendations which provided for military instruction being incorporated in the curriculum of every school in the United States, and proposed that a corps of instructors from the army should teach the gymnastic and elementary part of the military education in every school in the United States. Such a program, as outlined by the committee, was expected to reach every child attending school.

In proposing the use of the schools for military instruction, the committee sought to reach youth at an early age. This was considered to be an essential phase of the program. The Knox Plan of 1790 had proposed training for youths as early as eighteen years of age, but Mr. Harrison thought that although the Plan concerned non-age youth, it was too late in their lives.

No action was taken by Congress on the report of the Committee, nor was any action anticipated. The object was merely to get the idea of the proposals before Congress, to give members an opportunity for cogitation on the matter, and then to reintroduce the plan. In order to afford an opportunity to use this procedure, Mr. Harrison, at the close of his report, recommended the adoption of a resolution to require the Secretary of War to lay a plan before the House which would provide military instruction to all the youth of the United States. This was to be accomplished with as little distraction as possible from the ordinary course of education. What action was taken on this resolution was not recorded.

The legal right of Congress to prescribe a course of training for the militia had arisen as a question of technicality. Congress held this power only when the militia were in the service of the United States. The jurisdiction of the preliminary training belonged to the State government. In order to provide for this detail of law, Mr. Harrison, for the Committee, proposed an amendment to the Constitution of the United States in the form of a resolution. It was advanced that Congress, concurrently with the States, should have power to provide for the training of the militia, and also to provide for teaching in the primary schools. The system for the purposes of pre-military training of the non-age group appears to have died in committee with the close of Mr. Harrison's term of office on March 3, 1819.

Extensive perusal of official documents disclosed no further records of formal proposals made to Congress in this early 19th century period. However, in a speech before the House on May 31, 1984, on the subject of the bill making appropriations for the support of the Army and the military academy for the year 1842, Mr. Aaron Ward, of New York, directed his remarks to the difficulties encountered in training the militia. He referred to an Act passed in 1792, which called for the enrollment of every free, able-bodied citizen and the demand that these men be present on exercise days. Since the states held the power for the training of the militia, there were unequal exercise periods: some states held annual rendezvous; while others assembled for review and martial exercise every second year; and still others only every third year. This was looked upon by Mr. Ward as inequality which had no justification. No action was taken to alleviate the conditions described by Mr. Ward, and it was some years later before Congress allied itself with a military training program.

Proposals for Pre-Military Training

The federal government acknowledged education as a national phase of American life, when, in 1785, Congress enacted legislation reserving certain township sections for schools. Two years later, The Northwest Ordinance contributed to this recognition by declaring a government policy encouraging schools and the means of education. The ordinances prefaced acts through which Congress extended the policy of federal aid for education to states. From the time of these early enactments to 1862, grants to education in the form of land or moneys were of a general nature. However, during the period of the

Civil War, when the war revealed a genuine need for physical conditioning, Congress invested itself with additional responsibilities.

The Morrill Act of 1862, passed at a time when the building of mechanical equipment had surpassed the progress of the agricultural phase of living, initiated the enlistment of federal funds for a specific type of education when it specified the teaching of agriculture, but included the provision that the institution concerned offer instruction in military tactics as well.

The force of the government sponsorship of military training was reflected in the physical training programs in the schools. During the Civil War there was a check on the gymnastic revival begun in the 1850's, and a growing prominence of military forms. There appeared to be general agreement that some form of bodily activity should be offered in the schools as physical conditioning: the strict militarists proposed military routine identical to that which was mandatory in the Army; and the physical educators proposed a training similar to that introduced by William Henry Harrison in 1817, which consisted of a program of games, exercises, and sports. The issue, national in scope, provoked discussion for some years. Allusions to the matter were made in newspapers and the governmental phase was opposed in the literature of the physical educators, who appeared to feel that Uncle Sam was an ardent supporter of military drill, but that the United States Government did not give the same encouragement to physical training. The federal government, however, did play an important role in fostering physical training by precept, if not through legislation. The United States Commissioner of Education, William T. Harris, presided over the Conference in the Interest of Physical Training held in Boston in 1889. The meeting was viewed as a great success in view of the prominent national educators who were in attendance, and the impetus the meeting gave to physical education in the schools of the United States.

The first formal attempt to enact national legislation affecting the physical education program in the public schools was introduced December 19, 1894. The proposal sought to permit the officers of the Army and Navy to be detailed as instructors to the public schools, and was an endeavor to extend the Act of 1866 which authorized officers of the Army to be detailed to colleges and universities. The Secretary of War and the Major-General commanding the Army believed that no better employment could be given to officers of the regular Army in time of peace than in a dissemination of elementary military education. In the subsequent revamping of the bill, there was considerable discussion on the number of schools which could qualify; one representative said fifty, while another thought there might be thousands. No one seemed to have the data, and no decisions were reached. It was clear that some persons thought there were more valuable things to learn in school than military tactics.

A new approach to the subject of military instruction in schools was initiated in 1896. Certain statistics on the number of rejections by the Army were used by the sponsor of a Senate bill as evidence of the need for new methods in the physical conditioning of youth. In the opinion of the sponsor, the emphasis should be on bodily conditioning through physical activities not of the formal military type. In order to meet the physiological requirements of growing youth, physical training should furnish a resistance to be overcome; should include activities performed with vigor and rapidity to use as many muscles as possible; should insure increased activity of the heart and lungs to improve the circulation and respiration; and should coordinate the action of the muscles and in so doing effect the training of the central nervous system.

In the period 1894-1897 nine bills and one House Resolution were introduced to enlist the support of the federal government in the physical conditioning of youth. Seven of the bills sought to amend certain Statutes so as to include public schools in the provisions; two bills attempted to establish a bureau of military education in the War Department; a House Resolution attempted to furnish equipment to public schools from the government ordnance supplies; and one bill permitting retired Navy and Marine Corps officers to teach in schools and colleges became an act.

Provisions for Pre-Military Training and Physical Training

Congressional considerations, which aimed to make it possible to detail officers of the Army and Navy to the public schools as instructors in military training, met with some direct opposition. The National Women's Christian Temperance Union, through its Department of Physical Education, declared that legislators were attempting to make the public schools a training-ground for war purposes. This society directed efforts against specific bills and, in an attempt to bring physical education to the attention of legislators and to the people, printed and distributed for general circulation over two million pages of pertinent literature written by specialists in the field of physical training. In addition, through their official publication, Mind and Body, the Turnverein sought to disseminate information supporting bodily conditioning through physical training as against that prescribed by the Army.

Simultaneously with the discussion of military training in the schools by Congress, the American Association for the Advancement of Physical Education (first Convention 1899) initiated a program designed to achieve a fuller recognition of physical training in the elementary, secondary, and higher educational institutions. The committee responsible for the work consisted of fifteen nationally known educators including Honorable William T. Harris, United States Commissioner of Education; President G. Stanley Hall of Clark University;

Dr. Edward Mussey Hartwell of the United States Bureau of Education; and the President of the Association, Dr. Dudley A. Sargent. The work of the committee was a stepping stone toward a national acceptance of physical education.

The attendance of educational leaders from the United States at The Congrès International de L'Éducation Physique, held in Paris in 1900, was effective in establishing the trend of thinking toward a scientific outlook in the matter of physical education. The conference, attended by representatives from all parts of the world, directed national attention to the physical fitness of youth. The object of the conference was to define the concept of physical education by associating it with the scientific conditions of human perfection and, as such, stimulate interest in this phase of education on a national scale.

The founding of the Playground Association of America in 1906 allied this recreational organization with physical activity on a national basis. This society held the initial meeting of its Board of Directors in the White House upon invitation of President Theodore Roosevelt. It was early identified with promotional work to encourage physical education in every school in the United States, and later played an important role in sponsoring the administrative phase of the Fess-Capper Physical Education Bills, as well as supplying funds to encourage the passage of the bills.

The need for legislation concerning physical education in all states was advanced at the National Teachers Convention in Minneapolis in 1902. It was contended that there was more money available for the education of school children in the United States than in any of the European countries, so that money should not be the determining agent; that enormous sums of money could be saved to the country every year if the hygienic and prophylactic values only were considered; that the educational and ethical values for building a self-controlling man and woman could not be estimated; and that everyone should keep working and agitating until physical education was established in every school.

Eighteen bills and resolutions, directed toward the improvement of the fitness of youth, were revealed in the official records for the period from 1898 through 1917. President Theodore Roosevelt lent his support to the movement through sending direct statements to Congress favoring the promotion of the teaching of military training in the schools of the United States. Secretary of War, Elihu Root, favored such a policy in 1902, as did Secretary of War, Luke E. Wright, in 1908.

Using the schools for the purpose of pre-military training was looked upon favorably by Congress, also. This is attested to by the

fact that bills directed to this end were passed in this period. House
of Representatives Bill 4742, proposed originally in 1899, passed
with amendments in 1901; Senate Bill 5918, introduced in 1902, was
virtually the same as the previous House Bill; Senate Bill 1399, in
substance the same as the previous bills, holding an added provision
for equipment, passed in 1904; and in 1909 Congress provided for
ammunition to be used for instruction in target practice. The 1909
Act was still contained in the statutes as listed in the United States
Code for 1940.

The initial proposal to provide for the physical fitness of youth
through a program of physical training was contained in a Senate Bill
in 1902. The bill proposed an executive department of physical culture. 1910 bills, introduced in both the Senate and the House, sought
to improve the physical efficiency of youth by originating a division
for the purpose in the United States Bureau of Education. A 1917
fourteen-page bill sought to promote physical culture through a plan
of cooperation with the states. Funds for the payment of teachers'
salaries were requested, and a plan for the training of teachers of
physical culture on a state-matching, dollar-for-dollar arrangement
was advocated. The bill carried provisions for awards and prizes.
No consideration was given to any bill during this period that was
specifically set up to aid in the physical fitness of youth through a
program of physical training.

Fifteen of the eighteen bills introduced into Congress between
1898 and 1917 were aimed toward the improvement of the physical fitness of youth through a program of military training, however. The
bills which failed of passage, with one exception, contained the approximate provisions of those that passed. They were lost in committee or tabled; none was actually voted down.

Proposals for Physical Education

That the youth of the United States were not physically fit when
their services were demanded in the First World War was brought out
in widely publicized draft statistics. The United States was a nation
unprepared to meet the physical responsibilities placed upon her.
The State laws which did exist had no way of bringing enforcement,
and many programs of physical education placed no particular emphasis on conditioning. In response to public interest, the United States
Commissioner of Education organized a working committee for the
purpose of sponsoring a federal bill directed to improve the situation.
The Playground and Recreation Association of America, through its
National Physical Education Service, acted as the central agent for
the work. Using the names of the sponsors, the Fess-Capper Physical Education House Bill and the companion Senate Bill were introduced in February 1920. These bills were afforded committee hearings and were the only bills entered on behalf of physical education to

receive even this amount of consideration. However, n
ever came to a vote. The bills were revised and re-in
the Revised Fess-Capper Physical Education Bills, but we
committee with the close of the respective Congress.

During the time the Fess-Capper bills were in committee, a
series of Department of Education bills, carrying in their provisions
a section on behalf of physical education to the amount of $20,000,000,
was under consideration. A number of revisions were made to these
proposals, but the section providing for physical education remained
unchanged throughout. These bills were re-introduced several times,
but passage was never realized.

During the Great Depression of the 1930's, certain acts provided facilities for physical education. The Works Progress Administration, established by Executive order in 1935, rendered a service
to the program of physical education through many channels. By
1939 this agency had figured in the construction and repair of facilities to the following extent: playgrounds, $33,952,863; athletic fields,
$30,119,348; bathing beaches and outdoor swimming areas,
$6,236,317; and social and recreational buildings including indoor
pools, $47,697.146. The assistance given through direct projects of
the W.P.A. involved personnel in 15,288 communities in the United
States.

The National Youth Administration, established by Executive
order in June of 1935, supplied emergency scholarship aid to high
school and college students. Departments of physical education
realized thousands of hours of work in the keeping of records, cleaning, repairing and dispensing equipment, lining and general upkeep of
indoor and outdoor facilities, and clerical work in offices and miscellaneous jobs.

In 1940 the Schwert Physical Education Bill, backed by the
American Association for Health, Physical Education and Recreation,
made its appearance. Federal funds of $200,000,000 were requested
for the purpose of national preparedness through physical education.
Considerable promotional work was expended on behalf of the bill, but
it never emerged from committee. The same fate was afforded the
Revised Schwert Physical Education Bill of 1941. The non-passage of
the Schwert bills was a severe blow to many professional persons.
The Revised Bill seemed to have a chance of success, but hope was
gone with the sudden death of the sponsor.

In the period from 1918-1941 twenty-six bills with physical education or military training provisions were introduced. Six were directed toward military training; five were entered on behalf of general
education but included physical education provisions; and fifteen were
designed specifically to aid physical education.

Summary

From the time of the first Congress, the United States government has shown concern for the physical fitness of youth and has recorded the ideas of the legislators. Thoughts on physical education
appear not only in formal bills (although bills are interesting reading),
but also in comments and speeches from the floor. The latter provide exciting reading in Americana.

There is written evidence of the conflict of military versus non-
military training methods for conditioning, and a clear picture of
where Congress stood on money matters. Congress acted on military
training bills which involved no additional expense to the government,
and did not act on physical education bills which contained clauses for
federal funds. However, there was no positive expression on the part
of Congress, to 1941, which directly reflected unwillingness to provide for physical fitness through a program of physical training in the
schools. This much can be said, since no bill directly identified with
physical education reached a status commanding Congressional ballot.

CHAPTER 6

THE CONTRIBUTIONS OF LABOR LEADERS TO PHYSICAL EDUCATION

Arthur Weston
Brooklyn College of the City University of New York

To a surprising degree the growth of organized labor in the United States and the shaping and molding of American physical education have travelled parallel routes in the historical expansion of their roles on the American scene.[1]

From the vantage point of 1962, it is clear that the American people have come to accept trade unions as an essential part of the democratic way of life. However, the powerful labor organizations create serious problems that affect the whole economy. But the labor leaders have never been able to become an island unto themselves since they, too, are affected by all the pressures that interact in an expanding national economy.

To gain an insight into the attitudes, views, and contributions of labor leaders and their organizations to physical education, it is necessary to examine closely the following points. How is physical education interpreted by labor leaders; in other words, what is their conception of physical education as to the aims and contributions of physical education? Have labor leaders supported physical education as an essential part of the school and college curriculum? Have their views and activities concerning physical education changed with the evolution of American society? Has labor been a powerful cultural force that has had a marked effect on the development of American physical education?

To interpret correctly the actions of the labor leaders, one must examine the developments among the labor groups as they evolved from Colonial America to the present. In Colonial America

Editor's Note: This interesting paper about the contributions of labor leaders to physical education over the years was first presented at the AAHPER Convention in Cincinnati in 1962. Dr. Weston very kindly consented to our use of the essay in this particular volume.

[1] A paper presented at the AAHPER Convention, History and Philosophy Section, Cincinnati, Ohio, April, 1962.

the settlers had to devote nearly all their time and energy to securing food, clothing, and shelter and protection against a hostile environment. Organized health and physical education programs were not a part of their daily routine. It was not until the close of the eighteenth century that the shopkeepers began to form local trade societies which gradually evolved into the organized labor movement. This movement had an important influence upon physical education and recreation in the nineteenth century with the transformation of an agricultural economy into an industrial age which brought increased leisure to the laboring masses. But the laws of Colonial America were against play, pastimes, and leisure. Without stringent laws, the ruling fathers feared that the workers would frequent taverns and engage in sports and games. Participation in sports and pastimes was generally considered sinful and a dishonor to God, since leisure symbolized the triumph of evil over truly spiritual values. To condemn sports and pastimes was a vote for the moral and upright way of life.

The strength of labor became apparent in the 1830's, when the National Trades' Union secured a ten-hour day for the workers in many trades. "Our object in the formation of the National Trades' Union," declared its organ, The Union, on April 21, 1836, ". . . was to raise in the estimation of themselves and others, those who are the producers of the necessities and luxuries of life." John Ferral, the aggressive handloom weaver of Philadelphia, stated that this union promoted the activities of the German Turnverein with its physical activity which is essential for every family. This union was a powerful force behind German gymnastic programs in the Pennsylvania schools in the nineteenth century. Ferral, in backing the ten-hour day for the union, stressed the need for physical education instructional programs in the schools that would provide activity skills for family participation. Ferral's position on physical education was supported by Ely Moore, who was the first president of the National Trades' Union. Moore, originally a student of medicine, abandoned the medical field due to ill health and became a printer. He entered actively into the labor movement; he visited annually many schools in New York City, and is credited with stressing the need to participate in outdoor sports and games.

Thomas Wentworth Higginson asked in the Atlantic Monthly in 1858, "Who in our society really takes exercise?" Soon a renewed campaign was started to eliminate prejudice against sports and games as an idle diversion and encourage more active participation in outdoor sports and pastimes. Labor leaders quickly came to the support of outdoor exercise to conserve National health, and more barriers to leisure-time physical activity began to fall. Labor leaders were instrumental in promoting outdoor recreation as an important feature of American life.

A national labor union was created in 1866 with William H. Sylvis as President. Although this attempt to create a National union gained only a small measure of success, it promoted the need for an eight-hour day which was to have a direct bearing on twentieth century leisure and recreation. As William H. Sylvis completed his first year in office, an editorial in the New York Sun stated that "never has a labor leader been so devoted to the cause of improving the health and welfare of the people." In December of 1868, Dr. Edward Hitchcock invited William H. Sylvis to speak at the Amherst College general assembly. In this speech he stressed the need for good health and physical stamina and referred to statistics of the Civil War showing the poor state of health of the young men of the country. Sylvis travelled widely, and on numerous occasions addressed school and college groups on the subject of health education and the need for physical activity. Thus, William H. Sylvis, and numerous other labor leaders of that period, considered programs of hygiene and physical activity essential to the health and physical stamina of school children and stressed the need for these programs in the school program.

The depression of the 1870's brought unemployment and want to the workers. This period saw the growth of national labor group-- such as the Knights of Labor--which later combined to become the American Federation of Labor. The valuable reform measures sponsored by the labor leaders in this period bore valuable fruit for physical education and recreation in the twentieth century. The New York Times of January 27, 1884 carried a release from the Knights of Labor stating that a national effort should be made "to provide recreational activities for the unemployed workers." The leaders of the Knights of Labor urged school and college officials to make their recreational facilities and equipment available to these people whenever possible. This concern was a preview of the national support given by labor leaders for the recreational needs of the masses during the Great Depression of the 1930's.

The national labor movement was molded into the American Federation of Labor in 1886 with Samuel Gompers as the first president, a position he occupied until 1924. The first principle established by Samuel Gompers was that "the unity of labor was to be promoted through education, health, and the welfare of the working classes." The active support of labor leaders for the sports and pastimes helped bring to an end the Victorian repression of sports and leisure-time activities. The support given by labor leaders to the sports movement was reflected in the sports' pages of newspapers and magazines. The New York Tribune carried some 500 columns of sports in the summer of 1886, and a sports' page was started by William Randolph Hearst a decade later in the New York Journal. This period found the 12-hour day giving way to the 10 with a two-week vacation; and recreation and health soon became an important concern of the workers.

During the 1890's Samuel Gompers visited Dr. Dudley Allen
Sargent on several occasions at the Hemenway Gymnasium at Harvard
University to discuss "problems in health and the physical stamina of
the people." Information from the files of the A. F. of L. shows that
Samuel Gompers was strongly influenced by Sargent to place greater
stress on the need for better health conditions among the masses. On
at least three occasions, Gompers was invited by Sargent to speak at
the Hemenway Gymnasium on the "nature of personal health." In
addition Sargent discussed with Gompers the question of manufactur-
ing gymnasium equipment for physical education. In Sargent's personal letters, a note from Gompers in 1896 shows that Gompers
recommended that Sargent take out patent rights on his intricate physical education equipment. But Sargent never did, and consequently
any manufacturer who wished took over the manufacture of the equipment Sargent had designed for physical education.

During the early years of the twentieth century, industrial
recreation gained stature through strong support from many labor
leaders and their unions. Samuel Gompers stated in the Trade Union
Advocate that a carefully planned industrial recreation program for
the workers and their families will secure goodwill in the community
at large, teamwork on the playing fields, encourages teamwork in
the organization, and improves the physical and mental well being of
the workers. Further, it is a good medium for establishing a better
esprit de corps among the various branches of industrial work. In
1919 a study was made in the many plants of the Carnegie Steel
Corporation to see how industrial recreational programs benefited
the workers. The conclusions drawn were to the effect that such programs improved physical alertness, created a better spirit, and
brought about more friendly relationships. And the place to learn
these recreational activities, according to leading labor leaders, was
the school physical education program.

As the shadow of the First World War fell over the United
States, Gompers, still President of the A. F. of L., was appointed
to the Advisory Commission of the National Council of Defense. As
the principle spokesman for Labor, Gompers supported programs of
physical education in schools and colleges as essential to physical fitness for the youth of America. The Philadelphia Public Ledger
stated in an editorial in 1918 that Gompers' fight for health and physical stamina among the union members was applied to the war effort
to promote youth fitness.

Many labor leaders and labor organizations were shocked by the
thirty-three per cent rejection rate of men drafted for military service as unfit to serve. Out of the accusations came an aroused public
opinion which supported physical education, recreation, health and
hygiene. Swimming pools, gymnasiums, and athletic fields for intramural sports programs were built throughout the country. State

legislation in physical education was given strong support by the
A. F. of L., and also by the United Mine Workers through the effort
of John L. Lewis.

In scores of ways, workers were taking over the customs,
mores, recreational events, and aspirations of the wealthy classes.
Social democracy appeared to have attained a new validity as the
American way of life. The A. F. of L. as labor's national spokesman supported a short week, greater leisure and recreation for the
masses, and sports and games programs through industrial recreation programs and in the community. Local unions in nearly all the
large cities supported bond issues for community playgrounds, swimming pools, and athletic fields. Labor leaders happily agreed with
President Hoover in 1928 when he said, "we in America are nearer to
the final triumph over poverty than ever before in the history of any
land." But only a few months later a host of unemployed citizens
faced the grim problem of existence, and an equally great number
toiled with little return as "The Great Depression" swept across the
land.

Health and physical education as one of the so-called "special
subjects" had "hard going" to survive the depression. Some programs were retained through the support of outside organizations
such as the American Federation of Labor. For example, they were
able to bring about a restoration of physical education programs in the
Chicago schools where they had been eliminated because of drastic
curriculum retrenchments. The A. F. of L. was instrumental in
Michigan in saving the state physical education law, and also passed
a resolution favoring the continuance uninterruptedly and undiminished
of the health, physical education, and recreation programs. The
American Federation of Labor, influenced by the value of organized
recreational programs in improving the morale of the unemployed,
repeatedly advocated the necessity of public recreational movements.
Similar support came later from the Committee for Industrial Organizations. The Federal Government, through agencies such as the
W.P.A., provided money and materials so that many communities
were able to construct and staff new gymnasiums and community centers. Organized labor supported all these attempts by the Federal
Government to raise the morale of the unemployed.

In 1938, John L. Lewis promoted the final steps in the organization of the C.I.O. with concern for the needs of the unskilled workers. He was a staunch supporter of industrial recreation. Correspondence in the archives of the C.I.O. shows further that John L.
Lewis believed that physical education programs are necessary for
growth and development of children, and also for them to gain physical skills for later leisure activities.

Labor leaders and their unions supported the organization of the National Industrial Recreation Association in 1941 to promote employee recreation programs. Early issues of this organization's journal—Employee Recreation—shows important support from labor leaders to organize company teams in the physical activities of softball, bowling, and basketball. Both labor leaders and management leaders supported industrial recreation as conductive to understanding and good fellowship, and as an excellent medium for establishing a better esprit de corps among the various branches of industrial work.

The attack upon Pearl Harbor in 1941 created an urgent need for National unity. Following this attack, John L. Lewis, speaking for labor, stated that "when the nation is attacked every American must rally to its defense." In his statement he supported physical fitness as essential to the war effort, and to bring it about there must be strong programs of physical education, recreation, and athletics. Later in the war, William Green, President of the A. F. of L., stated before the War Labor Board, that greater support must be given to physical fitness in the schools and colleges through strong physical education programs. This statement was followed with a doorbell-ringing campaign organized by R. J. Thomas, newly-elected head of the United Automobile Workers, to stress war-time responsibilities. As one aspect of this campaign, emphasis was placed upon physical fitness through physical education and athletics.

In synthesizing labor groups as a cultural force in American society, and their understanding and support (or lack of support) for physical education, we have seen extremely interesting developments. It is widely accepted that labor leaders and unions form one of the most powerful culture groups in our society. Even the most conservative business leaders accept the basic role of the unions in the National economy. The editors of Fortune Magazine recently state "the growth, power and prestige of the unions is one of the significant features of the modern free enterprise system, and is playing on increasingly important role on the political scene." The latter point was outlined in a U. S. News and World Report article of February 26, 1962 entitled "How Congress Sizes Up President Kennedy." One question asked members of Congress was, "what group in your judgment is the most influential with the President?" The group chosen was labor leaders. There was the feeling among the Congressmen that it was obvious that we now have a labor government, and labor leaders are having tremendous influence; after all, stated numerous members of both parties, the President owes his election to labor groups.

As far as the labor leader's understanding of physical education is concerned, it means sports and games, recreation, athletics, and physical fitness. The available literature in the field of labor shows quite clearly that labor leaders support physical education programs as necessary in the learning of sports and games skills for industrial and municipal recreation programs, and as an important medium for promoting physical fitness in time of national emergency.

Labor leaders see future advancements in automation resulting in more and more leisure time. At the A. F. of L.--C.I.O. convention in Miami Beach in December of 1961, a resolution was adopted by the delegates to promote a 35-hour work week to ease the problems of automation. In January of 1962, the Brotherhood of Electrical Workers in New York City responded by winning a 5-hour day as part of a 35-hour work week. Following this development, Arthur Goldberg, Secretary of Labor, stated in Washington that a shorter work week is absolutely essential to combat the ills of automation. The National Advisory Council of the A. F. of L.--C.I.O. then went on record with a statement concerning automation which had one section pertaining to leisure. The statement was "Labor leaders have a responsibility to help mobilize recreation resources and to support physical education programs." Walter Reuther stated that labor leaders will be the most powerful influence in shaping leisure time programs during the coming years of this century. He went on to emphasize that labor leaders as a group are giving careful attention to the report of the Outdoor Recreation Commission which was recently made public. This study--commissioned by President Eisenhower in 1956 and directed by Lawrence Rockefeller--analyzed the recreational needs of the American people through the year 2000. Among their many findings was a special emphasis upon increased leisure and more spending money; and a much greater need for sports and games programs that will become the medium of recreation programs.

While labor leaders have not usually spoken in the vein of the well-qualified physical education teacher concerning physical education in the school curriculum, labor leaders have, nevertheless, been a powerful force in supporting physical education for recreation and physical fitness.

CHAPTER 7

NATIONALISM IN AMERICAN PHYSICAL EDUCATION
(1880-1920)

Harold J. VanderZwaag
University of Massachusetts, Amherst

The nineteenth century was a period during which the United
States went through several stages in the development of its nationalism. The first half of the century was characterized by the growth
of both national and sectional feelings in this country. However, the
ties with the "old world" remained strong during this period.
Following the Civil War, our nation set about to re-establish itself on
a firm national basis. By the end of the century, this nationalism had
been extended to a type of internationalism, in which the United States
sought to exert its influence upon other nations through its newly
formed institutions.[1]

This process of development was not restricted to political
institutions. Other forces were at work developing our economic,
religious, social, and educational institutions along a similar course.
The changes in these areas did not always occur at the same time or
at the same rate, but the interacting of these major historical forces
was always evident.

In light of our nineteenth century historical development, it is
not surprising that many of the roots of our present-day programs of

---

Editor's Note: Chapter 7 was contributed upon the Editor's
request by Professor Harold J. VanderZwaag, University of
Massachusetts. This essay explains most succinctly some of the elements of nationalism present in developing American physical education between the years of 1880 and 1920. Dr. VanderZwaag tells how
by 1920 "it was evident that the United States had evolved a program
of physical education which was characterized by informality and emphasis upon national sports."

---

[1] A paper presented originally at the 69th Annual Meeting of the
National College Physical Education Association for Men, Philadelphia,
Dec. 27-29, 1965. This topic is discussed further in Foundations and
Principles of Physical Education by Karl W. Bookwalter and Harold J.
Vander Zwaag (Philadelphia: W. B. Saunders Company, 1969, pp. 67-
73).

physical education are to be found in the closing years of that century.
This was another manifestation on the part of the nation to cement its
national unity by making our institutions more distinctly American in
nature. This was stated in 1881 as follows:

> The first use we should make of our regained liberty is, there-
> fore, the re-establishment of those institutions to whose influ-
> ence the happiest nations of antiquity owed their energy and
> their physical prowess, their martial and moral heroism, their
> fortitude in adversity.

Before considering the relationship between nationalism and
physical education, it will be necessary to clarify what is meant by
the terms "nationalism" and "physical education" in this context. It
is evident that the term "nationalism" could lead to varied forms of
inquiry due to its abstract nature. However, it will be used here to
include those composite unifying forces of a nation, as compared to
sectionalism and internationalism. Physical education would not be
classified as an abstract term, but it is frequently misunderstood as
to its content and scope. In our consideration here, it should be
understood to include all those motor activities which are carried out
predominately for education of and through the human body.

Viewing physical education and nationalism in these contexts, it
appears that the years 1880-1920, roughly speaking, were somewhat
of a watershed in the history of physical education in the United
States. For it was during this period that many of the international
and sectional ideas on physical education were considered, modified,
and merged into programs which make up our present-day bases of
physical education.

The earlier history of physical education in this country was
characterized by slow and sporadic development. Quite naturally,
the earliest interest was largely in physical training of a military
nature. However, Benjamin Franklin, possibly influenced in this respect by his contact with the royal courts of Europe, was one who
envisioned a broader scope of physical education. Interest in physical education arose from several sources during the first eight years
of the century, but the evidence seems to indicate that little progress
was made on a national level:

> In 1825, Professor Beck opened, in Northampton,
> Massachusetts, the first American school where gymnastics
> formed a branch of the regular curriculum. He has followers,
> but, considering our progress in other directions, his wheat
> cannot be said to have fallen on a fertile soil. Taking
> Massachusetts, Ohio, and North Carolina as representative
> States of their respective sections; it seems that at present

(1881) an average of three in every thousand North American schools pays any attention to physical education.

However, during the interim, there were periods in which physical education flourished on a sectional basis. An outstanding example was the wave of enthusiasm which accompanied the first introduction of the German Turnverein in this country at Cincinnati in 1848. Others followed rapidly in the North, mostly in the North-Central area. Members of the Turnverein were also active in support of the Union during the Civil War. But the Civil War years again, naturally, saw the popularity of gymnastics decline in favor of military drill. The situation noted above, as of 1891, can partly be accounted for by the lack of interest in physical education following the war:

> After the close of the war the ardor for military exercises naturally declined very perceptibly. Then, since the military exercises had in a great measure supplanted those of the gymnasium, there came a period of comparative quiet in both these lines of physical training. This did not follow immediately after the cessation of hostilities, for such a movement once underway rarely collapses suddenly; but before ten years had passed popular interest was at a low ebb; then, after a time, it began to rise slowly and gradually, but surely.

The earlier editions of <u>Mind and Body</u>, a national physical training journal first published in 1894, were much concerned about replacing military drill with a gymnastic system. In particular, the first managing editor, Hans Ballin, was a strong advocate of the German system of gymnastics. Following is an example of attitudes he expressed in some of his editorials:

> Militarism is concluded in this issue. A perusal of the answers to our inquiries will convince that there is a majority of teachers opposed to military drill, and an overwhelming majority prefers a graded system of physical training to military drill. It can also be observed that in cities and schools where German physical training is in use, the educators are strongly in favor of it, and opposed to the drill, while on the other hand, in schools where Swedish physical training is "claimed" to be in vogue, a sentiment for military drill is predominant, as in Boston.

In using the expression "graded system of physical training," Ballin was referring to a standard system of progressive exercise through gymnastic movements. The whole matter of gymnastic systems was one of the most pertinent issues of the time for physical educators. In fact, the Conference in the Interest of Physical Training held at Boston in November, 1889 was assembled largely for the purpose of discussing the various systems. The Swedish system of gymnastics had been recently introduced into the country, and its proponents were striving to compete with adherents of the revised German system for leadership. There was also the system introduced by Sargent at Hemenway Gymnasium of Harvard and various other "eclectic" systems. However, there was a great amount of disagreement as to whether there was or should be something which could be called an "American system."

Anderson of the Brooklyn School for Physical Training indicated that there was some form of an American system, which he would not change: "The so-called American system is as scientific as that of Ling. . . . We begin where he stopped. . . . I have much respect for the German and Swedish systems. . . . but taken as they are they will not suit the American people." Hitchcock of Amherst College was not entirely in agreement with the former: "The gentlemen have spoken of American methods. I have been working at physical culture for quarter of a century. . . . I do not, however, think that we have a system." Channing was one who expressed the viewpoint that there was too much discussion about systems: "I suppose we are all laboring for the same end, yet we have too much to say about systems. Who, I may ask, can lay claim to any special system?"

One of the leading spokesmen for those actively engaged in physical training was E. M. Hartwell. His opinions seem to be representative of those at the conference who felt that a change towards a more unified system of physical training was necessary in the United States:

> It is not within the scope of this paper to set forth the lesson to be learned from the best European system of physical training, or to show how fragmentary and defective our so-called American systems have been and are; but I remark in passing that a careful study of the German and Swedish systems of school gym gymnastics will be found an indispensable preliminary step for those who propose to organize a natural, rational, safe, and effective system of American physical education.

Writers of physical education history seem to be quite in agreement that the Boston Conference of 1889 was a landmark in the history of American physical education. Its participants included many of the leaders in the gymnastic world and many of the most prominent figures in American education. An interesting result of the conference is noted in the action taken by the Boston School Committee on June 24, 1890, when it ordered the introduction of the Swedish system of gymnastics in all the public schools of that city and appointed Hartwell as the Director of Physical Training in Boston.

It appears that a number of other cities in the East followed the Boston example, while the Germans strengthened their position in the Midwest. Thus, sectionalism was still a dominant force in our physical education. However, it would seem that the real significance of the Boston Conference is to be found in indications that there would be more changed in the future,--changes which would alter the course of physical education in the United States. For one thing, the papers and discussions had not been limited only to the area of gymnastics. Reference was made to athletics, and here possibly was the key to what the future would bring.

Rivalry among the various gymnastic systems continued throughout the 1890's with <u>Mind and Body</u> acting as the spokesman for the German system. A representative viewpoint of the time for that periodical is found in the August, 1897 issue:

> While I think that all advocates of thoroughgoing physical education ought to unite in a solid phalanx to win the great mass for their common cause, and that they should leave to time and to experience the decision whether any of the present systems shall gain predominance by assimilating from others, or whether at some future congress of physical educators the various systems shall be merged into one, an American system adapted to our national educational requirements,--I frankly say that upon the whole the German system, gradually developed and still developing by the thought and practical work of thousands of eminent pedagogies, surgeons, and other men of science of the highest standing in collaboration with the foremost physical educators, seems to be destined to form the substantial framework for the future, eclectic physical curriculum for the American school system.

Similar arguments were being presented by those advocating other systems. However, most seemed to be in agreement that some form of an eclectic system would be evolved. This was essentially the conclusion reached by James Boykin in the article written for the U. S. Commissioner of Education Report for the year 1891-1892:

> Furthermore each wave of popular interest which the history of physical training disclosed has left its impress upon the general character of physical training as it is today, and has contributed to make what will be at some future time the American system of physical training. Such a consummation has not yet been reached, or the German system, the Swedish system, and the Delsarte system, would not enjoy such high favor; but there can be no doubt that in its final development the American system will be a composite not of these three, as the "combination systems" of today generally claim to be, but of all combined

American experience in the field of physical training. The
progress of the evolution toward an American system even in
the last few years, may be distinctly seen, especially in school
gymnastics; for have not the Germans begun to adopt the
Swedish ideas of the day's orders and systematic progression,
and have not the Swedes aimed to make their gymnastics more
attractive, even going so far in one case as to use the German
bars, and in another to advocate the use of a combination of
systems for older pupils; and have not the professed followers
of Delsarte adopted exercises that are plainly muscle makers
as well as grace givers? And do not they all utilize much that
comes from the old English sports, from calisthenics, from
Dio Lewis, and from Sargent? And is not all this found side by
side and in harmony with military institutes after the plan of
Colonel Partridge, manual labor and manual training schools
after the manner of Dr. Cornelius and military drill in high
schools after the war-time ideas? And finally, there is reason
to believe that until this composition of forces, this amalgamation of system does take place, so that a well-defined and
well-established American system is produced, physical training will never rest upon a safe basis in this country.

There is evidence, however, that supporters of specific systems were not ready to agree with Boykin. A rebuttal to this article
was presented by Ballin in the March, 1896 edition of Mind and Body,
in which he pointed out that he saw little evidence of the trends referred to by Boykin. Ballin added that Americans were not prepared to
make a decision in this matter, because they had given neither the
German nor the Swedish system of physical training a fair test; they
had not yet accepted physical training as a necessary practice.

In spite of this apparent disagreement as to the status of physical education, as viewed by leaders in the 1890's, a trend toward more
centralization can be noted. The establishment of the (American)
Association for the Advancement of Physical Education in 1885 was an
evidence of this change. But it must be stressed that the change was
definitely not one which would establish a fixed system for the United
States; rather, it was more a recognition of a national need and a
national basis for physical education.

Again, it must be emphasized that this changing outlook was
entirely in keeping with changes that were taking place in other areas
in the lives of the American people. In the economic sphere, the
doctrine of laissez-faire capitalism was being challenged. This
meant that rugged individualism was losing ground to cooperative
enterprises that would eventually be extended to the national level.
Politically, with our western frontier closed, we found a new bond as
a nation in looking for new frontiers where the American way of life
could be spread. Socially, we were recognizing that the economic and

political changes were creating certain national problems that were
not present before. For example, the industrial revolution was
resulting in a population shift from rural to urban areas. The requirements for physical labor in this urban industrial life were found
to be quite different from the heavy physical labor of the farm. Some
people saw that new forms of physical activity for leisure time would
be required to meet the needs of this rapidly expanding urban population. At the same time, the shifting population had the effect of
promoting cooperation among divergent groups by bringing them into
proximity where more organization was both natural and essential.
Thus, the social individualism of the frontier was also rapidly being
altered.

It was in such an economic, political, and social setting that
the roots of our current programs of physical education can be found.
The nation was experimenting with a new nationalism and a new conception of democracy. Within such a framework, a philosophy of
physical education was developing which was to be distinctly American, although influences of the European background would always be
evident.

The foregoing provides the key to the central problem of this
paper: Has nationalism been the dominant force in the American
philosophy of physical education? We notice that the nineteenth century was characterized by sectional interests and struggles among
systems in physical education. This would not seem to be true today.
What was the turning point? We have already advanced the thesis that
the answer to this question is to be found in events which took place
between 1880 and 1920. But what were these significant events, and
why did they occur?

An answer to these questions is to be found in the steadily increasing interest in sports among the American people. The popularity of athletic contests was evident long before 1880. However, the
earliest interest was developed through athletic clubs and intercollegiate athletics. The mass of the people did not receive the educational benefits to be derived from such activity. Doerflinger incidentally alluded to this fact in his article for Mind and Body while
advocating an acceptance of the German gymnastic system:

> Athletic associations of all kinds have done a great deal to
> counteract the degenerative tendencies alluded to before. But
> their adherents form only a small fraction of the whole people.
> The great mass of the 70,000,000 inhabitants derive no benefits
> from them. National physical improvement can be accomplish-
> ed only through institutions that reach practically the whole
> people. In my estimation there is but one practical way to
> attain this: the introduction of physical education in the people's
> schools. . . .

Doerflinger was to be proven correct as to the means for gaining wider acceptance of physical education, but the emphasis in the physical education program did not take the form that he would have preferred. There is evidence that the English games exerted greater influence in the United States than any other elements of physical education from foreign countries:

> The Honorable Edward Littleton, an authority in English higher education, has written a notable article in the "nineteenth century" on "Athletics in Public Schools." He canvasses the system with some thoroughness, and arrives at independent conclusions regarding it, which will be of special interest on this side of the Atlantic, now that such vigorous efforts are being made to adopt the same policy in our higher schools.

Hartwell, a strong supporter of gymnastics, also made reference to the growing popularity of athletics on more than one occasion. In his concluding remarks at the Boston Physical Training Conference he stated: "We have at least established a department of athletics, if not a system. We have an inherited taste for out-of-door games that is not going to be squelched." This was confirmed in a later article found in the Report of the Commissioner of Education for the Year 1903: "On the whole, the advancement of physical education in America has been greater in the past twenty-five years than in any other period of its history. Obviously the most striking and rapid expansion has been in the department of athletics."

This trend reached a climax following World War I as a result of facts brought out during the conflict:

> Thirty-five per cent of the men in the first draft were rejected as physically unfit. . . . Only a minority of the men when they arrived at camp were possessed of the strength, endurance, agility, muscular control, and disciplined initiative necessary for the rigors of immediate intensive military training. This minority was made up largely of men who have had thorough and varied athletic experience under competent direction.

By 1920, it was evident that the United States had evolved a program of physical education which was characterized by informality and emphasis upon national sports. Such a program was entirely natural in view of our changing educational and political philosophies. Educationally, there was a growing recognition that a sound program of education must be based upon the needs of the child. This was also being recognized in physical education: "We are rapidly coming to a system of physical education for the public schools, which will be based upon the play activities of childhood." Politically, we were moving in the direction of more national government control while retaining state and local autonomy in some important areas. A parallel can be seen in physical education where we adhered to a national sports setting while retaining great divergence among local programs.

Such a program is entirely consistent with our concept of democracy, but at the same time it represents an interesting paradox found in the history of American democracy. Our institutions have moved in the direction of increased nationalism, while, at the same time, we have broadened the base of participation and retained individual freedom. For physical education, the years 1880–1920 were particularly significant in establishing its position as a representative institution of our democracy.

Bibliography

Ballin, Hans. Mind and Body. Vol. III. March, 1896.

Barrows, Isabel C. Physical Training (A full Report of the Papers and Discussions of the Conference held in Boston in November, 1889). Boston: Press of George H. Ellis, 1890.

Boykin, James. "Physical Training," Report of the Commissioner of Education for the Years, 1891–1892. Vol. I. Washington: U. S. Government Printing Office, 1894.

Doerflinger, Charles. "Physical Education in the United States: Retrospect, Systems and Aims." Mind and Body. Vol. IV. August, 1897.

Hartung, Henry. "Physical Training in Public Schools." Mind and Body. Vol. XVIII. September, 1911.

Hartwell, E. M. "On Physical Training." Report of the Commissioner of Education for the Year 1903. Vol. I. Washington: U. S. Government Printing Office, 1903.

Oswald, F. L. "Physical Education." Popular Science Monthly. Vol. XIX. May, 1881.

Small, Willard S. "The Nation's Need of Physical Education." Mind and Body. Vol. XXVI. March, 1919.

Underwood, C. M. "The Value of Organized Play in Physical Education." Mind and Body. Vol. XXVII. April, 1920.

CHAPTER 8

GERMAN TURNERS IN AMERICA: THEIR ROLE IN NINETEENTH CENTURY EXERCISE EXPRESSION AND PHYSICAL EDUCATION LEGISLATION

Robert Knight Barney
University of Western Ontario, London, Ontario

Introduction

One of the most fascinating aspects of viewing Americans in their cultural setting is witnessing their predilection for sport and physical exercise. Interest in sport and exercise in the twentieth century has grown enormously among Americans of every age, socio-economic status, and ethnic background. This exercise expression, viewed in collective fashion, is one which is underscored by the term "versatility," in perfect accord with the nation's so-called melting-pot society. The seeds from which this luxuriant foliage of physical activity grew were sown largely in nineteenth century American history. Among the more important of these seedling ingredients folded into America's emerging exercise culture was the German-American Turnverein experience. In fact, aside from the sports and games movement during the latter part of the period few developments rivaled those contributions made by Turners to nineteenth century physical education legislation and exercise expression – contributions which demonstrated elaborate organization and intense zeal and discipline, cast in the true spirit of Germanic thoroughness and efficiency.

The philosophy and resulting practices of Friedrich Ludwig Jahn, father of the Turnverein movement in Germany, placed the subject of physical exercise in clear focus during German social development in the first half of the nineteenth century. With a patriotic zealousness reminiscent of later German leaders, of which Adolf Hitler cannot be excluded, Jahn, almost singlehandedly, developed a vast network of Turnverein organizations, the very basis for which was the dedication toward raising the physical fitness and responsive

---

Editor's Note: A volume such as this would not be complete without a selection which explained something about the contribution of the German-American Turners to physical education and sport in the United States. Fortunately, the Editor's colleague and close friend has specialized in this area of historical investigation. It was very gratifying, therefore, to include this selection along with others describing what transpired in the nineteenth century. Our appreciation is extended to Professor Barney for his willingness to cooperate in this venture.

discipline of German youth. Stung to the point of utter humiliation by Napoleon's incursions into the Fatherland, Jahn sought to rehabilitate the spirit of those Teutonic virtues which he felt formed the very spinal column of Germanic culture. His success in that endeavor, in long term measurement, has contributed a vivid chapter to the social and political history of Western man. _Turnvereine_ spurred the liberal revolution in Germany for much of the nineteenth century, a revolution aimed at a closer union of the semi-independent German states and, even more importantly, the substitution of constitutional liberty for the absolutism of monarchical rule.

The German _Turnverein_ movement in America was one which was often implemented with the same spirit and dedication as had been the order of the day in Germany. Certainly the nineteenth century Turnverein experience in North America must be considered to have been secular in nature. German-American Turners, unlike many types of ethnic groups which emigrated to America from Europe and particularly those which came for reasons underscored by religious upheaval, immersed themselves in the public affairs of their new country in quite a natural manner because most of them had, in fact, emigrated from Germany in search of constitutional liberty. And certainly within the matrix of unrest exhibited by emigrating Germans was a deep-rooted concern for the proper education of their children. Since the Reformation in Northern Europe the subject of education had been one of particular interest and debate among the progressive and industrious Germans. Eighteenth and nineteenth century developments in the education of young people, including attention to the fostering of physical prowess in gymnastics, had made Germany a leader in the area of educational enlightenment. The education of their young in America continued to be a subject of intense interest to the emigrants, and their dedication to the task of developing such a process remained steadfast.

The Roots of the German Turnverein Experience in America

As early as 1825 the principles of German gymnastics and _Turnvater_ Jahn's _Turnplatz_ had begun to be applied in North America. The groundwork for the German expression of gymnastic exercise was laid initially by that distinguished trio of Carlsbad Decree exiles, Karl Follen, Karl Beck and Franz Lieber, whose collective work at Harvard College, the Round Hill School in Northampton, Massachusetts, and in the city of Boston, respectively, served as a springboard in launching the classical German _Turnverein_ experience in the western hemisphere. As a result of the failure of the liberal revolutionary movements of 1848 and 1849 in Germany, thousands of political and social refugees emigrated to the United States in search of a new life. Among the first of those "Forty-Eighters" to arrive in America was one Friedrich Hecker, popular hero of a defeated republican uprising in South Germany. By November of 1848 in Cincinnati,

Hecker had established a temporary home for the first German-American Turnverein. Other Turnverein societies followed in rapid succession, extending geographically from New England, New York and Baltimore on the eastern seaboard to the growing frontier cities of Milwaukee, St. Louis, Indianapolis, and bustling New Orleans. Even isolated California felt the Turnverein growth impetus of the 1850's, with flourishing organizations forming in San Francisco and Sacramento, and smaller but ambitious "satellite" groups in a number of small mining towns and villages along the Sierra Madre gold field corridor. By the eve of the Civil War over 150 individual Turnvereine existed in America, encompassing a membership of between 9,000 and 10,000 individuals of direct German origin (Leonard and Affleck, 1947, p. 295).

The German verb Turnen, meaning "to do gymnastic exercises," was the common denominator to all German-American Turnvereine, although social involvement and political activism often characterized the activities of many organizations with almost the same amount of fervor as the physical exercise variable. The form of exercise reflected was a combination of strict "Jahnistic" apparatus work and that type of free exercise expression closely akin to that espoused by Adolf Spiess, father of the free exercise movement in Germany.

German and American history in both the nineteenth and twentieth centuries leaves little doubt as to the effectiveness of Turner involvement with exercise. In those nineteenth century German military ventures following the Napoleonic Wars, Turners formed the backbone of the most physically fit and best disciplined units of the Germany army. From a statistical point of view the first such evidence of Turner fitness is reflected by the fact that in World War I, ninety-three per cent of all Turners examined for service in the American Expeditionary Forces were found to be physically fit, whereas the national average was not more than sixty-seven per cent (Leonard and Affleck, p. 313). No similar set of statistics are available for the Civil War but it has been substantiated that over 5,000 American Turners played prominent roles in support of President Lincoln's "cause," usually operating in the field as distinct Turnverein companies (Leonard and Affleck, p. 299).

Turnverein activity during the post-Civil War period and "Gilded Age" of American history (1865-1990) displayed vigorous growth and activity in terms of increases in membership, new societies, and in the preparation of gymnastics teachers. By the dawn of the twentieth century the number of Turners in America had increased to more than 34,000. This membership was distributed throughout 258 societies that employed 166 teachers of German gymnastics (Leonard and Affleck, p. 310). Stemming from the work of those pioneer teachers of German gymnastics in America evolved the vigorous efforts of <u>Turners</u> towards having their unique exercise expression accepted as the form of physical education most desirable for American school children.

The Turners and America's First Legislation for Physical Education

Turner enthusiasm and persistence played an important role in shaping the character of American public school physical education, particularly in the Midwest where large numbers of German immigrants settled along the length and breadth of the Ohio and Mississippi River valleys. However, it was in the then fledgling state of California that <u>Turners</u> first involved themselves in the business of forging legislation aimed at bringing about mandatory physical education in the public schools.

Prior to 1940, various investigators concerned with tracing the history of American physical education believed that the first State laws for the subject to be included in the public schools were enacted in Ohio in 1892, even though Pennsylvania had attempted to pass similar legislation in 1890, only to have the effort vetoed (River, 1926, p. 239). According to research done prior to 1940 only North Dakota joined with Ohio in actually passing state laws concerning physical education in the schools before the twentieth century.

The history of American physical education is indebted to the late Dudley Sargent DeGroot, eminent scholar and athlete, for pinpointing exactly the date of the very first state laws for physical education in the schools (DeGroot, 1940). According to his research, completed in 1939, the state of California, in 1866, enacted the first legislation in the country which dealt specifically with the subject of physical education in the public schools. This was more than a quarter of a century before the 1892 Ohio milestone previously reported by historians.

And what of the laws themselves? Today's student and professional practitioner of physical education might well be excused for thinking them to be quite humorous. Specifically, California's school laws for 1866 provided that: "Instruction shall be given in all grades of schools, and in all classes, during the entire school course in. . . the laws of health; and due attention shall be given to such physical exercises for the pupils as may be conducive to health and vigor of body, as well as. . ." (<u>Second Biennial Report</u>, 1866, Section 55). Under the "Rules and Regulations of the Public Schools of California," for the same year, is found an even more positive declaration: "In all primary schools, exercises in free gymnastics and vocal and breathing exercises, shall be given at least twice a day and for a time not less than five minutes for each exercise" (<u>Rules and Regulations</u>, 1866, p. 283). Inconsequential? Primitive? Perhaps. But every advanced, highly sophisticated piece of legislation had to originate from embryonic thought and governmental legislation relative to physical education has not proven to be any exception to that rule.

DeGroot's investigation of the history of physical education in California pointed specifically at John Swett, New Englander turned Californian, as the most important factor in the shaping of the historic 1866 legislation. DeGroot was at least partly correct in his assumptions pertinent to Swett. Certainly, the storied educator cannot be overlooked as a cornerstone figure in the history of public school physical education in California and other areas of the American West. Swett's role in that episode has been well documented (Carr, 1933, and Swett, 1876) and need not be amplified here.

Despite the saga of John Swett, the role of the early California Turnvereine in helping to formulate America's embryo physical education legislation was significant. By 1858 at least nine Turnvereine were known to have existed in Northern California alone. These organizations were nearly all located in communities situated along the corridor of Swett's educational and political activity--San Francisco, Sacramento, Oakland, Auburn, Stockton, Marysville, Dutch Flat, Sonora and Shasta (McCoy, 1962, pp. 67-68). As far as California's Turnverein history is concerned the first such organization was founded in San Francisco in 1852, even though two years earlier in the same city a German group devoted to vocalizing [Die Sänger am Stillen Meere] had been formed (The Sacramento Turn-Vereine, 1854-1954, p. 13). By 1860 western Turnvereine had banded together into the Pacific Turnerbund, the early leadership of which was provided mainly by the vigorous and energetic members of the San Francisco and Sacramento Vereine.

Even though there were some instances of attempts at strong political involvement on national issues among California Turners, the constitutions of the various western German organizations and their subsequent activity centered around social and physical expression rather than a focus on the psycho-politico efforts along the lines of the national Bund. Eastern and midwestern organizations, usually including high percentages of "Forty-Eighters" or "Greens," paid rapt attention to the political tone of the times and often applied their efforts towards affecting national policy (Hawgood, 1940). For instance, most Turnvereine in the East and Midwest steadfastly supported the position of President Lincoln and the enunciations of the Republican Party. Most Turners were staunchly anti-slavery in principle although not all were active abolitionists. In California and other areas of the West, political issues were sometimes lost in the stark realities of hard work to gain life's necessities. Florence McCoy, in her excellent study of the early years of Pacific Coast Turnverein activity in general, and that of the Sacramento Turnverein in particular, has concluded that, by the end of the first wave of

German migration to California in 1852, few individuals were present who were dedicated to the national political causes which heightened the fervor of so many of the "Forty-Eighters" in the East. On the subject of public education, however, German influence was nation-wide in importance in helping to spearhead local and state govern-mental legislation.

What then were the thoughts and activities of California Turners regarding physical education prior to the legislation under investi-gation? It is at least apparent that they could not be passed off lightly when the subject of physical education arose - a subject which many historians have felt formed the cornerstone of Turnverein activity. An examination of the constitution of the Sacramento Turnverein re-veals that gymnastics participation and instruction to its younger members was of paramount importance among the fundamental pur-poses of the organization: "The purpose of the society is to further most strongly, through word and deed, the way of the gymnast and socialism" (Second Constitution, 1854, p. 1). Socialism, if defined as active political involvement at the national level, was practically absent in the cases of California German organizations. Gymnastics occupied the front of the stage and membership in most societies consisted of four classifications, all of which embraced quite solidly the furthering of gymnastics "by word and deed." The Sacramento constitution, almost an exact copy of the San Francisco document of 1852, outlined its membership classes in the following manner:

(a) Active members - those who participate in all gym-nastic exercises and meetings.

(b) Inactive members - those who cannot fulfill the obligations of gymnastic exercise of the regular members, but who will interest themselves as much as possible in the furthering of the exercises.

(c) Honorary members - those who have given extra-ordinary service in the cause of gymnastics.

(d) Gymnastic students - those who have not yet reached their sixteenth birthday.

Augmenting the efforts of California Turnvereine in spreading the gospel of fitness through exercise were the public gymnasia, a few of which made their appearance on the Pacific Coast in the 1850's. By far the most successful of these, and quite possibly the only in-door facility of its type in the state, was the Sacramento gymnasium opened in the summer of 1856 by Frederick Van Vleck (The Sacramento Union, Sept. 8, 1856). Van Vleck, of German-Dutch par-entage, was not a member of the Turnverein, but simply an entrepre-neur in the city's German community who sought to profit financially from the growing appeal for gymnastic exercise. His enterprise was popular with the Sacramento townspeople and in 1857 the program was enlarged to accommodate women. Late in 1856 Van Vleck was appointed by the Sacramento school authorities to teach gymnastics to schoolboys. The cost of this program was one dollar per month for each boy, the fee to be paid by their parents (The Sacramento Union, Sept. 15, 1857). By 1957, far in advance of Swett's ascendancy to the position of State Superintendent of Public Instruction and the landmark 1866 physical education legislation, the Sacramento School Board of Education, in viewing the physical education activities of the Turnverein and Van Vleck's gymnasium, gave its formal approbation to the exercise movement as follows: "It is contemplated in this way (the work of the Turnverein and public gymnasium), it will be perceived to constitute gymnastics a regular branch in the course of education pursued in the schools" (The Sacramento Union, Sept. 28, 1857). The support for physical education in the school program, directed by German gymnastic influence in Sacramento, the state capital, was apparent. It is, therefore, to be expected that it was voiced strongly in the legislative chambers by various German representatives and citizens of Sacramento.

California newspapers of the 1850's and 1860's, particularly the San Francisco Chronicle and the Sacramento Union, covered Turner activity in breadth, underscoring the prominence of the German group in the pioneer society. And yet, not once in his prolific writing prior to 1866, did Swett mention the California Turners, or even the German people as a group, as having been an influence in helping to direct public consideration toward the need for physical education in the schools. This fact is difficult to fathom, especially since the German ethnic group in California between 1850 and 1865 formed both a considerable and influential portion of society. This was particularly apparent in the two most significant areas of the State relative to politics - San Francisco and Sacramento. The first California census, for example, reflected that in Sacramento County, one of the state's two "hubs" of political, social, and economic activity, there were far more Germans in residence than any other European-born ethnic group (California Census, 1852, Vol. 5). Further, the same census revealed that the number of Germans engaged in gold mining, unskilled labor, and other transient-like ways of living was proportionately small when compared to those Germans plying their efforts at trades which formed the bulwark of society. More than fifty per cent of all German men were engaged in professional, merchant, and skilled labor occupations. This figure represented a considerably larger percentage than that reflected by the second most prominent ethnic group - the Irish.

Germans were willing and able candidates for California's early legislatures as well. The various Turnvereine elected and heartily endorsed their own representatives for the state government. Their political presence was not negligible. The inference thus becomes quite clear that the Germans of Northern California, comprising a significant segment of not only the population itself, but the middle and upper classes of that population, and linked together in a new land by the traditions and heritages of the old country, of which Turnverein activity featuring physical exercise was most prominent, may well have been a formidable influence in activity and discussion leading to laws dealing with physical education in the schools, many of which were attended, or would be attended, by their children. Certainly education was a subject of great concern to Germans. Its development in the various German states prior to the period under discussion was perhaps unrivaled in all Europe.

Epilogue

In the years following the 1866 California legislation, Turners undertook a systematic campaign to acquaint American educators and the public in general with the merits of the German system of exercise expression. A normal school dedicated to preparing teachers of the German system was established initially in New York City in 1866. Later it "travelled" to Chicago, Milwaukee, Cincinnati and elsewhere. Emanating from the various normal school courses a steady stream of gymnastics teachers fanned out into those cities of the American midwest which had significant German-American populations. These teachers, located in such places as Kansas City, Chicago, Rochester, Louisville, St. Louis, Cleveland, Cincinnati and Dayton, among others, were ultimately successful in instrumenting regular instruction in gymnastics in the public schools of those cities well before the end of the century (Leonard and Affleck, p. 309). The Turnverein influence was felt nationally as well, since their delegates attended annual meetings of the infant (American) Association for the Advancement of Physical Education, outlining in strong terms all aspects of the Turnverein approach.

A distinguished historian of physical education, Dr. Edward M. Hartwell, who lived at a time during the nineteenth century when the German system of physical education rose to its zenith in America, identified the American Turners as being the most influential force in bringing about the introduction of gymnastic exercises into the public schools (Zucker, 1950, p. 109). No other individual or group did more to place the subject of physical education before the public's eyes than did the various Turnvereine of the United States. As Turnverein activity enlarged, so did an awareness of gymnastics on the part of lay people, an awareness which in no little way contributed towards support for governmental physical education legislation and personal involvement in physical exercise.

General Bibliography

California State Census of 1852, The. Vol. V (County of Sacramento).

Carr, William G. *John Swett – The Biography of an Educational Pioneer*. Santa Ana, California: Fine Arts Press, 1933.

DeGroot, Dudley S. "A History of Physical Education in California, 1848–1849." Ph.D. dissertation, Stanford University, 1940.

Hawgood, John. *The Tragedy of German-America*. New York: G. P. Putnam's Sons, 1940.

"Historical Sketch of the Sacramento Turnverein," *The Sacramento Turn-Vereine, 1854–1954*. Sacramento, California: Spilman Printing Co., 1954.

Leonard, Fred Eugene and Affleck, George B. *The History of Physical Education*. Philadelphia: Lea and Febiger, 1947.

McCoy, Florence. "History of the First Five Years of the Sacramento, California Turnverein." M.A. thesis, Sacramento State College, 1962.

Rice, Emmett A. *A Brief History of Physical Education*. New York: A. S. Barnes and Company, 1926.

Rinsch, Emil. *The History of the Normal College of the American Gymnastic Union of Indiana University, 1866–1966*. Bloomington, Indiana: Indiana University, 1966.

"Rules and Regulations of the Public Schools of California, 1866." Section 18.

Sacramento [California] *Union, The*. September 8, 1856, and September 15 and 28, 1857.

"Second Biennial Report of the State Superintendent of Public Instruction, 1866–1867." Appendix E, Revised school law, March 24, 1866, Section 55.

"Second Constitution of the Sacramento Turn-Vereine." Adopted July 20, 1854.

Swett, John. *History of the Public School System of California*. San Francisco: R. L. Bancroft and Company, 1876.

Zeigler, Earle Frederick. "A History of Professional Preparation for Physical Education in the United States, 1861-1948." Ph.D. dissertation, Yale University, 1950.

Zucker, A. E. The Forty-Eighters: Political Refugees of the German Revolution of 1848. New York: Columbia University Press, 1950.

CHAPTER 9

EDWARD HITCHCOCK, M.D., FOUNDER OF PHYSICAL EDUCATION IN THE COLLEGE CURRICULUM

J. Edmund Welch
West Virginia Institute of Technology, Montgomery

Edward Hitchcock was professor of hygiene and physical education at Amherst College, Amherst, Massachusetts, from 1861 until his death in 1911. As director of the first successful program of physical education in any American college, Hitchcock was, in fact, the "founder of physical education in the college curriculum." The example he set was followed by many colleges and universities in America, as well as in Japan. Amherst College was the first institution of higher learning to make physical education an integral part of the college curriculum.[1]

There had been sporadic attempts by other colleges and universities to start physical education programs during the period 1826-1830 and later during the 1850's, but in no case did the institution provide adequate facilities and competent instructors. President William A. Stearns of Amherst College pointed out the need for physical education in college in his inaugural address of 1854. From the very beginning of his administration, Stearns was plagued with problems of student health. He urged the trustees to build a gymnasium and appoint a competent professor of hygiene and physical education. Stearns was successful in his efforts. Barrett Gymnasium was begun

---

Editor's Note: It is a pleasure to be able to include a paper by Professor Welch which was abstracted from his earlier classic study about Edward Hitchcock of Amherst. In correspondence with Professor Welch, he told the Editor that this material had probably received sufficient exposure, but we emphasized that a volume of this type really should have information about Dr. Hitchcock in it. An excellent bibliography is included as well.

---

[1] An abstract of the author's book entitled, Edward Hitchcock, M.D., Founder of Physical Education in the College Curriculum, and which was published in cooperation with the East Carolina College Library in 1966. (This abstract was published originally in The Physical Educator, Vol. 24, No. 2:54-56 (May, 1967).)

in 1859, and John W. Hooker, a physician and gymnast, was appointed as the professor in 1860. Hooker served effectively, but his health broke and he resigned at the end of his initial year. In 1861, Hitchcock was appointed to the professorship, and he served Amherst College and the cause of physical education with great distinction for the next half century.

Hitchcock was born in Amherst, Massachusetts, on May 23, 1828, where his father was the third president of Amherst College and an eminent geologist. From his father Hitchcock gained many insights into science and teaching. Hitchcock was superbly educated for a man of his day. His preparatory work was done at Amherst Academy and Williston Seminary, and he graduated from Amherst College with a bachelor of arts degree in 1849. He also held a master of arts degree from Amherst. His medical degree was from Harvard University, and he spent four months in Paris and London studying medicine, natural history, and comparative anatomy. In London he was the private pupil of Sir Richard Owen, the outstanding comparative anatomist of the British Museum. Hitchcock's work under Owen was the high point of his professional preparation, for comparative anatomy was his favorite subject.

After graduating from Amherst, Hitchcock taught natural history at Williston Seminary from 1850 to 1860. During the early 1850's he took leave to secure his medical degree from Harvard. When he became professor of hygiene and physical education at Amherst, he was especially prepared to direct a program of student health. He lacked training in gymnastics, but he overcame this weakness while on the job.

The Program

The program which Hitchcock developed at Amherst comprised required exercises for all students; extensive health care, supervision, and instruction; and scientific measurement. It became known nationally and internationally as the "Amherst Plan" of physical education. Each of the four college classes was required to meet four times per week for thirty minutes of exercise under the direction of the professor. The students dressed in uniforms and elected their own class and platoon captains. These captains were trained by Hitchcock in the art of giving calisthenics and maneuvering the class in the gymnasium. The exercises consisted of calisthenics with light wooden dumbbells, and the students repeated the drills in unison in time to piano music. A portion of every class was given over to free exercise during which the students ran, used the heavy apparatus, sang, danced, or turned somersaults. Hitchcock felt this recreational portion of the class was important to allow students an opportunity to work off their boisterous instincts.

The trustees of Amherst were particularly desirous that the health of the students be a primary concern of the new professor of hygiene and physical education. Hitchcock carried out this mandate with the utmost skill and success. He gave regular medical examinations to the students, and he kept detailed health records. Each student could call on him for health care and counsel, and he made daily visits to the room of sick students. His dream of a student infirmary finally materialized in 1897 when the Pratt Health Cottage was built and endowed.

Health instruction was a vital phase of the Amherst Plan. Hitchcock gave regular lectures in hygiene to the freshman class. He covered such subjects as diet, exercise, care of the muscles, care of the eyes, alcohol, tobacco, and reproductive organs. A course in anatomy and physiology was given to sophomores.

Body Measurements

One of Hitchcock's most original contributions was his work in anthropometrics, or the science of bodily measurements. He desired to put his physical education program on a scientific basis. By keeping accurate measurements on all students, he was able to show that regular exercise and proper health supervision improved the growth and health of college students. Hitchcock was the first American physical educator to apply the science of anthropometry to problems of the profession. Through his efforts and those of Dudley A. Sargent, anthropometrics became the central foundation for the entire profession of physical education in America during the latter half of the nineteenth century. Hitchcock knew that detailed physical measurements over a period of years would be invaluable to anthropometrics in general. His work helped determine the average measurements of college students, and these statistics have been used in studies of human growth.

Publications

Hitchcock contributed only one book to the profession. This was a textbook in anatomy and physiology. However, a list of his published articles, papers, manuals, and reports covered eight pages in the American Physical Education Review. He ranks as one of the important writers in physical education in the nineteenth century, along with Sargent, Anderson, Hartwell, and Gulick.

Through his papers and news stories describing the Amherst Plan, Hitchcock influenced the development of physical education in many other American colleges. Three of his students, Edward Mussey Hartwell, Watson L. Savage, and Paul C. Phillips, made national contributions to American physical education. The Japanese government requested Amherst College to send a teacher to Japan to install the Amherst Plan. George A. Leland, another of Hitchcock's students, was selected tor the assignment, and he spent three years in Japan. He is credited as being the founder of modern physical education in that country.

National Leadership

Hitchcock was a prominent member of the two principal professional organizations of his time. He was the first president of the American Association for the Advancement of Physical Education, and he was chairman pro tem of the meeting at which the Society for College Gymnasium Directors was founded. Hitchcock was a charter member of both organizations and was particularly active in the affairs of the Association. In addition to being president for the first two years, he was vice president for six years, a member of the National Council or executive committee for ten years, and, as a member of the committee on statistics and measurements, he presented important papers on anthropometry at the national meetings. Of equal importance was the fact that Hitchcock served as a harmonizing agent during the critical, formative era of the Association. He never dodged a debate, but he was friendly to all, especially to the younger men in the profession, and he was successful in holding dissident elements together for the advancement of the profession.

Honors

Many honors and recognitions were bestowed upon Hitchcock. He was granted an honorary doctor of laws degree from Amherst College and an honorary master of physical education degree from Springfield College. A special dinner was given in his honor by the American Association for the Advancement of Physical Education. This dinner, held at a national convention in New York City, was in commemoration of Hitchcock's fortieth anniversary as professor at Amherst College and as leader in the profession. Later, the same organization made Hitchcock an honorary member, and this was his most prized recognition. Hitchcock is a fellow in memoriam of the American Academy of Physical Education. Hitchcock Memorial Field and Hitchcock Memorial Room at Amherst College were dedicated in his memory. In 1932 Amherst College was awarded the first certificate of high merit of the American Student Health Association. This award was in recognition of the pioneer work of President Stearns and Hitchcock.

Summary

Prior to 1860 there were no planned physical education programs in American colleges and universities. As a result of the outstanding work of Hitchcock at Amherst College, the way was opened for physical education to become an integral part of the college curriculum throughout the United States.

General Bibliography

The following materials are located in the Hitchcock Memorial Room, Robert Frost Library, Amherst College, Amherst, Massachusetts.

A. Addresses and Papers

"Discourses and Addresses at the Installation and Inauguration of the Rev. William A. Stearns, D.D. as President of Amherst College," Amherst College Inaugural and Valedictory Addresses of Presidents. Amherst, Massachusetts: J. S. & C. Adams, 1885.

Hitchcock, Edward. "Anthropometric Statistics of Amherst College." Paper read at a meeting of the American Statistical Association, 1893.

_____. "Hygiene at Amherst College." Paper read at a meeting of the American Public Health Association, Chicago, Illinois, September 26, 1877.

_____. "The Need of Anthropometry." Paper read at the second annual meeting of the American Association for the Advancement of Physical Education, Brooklyn, New York, November 26, 1886.

_____. "The Results of Anthropometry, As Derived from the Measurements of the Students in Amherst College." Paper read at the seventh annual meeting of the American Association for the Advancement of Physical Education, Philadelphia, April, 1892. Amherst, Massachusetts: Press of Carpenter & Morehouse, 1892.

_____. "What the College may do to Prevent Insanity." Reprinted from Proceedings of Twelfth Conference of Charities and Correction held in Washington.

Raycroft, Joseph E. "History and Development of Student Health Programs in Colleges and Universities." Paper read at the twenty-first annual meeting of the American Student Health Association, University of Michigan, Ann Arbor, Michigan, December 27-28, 1940.

Raycroft, Joseph E. "Presentation of Award to Amherst College."
Address given at the annual meeting of the American Student
Health Association, New York, New York, December 28, 1932.

B. Books

Hitchcock, Edward and Edward Hitchcock, Jr. Elementary Anatomy
and Physiology for Colleges, Academies and other Schools.
New York: Ivison, Phinney & Co., 1860.

Welch, J. Edmund. Edward Hitchcock, M.D., Founder of Physical
Education in the College Curriculum. Greenville, North
Carolina: East Carolina College Library, 1966. Out of print.
Available on microfilm from University Microfilms, Inc.,
Ann Arbor, Michigan, and on microcard from University of
Oregon, Eugene, Oregon.

C. Booklets and Manuals

Allen, Nathan. Physical Culture in Amherst College. Lowell,
Massachusetts: Stone & Huse, Book Printers, 1869.

"Gymnasium Handbook of Amherst College, 1899-1900."

Hitchcock, Edward. A Manual of the Gymnastic Exercises as Practiced by the Junior Class in Amherst College. Boston: Ginn,
Heath & Company, 1884.

_____. A Syllabus of the Health Lectures in Amherst
College, 1891-92. Third edition. Amherst, Massachusetts:
1891.

_____. "The Department of Physical Education and
Hygiene in Amherst College." Boston: Rand, Avery and Company, 1879.

D. Periodicals

Hitchcock, Edward. "A Perverted Will as a Factor in Insanity," The
Sanitarian, No. 174 (May, 1884), 381-393.

_____. "Athletics in American Colleges," Journal of
Social Science (June, 1885), 27-44.

_____. "Dangers of Overtraining," Men (March 13,
1887), 104-105.

Hitchcock, Edward. "The Gymnastic Era and the Athletic Era of Our Country," The Outlook (May 18, 1895), 816-818.

_____. "Physical Education," The University Magazine (September, 1891), 833-835.

_____. "Relation of the Student-life to Health and Longevity." Reprinted from the New Englander, July, 1877.

Johnson, Burgess. " 'Old Doc' Hitchcock, Creator of a System of Physical Education," The Outlook (April 27, 1907), 956-961.

Marsh, Allison W. "Physical Education at Amherst," The Amherst Graduates' Quarterly (November, 1929), 18-26.

Phillips, Paul C. "The Amherst Illustrious: George A. Leland," The Amherst Graduates' Quarterly (November, 1924), 29-33.

"Professor Hitchcock on Physical Education," Boston Medical and Surgical Journal (October 25, 1877), 480-482.

CHAPTER 10

DR. DUDLEY A. SARGENT AND THE HARVARD SUMMER
SCHOOL OF PHYSICAL EDUCATION

Bruce L. Bennett
The Ohio State University, Columbus

Origin[1]

The first summer school in the United States was started by
Louis Agassiz, a Harvard professor, in 1873 for zoology students at
Penikese Island in Buzzard's Bay off Newport, Rhode Island, although
the University of Virginia had a summer session of law as early as
1870 (Willoughby, 1894, p. 898-900). The Penikese Island school
was abandoned after a few years but summer schools in chemistry
and botany were started in 1874 (Willoughby, 1894, p. 953) and geo-
logy was added in 1883 (Harvard Catalog, 1883-84, p. 243). The financial risk of these schools was assumed by the instructors who
handled the receipts and paid the salaries through the Business Office
of the University. These courses did not give credit towards a degree but simply offered an opportunity for review or extra study.

The idea of a summer school of physical training came to Dr.
Sargent during a month's stay at Chautauqua, New York, in August,
1879 (Ledyard Sargent, 1927, p. 157). Soon after coming to
Hemenway Gymnasium at Harvard University, Sargent received applications for teachers familiar with his methods and apparatus. Since
many prospective teachers were busy during the year and could only
come in the summer, Sargent began to use some of his vacation time
to instruct them.

Editor's Note: A fine biographical study about Dr. Dudley A.
Sargent of Harvard was completed by Professor Bennett in the
summer of 1947. For a contribution to this book, we requested that
Dr. Bennett allow us to include a chapter from his earlier study at
Michigan. In this essay he describes the relationship between Dr.
Sargent and the now defunct Harvard Summer School of Physical Edu-
cation - a most successful venture that had significant impact on the
development of physical education in the United States at that time.

---

[1] This is a chapter from Bruce L. Bennett, "The Life of Dudley
Allen Sargent, M.D., and His Contributions to Physical Education."
Ph.D. dissertation, University of Michigan, 1947.

In a descriptive booklet which Sargent had published in 1882, he announced that a summer school would be opened in Cambridge, July 5, 1883, for a five-week session. The purpose was to train pupils in the theory and practice of health-promoting exercises to meet the growing demand for teachers in this department of education. The course, open to both sexes, would include a series of lectures on the "Care of the Body" by Sargent and practical instruction in calisthenics, gymnastics, and athletics (Dr. Sargent's System, 1882, p. 8). We have no evidence to show whether the school was actually held or how many attended. It was not connected with Harvard and the classes were undoubtedly held in Dr. Sargent's own normal school building. However, in 1884 Sargent advertised a summer session at his normal school (Hartwell, 1885, p. 59).

As the demand increased, Sargent wrote to President Eliot of Harvard and inquired about starting a summer school in physical training. Eliot approved the plan if Sargent cared to take the financial risk (Sargent manuscript, 1907). The first course, lasting five weeks, was given in 1887 and attended by a surprising total of fifty-seven men and women, only five less than the number enrolled in Chemistry, the largest course (Harvard catalog, 1887-88, p. 330). The plan and work of the first session is found in the catalog for 1887-1888:

> The aim of the course is to qualify men and women as instructors in the Harvard system of physical examination and training. The present need is for intelligent organizers and teachers rather than for skillful performers--for those who can arouse enthusiasm for health and bodily development rather than for gymnastic feats.

> The course consists of lectures by Dr. Sargent, examinations and exercises condensed from the winter course, and a new system of exercises adapted to the needs of school children.

> Certificates are given indicating the time spent at the school, the work done, and the nature of the service that each teacher is capable of rendering. A preliminary course of reading is prescribed for those who have entered their names for the course (p. 321).

The fee was fifty dollars and Dr. Sargent cleared about $1,500 the first year (Sargent manuscript, 1907). The success of this initial session was assured not only by the large number but also by the quality of the students, most of whom held regular positions and came from all parts of the country. Among those present were Dr. Delphine Hanna of Oberlin, Professor John B. Crenshaw of Randolph Macon, Helen Putnam of Vassar, Carolyn Ladd of Bryn Mawr, Belle Boveé, then at Brearley School in New York, Anna Bridgman of Rockford Seminary, Dr. Frank Whittier of Bowdoin, and Booker T. Washington of Tuskegee Institute (Harvard catalog, 1887-88, pp. 321-24).

Program

Beginning in 1888 the work of the summer school was divided into theory and practice. The theoretical work comprised lectures and recitations in applied anatomy and physiology, personal hygiene, anthropometry, physical diagnosis, prescribing individual exercises, massage, physical exercise in treatment of spinal curvature, and testing for normal vision and hearing. Practical work included free movements, calisthenics, light and heavy gymnastics, marching, gymnastic games, track and field, boxing, fencing, swimming, and the Monroe system of voice training. Each student attending the full course was given a general certificate indicating the manner in which his or her work was performed (Harvard catalog, 1888-89, pp. 341-42).

The curriculum of the summer school expanded and changed to include the latest work in physical training, games, dancing, and athletics. It was this elasticity and broad scope of the work offered which accounted for the wide appeal of the school, not only to young physical education students, but also to mature people from all walks of life. Thus, in 1890 the Delsarte movements, relaxing exercises, and Swedish gymnastics were added to the practical work (Harvard catalog, 1890-91, p. 351). The new aesthetic dancing was first taught in 1894 (Van Wyck, 1942, p. 411). The Harvard Summer School was the first to offer track and field instruction for women in 1896. The class was taught by James Lathrop, the Harvard track coach, who ordered the first pair of spiked running shoes for a woman (Ballintine, pp. 15-16). The Harvard Summer School played an important part in the introduction of English field hockey to this country. In 1901 Constance Applebee, who had just arrived from England, attended the summer school and demonstrated the game to the other students. Miss Harriet Ballintine, director of physical training at Vassar, was impressed by the game and invited Miss Applebee to come to Vassar in the fall. Other trips to Wellesley, Smith, Mt. Holyoke, Bryn Mawr, and Radcliffe followed. Dr. Sargent wrote a recommendation of Miss Applebee and the game for her book which was published in 1902 (Applebee, 1902, p. 58).[2]

---

[2] Field hockey was played by the men at Springfield College as early as 1897 and possibly also at Mt. Holyoke, according to McCurdy, quoted in Ballintine, p. 17. However, the continuous popularity of field hockey dates from Miss Applebee's visit.

An examination of the class schedule for 1906 shows that a wide range of courses were actually taught. In theory, histology, history of education, psychology, and philosophy of exercise were added to provide a broad background of training. Football, wrestling, fencing, hockey, and tennis were more recent additions to the practical work (Van Wyck, 1952, p. 427). Methods of teaching, philosophy of education, history of physical education and first aid were taught in 1910 (Van Wyck, 1942, p. 428). In 1915 four courses in playground work and a course in folk dancing reflected the rise of recreation activities in this country although the summer school had taught various games almost from the beginning (Van Wyck, 1942, p. 429). Even while recognizing the rise of athletics and recreation, the summer school continued to teach apparatus, Swedish gymnastics, tumbling, marching tactics, Indian clubs, and dumbbells as part of the necessary training of a well-rounded physical educator.

For the first ten years or so, the summer school was quite informal and course work was optional. Students attended whatever classes they liked for as long as they wishes. "The course of the summer school is entirely optional, the full list of exercises is laid before the students giving them the opportunity to select what they prefer or are best for them" (Letter to Miss Oldham, 1894). Beginning in 1899, two summers were required for a full certificate and courses were classified for the first or second year (Van Wyck, 1942, pp. 412-13). In 1902 at the suggestion of President Eliot, the program of graded courses was extended to four summers for a full certificate. This system was in effect during the rest of Dr. Sargent's administration which ended with his retirement from Harvard in 1919. Three years later by an arrangement with the Harvard School of Education, summer school students with a B.A. degree could complete four summers and receive the Master's degree in Education.

Faculty

No less important than the breadth of the courses was the quality of the instructors. Hartvig Nissen, a Norwegian who first brought Swedish gymnastics to the United States in 1883, taught that subject; Christian Eberhard, Francis Dohs, and Carl Schrader were all graduates of the Turnverein Normal School at Milwaukee; and Melvin Ballou Gilbert taught his own aesthetic and classic dancing for fifteen summers. The theory courses were taught by distinguished physicians of Boston and the Harvard Medical School. At one time or another, Dr. Henry P. Bowditch, Dr. Edward H. Bradford, Dr. Walter Channing, Dr. Robert W. Lovett, and Dr. Myles Standish were lecturers. Men like Dr. R. Tait McKenzie, Dr. Fred Eugene Leonard, Dr. George Meylan, and Dr. Edward M. Hartwell came first as students and later as instructors. In addition to Lecturers and Instructors who were in charge of the theory and practice courses respectively, Dr. Sargent used Student Assistants to help with the course work in return for free tuition. This plan induced many expert performers to enroll as students to acquire the prestige attached to the Harvard Summer School (Van Wyck, 1942, passim).

Administration

After the first year of operation, all the Harvard summer schools were placed under the supervision of a faculty committee (Willoughby, 1894, p. 954). This action may have been inspired by the great financial success of the first physical education session. As Sargent wrote to a former student, "Since you were here the University has taken the course under its sheltering wing and I am not quite as free as I once was. You see it appreciates a good thing" (Letter to Mr. Bell, 1889).

As a result of this new arrangement, Sargent was given a salary of $1,000 for the summer and his department was placed on a budget (Letter to Eliot, 1896). The physical training department generally showed a healthy surplus which was applied to the other expenses of the summer school. Sargent, therefore, vigorously objected to President Eliot when he received a check for $810 in 1895 and $837 in 1896 because he had exceeded his appropriation by that amount which was deducted from his salary (Letter to Eliot, 1896). Sargent claimed that he was never told what his appropriation was and that for 1895 at least the receipts for physical training exceeded expenses (Letter to Shaler, 1895). Eliot approved payment of the balance in 1895 and presumably the matter was settled to everybody's satisfaction the following year.

Up to 1900 enrollment at the summer school of physical education varied from 45 in 1888 to 124 in 1897. From 1900 on, registration never dropped below 111 and climbed to over 200 from 1912 to 1916. The war years of 1917 and 1918 caused a drop to 190 and 179, but an even 200 pupils attended Dr. Sargent's last summer in 1919 (Van Wyck, 1942, p. 426). The school operated until 1932 when it was discontinued.

While it is comparatively easy to consult catalogs concerning the summer school and to gather statistics, it is more difficult to catch the spirit of student life. The idea of men and women exercising together by no means met with popular approval, particularly when the women wore the rather daring divided skirts, as advocated by Dr. Sargent. In reply to a question on this subject, Sargent wrote:

The men and women exercise together at the Hemenway gymnasium, in the summer, and it is gratifying to see how freely they mingle together in their gymnastic costumes, with apparently no thought of anything but their work. I can see no reason why any ladies cannot admit gentlemen wishing to take the same exercises, if their costumes are proper to wear in view of each other, though they might sometimes object to certain individuals (Letter to Sanborn, 1890).

Most of the students worked hard and found that good grades did not come easily. Dr. Sargent set rigid standards for his pupils and in the history of the summer school only one student received a certificate with the special inscription for excellent work, "With honors in theory and practice" (Van Wyck, 1942, p. 419). Coincident with the four-year graded program in 1902, Dr. Sargent introduced a complicated credit point system. Each subject was given a certain number of points toward a diploma, based on its estimated relative importance in a liberal course of study (Editorial Note, 1904, pp. 217-18). The results proved thoroughly unsatisfactory to the students who never knew their exact status in relation to graduation. Through the efforts of some of the staff members with Dr. Sargent, a new system was organized in 1906 with specific course requirements for graduation (Van Wyck, 1942, pp. 415-16). The school day often lasted eight hours with additional study necessary in the evening.

Yet more important than the actual work accomplished was the free mingling and association of the pupils with their diverse backgrounds and experiences. Here was one place where exponents of the Swedish system could meet on equal grounds with the German gymnasts, or the football coach could talk sensibly and calmly with an Indian club specialist. Each learned to appreciate the value of the other's views under Dr. Sargent's broad philosophy, and the Harvard Summer School was of inestimable service in easing the bitterness engendered by "the battle of the systems" which split the physical education profession near the end of the nineteenth century. Every student of a worthwhile, sound system of physical training was assured a respectful and friendly, though critical, audience at the Harvard Summer School. Friendships were made and renewed each year and a professional camaraderie was encouraged.

Dr. Sargent soon realized the need of some type of recreational program for the students who worked hard during the year and then gave up a summer of leisure and rest to attend school. A reception and an exhibition were given at the end of each summer session and, about 1900, dances, organized by Dr. George L. Meylan, were held for the physical training students. These affairs drew envious appeals from other summer session students to the faculty committee for similar functions for themselves (Interview with Meyland, 1947). The entire school also went to the beach for an afternoon of recreation and fun which provided Dudley Sargent with one of his few moments of relaxation.

Problems of Summer Schools

The success of the Harvard Summer School was not inevitable. Many problems had to be solved, much hard work had to be done, and considerable foresight was necessary to establish its reputation. Springfield College started a summer session in physical training in 1887, the same year as the Harvard School; but it lasted only five years (Willoughby, 1894, p. 920). In 1904, Yale began a summer school of physical education which expired four years later (Yale catalogs, 1904 to 1908). These examples illustrate that the success of a summer school was not automatic. The Harvard School showed a decline in attendance for a couple of years after 1905 which Sargent attributed to the following reasons:

1. Growth and development of similar courses in other universities.

2. Increasing attractions offered by summer camps.

3. Competition of other schools not only for pupils but also for instructors trained in the Harvard Summer School.

4. The current belief, having full value at other institutions, that the so-called "Sargent System" is not approved or adopted by either Harvard or Radcliffe authorities.

5. The discouragement if not actual prohibition of students from Radcliffe and Boston Normal School of Gymnastics from attending.

6. The Director is not a member of the Harvard Faculty (Sargent manuscripts, 1907).

The first three reasons were doubtless significant in influencing summer school attendance at Harvard. The last three were of lesser importance and probably more the personal grievances of Dr. Sargent than potent forces in the registration decline. Another cause, not mentioned here by Sargent, may have been the unpopular credit point system in effect from 1902 to 1905. But whatever the effect of these factors, it was merely temporary, and 1908 marked the beginning of a steady upward surge in enrollment.

Influence

The Chautauqua Summer School of Physical Education, conducted by Dr. William G. Anderson and Dr. Jay Seaver, was by far the largest of all the summer schools and at times had nearly a thousand student (Morris, 1892, p. 367). The excellent work of the Chautauqua

School in popularizing physical education cannot be discounted or
overlooked, and in all fairness deserves recognition with the Harvard
Summer School. However, the smaller size of the Harvard School
was somewhat offset by the fact that approximately 75 per cent of the
students were regularly employed teachers and in an excellent position, therefore, to promote the teachings of the school and put them
into practice. In the first twenty-five years, 170 college instructors
and directors attended in addition to numerous high school, elementary, and private school principals and teachers from all over the
country as well as Canada, Cuba, Japan, England, France, and
China (Contributions of the Hemenway Gymnasium, 1913, i-xvi). One
is impressed by the large number of leaders in college athletics and
physical education who have attended the Harvard Summer School.
Dr. Sargent, who was a vigorous opponent of athletic evils, was encouraged by the influence of his summer school pupils in teaching
athletics with regard for fair play and the rights of others and in
interesting large numbers of youths in sports for sport's sake
(Sargent manuscript, 1907).

Van Wyck, who served as secretary to the school for many
years, has appropriately expressed the broad value of the Harvard
Summer School in the concluding sentence of his excellent history of
the school:

> During its life of more than three hundred years, Harvard
> University has rendered many services of great value to the
> community--not least in the list of these services is the contri-
> bution which was made to the physical welfare of the American
> people by the Harvard Summer School of Physical Education
> (Van Wyck, 1942, p. 426).

General Bibliography

Applebee, Constance M. K. English Field Hockey for Men and
    Women. New York: American Sports Publishing Company,
    1902.

Ballintine, Harriet I. The History of Physical Training at Vassar
    College, 1865-1915. Poughkeepsie, New York: Lansing and
    Broas, n.d.

"Contributions of the Hemenway Gymnasium to the Cause of Physical
    Education," Harvard Illustrated Magazine, Spring Athletics
    Number (Supplement), 14:i-xvi, May, 1913.

"Editorial Note and Comment," American Physical Education Review,
    9:217-18, September, 1904.

Hartwell, Edward M. Physical Training in American Colleges and Universities. Bureau of Education Circular in Information No. 5, 1885. Washington, D. C.: Government Printing Office, 1886.

Harvard Catalog. Issues for 1883-84, 1887-88, 1888-89, 1890-91.

Interview with Dr. George L. Meylan, March 27, 1947.

Letter from Sargent to Mr. Bell, June 7, 1889.

Letter from Sargent to President Eliot, September 18, 1896.

Letter from Sargent to Miss Margaret Oldham, June 21, 1894.

Letter from Sargent to George A. Sanborn, October 3, 1890.

Letter from Sargent to Dr. Shaler, September 20, 1895.

Morris, R. Anna. "Physical Education in Our Schools," National Education Association Journal of Proceedings and Addresses. 31:366-72, 1892.

Sargent, Dudley A. "Harvard Summer School." Unpublished manuscript, no date, but probably July, 1907.

Sargent, Ledyard W. (editor). An Autobiography. Philadelphia: Lea & Febiger, 1927.

Dr. Sargent's System of Developing Appliances and Gymnastic Apparatus. Cambridge, Massachusetts: John Ford & Son, 1882.

Van Wyck, Clarence B. "The Harvard Summer School of Physical Education, 1877-1932," Research Quarterly, 13:403-31, December, 1942.

Willoughby, W. W. "The History of Summer Schools in the United States," Vol. II, pp. 893-959, Report of the Commissioner of Education for 1891-92, 2 volumes. Wahhington, D. C.: Government Printing Office, 1894.

Yale Catalog. Issues from 1904 to 1908.

CHAPTER 11

A BRIEF CHRONICLE OF SPORT AND PHYSICAL ACTIVITY FOR WOMEN

Earle F. Zeigler
The University of Western Ontario, London

The great Aristotle believed that women had been fitted by nature for subjection to the male of the species because they had no ability for self-direction.* Generally speaking, he felt that they were weaker, less courageous, and incomplete. Plato held a different view; he believed that women should have all types of education similar to the pattern he prescribed for men, including even the highest type of liberal education and preparation for warfare.[14]

Certainly one of the significant social trends of the twentieth century has been woman's "emancipation." In past societies it had been erroneously concluded that women simply did not possess the intellectual capacity to profit from the higher types of education. Hence, girls and women were typically given no intellectual function and, on the whole, their duty has been to bear and rear children - and manage the home. This concept has certainly changed considerably for a percentage of women in the United States, Canada, and elsewhere. Equalitarianism has been fostered through such influences as the Industrial Revolution, the various wars, and through

---

Editor's Note: Chapter 11 is a brief historical summary of one of some fifteen "persistent problems" which have been identified over a period of twenty years by Professor Zeigler. It is hoped that this identification will not cause the Editor to be identified as a "male chauvinist"; in fact, just the opposite may be the case. The extent to which women achieve equality in this or other societies will undoubtedly have an influence on programs of physical education and sport.

---

* A paper presented at the Second Canadian Symposium on History of Sport and Physical Education, University of Windsor, Ontario, May 3, 1972. The writer considers the question of sport and physical activity for women as one of some fifteen persistent (recurring) historical problems that are deserving of further investigation. This exploratory chronicle obviously just "scratches the surface." Others are encouraged to study and report on various aspects of this topic in much greater depth.

more democratic theories of state. Women's physical education and
sport has been hampered not only by the place of physical education in
a particular society, but also by the place that women held in any
society under consideration - and to a considerable extent by the ideas
that men and women had about the limitations of women because of
their anatomical structure.[17,44]

Early Historical Background

In primitive and pre-literate societies, education took place
largely in the home where the mother nurtured the young boys and
girls until a division of labor took place. At this juncture the mother
began the education of the girl in household arts, and the father started the boy on preparation for manhood. The boy's training was designed to test his strength, endurance, skill, and courage. That
which might be called drudgery was assigned to the females in the
large majority of societies, although there is evidence that women
and young girls took part in minor amusements and played whenever
possible.

In early civilizations before the time of the Cretans and
Spartans, there are evidences that girls and women engaged in various physical activities and games. In the Egyptian Civilization, for
example, there is pictorial proof that women took part in simple ball
games, swimming, archery and dancing. Dancing was not considered
proper for members of the upper class, although certain priestesses
evidently performed religious dances. With the common people, however, dancing was practiced regularly, and there were numerous professional women dancers.[21,43,45,49,70,73,81]

China. Aside from simple childhood games and the popularity
of dancing, the large majority of people in ancient China got their
exercise from various types of physical labor. Time for recreation
was extremely rare. The emphasis on intellectual training was such
that physical training was deprecated. A few girls whose families
had means were educated, but physical activity was not a part of such
training. There were a few exceptions, but these were rarities indeed. A simple, yet devastating maneuver like binding the feet kept
women quite weak and useless for anything save household and decorative purpose. [12,13,73,81]

India. Although ancient India had a great many health problems,
history indicates that there was considerable concern for health prior
to foreign rule in the tenth century (A.D.), and that a number of
sports and games were practiced. Accompanying the decline in physical activities and physical culture were the restrictions laid down by
Buddha himself against the popular pastimes of the day. There was
often a military class which had to keep fit for combat. Dancing was
popular, but then fell into disrepute except for members of the lower

classes and professional dancing girls. Generally speaking, there
was a complete rejection of bodily activity for women (who were kept
in an inferior social position.[61,70,73,81]

Iran and Israel. In Iranian Civilization there is no mention of
physical education for women whatsoever, but in Hebrew Civilization
the situation was somewhat different. Women appear to have occupied an important place, especially in early times. Dancing was often
involved in religious worship, but subsequently continued only as a
form of recreation and for various secular celebrations. There was
a certain amount of physical labor for women in connection with the
routine chores of the camps, or perhaps with the flocks in the fields
or in vine culture on the hillsides. Particular health habits and recreational pursuits were considered desirable, the latter especially
on the Sabbath. As social life increased, the women were confined to
a greater extent to the home. They were not expected to possess
intellectual acumen. Many did involve themselves in simple games,
music, and dancing.[42,70,81]

Crete. The Cretan Civilization preceded that of the Greeks and
extended roughly for a period of several thousand years on the island
of Crete and at other points in the Mediterranean Sea. It was evidently the first society in which women assumed a relatively important role. Even their deity was a Mother Goddess, and there appears
to have been more equal status in marriage between the sexes. They
did other things like hunting, driving chariots, and even bull-grap-
pling - a most dangerous sport. There is evidence further that they
attended various celebrations and religious festivals. Because of the
proximity of the sea, they were active in boating and undoubtedly
knew how to swim.[21,81]

Classical Civilization

Greece. In the city-state of Sparta, presumably the most warlike of the various Greek city-states, the educational system was
carefully designed to fulfill their avowed goal of military supremacy.
Women received unusual attention, since it was felt that it was absolutely necessary for them to produce rugged children to be future
warriors. They took part in many of the activities of the boys and
young men and developed a concept of good health and their place in
life. They wrestled, ran, played ball, threw the javelin, swam, and
rode horseback. Some even won Olympic victories. Typically, they
continued public exercises until marriage and were probably on the
average the finest physical specimens that the world has seen to date.
There is some disagreement as to whether this training fully accomplished its purpose, although it is quite natural that the Athenians
would riducule these ladies because of the different standard held for
women by them. There is evidence, however, that the dancing of the

young Spartan maidens was graceful, and that their mien was appropriate to that typically expected of a woman.[22,42,45]

Contrasting Cultures. There were sharp contrasts between the Spartan and Athenian cultures; yet, the ideal of service on behalf of the state characterized Athenian life as well. The Athenians, however, did gradually develop a concept of education which envisioned harmony of development of all the aspects of man – physical, mental, moral, and aesthetic. They fostered, as perhaps never before or since, an ideal of liberal education for freemen that has been admired down through the centuries. And yet we find that women had virtually no part (immediately visible to the historian's eye) in the achievements of this civilization save for the function of child-bearing and care of the home. Subsequently, women achieved greater status as teachers of their children, but the boys were taken away from them when ready for the palaestras. Lower class women did have opportunity to become entertainers in such occupations as dancing, juggling, and the playing of various instruments. Properly modest Athenian women played games as children; learned household arts as young ladies; at times learned to read and write; married early; and were rarely heard of thereafter.[11]

Roman Culture. The status of women in Roman culture was very low initially, but changed considerably during the time of the Empire. In early Roman education the average woman was definitely considered inferior, and had little to say about her place in life. Her education came to an abrupt end when she married. Despite these limitations, her station is generally considered to be somewhat higher than her counterpart in Greece. She did learn how to read, write, and cipher and was responsible for the early education of her children. Presumably she took part in childhood games and, in some cases, learned how to swim.

In the later days of the Empire, women achieved a greater amount of independence including social and moral equality, as well as the opportunity to gain divorces from their husband and to own property. A developing laxity in morals took place, and adultery was much more common. Many women distinguished themselves in a variety of ways, however, and were trained in the various professions. Their pattern of education changed also, although there is doubt whether coeducation ever existed. Dancing, music, and literature were included, and then were banned later under the influence of Christian asceticism.[8]

The Romans never caught the Greek spirit of the total education of man, although they exercised for health and took part in a number of different sports, especially ball playing. Women went to the public baths, took part in the simple forms of ball playing, and watched the spectacles, but on the whole were not very active physically. The exercises of the gymnasium were simply not considered proper for women except in rare instances when such activity was tried and summarily rejected. [81]

The Middle Ages

The Middle Ages was a time when physical education sank to its lowest ebb except for the training of knights in the feudal period, and its appearance in some of the humanistic schools of the Renaissance Era. The Church gave very strong opposition to athletic and recreational excess during this time, and there developed a growing concept that the body was evil and its demands should be suppressed. The Romans in their final days so debased sports and games that such subsequent opposition was quite understandable. There were some exceptions to this belief, but they were rare indeed. There is very little, if any, mention made of women during the "Dark Ages." During the feudal period girls received training in the courtly graces in schools conducted at the various castles. There were, of course, the usual children's games which have persisted throughout history. During the transitional period now known as the Renaissance, the care and development of the body received greater emphasis. There does not appear to be evidence that the conception of all-round development was generally recognized, however, and this certainly held true in the education of girls and young ladies. It should be pointed out that the individual humanism of the early Renaissance gave great promise for physical education, but a growing spirit of intellectualism cut short this hopeful development. In the lands where the Protestant Reformation took hold, study of the classics was combined with that of Biblical literature with the result that the educational aim was somewhat more social than individual. These so-called social humanists promoted a much narrower concept of education and copied Greek and Roman classic writers slavishly. With this approach there was little room in the curriculum for physical education, music, or art. [12,13,20]

Early Modern History

During the sixteenth and seventeenth centuries there were a number of educators who rebelled against the formalism present in education at that time. These educators, known as Realists, have since been divided into three categories: (1) the verbal realists who desired a strong body for the help that it could give the mind as it strove for religious piety; (2) the social realists, who conceived of physical education as an important part of education for an integrated personality; and (3) the sense realists, who desired physical fitness for its contribution to sound health and as a basis for intellectual attainment. [73]

Very little attention appears to have been given to education for girls during this eara. Fénelon, Archbishop of Cambrai, provided some stimulus for the education of women by presenting his theories on the subject, but his main contribution appears to be in the direction of liberalizing educational method. Juan Luis Vives, a Spanish scholar, omitted such subjects as music, dancing, and drawing in his proposed curriculum, while including training in Latin and the vernacular, religion and moral conduct, and household and child management. John Locke, whose greatest contribution was made in the latter half of the seventeenth century, was greatly concerned with character development, as well as health and physical fitness as a necessary base. He stressed the need for recreational activity as well, mainly because of the refreshment from toil that it provided. His recommendations were made for boys and young men primarily.[12]

Eighteenth Century Europe

The eighteenth century is generally regarded as a transitional period insofar as political, social, religious, and educational ideals are concerned. It might be designated as a reactionary period in education, especially in the first fifty years. Formal discipline in education developed as a reaction against the realistic theories. The tendency toward universal education was retarded to a considerable degree, since rationalism became an important goal in education. The greatest influence on education in this century came in the latter half through the influence of Jean Jacques Rousseau.[24] He was the exponent of naturalism in education - an educational idea which represented a revolt against the corrupting influence of society and the absolute (dogmatic) authorities of the state and church respectively. His doctrine of naturalism gave unusually strong emphasis to the place of health and physical education in the child's education, because he evidently realized the interrelatedness or unity of the mind and body. But unfortunately for the women of his time, he did not appreciate the possibility that a woman might possess an individuality of her own. He felt that woman was destined to be a supplement to man. Hence she should be strong physically for the result that this might have on her offspring. She should also receive sound moral instruction, as this would get her children off to the right start in life. Furthermore, her education should include such skills as singing, dancing, and a variety of household abilities, since the possession of these talents would make life more comfortable and enjoyable for her husband.

The Influence of Nationalism. The influence of nationalism on education in both Europe and the United States in the nineteenth century was very strong, as it helped to bring about state-controlled and state-supported public school systems. In any national school system, physical training designed to maintain and improve the fitness of the populace will invariably find an important place, and this will usually

- 144 -

include girls and women as well as boys and men. Thus, w
various systems of universal, free, and compulsory educatio
veloped throughout the Western World to a greater or lesser ex
This secular and civic education typically included citizenship, ph
cal fitness, and vocational training.[12]

New Ideas in Elementary Education. Concurrent with the development of nationalism in education, another change was gradually
taking place in connection with the actual educational process itself.
Many concerned individuals began to realize that education should involve a type of control of the child's development according to certain
psychological principles resulting from the interaction of the individual and his environment. The results of these new ideas were felt
primarily only in the elementary school during this century, and subsequently extended to some degree to the other levels.[13]

Early Women's Physical Education in the United States

During the so-called "provincial period" following the "colonial
period" in American education, educational practices for girls and
women began to change. This change in practice was true in the
matter of exercise as well, which had previously been characterized
by formalism. The boys and men of the early 1800's were following
a German pattern as prescribed by Beck, Follen, and Lieber, but
there was some variation in the exercise patterns prescribed for
girls.[12,25,31,64,80]

✓ Typically, girls were considered to be quite frail, and it was
believed by many that calisthenics were much too strenuous. A new
type of wand drills known as Indian Scepter exercises was quite popular for a time. Another trend was the introduction of apparati to improve posture and develop strength. Women of this period, according
to fashion, were expected to have small waists and weak backs. It
was significant to note that - for the first time - walking, riding,
croquet, swimming, skating, and archery were being recommended
as desirable activities for women.

Other Developments. Around the middle of the nineteenth century, the Turners were promoting German gymnastics as the best
program for the schools. At this time, also, George Barker Winship
was declaiming that strength and health were synonymous. Furthermore, some colleges became concerned with the health habits and
practices of their students. Then along came Dio Lewis with his
"system" of light exercises designed for adult women, as well as for
the young and the old.[26,36,37,69]

Post Civil War Period. After the Civil War, the exercises
devised by Lewis, and those proposed earlier by Catherine Beecher,
continued to meet stiff opposition from German gymnastics, Swedish

patterns being devised by Hitchcock, Sargent,
st in athletic participation in various sports and
ineously. Greater freedom in activity (and
ly being accepted, although such "freedom" was
d in scope by the standards of today. In dancing
as well away from the so-called "fancy steps"
d movements with very little bodily action to a
of dance which involved all parts of the body. In
early health education, the emphasis had been on the unsatisfactory
environmental conditions in the schools. During this post-war period,
the concern was increasingly related to the harmful influence of
bacteria, along with physiology of the body (including the harmful influence of alcohol and narcotics on the body).[35,58,71]

Early Twentieth Century

At the beginning of the twentieth century, there was still a great
deal of opposition toward the idea of women taking part in interscholastic athletics, but the recommendations of women's organizations in favor of intramural sports did not discourage the women
basketball enthusiasts. The first standardized rules guide was
published on behalf of the American Physical Education Association
in 1901. It is noteworthy that professional women physical educators
made every effort to guard women's athletics from many of the difficulties that the men had encountered.[23,35,44,74]

The "Natural" Movement. Another innovation at this time was
the widespread effort to bring dancing into the curriculum. A new
conflict developed - the extent to which dancing and athletics should
supplant gymnastics in physical education programs. Folk dancing
became so popular that many felt it and athletics were receiving undue
attention. These trends were part of the growing "natural" movement
in physical education, of course, which attempted to relate the field
to current American educational theories. This movement undoubtedly had a relationship to the growing interest in play and recreation, as
well as to the competitive athletic trend.[6,7,17,60]

There is no question of the tremendous influence that Dewey's
philosophy of education had on the natural movement. Wood and
Cassidy's The New Physical Education, published in 1927, was designed to clarify this approach so that all who were interested might
understand what the naturalized program was intended to accomplish.
It was based upon a system of motor education to be implemented
through "learning while doing." The belief was that it was in agreement with "modern educational theory" and helped the student to
realize "concrete goals in activity." The major emphasis was to be
on exercise that was more natural, spontaneous, and enjoyable. Education through the medium of the physical was to supersede education
of the physical.[15,27,35,79]

1930 to 1940. In 1930 the American Physical Education Association elected Mabel Lee as its first woman president, and in the following year the Women's Division of the National Amateur Athletic Federation affiliated with the A.P.E.A. In 1940 this group (the Women's Division) merged with the National Section on Women Athletics (A.P.E.A.). This Section, now known as the Division of Girls' and Women's Sports, has exerted a strong, wholesome influence on all aspects of women's sport. The decade from 1930 to 1940 was dominated by the devastating financial depression, which incidentally gave impetus to the concept of education for wholesome use of leisure. Requirements for teachers were upgraded during this period.[10,34,35,74,76]

World War II

World War II dominated the decade from 1940 to 1950 and brought increased emphasis on physical fitness for both boys and girls. The time allotment for physical education was generally increased. The acceptance of women for enlistment in the various branches of the armed forces provided additional incentive for women to stress physical activity. Increased interest was shown in a large variety of individual, dual, and team sports, but competition for women was still confined almost completely to the intramural program with some emphasis on interscholastic competition in specific geographical areas (e.g., Iowa). Interest in all aspects of the dance continued to grow, with special emphasis on modern, folk, and square dancing.[35,40,65]

Women's Aims

Women physical educators have continued to emphasize the need for a broad program of health, physical education, and recreation. Where possible, they have encouraged a program of required physical education for all girls, as well as a remedial program for those who needed it. They have taken the lead in the elementary field, and many have made an effort to implement a concept of "movement education" into our field. They have stressed health education, instruction in carry-over activities, and voluntary recreational participation. Recommendations for improved physical fitness from the national level in the latter half of the 1950's and the early 1960's are undoubtedly having an influence on girls' programs at present. The extent to which the desire for increasing physical fitness has influenced the gradual upswing in the calibre of girls' and women's sports has yet to be determined.[3,4,27,35]

As educators, both men and women physical educators have a responsibility to bring all of the advantages to young people that the total field offers. In this regard girls and women are no exceptions.

They have the right to enjoy an outstanding, well-balanced program of physical education and sport.

References and Bibliography

1. Adams, Ruby A. "The History and Development of Women's Field Hockey." Master's thesis, University of North Carolina, 1952.

2. Ainsworth, Dorothy S. "The History of Physical Education in Colleges for Women." Ph.D. dissertation, Columbia University, 1930.

3. American Association for Health, Physical Education, and Recreation, Division for Girls' and Women's Sports. "State of Policies and Procedures for Competition in Girls' and Women's Sports." JOHPER, 28, No. 6:57-58, September, 1957.

4. American Association for Health, Physical Education, and Recreation, Division for Girls' and Women's Sports and Division of Men's Athletics. Values in Sports. Washington, D. C.: AAHPER, 1963.

5. Anderson, Julia M. "The Development and Growth of Sport Activities for Women in North Texas Teachers College from 1908 to 1938." Master's thesis, North Texas State Teachers College, 1939.

6. Ashton, Dudley. "Contribution of Dance to Physical Education, Part I," JOHPER, 26, No. 9, December, 1955.

7. _____. "Contributions of Dance to Physical Education, Part II," JOHPER, 27, No. 4, April, 1956.

8. Ballou, Ralph B. "An Analysis of the Writings of Selected Church Fathers to A.D. 394 to Reveal Attitudes Regarding Physical Activity." Ph.D. dissertation, University of Oregon, 1965.

9. Bennett, Bruce L. "The Life of Dudley Allen Sargent, M.D., and His Contributions to Physical Education." Ph.D. dissertation, The University of Michigan, 1947.

10. Bennett, Patricia. "The History and Objectives of the National Section for Girls' and Women's Sports." Ed.D. dissertation, Mills College, 1956.

11. Boslooper, Thomas. "Image of Woman in Classical Antiquity," Proceedings of the Second World Symposium on the History of Sport and Physical Education. Banff, Alberta, Canada, 1971.

12. Brubacher, John S. A History of the Problems of Education. Second edition. New York: McGraw-Hill Book Co., 1966.

13. Butts, R. F. A Cultural History of Education. New York: McGraw-Hill Book Co., 1947.

14. Cahn, L. Joseph. "Contributions of Plato to Thought on Physical Education." Ed.D. dissertation, New York University, 1941.

15. Caldwell, Stratton. "Conceptions of Physical Education in Twentieth Century America, Rosalind Cassidy." Ph.D. dissertation, University of Southern California, 1966.

16. Cobb, Louise S. "A Study of the Functions of Physical Education in Higher Education." Ph.D. dissertation, Columbia University, 1943.

17. Cozens, F. W. and Stumpf, F. S. Sports in American Life. Chicago: The University of Chicago Press, 1953.

18. Drew, A. Gwendolyn. "A Historical Study of the Concern of the Federal Government for the Physical Fitness of Non-age Youth with Reference to the Schools." Ph.D. dissertation, University of Pittsburgh, 1944.

19. Dulles, Foster R. A History of Recreation. Second edition. New York: Appleton-Century-Crofts Co., Inc., 1965.

20. Eby, F. and Arrowood, C. F. The Development of Modern Education. Englewood Cliffs, N. J.: Prentice-Hall, Inc., 1934.

21. Evans, A. The Palace of Minos at Knossos. 5 volumes. London: The Macmillan Company, 1921-1936.

22. Eyler, Marvin H. "Origins of Some Modern Sports." Ph.D. dissertation, University of Illinois, 1956.

23. Felshin, Janet. "Changing Conceptions of Purpose in Physical Education in the United States from 1880-1930." Ed.D. dissertation, University of California, 1958.

24. Frederick, Mary M. "Naturalism: The Philosophy of Jean Jacques Rousseau and Its Implications for American Physical Education." D.P.E. dissertation, Springfield College, 1961.

25. Goodsell, W. Pioneers of Women's Education. New York: McGraw-Hill Book Co., Inc., 1931.

26. Hall, Ann. "Women's Sport in Canada Prior to 1914." Proceedings of the First Canadian Symposium on the History of Sport and Physical Education. Edmonton, Alberta, Canada, 1970.

27. Harres, Bea. "Attitudes of Students toward Women's Athletic Competition." Research Quarterly, Vol. 29, No. 2:278-284, May, 1968.

28. Henry, William. An Approved History of the Olympic Games. New York: G. P. Putnam's Sons, 1948.

29. Hess, Ford A. "American Objectives of Physical Education from 1900-1957 Assessed in the Light of Certain Historical Events." Ed.D. dissertation, New York University, 1959.

30. Hileman, Betty Jean. "Emerging Patterns of Thought in Physical Education in the United States, 1956-1966." Ph.D. dissertation, University of Southern California, 1967.

31. Holliman, Jennie. "American Sports, 1785-1835." Ph.D. dissertation, Columbia University, 1931.

32. Jensen, Judith L. "The History and Development of Volleyball for Girls and Women." Master's thesis, Ohio University, 1959.

33. Langon, John. "A Historical Development of Girls' Basketball." Master's thesis, University of Wyoming, 1954.

34. Lee, Mabel. "The Case for and Against Intercollegiate Athletics for Women." Research Quarterly, Vol. 2, No. 2:93-127, May, 1931.

35. _____, and Bennett, Bruce. "This Is Our Heritage: Part Part I, 1885 to 1900; Part II, 1900 to 1915; Part III, 1915 to 1930; Part IV, 1930 to 1945; Part V, 1945 to 1960," JOHPER, XXXI (April, 1960), 26-85.

36. Lewis, Dio. Our Girls. New York: Harper Brothers, 1974.

37. Lindsay, Peter L. "Woman's Place in Nineteenth Century Canadian Sport," Journal of the CAHPER, Vol. 37, No. 1:25-28, September-October, 1970.

38. Locke, Margaret C. "A Biographical Study of Agnes Rebecca Wayman: Her Life and Contributions to the Field of Health, Physical Education, and Recreation." D.P.E. dissertation, Springfield College, 1959.

39. Lozes, Jewell H. "The Philosophy of Certain Religious Denominations Relative to Physical Education, and the Effect of this Philosophy on Physical Education in Certain Church-related Institutions." M.S. thesis, Pennsylvania State University, 1955.

40. Lynn, Minnie L. "Major Emphases of Physical Education in the United States." Ph.D. dissertation, University of Pittsburgh, 1944.

41. Malumphy, Theresa. "The College Woman Athlete, Questions and Tentative Answers." Quest, Monograph XIV, June, 1970, 18-27.

42. Marrou, H. I. A History of Education in Antiquity. Translated by George Lamb. New York: The New American Library of World Literature, Inc., 1964.

43. Mason, Otis T. Woman's Share in Primitive Culture. New York: D. Appleton and Co., 1942.

44. McCloy, C. H. Philosophical Bases for Physical Education. New York: Appleton-Century-Crofts, Inc., 1940.

45. McDonald, Margaret Anne. "A Study of Ancient Greek Physical Education with Emphasis upon the Dance, the Women, and the Professional." M.Ed. thesis, Woman's College, University of North Carolina, 1962.

46. Miller, Wilma K. "A Study of the History of Women's Sport Customs." Master's thesis, The Ohio State University, 1942.

47. Moolenijzer, Nicolaas J. "The Concept of 'Natural' in Physical Education: Johann Guts Muths and Margarete Streicher." Ph.D. dissertation, University of Southern California, 1965.

48. Morland, Richard B. "A Philosophical Interpretation of the Educational Views Held by Leaders in American Physical Education." Ph.D. dissertation, New York University, 1958.

49. Muller, Herbert J. _Freedom in the Ancient World_. New York: Harper & Row Publishers, 1961.

50. _____. _Freedom in the Modern World_. New York: Harper & Row Publishers, 1966.

51. _____. _Freedom in the Western World_. New York: Harper & Row Publishers, 1963.

52. Murray, Mildred C. "A Study to Document the Changes in Women's Gymnastics from 1940 through 1965." Master's thesis, Springfield College, 1967.

53. Nicollusi, Gayle F. "The Development of Competitive Track and Field for Women in the United States." Master's thesis, Ball State University, 1966.

54. Oberteuffer, D. and Ulrich, C. _Physical Education_. Third edition. New York: Harper & Row Publishers, 1962.

55. Peterson, Patricia M. "History of Olympic Skiing for Women in the United States: A Cultural Interpretation." Ph.D. dissertation, University of Southern California, 1967.

56. Phillbeck, Ellen. "The Development of Women's Golf in the United States." Master's thesis, University of North Carolina, 1960.

57. Phillips, Madge M. "Biographies of Selected Women Leaders in Physical Education in the United States." Ph.D. dissertation, State University of Iowa, 1960.

58. "Pioneer Women in Physical Education." _Supplement to the Research Quarterly_, XII, October, 1941. (Includes articles written by various authors about Amy M. Homans, Eliza Mosher, Celia Mosher, Delphine Hanna, Marien Carter, Harriet Ballintine, Senda Berenson, Jessie Bancroft, Anne Clapp, Ethel Perrin, Lillian Drew, Constance Applebee and Abby Mayhew.)

59. Price, Mary A. "The Role of the United States Women's Participation in the Modern Olympic Games." Ed.D. dissertation, Columbia Teachers College, 1953.

60. Rainwater, Clarence E. _The Play Movement in the United States_. Chicago: University of Chicago Press, 1922.

61. Rajagopalan, K. _A Brief History of Physical Education in India_. Delhi: Army Publishers, 1963.

62. Roose, Alice E. "Trends in Women's Sports as Reported in the Oregonian Newspapers, 1850-1900." Master's thesis, State College of Washington, 1941.

63. Sanborn, Marion A. and Hartman, Betty G. Issues in Physical Education. Philadelphia: Lea & Febiger, 1964.

64. Schwendener, Norma. A History of Physical Education in the United States. New York: A. S. Barnes & Co., 1942.

65. Searcy, Paulajean. "The History, Organization, and Function of the Division for Girls' and Women's Sports, 1940-1962." M.S. thesis, Smith College, 1962.

66. Shepard, Natalie M. "Democracy in Physical Education: A Study of the Implications for Educating for Democracy through Physical Education." Ed.D. dissertation, New York University, 1952.

67. Smith, Ronald A. "The Rise of Basketball for Women in Colleges." Proceedings of the First Canadian Symposium on the History of Sport and Physical Education. Edmonton, Alberta, Canada, 1970.

68. Somers, Florence A. Principles of Women's Athletics. New York: A. S. Barnes & Co., 1930.

69. Spencer, Herbert. Education: Intellectual, Moral and Physical. London: Watts & Co., 1949.

70. Steere, Julia. "The Woman Athlete: A Chronological Account of the Woman in Athletic Sports from the Days of Ancient Egypt to 1900." Master's thesis, Colorado State College of Education, 1928.

71. Trekell, Marianna. "The Effect of Cultural Changes on the Sports Activities of American Women, 1860-1953." Master's thesis, The Ohio State University, 1953.

72. _____. "Gertrude Evelyn Moulton, M.D.: Her Life and Professional Career in Health and Physical Education." Ph.D. dissertation, The Ohio State University, 1963.

73. Van Dalen, D. B. and Bennett, B. L. A World History of Physical Education. Englewood Cliffs, N. J.: Prentice-Hall, Inc., 1971. Second edition.

74. Von Borries, Eline. The History and Functions of the National Section on Women's Athletics. Washington, D. C.: National Section on Women's Athletics, 1941.

75. Wagemann, Jacqueline. "The Study of the Development of the Swimming Program for Women at the University of Illinois." Master's thesis, University of Illinois, 1960.

76. Watts, Doris P. "Changing Conceptions of Competitive Sports for Girls and Women in the United States from 1880 to 1960." Ph.D. dissertation, University of Calitornia at Los Angeles, 1960.

77. Weaver. R. B. Amusement and Sports in American Life. Chicago: The University of Chicago Press, 1939.

78. Weston, A. The Making of American Physical Education. New York: Appleton-Century-Crofts, Inc., 1962.

79. Wood, Thomas D. and Cassidy, Rosalind F. The New Physical Education. New York: The Macmillan Company, 1927.

80. Woody, Thomas. Life and Education in Early Societies. New York: The Macmillan Company, 1949.

81. Woody, Thomas. Women's Education in the United States. Volumes I-II. Lancaster, Pa.: Science Press, 1929.

82. Young, Mildred L. "The History of Construction, Selection, and Maintenance of Equipment Used in Women's Popular Sport." Master's thesis, The Ohio State University, 1941.

83. Zeigler, Earle F. "A History of Professional Preparation for Physical Education in the United States, 1861-1948." Ph.D. dissertation, Yale University, 1951. (Published by Microcard Publications, University of Oregon at Eugene.)

CHAPTER 12

THE EFFECT OF SOME CULTURAL CHANGES UPON THE SPORTS AND PHYSICAL EDUCATION ACTIVITIES OF AMERICAN WOMEN, 1860-1960

Marianna Trekell
University of Illinois, Urbana

The century between 1860 and 1960 was characterized by more social, political and economic upheavals than in any comparable time period in the recorded history of man. The phenomenal advances in scientific knowledge during this era was the all-pervasive factor which precipitated the ever-accelerating rate of change in all aspects of society. The changing patterns of participation by girls and women in sports and physical education activities during the past century clearly reveal a full cycle of change. Practices evolved from almost no acceptance of or participation in sports and physical education activities to almost complete acceptance to active promotion of participation by women in a wide variety of activities.[1]

Changing habits and attitudes regarding sports participation for women closely parallel progress made by women in other phases of American life--political, educational and economic--advancements which found them emancipated from the narrow bonds of home life. Changing patterns of participation in sports by women can best be understood against the backdrop of the entire women's rights movements of the past century, which clearly reflects the cultural climate of the times.

Editor's Note: Professor Trekell, the Editor's former colleague and personal friend at the University of Illinois, Urbana, has strengthened and extended an earlier study. This investigation concentrates specifically on the effect of cultural changes in the United States on sports and physical education activities for American women during the century from 1860 to 1960.

---

[1] This study, originally developed as a M.A. thesis at Ohio State University in 1953, covered the period from 1860 to 1953. Subsequently a paper covering the period from 1860 to 1960, was presented on March 18, 1965 at the AAHPER Convention in Dallas, Texas. Thus, this article represents an amalgamation of these previous works.

Only minor gains were made in increased participation in sports and physical education activities for girls and women during the first half of the nineteenth century. The preoccupation with expansion, the long hours of work both on farms and in factories, and the resurgence of religious opposition to play and recreation inhibited any swift acceptance of the idea of recreation, sports, and physical activities. Major changes in the picture of sports and physical education activities for girls and women slowly began to appear after the close of the Civil War.

Launching of Women's Rights, 1860-1880

If the American belief in the ways of democracy was to survive, progress in solving the problem of equality for women was certain to come. As America began to settle herself after her initial struggle for freedom, she began to see the inconsistency of her treatment of women in light of her democratic ideals.

The effect of the Industrial Revolution upon the place of woman in society was incalculable. For the first time there was an economic reason and a social opportunity for women to leave the home. Until the upheaval caused by the Industrial Revolution, this great natural resource, the female force, remained unreleased, unrecognized, and unappreciated.

This need for women's potential on the labor market had an important contribution to make to the advancement of higher educational opportunities for women. It was believed that some useful social end should be served by this reservoir of potentialities. By 1860 a number of colleges, believing that women were misjudged and neglected, opened their doors to the fairer sex.

Although the Civil War interrupted the organized efforts of women's strivings for equality, wartime conditions allowed women to display their unsuspected talents and abilities. Despite the accomplishments of women during the Civil War, however, their rights were still denied.

The status of women in the social life of the nineteenth century had a definite bearing on recreation.

> Before the Civil War, nice women exercised very infrequently; they work skirts when they ran and to be utterly proper, they didn't run at all. Sometimes a few bold spirits would go ice skating, although a contemporary book of etiquette urged them to hang onto the coat tails of their male partners, thus enjoying all the pleasure without incurring any of the fatigue of the exercise. (Jensen, 1952, p. 121).

The socially elite were beginning to approve of activities in which men and women could participate as partners. One of these was roller skating which was introduced in 1863 by James L. Pimpton. New York's social leaders had hoped that roller skating could be restricted to the finer class of people, but, before long, rinks were being built for all people. As a consequence the elite began to frown upon roller skating as a socially acceptable sport for women.

In 1874 another innovation for the emancipation of women from domestic life was the introduction of tennis to the United States by Mary E. Outerbridge. At first, tennis was confined to a few wealthy people in the East, but as time progressed more courts were built and many more people participated. Ice skating was another activity in which women could participate without being ridiculed, because it was thought to be socially acceptable for the fairer sex.

Two equally important crazes struck the American people in 1876: Edison's telephone and the bicycle craze. At this time 20,000 people were riding bicycles. Men were riding the high two-wheeled bicycles while the women rode high three-wheeled tricycles. Bicycling was considered to be on a higher social plane than playing on ball-fields or in rinks. This outdoor activity proved to be a step towards the emancipation of woman from her usually inactive life.

In the post Civil War era physical education programs for girls and women were restricted to activities which society defined as feminine and lady-like. If a member of the fairer sex exerted herself physically she was frowned upon. Because physical training curricula were dictated by the opinions of society, girls and women participated mainly in bicycling, ice skating, calisthenics, gymnastic exercises, and walking. By 1879 women were slowly progressing in their efforts to gain equal rights. With determination and perseverance women continued to struggle for those things they believed to be their full democratic prerogatives.

Progress in Women's Activities, 1880-1900

"Women's rights! What more rights do they want? My wife bosses me; our daughters boss us both, and the servant girls bosses the whole family. It's time the men were allowed some rights." (New York Daily Tribune, 1883, p. 5). One concludes that this Philadelphia man certainly was bitter, but not so much about women's rights as about women in general. Squire in her book, The Woman Movement in America, said, "Surely we women will have small reason ever to be thankful to politicians, statesmen, judges, legislators, or presidents or to men, no matter what they may in the future do for us." (Squire, 1911, p. 244).

The conflicts and feelings of the times were aptly expressed by these two people. Men had begun to feel that they were being dominated by women. Women believed that they were never going to gain their freedom, because men were not willing to accept them on an equal basis. In spite of and because of such feelings, and more doggedly than ever, the women continued their battle for woman suffrage.

Toward the latter part of the 1880's women were making more progress in their efforts for suffrage. Utah's new constitution included political equality for women. During the period of 1880-1900, Colorado, Idaho, and Kansas followed suit in granting women municipal suffrage.

Women who were working played an important part toward the advancement of woman suffrage. In 1880, 14.5 per cent of the total population of women, sixteen years of age and over, were gainfully employed. Ten years later in 1890, 16.5 per cent were gainfully employed.

By 1900 most colleges and universities had opened their doors to women. In spite of opposition, it was slowly being accepted that girls and women had the right to, and would benefit from, a higher education. Their curricula consisted mainly of teacher training and homemaking. Some people maintained that women were too delicate and could not survive a strenuous college program.

Most physical education activities for girls consisted of various systems of gymnastics and exercises. It was during this time that there was much concern for the health status of girls and women. Care had to be taken to avoid undue strain on the delicate female!

Until 1892 colleges had neither introduced nor popularized any sport, but in this year Senda Berenson introduced basketball to the girls of Smith College. In 1899 the first committee on basketball rules for women was organized.

Because of more leisure time and changes of attitudes, greater numbers of people were beginning to participate in recreational and sports activities. Tennis and golf were being enjoyed by the wealthier classes who could afford the equipment and money to join the country clubs, which were just coming into existence. In 1887 women first played in a national tennis tournament, but it was not until two years later that the United States Lawn Tennis Association officially recognized women tennis players. The first women's golf tournament was held October 17 and 18, 1894 at Morristown, New Jersey. By 1895 the United States Golf Association had sanctioned golf tournaments for women.

The increased interest in sports and amusementd during this
period brought with it a broad interest in recreation. Many people
felt the need for play. The previous Puritan influence was diminishing. Religion still maintained a vital place in the lives of people,
even though participation in many different forms of recreation was
generally acceptable.

Fashion designers indeed had a difficult time trying to produce
a riding habit for women. Godey's Lady's Book, "... advocated a
kilted skirt trimmed with fancy brandenburgs, jacket bodice and vest,
cloth cap and leggings. Other arbiters of fashion favored divided
skirts and top boots; there were suggestions that even bloomers
might be worn without offense to female dignity and modesty."
(Dulles, 1940, p. 266).

While the Women's Suffrage Movement was making only a dent
in the struggle for equal rights, women were participating in sports
and recreational activities in ever-increasing numbers. Women
were accompanying men to sporting events. Women and men were
active in the outdoor movement of walking, camping and sailing. Of
course, women could only be spectators at such activities as baseball, running, and boxing. Play, as the majority of people saw it,
was not to be frowned upon as a worldly pleasure. People considered play to be important, because it contributed to healthy bodies and
relaxed minds for both sexes.

Beginning of a New Century, 1900-1920

There was an increasing interest in liberality and a growing
belief in equal rights. It was difficult to crystallize the scattered
results into solid gains because of the diverse opinions concerning
women's right. Congress and state legislatures were against full
suffrage, while at the same time various labor unions were supporting women in their struggle to vote. Four Western states had already given women political equality. In spite of the many forces
against them, women continued lecturing, distributing literature,
working with legislatures and trying to build new interest.

During this period women increasingly entered the labor forces.
By 1905 some five million women were at work. Approximately one
million of them were working in factories. During World War I, as
men left to join the armed forces, women took jobs in munitions
plants, railroads, factories, offices, and other places. A few daring
women went to France as ambulance drivers and nurses. After the
war women lost many of these jobs, but in the interim they had
proven that they had many talents and were capable of doing a good
job.

Because of the increased number of women in the labor force, several significant events occurred. One was the enactment of the law already adopted by most states giving married women the right to collect and control their earnings, as well as to be held responsible for their own actions. Also, the Federal Government and many boards of education adopted the principle of equal pay for comparable work regardless of sex.

1900 to 1920 -- What a boom period this must have been for fashion designers because of the changes made in women's clothing. During the war women shed their old armor plates while the skirts climbed from the floor to reveal stockings. "The athletic vogue was growing; some women were putting on more sensible clothes for bicycling and swimming. The 'rainy day' skirt, a daring two inches above the ankle, was hailed as a symbol of the emancipation of women." (Jensen, 1952, p. 137).

About this time the motion picture burst upon the scene to leave its indelible imprint upon the modes of American society. According to some, the evil eye of the motion picture camera would lead to a laxity of morals. Even though not everyone approved of the early pictures, women tried to copy hair styles and fashions from the actresses.

Schools and universities were constantly growing. By 1900 there were 500 universities, 175 normal schools, and 6,000 public high schools. The University of Nebraska, one of the 500 universities in the United States, deserves special mention, because it was their Chancellor Canfield, who:

> ...was a pioneer in introducing competitive athletics for
> women. Since no girls could run, let alone bend over,
> in corsets and long skirts, he required a sensible
> costume for track and gymnasium. Even though men
> were not present, new girls at first would sink to the
> floor in shame over their bloomers--but in a week they
> generally got over it. (Jensen, 1952, p. 129).

In 1901 Spalding published the first basketball guide for women. The game of basketball which originated in the late nineteenth century was now enjoyed by many girls in colleges and universities. Field hockey for girls and women had a tremendous growing period from the time it was introduced in 1901 by Constance Applebee. After World War I, soccer was beginning to appear as a team game for girls and women.

The acceptance of women in sports was aided in a large measure by Margaret Curtis, May Sutton, and Eleanora Sears. Margaret Curtis, from Boston, was a three-time winner of the Women's Golf

Championship. May Sutton was America's first outstanding international tennis player. Eleanora Sears defied all conventional thinking and participated in such varied physical activities as tennis, golf, swimming, rifle shooting, squash, and motorboat and automobile racing. It is said that she was the prime liberator of women in sports.

Other women were active in the conventional type sports and some expressed a desire to participate in additional activities. In 1912, at the sixth Olympic Games in Stockholm, women were invited to compete in swimming and diving. In 1916 women took up the sport of trapshooting.

In the early part of the twentieth century women made definite gains in their struggle for the right to vote. By 1920 women were confident that their desire for suffrage would soon be realized.

Women's Victory, 1920-1940

Final victory in women's long struggle for the right to vote came on August 18, 1920, when Tennessee ratified the 19th amendment and it became the law of the land. Once they had gained suffrage rights, women turned their sights on participating in local, state, and national political campaigns.

The freedom to pursue their newly found gains was enhanced by technological advances. Between 1920 and 1940 many new conveniences appeared in the home which simplified women's household work. Such appliances as new stoves, laundering facilities, and cleaning equipment gave women time for leisure to take part in activities outside of the home without shirking domestic duties.

By 1920 women had made great strides by being granted political equality, and they were making a noticeable impact on the make-up of the labor force. The 1920 census showed that over eight million women were employed in the United States. By far the largest percentage of the total number of women workers were servants or domestic help, followed by the category of common farm laborers. Teachers formed the third largest group, followed by stenographers, clerks, laundresses, saleswomen, and bookkeepers.

The aforementioned gains by women were reflected in their styles of dress, which became less restricting. Some women during this period began to appear on the streets in pants or slacks; and nationally prominent women such as Marlene Dietrich wore mannish suits, both pants and jackets. Just as controversial as women wearing slacks was the proper attire for women who wanted to go swimming. At the beginning of the 1920's a woman wearing a one-piece bathing suit had to see that the neck of her suit was not too low, or the bottom of the suit too high. If it were suspected of being too brief, a policewoman measured her suit; when the suspicions were verified, the culprit could be arrested for being immoral. This ruling did not prevail for long, because styles and fashions fluctuated rapidly. In the 1930's everyone thought that the swimming suit styles then in mode were as brief as possible! (but--).

In the early 1920's schools were still having formal gymnastics, but in the latter part of this decade and the thirties other physical activities appeared in the schools. Many girl's and women's physical education programs included the fundamental skills of running, jumping, throwing, catching, climbing, team games, individual sports, dancing, self-testing activities such as combatives, stunts, gymnastics, and swimming. The major stated objective for participation by women in sports and physical activities centered on the benefits which would accrue in terms of health and vitality.

Growth of interest in sports and physical education activities in the twenties received considerable impetus from the dismal picture revealed about the health status of American youth, as a result of the medical examinations for the Armed Forces during World War I. It was believed that an organization should be formed to stimulate sports participation in an effort to cope with this national problem. In order to promote sports and recreation competition the National Amateur Athletic Federation was formed, holding its first meeting, February 21, 1923.

Mrs. Herbert Hoover assumed leadership for the girl's and women's section of the Federation. Believing that there were fundamentally different factors underlying the athletics of men and boys and of women and girls, she was the prime instigator in organizing a Women's Division of the National Amateur Athletic Federation. This organization, pioneering in establishing standards and policies for women participating in sports and athletic events, did much to promote favorable attitude changes for sports atcitivies for women.

In 1932 the Committee on Women's Athletics of the America Physical Education Association, dedicated to promoting a wholesome athletic program for all girls and women, changed its name to the National Section on Women's Athletics. This organization, now called the Division for Girls' and Women's Sports, carried major responsibility for rules and standards in most sports participated in by girls and women, especially in school and college programs.

Not only were women interested in participating in sports, but some wanted to engage in more highly organized competition. These women received their wish by taking part in the Olympic Games. One of the most outstanding women ever to participate in the Olympics was

Mildred ("Babe") Didrikson Zaharias. In 1932 she broke four
Olympic records. Between 1932 and 1950 the "Babe" was voted female athlete of the year five times.

Other outstanding women athletes flashed upon the American
scene. Tennis was advanced by Helen Wills. In 1926 Gertrude
Ederle swam the English Channel--as the first women to accomplish
such a feat--and she was greeted with a traditional ticker tape reception upon her return to New York. America's best woman golfer in
the twenties was Glenna Collett, who won six United States National
Amateur championships.

Between 1929 and 1937 America was engulfed in the Great Depression. In 1935 President Franklin Roosevelt established the
Works Progress Administration to assist the unemployed. The program included building government housing, repairing and building
roads and highways, establishing drama and art centers, and many
other projects. By the close of 1937 the WPA had allotted ten per
cent of its total expenditures for constructing recreation buildings,
parks, athletic fields, swimming pools, tennis courts, and golf
courses. This interest in establishing facilities to enable people to
participate in recreation and sports activities reflected a national
appreciation of the social, emotional, and physical values of such
pursuits.

Recreation had now become a part of everyday living of the
American people, both male and female alike. In fact, it might be
said that recreation was a symbol of the American way of life.

Expected Contributions and Acceptance of Women, 1940-1960

During the period 1940-1960, women were gradually playing a
more important role in shaping the pattern of government. This
trend did not gain momentum until after the Second World War, and
it was stimulated by the important contributions American women
made in industry, government, and the armed forces during the war
years. Women had been advancing in their social and economic positions before the war, but the need for their services and the quality
of their work during the war helped to advance their status.

In 1940, 26 per cent of the women were gainfully employed. By
1960 the number had risen to 35 per cent. (Highlights, 1960, p. 3).
Generally speaking women had been accepted as an integral part of
the total labor force. Women were now entering occupations that
once were forbidden to them. It is interesting to note that the average women worker of 1960 was married and 40 years old.

By 1960 most colleges and universities had not only opened their
doors to women, but also permitted them to enter any field of study

- 163 -

for which they were academically qualified. Even the Harvard Business School, one of the all-male sanctuaries, admitted graduate women in the Management Training Program. The favorite undergraduate major programs of college women were Education, English, Home Economics, Business, Commerce, and Social Studies. (Leopold, 1959, p. 3).

In spite of the continuing question and/or problem concerning the type of education women should receive, more women were graduating from colleges and universities. By 1960 women constituted 34 per cent of the entire higher education enrollment and 41 per cent of the entering class of that year. (Americana Annual, 1962, p. 233).

The emphasis on physical fitness, which grew out of a general concern for fitness during World War II, placed new demands on physical education programs. Schools and colleges sought to maintain quality programs of physical education and sports, rather than retreat to formal fitness and exercise programs. Physical education programs for girls stressed activities in which endurance, stamina, and skills could be developed. While lack of facilities precluded all schools offering some of the recreational, "carry over" activities, variety became the key word for high school girls' physical education programs.

Sports activities were not limited to educational institutions. Most city recreation systems had a division of sports activities for girls and women. They provided an opportunity for girls to participate in such activities as bowling, swimming, basketball, dance, softball, volleyball, tennis, golf, and personalized exercise or fitness programs.

In 1959 more attention was focused on skilled women athletes as they trained for Olympic team membership. The winter Olympics being held in Squaw Valley, California did much to build interest in winter sports activities for men and women.

As more and more women trained for the Olympics, the competition became keener and records were constantly being broken. The greatest runner since Mildred Didrikson Zaharias's time was Wilma Rudolph, from Tennessee State University, who won three gold medals in the 1960 Olympic Games held in Rome.

Through television more people were exposed to watching and understanding the Olympic Games. By 1960 people could view the Games in their own living rooms, and watch the skill, grace, strength, and endurance of the many Olympic competitors. Television played an important part in furthering an interest and understanding of competitive sports for both men and women.

Another important development during the post World War I era was the tremendous increase in informal and family-centered sports and fitness-oriented recreation. Increased leisure of workers, more money to spend on recreational activities, and interest in fitness, all from a health and cosmetic point of view, resulted in an emphasis on a variety of different activities. Increased spectator interest in sports, informal participation of women in non-competitive unorganized sports, family recreation togetherness, the popularity of backyard swimming pools, and the beauty or health salon approach to fitness represented important trends bearing on the cultural impact on sports and physical activities for women.

The world-wide symbol of the All-American girl--young, healthy, and beautiful--appeared to be a universal quality associated with women in the United States. American women continued in their efforts to achieve this quality. Television, movies, and magazines appealed to the feministic and vain sense of all women. Many women were evaluating themselves in regard to slimness, agility, hairstyles, facial appearance, and clothes according to famous television and movie stars, models, or the "top ten" women in the United States.

During the twenty year period from 1940 to 1960, women made definite strides in furthering their role as contributors to local, state, and national affairs, education, the labor force, professional occupations, family living, and society. This general acceptance of women in all walks of life was advanced by the contributions women made during World War II. The growing, more intelligent appreciation of women's potential in our culture was reflected in both increased numbers of participants and greater variety of recreational and competitive activities acceptable for women.

Conclusion

In the century under consideration we have seen complete change in every aspect of the American woman's life. The emancipation of women from 1860 to 1960 was inevitable in light of the rate and nature of the economic growth and the continued striving to fulfill democratic principles. This 100-year period gave rise to the acceptance and recognition of an entirely new role for women in society.

In conjunction with their emancipation, women also found themselves free to participate in a great variety of sports and physical activities. Schools, colleges, recreational and sports organizations encouraged women to actively participate in physical activities. It was and still is true that the kinds of activities in which women engage are basically influenced by the standards, values, and attitudes of the contemporary society.

General Bibliography

Americana Annual 1962. New York: The Americana Corporation.

Dulles, Foster Rhea. America Learns to Play. New York: Appleton-Century Company, 1940.

Highlights 1920-1960. Washington: U. S. Department of Labor, Women's Bureau, 1960.

Huelster, Laura. "Physical Education for Women in Coeducational Institutions." American Academy of Physical Education. No. 6, November 1958, pp. 45-54.

Jensen, Oliver. The Revolt of American Women. New York: Harcourt, Brace and Company, 1952.

Leopold, Alice. "Today's Women College Graduates." The Personnel and Guidance Journal. December 1959, pp. 280-284.

New York Daily Tribune. April 8, 1883, p. 5.

Squire, Belle. The Woman Movement in America. Chicago: A. C. McClure and Co., 1911.

Women in Gainful Occupations. Washington, D. C.: United States Government Printing Office, 1929.

Women's News Service Incorporated. Women of 1923. Philadelphia: John C. Winston Company, 1923.

CHAPTER 13

THE HISTORY OF PHYSICAL EDUCATION IN COLLEGES
FOR WOMEN (U.S.A.)

Dorothy S. Ainsworth
Professor Emeritus of Physical Education
Smith College, Northampton, Mass.

Early Days of Colleges for Women

Colleges for women in the U.S.A. were first established in the
second half of the nineteenth century. First was Elmira in 1855,
followed by Vassar 1865, Wells 1870, Smith 1875, and Wellesley
1876.[1] Prior to this there had been some very excellent seminaries
or secondary schools for girls such as Emma Willard in Troy, New
York, Mary Lyon in South Hadley, Massachusetts, and a school of
Catherine Beecher's in Hartford. All of these ladies for whom the
schools were named approved of some form of exercise for their students; so, it was not strange that the next step in the advancement in
the education of women to the college level would again make note of
the need on the part of the women students for activity. Indeed there
was concern and fear that women were entering upon higher education
which might be too much for their "delicate constitutions" (then considered a feminine characteristic). Even President Seelye reported
at the end of his first year at Smith College that he was happy to say
that the young ladies were none the worse for a strenuous year of
study and, in fact, he thought that most of them were in better health
and spirits than when they arrived.

Editor's Note: Chapter 13 is an essay that was requested from
Dr. Dorothy S. Ainsworth, Professor Emeritus and former Director
of Physical Education at Smith College. Many years ago Miss
Ainsworth's doctoral study was about the history of physical education
in colleges for women. Subsequently this material was reworked and
published by the A. S. Barnes & Company in 1930. Because of her
long experience in the field in the United States and all over the world
which has brought her both knowledge and wisdom, we were so
pleased when Dr. Ainsworth agreed to take time from her still busy
schedule to write on this subject.

---

[1] Ainsworth, Dorothy S. The History of Physical Education in
Colleges for Women. New York: A. S. Barnes & Co., Inc., 1930.

In a study completed in 1930 (Ainsworth, 1930, p. 30), the growth figures of several colleges for women between 1860 and 1930 were shown, and it is equally interesting to see today the much greater expansion and growth from 1930 to 1960. In the earliest period the person who was in charge of physical education was also the Director of Physical Education, or Gymnastics, or of the Gymnasium. In some institutions this person was also a Doctor of Medicine, which was natural as the main objective of the Department was the health of the students. The first teachers had been trained by Dio Lewis (1861) or Dr. Sargent (1881 on) for the most part, but Catherine Beecher ✓ was equally important because of her book on physiology and exercise. German gymnastics also appeared in the Middle West because of a great many German settlers who came to this country after 1848. They brought with them their Turnverein organizations and established branches in many cities and schools in the U.S.A.

Somewhat after this the Swedish system of gymnastics appeared and, after the great meeting in Boston in 1889 which was called by Mrs. August Hemenway where all types of gymnasts were invited to demonstrate their particular work, the Swedish system seemd to have made a great impression and was very thoroughly established in colleges for women. It remained the basic program for the physical education in colleges for women for the next 20 to 30 years.

The Beginnings of the Sport Program in Colleges for Women

At the same time in the "Gay Nineties" sports which were much beloved by the college students began to appear on the campuses. Tennis is mentioned in the early 90's, and the courts consisting of white tapes to mark the lines and, of course, a net stretched across the middle, were to be seen on many campus lawns. No special courts were built at that time. In 1892 Senda Berenson at Smith College heard of the new game of basketball for men invented by Dr. Naismith at Springfield College, and went to see if this could be used by women. She decided that with some modifications it could be and, with Naismith's consent, brought the game to Smith College where it was played amid terrific excitement and with such great success that it quickly spread to other colleges for women. It had been modified to some extent, but it was a very fast game even with the court divided in three parts and nine girls on a team. It was so popular that Miss Berenson had to have the guide of modified rules (that she had prepared) printed to distribute to other colleges for women, and she continued to be the editor of this guide for 20 years (until 1912).

Following this was the introduction of field hockey by Miss Constance Applebee from England, who on a tour of various women's colleges in 1901, established a strong place for this sport on the campuses of the women's colleges. Other sports followed or had been started before this; for example, boating in '76 by Vassar and Wells;

baseball and archery at Vassar in '76; tennis at Vassar and Smith in '79; swimming at Goucher in 1889; basketball as mentioned above; bicycling by Wellesley in '94; golf at Wells in '94; fencing at Smith in '95; track at Vassar in '94; lacrosse at Wellesley in 1901; volleyball at Smith in 1907; water polo and cricket at Bryn Mawr in 1907; and in 1919 soccer also at Bryn Mawr. These sports, however, were not as yet included in the required program, but there was usually some way of reporting that there had been exercise of some form during the week--i.e., there might be so-called exercise cards on which to write the number of hours spent on sports during the week. This was particularly true in the fall and spring. In the winter, gymnastics was required of all, though there were usually three gradations (the advanced group, which the students called "strong gym"; the middle group, designated as the "regular gym"; and corrective gymnastics called "weak gym").

The activities increased greatly from 1890 to 1920. There were as many as eight different activities in the colleges in 1890, while in 1929 there were anywhere from 12 to 25 in the colleges.

The Outing Club movement sprang up in the early 20's and was a very popular informal activity. A number of colleges actually secured their own outing cabins. The first to have a cabin was Smith in 1922, and this was followed by others at Barnard, Goucher, Mount Holyoke, Wells, and Vassar. These have continued for many years to serve a useful purpose in many colleges throughout the country, although they can no longer rival the ski outings.

World War I (1914-1918) affected the program to a certain extent in such ways as having company drills and the winning of efficiency and proficiency points at Radcliffe. Marching was stressed, and there was daily drill for all students at Elmira. Farm and garden work was a part of the Vassar program. But still the serious part, and definitely the required part, was a strong gymnastic program of anywhere from two to three and even four hours a week that was required of all students throughout the winter term from about mid-November to April 1. This was indeed the serious work! The gymnastic meets at the end of the season were very popular, and classes competed against each other to win the highly prized trophy.

During these early years the majority of the teachers of physical education had no academic rank. There were several teachers and a director. This may have been due to the fact that not all members of the department held even a bachelor's degree; they were undoubtedly excellent in their own field of activity, however. Of the ten colleges studied in 1929, it was only after 1928 that all of them required even a bachelor's degree for membership in the college faculty. The directors had the following degrees in 1929: two Ph.D's; three Master of Arts; four Bachelor of Arts; and two no degrees.

This does not mean that these were not all distinguished women.
They were, in fact, leaders in the field of physical education for women, but this listing shows a lack of insistence upon higher degrees
for teachers in the field of physical education for women, even in
1929. As for their faculty ranking in the ten colleges, there were
two professors, four associate professors, six assistant professors,
24 instructors, and six assistants in the faculties of the total colleges
studied. In the non-academic classification there was one chairman,
five directors, one assistant director, and one assistant medical director. To compare this with the years after 1930 (i.e., from 1930-
1960), you will find that the great majority of directors or chairmen
have the rank of full professor and also a doctoral degree of some
sort in education or in some arts or science field. Many in the lower
professional ranks also have their doctorate and very few, if any, on
the college level are without their master's degree (unless they are
in the process of obtaining a higher degree, of course). These
instructors not only have the basic scientific theory needed for a
teacher of physical education, but often also a specialist's training in
the area of the field in which they will teach. The main areas in
physical education in which a student will specialize are sports,
dance, the study of movement, gymnastics (general or corrective),
and perhaps recreation. As each of these divisions in the work of
physical education has developed there has been a tendency for them
to branch off into an area of specialty. Even in the sports area there
is a tendency to be particularly difficult because there are certain
times in the administrative process when all must be brought together
and coordinated for the benefit of the administration of the department.

Important Changes Appear in Physical Education Theory and Practice
from 1920 on.

        The great change in the program of physical education came in
the second and third decades of the nineteenth century when the
natural program developed. The great center for this was in New
York City, where Dr. Jesse Feiring Williams and Dr. Thomas D.
Wood sparked the Department of Physical Education at Teachers College, Columbia University, and Dr. J. B. Nash was at New York
University in the same city. These changes were carried out to many
parts of the country by the graduates from these institutions. In both
schools a more natural form of exercise was advocated. Williams
and Wood rested their theory on the psychology and teaching of
G. Stanley Hall, John Dewey, and William Kilpatrick, all great teachers at Columbia in Psychology or Philosophy of Education or Sociology
of Education. Dr. Wood and Dr. Williams applied their ideas to physical education and gradually caused a great change in the program of
physical education all over the country. Clark Hetherington was also
a great teacher at this time. A book by Rosalind Cassidy and Thomas
D. Wood called The New Physical Education published in 1927 was
extremely interesting and helpful in this new development. This was

followed by Principles of Physical Education by Dr. Williams in 1927.
Both of these volumes and the materials in them made a deep impression on the many students who flocked to New York at this time.
Also the works by other great leaders in this new field, J. B. Nash
and Hetherington, brought many more people to the belief that physical education should not consist primarily of gymnastics, but of activities which were more natural and useful in everyday life. The
new school of thought felt that there were two general objectives:
"(1) the harmonious development, the interest, capacities and
abilities of the individual by means of natural activities during childhood and (2) abundant interest, ideals, and habits for a healthy, useful, and, therefore, happy adult life. The first will lead naturally
into the second." (Wood and Cassidy, 1927, p. 65). The new leaders
believed that physical education should not aim only at physiological
values in a field where the possibility for the development of social,
moral, spiritual and intellectual values is unlimited and indispensable. (Wood and Cassidy, 1927, p. 30). This same group worked
with the same conceptions in the theory of teaching as did others at
Teachers College, and brought physical education much closer to the
field of education than it had been before. The general theory was
that the command-and-obey theory used in formal gamnastics did not
train a child or a person to think for himself, or to contribute anything to his own creativity. These were very exciting days in the
early 20's and in the second decade as well, and there were many
interesting experiments in teaching. These new ideas gradually
caused a great change in physical education programs all over the
country.

Changes in Programs at Colleges for Women

At the same time the women's colleges had been developing
important programs in sports, but in many cases it was purely the
volunteer or elective side of the program for the student. Wellesley
and Bryn Mawr began as early as 1906 to 1907 to include sports in the
required program, and Barnard later (1918) permitted them as a result of physical efficiency tests initiated by Agnes Wayman (i.e., as a
substitute for gymnastics when the physical efficiency tests had been
passed). Many other colleges for women accepted this arrangement
in the second or third decade of the twentieth century. This change
was well established after 1925, though some aspects of gymnastics
have remained in the program permanently such as basic motor
skills or the study of movement (which has been added as a replacement for the old gymnastics). But nowhere has a straight exercise
program been retained as the one basic part of the program. It is
now only a small requirement within a more general one of basic education for sports and technique for the dance. Dr. Gladys Scott of
the University of Iowa and others developed scientific tests by means
of which students could be classified as to their various skills. These
tests permitted exemptions from certain required activities.

Meanwhile the corrective or adapted exercise program was followed in all the colleges for those students who had certain deficiencies for physical handicaps. Through these exercises the students, where possible, were helped to regain their motor ability and efficiency of movement. Lillian Drew was a pioneer in this area and worked in the Central School of Hygiene and Physical Education at the Y.W.C.A. in New York City which had been founded in 1909 by Miss Helen McKinstry. This school was later moved to Troy, New York and became a part of Russell Sage College. Miss McKinstry also formed a connection with the Nils Bukh School of Physical Education in Ollerup, Denmark, and was instrumental in sending several groups of teachers from the U.S.A. to this school for some study in Danish gymnastics.

Another form of activity which has interested women in physical education continuously in this country is the study of movement developed earlier in England. This is an adaptation of the Laban method of teaching movement for dance. The principles of Laban were taken by expert teachers of physical education, Ruth Morison of the I. M. Marsh College and Ruth Foster who was formerly Her Majesty's Inspector of Physical Education for Girls in England, who have very successfully made the adaptation from dance techniques to educational gymnastics. They have helped to spread this new method throughout the colleges for teachers of physical education of England. Miss Morison has also visited very recently in the United States and been most helpful in showing this work to women teachers in this country. Her new book called A Movement Approach to Educational Gymnastics[2] is also most helpful. Dr. Liselott Diem of Cologne, Germany, has also taught her fine work for children to teachers in the the U.S.A. most successfully.

Organizations to Further Physical Education for College Women

As early as 1910 Miss Homans of Wellesley College invited the women directors of physical education in New England to meet at her college. Those directors which came represented Wellesley, Mount Holyoke, Colby, Bates, Smith and Radcliffe. The purpose of the meeting was to discover the status of physical training in New England England colleges for women. As a result of this session they formed an organization of directors of physical training in women's colleges of New England. In 1915 they met at Wellesley with 16 directors present and one lady came from as far South as Randolph-Macon College, Lynchburg, Virginia. A stand was taken against sending U.S. women to compete in the Paris Olympics, and in 1930 they voted against

---

[2] Morison, Ruth. A Movement Approach to Educational Gymnastics. London, England: J. M. Dent & Sons, Ltd., 1969.

intercollegiate athletics for women. They endorsed the women's division of the National Amateur Athletic Federation (NAAF) and adopted a platform for the purpose of developing the play attitude in athletics rather than the highly competitive attitude which makes records its goal. The Eastern Society also discussed affiliation with the mid-Western and Western Societies in 1923 and earlier. However, it was in 1923 that a meeting for the formation of a National Association of Directors of Physical Education for Women in Colleges and Universities was held at Wellesley from April 9-11. There were some complications because of different regulations for membership, but basically the group functioned as a whole. Later the name was changed to the National Association of Physical Education for College Women (NAPECW). The actual vote which changed the name of the eastern group came in 1944 when the name of Directors Association was dropped and replaced by the Eastern Association of Physical Education for College Women. This move admitted staff members to associate membership. Later it was changed to full membership. The East was slower in doing this than the mid-West and Western groups who had carried out such a change much earlier and enjoyed the help of many younger persons.

In conclusion the NAPECW has developed tremendously and comes into the picture again in connection with other organizations concerned with women and sports. A very good survey of this was made by Paulajean Searcy in June 1962 as her thesis for her master's degree at Smith College. She feels that the reason basketball was accepted as a sport suitable for women was due in a large measure to changes in the social climate. Women were continuing to think differently, to behave differently, and their role in American life was rapidly shifting. There was a great suffrage revolution when women won the right to vote, to hold public office, to speak publicly, to obtain an education equal to that of men, and to enter certain heretofore exclusively male professions (Searcy, 1962, pp. 15, 16).

Undesirable practices in basketball competition became obvious, and these problems were soon apparent in other sports for women. In 1916 Florence A. Somers wrote "it would be wise or practical to have a national body or committee for the purpose of standardizing and controlling athletics for girls and women." (Searcy, 1962, p. 16). In 1917, William Burdick, President of the American Physical Education Association, later AAHPER, appointed a Committee on Women's Athletics largely for the investigation of a full and varied program of activity for girls and women. Elizabeth Burchenal was the Chairman. This committee promptly named a sub-committee at the request of Senda Berenson to take over the task of compiling basketball guides (rules) that had been previously prepared by Miss Berenson's committee. By 1922 similar committees had been appointed for such other sports as hockey, swimming, track and field, and soccer. More were added later. The women were indeed eager to have their own rules rather than using regulations that had been established for men players. This, says Searcy, complemented advances in the social field and in freedom of the press. In 1920 it was an age of youthful gaiety; women bobbed their hair, wore skirts to the knee, publicly smoked, drank, and held many more jobs. Their woolen gymnasium suits were replaced by middies over pleated bloomers at first; later these were replaced by the more narrow, fitted bloomer.

The Women's Athletic Committee formulated resolutions condemning participation by women in the Olympic Games of 1922 and 1926. The NAPECW also worked on good practices of the conduct of sports. The Olympic question brought out much criticism and pointed up the fact that a more influential committee of women's athletics was needed. In 1920, the Women's Athletic Committee became the Women's Athletic Section. This group took part in convention programs of the A.P.E.A. of 1917 and those of every year between 1922 and 1930, thereby gaining recognition and sympathy for its efforts. They also gained a seat on the Association Council and were called the "Executive Committee of the Women's Athletic Section." In 1923, the National Amateur Athletic Federation was organized and set up definite standards which prevented a disorganized and unofficial growth of intercollegiate sports for women. The women's committee was now a section of the A.P.E.A. and did not approve of the encouragement of intercollegiate sports. They worked conversely to give opportunity for the less-skilled girl to participate in sports. Out of the Women's Athletic Committee in 1920 the Women's National Official Rating Committee was developed. By 1927, there were eight existing official boards which became the Women's National Official Rating Committee and sub-committees.

There was a complete reorganization of the AAHPER in 1930-1931, and this change affected the structural pattern of the Section on Women's Athletics (NSWA). Mabel Lee was at this time the first woman president of the A.P.E.A. The new constitution gave formal recognition to the National Section on Women's Athletics (NSWA). The Section promoted a wholesome athletic program for all girls and women stating guiding principles and standards for the administrator, leader, official, and player. Also stressed were the publication of rules, the dissemination of accurate information in publications and program, and the stimulation and valuation of research in the field of women's athletics. The 1930's brought a depression but relatively little effect on the physical education program. In 1938 the N.A.A.D. became a part of the N.S.W.A. after having performed a very fine and arduous task. In 1936 state representatives were appointed. In 1937 A.P.E.A. also became a department of the National Education Association, and then in 1938 added an "R"--i.e., "Recreation" to its title. In the 1930-1940 decade the N.S.W.A. printed Standards in Athletics for Girls and Women, a very influential statement.

With World War II there was more freedom for women who were entering another era and an intensification of the fitness pro gram for everyone. The Office of Education published a manual called Fitness Through Education. Possibly the best effort of the war years was the encouragement of intercollegiate sports, but they worked together also to give opportunity for the less-skilled girls to participate in sports. This subsequently led to a further development of intramural and intercollegiate sports.

The work of the National Section on Women's Athletics expanded to such an extent that it was made a Division in 1958, and one of its functions was the further development not only of "sports for all," but also of intercollegiate sports. The D.G.W.S. has since become instrumental in the establishment of national tournaments for six different sports. These are to be held in different parts of the country and on alternate years. The program for the Division has become extremely complex, and there have been a number of important conferences for the development of sports for women. Many college teachers have benefitted from these meetings.

The latest statement concerns the scheduling of national tournaments for 1969-1970 and a 1970-1971 (Beauman, Mary, D.G.W.S. Spring Newsletter, May 1969, p. 4). This is a new feature of sports for women, and may not affect the fine general program of physical education in the different colleges for women (but it is a possibility!). The girls who would be most affected by this might be those on the Athletic Association Board, who have given their services so long and faithfully for the promotion of physical education for the total college group. It is hoped that the new plans will stimulate their interests and their work in relation to the Department of Physical Education in colleges for women. Without their services and their great contribution of interest, energy, and enthusiasm, in the past, large general programs for physical education for all girls would have fared much less well than they have done. With their help the program has been a joy and a great satisfaction to the teachers of physical education in colleges for women. The benefits to sports for women through the work of Florence Somers and Helen Hazelton and the various committees throughout these years cannot be over-estimated. They have given their thought and wisdom to the careful development of sports for college women. Rachel Bryant, as Consultant of Women's Sports at the Office of the AAHPER, should also be given great praise for her careful, intelligent, and continuous work with this Committee.

As sports experiences for women were expanding, interest in dance was developing along new paths and bringing much more emphasis in this area as well. The change in the educational theory in the second and third decades of the twentieth century affected the dance in various parts of the country. In the colleges for women there had been a form of dance and folk dancing for many years. From about 1900 to 1910 this was influenced by the work of Gilbert and also Chalif and other modified ballet techniques. These were taught at summer schools for teachers and in studios, and this type of dance was known as "Aesthetic Dance." It was definitely modified ballet technique, and was a part of most requirements in physical education in many colleges from the early 1900's on. There was also some work under special rhythmic instructors (e.g., Dalcroze and Delsarte), but from 1910 to 1920 the new philosophy of "teaching the whole child" as proclaimed in Teachers College and New York University favored the dance as never before and thus it was given a more important place.

At Columbia Teachers College Gertrude Colby worked on natural movement and self-expression. She had worked with Dalcroze and Delsarte, but it was from Isadora Duncan that she found her insight into the development of "Natural Dance." She had also worked with Alys Bentley. In 1915 Marjorie H'Doubler came to New York City and devoted much of her efforts to educational dance. She, too, studied with Alys Bentley who was teaching music through movement. In 1917 Miss H'Doubler returned to the University of Wisconsin and started her dance program through which she relied on music for motivation. She was concerned in developing the body as an instrument of expression. She developed a basic teaching program that it was possible to understand, use, and thoroughly enjoy. It was adaptable and adapted to different personalities. She trained many teachers of dance at the University of Wisconsin, who were in great demand and spread out through the country.

In 1920 to 1930 the natural movement in physical education advanced rapidly. Sports, swimming, and dance were replacing the former gymnastics. This new educational environment favored the growth of dance, and in 1926 a dance major for the preparation of teachers was introduced both by Miss Colby at Teachers College and Miss H'Doubler at Wisconsin. During the 1920's dance clubs or dance groups sprang up all over the country in colleges for women, and in universities and co-educational colleges as well. The May Day pageant became the climax of the dance year.

In the meanwhile the professional dancers such as Martha Graham, Doris Humphrey, and Charles Weidman were revolting against the established professional dance. In 1923 Graham left Denishawn, and in 1928 Humphrey and Weidman also followed. Their purpose was to explore dance as a medium of expression as well as new forms of movement. They began the modern dance. Graham sought to center and integrate movement within the body space of action and used percussive movement for this. Weidman invented new forms of dance for men. Thus, they all began to create new forms of dance and evolved principles of movement and techniques. In 1931

Hanya Holm came to the United States. She had worked with Mary Wigman in Germany and, in her "automatically sound technique and sensitive use of space" (Hawkins, 1954, p. 12), she was a fourth exponent of modern dance.

In the colleges Mary O'Donnell of Teacher College and Martha Hill at New York University were important links between professional dance and educational dance. In 1932 Agnes Wayman of Barnard arranged a dance symposium for the exploration of the new methods. Vassar, Wellesley, Smith, New York City, and Barnard were all represented, and Oscar Becque and Mary Wigman participated.

Between 1934 and 1941, there was a Bennington Summer School of Dance bringing a special program to the teachers of dance in the colleges. Also in 1935 Humphrey and Weidman took their newly formed dance group to many colleges and universities. The success of these tours was largely due to the college audiences. By 1938 practically every major dance company had completed a continental tour of the United States, and often there were some dance lessons as well as performances. There were also Christmas classes in New York, summer schools at Mills College, the University of Colorado, and at the Perry Mansfield Camp.

A powerful influence on the dance was the AAHPER Dance Section which sponsored District and National meetings. Leading artists participated in these both as speakers and in performances. There were some pre-convention sessions for this purpose.

Between 1940 and 1950 professional dance had reached a point where they no longer needed to look to education and their students as a major source of true understanding, and they were eager to settle down in New York City and concentrate on concert dance. Dance educators had succeeded in establishing modern dance in these colleges and as part of the college program. Up to this point college teachers in general (after the very early teachers) had thought of dance in terms of professional dance. In the early 1940's, however, they gave thought to dance in relation to general educational goals rather than purely concert work. Several people had written on this subject and brought out the idea that the development of the student as a total personality was of primary importance (Deane, February 1940, JOHPER, p. xi, 81). And H'Doubler in 1945 declared that educational dance is a process not an end in itself, and its aim is indeed the integration of personality (Hawkins, 1954, p. 21). Others expressed this same point of view, but there was disagreement between those with a truly educational view concerning their students and those who thought all that mattered was the teaching of dance.

The general tendency seems to be to have dance develop into a separate part either of the physical education or the theater or art department, or even to evolve into a completely separate department. All these possibilities are now being explored, and it will take some years before the most effective type of organization and the place of the dance will be found in women's colleges. Dance may move definitely toward the art side of the liberal arts program, or it may continue its very effective work within physical education. In any case, this is a growing and stimulating force in the field of activities, and one which offers promise of growth and development.

Conclusions

The place of physical education as a part of the college program for women has not been questioned, but the place of the requirement in physical education has been by both students and faculty. Some colleges have lost their requirement and have had a very satisfactory continuation of volunteer participation in sports, dance, conditioning, and recreational work. Other colleges continue their requirement in physical education with greater freedom of choice of activity and much greater extension of the program as to possibilities of selection. This question of the requirement does not affect the undergraduate major courses nor graduate courses. All work leading to a degree in physical education is credited and leads on to a substructure for advanced degrees in this field. But the general work in the requirement is another matter. This is a particularly pressing situation, but it is our hope and belief that the values and the training and the interest will continue in the programs of today.

General Bibliography

Ainsworth, Dorothy S. The History of Physical Education in Colleges for Women. New York: A. S. Barnes & Co., Inc., 1930.

Carson, Mary R. A History of Physical Education at Smith College. A thesis submitted to the faculty of Smith College in partial fulfillment of the requirements for the degree of Master of Science in Physical Education, 1951.

The Committees on Dancing of the American Physical Education Association for the years 1931 and 1932. Dancing in the Elementary Schools. New York: A. S. Barnes & Co., Inc., 1933.

Erdman, Jean. What Is Modern Dance? New York: Lawrence R. Maxwell at the Sign of the Dancing Bear, 1954.

Halsey, Elizabeth. Women in Physical Education: Their Role in Work, Home, and History. New York: G. P. Putnam's Sons, 1961.

Hawkins, Alma M. Modern Dance in Higher Education. New York: Bureau of Publications, Teachers College, Columbia University, 1954.

Journal of Health, Physical Education, and Recreation. "Selected Articles on Dance." Washington, D. C.: American Association for Health, Physical Education, and Recreation.

Leonard, Fred Eugene and McKenzie, R. Tait. History of Physical Education. Philadelphia, Pa.: Lea & Febiger, 1927.

Marks, Joseph E. III. America Learns to Dance. New York: Exposition Press, 1957.

Meadows, Jo Ann. A History of the Eastern Association for Physical Education of College Women, 1910-1963. A thesis presented to the faculty of the Department of Physical Education, Smith College, in partial fulfillment of the requirements for the degree Master of Science in Physical Education, 1964.

Rice, Emmett A., Hutchinson, John L. and Lee, Mabel. A Brief History of Physical Education. Fourth edition. New York: The Ronald Press Company, 1958.

Rogers, Frederick Rand. Dance: A Basic Educational Technique. New York: The Macmillan Company, 1941.

Sanford, Barbara Ellen. The Administrative Climate of Women's Physical Education Departments in Eastern Colleges and Universities. A thesis presented to the faculty of the Department of Physical Education, Smith College, in partial fulfillment of the requirements for the degree Master of Science in Physical Education, 1969.

Searcy, Paulajean. The History, Organization, and Function of the Division for Girls and Women's Sports, 1940-1962. A thesis presented to the faculty of the Department of Physical Education, Smith College, in partial fulfillment of the requirements for the degree Master of Science in Physical Education, 1962.

Smith, Nancy W. Focus on Dance (IV). Washington, D. C.: American Association for Health, Physical Education, and Recreation, Department of the National Education Association, 1967.

Stodelle, Ernestine. <u>The First Frontier: The Story of Louis Horst and the American Dance</u>. Cheshire, Conn.: Ernestine Stodelle, 1964.

Wood, Thomas Denison and Cassidy, Rosalind Frances. <u>The New Physical Education</u>. New York: The Macmillan Company, 1927.

CHAPTER 14

A BRIEF HISTORY OF DANCE IN PHYSICAL EDUCATION
AND RECREATION

Earle F. Zeigler
The University of Western Ontario, London

Introduction[1]

The place of dance in physical education and recreation has
been a persistent problem throughout history. People have danced
for personal pleasure, for religious purposes, for expression of the
gamut of emotions, for exercise, for money and for the pleasure of
others in all ages. As both an art and a social function, dance will
probably always be with us and will reflect the dominant influences
of the age in which it is taking place. Consequently, the statement
that it is possible to distinguish the "pulse beat" of a civilization by
an analysis of its dance forms can probably be well substantiated.

As Woody has indicated:

> There is probably no better example of the survival of
> primitive practices in modern life than dancing. What
> causes this survival, long after certain of the previously
> assigned reasons for it have ceased to exist? The

Editor's Note: A further "persistent problem" traced historically by the Editor is included at this point to lend balance by the
inclusion of a discussion of a significant form of human movement -
dance. This treatment represents a preliminary effort to interest
people in the field to the importance of this aspect of the field's professional effort. Young men especially are typically not receiving a
movement experience in an activity like dance, and yet nothing is
done about it (save by the young themselves in the gyrations they have
developed most recently!)

---

[1] Sincere appreciation is extended to Professor Esther Pease,
The University of Michigan, for her careful and expert criticism of
portions of that which appears in this paper. Any inadequacies in this
brief treatment, however, must be attributed to the relative inexperi-
ence of the writer in this area. (See also Compilation of Dance Research, edited by Esther E. Pease, available through the AAHPER in
Washington, D. C., 1965.)

answer lies in human nature. Insofar as any activity satisfies some original or 'instinctive' demand of man it has, and will continue to have, adequate reason for its existence, though some of its earlier ideological associations and justification may have faded from his mind completely. Such an original satisfier rhythm seems to be. Life is a rhythm; dancing is life, as Havelock Ellis maintains in The Dance of Life . . . (Woody, 1949, pp. 22-23).

In primitive societies certain types of rhythmic expressions were "instinctive satisfiers" of man. The ancients pleaded to their various spirits and deities through the medium of different types of ritualistic dances. When they decided to fight their enemies, war dances helped them to achieve the necessary frenzy for the battle. If food was needed, other types of dances were employed to guarantee the success of the hunt. If they were victorious in battle, or successful on the hunt, they danced for pleasure and joy. When the vagaries of climate plagued them and their crops were failing, dances were used in the hope that they would bring more rain or more sunshine as the occasion demanded. And when disease and other illness struck, as so often happened, they danced to exorcise the "evil spirits" which brought these misfortunes. To these early people, therefore, dance was most often serious in nature and only incidentally served physical fitness, health, and recreation. In conclusion, we can safely say that the evidence of anthropologists, archaeologists, and historians points strongly to the belief that dance was a strong factor in Paleolithic culture, which was the first recognizable era of human civilization, and carried on its various forms into pre-literate societies.

Early Societies

Egypt. In some of the early societies, there was a tendency to curb the emotions; thus, an element of restraint was often present that gave some forms of dance an aesthetic quality, perhaps for the first time. When an element of drama was introduced, dance rose to the status of an art form and was accorded greater esteem by the more cultured people in that society. In Egypt, for example, dance developed both as an art and as a profession. A religious caste was established which consisted of dancers and singers who were affiliated with particular shrines. Egyptian professional dancing, contrary to popular opinion, was extremely flexible and acrobatic in nature. This class consisted of both men and women who danced for the entertainment of the upper classes at celebrations and other festivities. The lower classes took part in the folk dances of their regions.

Hebrew. From the Old Testament we learn that dancing was part of the life of the early Hebrews. It was an important feature of the many religious ceremonies and celebrations, along with singing and various type of instrumental music. Such dancing of an informal nature, along with the more stylized folk dances, continued to play a role in Hebrew Life, but the earlier emphasis on dancing at religious rites evidently waned in later centuries.

China. In ancient Chinese upper-class families, dancing evidently occupied an important place in the education of youth, and particularly the boys. Many different kinds of dances were developed for various purposes such as worship, war, and the driving-out of evil spirits. These dances seem to have varied somewhat under the different dynasties, but were usually accompanied by music and the recitation of poetry. This development of a written philosophy of dancing was, of course, a distinct advancement over the dances of the primitives. Kings recognized the power and importance of music, dancing, and formal ceremonies in the lives of the people; it has been said that the worth of rulers was often adjudged by the quality of the dance prevalent during their periods of control. Chinese dance is said to have begun more than two thousand years before Christ, but it should be mentioned for our purpose here that woman seem to have danced much less extensively than men; that their role in life seems to have revolved around decorative and household purposes; and that the seemingly ridiculous custom of foot-binding limited their physical exercise, including participation in the dance, most severely.

India. Ancient Indian dance was very closely associated with religious practices and was evidently held in high favor. This admiration for the expression of "rhythmic energy" continued up into the sixth and fifth centuries before Christ, and dance and music were included in the education of youth. But for various reasons, including more class-consciousness and the fact that it became professionalized, dance soon became an activity that only lower-class individuals took part in. It was difficult to erase its popular appeal, however, and men and women still enjoyed it on many occasions. There were still many temple dancers, and, as so often seemed to have been the case, professional women dancers and musicians were popular for the entertainment of guests at the homes of the wealthy.

Crete. Dancing was very much in evidence in ancient Cretan civilization--a culture that preceded the Greeks by several thousands of years on and around the Island of Crete. Along with music and sport, it played an important role in the religious life of these people. Women achieved a relatively high status in this society and were prominent in religious ceremonies including dance as a form of worship. There were gay, spontaneous folk dances, religious ceremonial dances of a stately nature, lively dances including outstanding tumbling routines, and war dances for various male purposes.

Sparta. Spartan Greek girls and young women were extremely active in their physical exercise, and it is to be expected that they would be involved in dancing as well. This activity is considered to be as strenuous as that for any girl in any society before or since. Dressed in what even today would be considered rather scanty attire, they danced on certain occasions while the young men watched. Dancing and music were regarded as basic to the education of youth, as both had a basic relationship to religion and war. Their national heritage was very important to the Spartans, and many dances related to the ongoing culture were conducted with great dignity. There were a number of dances, however, which we today would characterize as gymnastic dancing.

Athens. Athenian girls and women led a much different life than their counterparts in Sparta; they were regarded as inferior, and they stayed that way. They did engage in certain types of dance, however, at different stages of their lives. Certainly children of both sexes took part in a variety of informal dances. Dancing and music were also part of the education of young ladies in the more wealthy homes. Many of the slave girls did acquire great facility in the dance, but this type of activity would not have been proper for the Athenian maiden.

It is very interesting to note the extent to which both Spartan and Athenian men took part in the dance in its many forms. There was theatrical dancing, gymnastic dancing, and folk dancing, not to mention dance which was more specifically religious and that which was related directly to war and peace. If anything, it could be said that the Athenians were more dance-conscious than the Spartans. This was because their whole conception of education was pointed toward the harmonious development of all aspects of man's nature-- physical, mental, moral, and aesthetic. When the Hellenic Civilization declined, the quality of the dance retrogressed concurrently with the fading idealism in the culture.

Rome. Dancing served a purpose in Roman civilization, but its status was below that given it by the Greeks. In the early days it was associated with religion and war. Later, during the reign of Nero, it was held in high esteem. Thereafter, dance experienced a decline, as it became a matter of tricks, acrobatics, and feats of juggling often performed by slaves to provide entertainment. When this happened, it was naturally considered an unworthy activity for a true Roman. When this attitude developed, it is little wonder that no further progress was made in the art of dance. It still continued as a popular activity for the lower classes, but then waned in popularity with the advent of Christian asceticism. In general it can be said that the Romans saw some purpose for dance in religious festivals, did not understand the role that it had played in Greek life, and would not have accepted it anyhow because of its Grecian origin.

The Middle Ages

Early Period. During this period dance had very low status probably due to the corruption of dancing in the Roman era. The Christian Church accepted dance at first as a means of liturgical expression, but subsequently banned this form of dance because of its pagan origins. Folk dance did continue in the Middle Ages; in fact, it appeared to be one of the few opportunities that people had for freedom of expression. Typically, the so-called "Dark Ages" of the Middle Ages were characterized by Christian asceticism, and dancing as a natural activity was considered "of the body" and, therefore, evil.

Renaissance. The Renaissance Period rediscovered initially the grace and dignity of the earlier Classical Civilization. Because of this early emphasis, the place of dance in the culture began to rise again as it developed as an art form. The traditional folk dances were refined by dancing masters who devised various forms of the dance which became socially acceptable. In this period we see the beginning of dance theory, albeit very elementary. During this time men and women danced together at court activities. There were solo dancing routines, dances for couples, and dances for small groups. So-called European court ballet became fashionable, and then declined toward the end of the sixteenth century. During this time professionals performed what was known as pantomimic dance for the enjoyment of the people. At the end of the sixteenth century, also, a closed couple dance known as the volta came into existence, and it was regarded as highly questionable by many; yet, it did have an influence on future dance composition.

Dance in Modern History

Seventeenth Century. In 1661, the National Academy of Music and Dance opened in France, and dance gradually became a real art. Only men appeared in the ballets and wore masks when feminine roles were depicted (women did not take part until 1881). The minuet started as a dance of the peasants and achieved great popularity as it was gradually refined and became a "dance of courtship" in polite society. During this time the English rounds and longways dances were engaged in frequently, although they were really not new developments--the circles and files being merely adaptations of basic forms of many earlier societies.

Eighteenth and Nineteenth Centuries. Changing social conditions appear to have caused a decline in the popularity of the minuet toward the end of the eighteenth century. French leadership in the dance was superseded by the many variations of the German waltz in the so-called "Romantic Period" of European history. The whirling Viennese waltz has remained as the classical dance of the latter half of the eighteenth century and only began to wane about 1830 when numerous variations developed. The polka was really the only popular dance that rivalled the waltz in any way.

With the onset of a radically new, revolutionary attitude toward the rights of individuals, dance could not help but be affected and change accordingly. Transitional changes were taking place in the traditional ballet which started on its way toward becoming a theatre art in its own right. Costume changes became increasingly frequent, and scenes depicting contemporary social developments were displayed often. Further reforms in the ballet were characteristic of the nineteenth century, a time in which the potentialities of the "natural man" were being realized. The Romantic Period saw the birth of the romantic ballet, and a new role for women was envisioned. The ballerina achieved great esteem as a solo performer, and the male dancer found himself in a supporting role for one of the first times in history. By 1850, however, the "golden age" of ballet had passed-- at least for the time being.

The United States. To say that the introduction of dance in its various forms into the physical education curriculum in the United States has been an uphill struggle would be to put it mindly. In pioneer life many forms of recreation were viewed suspiciously. Children's dances and folk dancing brought over from the "old country," however, were impossible to suppress and gradually became increasingly popular. As a type of "society life" developed, the parties became gayer and more sophisticated in the eastern cities, and "polite" dancing was generally accepted. The recreational life of the westward-moving frontier group developed as well, and social dancing, of a folk- and square-dance nature, was increasingly evident despite the warnings of the religious circuit riders.

The nineteenth century was actually a transitional period in attitudes toward play and recreation. The first use of anything resembling dance in physical education came around 1850, when some of the calisthenics recommended were really elementary dance forms. In one of the handbooks published for young ladies, John Locke and others are quoted as being in favor of dancing instruction for children because of the "graceful motion" and "confidence" which it gave. Girls were not, however, supposed to be "brilliant" in their performance of any of the dance figures. Three names may be mentioned for the part that they played in the development of dancing as an integral part of physical education: ✓(1) Catherine Beecher, who introduced some elementary dance figures into her system of calisthenics; (2) François Delsarte, who actually developed a "couple dance" without calling it that, and whose Eurhythmics became a world-wide movement of aesthetic, systematized rhythmic training; and (3) Melvin B. Gilbert, who began the era of the so-called aesthetic dance in physical education in the 1890's. His teaching at the famous

Harvard Summer School of Physical Education did much to spread its popularity throughout the country.

The Twentieth Century. The twentieth century has witnessed a truly remarkable development in the dance. Many would say that the body has been rediscovered as a means of communication through the dance medium. The great Isadora Duncan, who had made a study of Greek culture, introduced a spirit of individualism and freedom with emphasis on a natural form of expression. This development symbolized a revolt against three centuries of more or less formalized ballet technique. Working from the premise that emotional states are typically expressed through movement, the early natural dance broke away from tradition and attempted to convey the gamut of emotional experiences through bodily movement. The main purpose of this concept was not to create a spectacle as much as it was a desire to communicate and to put self-expression into the dancer's movements--movement in which the performer was free to respond to various emotional states without necessarily being limited to a particular musical form.

Miss Duncan seemed to enter into the spirit of the twentieth century as an era in which the very tempo of civilization was increasing as many false traditions were being swept aside almost overnight. Her work was ably carried on by such outstanding dance teachers as Gertrude Colby, Margaret H'Doubler, Mary P. O'Donnell, Martha Hill, and Martha Graham, to mention only a few. Gertrude Colby saw natural dance as a dance form indigenous to the American culture--a form in which the body is used correctly and which is also based on established psychological laws. It became an art form which could draw on drama, music, color, design, and pantomime for its full fruition. It paved the way for later "modern" dance and, fortunately, served as a means of unifying various somewhat diverse approaches to the teaching of the dance.

In the early years of this present century, Louis Chalif came to New York from Russia and offered a course in dance for teachers. From a background in ballet and a developing interest in aesthetic dance, he applied a certain amount of this influence to the teaching of folk dance in this country. He was an outstanding teacher himself and evidently an indefatigable enthusiast as evidenced by the short courses he conducted in many centers across the country. Although some questioned the educational soundness of his type of dance instruction, there is no question but that he was a great influence in the establishment of dance in America. Elizabeth Burchenal is credited with helping to establish folk dance more soundly within the educational system along with Mary Wood Hinman.

Another interesting development was the advent of clog dancing and subsequently tap dancing within physical education programs in the United States. The above-mentioned Mary Wood Hinman recognized the worth of this dance form, and she continued to promote it despite a good deal of early criticism about its worth as a dance form in education. This trend in dance was not to be denied, however, and for a period tap dancing was tremendously popular and became known in other countries as an American contribution to the art of dancing. Marjorie Hillas and Anne Schley Duggan have been prominent in applying this dance form to education.

After 1912 a new era of social dancing began in the United States which reflected the social attitudes of a vigorous, thriving country. America broke away from the traditional, standardized European dance forms which had dominated up until this time. This new wave of interest owed much to the influence of Vernon and Irene Castle who popularized the movement. The beginnings of jazz and ragtime soon resulted in a variety of popular dance steps which were doomed to extinction almost before they started. The Turkey Trot, the Bunny Hug, the Charleston, and innumerable other dance crazes (such as The Twist and The Frug, etc. in the 1960's) have superseded each other in fairly rapid succession since the early years of the century, and each has been typically enjoyed by teenagers and young adults. They have been counteracted to a degree by the efforts of professional ballroom dancing instructors, who have made an effort to offer more refined dance steps for public entertainment such as the Tango, the Hesitation, the Waltz, the Fox Trot, the Lambeth Walk, the Rhumba and others.

Modern Dance. Modern dance grew from natural dance in the late 1920's and made rapid strides in the following decade. For a while in the 1930's the influence of Mary Wigman and her German modern dance as a further development of earlier expression gymnastics can be noted, but it was fairly soon absorbed by the rapidly growing and expanding American modern dance. A dance section was established in the American Physical Education Association in 1932, and various outstanding summer schools of the dance were inaugurated at Bennington College, New York University, Connecticut College for Women (during World War II), and other institutions. As early as 1926 the first major program in dance had begun at the University of Wisconsin under the leadership of Margaret H'Doubler, and many others have started since that time. In 1951, the Juilliard School of Music in New York City organized a dance department, and recognition by this noteworthy institution tends to indicate its recognition as an art form still further.

Despite the advancement of modern dance and its acceptance in modern education as witnessed by the development of dance education, teacher preparation programs across the country, there is still much room for progress. A significant body of research knowledge is lacking, although the American Association for Health, Physical Education,

and Recreation has a research chairman in its Dance Division and has
published bibliographies of research in recent years. The Committee
on Research in Dance sponsored a Preliminary Conference on Research in Dance at the Greyston Conference Center, Riverdale, New
York, New York from May 26-28, 1967. The Proceedings are entitled "Research in Dance: Problems and Possibilities." CORD--
the Committee on Research in Dance--is a group established in 1964
on the basis of ideas expressed by some members of the U. S. Office
of Education to some dancers who were members of AAHPER, the
National Dance Guild, and the Dance Notation Bureau.

A certain amount of curriculum standardization for prospective
teachers seems desirable, and an improvement of the interaction between the dance teacher and the professional performer would add
further strength to the development. Articulation within the dance
curriculum at the various levels within the school system is needed
as well. Further analysis must be made of the reasons why modern
dance especially, and many of the other dance forms, seem unacceptable to the majority of male physical education teachers on this
Continent. Square dancing and social dancing continue to be popular
throughout many parts of the country with the masses, and a certain
amount of folk dancing remains. Tap dancing is on the wane, and
interest in ballet is limited except in certain areas. Most interesting
recent developments are the proposed National Academy of Music,
Drama, and Dance in Washington, D. C., and the Lincoln Center in
New York City. Such activity indicates a rebirth of interest in the
arts including dance.

General Bibliography

Ainsworth, Dorothy S. "The History of Physical Education in Colleges for Women." Ph.D. dissertation, Columbia University,
1930.

Ashton, Dudley. "Contributions of Dance to Physical Education,
Part I." JOHPER, 26, No. 9, December, 1955.

_____. "Contributions of Dance to Physical Education,
Part II." JOHPER, 27, No. 4, April, 1956.

The Bible. See: Psalm 149:3, Psalm 150:4, II Samuel 6:14, 6:16,
I Chronicles, 15:29, Exodus 15:20-21, I Samuel 10:5-6, I Kings
18:26, 28.

Catlin, G. Letters and Notes on the Manners, Customs, and Conditions of the North American Indians. 2 volumes. London:
1841.

Duncan, Isadora. Art of the Dance. New York: J. J. Little and Ives Co., 1928.

Edman, Irwin. The World, the Arts, and the Artist. New York: W. W. Norton and Company, 1928.

Ellfeldt, Lois E. and Metheny, Eleanor. "Movement and Meaning: Development of a General Theory." Research Quarterly, 29, 264-73, October, 1958.

Ellis, Havelock. The Dance of Life. New York: Modern Library, 1929.

Engels, Karl. "Why Do We Dance?" Musical Quarterly, 6, 510-31, October, 1920.

Evans, A. The Palace of Minos at Knossos. 5 volumes. London: The Macmillan Company, 1921-1936.

Fowler, William Warde. Social Life at Rome. New York: The Macmillan Company, 1909.

Freeman, Kenneth J. Schools of Hellas. London: The Macmillan Company, 1922.

Gage, Margaret. "The Greek Choral Dance." Theater Arts, 13, 560-78, 1929.

Geiger, George R. "An Experimentalist Approach to Education," in Modern Philosophies and Education, edited by N. B. Henry. Chicago: The University of Chicago Press, 1955.

_____. "A Study in American Modernism." Theater Arts, 14, 229-32, March 1930.

Giles, H. A. Adversaria Sinica. Shanghai: Kelly and Walsh, 1914.

Grasberger, L. Erziehung Und Unterricht Im Klassischen Altertum. Würzburg: Stahel'schen Buch-und Kunsthandlung. 3 volumes. 1864-1881.

Grove, Lily. Dancing. London: Longmans, Green and Company, 1907.

Hambly, W. D. Tribal Dancing and Social Development. London: Witherby, 1926.

_____ and Hose, C. Origins of Education Among Primitive Peoples. London: The Macmillan Company, 1926.

Harrison, Jane. Ancient Art and Ritual. New York: Henry Holt and Company, 1913.

H'Doubler, Margaret. Dance, A Creative Art Experience. New York: F. S. Crofts and Co., 1940.

_____. The Dance and Its Place in Education. New York: Harcourt, Brace, and World, 1925.

Hirth, F. The Ancient History of China. New York: Columbia University Press, 1911.

Karsten, R. The Civilization of the South American Indians. New York: Alfred A. Knopf, Inc., 1926.

Kees, H. Der Opfertanz des Ägyptischen Königs. Leipzig: J. C. Hinrichs'sche Buchhandlung, 1912.

Kraemer, C. J. "A Greek Element in Egyptian Dancing." American Journal of Archaeology, 35, 125-38, 1931.

Lampkin, Lucy. "Dance in Art." Research Quarterly, 7, 138, May, 1936.

Lawton, W. C. Introduction to Classical Latin Literature. New York: Charles Scribner's Sons, 1904.

Lexová, I. Ancient Egyptian Dances. Translated by K. Haltmar. Praha: Oriental Institute, 1935.

Marquardt, J. Das Privatleben der Romer. Leipzig: Lirzel Buchhandlung, 1886.

Martin, John. The Dance. New York: Tudor Publishing Co., 1946.

Metheny, Eleanor. Connotations of Movement in Sport and Dance. Dubuque, Iowa: Wm. C. Brown Company, Publishers, 1965.

Mosso, A. The Palaces of Crete and Their Builders. London: Unwin, 1907.

Müller, F. M. (editor). The Sacred Books of the East. 50 volumes. Oxford: Clarendon Press, 1879-1910.

Pease, Esther E. (editor). Compilation of Dance Research. Washington, D. C.: AAHPER, 1965.

Plato. Laws. Volume 7, 815.

Raffe, W. G. Dictionary of the Dance. New York: A. S. Barnes & Co., 1965.

Reed, V. Z. "The Ute Bear Dance." American Anthropologist, O.S. IX, 237-44.

Sachs, Curt. World History of the Dance. New York: W. W. Norton & Company, Inc., 1937.

Selden, Elizabeth. The Dancer's Quest. Berkeley: University of California Press, 1935.

_____. The Elements of the Free Dance. New York: A. S. Barnes & Company, 1930.

Sonnenschein, E. A. What is Rhythm? Oxford: Basil Blackwell, 1925.

Stevenson, M. C. The Zuni Indians. Washington, D. C.: Government Printing Office, 23rd Annual Report American Etymology 1901-02, 1904.

Tan, George G. "The Place of Dancing in Physical Education with Special Refreence to China." Physical Education Today, 7, No. 2 & 3: June-September 1960.

Van Loon, H. W. The Arts. Simon and Schuster, 1937.

Vuillier, Gaston. History of Dancing. New York: Appleton-Century-Crofts, 1897.

Weege, F. Etruskische Malerei. Halle: Niemeyer, 1921.

Westermann, W. L. "The Castanet Dancers of Arsinoe." Journal of Egyptian Archaeology, 10, 134-44, 1924.

Wilkinson, J. G. The Manners and Customs of the Ancient Egyptians. 3 volumes. Boston: Cassino, 1883.

Williams, Jane E. Ancient Art and Ritual. London: Oxford University Press, 1943.

Woody, Thomas. Life and Education in Early Societies. New York: The Macmillan Company, 1949.

CHAPTER 15

THEODORE ROOSEVELT'S ROLE IN THE 1905
FOOTBALL CONTROVERSY

Guy Lewis
University of Massachusetts, Amherst

Abstract

In 1905, intercollegiate football was tremendously popular, but contests were dull and dangerous affairs in which offensive players rushed the ball through massed defenses. Efforts to improve the sport for spectator and participant met with failure because the Intercollegiate Football Rules Committee refused to adopt reform legislation. Although it represented only a few of the large number of colleges participating in the sport, the influence of the Rules Committee was so great that attempts to establish rival legislative bodies were unsuccessful. In 1905, dissident elements again challenged the authority of the Rules Committee but the movement was in jeopardy until President Theodore Roosevelt used his influence to secure for it the necessary recognition.*

Introduction

Many college coaches and administrators had long favored changes in the rules which would reform the game of football, but it was not until 1906 that they were able to secure the adoption of necessary legislation. Earlier sectional or individual efforts to modify the sport had failed largely because the Intercollegiate Football Rules Committee opposed changes in the rules. Events during the 1905 football season provided colleges not represented on the Rules Committee with an opportunity to challenge the authority of the existing

---

Editor's Note: We are in Professor Lewis' debt for his willingness to share this scholarly effort with the reader. In this essay he explores what has hitherto been a rather hazy incident in most minds – the extent of President Theodore Roosevelt's involvement in the plight of intercollegiate football at the turn of the twentieth century.

---

* This historical study appeared in the October, 1969 issue of the Research Quarterly of the American Association for Health, Physical Education, and Recreation, and is reprinted here with the kind permission of the author and the AAHPER.

legislative body. Although the reform movement enjoyed widespread support, its complete success was not assured until the Rules Committee agreed to sit in joint session with representatives of the new group. President Theodore Roosevelt was involved in the controversy, but the nature and extent of his participation has not been established by previous investigators.

Review of the Literature

The concluding statements of historians regarding President Roosevelt's role in the controversy range from extreme caution to gross exaggeration. Danzig (5:29), Van Dalen, et al. (26:347), Weyand (28:82), Davis (6:111 and Krout (12:246 wrote that the President did nothing more than call a conference of representatives from Harvard, Yale, and Princeton, and suggest to them the desirability of having the objectionable features removed from the game. Other authors have given President Roosevelt credit for issuing an ultimatum which saved the sport. Brubacher and Rudy wrote that President Roosevelt called a White House conference in response to public outrage after the report of a large number of deaths and injuries attributable to football appeared in the Chicago Tribune at the conclusion of the 1905 season. The result of this meeting, the authors decided, was the adoption of reform in intercollegiate athletics throughout the country. (3:129) In his history of higher education, Rudolph informed readers that after viewing a newspaper photograph of a badly mangled football player the President threatened to abolish the sport unless the colleges reformed it. (22:376) While the studies contain an element of truth in that the President was concerned about the football question, an accurate reconstruction of his involvement must focus upon the primary issue in the controversy.

Statement of the Problem

The controversy was composed of many facets, but the most important one was the confrontation between the Rules Committee and the rival legislative body established by the new national group. Such concerns as the spirit of the rules and the adoption of restrictions to place football in proper perspective were only minor concerns of the reform element. Finally, while there was abolitionist sentiment and some administrators actually banned the sport, the threat of football being outlawed was never a serious one. The central issue was authority to draft the rules. Resolution of the dispute came when rival legislative groups agreed to sit in joint session, a decision influenced by the President of the United States, Theodore Roosevelt.

The Intercollegiate Football Rules Committee

In 1905 the sole rules-making body was the Intercollegiate Football Rules Committee. This was an association, with the exception of

Chicago's Amos A. Stagg, of representatives from Eastern institutions. The power to regulate its own membership made it a self-perpetuating group and, therefore, a society which was accountable to no one for its decisions or lack of action. While the Rules Committee could not force outside institutions to abide by the code it adopted, the very nature of intercollegiate competition, especially intersectional contests, compelled the colleges to adhere to a common set of rules. This action was taken even though various members of the group repeatedly stated that they had no desire to legislate for others.* The Committee's most powerful figure was Walter Camp, who, as secretary, directed its activities and virtually decided its membership. Camp, "the father of American football," had formulated most of the game's rules and fostered its development, and, as patriarch, he was willing to entertain suggestions for change but refused to adopt them unless the proposed alterations were in agreement with his concept of the game. In 1905 Camp and his fellow committeemen were satisfied with their game.**

Until late in the 1905 season those associated with Camp agreed that devotion to the game rather than self-interest motivated him. Although he was the person most responsible for the unequaled success of Yale teams, no one questioned the position he assumed on various legislative matters. His image was one of a perfect gentleman; a man with such ethical standards that he could negotiate and legislate on matters in which Yale was involved without permitting personal consideration to affect his conduct. This regard for Camp had developed over the years because of the manner in which he had settled numerous disputes between schools, instituted successful promotional plans, and thwarted the abolitionists. (6:88--110)

While order and unity prevailed among members of the Rules Committee, there was outside opposition to the body in general and Camp in particular. Coaches in the Middle West had been attempting to secure changes in the rules that would make contests more exciting:

---

* For example, the desirability of a uniform playing code became perfectly clear to members of the Rules Committee in 1895 and to a Middle West group in 1897. A dispute over momentum plays in 1895 forced a split in the membership of the Rules Committee and they adopted a dual code. The resulting situation was so unsatisfactory that they compromised their differences after one season of play. After repeated unsuccessful attempts to secure rules reform through the Rules Committee, institutions in the Middle West appointed their own rules committee in 1897. The code they drafted was never adopted because one of the schools had games scheduled with important Eastern teams.

** See the Camp papers, Yale University Library, for expressions of this sentiment.

games featuring long runs, spectacular plays, and more touchdowns. These professional coaches derived their livelihood from the sport and felt that the open-game they advocated would attract more spectators. (13,2:2). In 1897, when the Rules Committee refused to adopt their suggestions, the Middle Western coaches threatened to formulate their own code. Although the revolt failed to materialize, they continued to exert pressure upon the Rules Committee. After years of charges and threats, Camp, in an effort to placate the dissenters, agreed to seat a representative from the Middle West on the Rules Committee, provided they nominate Amos A. Stagg.* In 1904, Stagg (a former Yale athlete) assumed the role of spokesman on the Rules Committee for all those outside the select group, but coaches recognized the franchise as token and not something that would provide a solution to their problem.

Roosevelt and Football

In dealing with the football question, President Roosevelt was guided by two values: a belief that football was a valuable educational experience for participants and a desire for Harvard teams to be successful. According to President Roosevelt the qualities most essential to success were morality and virility, and these could not be developed unless boys avoided a life of effeminacy and luxury and engaged in the "rough sports which call for pluck, endurance, and physical address." (21:156). Football, he reasoned, was the most valuable of all team sports because it provided each individual with opportunities to test his courage. Harvard football was a special concern of President Roosevelt's. He participated in the formation of an organization founded for the purpose of securing highly qualified coaches. He also frequently sent the team measages of encouragement. (15:V. 3, 653)

The White House Conference and the President's Position

On October 9, 1905, President Roosevelt conducted a conference at which representatives from Harvard, Yale, and Princeton discussed the importance of the spirit of the rules. He called the meeting in response to a request from the Conference of the Masters of Church Schools of New England and the Middle States. Members of the Conference were concerned because their students had adopted dishonest practices employed by college players.** Camp made public the resolution adopted by the representatives.

---

* Letter from Walter Camp to Julian W. Curtis, December 5, 1905, Camp Correspondence, Yale University Library.
** Letter from Endicott Peabody to Theodore Roosevelt, September 16, 1905, Roosevelt Collection, Letters Received, Vol. 97, Library of Congress.

At a meeting with the President of the United States it was agreed that we consider an honorable obligation exists to carry out in letter and spirit the rules of the game of football relating to roughness, holding, and foul play, and the active coaches of our universities being present with us pledged themselves to so regard it and to do their utmost to carry out that obligation. (27)

The President was extremely pleased with the attitude of the representatives, especially Camp's. "I can not tell you," he wrote, "how pleased I am at the way you have taken hold. Now that the matter is in your hands I am more than content to abide by whatever you do."*

One college president and a coach from the Middle West, among others, asked President Roosevelt to take an uncompromising stand on the reform issue. Some groups and individuals asked him to endorse statements calling for abolition of the sport. In each case, the President made it clear that he was neither reformer nor abolitionist.**

He did not alter his position when reports of the Yale-Harvard freshman game revealed that his son, Theodore, Jr., had been injured in the contest. President Charles Eliot of Harvard declared the injury another example of the win-at-any-cost philosophy. He insisted that the repeated rushes at "Ted's" position were planned to weaken the defense at a strategic point and then take advantage of it.*** President Roosevelt, after receiving assurances from Camp, decided that the repeated attacks were a reflection of the respect the Yale team had for "Ted's" playing ability. (15:V. 5, 81 & 82). Although his son was suffering with a broken nose, cuts, and bruises, the President was still certain that Camp was motivated by higher ideals than Yale victories (15:V. 5, 93 & 94). Favorable reports of the Yale-Harvard varsity contest prompted the observation: "It seems to me

---

* Letter from Theodore Roosevelt to Walter Camp, October 11, 1905, Roosevelt Collection, Vol. 151, Letterbook 28, Library of Congress.
** For example: Letter from Theodore Roosevelt to William R. Harper, December 4, 1905, Roosevelt Collection, Vol. 151, Letterbook 29, Library of Congress and his letter to Henry L. Williams, December 11, 1905, Vol. 152, Letterbook 30.
*** This opinion was expressed in several exchanges between Roosevelt and Eliot. See the Letterbooks and Letters Received, Roosevelt Collection, Library of Congress.

that this year Harvard, Yale, and Princeton have played absolutely straight and clean games."*

The National Conference

Chancellor Henry B. McCracken of New York University proposed that Harvard's President Charles Eliot call a meeting of college and university administrators for the purpose of either abolishing or reforming football, after a player received a fatal injury in the Rochester-Union game. President Eliot refused to participate because he did not have the authority to abolish the sport, and it was impossible to reform it. "Deaths and injuries are not the strongest arguments against football," he informed McCracken. "That cheating and brutaility are profitable is the main evil." (19)

President Eliot's attitude failed to deter the Chancellor. "I would not," he declared, "intrust the reformation of the game to the present Rules Committee." (1) As an initial step in his plan to form a body which would be responsible to the university authorities, he invited the presidents of institutions whose teams had opposed those of New York University to send representatives to a meeting in New York City.

On December 8, 1905, with thirteen institutions represented, McCracken's conference convened in New York. (7) There was no opposition to the proposals that the group endorse football and initiate a reform movement. Delegates sanctioned the suggestion that colleges without representation on the Rules Committee establish a second such body. In order to gain popular support for the reform movement, they voted to invite all institutions to send representatives to a meeting. (8)

Sixty-two colleges from all sections of the country sent delegates to the national session on December 28. They organized the Intercollegiate Athletic Association of the United States and, following the election of Pierce of West Point as chairman, appointed a rules committee. The remainder of the "stormy" nine-hour session was devoted to the question of the Rules Committee. Some felt that cooperation of Camp's committee was essential to the success of the reform movement; others were certain that the Rules Committee would destroy or impede efforts to change the rules. The delegates finally adopted a resolution that instructed members of the new rules committee "to communicate with . . . the committee that has formerly governed football and propose that the committees be amalgamated

---

* Letter from Theodore Roosevelt to Alexander D. Lambert, November 27, 1905, Roosevelt Collection, Vol. 151, Letterbook 29, Library of Congress.

into one which shall formulate rules under which football shall be played." (12:2) In the event the amalgamation effort failed, the committee was to adopt a code for colleges represented at the conven tion.*

President Roosevelt Rejects Camp

A few days after the Yale-Harvard game President Roosevelt began to receive reports alleging that Yale had gained the victory by deliberately injuring Harvard's leading player. One writer accused Camp of destroying the gentlemen concept of sport with an "anything to win philosophy," (11:216-23), and Eliot presented the President with signed affidavits asserting that the Yale player struck the Harvard player with his fist.** After an exchange of letters with the game's official, Dashiell, and Camp, President Roosevelt concluded that the act was a perfect example of profitable brutality because it probably gave Yale the game or "it at least prevented all chance of Harvard winning."***

On December 9, the day after McCracken's first meeting, the Rules Committee met in Philadelphia. (9) Delegates adopted reform proposals that included changes in the rules, severe punishment for unnecessary roughness, and the establishment of a board to appoint officials. Camp, without success, solicited President Roosevelt's endorsement of the proposed reforms. He informed Camp and Harvard's coach, William Reid, that he was opposed to any plan which

---

* For accounts of the first meeting consult: Palmer E. Pierce, "The Intercollegiate Athletic Association of the United States," Intercollegiate Athletic Association, Proceedings, 1907, pp. 27-32; Walter R. Okeson, "E. K. Hall - An Appreciation," National Collegiate Athletic Association, Proceedings, 1930, pp. 132-36; Intercollegiate Athletic Association, Proceedings, 1906, pp. 22-23; Paul Stagg, "The Development of the National Collegiate Athletic Association in Relationship to Intercollegiate Athletics in the United States," (unpublished doctoral dissertation, New York University, 1946), p. 32; "Football Solons Getting Into Tangle of How to Change Game," Philadelphia Inquirer, December 28, 1905; and "Football Convention Wants One Rule Code," New York Times, December 29, 1905.
** Eliot included statements by R. H. Dana and F. J. Stimson in a letter which President Roosevelt sent in its entirety to Paul Dashiell, December 5, 1905, Roosevelt Collection, Vol. 151, Letterbrook 29, Library of Congress.
*** Letter from Theodore Roosevelt to [Paul] John Dashiell, December 21, 1905, Roosevelt Collection, Vol. 152, Letterbook 30, Library of Congress.

would leave the selection and control of game officials with the Rules Committee.*

On December 29, members of the Rules Committee held as informal meeting in Philadelphia to consider their position in light of developments brought about by the creation of a new rules committee. (8,10) Although one writer warned that the group "had better amalgamate or be devoured," committee members decided not to act without formal instruction from their schools. (25,20,17,18)

The Harvard-Yale Power Struggle

At the invitation of the Athletic Association, a group of Harvard graduates, "football experts," gathered at Cambridge for a long series of meetings. Although they adopted a number of reform suggestions, the playing code was not their major concern because the changes they proposed differed little from the ones sanctioned earlier by the Rules Committee. The crucial issue was how to deal effectively with Camp for, as they viewed the situation, Harvard had never received fair treatment from the Camp-dominated Rules Committee.** Thus, the questions before the Harvard Athletic Association was whether to remain loyal to the Rules Committee--an act that would be tantamount to an endorsement of Camp--or to affiliate with the new Intercollegiate Association--a course which would result in a loss of status unless other members of the Rules Committee joined the revolt. The decision was a difficult one, but Reid, who had been in contact with Roosevelt throughout the controversy, received an assurance from the President that he would exert his influence in behalf of a joint committee.***

_____

* Letters from Theodore Roosevelt to Walter Camp, December 11, 1905 and William T. Reid, December 11, 1905, Roosevelt Collection, Vol. 152, Letterbook 30, Library of Congress. Roosevelt had decided that Camp was responsible for starting the "crooked ways in football," but he was certain that Harvard and Princeton had also adopted the practices. Letter from Endicott Peabody to Theodore Roosevelt, January 25, 1906, Roosevelt Collection, Vol. 5, Letterbook 30, Library of Congress.
** See: Report of the President and Treasurer of Harvard College, 1905-06, pp. 119-30, "Athletic Sports"; "Athletics-Committee Minutes," Harvard Graduates' Magazine, 14:484-85, March, 1906.
*** Letter from Theodore Roosevelt to William Reid, Harvard's coach, January 11, 1906, Roosevelt Collection, Vol. 152, Letterbook 30, Library of Congress.

President Roosevelt Supports the National Committee

The President encouraged and supported developments which destroyed the unity of the Rules Committee. This change of condition was the most important factor in bringing about the merger of the rules groups. There was no evidence of disagreement among members of the Rules Committee prior to the time President Roosevelt not only refused to endorse the reform proposals adopted on December 9, but also denounced the Rules Committee. Following this, the President held a series of meetings with Coach Reid, and eventually Harvard graduates conducted a conference for the purpose of considering the football question. Although the Harvard graduates felt it advantageous to identify with the committee of the Intercollegiate Athletic Association, they were reluctant to sanction a halt of the Rules Committee without assurances that the Harvard representative would not be the lone dissenter among members of the Rules Committee. President Roosevelt was able to provide this assurance because Navy's representative, Dashiell, due to the roughness incident, was obligated to demonstrate to the President that he genuinely wished to secure impartial officials for contests. President Roosevelt insisted that Dashiell actively support the proposed merger of the committees. *

The Rules Committee Recognizes the Intercollegiate Athletic Association

On January 12, 1906, the two rules committees held independent sessions at the Hotel Netherland in New York City. Reid, on instructions from his Athletic Association, left the meeting of the Rules Committee and joined the group representing the Intercollegiate Athletic Association. ** An exchange of notes brought the two groups into agreement for a joint session. A member of the Rules Committee served as chairman and Reid assumed the duties of secretary. The move gave Harvard the position in the joint session which Camp

---

* Letter from Theodore Roosevelt to Paul J. Dashiell, January 10, 1906, Roosevelt Collection, Vol. 152, Letterbook 30, Library of Congress. Although the letter to Reid wasn't written until the eleventh (one day prior to the meeting) and the one to Dashiell on the tenth, Roosevelt had been in close touch with both men (personally and through correspondence) prior to the two communications.

** "Harvard on New Committee," New York Times, January 11, 1906.

had used to exert his influence over the activities of the Rules Committee.* That Yale authorities did not approve Harvard's action was revealed by the institution's president, Arthur Hadley." "It looks to me," he wrote Camp, "as though Reid were not playing fair . . . . we treated Harvard courteously in the December meetings, and they have tried to take advantage of it. This ought to be a lesson to us for the future."**

Amalgamation produced a more representative rules group, but it did not bring an immediate end to Eastern control. Although the Intercollegiate Athletic Association succeeded only in gaining representation on the joint committee that was equal to that of the Rules Committee, the new arrangement was far more equitable than the former one. "The closed corporation policy of the old committee," one observer wrote, "has long been like a red rag before the Western universities who had but one representative on the committee, and until two years ago none at all." (4:17) The rules committee of the Intercollegiate Athletic Association and the Rules Committee continued the policy of a joint session for the purpose of drafting rules until Yale joined the national body in 1915. (24:33,111,112) In 1906, Pierce, in an effort to make affiliation attractive, guaranteed members of the Rules Committee a place on the rules body if their institutions would join the Intercollegiate Athletic Association. Despite the offer, the "old guard" schools were slow to accept membership. Pennsylvania jointed in 1906 but Navy remained outside until 1920. Harvard became a member in 1908. (24:111)

The Intercollegiate Athletic Association of the United States became a positive force in the development of intercollegiate sport. On March 31, 1906, the members adopted a constitution and by-laws and, although the Association possessed neither legislative nor executive functions, its crusade for faculty control of the programs at member institutions "lent force to the rallying-cry that athletics are 'educational'." (23:22) Four years later the name of the Association was changed to the National Collegiate Athletic Association. (14:34)

Conclusion

President Roosevelt's role in the 1905 football controversy, probably the single most important event in the history of intercollegiate sport, was a significant but not a crucial one. His action did

---

* [James] Murphey, University of Pennsylvania Athletic Association to Walter Camp, January 24, 1906, Camp Correspondence, Yale University Library. Murphey reconstructed the recent events and reached the conclusion that Reid supported the Association because Camp controlled the Rules Committee.
** Letter from Arthur T. Hadley to Walter Camp, February 2, 1906, Camp Papers, Box 96, Yale University.

determine the direction of football, but he did not save the game because its existence was never threatened, nor did he bring about reform in either rules or conduct by issuing an ultimatum. In rejecting Camp, he encouraged the discontent that resulted in the destruction of unity among members of the Rules Committee. His major contribution to solution of the controversy came when the new organization was attempting to secure an agreement to negotiate from the Rules Committee. At that point, in the interest of securing impartial officials and protecting Harvard's welfare, he used his position in government and his personal power of persuasion to force the Rules Committee to recognize the national organization. The development enhanced the position of the Intercollegiate Athletic Association of the United States. Thus, President Theodore Roosevelt should properly be viewed as one of the founding fathers of the National Collegiate Athletic Association.

References
(As they appeared in the original publication)

1. Abolition of Football or Immediate Reforms. New York Times, November 28, 1905.

2. Baird, Charles. Football Coaching and Play in East and West. Illustrated Sporting News. 4:2, 18; February 4, 1905.

3. Brubacher, John and Rudy, Willis. Higher Education in Transition. New York: Harper and Row, 1958.

4. Bushnell, Edward R. With the College Athletes. Illustrated Outdoor News. 5:17; January 20, 1906.

5. Walter Camp's Statement. New York Times. October 12, 1905.

6. Danzig, Allison. History of American Football. Englewood Cliffs, New Jersey: Prentice-Hall, 1956.

7. Davis, Parke H. Football: The American Intercollegiate Game. New York: Charles Scribner's, 1911.

8. Football Conference Called for Next Week. New York Times, November 28, 1905.

9. Football Convention Wants One Rule Code. New York Times, December 29, 1905.

10. Football Men Arrive in Town for Big Meeting. Philadelphia Inquirer, December 9, 1905.

11. Football Solons Getting Deep into Tangle of How to Change Game. *Philadelphia Inquirer*, December 28, 1905.

12. From a Graduate's Window. *Harvard Graduates' Magazine*. 15:216-23; December, 1905.

13. Krout, John A. *Annals of American Sport*. Vol. 15. The Pageant of America. 15 volumes. New Haven: Yale University Press, 1929.

14. Letter from Charles F. Mathewson to Walter Camp, March 19, 1895, Camp Papers, Box 44, Yale University Library.

15. Miscellaneous Business. *Proceedings*, p. 34, national collegiate athletic association, 1910.

16. Morison, Samuel E. and Blum, John M. (editors). *Letters of Theodore Roosevelt*. 8 volumes. Cambridge: Harvard University Press, 1951-54.

17. New York's Conference. *Illustrated Outdoor News*. 5:2; Jan January 6, 1906.

18. No Football Reform; Delay by New Body. *New York Times*, December 30, 1905.

19. Okeson, Walter R. E. K. Hall – An Appreciation. *Proceedings*, pp. 132-35, national collegiate athletic association, 1930.

20. Pierce, Palmer E. The Intercollegiate Athletic Association of the United States. *Proceedings*, pp. 27-32, intercollegiate athletic association of the United States, 1907.

21. President Eliot won't act. *New York Times*, November 28, 1905.

22. Roosevelt, Theodore. *The Strenuous Life*. New York: Century, 1902.

23. Rudolph, Frederick. *The American College and University: A History*. New York: Vintage, 1962.

24. Savage, Howard J. and others. *American College Athletics*. Bulletin 23. New York: Carnegie Foundation for the Advancement of Teaching, 1929.

25.   Stagg, Paul. The Development of the National Collegiate Athle-
       tic Association in Relationship to Intercollegiate Athletics in the
       United States. Unpublished doctoral dissertation, New York
       University, 1946.

26.   Stauffer, Nathan P. There is Handwriting on the Wall for the
       Rules Committee to Read. Philadelphia Inquirer, December 29,
       1905.

27.   Van Dalen, Deobold and others. A World History of Physical
       Education. Englewood Cliffs, New Jersey: Prentice-Hall, 1953.

28.   Weyand, Alexander. The Saga of American Football. New
       York: Macmillan, 1961.

CHAPTER 16

A HISTORY OF RELATIONS BETWEEN THE NCAA AND
THE AAU, 1905-1968

Arnold W. Flath
Oregon State University, Corvallis

While many American sports fans have been basking in the
reflected honors of American athletes and their outstanding performances in recent Olympic Games and international athletic competition,
those close to amateur sports have not been surprised that the controversy between the National Collegiate Athletic Association and the
Amateur Athletic Union continues to plague those involved in "amateur" sports in the United States.

Many fans, athletes, and athletic administrators know little and
care less about the relations between the NCAA and the AAU than
perhaps any other aspect of sports; yet, there is nothing in sports
today that will have as much to do with the quality and kind of representation the United States will have in international competition in
the future as does the persistent controversy between the NCAA and
the AAU over the administration of amateur sports.

Even though the struggle for control of amateur sports has been
a part of the history of sports ever since the AAU was formed in
1888, the AAU has only been seriously challenged to make changes
since 1905 when the NCAA was founded. It was at this time that
NCAA leaders began to express the need for a more democratic method of selecting athletes for international competition than that existing under AAU control.

Those desiring a greater voice in the control of amateur sports
pointed to the fact that, while athletes representing athletic clubs
under AAU control were the primary source of athletes for national

---

Editor's Note: In Chapter 16 is presented a paper that was
obtained from Professor Flath. His earlier study, which was published as a monograph as well, traced the history of relations between the
National Collegiate Athletic Association and the Amateur Athletic
Union from 1905 to 1963. For the purposes of this volume, Dr.
Flath has extended the period of discussion down to 1968. It should
be pointed out that no conclusions were drawn at the end of the earlier study because of the extremely controversial nature of the topic.
The avoidance of the presentation of conclusions was thought advis-
able to prevent charges of extreme bias (because of the presence of
two prominent NCAA officials on the doctoral committee).

and international competition prior to the revival of the Olympic
Games in 1896, the high schools, colleges, military services, and
many social and fraternal groups in the United States soon were producing nearly all the athletes representing the United States. With
those groups affiliated with the AAU producing fewer competitors and
yet continuing to play the dominant role in the administration of international competition, it was no wonder that dissatisfaction with AAU
control broke out.

The Origin of the AAU

Although a few athletic contests were held in the United States
during the period between the Revolutionary War and the Civil War,
little progress had been made in the development of competitive
athletics, and there was little concern about the amateur status of
participants in athletic contests. Most of the development in amateur
athletics took place after the Civil War at a rate so rapid that some
means of control became necessary. Leaders in developing this control were the athletic clubs, particularly in the East. These clubs,
the product of urban development, strove to stimulate amateur athletic competition. The first of these clubs was the San Francisco Club
founded in 1860 as a social and gymnasium club, but probably the
most influential of these athletic clubs was the New York Athletic
Club. Organized in 1866, the New York Athletic Club's form of
organization, constitution, and by-laws, patterned after the Amateur
and the London Athletic Clubs of England, served as models for many
of the hundreds of athletic clubs which soon developed.

The National Association of Amateur Athletes of America, the
first organization to attempt the control of amateur athletic clubs,
was formed in 1879. The strength of the NAAA was in the New York
City area, where the Association conducted athletic competitions for
nearly ten years before it was forced out of existence by the development of the AAU.

The AAU was formed in 1888 after a group of fifteen athletic
clubs, led by the Athletic Club of the Schuylkill Navy and the New York
Athletic Club, withdrew from the National Association of Amateur
Athletes. Originally, the AAU was a union of athletic clubs, but at
the annual meeting in 1890 the need for local autonomy was satisfied
when the AAU was changed from a union of individual clubs to a union
of district organizations. Pressure was brought to bear on organizations by the AAU's development of sanctioning and jurisdiction
policies. All athletic sporting events had to be sanctioned by the AAU,
or else athletes competing in an unsanctioned meet would be prohibited
from participating in any athletic sporting event sanctioned by the
Union. The AAU claimed jurisdiction of twenty-three sports, and

athletes competing in those sports, over which the AAU claimed jurisdiction, had to register at a small fee and certify their amateur standing.

Even though the AAU was to change its policies as the result of conflict with colleges and other organizations sponsoring athletic competition, the Amateur Athletic Union's requirements for the sanctioning of games and for the registration of athletes, two of the primary methods of controlling amateur athletics and raising revenue, were to become the sources of controversy and misunderstanding in the years to come.

The Origin of the NCAA

While athletic clubs and colleges were attempting to raise athletic competition to a higher plane after the Civil War, amateur athletics were not above reproach. To counteract the professionalism and commercialism that threatened to dominate athletics, the Olympic Games were revived in 1896. Under the leadership of Pierre de Coubertin, the revival of the Olympic Games was the result of the desire of many sportsmen to rekindle the Olympic spirit and to develop international competition as a means of promoting peace and friendship between nations.

Even though the Olympic spirit had been "fanned alive" at the Olympic Games in Athens, Paris, and St. Louis, college athletics come under severe criticism, especially during the first few years of the twentieth century. The year 1905 was memorable in the world of college athletics because of the campaign waged against the various college sports. The game of football was under particularly heavy criticism. Public sentiment against football reached such a peak that President Theodore Roosevelt felt it necessary to begin a campaign for the reform of football and for the development of uniform eligibility codes for all American colleges and universities. In 1905 representatives of sixty-eight institutions met to resolve the problems facing intercollegiate athletics. The work of these delegates resulted in the founding of the Intercollegiate Athletic Association of the United States--a title that was to be changed to the National Collegiate Athletic Association in 1910. Early in its history, the NCAA was organized as an advisory body with no executive function except through its committees. This principle was followed until 1947, when the NCAA instituted an enforcement program. The NCAA expanded its influence through actions of its various committees, through resolutions at conventions, and through its championship events which began in 1921 with a track and field championship.

With the founding of the NCAA in 1905, there have been several persistent areas of conflict between the collegiate group and the AAU:

1. The AAU's rules requiring sanctioning of participants and claims of jurisdiction over certain sports;

2. The question of the rights of the colleges to compete internationally without permission of the AAU;

3. Representation in the Olympic organization.[1]

Past Conflicts between the NCAA and the AAU

Following World War I, there was a great revival of interest in athletics. The NCAA expanded its function and took an interest in athletic programs that had been primarily the interest of the AAU. Most of the conflict revolved around representation in Olympic and international competitive organizations.

An attempt at forming a national association composed of all existing amateur sports organizations, as suggested by Secretary of War John W. Weeks in 1921, was strongly supported by the NCAA and other sports bodies in sympathy with the attempts to broaden the base of support and control beyond that of the AAU and the American Olympic Association. The struggle in the 1920's nearly disrupted American Olympic efforts, and an all-out war between the sports bodies was avoided only through changes in the American Olympic Association's constitution giving a greater voice to the colleges, not to mention the appointment of General Douglas MacArthur as President of the American Olympic Committee in 1927.

With the AAU in control of certain sports which they held to be under their jurisdiction through membership in a number of international federations administering each sport, grievances accumulated steadily over the years. The major point of dissension was in what the NCAA termed "the dictatorial attitude of the AAU with reference to established policy in sports in which it is the international representative."[2] Because there did not seem to be any sincere AAU intent to make some correction of these grievances, the NCAA's Council voted at its April, 1960 meeting not to respect suspensions of the AAU unless agreement on rules and procedures could be obtained.

---

[1] Paul Stagg, "Background of the Conflict between the NCAA and the AAU," Proceedings of the National College Physical Education Association (Dallas, Texas, Jan. 8-11, 1964), p. 72.

[2] Prevalent grievances and points of dissatisfaction that exist regarding the AAU. A photostatic copy of a typewritten document compiled by the National Collegiate Athletic Association, Kansas City, Missouri.

The Council went on to authorize the NCAA officers to cancel the Articles of Alliance between the NCAA and the AAU which had been in effect since 1946.

The impact of the cancelling of the Articles of Alliance between the NCAA and the AAU went virtually unnoticed because of the attention given to the 1960 Olympic Games in Rome, but already movements were underway which resulted in the formation of new federations in track and field, baseball, basketball, gymnastics and wrestling. Each of these federations was supported by organizations, including the NCAA, and were composed of colleges, junior colleges, and high schools. Provision was made for the AAU to play an important part in the federations. Realizing that this development would mean a diminishing of their power to control, the AAU denounced the federations and looked upon them as usurpers of its authority. With this split made known to the sporting public in an article written by Tex Maule in the September 25, 1961 issue of Sports Illustrated, the controversy over the administration of amateur sports erupted onto the daily sports pages all over the world. As AAU attempts failed to bring the NCAA and its supporters back into the AAU, and NCAA attempts failed to enlist the AAU in the federation form of control, it became evident that the sports bodies were on a collision course with neither side willing to temper their demands.

By the fall of 1962 the NCAA-AAU fight had become very serious. Attorney General Robert Kennedy acknowledged to the press that the federal government was concerned that the dispute would interfere with Olympic preparations for the 1964 Games in Tokyo. A meeting of the warring sports bodies followed, and this resulted in an alliance that would serve as a truce to last until November 1, 1964. With both sides coming out of the meeting with extremely different opinions about how the agreement was to be put into practice, the gulf between the NCAA-sponsored federations and the AAU led to a two-day arbitration session in New York on January 18, 1863 with General MacArthur once again playing a major role in settling a dispute between the two bodies by serving as arbitrator at President Kennedy's request.

At these meetings the federations and the AAU adopted what has come to be known as the MacArthur Plan. The MacArthur Plan served to (1) reinstate athletes who had been disqualified from Olympic competition for reasons other than those which were purely personal to the individual; (2) required the lifting of a ban by the NCAA on use of college members' facilities and athletes in meets not sanctioned by the federations; (3) called for the formation of an Olympic Eligibility Board that would decide on the American representation to the 1964 Olympics, and (4) recommended to the President of the United States that an athletic congress be called following the 1964 Olympics to devise a permanent plan under which all amateur sports bodies might cooperate in providing the United States with its strongest possible representation in international sports competition.

MacArthur's function as an arbitrator was put to a test on a number of occasions in 1963, and in each instance his decisions were accepted by the NCAA-supported federations and the AAU. All indications pointed to a solution of the problem along the lines outlined in the MacArthur Plan, but with the assassination of President Kennedy on November 22, 1963, and the death of General MacArthur on April 5, 1964, the element of uncertainty in reaching a solution was once again injected into the controversy. Even so, neither side seemed anxious to make any move to upset the existing plans for Olympic Games.

Within days after the conclusion of the 1964 Olympic Games in Tokyo, it became evident that the Kennedy-MacArthur inspired truce had come to an end. The NCAA announced a rule banning NCAA athletes from competing in open meets not sanctioned by the United States Track and Field Federation after March 1, 1965.

Since the 1965 ban, the NCAA and the AAU have gone through a series of bans, amelioration of differences, and restoration of relations. The 1968 Olympic Games were threatened by the actions of the two organizations, but as in the past the differences between the NCAA and the AAU were resolved long enough to permit the United States to compete in the 1968 Games in Mexico City. In June, 1969, the NCAA again instituted its ban on international competitions in meets not sanctioned by the United States Track and Field Federation.

The Nature of the Differences between the NCAA and the AAU

The differences between the NCAA and the AAU have been the result of differences in administrative philosophy and their understanding of the role of competitive athletics in the American society. The AAU has traditionally held that:

1. Most amateur athletics in the United States should be administered by a central "umbrella" administrative body.

2. The AAU, as a result of its early beginning and the services already rendered in behalf of amateur athletics, should be the organization to control athletics.

3. The AAU is already recognized by international organizations as the official governing body for the majority of amateur athletics in the United States.

4. Administrative structure, policy, and practice is already established and functioning; therefore, no new organization is needed.

5. A system that includes registration and certification of athletes and sporting events is the best way to ensure amateur athletics.

6. The NCAA colleges should join the AAU and make it the national controlling body.

On the other hand, the NCAA has traditionally held that:

1. Amateur athletics should be administered on the basis of specialized and singular sports organizations, i.e., track, basketball, wrestling, etc. rather than the "umbrella" approach. Federations of the separate sports would administer the programs for international competition.

2. The colleges have the highly competent staffs and the expensive facilities necessary for the conduct of athletic programs.

3. The colleges chose to conduct their own programs, rather than to subordinate themselves to representatives who may be college men (but not representatives selected by the colleges).

4. The NCAA questions the right of the AAU to require sanctioning of all open meets.

5. The NCAA does not accept the AAU as the governing body for international athletics. It recommends instead national federations in basketball, track and field, baseball, gymnastics, and wrestling.

6. The NCAA does accept the American Olympic Association as the governing body for the American participation in the Olympic Games. It does feel, however, that this organization, as constituted, is controlled by the AAU and is not representative of the athletic interest of amateur athletics as they are conducted in the United States.[1]

---

[1] Stagg, op. cit., pp. 76-77.

The AAU has been able to capitalize on its advantages in the dispute. They have been accepted as the controlling body for amateur athletics in the United States by the International Federation. This relationship permits the AAU to threaten ineligibility for the Olympic Games and international competition. Without this threat the AAU would have no control over the colleges. In addition to the long-time, amenable relationship between the AAU and the international sports governing body (IOC), the AAU recognizes the advantage it holds since the conflict operates only during the period between the Olympic Games. Public pressure forces the NCAA to relent in its struggle in order to permit college athletes to compete in the Games.

The NCAA capitalizes on the power it can exert in that it exercises some control over a large proportion of the coaches, athletes, and athletic facilities of its member institutions. Since many top-class athletes in all sporting events are from NCAA institutions, any ban that withheld them from AAU competition would be a serious blow to the AAU. The AAU needs the coaches, the athletes, and the facilities of the NCAA-related institutions for their programs, but the colleges have developed enough competition to satisfy their needs. The colleges do not need AAU competition to develop high level performances.

Future Relations between the NCAA and the AAU

The nature of past relationships between the NCAA and the AAU would indicate that the positions of the two organizations are becoming polarized, and that only a thorough reorganization of the control of amateur athletics in the United States will ameliorate the existing differences. The possibility of any significant alteration in relationships is most unlikely, unless the International Federation alters its recognition of the AAU as the amateur sports governing body in the United States. The possibility of the International Federation changing its position in this regard is practically non-existent. The NCAA will continue to press for greater representation in Olympic and international competition. The AAU will continue to withstand the pressures, insofar as possible, altering its stand only when compelled to do so. It is very likely that this controversy will continue until one of the organizations succumbs, or until attempts are made to fulfill the part of the MacArthur Plan, which recommends to the President of the United States:

"That, if desired......an athletic congress be called ....to devise a permanent plan under which all organizations dedicated to amateur athletics and all individual men and women aspiring to represent our country in international games be able to pool their resources so that by a united effort we may be able successfully to meet the challenge from any nation in the field of athletics and sport."[1]

Selected References

With the exception of the weekly newspaper, The Spirit of the Times, and The New York Times, the early history of amateur athletics in the United States may be traced through information gathered from sources such as: Robert Korsgaard's, "A History of the Amateur Athletic Union of the United States," (unpublished Doctor of Education project, Teachers College, Columbia University, 1952); John Allen Krout's, Annals of American Sport, Volume 15: The Pageant of America (New Haven, Connecticut: Yale University Press, 1929); Howard J. Savage et. al., American College Athletics (New York: The Carnegie Foundation for the Advancement of Teaching, 1929); Victor Paul D. Dauer's, "The Amateur Code in American College Athletics," (unpublished Ph.D. dissertation, School of Education, The University of Michigan, 1950); and Paul Stagg's, dissertation, "The Development of the National Collegiate Athletic Association in Relationship to Intercollegiate Athletics in the United States," (unpublished doctoral dissertation, New York University, 1946).

From the annual NCAA Proceedings beginning in 1905 to the present, much information concerning the relationship between the NCAA and the AAU may be found. The careful reader may find some information in the Minutes of the Annual Meeting of the Amateur Athletic Union of the United States. More important minutes of both Associations are to be found in the national offices of the AAU in New York City and of the NCAA in Kansas City.

Much recent material in regard to the dispute is to be found in NCAA-AAU Dispute, Hearings before the Committee on Commerce of the United States Senate, Eighty-ninth Congress, First Session on the Controversy in Administration of Track and Field Events in the United States, August, 1965 Serial No. 89-40, U. S. Government Printing Office: Washington, D. C., 1965.

---

[1] The MacArthur Plan. A mimeographed copy dated January 19, 1963 presented to representatives of the federations and the AAU at the outset of the arbitration meeting held on January 18, 1963 in New York City.

CHAPTER 17

THE GROWTH OF THE INTERSCHOLASTIC ATHLETICS
MOVEMENT IN THE UNITED STATES, 1890–1940

James A. Montgomery
Millsaps College, Jackson, Mississippi

A study of the interscholastic athletics movement in the United
States should be prefaced with a review of the origin and growth of
the high school itself in the United States. Further, the development
of interscholastic athletics, such as it was before 1890, should be
examined for trends and tendencies which give some indications of
the direction taken in the development of the interscholastic athletics
movement in the United States.

Growth of the High School in the United States

The high school in the United States may be said to be "the
child" of the middle classes. During the early history of the United
States, instruction in Latin, Greek, and the Bible was considered
sufficient education for most people. But as the country grew, the
tradespeople, merchants, and others demanded a more enriched approach to education than just reading, writing, and arithmetic. A
larger number of people eligible to pay taxes, caused by an increase
in the number of people in the merchant class, increased the political
strength of that group.

The reasons for the establishment of the high school are given
legal, political, and social overtones by some historians. Noble
indicated that:

> The establishment of the nonsectarian, free, day high
> schools, open alike to both sexes, may be termed an
> 'upward thrust of Jacksonian Democracy,' for the temper
> of the times demanded the removal of the stamp of class
> rigidity, sect, and charity from the training of the mass-
> es. (Noble, pp. 809, 813)

Editor's Note: Continuing the discussion of sport and athletics,
an essay by Professor Montgomery was obtained. His willingness to
allow the use of the results of his study about the growth of the interscholastic athletics movement in the United States from 1890 to 1940
is sincerely appreciated. The athletics program at the high school
level has influenced the field of physical education profoundly, and it
is wise to make every effort to understand the development of the
"athletics phenomenon."

The public high school movement at first was largely confined to the major centers of population in the East and in the rapidly growing Middle West. By the beginning of the Civil War there were 300 or more high schools in the United States, and during the last years of the nineteenth century the expansion in number was enormous. (Butts, p. 489)

The rapid expansion of the high school movement toward the end of the nineteenth century was due to a number of things, not the least of which was a ruling by the Michigan Supreme Court in 1872 establishing a legal precedent that overrode the existing permissive legislation on the maintenance of public high schools. This ruling concerned the legality of spending school tax money for high schools, since high schools were not specifically mentioned in the laws of the state. The court ruled that the high school was a proper part of the public school system. (Knight, p. 386) In so doing,. it established the basis for the legal and financial system of support for high schools that exist today.

By the end of the century the aims of the high school had changed greatly. Secular aims had superseded the religious-moral aim; the old classical aims had given way to informational, social-civic, vocational and practical, and individual-development aims. The vocational and practical aims gave impetus to subjects in the curriculum, such as industrial arts, home economics, social studies, and agriculture. The values inherent in individual development stimulated the arts and physical education. (Butts, pp. 506-510)

Knight pointed out in 1929 that since 1890 the rate of increase in public high school enrollment had been twenty times greater than the increase in the population of the country during that period. (Knight, p. 17)

Subject matter and courses had continued to be a problem to the growing high school. The evolvement of the two-track curriculum led to problems in meeting college entrance requirements. To resolve some of these problems, a Committee of Ten (mostly college officials) was set up in 1893 with President Eliot of Harvard as chairman. This committee stated as a principle that subjects studied for the same length of time were educationally equal. (Dixon and others, p. 127)

In the early part of the twentieth century, several factors became evident that led educators to believe a thoroughgoing revision of the secondary school curriculum was needed. (Butts, p. 647) Inglis listed these factors as:

1. Change in the character of the secondary school clientele;
2. Introduction of the new subjects for study;

3. Reorganization of grades 7-9;
4. Development in the field of educational psychology, such as new light on the laws of learning, the psychology of individual differences, and the nature and measurement of intelligence;
5. The disclosure of prevailing defects (in the curriculum) by means of objective measurement;
6. Changes in our conception of the functions to be performed by the secondary school (Inglis, p. 259).

John Franklin Brown pointed out that it was the function of the school to provide some things for the pupil that were not academic subjects:

> . . . there are certain specific things more or less apart from scholarship that it should do for him. First of all, it should develop his physical powers. . . . The development and maintenance of the highest practical degree of physical health and vigor on the part of the pupil should not be merely an individual but a definitely conscious purpose of the school, and proper provision should be made for realizing it. (Brown, pp. 72-73)

Interscholastic Athletics in the United States Prior to 1890

The origins of school athletics are not completely shrouded in mystery, because we know people have played vigorous games throughout recorded history, especially during the days of the classical western civilization. (Kilzner, Stephenson, and Nordberg, p. 175) However, since most of the earliest settlers in this country came from England, it is only natural that they would introduce English customs and games to the New World.

Most of the English games were played in their schools and colleges, and since English schools and colleges were copied in America, the English games were copied, too. The English had long been devotees of sports and ".... it is generally held out that this rich tradition of sport in England has developed the games and athletics of American schools and colleges." (Williams and Hughes, pp. 24-25)

A gradual change in the attitude of many people toward school athletics was evident beginning in the 1870's. There was an increasing interest on the part of the students, also. Elmer Ellsworth Brown, using Central (Philadelphia) High School as an example, said that before the Civil War there were no organized athletics at the school, though there was a lively playground interest in townball--a forerunner of baseball. A change-over to organized athletics came slowly and had hardly begun until the seventies. (Brown, pp. 434-435)

- 219 -

There is no doubt as to how athletics got into the high school program, though some of the reasons why are rather obscure. That athletics were introduced into the high school by the students is certain. (Mitchell, xvi) Some feel that athletics were literally forced into the high school program, and primarily because the boys desired physical activity and a method of self expression. Most school administrators did not see athletics as an educational tool for a long time. (Shepard and Jamerson, p. 2)

Some writers feel that athletics developed from community life as an expression of community needs and came into the schools this way, rather than as an expression of educational philosophy. (Scott, p. 49) This feeling, and also the growth of the high school itself, gave impetus to the introduction of athletics into the high school program:

> This development of high schools was of tremendous importance to the growth of competitive sports. Since the high schools were institutions of and for the people, community interests were of necessity reflected in the educational curriculum. Games and sports had come to play a prominent part in the life of the community and it was inevitable that sooner or later the activities would become part of the curriculum of the school. (Scott, p. 13)

However, because of the enthusiasm of high school youth, athletics grew to such proportions that high school administrators were forced either to stamp athletics out or to control them. The administrators chose the latter course, and thus set the stage for future developments in interscholastic athletics. (Morland, pp. 1-2) Emmett A. Rice, historian of physical education, pointed out two other reasons why athletics were brought into the high school. The first was the emphasis put on the values of play in the 1880's. This emphasis on the value of play created a permissive atmosphere in which athletics developed rapidly. The second reason was that high school boys imitated college athletic teams and sought to bring athletics into the high school just as they had been brought into the colleges. Rice also mentioned that interscholastic athletic teams were an outgrowth of the intramural or playground teams. (Rice, p. 236)

Trends, 1890-1940

During the decade 1880-1890, educators began to realize the value of play and to emphasize it in the schools and on the play grounds. One of the results which accrued from this emphasis was an extension into the lower schools of a highly organized system of competitive athletics that already existed in the colleges and universities. The history of athletics in the colleges then began to repeat

itself in the high schools, going through the same processes of
(1) intramural (or playground) athletics which developed into interscholastic athletics; (2) the rise of the student manager; (3) the advent
of the professional coach; and finally (4) faculty control of athletics.
(Rice, p. 236)

This imitation of college athletics by the high schools led one
writer in 1927 to say, "The craze of the day is competitive athletics.
Twenty years age the competitive sports were confined to colleges
and universities, but now they have spread to the high school."
(Foster, p. 33) To be sure, the same games that were played in the
colleges were played in the high school community, because then, as
now, youth wanted to imitate what it admired. Needless to say, college boys and college sports were more admired by the youthful mind
than were the boys and the sports played in the local community.

The development of athletics in the programs of the high schools
of the United States followed a well-defined pattern as follows:

1. Athletics were first sponsored by the students, with
    the school administrators and faculty being unsym-
    pathetic or hostile.

2. The community assisted the students in the form of
    finances and coaching aid, with school administrators
    and faculty being either indifferent or intolerant.

3. The administrators and faculty recognized the mal-
    practices in athletics and moved toward faculty con-
    trol and guidance.

4. Athletics were accepted by school administrators and
    faculty as an essential part of the school program.
    (Shepard and Jamerson, p. 3)

From 1900 to 1910 the interscholastic athletic movement burst
into full bloom. Development, organization, and supervision of high
school athletics grew almost overnight into a program that drew much
criticism from educators and laymen alike. The chief objection to
the new athletics activities was that they neglected the many to train a
few to insure victory in interscholastic athletics contests. (Rice,
p. 272) This athletics movement during the first ten years of the
twentieth century was considered by some experts to be strictly a physical education movement that had gotten out of hand. (Rogers,
p. 554)

Perhaps one of the reasons why interscholastic athletics grew
so fast was that, at the time, many educators were asking for new activities to be introduced into the high school program. Athletics and

collateral activities, as many as could be handled by the students and faculties, were asked to be under faculty control and supervision. (Boynton, pp. 206-214) The educational worth of the formerly extra-curricular activities was beginning to be recognized.

Some writers felt that the rapid spread of interscholastic athletics was due to a revolt on the part of the students, and perhaps many of the faculty as well. The school curriculum of the early part of the twentieth century was determined mostly by the faulty philosophy of a curriculum that embodied a rigid program of formal discipline. This rigid discipline the students did not like; so, they brought into the curriculum other activities that satisfied their needs. (Williams and Brownell, pp. 205-206)

The acceptance into education of the methods of science during the first decade of the twentieth century brought about new activity areas of which games and sports were a part. (Scott, p. 164) The development and adoption of John Dewey's ideas on educational philosophy caused physical education student activities to move away from the formal programs toward individual programs and education for leisure activities. (Dixon and others, p. 164)

When the question of why athletics should take place in the high schools was raised, the idea was put forth that competition was firmly embedded in the American way of life and was something to hold as a heritage, to love, and to practice. (Orr, p. 52) By the beginning of the twentieth century, high school athletic associations began to be accepted as having real worth in building higher standards for athletics in the high schools. Nevertheless, the high school administrators' neglect in setting up machinery for controlling interscholastic athletics caused the program to be seriously challenged.

It became apparent that external control of interscholastics depended, in large measure, upon the strength of the athletics control system within the individual school. The tendencies toward evil in interscholastic athletics were found to be in ascending ratio with the increase in complexity of the athletics organization. Organizations alone, it was found, could not control athletics satisfactorily--leadership from and control by the institution were needed also.

The state high school athletics associations were formed to promote clean, wholesome athletics participation between state high schools, to guarantee good faith in matters of rules and eligibility, and to provide a means of redress for violations. The function of the National Federation of State High School Athletic Associations were defined as being to protect and supervise the interstate athletics interests of member schools belonging to the state associations.

By comparing the aims and objectives of interscholastic athletics and physical education during the period from 1890 to 1940, it was found that, while the aims of field of physical education changed with the educational trends of the times, the aims of interscholastic athletics changed more slowly, gradually espousing the aims of education in a moral and social sense.

General Bibliography

Boynton, D. "Athletics and Collateral Activities in Secondary Schools," Proceedings of the Forty-third Annual Meeting of the National Education Association of the United States, St. Louis, Missouri, June 27–July 1, 1904, XLIII. Winona, Minnesota: The Association, 1904.

Brown, Elmer Ellsworth. The Making of Our Middle Schools. New York: Longmans, Green, and Co., Inc., 1903.

Brown, John Franklin. The American High School. New York: The Macmillan Company, 1910.

Butts, R. Freeman. A Cultural History of Western Education. First edition. New York: McGraw-Hill Book Company, 1947.

Dixon, J. G. and others. Landmarks in the History of Physical Education. London: Routledge and Paul Kegan, 1957.

Foster, William T. "An Indictment of Intercollegiate Athletics." Mind and Body, 34, 33, April, 1927.

Inglis, Alexander J. "Secondary Education," in Twenty-five Years of American Education. Edited by J. L. Kandel. New York: The Macmillan Company, 1924.

Kilzer, Louis R., Stephenson, Harold H. and Nordberg, Orville. Allied Activities in the Secondary School. New York: Harper & Brothers, 1956.

Knight, Edgar W. Education in the United States. Boston: Ginn and Company, 1929.

Mitchell, Elmer D. "Editor's Introduction," in Administration of High School Athletics. By Charles E. Forsythe. Second edition. New York: Prentice-Hall, Inc., 1948.

Morland, Richard Boyd. "Trends in the Policies of State High School Athletic Associations of the United States, 1929-1947." Unpublished Master's thesis, Springfield College, 1947.

Noble, S. G. "How We Came To Have High Schools." School Review, 43, No. 2:100, 102, 103, 1945, citing Charles A. Beard and Mary R. Beard, The Rise of American Civilization (New York: The Macmillan Company, 1927), 809, 813.

Orr, W. "The Place of Athletics is Secondary Schools." American Physical Education Review, 12, No. 1:52, 1907.

Rice, Emmett A. A Brief History of Physical Education. Revised and enlarged edition. New York: A. S. Barnes & Co., Inc., 1929.

Rogers, Frederick Rand. Educational Objectives of Physical Activity. New York: A. S. Barnes & Co., Inc., 1930.

Scott, Harry A. Competitive Sports in Schools and Colleges. New York: Harper & Brothers, 1951.

Shepard, George E. and Jamerson, Richard E. Interscholastic Athletics. New York: McGraw-Hill Book Company, Inc., 1953.

Williams, Jesse F. and Brownell, Clifford Lee. The Administration of Health Education and Physical Education. Fourth edition. Philadelphia: W. B. Saunders Company, 1951.

_____ and Hughes, William L. Athletics in Education. Philadelphia: W. B. Saunders Company, 1931.

CHAPTER 18

A HISTORY OF UNDERGRADUATE PROFESSIONAL
PREPARATION FOR PHYSICAL EDUCATION IN THE
UNITED STATES, 1861-1961

Earle F. Zeigler
The University of Western Ontario, London

Introduction[1]

The history of physical education in the United States may be
divided into four fairly distinct periods: (1) The Colonial Period
(1609-1781); (2) The Provincial Period (1781-1885); (3) The Period of
the Waning of European Influence (1885-1918); and (4) The Period of
American Physical Education (1918-)(Schwendener, 1942, see Table
of Contents).

The years from 1830 to 1860 are sometimes called "The Architectural Period" of American public education. It was during these
years that the struggle for state-supported schools took place. The
problems of getting tax support, of eliminating the pauper-school
idea, and of doing away with pro-rated tuitions were all difficult in
themselves to solve. The elimination of sectarianism as a controlling
factor in the schools and the appointment of public officials to run
school affairs were major problems of the period. By 1860 the
American education ladder as a one-way system was fairly complete.
The first compulsory attendance law was passed in Massachusetts in
1852. With this development of the public school system, it was quite

---

Editor's Note: The essay in Chapter 17, and the following three
chapters, trace from different approaches the history of professional
preparation for physical education in the United States at both the
undergraduate and graduate levels. This first essay is by the Editor,
and grew out of a doctoral study completed at Yale University during
the late 1940's. It was abstracted and updated to serve as a background paper for the AAHPER Conference in 1962 (the report of which
was entitled Professional Preparation in Health Education, Physical
Education, and Recreation Education).

---

[1] This chapter from the 1962 Professional Preparation Conference Report of the American Association for Health, Physical Education, and Recreation is printed here with the permission of Mrs.
Nancy Rosenberg, Director of Publications.

natural that attention turned to the quality and type of teacher hired
for so important a task as the education of the coming generation.

In the field of physical education, after the introduction of gymnastics at the Round Hill School in Northampton, Mass. in 1823,
Harvard College started the first American college gymnasium in
1826. The year before, in New York City, physical training had been
introduced as one of a number of innovations in the school curriculum.
Yale followed Harvard's lead and established ground for gymnastics in
1826, and one year later Amherst, Brown, and Williams made such
areas available. Perhaps another dozen schools soon followed the
early example of the Round Hill School and Harvard College. Beck,
Lieber, and Follen did not continue their active roles in guiding the
teaching of gymnastics, however, and because competent instructors
were lacking to carry out the aims of this type of physical training,
the whole movement quickly waned within a few years after its beginning (Van Dalen et. al., 1953, pp. 369-370).

Although physical education was not yet generally part of the
school's curriculum, interest was developing in recreation and exercise. Many elementary schools were springing up in the newer parts
of the country, and the older public schools in the Eastern and Middle
States were being greatly improved in both organization and administration. Insofar as hygiene and health instruction were concerned,
some early educators showed an interest in the health and the comfort of their students. There were many articles and resolutions in
the literature of the time discussing physical education in the sense
of personal and school hygiene. This resulted in the publication of a
number of textbooks of physiology and manuals of calisthenics.

The Period from 1860 to 1890

Difficult days were in store for the American people after the
Civil War conflict which had wrought a tremendous change in the life
of the entire country. The population doubled rapidly. During this
period industrial capitalism became concentrated in the hands of a
few.

The development of urban society brought about a greater interest in social affairs than heretofore. Polite society became more
interested in music and literature. This period must be described as
one of literary sterility, however, even though several art galleries
and museums were founded. But the majority of the people had little
understanding of the aesthetic. The architecture of the period was
eclectic. Evolutionary theories and pragmatism left their marks on
traditional religious thought.

In education the idea of equality of educational opportunity had
made great strides. The educational ladder was gradually extending

upward. The number of high schools increased 500 per cent between 1870 and 1890. The state eventually took a position of prime importance in public education. State universities turned their attention to advancing the welfare of their own states with a resultant increase of revenues and attendance. In 1888 President Eliot of Harvard called for educational reform. One of his main points was the need for better training of teachers.

There were evidences of much life and vigor in the colleges and universities in the areas of athletics and gymnastics. Generally speaking, sports became increasingly popular in this era as well. Athletic clubs and associations of all types started with a subsequent increase of newspaper publicity to these activities. Harvard, Yale, and Amherst erected gymnasia in 1860, and this example was followed by many other institutions after the close of the War.

In schools the main emphasis in hygiene seemed to center around the environment provided for the students. Cleanliness and ventilation were primary concerns. The matter of communicable disease became a most important consideration. In the area of health instruction a rather dull system of pedagogy, combined with the social taboos of the time, presented a severe handicap to progress. Medical science had not yet achieved the necessary status to overcome these difficulties. For example, the American Public Health Association held its first meeting only in 1872.

In the area of general teacher training, improvement in the status of teachers came slowly in this period. Many state normal schools started at this time and were well distributed over the country as a whole. Although the facilities and courses of these institutions were poor at first, there has been a gradual improvement down through the years. Professional courses of the time were not too effectual, mainly because scientific method had not yet been applied to educational research.

In addition to the state normal schools, there was quite a rapid growth of city normal schools and classes, which paralleled the enlargement of cities. The college and university normal departments of this period were not very good by our present standards. After 1879, so-called departments of pedagogy began to develop with the aim of training secondary teachers. Quite naturally the demand for teachers trained in these departments was very slight.

The growth of in-service teacher education began about this time. By 1890 such activities as reading circles, professional teachers' organizations and institutes, and summer schools and extension work were contributing to the gigantic task of raising the levels of preparation of teachers in service.

It has been said that the gymnastic revival of 1860 grew out of the movement to disseminate knowledge of the laws of health (Hartwell, 1903, p. 750). Subsequently the desire grew to have these "laws" included in the program of school instruction. Dio Lewis gave great impetus to this movement when he lectured before the American Institute of Instruction in Boston on August 21, 1860. Lewis' Normal Institute for Physical Education was the first attempt to prepare teachers of physical education in the United States. The first course opened July 5, 1861 and ran for a ten-week period (Lewis, 1861, p. 665). Instruction was provided in anatomy, physiology, hygiene, and gymnastics. Special work was given explaining Ling's methods for treatment of chronic diseases. It was emphasized that each student would be able to use two hundred different exercises at the end of ten weeks. Another feature was a type of student teaching with each participant having the opportunity to lead a small class. During the seven years of the school's existence, 221 men and women graduated from the course (Eastman, 1891). These people met much of the demand for instructors in the new gymnastics which came first from the New England cities, and later from all over the country.

The Societies of the North American Turnerbund passed a resolution at their Pittsburgh Convention in 1856 recommending the inauguration of a teacher training school, but, for several reasons, including the outbreak of the Civil War, the Normal School was not opened until November 22, 1866 in New York City with an enrollment of nineteen men (Metzner, 1924). It was a travelling school and was conducted subsequently in Chicago, Milwaukee, and Indianapolis (Brosius, 1896, pp. 165-168).

The course offered by the Turnerbund was designed to include lectures on the history and aims of German Turnen, anatomy and aesthetics in their relation to gymnastics, and first aid. Other course work included gymnastic nomenclature, the theory of the different systems, and practical instruction with special regard to the training of boys and girls. By 1885 this curriculum had expanded to include the history and literature of physical training, a bit of the history of civilization, the essentials of physiology, some of the principles of education, and something about the German and English languages and literature. A little time was spent also in fencing and swimming (Rathmann, 1886, pp. 22-27).

Although the first schools for the training of physical educators started in Boston and New York City respectively, California was the first state in the United States to pass a statewide mandatory physical education provision in 1866. With the adoption of a new constitution in 1879, this provision was abolished; nevertheless, it is evident that the worth of physical education was recognized in the far West as early as the era immediately following the Civil War (Degroot, 1940, pp. 63-65).

Very little information has been published about the early efforts of the various state normal schools in training teachers of physical education. The beginnings were naturally unimpressive; yet, they are deserving of mention. The Mankato State Teachers College of Minnesota offered a type of teacher training course in physical training in 1868. West Chester State Teachers College in Pennsylvania is said to have had a two-year normal course (minor to a select group) in physical training in 1871. The first gymnasium was not erected at West Chester until the early 1890's with Dr. and Mrs. Ehinger in charge (Bramwell and Hughes, 1894, pp. 130-131).

From 1880 to 1890

The first important decade of American physical education was, from many standpoints, the period from 1880 to 1890. It was especially significant because so many sound teacher training programs were established. A growing conviction had developed that teachers of physical training needed to be carefully and thoroughly prepared for their work. Hartwell spoke of the measure of success attained by a few normal and training schools for the teaching of the principles and practice of physical education (Hartwell, 1899, p. 550). In this connection he mentioned Sargent's Normal School at Cambridge (1881); Anderson's Normal School at Brooklyn (1886); The Physical Department of the International Young Men's Christian Association Training School at Springfield, Mass. (1887?); The Boston Normal School of Gymnastics (1889); and the Posse Normal School of Boston (1890); as well as the Turnlehrer Seminar in Milwaukee (discussed previously). Each of these schools, at the time of the report, offered a course of theoretical and practical work covering two years. Summer schools were conducted, also. Especially prominent were those of the American Gymnastic Union, The Chautauqua School of Physical Education (1886), The Harvard Summer School of Physical Training (1887-1932), and the summer course of the International Young Men's Christian Association Training School (later Springfield College).

Prior to this decade and to the growth of the public high schools, there was the problem of special certification. The early California school teacher, for example, taught all subjects. In 1881 the California State Board of Education legalized the issuance of the first special subject certificates in city high schools. It was under such provisions that a number of the cities there first employed special teachers of physical education. It wasn't until later that California adopted the policy of accrediting properly qualified institutions to prepare and recommend their own graduates for teaching credentials (Degroot, 1940, pp. 436- 37).

Wayne State University of Detroit, Michigan offered one of the early teacher-training courses in physical education for elementary school teachers. This course began in 1881 when the College of Education started there. Wayne was actually a unification of a number of institutions of higher education, and was operating under the authority of the Detroit Board of Education.

The Corporation of Harvard College had appointed Dudley Allen Sargent (M.D.) an assistant professor of physical training and director of the recently completed Hemenway Gymnasiun in 1879 (Van Dalen, et.al., 1953, p. 392). In 1881 Sargent began to train teachers of physical training. Oddly enough, this did not take place with men or in connection with Harvard. The beginning was in the "Sanatory Gymnasium" opened for the benefit of the young women studying in the "Harvard Annex," which is now called Radcliffe College. From 1882 until 1904 a total of 261 women completed the regular course in theory and practice.

Miss Delphine Hanna closed out her program of studies at Sargent's Normal School in 1884 and went to teach at Oberlin College. She is reported to have taken with her a deep conviction that the teaching of gymnastics should be founded in science with resultant genuine body-building. This belief resulted in early teacher-training courses in physical education at Oberlin beginning in 1886 (Zeigler, 1950, p. 40). Although Luther Halsey Gulick, later of Springfield College, had known her but a short time, her acquaintance and influence became the determining spark of his life (Gulick, 1892, pp. 25-26). The propagation of her ideas found such fertile ground that Gulick left Oberlin immediately to study under Sargent at Boston.

The developing interest in physical education resulted in the founding of the Association for the Advancement of Physical Education at Adelphi Academy, Brooklyn, New York on November 25, 1885. William G. Anderson (M.D.), later founder of what was to be eventually called Arnold College and also Director of the early Yale Gymnasium, had the inspiration to start the organization that was later designated as The American Association for Health, Physical Education, and Recreation. Among those present at this first meeting were Anderson, Sargent, Edward Hitchcock of Amherst, William Blaikie (author of How to Get Strong), Dio Lewis, R. J. Roberts (later of Springfield College), W. L. Savage (founder of another training school), J. W. Seaver of Yale, and other interested people making a total of sixty (Proceedings of the AAPE, 1885, pp. 2-3). The succeeding meetings of this group until 1890 were characterized by reports from various members of the group. The topics of these reports ranged from a discussion of military drill to the use of the sphygmograph (Proceedings of the AAPE for 1886-1888).

Carl Betz proposed the introduction of physical education into the Kansas City public schools in 1885. Betz, a graduate of the Normal School of the American Gymnastic Union, directed the work

there himself during the next thirteen years (Leonard, 19
In the period from 1886 to 1896 physical training was intr
the public schools of many cities by graduates from the No...
School of the Turnerbund. The Turnvereine are reported to have
provided classes for 13,161 boys and 3,888 girls in January of 1886.
Ten years laters this figure had almost doubled (Leonard, 1915,
p. 115). Pioneer efforts such as this helped to create the early need
for physical education teachers.

Another milestone in the history of physical education in this
period was the organization of the noteworthy "Conference in the
Interest of Physical Training" by Mrs. Hemenway and Miss Homans.
Four sessions were held in Boston on November 29-30, 1889
(Barrows, 1889). Several thousand interested persons attended these
meetings which were presided over by William T. Harris, United
States Commissioner of Education. Representatives of the various
physical training systems in vogue at the time presented papers.
Heinrich Metzner, one of the first instructors in the Normal College
of the American Gymnastic Union, discussed the German system of
gymnastics. Baron Posse explained the Swedish system's chief
characteristics in the second session. Then Edward Hitchcock of
Amherst College discussed the essential principles for the direction
of a college department of physical education and hygiene. The third
session was highlighted by Dudley A. Sargent's presentation of the
system of physical training which he used at Harvard's Hemenway
Gymnasium. Spirited discussion followed all four addresses.

The Period from 1890 to 1920

Introduction. In the period from 1890 through 1919 the standard
of living in the United States was gradually improving. Although
twenty per cent of the population was foreign born, the culture was
gradually becoming almost completely Americanized. Both religion
and education found that it was necessary to change the prevailing
interpretation of their raison d'etre. Religious groups were considering the validity and impact of Darwin's theory of evolution.
Sabbath observance was lessening across the country.

American educators were becoming more critical of the method
of instruction as well as the content of the curriculum. John Dewey
led the way in socializing the school program more than had been
possible heretofore. Inasmuch as all school levels were changing
their ways, physical educators rapidly began a search for their field's
place in the curriculum. Such leaders as Sargent, Hartwell, and
Anderson gave continued impetus to the movement.

Various types of institutions offered preparation for teaching in
1890. There were the normal schools, either state or private, certain
high schools which maintained classes for teachers, and departments

of pedagogy or normal departments in the colleges and universities. The normal school was a well-established part of the American school system by the end of the nineteenth century. The normal schools admitted students of secondary rank and usually scaled their offerings to the ability of the students. The program aimed to give command of elementary subject matter, academic secondary studies, and professional education work. This latter area included the history and science of education along with courses in methods. The normal school had become the main agency for elementary teachers, and was beginning to enter the field of training teachers for secondary education as well. A very difficult task confronted these schools before they were accepted as qualified for this latter endeavor. The length and quality of their training had to be raised. In 1890 it was the rare normal school which extended more than two years past the high school level. The eventual transformation of this institution to full collegiate status has taken place since the beginning of the present century.

In this early period, teacher training in the colleges and universities was in most cases no better than the normal school training. Over a period of time, chairs of pedagogy had been introduced to provide college level instruction for beginning teachers. Unfortunately these programs were almost completely theoretical in nature with no provisions made for practice teaching. The colleges and universities were uncertain about the role in teacher education that they should play. Many of these institutions had traditionally neglected the technical phases of teaching, as this subject was considered unscientific, and consequently unnecessary. This belief still exists to a considerable extent in the minds of many college and university professors.

It was with trepidation, in this decade from 1890 to 1900, that certain colleges and universities authorized departments of physical training to offer teacher education courses. A demand for this service came about because of the tremendous growth in the number of public high schools. At this juncture of time many normal schools devoted solely to the training of "gymnastics teachers" sprang up, but they could not solve the problem for long. It was during this period that the Swedish gymnastics movement started in the United States. Organized camping began at this time, as did the playground movement. Sports and athletics continued their rapid rise to popularity with a consequent lessening of interest in formal gymnastics. Such activities as golf, tennis, and handball were introduced. Football and baseball enjoyed great popularity both as games to be played and as spectator sports. Basketball, invented in 1891, was on its way toward a very high goal--the country's foremost indoor team sport.

Physical education became identified with the movement that included vocational training and household arts in the school curriculum.

Because of a surge in interest in gymnastics caused by the Spanish-American War, physical education made definite advances. At the beginning of the twentieth century, this position was strengthened by such leaders as Thomas Dennison Wood, Luther Halsey Gulick, and Clark Hetherington.

Entrance Requirements. Selective admission, guidance, and placement were unheard of in the period from 1861 to 1890.[2] No mention was made of any entrance requirements in the programs of the Normal College of the American Gymnastic Union and Oberlin College, although Springfield College did state that its course was open only to Christian young men, who had "already shown some ability" (Catalogue of School for Christian Workers, 1886-1887). At least a fair English education was necessary, and business experience was desirable, but not absolutely essential.

But from 1890 to 1920 a great change took place in the entrance requirements of the various schools, colleges, and universities offering professional training. They were no longer vague and provincial. By 1910 most institutions specifically required that the applicant be a graduate of an approved high school, or be able to pass a satisfactory examination in the required entrance subjects. Entrance requirements for the University of Wisconsin, which started a professional program in 1911, mentioned also the necessity of sound health, organic vigor, aptitude for a high degree of motor efficiency, and evidence of strong leadership (Catalogue, University of Wisconsin, 1911-1912).

Methods. Important changes were evident in regard to the aims and methods of the various curricula. In the 1890's the aims were evidently only loosely formed, although some leaders predicted great happenings for the future. The general aim seemed to be to provide a normal course in physical training for persons interested in this "new crusade."

In some instances, as in the International Young Men's Christian Association Training School (later Springfield College), a distinct Christian emphasis was evident throughout this entire second period. The University of Wisconsin aimed to train teachers of physical education and directors of playgrounds and/or municipal recreation systems.

---

[2] The narrative is told fairly chronologically in the period from 1861-1890. This was possible because the number of professional programs described was relatively small. In this second period from 1890-1920 more of a topical approach will be followed so that the various changes will seem clearer.

The methods of the program continued to vary greatly in this second period, although the influence of the foreign systems upon the United States program was on the wane. Some leaders were asserting that their method was the "eclectic system," while others clung with great pride to that which they knew best.

Length of Program. The first course for training teachers of physical education extended for a period of ten weeks. Upon completion of this program, the student received a diploma. Today the professional student in physical education may be awarded the Doctor of Philosophy degree or the Doctor of Education degree upon successful completion of a program extending over a period of seven years or more.[3]

In this period from 1890 to 1920, the length of the different curricula varied greatly. From 1890 to 1900 the programs extended over a two-year period on the average, although certain normal schools of physical training still offered a one-year course.[4] Summer course "wonders" were causing distress in some quarters, because they were obtaining positions on the strength of one or two six-week summer sessions. Springfield College, to cite one example, discontinued its summer course, because many of these inexperienced people were passing themselves off as "Springfield men."

It was in this decade that a few of the first four-year programs leading to baccalaureate degrees began. In the first ten years of the twentieth century, four-year programs were introduced in all sections of the country. Teachers on the faculties of these institutions began to appear with various degrees, although many possessed only diplomas from one or another of the better-known normal schools of physical training. Perhaps the outstanding innovation of this era was the farsighted program introduced at Wellesley College after the Boston Normal School of Gymnastics had been transplanted to that campus. This program extended over a five-year period with the student receiving the traditional Bachelor of Arts degree at the end of four years, and a certificate bespeaking competence in physical education at the conclusion of the fifth year.

Curriculum. During this second period the subject matter of the curricula continued to expand. The normal courses were seemingly organized excellently from the standpoint of emphasis in the

---

[3] In some instances the degree is Doctor of Physical Education (either P.E.D. or D.P.E.).

[4] As this article is going to press, new evidence has just become available regarding early degree courses. Please see note at end of bibliography.

sciences and in the practice and theory of professional physical education. At Oberlin College no formal work whatsoever was given in professional education, but practice teaching was required of all in both the college and local schools. Instruction in the "academic" courses was almost completely lacking before the baccalaureate degree course began. The curriculum at Springfield College included a good amount of religious training over and above the usual courses of the time.

Around the turn of the century, the courses of study began to take on a broader aspect. In the final (second) year at the Boston Normal School of Gymnastics, professional courses in educational psychology and in the history of education were offered. In 1910 after the affiliation with Wellesley, the curriculum included a broad general education. The only professional education course offered in this curriculum was one called "Education and Psychology (for physical education students)." The Oberlin physical education curriculum was extended to four years in 1898, and was quite extensive in scope since the A.B. degree was awarded upon graduation. The student received a diploma as a result of the physical education specialization, also. No professional education work was included there at this time. Practical work was required throughout the four years of study. The University of Nebraska became the first state university to graduate a woman from a four-year major curriculum in 1900.

The University of Wisconsin gave evidence that it was abreast of the most advanced thinking in the preparation of teachers in general, and physical education teachers in particular. A degree program was offered which extended over a four-year period. The curriculum was well-rounded and included a reasonable distribution over the general academic, basic science, professional education, and professional physical education courses. Along with the theoretical work, a sound succession of practice courses was integrated in the curriculum offerings. Both a major unit (forty credits) and a minor unit (fourteen credits) were available to the students.

Curricula changed within this period from a one-year course of study, in one case, to a quite well-rounded course extending over a five-year period with the student receiving the A.B. degree at the end of the fourth year and a certificate in physical education at the end of the fifth year. The struggle for sound professional training was far from over; yet, it is possible to say that immeasurable progress was made in the area of the professional physical education curriculum during this period.

Teaching personnel grew in number from one in certain teacher education institutions to fifteen or twenty full-time and part-time instructors by 1920. The usual procedure was for an institution to engage one person for the new experimental program. This individual typically hired an assistant to work with members of the opposite sex in gymnastic classes. The private normal schools of physical education and the summer schools followed the practice of employing visiting lecturers who were experts in particular areas of specialization. This lent prestige to the programs, and also saved the expense of hiring such people as regular full-time staff members--which expense they could ill afford.

Faculty. The teachers in this new field received more academic preparation and earned advanced degrees gradually as time went by. It was common practice for the director of the normal school or department to hold the M.D. degree at this time. Toward the end of the second decade of the twentieth century, this practice was questioned seriously.

The director would then gather about him either graduates holding diplomas from his own program or from other well-known normal schools of the time. Gulick, during his fourteen years at Springfield College, practiced "inbreeding" to an extreme with his staff, but with good results seemingly. Sargent, of the Harvard Summer School of Physical Education, invoked a system whereby he made available to his students the best instruction to be found in the entire United States. To cite one other case, Miss Homans, of the Boston Normal School of Gymnastics (later joined with Wellesley College), added six science courses to the curriculum in 1893. These courses were given at the Massachusetts Institute of Technology, and were taught by regular members of the Institute faculty.

As the various programs grew and developed, it became necessary to add many new faculty members to the different departments and schools. It was increasingly important that these people have better preparation and hold baccalaureate degrees rather than just diplomas from two-year normal courses.

A tremendous growth took place during the period from 1890 to 1920 in the number of institutions offering professional preparation for teachers of physical education. Whereas seven private normal schools of physical education; several summer schools including the Harvard Summer School of Physical Education and the Chautauqua Summer School of Physical Education; and a small number of state normal schools, colleges, and universities had offered preparation of a professional nature for physical education from 1861 to 1890, this period from 1890 to 1920 witnessed the establishment of training programs of all types in all kinds of educational institutions. This was the period when the colleges and universities began to take notice of the great need for trained teachers in all fields, mainly because of the growth of the American high school. Altogether approximately 175 training programs, ranging from fifteen or twenty six-week summer courses to a five-year program granting an A.B. degree and a certificate in physical education, began within this span of thirty years (Zeigler, 1950, p. 136).

The Period from 1920 to 1961

Introduction. The years from 1920 to 1930 were filled with great changes in the way of life for many Americans. After a slight period of unemployment and depression in 1921-1922, the years immediately following were very prosperous. Education benefited greatly from this, and building programs were soon in evidence all over the country. The philosophy of Dewey had considerable weight in determining the child-centered aim of progressive education in this decade. In general there was an increasing interest in individual development because of the growing power of the psychology of individual differences. Testing and measuring assumed great importance in education, as efforts were made to classify students in groups according to their abilities. By 1929 some seventy per cent of the cities in the United States followed some form of homogeneous grouping.

A number of new types of schools developed at this time. The Dalton Plan in Massachusetts under Helen Parkhurst, the Country Day School, the Child Center School, the Play School, the Winnetka Plan, and many others appeared. California legislation reduced the number of elementary subjects from twenty-seven to fifteen, with twelve prescribed and three optional. The development of the junior high school was rapid. There were sixteen thousand public high schools established by the year 1925. It is interesting to note that eighty-five per cent of the public school teachers were women. From 1920 on, the Junior College Movement grew rapidly in the western part of the country. Farther up the educational ladder the trend toward teachers' colleges and away from the normal schools became apparent. For those who may or may not have had the benefits of formal education, adult education activities were being increasingly sponsored. In 1926, the American Association for Adult Education was formed.

The trend toward equalization of educational opportunity was given further momentum by restrictions against child labor and a stronger set of laws about compulsory school attendance. Although it was pointed out that federal aid was necessary for full realization of America's educational ideal, such backing did not come to the extent desired by its proponents. As the depression began to drain college and university endowments, public funds became more significant in the operation of higher education.

A rather strong reaction against the aims of progressive education set in about this time, but industry and technology continued to make many educators think of democracy in social rather than in individual terms. Despite the fact that the progressive schools of the preceding decade began to feel the influence of conservative opinion, educational process appeared to many to be becoming increasingly a social process. Much of the experimental school experience was having certain effects on school practice. The phrase "conservatively progressive" was at times used to describe such innovations as "regard for the whole child." Teachers became more concerned with the development of attitudes and the importance of accompanying emotions. Curricula continued to expand along with greater emphasis on "activity" or laboratory experience. The matter of individual differences had become a concern for many teachers. From the depression onward, the social emphasis of education seemed assured. By way of contrast, Robert M. Hutchins of the University of Chicago was organizing and administering the gradual growth of what has since been termed the "aristocratic wing" of higher education.

Expanding Programs of Physical Education. Physical Education, in this period after the first World War and before the Global War, found its scope increasing in many ways. Individual, dual, and team sports had been accepted almost universally during the war period, and the various types of dance had become very popular. A considerable struggle was waged between the proponents of the informal and formal systems of physical education. Due in large measure to the changing American scene, and probably also to the greater functional aspects of the natural program, the more formal systems continued to wane. The apparent possibility of greater learning both direct and concomitant, the opportunities for use of such learning during leisure, and the "cultural background" of the informal program made the battle very unequal.

It was at this time that a new idea appeared in connection with sports participation. The element of competition, long accepted for varsity squads, now became available on a somewhat modified scale for a larger number of students through the intramural athletic program. This additional phase, added to the concept of a total physical education program, grew faster in colleges and universities than it did at the high school level. The idea did find a very favorable reception with both teachers and administrators at all levels of the educational system, but unfortunately staff and facilities have only slowly and incompletely "caught up" with the impetus of the movement. Remedial or corrective physical education (now designated as "therapeutic," "individual," "adapted," or "adaptive" physical education), aquatics and water safety in general, and health education have been included as basic to the newer program. Still later, safety education (and then driver education) were added to the responsibility of the field of physical education.

A marked change took place in physical education when the financial depression of the 1930's began to be felt in the schools. Many schools discontinued the teaching of this subject, or combined physical education teachers' duties so that other subjects were added to the typical teacher's workload. Few new people were hired, which soon resulted in an oversupply of physical education teachers. Many teacher education institutions revised their curricula and began to select students more carefully. Several states raised their certification requirements during this trying period. It was inevitable that these measures would improve the calibre of teacher preparation.

The need for a broad cultural education became apparent at this time. Although increased emphasis was placed on this phase of the major curriculum in some institutions, the field as a whole had not caught up. In 1934 Peik and Fitzgerald pointed out this deficiency in their analysis of twenty-one universities and six colleges. They states that: "Physical education majors stood at the bottom of all teaching fields in the range and depth of their academic training (Peik and Fitzgerald, 1934, pp. 18-26)." Since then there has been a continuing emphasis on the importance of a sound general education along with a more thorough training in the foundation sciences and professional physical education courses. These emphases seem to have taken place despite the addition of a gradually greater amount of work in professional education. There is still room for improvement in this matter of "cultural heritage" in respect to the preparation of the physical education teacher.

After the Japanese attack on Pearl Harbor late in 1941, the entire nation was mobilized. Federal funds were made available through the U. S. Office of Education to train defense workers in schools and colleges. Actually, governmental subsidization brought many schools through the war. An all-out effort was demanded in order to wage war successfully.

Physical training programs with a broader scope were initiated in the armed forces, and there were improved rehabilitation programs for injured service men. Draft statistics again pointed up the need for improved programs of school health, physical education, and recreation. Since the beginning of the "Cold War" in about 1947, there has been an increased emphasis upon health and physical fitness that has been growing in intensity. Health programs appear to be improving steadily, and many leaders and citizens recognize the need for leisure education to meet this society's growing problem of automation.

The current drive for the physical fitness of youth started in 1954 when President Eisenhower heard about a set of "motor fitness" tests that were given to some American children and compared to test results obtained from administering the same items to a relatively small group of European children. Since he was shocked at the results, he called a meeting in Washington, D. C. that resulted ultimately in a President's Conference on Fitness of American Youth.

The American Association for Health, Physical Education, and Recreation, voice of more than 25,000 teachers in the profession, moved rapidly after Mr. Eisenhower expressed his concern. From September 12-15, 1956 a National Conference on Fitness was held in Washington, D. C. At this meeting the profession mobilized its efforts to meet the challenge and offered all possible assistance. In 1958, after considerable preparation and with the help of its Research Council, the A. A. H. P. E. & R. sponsored a national youth fitness study. Dr. Paul A. Hunsicker, of the University of Michigan, guided this effort. For the first time a reliable sampling of American youth was obtained, and a set of national norms (not standards!) was established in such tests as pull-ups, sit-ups, and the 600-yard run, to mention just a few. Some foreign comparisons with these United States' norms have been made, and the evidence seems to indicate that American youngsters are deficient in many of these test items.

Immediately after his election in 1960, President John F. Kennedy published an article explaining his belief in the importance of physical fitness for youth. He followed his beliefs with action. The President's Council on Youth Fitness guided itself by these words taken from a "Presidential Meesage to the Schools on the Physical Fitness of Youth":

The strength of our democracy is no greater than the collective well-being of our people. The vigor of our country is no stronger than the vitality and will of all our countrymen. The level of physical, mental, moral, and spiritual fitness of very American citizen must be our constant concern.

The need for increased attention to the physical fitness of our youth is clearly established. Although today's young people are fundamentally healthier than the youth of any previous generation, the majority have not developed strong, agile bodies. The softening process of our civilization continues to carry on its persistent erosion.

It is of great importance, then, that we take immediate steps to ensure that every American child be given the opportunity to make and keep himself physically fit--fit to learn, fit to understand, to grow in grace and stature, to fully live (Kennedy, 1961, see inside cover).

"Operation Youth Fitness" (a phrase coined by the A.A.H.P.E. & R.) was begun at this time.

Entrance Requirements. Returning to a consideration of the history of undergraduate professional preparation for physical education (from 1920 to 1961), it can be said that the actual development of such features as selective admission, guidance, and placement came about during this present period. By 1920 a "new plan" had been instituted at Wellesley College combining the best elements of the certificate system and of the examination system. Columbia Teachers College had made some changes in its entrance requirements as follows: a student could be admitted by (1) examination of Columbia or the College Entrance Examination Board; (2) certificate from an approved secondary school including the diploma and the principal's statement about the requisite fifteen units and his health, character, and general scholarship; or (3) presenting credentials from the Education Department of the State of New York listing the approved entrance units. The need for teachers at this time was so great that the admission procedures could not be too strictly enforced at many institutions.

Toward the end of this decade (1920-1930) the supply was beginning to catch up with the demand. The need for immediate raising of the entrance requirements became apparent. Such qualifications as participation in athletics, recommendations, a series of ability and proficiency tests, an intelligence test, a medical examination, and a probationary period of one year were recommended for each prospective student (Neilson, 1930, p. 9). In 1933 the National Survey of the Education of Teachers suggested that teacher-preparing institutions should agree on certain principles. It was evident that a research program was necessary to develop more accurate measuring instruments of teaching success, personal traits, and scholarship attainments. It was recommended further that: "a progressive program of selection, admission, elimination, and final recommendation for teaching should begin with matriculation and carry through to certification (Rugg, 1933, pp. 29-31)."

By 1940, many colleges and universities showed a definite trend toward consolidation of entrance requirements in an effort to standardize the situation across the country. Springfield College, for example, selected 160 men each year who seemingly possessed the greatest promise for success. It was stated that admission officers obtained their evidence regarding the candidates from application forms, school officers, the examining physician, personal and character refrrences, personal interviews, and aptitude tests. Of the fifteen units still required for admission, nine had to be from English (3), history and social studies (2), algebra and plane geometry (2), and science (2), while four of the remaining six elective units could be in non-academic subjects (Catalogue, Springfield College, 1940-42).

There has been a gradual tendency to include student guidance and subsequent placement along with selective admission as one phase of the total preparation effort (Zeigler, 1950, p. 182). This approach seemed fundamental to the production of superior teachers of physical education. Unfortunately there has been little agreement as to the bases upon which prospective teachers should be admitted because of the difficulty of securing valid criteria.

Very definite pre-admission requirements seem to have given way to a continuous long-range program of selection. At this juncture in the history, administrators were considering such qualities as personal integrity and sincerity, moral influence over pupils, willingness to cooperate with superiors and associates, personal health and vigor, knowledge and understanding of the nature of pupils, initiative, and self-reliance of prime importance in selecting teachers for their schools (Graybeal, 1941, pp. 741-744).

The trend toward generalization of entrance requirements is readily apparent upon examination of college and university announcements from 1950 on. The lack of standardization for entrance into the physical education field appears to be unfortunate. Some progress has been made, but there is still great room for improvement.

Curriculum. The aims, methods, and content of the various curricula underwent many changes in this period from 1920 to 1960. A unique American philosophy of physical education was beginning to exert its influence on the teacher preparation in the field. Sports, athletics, and team games had been greatly implemented by the war experience. The "natural" program of physical education, as so admirably propounded by Wood and Williams, began to make itself felt, but not without a struggle and much misunderstanding.

The results of the army draft medical examinations had come as a distinct shock to the American people. Because of this, legislation appeared for improved health education as well as for physical education. Wood's strong leadership helped to bring the status of a special subject field to the teaching of health. Health education had been previously considered the same as physical education (Williams, 1927, pp. 330-340).

These developments within the field as a whole soon made themselves felt in the various professional curricula. Leaders in the teacher education area of physical education began to envisage the physical educator as a man of more professional stature (Hines, 1920, pp. 52-56).

Approximately seventy-five institutions started four-year degree courses in physical education in the years from 1920 to 1925 alone, although some colleges still held out for a three-year course.

As the field continued to broaden in scope, such programs gradually succumbed (Zeigler, 1950, p. 227).

In 1926, statistics showed that there was a definite trend away from medical training for college directors. There were two distinct types of physical directors in colleges: (1) those who administered intercollegiate athletics, and (2) those who were concerned with the required physical education program and the teacher preparation program. A tendency toward the centralized department including everything was becoming more evident (Metcalf, 1926, pp. 45-47).

The most prevalent specialized curriculum in physical education for men in 1927 was that of athletic coaching! It was evidently felt that, due to the broadening scope of the field to include coaching of athletic sports and health service, such an opportunity for specialization would help to fulfill the need for qualified men as directors of physical education, athletic coaching, and health education.

The Division of Girl's and Women's Sports of the American Association for Health, Physical Education, and Recreation has exerted a strong and beneficial influence on professional preparation in physical education for women since its inception as a Standing Committee on Women's Athletics of the American Physical Education Association in 1916. This contribution has ranged from the establishment of high standards for the conduct of girls and women's sports to the development of sports guides and other important publications relating to this area. Further opportunities have been provided through the work of this Division for a variety of in-service experiences in the area of girls and women's sports.

As early as 1925 a conference of institutions offering professional training in physical education was arranged by the United States Bureau of Education at which the aims and objectives of professional training and other subjects were discussed. Committees were appointed to consider these topics and report at a future meeting. The second conference of these colleges and universities assembled in Washington, D. C. on March 30, 1927. The problem of the "coach" versus the "physical educator" came in for much discussion at this time. Some felt that one person could not be both an athletic coach and a physical educator at the same time; the majority opinion seemed to favor the idea of selling the concept of a broader physical education training, including all aspects of the field, to the professional schools in existence (U. S. Bureau of Education, 1927, pp. 38-41).

At this time leaders urged that a standardized course nomenclature be adopted so that progress might be made toward a standardized curriculum. A committee, with McCurdy of Springfield College as chairman, was appointed to study the terminology and to construct a list of the most suitable generic names for curricular subjects.

Those in attendance at the two successive conferences had requested unanimously that a committee study the existing curricula within the field. After Bowen's death (W. P. Bowen of Michigan State Normal College in Ypsilanti), McCurdy was asked to take over the responsibility of this committee, as well as the one studying course terminology. The report of this study group was published in 1929. It gave detailed information about the hours required in all courses in each of 139 institutions. The study made clear that the terminology attached to courses often gave no idea of the course content. This committee recommended a definite distribution of courses which totalled 136 semester hours (U. S. Bureau of Education, 1929).

An attempt to bring order into the existing situation originated within the profession itself. At a meeting of the Department of School Health and Physical Education of the National Education Association held in Los Angeles, California in July, 1931, a resolution was passed authorizing the appointment of a national committee for the purpose of establishing standards to be used in evaluating teacher education institutions preparing health and physical education teachers. Neilson of California was appointed chairman. The entire problem was divided, and subcommittees were assigned to recommend the following: (1) basic characteristics of the secondary school program; (2) general standards; (3) standards for the selection of students to be trained; (4) course standards; (5) standards for staff; and (6) standards for facilities. In 1935 the National Committee Report on Standards was publishing in the <u>Research Quarterly</u> of the American Physical Education Association. The standards recommended by Subcommittee A-4 (Course Standards) divided the courses comprising the total curriculum into the four basic areas which have been used to a large extent since that time for the classification of the subject matter considered necessary to prepare a physical education teacher adequately: (1) academic courses required by the institution (other than foundation sciences); (2) foundation sciences required; (3) courses in general education (professional) required; and (4) courses in health and physical education required. A standard four-year curriculum was recommended, but a complete seven-year course was listed (Neilson, 1935, pp. 48-68). In the previous year, a five-year integrated curriculum had been recommended to complete adequate gener-general education, specialization in physical education, a second teaching field, thorough orientation in education and psychology, and training at the elementary school level as a background for teaching.

Scott, then of The Rice Institute, urged the adoption of a unit plan of instruction in 1935 as employed at his school. He recommended that scientific method only should determine the nature of the professional curriculum in the future. He suggested that the student should be encouraged to start thinking professionally as soon as possible. The nature and importance of the subject matter should determine the length of the unit, not the traditional semester and semester-hour format (Scott, 1935).

Those physical educators who administered the curricula of the various teacher-training institutions in physical education began to realize that a gradual shift in emphasis had come about in connection with the biological sciences (i.e., zoölogy and physiology). It seemed logical to teach them as tool subjects rather than as ends in themselves. Other leaders, such as Bovard, advised the revamping of the curriculum in the direction of a greater affiliation with the social sciences (Bovard, 1935).

Length. The various trends evident in connection with the aims and methods of the professional physical education curriculum were not peculiar to the field of health education, physical education, and recreation alone. The teachers colleges generally wished to provide adequate acholarship in the various other fields of the entire teaching profession. Requirements in professional education had been decreased slightly and had been more carefully defined. A trend away from formal academic courses seemed to be developing with increases in functional courses stressing contemporary life. It seemed that the professional objectives of teaching itself were becoming more clearly defined as a marked increase in the prescription of courses was noticed. Inasmuch as broader majors for specialization purposes had been developed, more time would be necessary for the entire program. When the time elements involved under these different curriculum headings were totalled, it became obvious that teachers colleges were tending toward a five-year program for the realization of adequate and broad preparation of secondary school teachers (Sprague, 1940).

While this move for a five-year curriculum (resulting in either a teaching credential or a master's degree) has been gathering momentum gradually and is seemingly receiving support from the experience of institutions of higher education, there has arisen a minority in physical education that is asking whether the lengthening of the curriculum will provide the answer to the problem. Some have felt that a new type of approach to the problem of the curriculum was needed. This group working within the structure of the College Physical Education Association suggested further experimentation. The suggested plan was first to improve what was being done and then to lengthen the curriculum if necessary (Fredericks, 1938, p. 123).

Raising Standards. The Cooperative Study in Teacher Education, sponsored by the American Council on Education, 1938-1943, devoted considerable time to the matter of procedures and conditions conducive to continuous teacher education. Four basic conclusions of this study were as follows: (1) those schools made most progress where there was a conscious and studied effort by the faculty to become more democratic in their relationship; (2) by and large, the most successful programs were those that started with problems that the teachers believed important; (3) teachers and administrators work together most effectively when they work on problems on which they can make progress; and (4) adequate resources in personnel and materials should be available (Troyer, 1945, pp. 542, 582-584).

Although two major attempts to improve the quality of professional education in physical education had been to a certain degree successful, the objective was still not considered hopeless. National standards had not been realized, but further efforts were to be made subsequently. After the Global War was over, the College Physical Education Association revived an earlier Cooperative Study Committee of the A. A. H. P. E. & R. that had been curtailed because of the War. The original idea was to include representatives from the National Association, The College Physical Education Association, The National Association of Directors of Physical Education for College Women, The City Administrative Directors Society, The Society of State Directors of Health and Physical Education, and others at the discretion of the Committee and the President of the National Association (AAHPER). This group established its purpose at the outset, but decided to take no definite stand on the question of ideal standards for teacher preparation. It was felt that it would be unwise to try to rate institutions as had been recommended by the earlier National Study in the 1930's. The main objective was to seek out "desirable practices" for teacher education institutions (Scott, 1947, pp. 97-101).

In 1947 the organized teaching profession sent its leadership from all parts of the country to Miami University, Oxford, Ohio for the National Conference for the Improvement of Teaching. In presenting the qualifications of a good teacher, twelve abilities, attributes, and understandings were listed which the excellent teacher should possess. A very high standard was set in regard to specialized professional training as well as in general education and in the personal and social qualities required (The NCTEPS, 1947, p. 51).

The American Association of Teachers Colleges completed an extensive study in 1948. Attention was called to the lack of a well-organized training program for teachers, which once again demonstrated that the criticism which the physical educators leveled against themselves can be made about the teaching profession as a whole. Again the need for a broad background of general education was emphasized. Student teaching possibilities were not being fully used in many institutions. The charge was made that many teacher education programs focus attention on preparing teachers as technicians to the exclusion of developing them as responsible society members. It was suggested that students need the opportunity to share in developing plans for their own guidance. Some students should receive more preparation along certain lines than others. Such factors as intelligence, mental and physical health, social development, and emotional maturity should be taken into consideration when programs for the individual are planned (The AATC, 1948).

Professional Preparation Conferences. Physical education has continued to make progress toward improvement of the aims and methods of teacher preparation. The Committee of Teacher Education of the College Physical Education Association now the (NCPEAM) cooperated with eighteen organizations in sponsoring and participating in a National Conference on Undergraduate Professional Preparation in Health Education, Physical Education, and Recreation held at Jackson's Mill, Weston, West Virginia, in May, 1948. The Athletic Institute financed this important venture. This group re-emphasized the necessity of a cultural background for successful teaching. It was asserted that many teachers of physical education were going out into the field without a "frame of reference" upon which to base their work. It was quite evident that many institutions were allowing their students to overspecialize. The exact amount of time required to produce a competent teacher and cultured citizen will vary with individuals and with institutions. A general curriculum plan was considered essential, and competency in achieving the objectives of the curriculum should be the criterion for graduation rather than a definite number of years or a certain number of specific courses (The National Conference on UPPPEHE&R, 1948).

Those attending the Jackson's Mill Conference placed the burden on the teacher preparation institutions to develop teachers who are masters of many "knowledges" and skills. To accomplish this aim, superior instruction is needed under conditions where facilities and equipment are excellent. An unusually large number of colleges and universities have entered the field recently, but they cannot possibly have adequate staffs and facilities for the task at hand. Many leaders felt that standards for accrediting would come as an aftermath of the Jackson's Mill Report. Some states (e.g., Pennsylvania) have already acted to prevent colleges with inadequate facilities and staffs from offering major programs in this field.

The American Association of Colleges for Teacher Education served as one of the sponsoring agencies of the Jackson's Mill Conference. This body was formed in 1948 by a merger of the American Association of Teachers Colleges, schools of education in universities, and municipal universities engaged in teacher preparation. Its primary purpose was to improve the quality of teacher education. It "assumed the role of a voluntary accreditation agency, developed Evaluation Schedules for that function and held a series of evaluations of teacher education programs to familiarize college representatives with the schedules . . ." (Nordly, 1959, p. 4)

Evaluative criteria for the rating of professional programs in physical education were developed, and a number of institutions expressed their willingness to have their programs rated. These criteria were made available inexpensively by the American Association for Health, Physical Education, and Recreation. Professional leaders called for departments of physical education to undertake self-evaluation of major programs as a first step.

Accreditation. The American Association of Colleges for Teacher Education relinquished its accreditation functions to the National Council for Accreditation of Teacher Education in 1954. In 1957 the A. A. H. P. E. & R. held a workshop to revise the evaluative criteria for physical education in light of the changes which were made by the N. C. A. T. E. in the former general criteria developed by the A. A. C. T. E. It seems evident that, "General public respect for our profession and the effectiveness of our unique contribution to education are dependent upon the standards attained through cooperative efforts" (Nordly, 1959, p. 7).

Number of Programs. In the period from 1920 to 1960 the growth in the number of institutions offering professional preparation for physical education has been phenomenal. In the decade after World War I, which conflict exerted a tremendous influence upon the field forcing a flood of state physical education laws, some 137 colleges and universities began to offer teacher preparation in health and physical education. From 1930 through 1939, despite the severe financial depression which affected the entire educational field greatly, approximately ninety-seven more institutions entered the field. As had its predecessor, World War II exerted a great influence. From 1940 to 1950 over 100 colleges and universities decided to offer programs designed to prepare teachers of physical education. An exact figure for this decade immediately past (1950-1960) is not available, but a safe estimate would be that there are now over 635 colleges and universities offering teacher education in physical education (Undergraduate and Graduate Professional Preparation in HEPE&R, 1954).

Brief Summary

In the 100 years since the inception of professional preparation for physical education, very significant changes have taken place. In many instances early schools were owned by the individual or society sponsoring them. Subsequently these normal schools underwent a distinct transformation. Names were changed, curricula were expanded, staffs were increased greatly in number, degrees were offered, and eventually affiliation with colleges and universities took place.

The field has been influenced by a variety of societal forces as the American scene changed. Foreign traditions and customs held away initially, but gradually a fairly distinct American philosophy of physical education emerged. Such occurrences as wars and periods of economic depression and/or prosperity brought about sweeping changes.

In the period from 1900 to 1920, educators began to take the place of physicians as directors of professional programs. Many publicly-supported colleges and universities entered the field. A significant development was the awarding of academic degrees upon the completion of major programs in physical education. Specialized curricula were developed usually within schools of education. In many instances, the subsequent establishment of separate schools and colleges of physical education within universities has had a notable influence on professional preparation.

Down through the years of the twentieth century many leaders have urged a stronger "cultural" education for prospective physical education teachers. They have expressed further a desire for an improved background in the foundation sciences. Until somewhat more recently there has been a definite trend toward increasing the number of hours required in general professional education courses. A number of studies have indicated a lack of standardization in course terminology within the specialized area of Health, Physical Education, and Recreation.

There have been many attempts to improve the quality of professional preparation through studies, surveys, research projects, national conferences, and accreditation plans. A significant text recommending a "competency approach" to the preparation of teachers in this field has been published (Snyder and Scott, 1954). The field seems to be moving toward self-evaluation and self-improvement. The American Association for Health, Physical Education, and Recreation has been a great influence in this historical development aided by such affiliated groups as the College Physical Education Association (NCPEAM) and the National Association of Physical Education for College Women.

General Bibliography

American Association for the Advancement of Physical Education. Proceedings for 1886, 1887, and 1888.

American Association of Teachers Colleges, The. Report on Teacher Education. Washington, D. C.: 1948. 340 pages.

Association for the Advancement of Physical Education. Brooklyn, N. Y.: Rome Brothers, 1885. (This is the Proceedings of the first meeting of the Association.)

Barrows, I. C. (reported and edited by). Physical Training (a full report of the Conference held in Boston, November, 1889). Boston: Press of G. H. Ellis, 1899 (sic). 135 pages.

Bovard, J. F. "Some Trends in Teacher Training Curricula." Journal of Health and Physical Education, V, No. 4, April, 1935.

Bramwell, A. B. and Hughes, H. M. The Training of Teachers in the United States of America. London: Swan, Sonnenschein & Co., 1894.

Brosius, George. "The Rise and Growth of the North American Normal School of Gymnastics at Milwaukee." Mind and Body, 3, No. 33:165-168, November, 1896.

Degroot, Dudley S. "A History of Physical Education in California (1848-1939)." Ed.D. dissertation, Stanford University, 1940.

Eastman, Mary S. The Biography of Dio Lewis. New York: Fowler & Wells Co., 1891.

Fredericks, J. W. "Final Report of the Committee on the Professional Curriculum." Proceedings of the College Physical Education Association, 1938.

Graybeal, E. "A Consideration of Qualities Used by Administrators in Judging Effective Teachers of Physical Education in Minnesota." Research Quarterly, 12, No. 4:741-744, December, 1941.

Gulick, Luther H. "Professor T. D. Wood," Physical Education, 5, No. 1:25-26, April, 1892.

Hartwell, E. M. "On Physical Training," in Report of the Commissioner of Education. Washington, D. C.: Government Printing Office, 1903.

Hines, L. N. "Personal and Professional Qualifications of the Physical Training Teacher." American Physical Education Review, XXV, No. 2:52-56, February, 1920.

Kennedy, John F. "A Presidential Message," in Youth Physical Fitness. Washington, D. C.: U. S. Government Printing Office, 1961.

Leonard, Fred E. Pioneers of Physical Training. New York: Association Press, 1915.

Lewis, Dio. "New Gymnastics." Barnard's American Journal of Education, 12:665, 1861.

Metcalf, T. N. "Professional Training for Directors of Physical Education." Proceedings of the Society of Directors of Physical Education in Colleges (30th Annual Meeting), December, 1926.

Metzner, Heinrich. A Brief History of the American Turnerbund. Pittsburgh, Penna.: National Executive Committee of the American Turnerbund, 1924.

National Commission on Teacher Education and Professional Standards, The. The Improvement of Teaching. Washington, D. C.: National Education Association of the United States, 1947.

National Conference on Undergraduate Professional Preparation in Physical Education, Health Education, and Recreation. Chicago, Ill.: The Athletic Institute, 1948.

Neilson, N. P. "Job-Analysis Technique Should Be Applied to Physical Education." Journal of Health and Physical Education, 1, No. 1:9, January, 1930.

Neilson, N. P. (Chairman). "National Study of Professional Education in Health and Physical Education." Research Quarterly, vi, No. 4:48-68, December, 1935.

Nordly, Carl L. "The Development of the Standards and Guide," in Evaluation Standards and Guide. Washington, D. C.: American Association for Health, Physical Education, and Recreation, 1959.

Peik, W. E. and Fitzgerald, G. B. "The Education of Men Teachers of Physical Education for Public School Service in Selected Colleges and Universities." Research Quarterly, 5, No. 4:18-26, December, 1934.

Rathmann, C. G. "German System of Training Teachers at the Milwaukee Normal School," in Proceedings of the American Association for the Advancement of Physical Education, Brooklyn, New York, 1886.

Rugg, Earle U., et. al. "National Survey of the Education of Teachers (1933 Bulletin)," in Teacher Education Curricula, Vol. III, No. 10.

School for Christian Workers. Catalogue, 1886-1887.

Schwendener, Norma. A History of Physical Education in the United States. New York: A. S. Barnes & Co., 1942.

Scott, Harry A. "Report of the Committee on Teacher Education," in Proceedings of the College Physical Education Association, 1947.

Scott, Harry A. "The Unit Plan of Instruction as Employed in Professional Preparation of Teachers in Health and Physical Education at Rice Institute." Research Quarterly, VI, No. 4, December, 1935.

Snyder, Raymond and Scott, Harry A. Professional Preparation in Health, Physical Education, and Recreation. New York: McGraw-Hill Book Company, Inc., 1954.

Sprague, H. A. A Decade of Progress in the Preparation of Secondary School Teachers. New York: Teachers College, Columbia University, Contrib. to Educ., No. 794, 1940.

Springfield College. Catalogue, 1940-42.

Troyer, M. E. "Trends in Teacher Education." Journal of Health and Physical Education, XVI, No. 10:542, 582-584, December, 1945.

U. S. Bureau of Education. "Professional Courses in Physical Education for Teachers," in Circular, April 15, 1929.

U. S. Bureau of Education. Professional Training in Physical Education. Washington, D. C.: Physical Education Series, No. 9, 1928.

U. S. Department of Health, Education, and Welfare. Undergraduate and Graduate Professional Preparation in Health Education, Physical Education, and Recreation. Washington, D. C.: Office of Education, Circular No. 403, 1954.

University of Wisconsin. Catalogue for 1911-1912.

Van Dalen, D. B., et. al. A World History of Physical Education. Englewood Cliffs, New Jersey: Prentice-Hall, Inc., 1953.

Williams, Jesse F. "Nature and Purpose of Health Education and
    Physical Education Viewed from the Standpoint of General Edu-
    cation." American Physical Education Review, XXXII, No. 5:
    330-340, May, 1927.

Zeigler, Earle F. A History of Professional Preparation for Physi-
    cal Education in the United States, 1861-1948. Eugene,
    Oregon: Microcard Publications, 1951. (This was a Ph.D.
    dissertation completed at Yale University.)

(Note: Through the efforts of Professors Walter Kroll and Guy Lewis
of the University of Massachusetts at Amherst, we now have evidence
indicating that an A.B. degree with a major in physical education became available at Stanford University in 1892-93, and that Walter
Wells Davis received this degree in hygiene and organic training in
1897. The program was started under the direction of Dr. Thomas
D. Wood.

    But even more surprising than the above data is the evidence
that "the first academic four-year degree recipient in physical education" was James F. Jones, and that the program was developed at
Harvard College by George Wells Fitz. He began a Department of
Anatomy, Physiology, and Physical Training in 1891 at Harvard College. Thus, Jones received a B.S. degree with cum laude honors in
Anatomia, Physiologica, et Corporis Cultu in June, 1893! For
further information, please see Kroll, Walter, and Lewis, Guy, "The
First Academic Degree in Physical Education." JOHPER, June,
1969 under the section entitled "History and Archives.")

CHAPTER 19

A HISTORY OF PROFESSIONAL PREPARATION IN PHYSICAL EDUCATION IN SELECTED NEGRO COLLEGES AND UNIVERSITIES TO 1958

Armstead A. Pierro
Southern University, Baton Rouge, Louisiana

Introduction

The Negro athlete has been a formidable contender in the field of college athletics since the latter part of the nineteenth century, and yet there seems to be relatively little in the literature to record the exploits of this minority group. But from time to time new records and instances of Negro participation are revealed or uncovered quite by accident, even though the complete account of his exploits lies buried in the mass of "news-print" materials or otherwise unpublished information which repose in newspaper morgues or library archives. Negro athletes are known to have been involved in college athletics as early as 1860. Even though there have possibly been some unnamed heroes prior to that time, their identities have never reached national notice.

Prior to the turn of the twentieth century the Negro's formal experience in physical education was primarily in intercollegiate athletics. The first director of Harvard University physical education was a man of color (Higginson, 1959, p. 38). Abram Hewlitt was employed as an instructor and director of the first gymnasium in 1859 and held that post until his death in 1871. In 1875 W. G. Higginson, gave the following account and description of Hewlitt:

> The first teacher of gymnastics at Harvard College was Abram Molineaux Hewlitt. He was a professional teacher of boxing, and had established a gymnasium of his own in Worchester, Massachusetts, where he was highly esteemed. He was a mulatto, of very fine physique, and of respectable and estimable character.... He was moreover a fair gymnast and a

---

Editor's Note: This historical essay represents the essence of a doctoral study completed in the 1950's at Michigan (Ann Arbor) by Professor Pierro. The historical investigation was carried in a most careful and painstaking manner by Dr. Pierro, and employs a "persistent problems technique" that can be used most effectively by others. The reader will be interested to learn about his findings and conclusions.

remarkable good teacher of boxing. In the first years of his
term of service there was a good deal of activity in the gymnasium and regular class-exercise went on.

In the final decade of the nineteenth century, names of Negro
athletes began to appear on the rosters of college teams in the eastern section of the country. In the early 1890's two Negro athletes,
William Tecumseh Sherman Jackson and William H. Lewis, from
Virginia appeared on the rosters of Amherst College and Harvard
University. Jackson and Lewis went from Virginia Normal and Collegiate Institute at Petersburg, Virginia (Henderson, 1939, pp. 5-10)
to Amherst where each became a star on athletic teams. Lewis later
attended Harvard where his exploits in football were sufficient to
cause him to be named to Walter Camp's "All-American" teams in
1892 and 1893 (Menke, 1944, p. 444). In 1904 the New York Evening
World which published its All-Time, All-American team gave Lewis
the center berth.

By the early 1900's, Negro athletes began to gain recognition,
in increasing numbers, in many of the white schools in the country.
Howard Drew of Southern California who was co-holder of the 100-
yard dash record in 1914, Eddie Tolan of the University of Michigan,
Ralph Metcalfe of Marquette, and Jesse Owens of the Ohio State University were names of Negro athletes which were written into track
and field records (Menke, 1944, pp. 927-956) during the first third
of the twentieth century.

Early Physical Education in Negro Colleges and Universities

The growth and development of professional preparation for
physical education in the Negro schools and colleges did not follow
the same evolutionary pattern as in the white colleges and universities. Professional preparation for physical education in Negro
institutions of higher learning was added to the curricula in those
schools which had teacher-training programs already established.
There were no special training schools for Negro physical education
teachers such as those established by Dio Lewis, Dudley Sargent,
William Anderson and Watson Savage (Van Dalen, 1953, pp. 420-68).

In the Negro colleges no thought was given to physical education
as a teaching field until well into the twentieth century. However,
just before the turn of the century Hampton Institute offered special
training in gymnastics (Hampton Catalog, 1894, p. 29), and students
who satisfactorily completed the courses received a certificate recommending them as "fitted to teach gymnastics." Although Negroes
attended white colleges and universities in certain parts of the country prior to the turn of the century, there is no evidence available
which indicates that any of them were prepared to teach physical

education. By 1900, a total of 390 Negroes had graduated from seventy-three white colleges (Dubois, 1903, pp. 28-37); none of these were identified as physical educators. It is also interesting to note that Dubois does not mention any of the normal schools of physical education in his list of seventy-three schools. It is, however, possible that some Negroes may have attended some of these normal schools. Some few did attend the Harvard Summer School and, when the Harvard Summer School closed its doors (Rice, 1958, p. 307), many Negroes attended Springfield International YMCA College and the Sargent School of Boston University. George Williams College later graduated some Negro males, and Sargent graduated many Negro women.

A search into the beginning of Negro institutions revealed that there was an awareness of the necessity for including physical education in their programs (Thrasher, 1901, pp. 209-10), but it appeared that their concept of physical education was vague and quite provincial. Some schools considered physiology, hygiene, and a general program of calisthenics as satisfying the general physical education requirement (Catalogues and Bulletins, Tuskegee Institute, 1881, p. 10 and Hampton Institute, 1886, pp. 6-9).

Although Howard University is credited with offering the first four-year degree course in physical education in 1924, Hampton Institute also launched a four-year course organized for physical education majors in the School of Education that same year (Hampton Catalog, 1924-25).

Howard University had required physical education from the beginning, but it was primarily for the benefit of the individual person. The aims of the program were good physical conditioning, health, and participation in activities which had implications from military science. Teaching, as a profession, was evidently not considered as far as men were concerned, because most of the trained physical education teachers in Negro schools during that time were women. Little was done in the way of physical education for women at Howard before the major program was started in 1924. Except for a bit of calisthenics, gymnastics, and (for men) running around the city reservoir, the entire physical education program was expressed in terms of intercollegiate athletics. It is mainly for this reason that the department was later divided, and separate departments for men and women came into existence.

In 1921, Louis L. Watson, a graduate of Howard University who had gone to Springfield and earned a physical education degree, returned to Howard and was appointed the director of the physical education department and athletic coach. Prior to Watson's coming to Howard, the director of physical education at the University was Edward Morrison, one of the leading dentists in the community.

Morrison had been a famous Negro football player at Tufts College in 1914-16. His interest in Howard's program was wrapped up in his fondness for football and athletics. This, therefore, became the major emphasis in physical education at Howard until Watson and Maryrose Allen came on the scene in 1924-25.

Unlike the programs at most other schools, the early program at Hampton was designed for women. Young women were required to take gymnastics for three years. The gymnasium was a room on the fourth floor of the academic building and was equipped with Swedish apparatus. The course included exercises on apparatus, floor work, and gymnastic games. Williams points out the aims of the program during this period:

> It is the purpose of the gymnastic games to train the swiftness and exactness of both the mind and body, and at the same time afford a pleasant relaxation from military discipline in other parts of the drill. The popular game of basketball has been introduced. Muscular development is not the aim of gymnastics,... We do not strive for athletes, but rather to train the muscular and nervous system together, and strengthen the heart and lungs upon which all other organs of the body depend.

At Tuskegee Institute, the evolution of the program followed closely the pattern at Hampton. There wes very little done in the way of physical education for men except the drills and exercises connected with the military program. When Booker T. Washington became Principal of Tuskegee in 1881, he set out to develop attitudes of industry and honesty in the backward and underdeveloped country youth of Alabama. His aim was to develop specific skills in definite crafts, and to prepare teachers for the public and private schools in the south. Although no details could be found about the recreation, play, or frivolities of the early students, the name of Michael B. Stephens is listed as the Sociology-Gymnastic teacher in 1900 (Thrasher, Appendix, pp. 209-10).

The very first catalog published by Tuskegee listed physiology and hygiene and calisthenics as requirements and the name of Azalia Thomas appears as the first gymnastic teacher (Catalog of Tuskegee State Normal School, 1881, p. 10). So it seems that in spite of his "vocational emphasis" Mr. Washington did consider exercise or gymnastics significant, even though the program was provided only for women. Actually, physical education did not flourish at Tuskegee until Robert R. Morton became president in 1916.

Early physical education for men at Tuskegee was primarily an athletic program involving football and baseball. Basketball and track and field were considered minor sports. The first athletic coach was J. B. Washington (1894-1897), who worked in the post office department. From 1897 to 1907 Charles Winter Woods, of the English department, served as coach. Physical education for men came under the ROTC program, while the women had an organized program of calisthenics and exercises which were carried on in the gymnasium (a room set aside in the academic building) under the direction of Amelia Roberts, who had a diploma from Sargent, and came to Tuskegee in 1905 (Tuskegee Bulletin, 1905).

An organized physical education program for men really began in 1923 with the coming of Cleveland L. Abbott, a graduate of South Dakota College with a major in agriculture. He organized the intramural football team within the agriculture department, and his team defeated the varsity football team that year. He became director of physical education and brought in Louise Atkins to bolster the women's staff and to teach tennis. Ross Owens was lated added to the men's staff, and by 1927 Tuskegee was well on the way to developing a physical education program for both men and women (Taped Interviews, Mrs. Cleveland Abbott, April 27, 1960). In 1931 the gymnasium (Logan Hall) was completed, and the program expanded to a professional preparation program in 1933.

As early as the last quarter of the nineteenth century, intercollegiate athletics was beginning to have a definite place in the student life at Wilberforce University. The athletic association was organized and sanctioned to promote the typical program carried on by the Negro colleges during this period (McGinnis, 1941, p. 173). By 1900 physical education was offered in the university program, and a department of health and physical education had been organized. Between 1900 and 1927 athletics played an important part in the advertising of Wilberforce. Football, basketball, and baseball were given utmost attention (Minutes of Meetings of the General Faculty – Reports on Athletics, 1900-1930). In her zeal to achieve recognition in the field of athletics Wilberforce went "all out" for sports. The desire to develop a department of health and physical education was one cause for this over-emphasis, and the desire to develop championship teams was another. There was constant debating among faculty members about this over-emphasis given to athletics (Wilberforce University: Minutes of General Faculty, March 7, 1910).

Although there was a department of physical education as early as 1910, there was no listed physical education instructor unitl 1915 (Wilberforce University Bulletin, 1915, p. 127). The first instructor was Horace Preston, who held a bachelor of science degree in physical education, and in 1917 Charles Blackburn was added to the staff.

By 1923 the physical education department had expanded its offerings, and was bidding strongly to offer professional preparation for physical education. The lack of adequate facilities for conducting a full scale program had been corrected with the construction of

Beacon Gymnasium, a structure which was more than adequate for the student enrollment and the program at that time. To strengthen the program, the department employed a woman instructor, Miss Carlynne Payne, a graduate of Sargent School, and also Mr. Dean Mohr from Ohio State University (Wilberforce University Bulletin, 1924-5, p. 97). Among the eight course offerings for men, and six for women, was a course which dealt with teaching physical education in the elementary grades. Instruction was also given in taking measurements and the organization and administration of meets and festivals (Ibid., p. 98).

At Morehouse College, which was founded in 1867, as Atlanta Baptist College, the program was much the same as that followed by Wilberforce. Intercollegiate athletics, which began with baseball in 1891 (Catalog of Atlanta Baptist College, 1891-92, p. 12), constituted the physical education program. A. D. Jones, a physician, became the first athletic coach in 1902. Prior to this time the team captain did the coaching. When Jones left the coaching job at Morehouse, this responsibility fell to Samuel Archer, who was a graduate of Colgate and had come to Morehouse to teach mathematics. Archer was destined to become the Dean of the College and later the president. When his administrative duties become too heavy, the coaching responsibility was taken over by B. T. Harver, another Colgate graduate, who had come to Morehouse to teach chemistry.

Although Morehouse intercollegiate athletics was continued without interruption from its beginning in 1891, there was no organized physical education at the school until 1932. At this time the Division of Athletic Sports and the Service program were centralized under one title - The Department of Physical Education - and Franklin Forbes, who had graduated from Morehouse in 1928 and attended Springfield for several summers, was placed in charge of the physical education department (Morehouse College Bulletin, 1933, p. 9).

Lincoln University, like Morehouse College, was an institution which trained men only. Located in southern Pennsylvania, Lincoln was one of the two institutions in the north which was founded before the Civil War primarily to train Negro students. Today Lincoln is a non-sectarian four-year senior college, privately controlled and state aided. Its doors are now open to all races and both sexes. Unlike most of the other Negro schools, Lincoln did not require the students to take physical education. Required physical education began when Manuel Rivero, a graduate of Columbia University, became physical director in 1934. Students were encouraged, however, to participate in activities which would contribute to their physical development. In one of the President's annual reports to the board he advised:

The health of the students has suffered for the want of proper conveniences for healthful regular exercises. The lot assigned for their use has been a great advantage, but is too rough for safety in rapid running. It ought to be ploughed and leveled and thoroughly rolled. A small appropriation for this purpose is desirable. (Annual Report of the President, Lincoln University, 1872, Book I, p. 187).

Before 1924 most of the Negro colleges in the country either had no physical education dequirement or interpreted such activities as physiology, hygiene, and athletics as physical education in order to satisfy the requirements of the few states which required physical education for certification. After 1917 many Negro land-grant and private colleges included the teacher-training program in their curricula and consequently had to include physical education as a requirement (Cook, Bulletin No. 19, 1927, pp. 280-85). This was usually done with a minimum amount of organizational change. Among more than thirty schools investigated, only three indicated that they had instructors with physical education degrees when their teaching-training program began. One possible explanation for this is that prior to 1924 no Negro institution offered professional preparation for physical education, and the few persons who had received training in this area had attended Harvard Summer School, Springfield, or Sargent.

The need for professional preparation for physical education in the Negro schools became apparent in 1927 when all of the states began to require physical education for teacher certification. There simply were not enough Negro physical education teachers to go around.

Staff Evolution

Since intercollegiate athletics preceded professional preparation for physical education in all of the Negro institutions, the one person who was on the scene when the professional program began was the athletic coach. This meant that he was usually designated as head of the physical education department. Prior to 1930 only two schools began their professional program with trained physical educators appointed to direct the department. In most instances the staffs were composed of persons who were trained in other academic fields and began to qualify in physical education on a piecemeal basis by attending summer school or in-service programs.

Between 1924 and 1958 physical education teaching personnel grew in number from one, in some institutions, to as many as fourteen in others. The usual procedure for developing a physical education staff was to appoint one, two, and sometimes three persons from other departments who were already on the teaching faculty, and then bring in as many new people as was absolutely necessary. As the persons already employed were usually male coaches, one or more women were brought in to handle courses for women.

By the end of 1958 the staffs in all of the Negro schools, Wilberforce excepted, had increased significantly beyond their size prior to World War II, and the quality of academic preparation among physical education teachers had improved. In 1958 more than two-thirds of all persons engaged in the physical education instructional program in Negro colleges and universities had earned master's degrees, and more than half held a rank above that of instructor. It is not so gratifying, however, to note that there were only eleven persons with doctoral degrees, and there were still many schools which had departments in which not a single person had earned this terminal degree.

Physical Facilities

When the major programs in physical education were started in the Negro colleges and universities, the facilities available for conducting the programs were considered to be better than those which other departments had available to them when they began. This was primarily due to the fact that intercollegiate athletics, which had preceded the professional physical education program, had some semblance of facilities for operational purposes which became immediately available for use in the professional programs. It was very soon discovered, however, that these facilities were far too inadequate to serve the minimum necessities of a major program.

By 1939 Hampton Institute provided better facilities and more equipment for physical education than any other Negro college in the United States. Even before the turn of the twentieth century, Hampton had a large room located on the fourth floor of the academic building, which was equipped with Swedish apparatus consisting of stall bars, benches, straight and slanting ropes, double boom, balance beams, and vaulting standards. There was enough space for floor work which consisted of twisting, jumping, marching, and running (C. H. Williams, p. 2). There was in addition some space for outdoor courts and activities (Klein, p. 887). By 1928, a gymnasium had been built to serve a wider range of activities than the earlier had provided. Much of the unimproved land space had been developed into modern play courts and fields.

Howard University also provided facilities for carrying on physical education well in advance of the advent of the major program. The situation, however, did not favor Howard as it had Hampton. The entire physical education plant consisted of a compact plot of twenty-five acres, and there was very little land available to allocate as open space where out-of-doors activities could be conducted.

Therefore, prior to 1925, physical education was conducted in the basement of two dormitories on the campus. The outdoor activities for men consisted largely of military exercises and running around the reservoir of the water department of the District of Columbia. The athletic and sports activities were conducted at Griffith's Stadium, a major league baseball park adjacent to the campus, and Banneker Field, a district recreation facility across the street from the university.

In 1925 a new up-to-date gymnasium was erected. This building contained all modern facilities with an overhead running track, showers, swimming pool, gymnastic equipment, and rooms for recitation and military science tactics. By 1926 a new football field was added.

Within the next fifteen years the physical education department had outgrown the facilities and equipment. Both the men and women were obliged to use the same gymnasium, field, and pool. But after World War II Howard showed a tremendous increase in facilities, staff and program.

The situation at Wilberforce University was quite different from that at Hampton and Howard. Wilberforce was not entirely dependent upon church appropriations, endowments, philanthropy and student fees for income as were Howard and Hampton. More than half of the school's income was derived from appropriations from the state of Ohio to support the Combined Normal and Industrial Department (Wilberforce University Bulletin, 1924-25, p. 16). The physical education department was maintained entirely on the state side of the university, where adequate space was available for the development of courts and fields which were necessary to meet the demands of the school's physical education program. Of the 347 acres of land which constituted the physical plant, the state of Ohio owned nearly two-thirds (Klein, op. cit., p. 605). The outdoor activities at Wilberforce during the early part of this period were largely baseball and football. For indoor physical education, Beacon Gymnasium, built in 1922, was modernly equipped. It was a commodious structure which afforded ample space for all of the indoor sports and gymnastics conducted at Wilberforce at this time.

At Tuskegee Institute, the physical education program and training for men was confined to courses in health, hygiene, military drill, and outdoor athletic games. The program for women involved gymnastics, floor work, and calisthenics, all of which were conducted in a basement room of the laundry building. In 1931, Tuskegee completed the erection of Logan Hall. This building, which was an auditorium-gymnasium, was then the largest and most complete gymnasium in all of the Negro schools. The fact that it was large and complete made it an obstacle to the development of the physical education program. Logan Hall was designed large enough not only to accommodate the entire student body at one gathering, but also to provide a meeting place for the entire population of the Negro community at Tuskegee. So occasionally the physical education program had to give way to the "higher priority" farmer's conference, community gathering, general school movie or dance.

In 1939, because of the improved quality and quantity of the staff, and the change in the concept of professional preparation held by "Cleve" Abbott, there began a gradual expansion of the facilities necessary to conduct the professional program as well as athletics. By 1958, tennis courts, game areas, and sports fields had been added or developed, and the gymnasium had become the nerve center of the physical education program.

Early physical education at Virginia State College consisted mainly of intercollegiate athletic sports, some gymnastics, and a fairly good athletic program; the facilities consisted of an athletic field which was used primarily for football and baseball. But there were several tennis courts and a small gymnasium which was a large room in Virginia Hall, a classroom building built in 1888. In 1927 the college initiated an expansion of the physical education department to include the professional preparation of teachers. This action called for expansion of the physical facilities as well (Virginia State College Gazette, 1883-1934, p. 34).

A new structure was built and well equipped with ample facilities to conduct activities which were demanded of Negro teachers in physical education as well as white teachers during this time. Additional tennis courts were built, and a soccer field for women was constructed on the front of the campus. By 1932 the enrollment had outgrown the facilities made available earlier. A swimming pool was added to the gymnasium, and later several classrooms and administrative offices were added.

Very early in her history, Southern University, Baton Rouge, Louisiana, participated in intercollegiate athletics, and except for the facilities necessary to promote intercollegiate athletics she had little in the way of physical education facilities. Until 1938 the lack of physical education facilities was not a serious problem for the administration nor the physical education department, because the physical education requirements of the university, as well as those of the State Board for Certification, could be very easily satisfied without any special equipment other than the playfields and classroom spaces which were a part of the existing physical plant.

By 1938 the professional preparation program was well under way, and some attention was being given to improving and increasing the facilities and the staff as well as course offerings. A modern gymnasium-auditorium was completed in 1939, and a football stadium as well as a quarter-mile running track was added. Three new tennis courts were added to supplement the already existing two, and a new baseball field was constructed. By 1958 Southern had built an additional gymnasium complete with a swimming pool and seven classrooms, in addition to the main auditorium.

Morehouse College and Lincoln University in Pennsylvania were both schools for male students only. Neither was a state-supported school, and, therefore, they were obliged to depend upon their own resources and the supporting churches for procurement of all facilities necessary to carry any program. Morehouse was located in a large urban community, but her physical plant was limited to a small plot of ground, a mere seven acres, and this among other things accounted in part for the limited amount of facilities for physical education. Prior to 1930, the main teaching station was a large playing field on campus which served as the field for intercollegiate football and baseball as well as the service program in physical education. By 1930 a gymnasium for basketball and indoor activities was constructed, and in 1933 two tennis courts were added to the campus. The gymnasium was barely large enough for a regulation-sized basketball court, and its usefulness was further limited by spectator bleachers which were built in as permanent structures. The gymnasium equipment would have to be classified as very meager. There was some gymnastic equipment such as a side horse, parallel bars, and several tumbling mats. The gym floor afforded sufficient space for volleyball and gymnastics when not being used for basketball.

Since no professional preparation courses were offered during these years, and the student body was small, the greater part of the physical education program included outdoor activities. In 1932 the facilities of the Atlanta University athletic field were made available to Morehouse for use in conducting certain phases of her program. This athletic field was spacious enough to provide a quarter-mile, oval running track with a grassy infield which could be organized for soccer, speedball and softball. There were, in addition, two clay tennis courts and a regulation-sized baseball field far enough removed from the other activities to create a safe atmosphere, and a new health and physical education building was constructed. This structure was complete with a swimming pool, four bowling alleys, a game room and an all-purpose auditorium.

When Morgan College moved to its present site in Baltimore in 1919, a barn already on the property was converted into a gymnasium for indoor gymnastics, stunts and tumbling, calisthenics, and marching (Wilson, loc. cit.). Although these activities were known to have existed on campus, the course offerings were announced for the first time in 1932 (Morgan College Catalog, 1923-24, p. 58).

Unlike the other institutions previously discussed, Morgan did not have facilities for carrying on the intercollegiate athletic program during the early years of her existence. She did, however, have an intercollegiate program, and by 1935 a major sequence in physical education was offered (Morgan College Bulletin, 1935-36, pp. 13-15).

The professional preparation courses were conducted at the old Douglas High School. In addition to using the high school gymnasium, an instructor from the public school system served as a teacher. The athletic teams had to use one of two available facilities for practicing: a vacant lot which was located some distance from the campus on the high school athletic field across town. Because of the lack of available facilities, their intercollegiate games had to be played in rented facilities in Baltimore, Maryland.

Although the physical education facilities at Morgan were non-existent prior to 1935, Mr. Bowman, the supervisor of health and physical education for the public schools of Baltimore, stated:

> To be educated physically we do not need to have a complete modern plant, although it would be appreciated and used to its fullest extent. It is my feeling that we at Morgan College should first take advantage of the many opportunities for physical education that the college now offers. A new complete and modern gymnasium will come in time. Let us do our part to bring this to our campus (Morgan College Bulletin, 1935-36, pp. 13-15).

While Mr. Bowman's prophecy eventually did come to pass, the program had to develop without a new gymnasium for many years. In the meantime, the playing field was a "driveway" between the two buildings on the campus. On inclement days the classes were moved into the chapel where the physical education program was carried on as usual. In 1937 Morgan acquired her own athletic stadium, and in later years a gymnasium was built on the campus. Between 1939, when the Methodist Episcopal Church sold Morgan to the State of Maryland, and 1958 the school continued to show improvement in program and facilities.

Discussion

Negro colleges and universities, like all other institutions of society, reflect the culture of the region in which they exist. With a very few exceptions, all of the predominantly Negro colleges and universities in the United States are in the south, where the Negro's ascribed status as subordinate and inferior has been accepted as inevitable by members of both races. While this concept has been the source of much discontent, until recently it has not created a great amount of conflict. It remains a fact that the Negro schools, public and private, have not measured up to accepted standards for American schools.

In the public colleges and universities the physical education programs have been below standards for several reasons, not the least of which has been the lack of sufficient funds and facilities and the lack of properly trained personnel. The failure to allocate funds for schools maintained exclusively for colored people has resulted in an inferior quality of schools at every level from the elementary school to the university.

For many years now the physical education programs in Negro schools have had to content themselves with little or no facilities with which to carry on an indoor program. In most of the schools there has been little equipment available to conduct the most meager activity courses. While there has usually been some space available for outdoor activities, this has commonly been an underdeveloped area, or an improvised section of the campus yard.

In the Negro schools it seems that there has not always been a great concern for the quality of physical education instructors. Certifying boards have sometimes permitted persons to teach without the proper credentials; teachers have sometimes been hired for reasons other than their abilities to teach physical education; and in many instances they are paid on a scale which is lower than that of their counterparts in white institutions. This dual system has probably been an important cause of the low status of the Negro schools.

The gymnasium is the most important facility for conducting an indoor program in physical education. In many of the Negro colleges this facility is still non-existent, inadequate, or too poorly equipped to be adapted functionally. In too many instances this facility is still a dual or multi-purpose building which limits the types and numbers of activities which can be conducted.

In the public-supported Negro institutions the budget usually is not sufficient to provide the necessities for conducting the professional preparation program. There is usually not as much concerted public pressure placed upon schools or the boards of trustees to provide facilities for physical education as that exerted for the so-called "fundamental" subjects such as science, agriculture, and the vocational arts.

In private institutions the situation is, and has been, much the same. Presidents of private colleges have the primary responsibilities to "raise" money for operation. It is logical to presume that this can best be done by favoring the tastes of those persons who have money to give. Unfortunately, people or organizations that are sources of these monies have not been those who have seen the value of physical education as a part of the school program. So the request is made for a building which is first an auditorium or assembly hall and, secondly, a gymnasium.

Finally, those who are engaged in professional preparation in the field of physical education must share some of the responsibilities for the situations in Negro institutions. It appears that the people in physical education, with some exceptions, of course, have not professionalized the field to the extent that it commands the dignity and respect that other disciplines have. There are still too many persons engaged in physical education who barely have the academic qualifications and skills to teach professional courses. There seems to be too little individual initiative to take actions which will lead to professional growth. There are still many Negro colleges and universities which offer professional degree programs without a single staff member with a doctorate degree (even though the staff may be large). It is, however, gratifying to note that increasing numbers are moving up to the master's degree level. But past experience indicates that, for most of them, this will signal the end of their formal education.

The fact that many physical education teachers who are not qualified to conduct professional courses are actively engaged in the profession may be due to the indifferent attitudes of persons in the field. Unlike secondary and elementary school teachers, the college teacher is not required by law to meet certification standards. Most Negro colleges do not have rigid policies which govern the employment of a teacher, and employment becomes a "bargaining activity" between the employer and employee. More often than not the teacher is employed for reasons other than his academic ability.

Since his liberation from slavery the Negro has been waging a fight for more and better educational opportunity. The positive outcome of this struggle seems inevitable. In spite of integration the Negro colleges and universities in the south must be prepared to provide the education for the bulk of the Negro high school graduates for some time to come. In view of this probability, it is of utmost importance that serious attention be given the quantity and quality of these institutions, and every effort must be made to bring them up to professional standards.

Bibliography

Books

Brubacher, J. S. A History of the Problems of Education. New York: McGraw-Hill Book Company, 1947.

DuBois, William E. B. Souls of Black Folk. Chicago: A. C. McClurg and Company, 1903.

Henderson, Edward Bancroft. The Negro in Sports. Washington: Associated Publishers, 1939.

McGinnis, Frederick A. A History and Interpretation of Wilberforce University. Wilberforce: Brown Publishing Company, 1941.

Menke, Frank G. The New Encyclopedia of Sports. New York: A. A. Barnes and Company, 1944.

Rice, Emmett A., Hutchinson, John L. and Lee, Mabel. A Brief History of Physical Education. New York: The Ronald Press, 1958.

Thrasher, May Bennett. Tuskegee, Its Story and Its Work. Boston: Small, Maynard and Company, 1901.

Van Dalen, Deobold, et. al. A World History of Physical Education. New York: Prentice-Hall, Inc., 1953.

Woodson, Carter G. Education of the Negro Prior to 1861. New York: The Knickerbocker Press, 1915.

Bulletins

Hampton Institute Bulletins, 1886-1958.

Harvard Magazine, Vol. VI, 1859.

Howard University Bulletins, 1869-1959.

Lincoln University Bulletins, 1926-1952.

Morehouse College Bulletins, 1878-1957.

Morgan State College Bulletins, 1921-1959.

Southern University Bulletins, 1937-1952.

Tuskegee State Normal School Bulletins, 1881-1958.

Virginia State College Gazettes, 1883-1958.

Wilberforce University Bulletins, 1910-1949.

Periodicals

Cook, Katherine M. "State Laws and Regulations Governing Teacher's Certificates." Bureau of Education, Bulletin No. 19. Washington, D. C.: Government Printing Office, 1927.

DuBois, William E. B. "The College Bred Negro." Atlanta University Conference. Atlanta: Atlanta University Press, 1900.

Fitzgerald, G. B. and Peik, W. E. "The Education of Men Teachers of Physical Education for Public School Service in Selected Colleges and Universities." Research Quarterly, Vol. 5, No. 4 (December, 1934).

Frazier, W. B. "National Survey of the Education of Teachers." Bureau of Education, Bulletin No. 10. Washington, D. C.: U. S. Government Printing Office, 1933.

Jones, Thomas Jesse. "Negro Education: A Study of Private and Higher Schools for Colored People in the United States." U. S. Bureau of Education, Bulletin No. 39. Washington, D. C.: U. S. Government Printing Office, 1916.

Louisiana State Department of Education, Certification of Teachers (Negro), Bulletins Nos. 104, 219, 397 (1931-1939).

Troup, C V. "Building Construction on Negro Campuses." The Journal of Negro Education, XXIII, No. 1 (Winter, 1954).

Proceedings

American Association of Teacher College Yearbook, 1924.

American Physical Education Review, XXXIII, No. 5 (May, 1927).

Annual Report of the President of Tuskegee Institute to the Trustees, 1951-52. (On file in the Tuskegee Library).

Fifty-seventh Annual Report of the Principal to the Board. Hampton Institute, 1924.

<u>Memorandum from the Director of Physical Education to the President of Morehouse College Regarding the Weaknesses of the Department</u> (March 26, 1943). (On file in the Departmental Office.)

Metcalf, T. N. "Professional Training for Directors of Physical Education." <u>Proceedings</u>: Society of Directors of Physical Education in Colleges. Thirtieth Annual Meeting (December 28, 1926).

<u>Minutes of Meetings of the General Faculty</u>. Wilberforce University, 1900-1930.

<u>Minutes of the General Faculty</u>. Hampton Institute, October 9, 1924.

Unpublished Material

Williams, C. H. "The History of Physical Education and Athletics at Hampton Institute." Hampton: Department of Physical Education, Hampton Institute, 1960. (Unpublished research paper.)

Zeigler, E. F. "A History of Professional Preparation for Physical Education in the United States (1861-1950)." (Unpublished Ph.D. dissertation, Yale University, 1950.)

CHAPTER 20

A BRIEF DESCRIPTIVE HISTORY OF GRADUATE STUDY IN PHYSICAL EDUCATION IN THE UNITED STATES TO 1950

Earle F. Zeigler
The University of Western Ontario, London

Introduction[1]

Graduate study in physical education had its very early beginnings in the United States during the last decade of the nineteenth century and the early years of the present century. Prior to the presentation of a brief narrative presentation of this development, early graduate study - generally speaking - will be reviewed, and a few statements will be made about the beginning of undergraduate professional preparation for physical education as well.

It was toward the middle of the nineteenth century that some formal graduate work was offered to students in the United States for the first time. At the undergraduate level, America had borrowed the English system, but it was the graduate school pattern of Germany that was superimposed on the collegiate structure of the time (Ryan, 1939, pp. 1-8). At the University of Halle (Germany), a basic change in approach had been introduced - an approach which

---

Editor's Note: A third essay prepared by the Editor traces briefly the history of graduate study in physical education in the United States to 1950. It is a preliminary investigation, and it is the Editor's hope that further studies on this subject will be carried out. The period from 1950 to 1970 needs to be investigated historically (to the extent that historical perspective can be obtained).

---

[1] A paper presented at the International Seminar on the History of Sport, ENSEPS - 92 - Chatenay-Malabry, France, May 17-20, 1972. Professor Zeigler will become Dean of the new Faculty of Physical Education at The University of Western Ontario, London 72, Canada on May 1, 1972. He has been concerned with the history of professional preparation since the late 1940's when he traced the history of undergraduate study as a doctoral investigation. A paper on the history of the professional master's degree is appearing this spring in the Canadian Journal of History of Sport and Physical Education. This journal is edited by Dr. Alan Metcalfe, University of Windsor, Ontario, Canada.

involved a newer philosophy based on significant advances in science and mathematics. Such an interest in research and scholarly endeavor was actually characteristic of early programs in the United States generally, but in 1876 Johns Hopkins University was the first institution to pattern itself directly after the model of the German universities (Ryan, p. 28). The first Ph.D. program had been established sixteen years earlier by Yale University (Rosenberg, 1966, p. 34).

The master's degree, typically the second degree, become available at Harvard College only six years after it was founded in 1636. The student was required to take an additional year of study beyond the bachelor's degree, prepare a thesis or "synopsis" for presentation prior to commencement, and pay the additional fees for that period. These disputations were typically quite theological and unscientific in nature. During the eighteenth and nineteenth centuries many colleges awarded master's degrees which were honorary – more or less. Truly earned degrees under reorganized academic councils didn't appear until the 1870's (Knight, 1940, pp. 426-432).

Despite this seemingly meagre beginning, somehow by the beginning of the twentieth century at least fifty universities were offering the doctoral degree – the earned Ph.D. At that time there was an effort to standardize and accredit these programs, but only twenty or so of the universities seemed to be really concerned with this type of evaluation (Good in Henry, Graduate Study in Education, p. 6). In both 1908 and 1916, committees representing associations of universities made recommendations about the maintenance of standards. A similar statement was made concerning the status of the American master's degree in 1932 (Knight, pp. 436-437).

Graduate programs built upon a reasonably sound base developed steadily in these early years. There was an attempt to meet the needs of the time; the quality of faculty and students was quite high; and the administrative leaders of the period were of high calibre. From a most modest number of only 198 graduate students in the entire country in 1871-1872, the figure rose to a total of 47,255 men and women in 1930 (Edwards, 1935, pp. 469-470). Such an expansion could not have taken place without the incidence of a great many problems involving a great number of considerations. One recurrent problem, as repeated time and again in the literature over the years, revolved around the concept of research – as opposed to teacher preparation – as the basic responsibility of the graduate school (Dale, 1930, pp. 198-202).

Social forces within the country between 1920 and 1940 could not not help but influence graduate study significantly. Enrollments were rising sharply, and the character of a considerable percentage of

these students was changing. Graduate degree programs were established in a great many professional schools, and thus it became difficult to maintain high standards of scholarship. A change in emphasis
with a necessary broadening of the content of graduate programs was
considered justifiable by Edwards in the mid-thirties because of the
increased demand for teachers and administrators. From another
standpoint, it became almost impossible to provide intensified preparation for research specialization when the graduate schools were
graduating 3,000 Ph.D.'s and 25,000 master's candidates annually
(Edwards, 1935, pp. 469-470).

The master's degree in education was offered initially in the
latter part of the nineteenth century. In the year 1900 some thirty-
one master's degrees were awarded by a total of twelve leading universities. To give some idea of the growth of graduate study in professional education - for these same institutions alone - some 134
degrees were awarded in 1910; 678 by 1920; and 3,231 in 1930 (John,
1935, p. 450). By 1949-1950, this number had grown sixfold to
18,311 master's degrees in education by all colleges and universities
in the country offering such programs (Story, 1950, p. 78). It is
generally accepted that within this divergent group of study patterns
there is a "wide diversity of standards relating to entrance and degree requirements . . ." (Snyder and Scott, 1954, p. 205). Thus, it
becomes somewhat obvious why the Council of Graduate Schools in the
United States points out that a master's degree program should be
inaugurated by a university only when the "resources and special
traditions available" would seem to make such a degree program
desirable (Council of Graduate Studies in the U. S., "The Master's
Degree," p. 4).

While this development was taking place at the master's level,
graduate education generally was completing what Berelson has designated a "growth and diversification" phase from World War I to World
War II, and beginning on another period called "revival and reappraisal" since World War II (1960, pp. 24-42). It was during the
former of these two periods that the doctoral program was made
available in many more fields within the traditional arts and science
unit, but also in a great many professional fields including education
(p. 27). The persistent problem of "purpose and quality" was considered time and again (p. 28). According to Berelson,

> The demand for training and the supply of students, the institu-
> tions offering graduate work, the body of knowledge to be
> communicated, the professionalization of graduate study, the
> debate over the entire enterprise - all of these familiar trends
> were back in high gear by 1950 . . . (p. 32).

About this time also, both general and special professional education, as units related to schools and colleges of education within

universities, were confronted with a most serious problem.[2] One might say that young teachers were "damned if they did, and damned if they didn't." If the teacher elected the master's degree in education, there was every likelihood that he would not have enough so-called substantive courses in academic areas in his curriculum. Conversely, if he elected to pursue the M.S. degree program in, say, chemistry, he could well be criticized because of inability to give evidence of "master teacher" qualifications. These two examples were really not extreme cases, and they did represent a serious problem at this juncture of American graduate education.

This dilemma was brought more sharply into focus by the fact that the "body of knowledge" in each subject matter was increasingly so rapidly. Many knowledgeable people were recommending a fifth year of undergraduate preparation, and some states were actually requiring this extra work for teacher certification. Thus, a concern developed over the articulation of undergraduate programs with professional and graduate schools. Should the program of study in this fifth year be advanced undergraduate work, or should it be what might be called true graduate study involving the development of research competency? And more specifically, what is the exact progression of course experiences required to obtain the greatest advantage from this extended undergraduate program of the fifth year (if this were the approach taken)?

Undergraduate Professional Preparation for Physical Education. In order to understand why and how graduate study in physical education got its start, a brief outline of the history of undergraduate professional preparation for physical education should be considered. Such preparation began first in the United States in 1861 when Dio Lewis started the first ten-week diploma course. In the slightly more than one hundred years since that time, some highly significant changes and developments have taken place in the field. A variety of social forces in the changing American scene have influenced it almost unbelievably. Foreign traditions and customs held away initially, but gradually a fairly distinct American philosophy of physical education emerged. This has since been blurred considerably, especially since it has become possible to delineate the various educational philosophical trends (and more recently with a developing interest in critical analysis of a philosophical nature).

---

[2] "General" professional education refers to those courses in schools of education which are required typically for state certification. This might include history and philosophy of education, educational psychology, and others. "Special" professional education would be professional preparation for the teaching of physical education, or art education, etc.

In the period from 1900 to 1920, physical educators – trained as educators and not as physicians – were selected more frequently as directors of professional programs. During these two decades many publicly-supported colleges and universities entered the business of preparing physical educators. It thus carried further the new trend began in the 1890's to award academic degrees upon the completion of major, four-year professional programs in physical education. It was at this time also that some of these curricula were developed within schools of education, whereas others were in arts and science units (or various subdivisions thereof). The subsequent establishment of separate schools and colleges of physical education within universities has had a most notable influence on professional preparation and on the status of the physical education field as a whole.

Down through the years of the twentieth century, many educational leaders – both within and outside of the field – have urged that there should be a stronger "cultural" education for prospective physical education teachers. There has been a further desire expressed for these majors to have an improved background in the foundation sciences. Until recently there has been a definite trend toward increasing the number of hours required in general professional education courses. A number of studies have indicated a lack of standardization of course terminology within the specialized area of Health, Physical Education, and Recreation.

In the decade after World War I – a conflict which exerted a tremendous influence upon the field forcing a flood of state health and physical education laws – some 137 colleges and universities joined those already offering professional education in health and physical education. As a result school health education and physical education were interwoven in such a way that it became quite complex. Then, too, professional courses in recreation, camping, and outdoor education were introduced as well. In an attempt to improve the professional preparation experience, and also to aid in the establishment of quite separate professional endeavors, separate curricula in school health and safety education and in recreational leadership were gradually developed in a number of the leading colleges and universities functioning in this field. A series of national conferences further helped to bring the various objectives of the separate areas into focus for the professional leaders concerened. The trend toward specialization of function is now well established, and this development will undoubtedly continue to take the various subdivision schools and colleges of health, physical education, and recreation still further apart. Most recent developments include the addition of curricula in park administration, the establishment of minors in coaching, the removal of dance from the physical education unit to fine arts in some cases, and the addition of public health concerns into the health education department's purview. To a certain extent, possible agreement in philosophy of education within the field will determine the outcome of this most urgent problem. The American Association for Health, Physical Education, and Recreation, the largest single department of the National Education Association, has held meetings on this subject and has featured the various issues of the unification – separation – affiliation – federation matter within the profession. The Association itself has served as a great unifying force in the total movement. Over the years there have been many attempts within the field to improve the quality of undergraduate professional preparation through studies, surveys, research projects other than normative surveys, national conferences, and accreditation plans (Zeigler, 1962, pp. 116-133).

Early Graduate Study

Very little graduate study of a truly scientific or scholarly nature was conducted prior to the third decade of the twentieth century, although a number of colleges and universities had entered the field – or were planning to begin such programs. It wasn't actually until 1935 that a Master's thesis by Clarke was completed as a survey of the requirements for the Master's degree in physical education (Clarke, 1935). Norris and Sweet, in 1937, undertook a survey to determine the status of graduate study in this field.

Springfield College offered the first "graduate" course in the fall of 1891 with a one-year program superimposed on the regular two-year undergraduate curriculum. The M.P.E. degree was authorized there in 1905 (Doggett, 1943, pp. 104, 129). In 1901 Columbia University is reported to have established the first major program in physical education within education leading to the Master's degree.[3] Clarke stated further that Oberlin followed Columbia closely with its first student receiving the M.A. degree in physical education in 1904 (Clarke, 1934). Other institutions entered the field of graduate study in a chronologically sporadic pattern thereafter (e.g., The Normal College of the American Gymnastic Union in 1907, Wellesley in 1917, the University of Southern California in 1918, and the University of Oregon in 1920) (Zeigler, 1951, pp. 275-276).

A most important step was taken both by Columbia Teachers College and New York University in 1924 with the establishment of programs leading to the Doctor of Philosophy degree with concentration in physical education. Zeigler had reported earlier that the Doctor of Physical Education degree (D.P.E.) had been offered earlier by the Y.M.C.A. Graduate School of Nashville (Zeigler, 1951,

---

[3] It is believed that this became possible at this time under the jurisdiction of the educational faculty. Much further investigation is needed in this entire area.

(p. 276), but it remained for Welch of the West Virginia Institute of
Technology to uncover the fact that four D.P.E. degrees were awarded there between the years of 1925 and 1929 (Welch, 1968, pp. 9-10).
Thus, it would appear that the first doctoral degree in physical education was not completed in New York City! The intention of the
reporting of Welch's finding is not to detract from the early pioneering effort carried out by both Columbia Teachers College and New
York University. It is worthy of note that Ethel J. Saxman received
the first Ph.D. degree from Columbia Teachers College in 1926,
while in this same year James G. Bliss completed his work for a
similar degree at New York University. In 1927, David K. Brace,
Ruth Elliott, and G. B. Johnson received doctorates in physical education from Columbia, and they were followed by Clifford L. Brownell
in 1928.

Clark Hetherington, the organizer of graduate study in physical
education at New York University, addressed himself to the professional training problem in a talk to The Society of Directors of Physical Education in Colleges in December of 1924. Believing that this
problem was of the greatest importance and urgency, he expressed
his fear that many institutions would merely list their undergraduate
courses as graduate ones in the transition to the offering of graduate
study in physical education. He realized that the four-year period of
preparation was not sufficient for the task, and stressed that the
essentials could barely be covered in a program of that length. It
was in the graduate curriculum that a prospective teacher could be
prepared to perform the full functions of his work with some opportunity for specialization, he asserted, but only if the undergraduate
curriculum was well-planned, integrated, and articulated from year
to year (Hetherington, 1925).

Between 1926 and 1949, some fifty-four colleges and universities began Master's degree programs in physical education with a
rather equal distribution between Master of Arts and Master of Science nomenclature. Since 1940, however, the large majority of
institutions reporting entrance into graduate study in physical education offered the Master of Science degree (Zeigler, unpublished survey, 1948-49). Viewed somewhat differently, Hewitt, in his assessment of graduate study, reported that in 1942 that "56 institutions
offer major work in physical education" (Hewitt, 1942, p. 255).

The basic differences between undergraduate and graduate
courses seemed to revolve around greater emphasis on problems
courses, the concept of seminar, the addition of a thesis based on research, and the inclusion of a methods of research course (Norris
and Sweet, 1937, pp. 3-10). In 1938, Lloyd reaffirmed the need for
increased effort along the lines of research (Lloyd, 1938, pp. 33-37).
The literature on the subject of graduate study in physical education
was most certainly sparse, but there were some studies employing

descriptive analysis of existent programs carried out as doctoral projects at this time. Frederick developed principles which might be used as guidelines for the reformulation of requirements for the Master's degree (1938). Her study related to programs for women, and then it was followed by Shaw's similar study that applied to men's programs (1939).

In addition to his very detailed listing of institutions offering all types of graduate degrees in physical education, Hewitt raised some extremely interesting questions about the graduate program itself. (In fact, many of the questions he posed may still be asked with good reason a quarter of a century later.) He inquired whether physical education at the graduate level was becoming more closely associated with schools of education because it truly belongs there as an integral phase of professional education. Then, as a corollary question, he wonders whether physical education must continue to combine itself with professional education schools because it was "such a new and growing profession" and because it lacked "the respect of an old, established profession." He asked further whether the pattern being established would hinder physical education's future growth and might prevent it from "becoming an upstanding body comparable to other established professions" (Hewitt, 1942, pp. 252-256).

In an article published in 1945, Hewitt turned his attention specifically to the various requirements for the Master's degree in physical education. In forty-five of the fifty-six institutions studied, it was recommended that an undergraduate major in physical education was needed as an entrance requirement for graduate study in the field. Thirty-six of these institutions required no skill competence test for admission to the graduate level. This would seem to indicate that these universities viewed graduate study as being more theoretical and research-laboratory oriented. Presumably it could be postulated further that those in charge of the remaining twenty programs (out of a total of fifty-six) may have felt that the demonstration of such physical skill was a necessary prerequisite for the second professional degree. Interestingly enough, at that time admission to the graduate school was not typically the same as admission to candidacy for the Master's degree.

Five years was the maximum time allowed on the average for completion of the degree requirements. Forty of the fifty-six schools studied required some sort of a final comprehensive examination. There was a sharp division of opinion expressed as to whether a thesis should be required. Generally speaking, the thesis, if required, did not have to be a contribution to knowledge. Along the line of research orientation, the main purpose at this level was that of testing the individual's ability to use the tools of research (Hewitt, 1945).

In a second study on this subject published in 1945, this one of the status of the graduate faculty in physical education, Hewitt learned that the majority of the universities offering graduate study in this field did not specify any prerequisites for the teaching faculty. Seven of the fifty-six higher institutions studied required graduate instructors to have at least the rank of Assistant Professor. Eight insisted that a person should hold a Master's degree to teach at this level, and eight others required the possession of a doctoral degree. Hewitt concluded that, if the possession of a higher degree - or working for an advanced degree - is an indication of proper background for graduate instruction, graduate staffs in physical education were, or soon would be, well prepared for the task. Basically, however, the existing standards for graduate faculty in effect at most of the schools surveyed fell below those recommended by the national professional associations and various accrediting agencies (a situation probably not peculiar to physical education at that time) (Hewitt, 1945, October).

A further contribution had been made to our knowledge about this level of education by Hewitt in 1946 in an article in which he presented the results of an investigation of the status of the doctoral program. At that time some twenty institutions offered a major in physical education for a doctoral degree. Proceeding alphabetically by state, they were California (Stanford and the University of Southern California); Indiana (Indiana University); Iowa (State University of Iowa); Kentucky (University of Kentucky); Louisiana (Louisiana State University); Massachusetts (Boston University); Michigan (University of Michigan); Missouri (University of Missouri); New York (Columbia Teachers College, New York University, Syracuse University); Ohio (Cincinnati University and Ohio State University); Oregon (University of Oregon); Pennsylvania (Pennsylvania State College and University of Pittsburgh); Tennessee (George Peabody College for Teachers); Texas (University of Texas); and Wyoming (University of Wyoming) (Hewitt, 1946).

There were three types of doctoral degrees available with specialization in physical education in these twenty universities. They were (1) the Ph.D. degree in physical education; (2) the Ph.D. degree in education; and (3) the Ed.D. degree in education. Hewitt felt that the standards recommended for advanced degrees by professional associations were being quite well met by the twenty institutions surveyed. For example, the programs were quite uniform in that one year in residence was required and three years beyond the bachelor's degree were necessary. All of the universities required a qualifying examination of some sort to determine the candidate's ability to proceed forward into actual candidacy for the degree. Generally speaking, the doctor of philosophy degree program was one which emphasized research in an area of specialization, while the doctor of education degree program stressed development of professional competence and scholarship.

A reading knowledge of two foreign languages was required in almost all instances for the Ph.D. program, whereas standards concerning language background for the Ed.D. degree were not uniform. A comprehensive test on measurement in education was required in almost all cases. In all institutions the candidate had to defend his thesis or project before a faculty committee. Interestingly enough, Hewitt was anxious to see the doctoral programs in physical education sever their connections with schools of education. He believed that the profession of physical education would become well established and recognized only if such separation occurred.

In 1947 at the Teacher Education Section Meeting of the College Physical Education Association, papers were addressed to the graduate program in physical education, and they give some insight on the developments of the time. The late Dr. William Meredith of the University of Pennsylvania discussed the five-year program for the preparation of physical education teachers begun there in 1933. (This program was dropped subsequently - a most unfortunate development for the profession.) Harry Scott of Columbia Teachers College also chaired a panel discussion in that meeting in which it was decided that there were at least eight characteristics of graduate level instruction (as over against undergraduate level study) which were as follows: (1) the development of the ability to do critical thinking; (2) a broader field of preparation emphasizing expansion of one's knowledge both horizontally and vertically; (3) development of research tools for independent investigation; (4) the ability to do independent thinking; (5) specialization; (6) an opportunity to sense and apply relationships between the various areas of knowledge and human experience; (7) a greater amount of individualized instruction; and (8) a period of at least one academic year beyond the bachelor's degree should be required for the Master's degree (Nordly, 1947, pp. 58-61).

At this same meeting, further discussion was held as to the possible unique characteristics of the doctoral program over and above the program for the Master's degree. There was agreement that the student was both "broadened" and "sharpened" with this further preparation, and that maturation was important to the candidate for the doctoral program. (It should perhaps be considered that the people on the panel held both Ph.D. and Ed.D. degrees themselves.) Still further, it has never been completely decided that a Ph.D. degree program concentrates on "sharpening" only, as opposed to "broadening" - and indeed that exactly the opposite is the case for the Ed.D. program.) Generally speaking, the program leading to the doctorate was thought to be more leisurely than an intensive thirty-week master's program (that is, in those institutions where courses could be substituted for the thesis project, and the summer was therefore not needed to complete the write-up of the project.) Because of this "more leisurely approach" in the doctoral program, presumably a greater opportunity existed for individual investigation and independent study.

At this same point, 1948, Jones reported on the results of a study to determine practices relative to minors taken in other fields by graduate majors in physical education, and also minors in physical education taken by other graduate students outside of physical education on the Master's level. It was quite evident, according to his findings, that there was no uniformity among the various universities surveyed in the administration of such programs. Only sixty per cent of the institutions reported that a minor in physical education was, in fact, offered, and a large percentage of the individuals electing such a program were officially registered in departments of education. Interestingly enough, only four institutions required that graduate students in physical education take a minor in another field. Education, sociology, and biology were reported most frequently as the minors selected by student in those four universities (Jones, 1948, pp. 18-21).

As the end of the time period for this present paper is approached (1950), the first steps were taken to hold graduate study meetings in physical education. The first of these meetings was called in 1946 by Dr. Seward C. Staley of the University of Illinois "to discuss ways and means of upgrading graduate study in physical education" (Nat. Conf. on Graduate Study, 1950, p. 5). This initial session was followed by similar, but larger, meetings in 1947 and 1948. At the third session, standards were considered for the accreditation of institutions offering graduate work in the field. These included such subdivisions as (1) minimum standards; (2) history and accreditation of parent institution and physical education unit; (3) financial status of university; (4) faculty qualifications; (5) admission requirements; (6) course offerings; (7) scholarship standards; (8) degree requirements; (9) library facilities; and (10) laboratory facilities (Staley, 1948).

As a result of these early meetings, it became apparent that a larger and more nationally representative conference was needed to begin to provide some answers for the many and involved problems facing those professors concerned with graduate work in physical education in the United States. The final result was that the Athletic Institute was asked to finance a meeting of the Organizing Committee in Chicago on January 15-16, 1949 in Chicago. Thus, as this short, narrative history of graduate work in physical education in the United States is brought to a close, a national conference on graduate study was planned for January, 1950, at Pere Marquette State Park in Illinois.

This is probably a fitting place to stop this brief historical statement. It began with Springfield College offering a one-year course superimposed on the regular two-year undergraduate curriculum. It ends with the announcement of a national conference on graduate study in physical education with representation from people at all levels of the profession. At this point, some ninety-one colleges and universities offer graduate programs leading to a variety of degrees and culminating with the doctor of philosophy degree. This development represented a great deal of change and very definite progress. The end was not in sight, but no one can deny but that a reasonably good beginning had taken place.

General Bibliography

Berelson, Bernard. Graduate Education in the United States. New York: McGraw-Hill Book Company, Inc., 1960.

Clarke, H. H. "The Extent of Graduate Study in Physical Education in the United States." Journal of Health and Physical Education, 5, No. 4:33, April, 1934.

_____. "A Survey of the Requirements for the Master's Degree in Physical Education." Master's thesis, Syracuse University, 1935.

Council of Graduate Schools in the United States, The. The Master's Degree. Washington, D. C.: The Council, n.d. (Pamphlet).

Dale, Edgar. "Training of Ph.D.'s." Journal of Higher Education, No. 4, 1:198-202, 1930.

Doggett, Laurence L. Man and a School. New York: Association Press, 1943.

Edwards, Norton. "The Reorganization of Graduate Study in the United States." School and Society, 42:469-472, 1935.

Frederick, P. M. "A Study of the Requirements for the Master's Degree for Women Students Majoring in Physical Education." Ed.D. thesis, Teachers College, Columbia University, 1939.

Good, Carter V. "History of Graduate Instruction in the United States," in Henry, Nelson B. (editor), Graduate Study in Education. Chicago, Illinois: The National Society for the Study of Education, 1951.

Henry, Nelson B. "Summary of Reports from Eighty-five Universities and Colleges," in Henry, Nelson B. (editor), Graduate Study in Education. Chicago, Illinois: The National Society for the Study of Education, 1951.

Hetherington, Clark. "Graduate Work in Physical Education."
   American Physical Education Review, 30, No. 4:207-211,
   April, 1925. (This was continued in the May, 1925 issue, and
   had been presented earlier as an address to the Society of Directors of Physical Education in Colleges in December, 1924).

Hewitt, J. E. "The Doctoral Progaam in Physical Education." Research Quarterly, 17, No. 2:82-95, May, 1946.

_____. "The Graduate Major in Physical Education." Re-
   search Quarterly, 13, No. 2:252-256, May, 1942.

_____. "Requirements for the Master's Degree in Physical
   Education." Journal of Health, Physical Education, and Recreation, 16, No. 7, 369-370, 410-413, September, 1945.

_____. "Status of the Graduate Faculty in Physical Education."
   Research Quarterly, 16, No. 3:231-240, October, 1945.

John, W. C. Graduate Study in Universities and Colleges in the
   United States. Washington, D. C.: Office of Education Bulletin, No. 20, 1935.

Jones, Lloyd W. "The Graduate Minor in Physical Education." Research Quarterly, 19, No. 1:18-21, March, 1948.

Knight, Edgar W. Twenty Centuries of Education. Boston: Ginn and
   Company, 1940.

Lloyd, F. "The Research Specialist." Research Quarterly, 9,
   No. 4:33-37, December, 1938.

Nordly, Carl L. "Teacher Education," in Proceedings of the 50th
   Annual Meeting of the College Physical Education Association,
   1947.

Norris, J. A. and Sweet, D. C. "A Survey to Determine the Status
   of Graduate Work in Physical Education." Research Quarterly,
   8, No. 4:3-10, December, 1937.

Rosenberg, Ralph P. "The First American Doctor of Philosophy Degree." Ventures, 6, No. 1:31-37, Spring, 1966.

Ryan, W. Carson. Studies in Early Graduate Education (Bulletin #39).
   New York: Carnegie Foundation for the Advancement of Teaching, 1939. (For a more up-to-date treatment of graduate education, see Bernard Berelson, Graduate Education in the United
   States. (New York: McGraw-Hill Book Company, 1960).

Shaw, J. H. "A Study of the Requirements for the Master's Degree for Men Students Majoring in Physical Education at Teachers College." Unpublished Ed.D. thesis, Teachers College, Columbia University, 1939.

Snyder, R. A. and Scott, H. A. Professional Preparation in Health Education, Physical Education, and Recreation. New York: McGraw-Hill Book Company, 1954.

Staley, Seward C. "Report on the Pere Marquette Physical Education Graduate Study Conference." Proceedings of the College Physical Education Association, Dec. 27-28, 1948.

Story, R. C. "Earned Degrees Conferred, 1949-50," in Higher Education, U. S. Office of Education, Vol. 7, No. 7:77-78, December, 1950.

Welch, J. Edmund. "The YMCA Graduate School of Nashville." (A paper presented to the Research Section of the National Convention of the American Association for Health, Physical Education, and Recreation, St. Louis, Missouri, March 30, 1968.)

Zeigler, Earle F. "A History of Professional Preparation for Physical Education (1861-1961)," in the AAHPER Professional Preparation in Health Education, Physical Education, and Recreation Education. Washington, D. C.: The Association, 1952, 116-133.

_____. "A History of Professional Preparation for Physcial Education in the United States, 1861-1948." Ph.D. dissertation, Yale University, 1951. (This study has been published in microcard form through Prof. H. H. Clarke, Microcard Publications, University of Oregon, Eugene.)

_____. An unpublished survey of the teacher education programs in physical education in selected state universities in the United States in the late 1940's.

_____ and McCristal, King J. "A History of the Big Ten Body-of-Knowledge Project." Quest, 9, 79-84, December, 1967.

CHAPTER 21

A HISTORY OF THE BIG TEN BODY-OF-KNOWLEDGE
PROJECT IN PHYSICAL EDUCATION

Earle F. Zeigler
The University of Western Ontario, London
and
King J. McCristal
University of Illinois, Urbana

In 1930 the first meeting of the Big Ten (Western Conference) Physical Education Directors was called by Seward C. Staley of the University of Illinois.[1] This male group, now composed of deans, directors, and department heads--three official representatives from each institution--has met annually ever since for the past thirty-six years. The organization has no official status nor constitution, dues, or officers. Responsibility for calling the meetings is simply rotated alphabetically among the universities starting with Illinois and continuing through Indiana, Iowa, Michigan, Michigan State, Minnesota, Northwestern, Ohio State, Purdue, and Wisconsin.

The 1964 Western Conference Physical Education Meetings

The program for the annual meetings is in the hands of a different chairman each year--usually the chief administrative officer of the institution whose turn it is to organize the meetings. Typically the members have gathered to discuss common problems, assess

---

Editor's Note: The last of the four essays treating professional preparation - and the recent disciplinary emphasis - presents briefly the history of the Body-of-Knowledge Project in Physical Education in the Big Ten. This paper was prepared by Professor McCristal and the Editor. The late Arthur Daniels of Indiana University and King McCristal both played highly significant roles in this project developed by the Big Ten Directors of Physical Education group.

---

[1] The junior author of this article (EFZ) suggested this topic to the Quest editor. Because of Professor McCristal's active involvement with this project since its inception, he had hesitated to undertake the article. Editor Eyler and E. F. Zeigler felt that it should be reported, however. The basic material was obtained from Professor McCristal and the statement was written.

trends, and compare techniques for furthering the advancement of physical education in all of its aspects within the Western Conference.

In 1964 the sessions were held on the Urbana campus of the University of Illinois. King J. McCristal, as Dean of the College of Physical Education at the host institution, was, therefore, responsible for the planning of the program and discussed the matter at length with Arthur S. Daniels (now deceased), who was Dean at Indiana University. The "body-of-knowledge" topic had received some attention at the two previous annual meetings, and it was obvious to both of them that the theme held great interest for professors from the Big Ten institutions. The fact that the American Academy of Physical Education had also conducted sessions on this topic presented additional evidence of the importance of this topic to everyone in the profession.

Thus, as a result of a meeting between McCristal and Daniels in Champaign in July of 1964, the program was outlined for the December meeting. The conference theme was "The Body-of-Knowledge in Physical Education," and the following people were selected to make presentations at the second, third, and fourth general sessions, respectively:

1. Arthur Daniels (Indiana) - "Recent Efforts at Definitions and Boundary Lines: Current Status of the Profession."
2. Earle Zeigler (Illinois) - "History of Physical Education and Sport."
3. T. K. Cureton (Illinois) - "Exercise Physiology."
4. John Lawther (Penn State) - "Motor Learning."
5. Coleman Griffith (Illinois) - "Sport and the Culture (or Cultural Anthropology)."
6. Lawrence Rarick (Wisconsin) - "Human Growth and Development."
7. James Counsilman (Indiana) - "Biomechanics of Human Movement."
8. Arthur Daniels (Indiana) - "Implications These Reports Hold for Undergraduate Professional Preparation."

In his opening remarks at the Second General Session, Professor Daniels said,

If we are to gain greater recognition in the academic world, we must follow pathways similar to that traversed by other disciplines. This means a greatly expanded program of scholarly research and development in which the body of knowledge in physical education is defined as nearly as possible in terms of its fundamental nature, and in its relationships with other disciplines.

The Fifth General Session of the 1964 Meetings, chaired by Professor McCristal, was devoted to "Future Planning." The delegates agreed to appoint a steering committee to insure the continuity of program planning. Arthur Daniels, as the administrative head of physical education at Indiana University (the next institution in alphabetical order after Illinois), was named Chairman, and other committee members were Louis Alley (Iowa), Wellman France (Purdue), and King McCristal (Illinois). The plan was that each year a representative from the next host institution would be added to the Steering Committee, and thus would become responsible for the arrangements for the next annual meeting. The following year the pattern was changed. The representative of the host institution was still to be placed on the Steering Committee, but it was felt that the original nucleus of members should continue to function in order to keep the project aligned with the original plan.

In January of 1965 the first of a number of "on-call" meetings was held during the Annual Meetings of the National College Physical Education Association for Men in Minneapolis. A second meeting was held in July in Chicago at which time the plans for the 1965 meetings in Iowa City were completed. Dr. Stanley Salwak, Director of the Committee on Institutional Cooperation,[2] was invited to attend this meeting. When the development was explained to him, he agreed to provide a seeding grant of fifteen hundred dollars so that the developmental plans for the Body-of-Knowledge Project might be continued.

The 1965 Western Conference Physical Education Meetings

In 1965 the Western Conference Physical Education meetings at Iowa City, chaired by Louis Alley, followed a similar format but with certain changes in regard to the subject matters or sub-areas under consideration. Initially Arthur Daniels (Indiana) presented a "Progress Report on Developing a Blueprint for an Academic Discipline in Physical Education." Then King McCristal (Illinois) spoke to the subject "On Becoming an Academic Discipline." He explained that many established academic disciplines had rather modest origins, and he pointed out that,

> . . . it wasn't easy for the 'old guard' to achieve the coveted positions they now hold in the academic community. The road to unquestioned status as a discipline is far from being all down hill with a tail wind. The present interest of Physical Education in disciplinary

[2] The Committee on Institutional Cooperation was formed in 1958 to encourage voluntary cooperation within a variety of programs in a federation of midwestern universities composed of Big Ten institutions and the University of Chicago.

status closely parallels the historical controversy which accompanied admission of other areas to the charmed circle of academic disciplines.

After these two presentations which oriented the members present to the task at hand, five papers were presented which explained the status of the "body-of-knowledge" in additional sub-areas:

1. Louis Alley (Iowa) - "Biomechanics."
2. Bruno Balke (Wisconsin) - "Exercise Physiology."
3. Leon Smith (Iowa) - "Psychology and Motor Learning."
4. Earle Zeigler (Illinois) - "Philosophical Research in Physical Education and Sport."
5. Arthur Daniels (Indiana) - "Sport and the Culture."

Upon the conclusion of presentation, Stanley Salwak, Director of the Committee on Institutional Cooperation, spoke on the topic "The C.I.C. and Developmental Plans for Physical Education."

Papers and both formal and informal discussions at both the 1964 and 1965 meetings tended to substantiate the belief that there is a body of knowledge--and a potential body-of-knowledge--that may well comprise the academic discipline of physical education, sport, human movement, kinesiology, human motor performance, or what have you? Portions of this body-of-knowledge are in related disciplines, and portions of it sre unquestionably, uniquely, "physical education" in character. We are not completely certain what is pure and what is applied.

Delegates at Urbana in 1964 and Iowa City in 1965 agreed to retain the "body-of-knowledge" format for future meetings. No time limit was specified, and it was presumed that such a declaration meant a period of at least five years to insure continuity. In fact, there is no reason why a portion of the time allotment at future annual meetings cannot be allotted to a continuation of the project indefinitely.

Following the untimely death of Arthur Daniels in July of 1966, the Steering Committee decided that the C.I.C. seed grant funds should be transferred to the University of Illinois. King McCristal, then the senior member of the committee, was to administer them as the project developed. The 1966 meetings were planned in late August during a two-day meeting in Chicago. The University of Michigan, through Paul Hunsicker, was the host institution, but the actual meetings were held through the cooperation of Sheldon Fordham at the Chicago Circle Campus of the University of Illinois. At the August meeting of the Committee, it was decided to organize the academic content--at least initially--into six specific areas of specialization as follows: (1) Exercise Physiology; (2) Biomechanics; (3) Motor Learning and Sports Psychology; (4) Sociology of Sport

Education; (5) History, Philosophy, and Comparative Physical Education and Sport; and (5) Administrative Theory. There has been considerable debate as to what these areas are--or should be. For example, it can well be argued that Administrative Theory as a topic is not basic to the discipline--if it is indeed a discipline and whatever it may be named. Conversely, it can be stated that the managing of organizations within the field is becoming so complex that pure and applied research in this developing social science may be warranted.

The 1966 Western Conference Physical Education Meetings

At the August 1966 meeting it was decided to bring together work groups of two or three Big Ten faculty members in each of the six areas of specialization designated. Instructions were prepared and distributed to the chairmen and members of each of these groups and each group was asked to be responsible for the presentation of a paper by one member, the leading of a discussion by a second member, and the third member would be expected to serve as recorder. More specifically, each group was to undertake the following specific assignments:

1. Identify the related disciplines in its work area.
2. List in topical form the primary concepts in each related discipline (those that comprise what might be regarded as the body-of-knowledge for physical education in this area).
3. Supplement the primary concepts from the related disciplines with any additional primary concepts that seem unique to physical education.
4. State the prerequisites to the study of these concepts.

Thus, from a long-term standpoint, the intention was that any such concepts would be integrated where deemed necessary and desirable into all levels of our curricula (basic instruction, undergraduate professional, and graduate programs). During October and November of 1966 the work groups met in Chicago and elsewhere at their convenience and distributed the work load in what seemed to be the best manner in relation to the specific sub-area concerned. For example, inasmuch as Professor Zeigler had presented earlier papers (in. 1964 and 1965) on history and philosophy, respectively, it was decided that Professors Bruce Bennett (Ohio State), Harold VanderZwaag (Illinois - now Massachusetts), and William Johnson (Illinois) would present aspects of history, philosophy, and comparative physical education in that order.

At the December annual meeting the first presentation was a progress report on the C.I.C. project by King McCristal (Illinois). The committee reports were then presented, and the presentation of each paper by the respective chairman elicited animated discussion. The titles of the topics presented and the names of those who made presentations, chaired the ensuing discussion periods, and served as recorders are as follows:

1. Sociology of Sport and Physical Education
   (G. Kenyon, Chairman - Wisconsin; G. Lüschen - Illinois;
   H. Webb - Michigan State)
2. Administrative Theory
   (K. McCristal, Chairman - Illinois; R. Donnelly -
   Minnesota; W. Helms - Michigan)
3. History, Philosophy, and Comparative Physical Education
   and Sport
   (E. Zeigler, Chairman - Illinois; B. Bennett - Ohio State;
   H. VanderZwaag - Illinois; W. Johnson - Illinois)
4. Exercise Physiology
   (J. Faulkner, Chairman - Michigan; F. Nagle - Wisconsin;
   G. Tipton - Iowa)
5. Biomechanics
   (L. Alley, Chairman - Iowa; J. Cooper - Indiana;
   J. Counsilman - Indiana)
6. Motor Learning and Sports Psychology
   (L. Smith, Chairman - Iowa; R. Herron - Illinois;
   A. Slater-Hammel - Indiana)

Present Status and Future Plans

Immediately following the Big Ten meetings in Chicago, the augmented Steering Committee--now consisting of the chairmen of all six areas--met to lay plans for further development of the Project. On January 28, 1967, the Committee assembled in Iowa City, and after a two-day series of sessions a "symposium project" was outlined. The purpose of this proposed project was to develop and clarify still further the basic philosophic and scientific concepts of Physical Education. Still further, the Committee felt that it would be desirable to enrich the quality of the present Physical Education graduate programs in C.I.C. institutions (except Chicago) by providing selected faculty members with opportunities to exchange ideas about our developing discipline with recognized authorites from related disciplines. This continuing project seemed to be absolutely necessary, because the three-year effort had carried the Steering Committee's original plans about as far as they could progress--without active involvement in the process of attempting to discover avenues and approaches that might lead to the creation of new knowledge.

All members of the Steering Committee now believe that the success of the Symposium Project will hinge on the ability of the group to secure a sizeable monetary grant from a foundation or public agency. King McCristal, as Chairman of the Steering Committee, has explored many sources of grants. The Dean of the College of

Education at Illinois feels that the greatest opportunity for support of the proposal seems to rest with the United States Office of Education. Changes are now being made in the research proposal to conform to the usual specifications of the U. S. Office of Education. A telephone conference was held on September 27, 1967 to discuss the final format of the research proposal. This material has now been forwarded to Dr. Salwak at the office of the Committee on Institutional Cooperation in Lafayette, Indiana. He may be willing to co-sponsor the project with the members of the Steering Committee, and an approach will be made shortly to prospective sponsoring agencies.

The Steering Committee does not believe that the Western Conference Physical Education Directors are "trespassing upon territory" that ought to be the particular province of the American Association for Health, Physical Education, and Recreation or the American Academy of Physical Education. There would be some overlapping of personnel; this is granted. The Big Ten Body-of-Knowledge Project, which has been underway for more than three years already, would seem to be a "natural" by virtue of the long-standing association the institutions concerned, as well as the means for mutual cooperation that is provided through the structure of the Committee on Institutional Cooperation. It is quite possible that multiple approaches to this matter of a body-of-knowledge and a possible discipline are desirable. Obviously, too great proliferation of such ventures would dissipate readily available "strengths." At present a certain amount of consensus has been reached--a level of agreement which might not be possible at the national level--and the present Symposium Project is distinctly an effort to provide high level opportunities for our graduate professors to improve their understandings and sharpen their research techniques in relation to the developing body of knowledge.

CHAPTER 22

A HISTORY OF PHYSICAL EDUCATION IN THE Y.M.C.A.

Elmer L. Johnson
California State College at Fullerton

Introduction

Physical education in the Y.M.C.A. when viewed in its proper historical perspective is marked as the most influential variant in the history of the American Y.M.C.A. Probably no other feature so largely affected its public image, expectancy, and its relationship with youth. The Y.M.C.A., because of its interest and concern for the health needs of young men, has contributed greatly to the development of the ideals, principles, and practices which undergird modern programs in health education and physical education.

PART I: THE FORMATIVE YEARS
1844-1880

The Early Beginnings

The Y.M.C.A., a voluntary non-sectarian lay organization, was founded in 1844 in London, where a group of young men banded together for a prayer meeting under the direction of its founder, George Williams, a young wholesale drygoods clerk. The Y.M.C.A. movement soon spread into Canada and the United States. The first North American Y.M.C.A.'s were established in the late fall of 1851 at Montreal, Canada, and at Boston - the latter through the efforts of Thomas V. Sullivan, a retired sea captain.

Editor's Note: Although the Editor must admit to some bias, primarily because of an association over a forty-two year period with the Y.M.C.A. in a variety of capacities, this essay by Dr. Johnson can be fully justified on the basis of the contribution that the Y.M.C.A. has made to the field of physical education. This article was solicited from Professor Johnson, and we are grateful for his willingness to abstract this report from a much longer study on the topic. It represents a fine contribution that catches - in the opinion of the Editor - the true spirit of the Y.M.C.A. movement.

First Gymnasiums

It was not until after 1869 that serious attempts to do physical work* were successful when "well appointed" gymnasiums were completed at Washington, D. C., San Francisco, and New York, respectively.

First Gymnasium Superintendent

William E. Wood, an Englishman born in December 1819, was called upon to superintend the new equipment and program in the New York Association Building on Twenty-third Street, where he remained for two decades (1869-1889). Wood bears the distinction of being the first Y.M.C.A. Physical Director, and was one of the first to speak out against heavyweight lifting and fancy acrobatics which characterized the post-Civil War period. His Manual of Physical Exercises published in 1867 was one of the first American textbooks of its kind. The first crude attempts of the Y.M.C.A. to do physical work were aptly described as the "circus period" since the program involved weight lifting, acrobatics, and trapeze work.

First Christian Physical Director

The first Y.M.C.A. Physical Director (gymnasium superintendent) to leave his permanent mark upon Y.M.C.A. physical education methods was Robert J. Roberts (1849-1920), who was employed in 1875 by The Boston Association to direct the old Tremont Gymnasium located at Tremont and Eliot Street which had been under Association control since 1872 (Whiteside, 1951, pp. 38-39). Roberts had been a member of the Tremont Gymnasium since 1864 when it was operated as a private gymnasium. Roberts' program consisted mainly of light exercises and dumbbell drills readily adapted to the needs of the unskilled masses. Roberts was a Christian man, an expert gymnast, and a staunch advocate for obedience to all the laws of health. His reference to gymnasiums as "Halls of Health" reflected this purpose (Watchman, 1883, p. 258).

Roberts' Contributions

Roberts' early efforts at introducing dumbbell drills in the old Tremont Gymnasium in the Boston Association were heartily ridiculed by some of its members. Yet Roberts was a stimulating and determined teacher, and his ideas eventually took hold as "Y" memberships increased from 49 to 680 during his first four years of service. (Association Men, 1897, p. 1349).

---

* A term synonymous with physical education.

Roberts is credited with developing the first indoor track which he had installed in the new building in 1883 upon its completion at the corner of Berkeley and Boylston Street. He also devised the first "ring shower bath" and introduced the indoor shot, jumping weights, medicine ball, barbell, and vaulting bar into Y.M.C.A. physical work methods (American Gymnasia, 1905, p. 248).

Roberts was active in leadership recruitment by training some twenty-five to thirty young men for careers in physical education during a three-year period (1885-1887). Among this group were such men as Dr. William G. Anderson, founder of the American Association for the Advancement of Physical Education (AAHPER) and Dr. Henry Kallenberg of the George Williams College faculty. Roberts' enthusiastic and common sense approach undergirded a distinctive style of physical education which was exceedingly simple, adapted well to large classes, and could be taught by men of average ability.

PART II: ESTABLISHING FOUNDATIONAL PRINCIPLES
1880-1900

Looking Ahead

The last two decades of the nineteenth century was a remarkable era for the American Y.M.C.A. This was a period of innovations and creativity. New games were invented and hundreds of gymnasiums and swimming pools were built. A philosophy and methodology of physical education emerged and new principles were established. Practically all phases of Y.M.C.A. physical education which had lasting value originated during this period. Though foreign systems left their mark on Y.M.C.A. physical education methods, a distinctive Y.M.C.A. program had emerged by 1900 through a process of accretion, synthesis, and modification.

The Need for Trained Leadership

The most urgent problem which faced the American Y.M.C.A. during this period was the need for trained leadership. The Yearbook of 1880 reported that fifty-one gymnasiums were in operation. By 1887 this number had increased to 168; yet, only fifty-three physical directors were actively engaged in Y.M.C.A. physical work. This need was in part met by the founding of the secretarial training schools at Springfield where a program of instruction started in the summer of 1887 under Luther Halsey Gulick (1865-1918) with twenty-four instructors enrolled, comprising almost one-half of all men engaged in Association Work.

Gulick's Impact on Y.M.C.A. Methods

The coming of Luther Halsey Gulick (1865-1918) marked a change in Y.M.C.A. philosophy and methodology. He was an aggressive, volatile, and restless man filled with ideas well in advance of his time – the avant garde of his profession. Born of missionary parents in Honolulu on December 4, 1865, he attended Oberlin College and Dr. Dudley Sargent's School of Physical Training at Cambridge, Massachusetts, after which time he served briefly as the gymnasium superintendent at Jackson, Michigan (spring and summer of 1886).

Springfield College Founded

In the fall of 1886, Gulick left Jackson to study medicine at New York University. In 1887 he was employed, along with Robert J. Roberts, as a regular faculty member at the Springfield Training School, which opened a two-year training period in September of that year.

Gulick envisioned a department that would embrace the theoretical and the practical. Gulick chose to teach the former which included courses in philosophy of exercise, psychology of play, physical diagnosis, and hygiene. Roberts, on the other hand, was by inclination and training best suited to teach the practical floor work consisting of gymnastics, marching, and dumbbell drills.

Gulick received a medical degree in 1889. Meanwhile, he had assumed additional part-time duties of International Secretary for Physical Work with the International Committee (1887-1903). He served in this dual capacity up until 1900 when he resigned to become the principal of the Pratt Institute High School in Brooklyn.

Gulick's Contribution to "Y" Work

Gulick, during his brief but active career at Springfield, was instrumental in developing a system of measurement for the Y.M.C.A. He standardized physical work methods, and was one of the outstanding spokesmen for clean sports and a rational program of competitive athletics consistent with Y.M.C.A. principles and ideals. Gulick was a prolific writer. Some of his published works include the Gulick Hygiene Series consisting of no less than eight books on such topics as measurement, philosophy, physiology of exercise, and the medical inspection of schools.

Gulick served as secretary for the American Association for the Advancement of Physical Education 1892-'93 and as its president from 1903-'06. He was a member of the committee which organized the Boy Scouts of America. In 1906 he was elected the first president of the Playground Association of America; and, in 1911, working in conjunction with his wife, Charlotte, he was active in the founding of the Campfire Girls. Gulick's life was characterized by unusual vision, daring, and imagination. He remains as one of the most unique figures to leave his mark upon American Physical Education in the twentieth century.

George Williams College Founded

In the summer of 1890, The Young Men's Christian Association's Training School (now George Williams College) was established at Chicago. A two-year secretarial training course was initiated in September in rooms provided by the Central Y. M. C. A. on Madison Street with Dr. E. L. Hayford as "principal of the physical department." George W. Ehler served as principal from 1892-1897; John W. Shaw from 1897-1900; and Dr. Winfield S. Hall, 1900-1903. Henry F. Kallenberg, M.D., who had been with the Training School since 1896 serving as assistant principal, took over the duties as director of physical training in 1903, where he remained until 1917 when Martin I. Foss succeeded him.

First Swimming Pools

The first Y. M. C. A. swimming pool (forty-five feet by fourteen feet and five feet deep) was part of the magnificent new building completed at the Brooklyn Central Association in 1885 (Watchman, 1885, pp. 44-45).

The Montreal Association completed one of the most elaborate and ornate pools of this era some five years later in 1891. By 1895 seventeen Y. M. C. A. pools were reported in operation (Brown, I. E., 1895).

The first pools, known as "swimming baths," were crude in design and lacked the sophisticated systems of heating, filtration, and germicidal control - typical of modern swimming pools.

Origin of Leaders' Corps

During this period the first official Leaders' Corps Training Program was initiated by Dr. J. Gardner Smith of The Young Men's Institute Branch of the New York Association. He assembled a group of volunteers in the winter of 1885-'86, each of whom he instructed in methods of teaching various groups in his heavy apparatus class (Smith, 1899, p. 305). Smith's pioneer program marked the real beginning of lay leadership involvement, and this became one of the major approaches in physical education methodology throughout the history of the movement. The first Canadian Leaders' Corps was organized in 1892 at the Montreal Association under the direction of

William H. Ball, a young graduate fresh from the new training school at Springfield (Quebec Report, 1894, p. 19).

Early Health Education Programs

The Y.M.C.A. also embarked on a program of health education mainly through its involvement and the support of the White Cross Movement, which had as its prime target the elimination of sensuality in all its forms. Its major efforts were directed toward the removal of brothels and curbing the sale of obscene literature at city news-stands. A Handbook for Young Men written by Dr. Charles Scudder for the White Cross Committee (1892) served as a guide on sex and morality for the youth of that period and was widely distributed in Y.M.C.A. circles. Luther Gulick, writing for Association Outlook, began a series in the fall of 1897 which attempted to enlighten young men by interpreting sex in relation to anthropology, psychology, sociology, and medicine. First aid classes, then known as "surgical lectures," were taught by volunteer physicians. Dr. Frank Seerley, who later became the Dean of the International Training School at Springfield, gave talks in behalf of the Society for Sanitary and Moral Prophylaxis to various Y.M.C.A. and church groups in the New York area. With these approaches the Y.M.C.A. achieved its Christian emphasis through a broader service to the whole man. Such service eventually became the base for a more extensive program of health education after 1900 when boys' work was pursued with greater enthusiasm.

The Invention of Basketball

Probably no other event brought more recognition to the Y.M.C.A. than the invention of basketball. The first game was played informally at the Springfield Training School in early December 1891 under the direction of Dr. James Naismith, the game's originator, who had upon the suggestion of Gulick been urged to devise a game which would be interesting, easy to learn, and adapted to indoor playing conditions under artificial lights.

The first game was played with a soccer ball with nine men on a side. During the following month (January, 1892) when the first formal game was played, teams had been reduced to seven players. Peach baskets attached to the overhead running track served as basketball goals.

The game was accepted throughout the country very quickly. The Providence, Rhode Island Association was the first to adopt it outside of Springfield. (Association Seminar, 1904, p. 52). Geneva College of Beaver Falls, Pennsylvania and the University of Iowa were were the first colleges to play basketball in 1892. Duncan Patton, who who played on Naismith's original team, brought the game to India in

1902; Emil Thies introduced it to France in 1895; and C. Herek carried it to Persia in 1901.

The Origin of Volleyball

Volleyball followed a similar pattern of development. This game was invented in 1895 by William G. Morgan, the physical director at the Holyoke, Massachusetts' Y.M.C.A., and was envisioned as a game "not so rough as basketball and yet one in which the same degree of activity was required" (Physical Education, 1896, p. 50). During the first two decades following its invention, the game spread rapidly into other countries. Franklin H. Brown introduced the game to Japan; Elwood S. Brown to the Philippines; Robert E. Thompson and Jesse T. Hopkins to South America; J. Howard Crocker (a Canadian) to China; and Dr. John H. Gray to India.

The Red Triangle

The Y.M.C.A. red triangle, an emblem symbolizing the threefold nature of man - mind, body, and spirit - originated during this period. Luther Gulick's first proposal for its adoption was voted down at the International Convention in Philadelphia in 1889, and was rejected again at a similar gathering at Kansas City some two years later (Dorgan, 1934, p. 47). In fact, the triangle did not receive the official approval of the International Committee; the delegates at the International Convention at Springfield in 1895 authorized the preparation of an official Y.M.C.A. badge in that form (Young Men's Era, 1895, p. 330).

Formation of the Athletic League

The formation of the Athletic League of the Young Men's Christian Associations of North America was also approved at the International Convention at Springfield in 1895. Competitive athletics, at this stage in history, was in a state of flux and turmoil. The Y.M.C.A. had since 1888 given some thought to the establishment of a central controlling athletic body. Playing rules were not well defined nor clearly interpreted; officiating was lax, and eligibility requirements were not always enforced. Professionalism in sports was a concern of Luther Gulick who pushed for the formation of The League which became a reality in 1895. Thereafter, the League formulated rules, arranged for championship meets, arbitrated protests, and upheld the amateur code.

A League Handbook was authorized in April 1896. In June, that same year, By-Laws were adopted, and on October 3, 1896 the Articles of Affiliation with the A.A.U. were signed. The following January (1897) the A.A.U. adopted the Y.M.C.A. basketball rules as the Official Rules, and League memberships had now increased to 151 associations (Barnes, 1907, pp. 5-13).

The Y.M.C.A. Pentathlon

One of the events, which had earlier been developed by Luther Gulick and Dr. James H. McCurdy of the Twenty-third Street Branch of the New York Association and promoted by the Athletic League, was the Y.M.C.A.'s "Pentathlon Test" consisting of the one-hundred yard dash, twelve-pound hammer throw, the running high jump, the pole vault, and the one-mile run (Young Men's Era, 1890, p. 378). An indoor version of the Pentathlon was approved in 1893, making it possible to promote athletics on a year-round basis (Association Seminar, 1904, p. 62).

As this report came to a close, a philosophical orientation of physical education methods into the work of the Movement as a whole had been achieved. The physical directorship was now coming of age. The tools for doing Movement work had now been created, and the word was "forward" in all areas of defined service.

PART III: STANDARDIZATION AND EXPANSION
1900-1920

The Y.M.C.A. at the turn of the century stood amidst a setting still influenced by the events of the Spanish-American War. The United States was rapidly moving into a position of world power. In the Y.M.C.A. the prevailing mood was expansion into all phases of program including foreign work.

Physical Directors' Society Formed

The formation of the Physical Directors' Society was actualized at a conference at Lakewood, New York, in 1903. George W. Ehler of the Chicago Central Association was elected its first president (Physical Training, 1903, p. 275). Physical Training, with Luther Gulick as editor, came out with its first issue in November, 1901. These two developments had the effect of standardizing physical education in the Movement. In 1913 the Society initiated a plan of "Titles and Qualifications," which essentially attempted to upgrade the qualifications of men in the physical directorship (Physical Training, 1913, p. 246).

In 1903, Gulick resigned from his position at Pratt Institute in Brooklyn to become Director of Physical Training in the New York Public Schools; meanwhile, Dr. George J. Fisher assumed the position of International Physical Work Secretary as replacement for Gulick. Fisher's main thrust was in extension work where Y.M.C.A.

expertise was brought into community playgrounds, public schools, churches, and rural areas. Industrial work, consisting mainly of health talks, became a defined field of service after 1910. Sunday school athletic leagues, under lay direction, promoted competition in baseball, basketball, gymnastics, and track and field. The most famous was The Brooklyn Sunday School League which was formed in 1904 with a charter membership of sixty (Association Men, 1910, p. 224).

Various schemes of athletic promotion continued in vogue. The Cook County Amateur Athletic Federation was formed in 1908 in the Chicago area under the direction of Dr. Henry F. Kallenberg of the Association College (now George Williams).

Learn-to-Swim Campaigns

In September 1910, William H. Ball, the former physical director of the Detroit Association, was employed by the International Committee to promote a "Learn-to-Swim Campaign" for the Y.M.C.A. Ball enlisted the services of George Corsan, "The Billy Sunday of Y.M.C.A. Swimming," to launch the program. Using land drills, Ayvad water wings, and his "mass assembly line" method of teaching, Corsan was immediately successful. Thereafter, the number of persons taught to swim in the Y.M.C.A. rose steadily from 15,778 in 1909 to 63,438 in 1920.

Growth of Summer Schools

The most prolific period in the development of Association summer schools occurred between 1903 and 1915 when no less than seven were established. The Lake Geneva Wisconsin Summer School had already been operating since 1890. The Silver Bay, New York, School opened in 1903. The Southern School at Blue Ridge, North Carolina got underway in 1912.

Foreign Work

During this period great advances were made in extending physical education into foreign fields. Max J. Exner arrived in Shanghai, China, in November 1908 to establish a training course for physical directors. He was followed by Dr. J. Howard Crocker (Canada) (1911); Dr. Charles H. McCloy (1913); Dr. David K. Brace (1916); and Dr. John H. Gray (1920), who had previously served in India (1908-20). Franklin H. Brown arrived in Japan in 1913, where he introduced volleyball and Y.M.C.A. physical education methods. Elwood S. Brown served in the Philippines for a period of eight years (1910-1918). Foreign work in South America was initiated by Maurice C. Salassa in Rio De Janeiro in 1911 and Harry J. Sims, who succeeded Salassa in 1912. In 1912 Jesse T. Hopkins began his work at

Montevideo where a decade later (1922) the Instituto Tecnico (Technical Institute) was established through the joint efforts of Hopkins, James S. Summers, an Australian, and Phillip Conrad, the general secretary.

Service Overseas World War I

During World War I, Y.M.C.A. physical directors worked under the National War Work Council to provide an extensive program of recreation and athletics for men in the armed services. During the first year (1917-18), 1300 recreational centers were established with George Meylan, a Y.M.C.A. physical director, in charge. Among the most notable who saw wartime overseas service were Elmer Berry, Fred B. Messing, Dr. George J. Fisher, Elwood S. Brown, Dr. Luther Gulick, Amos Alonzo Stagg, Dr. James Naismith, and Dr. James H. McCurdy. The organizational genius of Y.M.C.A. physical directors reached its finest hour during the Inter-Allied Games which were held in Paris in the summer of 1919 under the direction of Elwood S. Brown, a Y.M.C.A. physical director.

PART IV: SEARCHING FOR NEW BASES

Following World War I the Y.M.C.A. was faced with the task of regrouping and assimilating its widely dispersed professional staff which included literally hundreds of "Y" secretaries and physical directors deployed at home and abroad. Such men as George E. Goss, Fred B. Messing, and Louis C. Schroeder, among others, remained on in the European theater to assist in post-war reconstruction.

National Physical Education Committee Formed

The Y.M.C.A.'s international outreach continued as new relationships were established with international sports federations and groups. Coed activities began to appear, and a program of internal reorganization made the "Y" more democratic. The Athletic League was dissolved in 1925, and its functions were placed in the hands of the National Physical Education Committee chaired by John H. Brooks (1872-1945), a layman. A nationalist volleyball championship, the first of its kind, was held in April, 1922 at the Brooklyn Central Y.M.C.A. This was the period when the "industrial physical director," best typified by the work of Dr. Robert A. Allen, who reactivated the Cook County Amateur Athletic Federation after the war, came into prominence (1919-1925).

Impact of the New Psychology

The impact of the new psychology, which tended to break down the rigid approaches in physical education methodology caused some internal conflicts between the old guard and the new breed of younger physical directors. Concomitant learnings and carry-over values were emphasized equally with the acquisition of primary sport skills. Physical education was now charged with providing beyond the "physical welfare" principle.

Y.M.C.A. Aquatic Program Upgraded

Summer school attendance declined during the decade following World War I. By the summer of 1929 enrollments at Lake Geneva, Wisconsin, had dwindled to fifty-one students. The first World Y.M.C.A. Physical Education Consultation was held in 1936 at the Berlin Olympics. Despite the Depression, Y.M.C.A. aquatics flourished. Dr. John Brown, Jr., National Secretary, reported that in 1932 "more than a million swimmers" had been taught in the Y.M.C.A. (Brown, J., Jr., 1932, pp. 16-17). In 1938 The New Y.M.C.A. Aquatic Program, Volume I, was published under the leadership of Dr. Thomas K. Cureton, then a faculty member at Springfield College, who has for a period of over three decades made the greatest contribution to Y.M.C.A. aquatics in the history of the Movement.

Effects of the Depression

The period of the mid-1930's were trying years for the Y. Y.M.C.A. Budgetary curtailments led to reductions in staffs and program. Many Y.M.C.A.'s opened their doors to the unemployed and provided free memberships. Softball, "a child of Depression," became popular in Y.M.C.A. industrial leagues as more free tax-supported recreational facilities built by W.P.A. funds competed for the attention of the youth. In 1938 The New Physical Education in the Young Men's Christian Association, the results of a three-year study under the chairmanship of John R. McCurdy, was published. Throughout this period, national leadership was dominated by Dr. John Brown, Jr., who served as the National Secretary for Physical Education (1919-1939).

PART V: THE MODERN ERA
1940-1969

The 1930's had been one of the gloomiest decades in modern history and was characterized by unemployment, federal relief programs, and bitter labor struggles. The Depression years had been a sobering experience. As economic conditions improved, Americans shrugged off their "Depression Blues" and looked forward with a new sense of confidence despite a sense of uneasiness caused by Hitler's invasion of Poland.

Wartime Physical Fitness Program

The Y.M.C.A.'s of the United States and Canada were quickly drawn into their traditional historic roles by becoming active participants in the United Service Organization (USO). Y.M.C.A.'s opened their facilities to men in uniforms, which included the free use of swimming pools, shower rooms, and gymnasiums for informal workouts. A National Wartime Physical Fitness Program which emphasized pre-conditioning of young men and a broadened program of health and physical education was implemented in the summer of 1942.

Harold Friermood, Senior Secretary, Arrives

In May 1943, Dr. Harold T. Friermood of the Dayton Association was obtained to fill the position of Senior Secretary for Physical Education, a post left vacant since 1939. Through his leadership the Wartime Program was intensified, and volunteers were trained to replace Y.M.C.A. staffs (forty per cent of whom had moved into war-related services).

Wartime Adaptations

A "back to body" movement which emphasized calisthenics, obstacle course running, combatives, and survival swimming tactics was popular. Sports and recreational programs in some Y.M.C.A.'s were scheduled on a "round the clock" basis in order to accommodate the "swing shift." Wartime Y.M.C.A. Fitness and Warfare Aquatic Conferences were held at Lake Geneva during the summers of 1943 and 1944. In 1946 the International Volleyball Federation was formed in Paris with the U.S.A. as one of the charter members.

A Period of Self-Examination

The 1950's was a period of self-examination for the American Y.M.C.A. Leaders. Assembled at the North American Centennial Conference at Cleveland in the summer of 1951, they eulogized the past and raised some questions as to the future role and direction of Y.M.C.A. physical education. In 1955 the National Board authorized a nation-wide study "to examine and make a critical evaluation of the Y.M.C.A.'s program in health education, physical education, sports and recreation. . ." The results of this survey came out in A New Look at Y.M.C.A. Physical Education authored by Robert E. Hamlin, the study director, in 1959.

The 1950's was truly a dynamic decade for the Y.M.C.A. Women and girls were welcomed into a fellowship that had been traditionally male. Memberships increased from 13.5 per cent in 1950 to 22.7 per cent in 1960. Dramatic changes occurred particularly in the age group for girls under twelve, which increased 265.3 per cent,

while boys in the same age group increased only 88.2 per cent.
Aquatic activities and gymnasium classes appeared to be most popular for women and girls. The family was seen as a prime unit for
character education. The annual report of 1959 indicated 220,005
members enrolled in 430 associations under family membership plans.
The number of Leaders' clubs increased 43.2 per cent, and a marked
advance in the quality and number of training institutes for volunteers
in physical education was evident.

The Last Decade

During the 1960's the Y.M.C.A. continued its emphasis upon
aquatics, physical fitness development, and testing for all ages and
both sexes. Skin and scuba diving instruction and certification became a defined field of service. Gymnasiums were redesigned to
accommodate new testing equipment and a dramatic resurgence of
"jogging" programs occurred.

Friermood Retires

This remarkable period of productivity and advances in health
and physical education draws to a close with the retirement of Dr.
Harold T. Friermood after forty-three years of outstanding service
in the Y.M.C.A. This included twenty-fives years as Senior Director for Physical Education for the National Council (U.S.A.).
Friermood, a tireless worker, catalyst, researcher, and prolific
writer that he is, takes his rightful place in the honored company of
Dr. Luther Halsey Gulick, Dr. George J. Fisher, and Dr. John
Brown, Jr., all professional leaders who have faithfully guided the
growth and development of the Y.M.C.A. health education and physical education program for a period of over eighty years. In 1943,
when Friermood assumed the postiion of Senior Director, there were
1,244 Y.M.C.A.'s with 674 of them reporting over twenty-three
million physical education "participation." By 1967 there were 1,718
Y.M.C.A.'s with 1,286 reporting over fifty-two million such activity
units. Friermood's influence was international in scope, and he
possessed rare ability in working with national and international
sports bodies. Among these were the Amateur Athletic Union, The
Olympic Committee, The United States Volleyball Association, The
Council for the National Cooperation in Aquatics, The Athletic Institute, The International Council of Sport and Physical Education, and
The American Association for Health, Physical Education and Recreation. Within the scope and framework of Y.M.C.A. physical education, Friermood had been active in nearly all major publications,
surveys, conferences, and other developments which have occurred
in Y.M.C.A. physical education in the past quarter of a century.
Friermood is one of the outstanding physical educators of the twentieth
century.

General Bibliography

American Gymnasia. May, 1905, p. 248.

Association Men. September 11, 1897, p. 1349.

Association Men. 35:224, February, 1910.

Association Seminar. 13:52, November, 1904.

Barnes, F. B., "History of the Y.M.C.A. Athletic League," in _Spalding's Athletic League Handbook_. New York: American Sports Publishing Company, 1907, pp. 5-13.

Brown, I. E. _Book of Y.M.C.A. Buildings_. Chicago: Published by the _Young Men's Era_, 1895, 122 pp.

Brown, John, Jr., "More Than a Million Swimmers a Year," _Swimming Pool World_, October, 1932, pp. 16-17.

Dorgan, E. J. _Luther Halsey Gulick, 1865-1918_. New York: Bureau of Publications, Columbia Teachers College, 1934, p. 47.

Fisher, G. J. (editor). _Official Volleyball Rules_. New York: American Sports Publiching Company, 1916, 90 pp.

Physical Education. 5:50, July, 1897.

Physical Training. 2:275, March, 1903.

Physical Training. 10:246, June, 1913.

Quebec and Ontario Convention Report, 1894, p. 19.

Smith, J. G., "History of Physical Training in New York City and Vicinity in the Y.M.C.A," _American Physical Education Review_, 4:305, September, 1899.

Watchman. November 15, 1883, p. 258.

Watchman. February 15, 1885, pp. 44-45.

Whiteside, W. B. _The Boston Y.M.C.A. and Community Need: A Century's Evolution, 1852-1951_. New York: Association Press, 1951, pp. 38-39.

Young Men's Era. June 12, 1890, p. 378.

Young Men's Era. May 16, 1895, p. 330.

CHAPTER 23

AMERICAN OBJECTIVES OF PHYSICAL EDUCATION FROM 1900 THROUGH 1957

Ford Hess
Humboldt State College, Arcata, California

Introduction

This discussion of the objectives of American physical education from 1900 through 1967 has been taken from the author's unpublished doctoral dissertation (New York University, 1959) in which the objectives were assessed in light of the major events in American history covering the same fifty-eight year period. The account which follows is written in summary style and includes but a few of the key references. Accordingly, a brief explanation is in order to make a meaningful transition from a four hundred and thirty-two page dissertation to a twenty-page review of same.

First, the objectives are not delineated but rather are discussed in context with the major events in the history of the United States during the fifty-eight year period. Secondly, a recapitulation of two questions, the answers to which formed the basis for the assessment of the objectives to meet the demands of the times as reflected in the significant events of the period, is presented at this point. The questions follow: (1) Were those objectives demonstrated to have been shaped by significant events in American history adequate to meet the demands of the times? (2) Were those objectives demonstrated to have been shaped by forces other than significant events in American history adequate to meet the demands of the times?

Editor's Note: It can be argued that philosophy results as a flowering process after a considerable amount of data collection, historical analysis, and historical interpretation have taken place. Or it could be - and the Editor leans heavily to this view - that philosophy is a "root-like" activity which assists us to analyze people's words and actions more effectively. Whatever the reader's position on this issue is, and it may be that both approaches have merit, the remaining three chapters, prior to the Epilogue, are historical-philosophical in nature. They treat (and trace) the questions that arise perennially in regard to values and objectives and how they influence physical education and sport. The first essay in Chapter 23 was requested from Professor Hess. It represents an abstracted presentation of an earlier investigation by him that traces the objectives of American physical education from 1900 through 1957 in a helpful and perceptive manner.

    The final paragraphs of this introduction present an overview of
the significant events in the 1900-1957 period. Included in this over-
view are brief references to recurring objectives of physical education.

    The 1900-1919 period witnessed such social and economic
changes as a marked increase in population, economic expansion,
and the beginnings of the labor problems. The United States became
actively engaged in World War I. Prior to 1900 there was a marked
European influence on American physical education, particularly
Swedish and German. Some of this influence may be traced to the
fact that the crest of both Swedish and German immigration occurred
within the middle and late 1800's. (Saveth, 1954, pp. 480-481).

    The 1920-1928 period has been described by some historians
as "The Decade of Prosperity." Such a title attests to the role of
economic advances as outstanding among the events of the decade.
As might be expected, the period saw increased offerings in physical
education, including new facilities and similar material gains.

    In direct contrast to the preceding period, 1929 through 1938
was marked by the title "The Great Depression." Toward the close
of the period World War II was fast becoming a reality. Domestic
events included the varied types of New Deal social and economic
policies. Physical education was among the many education functions
to feel the effects of the economic crisis that marked the period.
This was manifested by the curtailed budgets which had the effect of
reducing the various offerings but had come to be recognized as an
important part of physical education.

    World War II dominated the 1939-1945 period. The years be-
tween the outbreak of the war in Europe and America's entry in 1941,
along with the actual war years, witnessed an increased emphasis
upon the physical fitness objective of physical education.

    Post-war problems of every description occupied the early
years of the 1946-1957 period. This has probably been true following
every major war in which the United States participated. The last
few years, however, were marked by the Korean Conflict, the "Cold
War," industrial expansion, the development of atomic energy for
peace time use, and medical advances too new to evaluate their full
impact historically. During this period there was a return to the
peace time objectives of physical education, and a de-emphasis upon
the physical fitness objective that had characterized the war period.
A recent trend has been noted, motivated almost exclusively by the
Kraus-Hirschland Muscular Fitness Report (Kraus and Hirschland,
December, 1953, p. 17), toward what is being termed "total fitness"
as an objective of physical education.

Objectives and Events, 1900-1919

Throughout the greater part of the 1900-1919 period, the hygienic or health objective, along with the remedial, recreative, and educative, were acknowledged by leading physical educators as the prevailing purposes of American physical education. However, the health objective was considered singularly important, as attested to by Sargent in his statement that "it would be difficult to conceive how any system could be truly educative, recreative, or remedial which was not also hygienic." (Sargent, 1906, p. 69).

These objectives were shaped largely by two forces, namely, the prevailing medical knowledge of the period, and the purposes of certain European systems of physical education (especially Swedish and German).

During this 1900-1919 period America's leading physical educators acknowledged the population shift from farm to city that was underway, and directed the profession's attention to the effect which the crowded living conditions associated with city living imposed upon the health of children and youth in particular.

In addition to acknowledging the demographic forces of the period, these early leaders performed a similar service to their profession in respect to the demands of the times as reflected in advances in technology. They called attention to what they believed such tehcnological advances were doing to the health of America's labor force in limiting the opportunity for daily large muscle activity which the hand labor of the past had provided.

While American physical education leaders were stressing the need for objectives to direct the practices of the profession to meet the demands of the times reflected in changing demographic conditions and the advances in technology, American medicine was on its way to establishing unprecedented records in human conservation through the application of the modern principle of preventive medicine. Although medicine was credited with such advances that saw a striking decline in infant mortality and an increase in the adult life span, other disciplines made noteworthy contribution to these significant successes in human conservation. Chemistry and bacteriology made direct contributions through the immunization programs getting underway during this period. Public health, through federal and stage legislation, and health education, as a struggling service of public health, made contributions to human conservation.

While it is outside the scope of this review to account for the several disciplines contributing to the successes in human health and welfare, it is pertinent to disclose at this point what America's leading physical educators had to say about the contribution of their profession. For example, did they believe physical education could contribute to human conservation by emphasizing the singular importance of the health or hygienic objective? The answer to this query is a qualified "yes" insofar as the professional leadership of the late nineteenth century and perhaps as late as the first fifteen years of the twentieth century are concerned. (Sargent, 1906, p. 69).

Objectives and Events, 1920-1928

In the preceding period, the five objectives were identified singularly as well as in relation to one another, with the health or hygienic (objective) emerging as the underlying purpose of physical education. By the close of the first decade of the twentieth century, a trend in the objectives was well underway that was destined to change the status noted above. This trend was a shift in emphasis away from the objectives of the 1900-1919 period, based as they were upon the prevailing medical knowledge and Swedish and German systems, toward a type of educational objective that was based upon a body of knowledge gained from researches in the fields of psychology and the social sciences. This trend was readily identified by the end of the first world war, and was destined to become the prevailing force in directing the practices of American physical education during the 1920-1928 period.

Paralleling the shift in emphasis in the physical education objectives, marked changes were also taking place in the philosophy of the purpose of American education, changes that were based largely on the same advances in psychology and the broad social developments responsible for the shift in emphasis in the physical education objectives. These changes, related to the same forces and developing separately throughout the first two decades of the twentieth century, were formally linked when state laws forced physical education into the public school curriculum in the years immediately following the close of World War I. Physical educators hailed this formal union with education. Educators, however, were faced with a problem similar to that which they were up against when vocational education was forced into the public school curriculum; namely, they had little choice but to accept what the public demanded. As Snedden stated in 1920, "No educator of modern outlook dare now confess himself indifferent either to physical or vocational education." (Snedden, p. 240). The problem was somewhat eased for the educators when they were convinced that physical education leaders were, with a few exceptions, pledged to the same socially centered objectives as they, the educators were. Accordingly, this new union of education and physical education tended to reinforce the educational and social type objective that earlier physical education leaders had promoted on the basis of its relationship to advances in psychology.

Toward the end of the 1920-1928 period, this identity an
nition of the physical education objectives in context with broad
cational and social movements had progressed to a point where s
of America's leading physical educators even denied that health wa
the underlying purpose of physical education. (Williams, 1930,
p. 60). The school administrators who were responsible for providing a place for physical education in the public school curriculums
during this period encountered some difficulty in understanding just
what, if not health, physical education did contribute to education that
other school subjects did not. The schoolmen of this period, whether
right or wrong, had been led to believe that physical education was
brought into the public school curriculums because of its unique contribution to health--that American citizens, in their respective states,
had enacted legislation to force physical education into the curriculums in the sincere belief that the physical unfitness of American
youth, as disclosed in the draft findings of World War I, would not
plague the nation again should war break out.

War did not break out in the next ten years. With the exception
of the Panic of 1921 the nation enjoyed the most prosperous years of
its history between 1920 and 1928. The population shift from farm to
city continued at an accelerated pace during this period that saw
America's expanding economy geared to advances in technology. The
eight-hour day became a reality. Most everyone had more leisure
than they had ever enjoyed before.

In spite of the unprecedented prosperity and leisure of the
period, there were certain undesirable factors connected with the
population shift from farm to city and industrial expansion that was
geared to the advances in technology. These were noted in the foregoing discussion of the 1900-1919 period, namely, the effect which
crowded living in cities had upon the health of children and youth, and
the decreasing opportunities for large muscle activity in man's daily
labor which the new technology brought with it. However, these undesirable factors were somewhat offset by the positive contribution to
health made by the expanding services of the public health movement
that achieved prominence during this 1920-1928 period. Similarly,
the advances in preventive medicine continued to establish new records in human conservation.

However, leading physical educators of this 1920-1928 period
believed the profession had a more significant role to play in America's development than its unique contribution to the nation's health
status through large muscle activity. These leaders pointed out that
physical education was an integral part of education; that it had the
same objectives as education, and, in stressing the educational and
social objectives, such as worthy use of leisure time, physical education made a direct contribution to one of the cardinal objectives of all
education. In a similar manner these same leaders emphasized that

shared with other school subjects the responsi-
ity to contribute to the solution of the complex so-
iated with the period. This shared function with
 to help solve the complex social problems of
ed as the most emphasized objective of physical
The unique contribution which physical education made to
, through large muscle activity, emerged as a secondary objective during this period of prosperity. Even the highly emphasized objective, worthy use of leisure, was conceived in reference to social
and educational values. The idea of engaging in physical activity during one's leisure for health was even ridiculed by one leading American physical educator at the close of this period. (Williams, 1930,
p. 370).

Objectives and Events, 1929-1938

This new status of the physical education objectives, with its
emphasis clearly on an educational objective based on social and
psychological principles, had less than a decade in which to become
established before the impact of the Depression made itself felt upon
all phases of education.

Between 1929 and 1938 the nation faced up to the most severe
economic depression in its history. Every phase of the American
economy was put to the test of determining the bare essentials. Educators had to justify every subject in a curriculum that a decade of
prosperity had broadened considerably over any previous public school
school offerings. Essentials as opposed to fads and frills were to remain in the public school curriculums. The professional leadership
in physical education was quick to point out, in the face of searching
inquiries by taxpaying groups of citizens to weed out the "fads and
frills," that for the past decade physical education's objectives had
been squarely aligned with those of education. These leaders believed, and were generally assured, that their programs would be maintained as essential phases of the total education of America's children
and youth during this period of scarce money and widespread unemployment. The central theme of most of the writings published by
physical educators during this period of economic stress emphasized
that physical education shared with other school subjects the responsibility and opportunity for helping to solve the social problems connected with the times. According to this line of reasoning, physical education could not be viewed as a fad or a frill since it allegedly contributed to the same general objectives as all other school subjects. The
success of this reasoning was attested to in part by the fact that less
than five per cent of the schools in cities of 10,000 population and over
eliminated physical education from their school curriculums during
the depression years. Further evidence of the success of this reasoning is to be found in the fact that the American Association for Health,

Physical Education and Recreation became a department within the National Education Association in 1938.

Although the Depression was the most significant occurrence of the 1929-1938 period, it was not the only event to which Americans gave thought during this period. Developments abroad, not directly "under the lens" of the Depression, moved along with little opposition during the period when most Americans were understandably concerned with the Depression. Japan invaded Manchuria in 1931; Mussolini undertook his conquest of Ethiopia in 1935; and Hitler remilitarized the Rhineland in 1936. These developments we now know were singularly important links in a series of international events that took place during their period, and which eventually led to the outbreak of World War II in Europe in 1939.

While America's leading physical educators during this 1929-1938 period were vigorously justifying physical education as an integral part of general education on the grounds that its objectives were socially centered and educationally conceived, Japan and Italy were intensifying their physical education programs and justifying them on the grounds that they contributed to health and physical efficiency. As such they were indispensable to their political preservation. Similarly, England, France, and some of the smaller nations, whose borders were adjacent to Germany in particular, intensified their physical education programs during this period, and justified them on the grounds that they contributed to health and physical efficiency and, as such, were indispensable to their defense. Except for a few American physical educators who called the profession's attention to these developments abroad and identified them as threats to America's own security, it was the general consensus of the professional membership of this 1929-1938 period that the objectives of physical education should reflect and, in turn, emphasize the prevailing socially centered educational philosophy rather than the nation's health needs. It is noted here that Steinhaus, Rogers, and McCloy took some exception to these socially centered objectives of this period. They based their objections upon what they termed an undue emphasis on these objectives, and not upon the importance of the objectives per se. (Steinhaus, 1937, p. 345; Rogers, 137, p. 140; McCloy, 1938, p. 298).

Objectives and Events, 1939-1945

The first test of the adequacy of the socio-educational objectives to provide American physical education with the direction demanded by the times was foreshadowed by the outbreak of World War II in Europe in September of 1939. Within a brief span of two years (i.e., brief by comparison with the more than thirty years over which the change in status noted above took place), the professional leadership acknowledged, albeit reluctantly, that the health and physical objectives had been needlessly neglected and now demand, in a time of national peril, that physical education programs be immediately directed toward developing physical fitness, an objective deemed necessary in light of America's leadership position in world affairs. (Mitchell, 1940, p. 412; Cassidy, 1940, p. 409; Oberteuffer, 1941, p. 569; Hellebrandt, 1942, p. 119).

The enactment of the Selective Training and Service Act of 1940 by Congress marked the first time in the history of the United States that the nation was forced to adopt conscription in peace time. Among other things, this first peace-time draft law found America's political leaders officially linking the nation's security with the health status of its youth in particular. Physical education, historically associated with military preparation because of its unique contribution to health, was forced to shift its prevailing emphasis from practices that were directed by educational and social objectives towards solving complex social problems, to practices that were directed by health and physical objectives toward upgrading the physical fitness of all American youth. This emphasis continued throughout the war years and enabled physical education to make a specific contribution to the nation's civilian as well as military efforts to win the war.

Objectives and Events, 1946-1957

The years immediately following the close of World War II found America facing a wide variety of problems, ranging from the individual readjustment of the returning serviceman to the overall problem of reconverting a wartime industrial economy to a civilian industry economy. In the midst of these strictly national problems, the United Nations was struggling not only with its own organizational problems, but also with the more delicate problem of how best to function as a world agency to maintain world peace through the promotion of international understanding. Educational institutions throughout the United States responded to the ideals encompassed in the charter of the United United Nations. (AAHPER, 1951, ix).

In June of 1950 President Truman ordered American armed forces into the Korean conflict. This was six months after he had declared a state of national emergency to exist. In March of 1951 the AAHPER published its Report of the National Conference for the Mobilization of Health, Physical Education, and Recreation (1951, p. 21) in which it was categorically stated that the objectives of physical education for youth were the same in the emergency as they had been in peace time. The broadened educational and social objectives were to prevail. The unique contributions of physical education to health and in turn to national security, at a time when a third world war was imminent, were subservient to the broadened social and educational contributions which physical education now allegedly shared with countless other organizations devoted to the same broad purposes.

Physical education had lost its singular identity. (Oberteuffer, 1951, p. 53).

The war in Korea ended in 1952. By 1954 the profession was beset with still another challenge. (Kraus and Hirschland, 1953, p. 17). Only this time the challenge, instead of coming from war or the threat of war, was based upon America's advances in technology. This "new" challenge was described as automation. Automation, according to reports, limited the opportunity for large muscle activity for all Americans. Although the term automation was new, the challenge it posed to the profession was really an old one that had been expressed at least as early as 1908 in the physical education literature in connection with elevators, motor cars, carriages, and messenger services. The profession rose to meet the challenge of automation by proclaiming that the objective of American physical education was total fitness and, as such, encompassed social, health, and physical, emotional, and mental objectives. This new emphasis on total fitness was especially directed toward America's youth, and the term "youth fitness" became synonymous with total fitness as an objective of physical education. Total fitness (or youth fitness) succeeded in merging the two classes of objectives that had vied with each other, through their respective proponents, to provide the directing force for physical education's practices throughout the fifty-eight year period. While this merger was a compromise, it did apparently bring the two classes of objectives (i.e.,) the educational and social and the health and physical into a more stable relationship. Its ultimate success, however, will have to be judged by the demands of the times it served.

Conclusion

The author invites the reader to critically examine the current happenings at home and abroad and juxtapose such happenings with the prevailing purposes of physical education. The reader may then observe the relationship, if any, and, further, inquire if this relationship is serving as a positive force in shaping the objectives and in motivating the practitioners and consumers of physical education programs.

General Bibliography

Cassidy, Rosalind. "New Directions in Physical Education," _Journal of Health and Physical Education_. (September, 1940), p. 409.

Ekirch, Arthur A. _The Civilian and the Military_. New York: Oxford University Press, 1956, p. 280.

First Yearbook of the American Association for Health, Physical
Education, and Recreation, <u>Developing Democratic Human
Relations</u>. Washington, D. C., 1951, ix.

Hellebrandt, F. A., "The Contributions of Physical Education to Physical Fitness," <u>Journal of Health and Physical Education</u>, XIII,
(February, 1942), p. 119.

Kraus, Hans and Hirschland, Ruth P., "Muscular Fitness and
Health," <u>Journal of Health, Physical Education, and Recre-
ation</u>, XXIV, (December, 1953), p. 17.

McCloy, Charles Harold., "Physical Fitness and Citizenship,"
<u>Journal of Health and Physical Education</u>, IX, (May, 1938),
p. 298.

Mitchell, Elmer D., "A Challenge to Duty," <u>Journal of Health and
Physical Education</u>, XI, (September, 1940), p. 412.

Oberteuffer, Delbert, "College Physical Education for Peace and
Defense," <u>Journal of Health, Physical Education, and Recre-
ation</u>, XXII, (January, 1951), p. 53.

_____, "A Decalogue of Principles," <u>Journal of
Health and Physical Education</u>, XVIII, (January, 1947), p. 4.

_____, "May We View with Alarm," <u>Journal of
Health and Physical Education</u>, XII, (December, 1941), p. 569.

Rogers, Frederick Rand, "The Ultimate Imperative--Conservation
of Physical Fitness," <u>Journal of Health and Physical Education</u>,
VIII, (March, 1937), p. 140.

Rogers, James E., "Physical Education in Education," <u>Journal of
Health and Physical Education</u>, XIX, (December, 1948), p. 650.

Sargent, Dudley A. <u>Physical Education</u>. Boston: Ginn, 1906, p. 69.

Saveth, Edward N. <u>Understanding the American Past</u>. Boston:
Little, Brown and Company, 1954, p. 480.

Snedden, David, "Problems of Physical Education," <u>American Physical Education Review</u>, XXV, (June, 1920), p. 240.

Steinhaus, Arthur, "The Science of Educating the Body," <u>Journal of
Health and Physical Education</u>, VIII, (June, 1937), p. 345.

Williams, Jesse Feiring, "A Fundamental Point of View," <u>Journal
of Health and Physical Education</u>, I, (January, 1930), p. 11.

CHAPTER 24

THE IDEAS AND INFLUENCE OF McCLOY, NASH, AND WILLIAMS

Ellen W. Gerber
formerly Associate Professor
School of Physical Education, University of Massachusetts

In order to provide a proper setting for me to discuss the ideas and influence of Charles Harold McCloy, Jay Bryan Nash, and Jesse Feiring Williams, it seems appropriate to explain the philosophical framework from which my research was conceived and executed and the specific impetus to be involved in this particular study. Individualism, and the attendant historical view exemplified by Carlyle's dictum that "the history of the world is the biography of great men," went out of favor soon after the start of the twentieth century. Historians of this century have primarily espoused the social theory of history, accepting the view that great social forces have structured the events of man. Their view of man as a somewhat helpless figure, haplessly moved by the surrounding currents, is, I think, beginning to change. Man is flexing his muscles and finding ways to choose his own directions despite the social tides. As someone whose philosophical position is grounded in existentialism, I, of course, am imbued with a deep-seated belief in the power of the individual to frame his own directions on the basis of intellectual commitments. I accept the fact that major social forces such as the industrial revolution, the depression, and most recently the Vietnam War, have been almost overpowering factors in directing the course of human events. However, I also accept as an equally powerful force the influence of such major thinkers as John Maynard Keynes, John Dewey, and even John F. Kennedy. (Perhaps there is some transcendental magic in the name John!) Thus I cling to the perhaps refashionable theory that the study of the intellectual ideas, as promulgated by various influential figures, is a valid--and necessary--approach to the study of historical events.

Editor's Note: The second essay among this final group, Chapter 24, was prepared through the courtesy of Professor Gerber. Dr. Gerber explains the particular interpretations given to physical education's role in education by three great leaders of the twentieth century: Charles H. McCloy, Jay B. Nash, and Jesse F. Williams. There seems to be little doubt, even though true perspective is difficult at this point, but that the greatness of their contributions will stand up over the years.

It is an interesting feature of this particular study that in the biographical data of the men whose ideas were examined, evidence was provided to support my approach to history. By coincidence, all three men were born in the exact same year, 1886, in the same state, Ohio. Each received his baccalaureate degree from an Ohio institution, Nash and Williams from Oberlin and McCloy from Marietta College. All attended Columbia University, though only Williams and McCloy earned their terminal degrees there; Nash attended New York University, in the same city, for his degree. Although Williams earned an M.D., both McCloy and Nash were among the early physical educators to earn the Ph.D.

Their life parallels do not end there. As teachers, each served a single institution for more than twenty years, two of which were located in New York City. Within these universities each held primary responsibility for framing and developing that institution's first doctoral program in physical education. Each was an influential teacher and doctoral advisor, responsible for the work of numerous students who helped to extend his professional influence.

All three were prolific writers. McCloy's published works included twenty books, fourteen of which were in Chinese. He wrote twenty-seven articles for the Research Quarterly, twenty-four for the Journal of Health and Physical Education, as well as articles for other periodicals. Nash wrote nine books, edited a five-volume series, wrote seventeen articles for JOHPER and some for other publications. Williams' output can only be characterized as enormous. Between 1916 and 1964 forty-one different titles were published under his name, eight alone and thirty-three in co-authorship. Seven books were eventually published in multiple editions. He contributed eleven articles to the Journal, and two for the Quarterly, and wrote even more voluminously for other publications such as the Teachers College Record and School and Society.

Furthermore, they were all dedicated to the idea of professional service in various organizations. Each held the highest elective office, the presidency, of the American Association for Health, Physical Education, and Recreation, as well as in the relevant district association. Each was, in turn, awarded every major honor established by the profession.

And lastly, as I shall show in more detail later in this paper. Nash, McCloy, and Williams were in general agreement about the nature of man, holding fundamental assumptions congruent to the ideas of contemporary thinkers.

Given the fact that they functioned in the same point in time and their life circumstances were so remarkly similar, one might, if one were committed only to a social explanation of history, expect to find a uniformity of viewpoint about professional matters. But, in fact, this was not the case. These men were three individuals who operated within the same professional framework, shared similar modus operandi, experienced the same social forces, but responded differently to them. Each framed, as I intend to illustrate, a professional philosophy which was permeated by a strong centra theme.* They made different interpretations of their common beliefs, held a different hierarchy of values, placed emphases on different ideas, developed different concepts of programs, and, in sum, constructed different philosophies of physical education. Curiously enough, American physical educators did not choose among their contending viewpoints. As I intend to demonstrate in the final section of this paper, all three radically different viewpoints were accepted without any attempt to reconcile the contradictions.

My interest in these three men stemmed originally from an absorption with physical education in the period between 1930 and 1960. Atara Sherman, a doctoral candidate at the University of Southern California, had done a dissertation entitled "Theoretical Foundations of Physical Education in the United States: 1886-1930." In her study she examined the writings of professional leaders in an attempt to trace the significant concepts held by physical educators up to 1930, a time she characterized as the beginning of a new era in physical education. Other historians of the profession, including Mabel Lee and Bruce Bennett concurred with that judgment. The date 1960 also had significance in that it marked the seventy-fifth anniversary of the American Association for Health, Physical Education, and Recreation, an occasion used by the profession to make a general survey and summary of its accomplishments and directions. Furthermore, 1960 will, I believe, ultimately emerge as the end of an era in American thinking. The long period of intellectual stability and unity which this country had known since the depression, came, I think, to an end about this time, symbolically marked by the election of John F. Kennedy and his claim that "the torch has been passed to a new generation."

A cursory examination of the physical education literature of this this period revealed three main themes. These were clearly parallellleled by the writings of McCloy, Nash, and Williams which, by dint of of sheer quantity, dominated the literature. Furthermore, it was apparent that the profession itself had recognized the particular influence of these three men. They had been elected to office, given the highest awards, and were singled out in the few brief historical analyses of the period in which they worked.

---

* I have taken McCloy's viewpoints to be those expressed from approximately the late thirties. Prior to that time his writings did not exhibit a clarified or specific approach and some of his earlier statements were later contradicted.

Therefore, it seemed appropriate for me to study physical education for the period 1930-1960, to approach it via a study of the intellectual commitments held by physical educators, and to select for analysis the ideas of Charles Harold McCloy, Jay Bryan Nash, and Jesse Feiring Williams on the assumption that they were the most influential leaders of the period.

I

A philosophy of physical education, i. e. , a systematic, coherent set of consciously held theories about physical education, is contingent upon relevant and underlying conceptions about the nature and needs of man. McCloy, Williams, and Nash, in tune with their times, frequently cited the works of G. Stanley Hall, John Mason Tyler, and Edward L. Thorndike to amplify and support their beliefs about the physiology and psychology of man. Superficially their ideas were similar, but an analysis of the manner in which they interpreted their theories, as evidenced by applications to physical education, shows clear divergencies.

The Organic Unity of Man

Each man firmly believed in the organic unity of man; Cartesian dualism was emphatically rejected. Nevertheless, McCloy stated that "our organism is more body than mind, " (McCloy, 1936, p. 302, italics deleted) and, therefore, urged physical education to "re-think the whole problem of our more purely physical objectives, and... emphasize them more. " (McCloy, 1936, p. 303) Williams viewed "man as a unity of mind and body, with spirit or soul as an essential element of the whole" (Williams, 1922, p. 16), but, in direct contrast to McCloy, warned physical education that "too great a reliance on physiologic principles with resulting neglect of the social, moral, and spiritual elements in life produces the 'crude, vulgar, self-seeking individual' so obnoxious in human relationships and so dangerous to the state and nation. " (Williams, 1922, p. 16) Nash was the only one of the three to refuse to fragmentize the whole man by placing a higher value on one particular aspect. In fact, his attempt to avoid the trap of speaking dualistically, while proclaiming unity, led him to develop special terminology. Noting that "the very words 'physical' and 'mental' confuse thinking, " he stated that "therefore... the word 'organic' will be used in place of the word 'physical' and the words 'intrepretive development' or 'thinking' will be used instead of 'mental. '" (Nash, 1948, pp. 94-95)

The Instinctive Drives of Man

Darwin's theory of evolution was published in 1859. Some seventy years later, in the 1930's, the so-called instinctive drives of man were a subject of much study and speculation. "Ontogeny recapitulates phylogeny," a doctrine specified by Haeckel as early as 1868, and later popularized by G. Stanley Hall, was earnestly subscribed to by physical educators among others.

McCloy, Nash, and Williams all believed that the ancient need to hunt and engage in physical combat had instilled behavioral drives still present in contemporary man. But each used this so-called "fact" in a different way to support his theory about the role of physical activity.

McCloy reasoned that since physical activity was so primary in the human being, physical education should focus upon the physical as its first and fundamental concern. Thus he stated:

> But there is another type of expression that is found in physical competition; the desire for mastery, for self-assertion, the desire to cooperate loyally with others of one's own group, to express one's ego in leading others, in adventuring, in sheer physical striving, in feeling physically adequate, and in the joy-out perfection of movement. One sees this in the carefree dancing of the self-forgetful girl, in the joy of achievement of making a perfect smash in tennis, the making of a tackle in football, or the execution of a graceful dive....These physical cravings are deeply rooted in human nature and are more closely connected with those age-old urges which made for survival than are those of the more cultivated aesthetics. (McCloy, 1933, pp. 5-6)

Furthermore he saw hunting and fighting activities as a form of competition and, therefore, believed that competition per se was a natural human activity. This broad view of the ancient activities enabled him to state that sports were a natural outgrowth of man's biological inheritance--they were satisfying in themselves because they related to the inherited emotional drivers of the individual. In a rather poetic passage he established the cultural basis of sport competition and connected it to genetic inheritance:

> In spite of the tendency of the modern cultural dillettante to belittle the physical side of life and to talk vaguely of the values of packing his intellectual attic full of "cultural" secondhands-- artistic and otherwise, only a hundredth of which he will ever use except as something to brag about--we are primarily the descendants of a race of higher apes and prehistoric men whose functions were 90 per cent physical. Even our instincts, our fundamental interests, and our passions originate from these prehuman strata....Hence it seems to me that the first fundamental of physical education is that we should not get too far away from the physical itself. (McCloy, 1940, p. 96)

Williams, in recognizing these same sorts of drives, thought the activities they engendered inappropriate to modern man. Unlike McCloy, who thought that because of inherited tendencies modern man could find competitive physical activities satisfying, Williams urged that society's duty was to provide equivalent forms of activity which could better serve its own purpose. Thus Williams said that "necessity of providing an equivalent has been recognized....and physical education exists as a great constructive social force to guarantee to youth the fulfillment of these early adaptations." (Williams, 1942, p. 211) The expressions of underlying predispositions may, "under proper guidance...be made to serve high causes and noble ends." (Williams, 1927, p. 77)

Nash was closer to McCloy in accepting the urge to activity as a meaningful part of man's inheritance. "With this biological heredity as a base," he said, "we can mold these age-old activities into a social inheritance which can be passed on from generation to generation. As a means in this transportation 'the game's the thing.'" (Nash, 1928, p. 48) He also used this construct to help build the theory of "felt needs" (which will be discussed later in this paper), noting that:

> The basic drives of survival and belonging are so much a part of the subject matter of physical education that the natural motivation to participate in these activities is high....The right activity for the right age groups is enough incentive to participate. (Nash, 1951, p. 205)

Ideal of the Healthy Man

Consistent with their separate interpretations of a unified man impelled by certain primordial drives, they each delineated an ideal of the healthy man. As can be expected, McCloy's use of the term health was primarily in physical terms. He recalled that "from the earliest days of the profession, the physical educator has been interested in the health of the individual under his care," (McCloy, 1934, p. 51) and in urging his contemporaries to do likewise, detailed methods for appraising the physical health of the child.

Nash's view of the healthy man was consistent with his concept of the integrated man. He sought "a well adjusted, wholesome, self-directed individual meeting his responsibilities in the society in which he lives." (Nash, 1948, p. 225) Because of his broader view of health health, he believed that:

> Physical education has no monopoly on contributions to the health of the human organism...The very name, Department of Health and Physical Education carries some unfortunate connotations. One of them is that health and physical education are

- 324 -

synonymous or, even worse, that physical educati[ ]
ments should take over the responsibility for the h[ ]
school-age child. (Nash, 1948, p. 225)

Through a medical doctor and the author of numerous health
books, Williams' view was closer to Nash's, with greater and more
primary emphasis on the use to which good health was put, rather
than on its achievement. In fact, he defined health as "that quality of
life that enables the individual to live most and to serve best."
(Williams, 1951, p. 6) He thought that "the emphasis upon health in
education carries with it a fine idealism, a disciplining of self, a
training of one's powers, a regimen of preparation for worthwhile
causes." (Williams, 1933, p. 5)

Definition of Physical Education

In light of Williams', McCloy's and Nash's interpretations of
the nature of man, it is interesting to observe how their definitions of
physical education reflect their differing emphases. McCloy harks
back to the inherited tendencies, which, you will remember, he
characterized as deriving from functions which were 90 per cent physical. To him "physical education is an educational activity characterized by the doing of things of interest to individuals, most of which
are based upon the individual's original tendencies and inherited types
of emotions." (McCloy, 1940, p. 120) Nash, unable to separate physical and mental man, could not fragment man's daily life either. He
asked:

> How can a line be drawn between class time and the time
> spent in activity at noon, after school, or even during the long
> summer vacation? These are all times for physical education
> ....Physical education, as defined by time, is all the experi-
> ences children have in neuromuscular activities which are di-
> rected to the desired outcome. (Nash, 1951, p. 223)

Williams, in his definition, as usual placed primary emphasis on the
educational outcomes of the activity, rather than the activity itself.
To him

> ...physical education is the sum of man's physical activi-
> ties selected as to kind, and conducted as to outcomes. Since
> physical education is to be considered as a means of education
> through physical activities rather than an education of the phy-
> sical--how absurd the latter--the phrases selected as to kind
> and conducted as to outcomes assume considerable importance.
> (Williams, 1951, p. 10)

In accordance with a definite and deliberate commitment to physical education as an educational endeavor with aims congruent to those of general education, each agreed in general terms that the broad, overall objectives of physical education related to organic power, mastery of skills, recreation or leisure-time participation, personality development, and democratic concepts. However, there were decided differences in the significance which they placed on each of these objectives. Each established a definite hierarchy of values which reflected his interpretation of the nature of man and the emphasis in his definition of physical education. The varying degrees of concern held for each objective can easily be demonstrated.

At the top of McCloy's hierarchy were the objectives relating to organic power. He pointed out that "we (man) can do something for our organs...that the clothier cannot do. We can improve them to a certain degree after having received them from our parental germ plasm." (McCloy, 1937, p. 459) Therefore, he believed that the fundamental purpose of physical education was to assist the individual to develop his body, a position he stated in clear, certain terms:

> We need better-developed muscular systems that the current literature in our profession is demanding....Therefore, I should like to propose that as a profession we re-think the whole problem of our more purely physical objectives, and that we emphasize them more. I yield to no one in our profession in my belief in the educational importance of physical education when adequately organized and taught....But the basis of all physical education--developmental, educational, corrective, or any other aspect of our field--is the adequate training and development of the body itself. (McCloy, 1936, p. 303)

Furthermore, he regarded the development of the physical self to be an end in itself, a worthy objective for an individual or a profession because of its very naturalness to mankind. He said:

> Most men want to be well developed. Down in their hearts they would like to be strong and healthy. Those who do not react to such a developmental program either have it badly presented to them or feel that they would not succeed. (McCloy, 1934, p. 53)

McCloy thought that strenuous muscular exercise had energy-recharging effects which helped to alleviate the stresses of modern life, that it had an important effect on body tissues, including their rejuvenation and prolongation of physiological youth, and that increased strength and flexibility could and should be developed.

- 326 -

Close to physical development on McCloy's hierarchy, was the development of skilled performance in physical activity. As with the objective of organic power, McCloy basically conceived of the mastery of skills as being satisfying in and for itself, stating that a skilled performance was cultural in the motor field in the same sense that any learning which occurs in other disciplines may be cultural. "I believe," he said, "that any worthwhile activity executed skillfully enough to give the doer exquisite sensory pleasure is cultural." (McCloy, 1938, p. 480, italics deleted) But he reminded his readers that "skills must be mastered to the point where in these and subsequent situations the pupil may perform with such joy and satisfaction as to get from the activity its maximum educational effect." (McCloy, 1933, p. 4) He also acknowledged that mastery of skills, besides being an end in itself, was useful for future participation in sport (McCloy, 1927, p. 46), a position very close to Nash's. But McCloy did not stress the recreational objective as being of great importance, and, in fact, tended to see recreation as a means for exercising. He thought that "while education and recreation are important, organic health is notably more so." (McCloy, 1940, p. 293) In his earlier writing he underscored the possibilities inherent in physical education for developing character traits, provided that the leadership worked toward that end (McCloy), and he developed a conception of the interrelationship of the individual and the group in a democratic society (McCloy, 1940, pp. 122-24); but in later years he rarely mentioned either facet. Articles entitled "How About Some Muscle?" and "The Forgotten Objectives of Physical Education" made clear that his chief concern was man's physical development.

No man could take a more opposite position to McCloy than Jesse Feiring Williams. His interest in the organic objectives of physical education resided in his belief that health was a duty of good citizenship. In fact, he objected to the concept of physical fitness both in principle, because of its dualistic connotations, and as an objective of physical education. In the fourth edition of The Principles he swiped at McCloy in a section entitled "The Fallacy of the Back-to-the-Body Aim" and in a later edition he asserted that

> Physical education is brought forward as a great corrective, palliative, remedial agency, removing waste products, strengthening foot arches and abdominal muscles, enlarging chest capacity, and increasing strength of grip....These values, however, should come as by-products of motor activity designed to serve more vital needs. (Williams, 1964, p. 190)

The idea of the development of the physical being as a worthy end in itself was particularly repugnant to Williams. In a strong comment he asked the question:

What then, is to be said of the efforts of certain persons to develop large and bulging muscles or to pursue certain odd skills that have no useful function in life? The satisfactions derived from such exercises serve only whimsical values such as exhibitionism; at times they are outlets for maladjusted personalities. For example, the yoga devotee may finally acquire unilateral control over the rectus abdominus, but the evidence is lacking that this has in any way deepened spirituality. (Williams, 1964, pp. 186-87)

Williams supported the recreational objective of physical education by advocating the development of skills for future leisure-time pursuits, and for utilitarian use in the activities of daily living. (Williams, 1942, pp. 234-40) But, as he saw it, the primary objective of physical education related to character development. He believed that physical education activities were experiences through which children could learn the standards of conduct suitable to their democratic society. This is the basis of his famous statement that "physical education is education through the physical." (Williams) He declared that "physical education should identify at every opportunity the close relationship between the moral and the physical" (Williams, 1964, p. 151); that "physical education should gain increasing competence and expertness in guiding personality development" (Williams, 1964, p. 154); and that "physical education should help to establish the American Way of Life as a worthy ideal for all peoples." (Williams, 1964, p. 129) In the latter regard he stated that

Education must...show him (the citizen) how to apply in his whole life those moral principles of democracy that underlie the concept of government by free men....Some of these concepts will arise and must be taught in physical education. Four of these, equality of opportunity, personal worth, individual responsibility, and self-achievement, relate directly to physical education. (Williams, 1964, p. 57)

In contrast to Williams' position that the goal of physical education was to teach the individual to serve society. Nash's constant theme was that concern should be evidenced for the whole individual's own well-being and happiness. Thus in his hierarchy of objectives, the concept that assumes governing importance was the development of the integrated being, meaning "the bringing together of all the traits and powers of an individual into one personality which responds as a whole to lofty group ideals...." (Nash, 1948, p. 265) Beliefs that "integration and normality are achieved through meaningful recreational activity" (Nash, 1953, p. 200) and that "games...offer great opportunities for emotional development" (Nash, 1948, p. 191) led him to advocate that physical educators could help to secure this state-of-being by preparing the child for a life of active participation in recreational activity.

Nash proceeded from the point of view that man's life could roughly be divided into two categories, play and work, or time devoted to earning a living and time devoted to leisure. He maintained that it was within the province of the school to train children for life, and, therefore, that "education has a responsibility to prepare youth for the enjoyment of leisure." (Nash, 1953, p. 204)

Sports skills were an important element of physical education because "skills in youth are basic to the recreation patterns of later life." (Nash, 1953, p. 187) "The development of a rhythmic pattern of movement of grace and symmetry and the ability to judge objects in the environment--both physical and human--are the responsibility of physical education." (Nash, 1948, p. 184)

Nash did not stress the objective of organic power as being or primary importance, but he did include it as one of the few responsibilities of education to be achieved primarily in physical education. (Nash, 1948, p. 245) He argued for a concept of fitness that extended to all aspects of the person, rather than merely considering the physical. (Nash, 1942, p. 380) He agreed with Williams' position that the physical education program was a natural laboratory for democracy and specifically called attention to the fact that this also included play and recreation. He noted that "the practice of choice in play and recreation [should] become the great rehearsal for choice in a democracy." (Nash, 1953, p. 47)

It would be fair to say that all the previously cited objectives of physical education were embraced by Nash, inasmuch as they contributed to the ultimate well-being and happiness of the individual. He did not attempt to isolate any single one as having greatest importance to either the individual or the goals of education. However, he believed that preparation for the good use of leisure-time was the essential necessary to achieve well-being.

View of History

All three men reached back into history to find justification for their points of view. Their differing interpretations of history highlight their conceptions of physical education and serve as an adequate summary of their positions. It also serves to remind us of the many-sided truths of history and that our biases influence our interpretations.

McCloy said:

From about 500 B.C. until about A.D. 1900 the objectives
were reasonably simple, and the practice, while differing in
detail, was fairly uniform as to the goals sought. These goals
had to do largely with the development of strength, of an adequate physical development, and of appropriate skills. The
literature of physical education of those days sang the praises
of the physically competent, and individuals sought to emulate
the harmonious bodily proportions of the classic Greek statues.
(McCloy, 1937, p. 458)

Nash said:

Training, or "discipline of living," has been acknowledged throughout the ages as being beneficial. The Greeks
depended upon a system of gymnastics for the development of
strength, agility, rhythm of movement and beauty. Greek leaders considered training as a definite basis for the worthy use of
leisure. With training, leisure-time could be utilized for not
only physical but also mental betterment. (Nash, 1948, p. 94)

Williams said:

The achievements of the ancient Greeks in physical education lead us to inquire into the thinking of the Greek philosophers about this and related problems of physical education....
It is apparent that in Plato's conception of education, body and
mind are not simple opposites. For both Plato and Aristotle
the sum of physical education was not the education of the physical alone but rather the development of personality qualities
through the physical. (Williams, 1964, p. 147)

II

As McCloy, Nash and Williams attempted to translate their
views of the objectives of physical education into guidelines for educational programs, each dealt with the concepts of curriculum, method,
and evaluation in his own way and with varying emphasis. There
were several broad points of agreement among them, including the
belief that activities should be selected with regard to objectives; that
teaching methods should effectively bring about the fulfillment of
these objectives; and that measurement was a tool that potentially
could be used in evaluating the progress of the individual student.

Concepts of Program

McCloy revealed his deep-rooted bias toward a curriculum in which the development of organic power was foremost in the following comment about program organization:

> I have seen too many times project types of organizations which, while possibly educational, certainly wasted a lot of valuable time. I have repeatedly timed many pupils in gymnasium programs who in the twenty-five or thirty minutes of so-called activity, engaged in no more than three or four minutes of vigorous muscular work. Biologically, at least, this is certainly a minor. Until we obtain more time that we have now, I think we should compromise with "education" and obtain a little more for biology. (McCloy, 1937, p. 512)

Also illuminating, is his comment that "personally, I believe that a P.F.I. (physical-fitness index) of 120 would, at the present stage of physical education and recreation in our country, be of more value to more people than would be the skill to shoot eighteen holes of golf in 72." (McCloy, 1937, p. 512)

Nevertheless, he urged the development of a curriculum based upon a carefully graded program of skills suitable for each age group. He believed that "fundamental activities [such as running and throwing as found in track and field] should be stressed out of all apparent proportion to their direct values" (McCloy, 1927, p. 49) because they correlated with success in more complex sports. His main point though was that "a choice [should] be made of a few standard games and athletic sports...[and] these games [should] be thoroughly taught." (McCloy, 1940, p. 124)

Consistent with this approach was his stress on teaching the skills as efficiently as possible, particularly through use of the drill method. He reminded the profession that

> Good teachers concern themselves with the mastery of subject matter.... Stressing only the freedom of the child to develop tends to produce a large group of individuals who are badly educated and who possess little systemized knowledge.... (McCloy, 1940, p. 100)

The emphasis in McCloy's life work was certainly in measurement and evaluation; this was fundamental to all he advocated in terms of physical education programs and teaching. He believed that in order to promote the development of skill and strength, the educator had to know exactly what an individual child could and should be able to do. McCloy claimed that tests, properly administered, would yield information about the innate motor capacity and present motor ability of students, which in turn would aid in classification, grading, motivation, diagnosis of difficulties, and program evaluation. To further this work he developed an Athletic Quotient, Athletic Strength Index, and a General Strength Index, and he calculated formulas that yielded General Motor Capacity Scores and General Motor Achievement Scores. From these he derived a Motor Quotient which he claimed was "the motor analogue of the Intelligence Quotient in the mental field." (McCloy, 1939, p. 126) His naive hope was that each teacher would become a practical researcher, using tests and measurements to effectively increase teaching performance. As a result of these tests, students would be grouped homogeneously, exercised to certain levels of strength, flexibility, and endurance, and drilled in fundamental skills and a selected number of more complex skills which could be used in activities performed during their adult life.

Nash's concept of curriculum also included a belief in the development of power and the learning of skills for later life. However, his emphasis, unlike McCloy's, was really not on skill per se, but on the activity as a whole. Nash stated that "the student is not taught about a skill; rather he is taught to do the activity." (Nash, 1948, p. 55) He did a study which showed that "over 85 per cent of the recreational interests could be traced to below the age of twelve," (Nash, 1953, p. 187) and he urged that "future leisure-time needs should be a guide to curricular construction in our public school." (Nash, 1932, p. 125) "Sufficient opportunity for experience in a number of individual and dual sports is equally important at the secondary level. This is particularly true in the later senior high grades because of the recreational, coeducational and carry-over values." (Nash, 1928, p. 291)

Essential to a physical education program which was meant to insure effective participation throughout life was the child's interests or "felt needs":

The real issue is neither that which the child needs nor that which he can do. Rather is it some felt need, some want "half-formed in the dawning of his consciousness" that is the basis of attitudes which, in turn, become the all-determining factor. (Nash, 1928, p. 195)

The "felt needs" served both as motivators to learning and as guides to the kind of activities the child would later enjoy. Carrying this one step further, he said. "It becomes unnecessary to teach all children all of the traditional progression in the learning of motor skills, as many of these will have been acquired already because of a child's inherent interest in learning." (Nash, 1951, p. 204)

Nash did not share McCloy's enthusiasm for testing because:

> All types of testing encroach upon the too-limited time
> which is scheduled for activities. Few teachers at present
> have the educational background to conduct tests and to evaluate
> the results. To base conclusions about the whole physical edu-
> cation of an individual upon tests of one small aspect of physical
> efficiency is dangerous. (Nash, 1951, p. 181)

Throughout Nash's writings was an emphasis on the curricular relationship between physical education, recreation, and play. He envisioned a program largely determined by the child's interests or "felt needs," consisting of whole activities which would be suitable for carry-over into lifelong leisure-time participation.

Williams' suggestions for the physical education curriculum are centered in a rejection of formal gymnastic drills as being inimical to the fulfillment of the objectives of a democratic society, and in the endorsement of a program of natural activities. In this respect he was beating a dead horse since even his earlier works were written long after Thomas Wood and Clark Hetherington laid the ghosts of European gymnastics to rest. In general, Williams advocated a wide variety of activities in sports, games, dance, camping, fundamental skills, equitation, and aquatics. However, his obsession that "the focus of the individual should be in society, and not in his muscles," (Williams, 1964, p. 363, boldface deleted) led him to recommend that "it is important to eliminate from the program all purely muscle-centered activities in favor of a program of functional activities." (Williams, 1964, p. 352) He also stressed choosing activities that contributed to the personality development of the participant. For ex-ample, "athletic sports and games furnish very desirable material be-cause of the instinctive appeal in such plays and the opportunities they present for the development of moral and social values." (Williams, 1922, p. 61)

In the area of teaching methodology McCloy and Williams fre-quently seemed to be directly criticizing each other's viewpoint. Williams advocated the project method as most suitable for precisely the reason that McCloy came to reject it: because it was more suit-able for developing individual character traits than for presenting sub-ject matter. For instance, Williams favored an increase of discussion time, stating "the time is past when a physical education period is ad-judged good or bad depending upon the amount of physical activity ob-tained during the period." (Williams, 1932, p. 81) While McCloy found the drill method the most efficient means of teaching, Williams countered that

> The notion that formal drill was a good "discipline" for
> youth is correct if regimented persons who implicity obey the

order of the State are desired. But in a democracy, where initiative, self-discipline, and ability to take charge of oneself are educational goals, then formal drill for the general development of the citizen is a mistake and a waste of time. (Williams, 1964, pp. 62-63)

This paragraph was added in the last edition of The Principles, though even there he conceded that drill was a requisite for learning complex skills.

Like Nash, Williams was dubious about the use of testing. First, because "in the field of health, physical education, and recreation, there are a number of objectives...which do not lend themselves to the statistical approach" (Williams, 1964, p. 474), and, of course, this included the objectives in which he was most interested. Secondly, he noted that

In the face of devoted efforts to secure measurable outcomes, such as speed in running or height in jumping, there is the tendency to neglect the social justifications for running and jumping....Statistical averages or percentages may completely obscure standards of educational worth based on ideals. (Williams, 1942, p. 345)

However, he was willing to support a limited use of tests, especially for purposes of classification.

Williams' conception of a physical education program was one in which activities were selected which could best be used as tools through which the child might learn the socially approved values of his society, and to adjust his individual personality and desires to the group welfare. The physical educator's responsibility was to teach for optimal fulfillment of these goals by means of discussions or other methods.

III

McCloy, Nash, and Williams, in delineating fully developed and integrated concepts of physical education, influenced and guided members of the profession in their attempts to implement programs in accordance with newly stabilized professional goals. In 1938, with the addition of the term "recreation," the American Association for Health, Physical Education, and Recreation assumed its present name. A year earlier the American Physical Education Association had become a department of the National Education Association and had added the term "health" to the title. Thus, by 1938 the major interests and objectives of the profession had symbolically been consolidated in the association's name and affiliation with the country's major educational organization. Though the origin of this state-of-being harked back to the work of men like Thomas Wood and Clark Hetherington, the work of McCloy, Nash, and Williams was essential in spelling out professional direction. They detailed a concept of the role of physical education within education. They provided physical educators with clear, logical arguments, bolstered by evidence from contemporary intellectual thought, to support the validity of their beliefs about the objectives of physical education. Furthermore, they constructed explicit curriculums, methodologies, and evaluative techniques in relation to the emphases in their objectives.

But a problem was created because the ideas of these men, as I set them forth in the preceding pages, were in some ways diametrically opposed. This point is very crucial when considering programs in relation to the time allotment for physical education. Each man's primary objective demanded a total program commitment to achieve its fulfillment. Sixty to ninety minutes a week is hardly enough time to increase muscular strength, cardio-vascular endurance, and flexibility as well as develop high level skilled performance in some activities. Any athlete or coach will testify to the need for at least two hours of work a day to develop excellent skills and peak physical condition. Sixty to ninety minutes a week is hardly enough time to be introduced to a significant number of activities and to learn them well enough to provide a basis for carry-over into adult leisure-time. Every semi-serious golfer, tennis player, fisherman, skier, surfer, or bowler can testify to the need for prolonged and concentrated practice before a sport becomes pleasurable enough to be considered recreation. Sixty to ninety minutes a week is hardly enough time to effect changes in attitudes, inculcate social values and standards, and learn to subjugate one's desires for the welfare of the group, all while performing physical activities. Any psychologist or social worker will testify to the need for continuous and intensive counseling before an individual is willing and able to make basic changes in his beliefs and personality. Yet, physical educators have believed that in the duration of their programs, each of these aims could simultaneously be accomplished.

Nash, Williams, and McCloy knew better. By developing a hierarchy of objectives, each focused on a single belief that, in the words of Ortega, was "fundamental, decisive, sustaining and breathing life into all the others." (Ortega y Gasset, 1962, p. 168) Pointing out that programs had to be developed in keeping with objectives, they each advocated different programs. McCloy would have had students exercising, drilling on fundamental skills; Nash would have had students learning individual or carry-over sports according to their individual interests; Williams would have had students primarily playing team games and having group discussions. For the objectives to have even a remote chance of accomplishment, a student's entire school career in physical education would have had to be along a single program line.

But physical educators adopted all three modes and believed they they could effectively conduct all three types of program simultaneously. Although there were vague ideas advanced which suggested that in the lowest grades body development and fundamental skills should be the basis of curriculum, followed in the middle school years by games and team sports, and culminating in individual activities, in actual practice a little of everything was done at almost every level. As the fifties drew to a close, generally even the colleges still required that each student take some courses in fundamental activities or body development, plus one team sport, one individual sport, and perhaps a class in dance or aquatics.

Admittedly, during the course of this time period there were subtle practical variations. During times of national stress, such as that occasioned by World War II, or the findings of Kraus-Weber which, according to their standards, suggested that American children were physically inferior to others around the world, the profession veered toward placing greater emphasis on physical development. In later years, with a push from commercial sporting interests, always present in abundance at conventions, and with sufficient national wealth to allow many school systems larger investments in facilities and equipment, greater emphasis was directed toward lifetime sports. But through all this the socializing objective was never diluted in intent.

It is my belief that physical educators attempted the analytically and existentially impossible task of achieving all three aims in any single program. As a result, physical education projected itself into the anomalous situation of holding classes in accord with McCloy's suggestions, of advocating the activities urged by Nash, and of committing itself to accomplishing the social goals delineated by Williams. McCloy, Nash, and Williams deliberately attempted to influence the direction of physical education in their time. It must be assumed that each hoped his "truth" would prevail. But an analysis of the period from 1930-1960 shows that what prevailed was an amalgamation of their three, somewhat incongruent theories.

References

1. Gerber, Ellen W. Innovators and Institutions in Physical Education. (Philadelphia: Lea & Febiger, 1971).

2. McCloy, Charles Harold, "The Case for Physical Education," Journal of Health and Physical Education, IV (April, 1933), pp. 3-6, 62-63.

3. _____, "Forgotten Objectives of Physical Education," Journal of Health and Physical Education, VIII (October, 1937), pp. 458-61, 512-13.

4. _____, "How About Some Muscle?" Journal of Health and Physical Education, VII (May, 1936), pp. 302-303, 355.

5. _____, "In Quest of Skills," Journal of Health and Physical Education, IX (October, 1938), pp. 478-80, 524-25.

6. _____. The Measurement of Athletic Power. (New York: A. S. Barnes, 1932).

7. _____, "New Wine in New Bottles," Journal of Physical Education, XXV (October, 1927), pp. 43-52.

8. _____. Philosophical Bases for Physical Education. (New York: F. S. Crofts, 1940).

9. _____, "Some Applications of Psychology to the Teaching of Physical Activities," Journal of Physical Education, XXXI (March, 1934), pp. 51-54.

10. _____. Tests and Measurements in Health and Physical Education. (New York: F. S. Crofts, 1939).

11. _____ and Young, Norma Dorothy. Tests and Measurements in Health and Physical Education. Third edition. New York: Appleton-Century-Crofts, 1954.

12. Nash, Jay Bryan. The Administration of Physical Education. (New York: A. S. Barnes, 1932).

13. _____, "Call to Service," Journal of Health and Physical Education, XIII (September, 1942), pp. 379-81.

14. _____. The Organization and Administration of Playgrounds and Recreation. (New York: A. S. Barnes, 1928).

15. _____. Philosophy of Recreation and Leisure. (St. Louis: C. V. Mosby, 1953).

16. _____. Physical Education: Its Interpretations and Objectives. (New York: A. S. Barnes, 1948).

17. _____, Moench, Francis J. and Saurborn, Jeanette B. Physical Education: Organization and Administration. (New York: A. S. Barnes, 1951).

18. Ortega y Gasset, Jose. History as a System. (New York: W. W. Norton, 1962).

19. Williams, Jesse Feiring, "Education Through the Physical," Journal of Higher Education, I (May, 1930), pp. 279-82.

20. _____, "Health, An Objective of Education," Journal of Health and Physical Education, IV (March, 1933), pp. 5-6.

21. _____. The Organization and Administration of Physical Education. (New York: Macmillan, 1922).

22. _____. The Principles of Physical Education. (Philadelphia: W. B. Saunders, 1927).

23. _____. The Principles of Physical Education. Fourth edition. Philadelphia: W. B. Saunders, 1942.

24. _____. The Principles of Physical Education. Eighth edition. Philadelphia: W. B. Saunders, 1954.

25. _____ and Brownell, Clifford Lee. The Administration of Health Education and Physical Education. Fourth edition. Philadelphia: W. B. Saunders, 1951.

66. _____, Dambach, John I. and Schwendener, Norma. Methods in Physical Education. (Philadelphia: W. B. Saunders, 1932).

CHAPTER 25

PERSISTENT HISTORICAL PROBLEMS OF PHYSICAL EDUCATION AND SPORT

Earle F. Zeigler
The University of Western Ontario, London

Introduction[1]

The presence of serious-minded men and women at this First International Seminar on the History of Physical Education and Sport --professional people assembled from so many different countries in the world--attests to the significance of such a meeting as this Seminar. Despite the fact that all of us considered it important to be here, it is probably true that there would be as many different interpretations of this field's function as there are delegates present here at the Wingate Institute in Israel. This should not concern us unduly, however, as there are undoubtedly some common denominators upon which we can agree (even if there is considerable concern by some as to what constitutes an acceptable name for what it is that we are).[2]

Editor's Note: As the last chapter (25), the Editor has included a paper prepared for presentation originally at the First International Seminar on the History of Physical Education and Sport in Israel in 1968. It represents an approach which he has been developing and expanding over several decades - a persistent problems approach to the history, philosophy, and international aspects of physical education and sport. It may be helpful, because it does serve as a summarizing effort (as do the other two essays presented in Chapters 23 and 24).

---

[1] A paper presented to the First International Seminar on the History of Physical Education and Sport, Wingate Institute, Israel, April 9-11, 1968.

[2] No apology will be offered for calling the field "physical, health, and recreation education (including sport)" at this moment. From one standpoint it could be explained that such a title reflects the philosophically progressivistic bias of the author. It does intimate that we are concerned with many aspects of the total education of man throughout life. If we grant the seemingly widely accepted unity of the human organism, then it follows that there is no such thing as physical education.

What are some of these common denominators in physical, health, and recreation education (including sport)? One stands out more clearly than any other--the belief of the large majority that regular physical education periods should be <u>required</u> for all school children through sixteen years of age (approximately). A second point of agreement is that a child should develop certain <u>attitudes toward</u> his own <u>health</u> in particular and toward community hygiene in general. Thus, certain <u>basic health knowledge</u> should be taught in the school curriculum. We can find agreement also on the <u>worthy use of leisure</u>.

Still further, professionals within the field would argue to a man that <u>physical vigor</u> is important. Beyond this we cannot go, however, since there would be no general agreement among the men, or between men and women, about what constitutes physical vigor or fitness. There are no world standards for physical fitness, only national norms in some cases which give us present status--nothing more.

Even the role of <u>competitive sports</u> for boys and girls is an area in which there is some agreement. We feel generally that boys and girls at some stage of their development should have an experience of this type. But we can find no general agreement at all beyond this rather meaningless statement; there is quite a difference between a ten-year old playing marbles competitively and a fifty-four year old man wrestling competitively at the national level.

The matter of <u>remedial exercise</u> for physical defects that can be corrected in this way offers us another opportunity for a bit of agreement, but we can't decide who should attend to this, or when or where. Lastly, we agree that the area of <u>character and/or personality development</u> is important, but substantive evidence as to the effect of physical education and sport on such development is relatively negligible. The time is long overdue when this field should be able to present to the public far greater agreement on what it is that physical educators accomplish for the education of youth! (Zeigler, 1964, pp. 287-88)

The Body of Knowledge Project

The world is on the threshold of an exciting, if also a highly frightening, time. But even though man may be looking both hopefully and fearfully ahead, there is an ever-present need to become increasingly aware of the past. It was to this point that René Maheu addressed himself in the Foreword to the <u>History of Mankind</u>, the first global history of mankind, planned and written from an international standpoint by experts of world-wide reputation, and produced under the auspices of UNESCO:

At a time when man is preparing to launch out from this planet into space, it is well that History should hold him in contemplation of his trajectory through the ages. Never before, indeed, has he shown so searching a curiosity about his past or such jealous care to preserve its vestiges. . . Be that as it may, never more than now, when man finds himself hurtling at vertiginous speed towards a wondrous future, has there been a great need for the function of memory to ensure for mankind the appropriation of its creative actuality. . . To evoke this retrospective awareness is the first thing that this work which we now have the honour of introducing to the public sets out to do; it is an attempt to sum up the heritage of civilization to which we owe our present élan. (Hawkes and Wooley, 1963, xi)

These statements about man "hurtling towards a wondrous future," "launching out from this planet into space," and yet "contemplating his trajectory through the ages" may well be applied to the situation of the field of physical education and sport at the present time. The effort to define the field as a discipline, so that a body of knowledge may be developed upon which the profession may practice and build its theory, may well assist man quite substantially to realize a "wondrous future" both on this planet and in space. Thus, the kinesiologists, exercise physiologists, psychologists, and sociologists within our field, for example, should be able to help us discover how man moves, and what happens to him when he moves. But it will be largely up to those interested in the historical, philosophical, and comparative aspects of physical education and sport to assist the profession to "contemplate the trajectory" of physical education, sport, human movement, kinesiology, or human motor performance through the ages. Some of you may be unwilling to accept responsibility for the inclusion of history, philosophy, and comparative (or international) education as applied to physical education and sport within your sphere of operation as a professional person. Naturally, this must be your own choice. The point beind made, however, is that it is extremely difficult, if not impossible, to consider history, or philosophy, or comparative education without automatically encountering knowledge from one or both of the other two disciplines.

A Need to Specialize. This dilemma should not frighten professional physical educators who by necessity have been perennial "jacks of all trades" from the very beginning. It does not mean that quasi-historians, for example, are going to be forced to master the disciplines of philosophy and comparative education as well. It does mean, however, that a sport and physical education historian will need to maintain a continual awareness about what is taking place in the other two fields--and especially in regard to the points where the disciplines may impinge on one another.

At the same time there is a great need for vastly increased specialization within history, or philosophy, or comparative and international education as applied to this field. If it is maintained that physical education and sport represent an important phase of man's culture, it is absolutely imperative that competent historians record faithfully and analyze carefully what has transpired in this area. As Woody has stated, those who have written about education and history seem to have slighted "physical culture" through bias:

> Despite the fact that lip-service has been paid increasingly to the dictum 'a sound mind in a sound body,' even since western Europe began to revive the educational concepts of the Graeco-Roman world, there is still a lack of balance between physical and mental culture, both in school programs and among those who write of education. This is evident in many quarters, even where a certain universality of outlook ought to reign. Turn where one will, it is impossible to find physical culture adequately presented in books dealing with the general history of education. Written in keeping with a dominant rationalism, these books have been concerned chiefly with intellectual movements and institutions for mental improvement. (Woody, 1949, vii)

If this assessment is even reasonably substantially true, the field of physical education truly has its work cut out for it.

And last the occurrence of this First International Seminar should tend to make those present even the least little bit self-satisfied about progress in this direction, several perhaps embarrassing questions should be asked: (1) What percentage of those present at this Seminar spend even one-quarter (25%) of their working time each week adding to the body of knowledge about the history of physical education and sport?; and (2) How many others throughout the world, not present here, could answer this question affirmatively? Still further, are educational historians now assisting physical education and sport historians--consciously or unconsciously? Or for that matter, what help is coming from historians? And beyond this, can the field continue to rely on those laymen, perhaps sportsmen of one type or another, who have an inclination to write sports history of varying quality?

The Cause Is Not Yet Lost. That there should be serious concern about the present need for a greater amount of historical investigation in this area is self-evident, and this concern grows somewhat greater when it is understood that there doesn't appear to be anywhere nearly full awareness of the need. There can be encouragement, nevertheless, from the knowledge that "as late as 1880 there were only eleven professors of history in American colleges," and as Muller also pointed out that:

> Our age is nevertheless more historically minded that any previous age, and has a much longer, wider, clearer view of the past. Its contribution to historical knowledge over the last hundred years, are among its most honorable achievements. (Muller, 1952, pp. 33-34)

Persistent Historical Problems in Physical Education

More careful description and delineation of some of the persistent historical problems of physical education and sport is perhaps the most important professional goal of this author. He would like to be able to say that the idea for this approach came to him in a brilliant flash of insight while standing on a high mountain top, but, alas, the derivation of the idea occurred in a much more prosaic manner. Although it is true that many of the ideas for the specific problems listed below did originate with him and some of his colleagues and graduate students, and that some adaptations have been made, the credit for this unique approach in educational history and philosophy must go to John S. Brubacher, long-time professor of the history and philosophy of education at Yale, and more recently at The University of Michigan in Higher Education. Thus, it is the adaptation of the approach, the selection of certain of the persistent problems, and the delineation of the implications for this specialized field that may possibly be considered as new contributions.[3]

Such an approach as this does not really represent a radically different approach to history. The typical major processes are involved in applying historical method to investigation in the field: (1) the data are collected from primary and secondary sources; (2) the collected data are criticized; and (3) an integrated narrative is presented which is based on critical inquiry for the entire truth. This approach does differ markedly, however, when the organization of the collected data is considered: it is based completely on the problem areas of the present and an effort to illuminate them for the student of physical education and sport. Thus, a conscious effort is made to keep the reader from thinking that the subject is of antiquarian interest only. The student moves back and forth from early times to the

---

[3] For further information the reader is referred to the following books: J. S. Brubacher, A History of the Problems of Education. New York: McGraw-Hill Book Company, 1966; and E. F. Zeigler, Persistent Problems in the History and Philosophy of Physical Education and Sport. Englewood Cliffs, New Jersey: Prentice-Hall, Inc., 1968.

present as different aspects of the subject are considered, say, in the chapters of a book--a "longitudinal" approach as opposed to a strictly chronological one. These persistent problems, then, are ones that recur again and again down through the ages, and they will in all probability continue to occur in the future. A problem used in this sense (from its Greek derivation) would be "something thrown forward" for man to understand or resolve. The following are persistent historical problems of physical, health, and recreation education (including sport) as seen by the author and his associates at the present time:

1. Values (Aims and Objectives) – throughout history there have been innumerable statements of educational aims, and almost invariably there was a direct relationship with a hierarchy of educational values present in the society under consideration. In general educational philosophy, values have been either subjective or objective (i.e., do values exist in the world whether man happens to be present to realize them or not?). Physical education and sport has been viewed as curricular, co-curricular, or extra-curricular.

2. The Influence of Politics – the kind and amount of education has varied throughout history depending upon whether a particular country was a monarchy, an aristocratic oligarchy, or a type of democracy. Experimentalism (pragmatic naturalism) in education, and this applies to physical, health, and recreation education as well, can flourish only in a type of democratic society. Educational essentialism, and this includes its implications for physical education and sport, may be promoted successfully in all three types of society.

3. The Influence of Nationalism – the influence of nationalism on this field throughout history is obvious. If a strong state is desired, the need for a strong, healthy people is paramount. There have been many examples of this type of influence as far back as the Medes and the Spartans, and as recently as some twentieth century European and Asian powers. In a democratic society, however, it is extremely difficult for a government in power to promote nationalism except by indirect and less effective means. During wartime, for example, the basic educational objectives are threatened when the government of a democracy attempts to dictate that physical education and sport be employed to promote physical fitness and national loyalty.

4. The Influence of Economics – in past times education has prospered when there was a surplus economy and declined when the economic structure weakened. Furthermore, educational aims have tended to vary depending on how people made their money and created such surplus economies. One of the problems of advancing industrial civilization has been the uneven distribution of wealth bringing educational advantages of a superior quality to some. Education "of the physical" can be promoted under any economic system. In largely

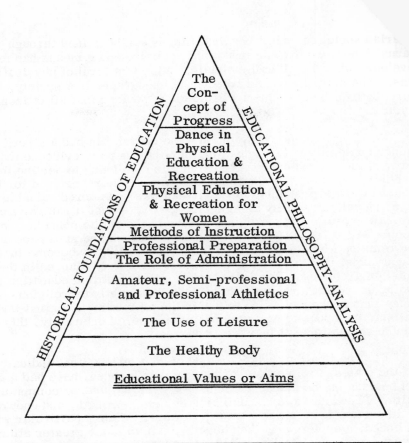

The
Con-
cept of
Progress

Dance in
Physical
Education &
Recreation

Physical Education
& Recreation for
Women

Methods of Instruction

Professional Preparation

The Role of Administration

Amateur, Semi-professional
and Professional Athletics

The Use of Leisure

The Healthy Body

Educational Values or Aims

HISTORICAL FOUNDATIONS OF EDUCATION

EDUCATIONAL PHILOSOPHY-ANALYSIS

HISTORICAL EVOLUTION OF SOCIAL FORCES
(Politics, Nationalism, Economics, Religion)

SELECTED, PERSISTENT, HISTORICAL PROBLEMS
OF PHYSICAL, HEALTH, AND RECREATION EDUCATION
(including SPORT)

eties, much physical fitness can be gained through
whereas in industrial societies some means has to be
reby __all__ will maintain a minimum level of physical fit-
re individual freedom is encouraged in a society, the
difficult a government will find it to __demand__ that all citizens be
physically fit.

5. __The Influence of Religion__ - the church has had a strong influence on education throughout history, but there is evidence that the
power of the church over the individual is continuing to decline in the
twentieth century. The Christian religion can be recognized for the
promulgation of principles in which man was considered valuable as
an individual. A society must decide to what extent it can, or should,
inculcate moral and/or religious values in the public schools. In
keeping with a trend toward separation of church and state, the question remains whether the church has the flexibility to become that
unique social institution needed to effect necessary changes in the
social environment. Physical, health, and recreation education (including sport) have not been supported significantly by religious organizations in the past. In fact, with the promotion of a mind-body
dualism, the opposite has often been the case. Fortunately, this
attitude seems to be changing to a degree.

6. __The Healthy Body__ - a study of past civilizations indicates
that the states of war or peace, as social influences, have had a direct bearing on the emphases placed on personal and/or community
health. Freedom from disqualifying defects, strength, and endurance
are important to men who want to win wars. When a particular war
has ended, a society may then be able again to focus greater attention
toward a more healthful environment at home. It is profoundly
disturbing that so many people in the world are not able to profit from
the outstanding progress that has been made in public health science.
There is still disagreement as to a definition of health and as to the
place of health instruction in the school curriculum. Which agency,
the home, school, or community agency, should play the greatest
role in this area?

7. __The Use of Leisure__ - this persistent problem has a relationship to the influence of economics on a society - both education
and recreation prospered in times past when there was a surplus
economy. In most of the world's twenty-one civilizations the average
man has had to work very hard to earn a meagre living. Certain
classes, rulers, priests, and nobles, were the first to enjoy anything
like extended leisure. Even in the Middle Ages life still held many in-
equalities for the masses, although recreation did begin to take on a
broader significance. Wars, the fact that times change slowly, and
the power of the Church prevented the concepts of political democracy and socialism from taking hold. Then, too, the natural sciences had to be advanced enough so that advanced technology could

lead men into an industrial revolution, which has lowered man's
working hours so markedly. Now we hear about cybernation and automation, and education for leisure would seem to warrant serious consideration. The extent to which such preparation is included in the
school's curriculum depends quite largely on prevailing educational
philosophy.

8. <u>Amateurism, Semi-professionalism, and Professionalism
in Sport</u> - the motivation behind participation in games and sports
through the ages has been so complex that there is really no general
agreement on the matter. Man has taken part for fun, for recreation, for self-expression, for health, for exercise, for competition, for money, and probably for other reasons not readily discern-
ible. There was even an early relationship of sport to religious ob-
servances. Even in the earlier days the aspect of over-specialization
because of the desire to win (and perhaps the material rewards) has
tended to "tarnish the lustre" of the amateur ideal. There are so
many different definitions of an amateur extant in the world today that
it is impossible to keep up with them. It may well be that we will
have to re-evaluate some of our treasured, basic assumptions about
the amateur code in sport, which views the matter on the basis of
polarities. There is need for a semi-professional category in which
the athlete will not be viewed as something "dirty and degraded."
There is a need further for professional sportsmen who will be taught
to devote his life to a social ideal--to serve his fellow man through
his contributions to the many phases of a sport's development. Under
the right auspices all types of sport can hold value for the individual.
Sport can be a "socially useful servant."

9. <u>The Role of Administration</u> - Social organizations, of one
type or another, are inextricably related to man's history as a human
and social animal. Superior-subordinate relationships evolved
according to the very nature of things, as man produced goods, fought
wars, organized his society politically, formed his churches, and developed a great variety of formal and informal associations. A central theme seems to have been that of <u>change</u>--change that was made
to strengthen the organization administratively. It was only recently
that "administrative thought emerged as a differentiated field of
sustained writing, conscious observation, abstract theory, and specialized terminology." (Gross, 1964, p. 91) Education has become a
vast public and private enterprise demanding wise management based
upon sound administrative theory. The "organizational revolution"
has meant that educational administrators have been forced to create
a greater amount of bureaucracy. Educational essentialists tend to
believe that there are valid theoretical principles of administration
that should not be violated. Educational progressivists, conversely,
tend to view administration as a developing social science--a science
that is gradually providing man with a body of knowledge about human

relations and the decision-making process. Administrators of physical education and sport organizations need to understand this development thoroughly.

10. <u>Professional Preparation</u> – the idea of professions (with accompanying preparation for this type of service) has its origins in antiquity in the very early societies. Professional preparation of teachers to any considerable extent is a fairly recent innovation. In early times the most important qualification for the position of teacher was a sound knowledge of the subject. In the Middle Ages there was no such thing as professional education to be a teacher, at least in the sense that certification is needed today to teach in the publicly-supported institutions at certain levels in particular countries. It was in Prussia where the most headway was made in improving teacher education in the late eighteenth and early nineteenth centuries. This system was copied extensively elsewhere. Significant advances in the theory of pedagogy occurred through the influence of Pestalozzi. In America, for example, the normal school became a well-established part of the educational system. In the twentieth century this organization has progressed to college and/or university status. Professional education eventually achieved status at the university level, but it is required for public school teachers only--not at the college or university level. Generally speaking throughout the world, professional preparation for physical education is included at the normal and/or technical school level. University recognition has been achieved at some institutions in England, Japan, and the United States, for example, but there is much progress to be made.

11. <u>Methods of Instruction</u> – The educational curriculum has been influenced strongly by a variety of political, economic, philosophical, religious, and scientific factors. In curriculum construction, therefore, a primary task is to determine which subjects should be included because of the recurring interest that has been shown among educators and laymen for their inclusion at some educational level. Primitive and pre-literate man undoubtedly learned through imitation and through trial and error. When writing was invented in the early civilizations, memorization played a large part in the educational process. Tradition and custom were highly regarded, and the importance of precept and proper example were significant aspects of both physical and mental culture. In the Near East Jesus was evidently a very fine teacher, but Christian religious leaders who followed him presumably employed less exciting teaching methods with an emphasis on formality and dogmatism. Toward the end of the Middle Ages, educational methodology is said to have improved considerably. With the onset of the Renaissance, there was greater recognition of individual differences, and the whole spirit of this period was much more humanistic. Physical educators need to understand that the concept of a mind-body dualism has prevailed in many quarters down to the present day. A physical educator should determine for himself what

influence that content has on method; do they go hand in hand? Shall physical education and sport (or whatever part of it is included in the curriculum) be taught formally, semi-formally, or informally. The persistent problem remains: how can the student be motivated so that learning will occur most easily, and so that it will be remembered?

12. <u>Physical Education and Recreation for Women</u> - throughout history women's physical education has been hampered not only by the concept of the place of physical education in a particular society, but also by the place that women themselves held in most societies—and by the ideas that men and women have had about the limitations of women because of their anatomical structure and their role in the reproductive process of the human race. Aristotle, for example, felt that they were generally speaking weaker, less courageous, and incomplete, and that they had been fitted by nature for subjection to the male. Plato held a different view; he believed that women should have all types of education similar to the pattern he prescribed for men (including the highest type of liberal education, and even preparation for warfare). Throughout history, with notable exceptions in the cases of Crete, Sparta, later Rome, and certain individual instances, practically all women were considered inferior. In the twentieth century, certainly one of the significant social trends has been woman's "emancipation." Many women are now conceived of as having as intellectual function depending in many cases upon her individual qualifications. More democratic theories of state have fostered equalitarianism. Many people feel that men's physical education and women's programs should more nearly approximate each other. The norm projected by society for women tends to be retrogressive; and it has been modified by what many consider to be unfortunate societal influences. For example, most women are quite concerned about the their appearance, but it is often maintained by artificial devices, and they are rarely physically fit. If our total field has advantages to offer to women, educators should see to it that they receive these opportunities.

13. <u>Dance in Physical Education and Recreation</u> - in all ages people have danced for personal pleasure, for religious purposes, for expression of the gamut of emotions, and for the pleasure of others. An analysis of the dance forms of a civilization can tell a qualified observer much about the total life therein. In primitive societies types of rhythmic expressions were "instinctive satisfiers" of man. Dance was most often serious in nature and only incidentally served physical fitness, health, and recreation. It served a purpose in Roman civilization, but its status was below that given it by the Greeks. During the Middle Ages dance had very low status probably due to its corruption in the later Roman era. The place of dance began to rise again during the Renaissance; different types and forms have waxed and waned over the centuries. The twentieth century has witnessed a truly remarkable development in the dance, as the body is

gradually being rediscovered as a means of communication through the dance medium. There is still much room for progress. For example, a significant body of research knowledge is lacking. Still further, an improvement of the interaction between the dance teacher and the profressional performer would add further strength to the development. Articulation within the dance curriculum among the various educational levels is needed. On the North American continent modern dance especially seems unacceptable to the majority of male physical education teachers (and hence to the boys and young men in their classes as well). As both an art and as a social function, dance will probably always be with us and will reflect the dominant influences of the age in which it is taking place.

14. <u>The Concept of Progress</u> - any study of history inevitably forces a person to conjecture about man's progress. Certainly there has been progression, but can this be called "progress?" To as ascertain if change may be called progress, it is necessary to measure whether advancement has been made from worse to better (for example). A criterion must be recommended by which progress may be judged. It is true that man has made progress in adaptability and can cope with a variety of environments. It is probably safe to assume that man on the whole is the pinnacle of evolutionary progress <u>on this earth</u>. Throughout the course of history until the Golden Age of Greece, a good education had been based on the transmission of the cultural heritage. During the Roman Empire and the Middle Ages such an educational pattern continued, despite the fact that from time to time certain educational theorists offered proposals of greater or lesser radical quality. Thus, when a society declined, those involved in the educational system had relatively few useful ideas about social rejuvenation. Despite the forces of the Renaissance and accompanying humanism, followed by the gradual introduction of science into the curriculum, the same traditional educational pattern kept the school from becoming an agent of social reconstructionism. In physical education and sport, it is vitally important to search for consensus among the conflicting philosophies of physical, health, and recreation education (including sport). The field had been proceeding "amoeba-like" for far too long considering the body-of-knowledge that is amassing. It is fortunate that there is more agreement in practice than in theory.

Conclusion

And so this discussion has proceeded full circle through brief summaries of some fourteen persistent historical problems back to the common denominators that were presented at the outset of this paper. Having stated these common denominators, it would appear that the time is long overdue when the field should be able to present fairly concrete evidence of far greater agreement to the public in relation to <u>what it is that we do</u>. The goal should be the discovery of what contributions physical education and sport can make to the development of man. Then, based upon its system of values, a particular society will accept or reject this evidence and promote that type of a program which the people will support. Based upon the scientific evidence from the discipline, and the enlightened support of intelligent laymen, the professional's task is to administer the program of physical education and sport so that maximum benefits will accrue to the greatest number of people possible. This task belongs to us alone.

Selected References

Gross, Bertram M. The Managing of Organizations. 2 volumes. New York: Crowell-Collier Publishing Company, 1964.

Hawkes, Jacquetta and Wooley, Leonard. History of Mankind. (Volume I, Prehistory and Beginnings of Civilization). New York: Harper & Row, Publishers, 1963.

Muller, Herbert J. The Uses of the Past. New York: The New American Library of World Literature, Inc., 1954.

Woody, Thomas. Life and Education in Early Societies. New York: The Macmillan Company, 1949.

Zeigler, Earle F. Philosophical Foundations for Physical, Health, and Recreation Education. Englewood Cliffs, New Jersey: Prentice-Hall, Inc., 1964.

EPILOGUE

THE IDEA OF PHYSICAL EDUCATION IN MODERN TIMES

Earle F. Zeigler
The University of Western Ontario, London

Introduction[1]

To express the "idea of physical education in modern times" is an exciting assignment, but one that seemed much simpler when first considered in a casual way. In the first place, it would be ridiculous to define the term in such a way that it might not apply for the entire world. Obviously, physical education "means many things to many people," and it may well be said that we are presenting a "blurred image to a bewildered public."

Thinking about this particular topic - the idea of physical education in modern times - "idea" will be taken to mean "the conception of" or "the nature of." "Physical education" will be accepted as a program which is offered by certain departments in schools and colleges throughout the world, as well as the activity carried on both formally and informally by parents, community leaders, and an individual himself. It can and does include health education, physical education, recreation, safety education, dance, sport and competitive

---

Editor's Note: Finally, in the Epilogue the reader will discover an essay largely philosophical in nature, but one that concludes with an historical allegory explaining the "basic nature" of sport, dance, exercise, and play over the centuries. In conclusion, the Editor would like to reiterate how truly thankful he is to so many of his professional colleagues who have made this volume possible. This is one of the first books of its type in the field of physical education and sport, and it probably would not have been possible to produce it before this decade. To the younger authors included in this book, and to those who are standing in the wings as future physical education and sport historians, keep up the good work. All of us are proud of recent developments, but we know that all of us working together and individually can do ever so much better.

---

[1] A paper presented to the Philosophical and Cultural Foundations Area of the Physical Education Division of the American Association for Health, Physical Education, and Recreation, St. Louis, Missouri, April 1, 1968.

athletics, and other types of activities. All of this leads one to think that perhaps "physical education" has become a highly unsatisfactory name - everything considered. And lastly, considering this paper's topic, "modern times," which may have begun about 1500 A.D. (McNeill, 1963, xii), will be defined as the twentieth century for the purposes of this presentation.

One last introductory statement should probably be made. With a topic like this it is difficult to determine where history leaves off and philosophy begins. Although the writer has a sincere interest in both aspects of the field, his preference is to place greater emphasis on the philosophical aspects of the topic. This will be done in the first half of this paper, but a historical summary in the form of an allegory will be included at the end. The assumption is that the major points to be emphasized will be made more forcefully that way.

Philosophical Analysis

The philosopher approaches his task typically in at least one of three ways: (1) speculatively, (2) normatively, or (3) analytically (Frankena, Philosophy of Education, 1965, p. 10). He may speculate about what we know and believe about the universe and our own sphere of human affairs within this framework. He may approach these questions normatively and evolve a systematic and coherent plan whereby a human may live. Lastly, and it should be stressed that there are a number of different methods and techniques within each of these three approaches, he may seek to analyze other philosophical approaches critically and to make comparisons. In this latter approach he will probably attempt to clarify concepts and to present evidence that seems to bear out one philosophical position or another. Finally, he may go so far with critical analysis that he will decide that language analysis and a type of semantics should be his primary task (Zeigler and VanderZwaag, 1966, p. 78).

Five Meanings of Physical Education

No matter which of the three approaches is employed primarily by a philosopher of physical education and sport, he should at least recognize the ambiguity of the term "physical education," and the fact that it may mean any one of five things:

    (1)   the activity of physically educating carried on by teachers, schools, and parents (or by oneself),

    (2)   the process of being physically educated (or learning) which goes on in the pupil or child (or person of any age),

    (3)   the result, actual or intended, of (1) and (2),

(4)   the discipline or field of enquiry that studies or re-flects on (1), (2), and (3) and is taught in depart-ments, schools, and colleges of physical education,

(5)   the profession whose members practice (1) above, try to observe (2) taking place, attempt to measure and/or evaluate whether (3) has occurred, and base their professional practice on the body-of-knowledge developed by those undertaking scholarly and re-search effort in the discipline (4). (Adapted from Frankena, <u>Three Historical Philosophies of Educa-tion</u>, 1965, p. 6, with some modifications).

Thus, without even considering "the idea of" physical education in relation to its objectives, the professional physical educator can readily see how important it is that he communicate more effectively with his fellow professionals. Where this problem in language leaves the layman is immediately obvious.

A Plethora of Objectives

That this field, whatever it is called by anyone, has had a ple-thora of objectives espoused by its leaders must be considered one of the "understatements of the year." Because of the field's "defensive posture" occasioned by many attacks against its gradual "intrusion" into the curriculum, leaders in physical education have claimed that an adequate physical education can cure everything from "soiled characters to chilblains." Notable among these leaders who have defined certain objectives, starting in the early 1920's, have been Hetherington (1922), Bowen and Mitchell (1923), Wood and Cassidy (1927), Williams (1927), Hughes (with Williams in 1930), Nash (1931), Sharman (1937), Wayman (1938), Esslinger (1938), Staley (1939), McCloy (1940), Clark (1943), Cobb (1943), Lynn (1944), Brownell and Hagman, Scott, Bucher, and Oberteuffer (all in 1951). There have been many other statements since that time, but 1951 seems like a good year to stop. One could categorize and then enumerate the vari-ous objectives proposed for the field, and the list would be really im-pressive. Fortunately, for this present paper, Hess assessed these objectives of American physical education from 1900 to 1957 in the light of certain historical events. The major objectives in the se-quence in which they appeared (according to Hess, 1959) were (1) the hygiene or health objectives (1900-1919); (2) the socio-educational ob-jectives, including worthy use of leisure (1920-1928); (3) the objec-tives of physical fitness and health (1939-1945); (4) the objectives were broadened to include the ideals of international understanding and the improvement of human relations, including an emphasis on coeducational activities (1950-1957); and, finally, broadened educa-tional and social objectives, encompassing the social, health, physi-cal, emotional, and mental aspects of total fitness (1950-1957).

The Need for Consensus

It seems quite obvious that the profession should take positive steps to plan and then work for consensus among the conflicting philosophies of physical education extant in the Western world. This is especially true, because our field now seems to be redoubling its efforts to relate to other countries in all parts of the world. One might well ask about the wisdom of attempting to export the present "mass confusion" on the matter of objectives. Not many people will be fooled for very long with such an approach. Delineation of one's own personal philosophy on the part of each physical educator will help, but the employment of optimum methods for the achievement of greater agreement with our colleagues at home and abroad must be carried out for the best possible outcome. Still further, the East and the West should meet--and just as soon as possible. (Burtt, pp. 272-273)

The Need for Verification of Objectives

Most recently, physical educators have realized the need for the development of a "body-of-knowledge" through a greatly expanded program of scholarly and research endeavor in a variety of sub-disciplines (Zeigler and McCristal, 1967). Some of our scientists had realized this earlier, especially in the physiological area and certain aspects of psychology. But now relationships are gradually being strengthened with such disciplines and sub-disciplines as anatomy, sociology, history, philosophy, comparative and international education, anthropology, and administrative theory (within the behavioral sciences and educational administration) as well (Zeigler, 1967).

As the "body-of-knowledge" increases, and inventories of scientific findings from the various sub-disciplines to which the field is relating improve in both quantity and quality, it will become increasingly possible to verify whether a planned program of physical education does actually result in the achievement of the many objectives which have been stated. Maybe then the field will be able to achieve consensus on certain "common denominators" in the "education of an amphibian" (Huxley, 1964) or a "naked ape" (Morris, 1967). What seems to be really important in regard to the classification of a "relatively hairless ape," in addition to the obviously still prevailing legacy from ancestors, is that man has now become "almost non-apelike" and that there remains ample opportunity for all sorts of differential development in the eons which lie ahead. (Simpson, 1968) Physical education has a significant role to play in this development, no matter what the field decides to call itself. The following allegory will perhaps explain the "basic nature" of physical education from both a historical and philosophical standpoint.

The Basic Nature of Physical Education (An Allegory)

Blank, sometimes designated as _____, but who really should be called tnemevom (which is quite difficult to pronounce), has had both a glorious and a shameful existence. He is a part of the very nature of the universe, a fact which is incontrovertible. He is involved with both the animate and inanimate aspects of the cosmos. His is a basic part of the fundamental pattern of living of every creature of any type that has ever lived on earth. Early man knew he was important, but he was often not appreciated until he was gone, or almost gone. Civilized man used him extensively in the early societies, as did the Greeks and the Romans and all others. Some used him vigorously, but others used him carefully and methodically. He was used gracefully by some, ecstatically by others, rigorously by many when the need was urgent, and regularly by most who wanted to get the job done. He was called many things in various tongues. But strangely enough, he was never fully understood.

The time came when he was considered less important in life, although people still admired him on innumerable occasions. Some seemed to understand him instinctively, while others had great difficulty in employing him well. He was eventually degraded to such an extent that well-educated people often did not think that he had an important place in their background and preparation for life. Many gave lip service to the need for him, but then would not give him his due. Others appreciated his worth, but felt that he was less important than many aspects of education. But he persisted despite the onset of an advanced technological age. Some called his calisthenics. Others called him physical training. A determined group called him gymnastics. A few called him physical culture, but they turned out to be men of "ill repute." Others felt that he had been neglected in the preparation of man for life; so, they did him a favor and called him physical education.

The Aftermath of a New Name. He prospered to a considerable degree with this name, although it caused him considerable embarrassment because it classified him as a second-class citizen. But he struggled on. Then a strange thing happened. As a result of this modicum of prosperity, he developed offshoots. (Two of these offshoots – his brothers – had, of course, been with him for thousands of years. They were known as dance and athletics.) These were two new offshoots. One soon became known as recreation, and the other was called health and safety education. Our hero helped to develop them quite a bit and, of course, they in their gratitude helped him, too (while maintaining the dependency of youth).

Then one day after some great wars and other strong social for forces had their influence on society, physical education, who was still a second-class citizen among educators, discovered that his offshoots (recreation and health and safety education) had grown large and important in the world. They were anxious to become first-class citizens, and they made loud noises on occasion to inform all men that they deserved priority in life--and men, at least a goodly portion of them at any rate, recognized that they were right. But times change slowly, and the education of men was not yet greatly affected by this recognition.

During roughly the same period of time, two other phenomena occurred which held great import for physical education. His brothers, athletics and dance, had been performing so well that they had over a period of time grown strong and powerful as well. Athletics (or sport, as it seems to be called on continents other than North America) looked at him and said, "What a dull clod art thou!" What athletics meant was that physical education, or blank, or _____, or tnemevom (which is quite difficult to pronounce) wasn't very exciting, as he usually involved repetitive exercises and endurance activities which promoted muscular strength, flexibility and cardio-vascular efficiency. Sadly enough, dance (his other brother) seemed to feel the same way. He realized that he had a responsibility to teach young people about himself in schools, but it was so much more thrilling to perform for the cognoscenti, and even the multitudes. Thus, he proclaimed that he was an art, and he wanted to join his brother arts in performing centers which were springing up in communities and on college and university campuses.

The Unhappy Plight of Physical Education. Physical education, or blank, or _____, or tnemevom felt very sad, and he became worried. He looked back at his long heritage, and he recounted to himself the tale that has just been told to you. He felt important--at least to himself. He figured that he had been misjudged, since his motives were pure. He wondered if he had been stupid, because people still needed him (hadn't a great president been shocked by his absence?), but his very name--physical education (both words thereof, in fact)--made many seemingly intelligent people's lips curl. Thinking about the proverbial rose, he wondered if he would "smell as badly" with another name. After all, the U. S. Tire and Rubber Company was now known as Uniroyal, and people didn't look down on it. What should he do?

Time for Reflection. And then he began to think deeply, as deeply as he, a second-class citizen, could think. His identical twin sister, that lowly female creature who was really part of him (but who often made different noises as she went her own way), had been telling him for some time that he couldn't see the forest for the trees. She said, "Physical education; blank; sometimes designated as _____; but who should really be called tnemevom (which is quite difficult to pronounce), we have really been fools, and we merit our plight. We have been so stupid that we haven't been able to spell what we really should have been called--<u>tnemevom</u> it is, to be sure, but we have had it completely reversed!

Crestfallen, but with a rising sense of elation, <u>tnemevom</u> came to life all at once. He saw the light as explained to him by his identical twin sister. He took a deep breath, tensed his muscles, and executed a back somersault with a half twist. He assumed new dignity almost immediately, as he realized that he now had a new name (that was quite simple to pronounce), and it was <u>MOVEMENT</u>! From that day forward, he vowed that he would carry out his function more purposefully than ever before. He recognized that he could still relate effectively to his brothers and/or offshoots, as well as to his own identical twin sister (the person known formerly as a woman physical educator). But, more importantly, he realized that there was more to him than push-ups and jogging, as truly important as these parts of him might be. He sensed that he had physiological aspects, anatomical aspects, historical aspects, philosophical aspects, sociological aspects, psychological aspects, and so many other aspects that he couldn't count them on the fingers of his two hands.

The Hard Road Ahead

This was an important realization for MOVEMENT (formerly spelled <u>tnemevom</u>), but he didn't rush off blindly to proclaim his glory to the world. He had learned his lesson. This time he would spell his name correctly, and he would rest his case for recognition on a sound scientific base. He defined himself to the best of his ability and decided that "the interaction of man and his movements" (Paddick, 1967, p. 70) described his function quite well. Thus, a disciplinary body-of-knowledge could conceivably come from the "human movement sciences" (Kenyon, 1968, p. 16), or perhaps the human movement arts and sciences. Having reasoned so deeply, our hero looked around for his twin sister (that lovely female creature who was really part of him, but who was fidgeting rather impatiently at the moment) and said, "It's a hard road that lies ahead, and we may be unfit for the task. But if it is to be traversed, we must do it together. If we deserve to reach the goal we have dreamed of, we may get there some day. But let's not debate the issue to long, since the sun is already quite high in the sky."

General Bibliography

1. Bowen, W. P. and Mitchell, E. D. The Theory of Organized Play. New York: A. S. Barnes and Company, 1923.

2. Brownell, Clifford L. and Hagman, E. P. Physical Education - Foundations and Principles. New York: McGraw-Hill Book Company, Inc., 1951.

3. Bucher, Charles A. Foundations of Physical Education. St. Louis: The C. V. Mosby Company, 1952.

4. Burtt, Edwin A. In Search of Philosophic Understanding. New York: The New American Library, Inc., 1965.

5. Clark, Margaret C. "A Philosophical Interpretation of a Program of Physical Education in a State Teachers College." Ph.D. dissertation, New York University, 1943.

6. Cobb, Louise S. "A Study of the Functions of Physical Education in Higher Education." Ph.D. dissertation, Teachers College, Columbia University, 1943.

7. Esslinger, Arthur A. "A Philosophical Study of Principles for Selecting Activities in Physical Education." Ph.D. dissertation, State University of Iowa, 1938.

8. Frankena, William K. Philosophy of Education. New York: The Macmillan Company, 1965.

9. _____. Three Historical Philosophies of Education. Chicago, Illinois: Scott, Foresman and Company, 1965.

10. Hess, Ford A. "American Objectives of Physical Education from 1900-1957 Assessed in the Light of Certain Historical Events." Ed.D. dissertation, New York University, 1969.

11. Hetherington, Clark. School Program in Physical Education. New York: Harcourt, Brace & World, Inc., 1922.

12. Huxley, Aldous. Tomorrow and Tomorrow and Tomorrow. New York: The New American Library of World Literature, Inc., 1964.

13. Kenyon, Gerald S. "On the Conceptualization of Sub-disciplines within an Academic Discipline Dealing with Human Movement." A paper presented at the Annual Meeting of the National College Physical Education Association for Men, Houston, Texas, January, 1968, and which will appear in the forthcoming Proceedings. It will appear also in the first issue of the new International Review of Physical Education and Sport that will be published in the spring of 1968.

14. Lynn, Minnie L. "Major Emphases of Physical Education in the United States." Ph.D. dissertation, University of Pittsburgh, 1944.

15. McCloy, C. H. Philosophical Bases for Physical Education. New York: Appleton-Century-Crofts, Inc., 1940.

16. McNeill, William H. The Rise of the West. Chicago: The University of Chicago Press, 1963.

17. Morris, Desmond. The Naked Ape. New York: McGraw-Hill Book Company, 1967.

18. Nash, Jay B. (editor). Mind-Body Relationships. Volume I. New York: A. S. Barnes and Company, Inc., 1931. (This was the first volume in the Interpretations of Physical Education Series; of interest, also, is Character Education Through Physical Education, 1934.)

19. Oberteuffer, Delbert. Physical Education. New York: Harper & Row, Publishers, 1951. (The Second Edition in 1962 was in collaboration with Celeste Ulrich.)

20. Paddick, Robert J. "The Nature and Place of a Field of Knowledge in Physical Education." M.A. thesis, The University of Alberta, April, 1967.

21. Scott, Harry A. Competitive Sports in Schools and Colleges. New York: Harper & Row, Publishers, Inc., 1951.

22. Sharman, Jackson R. Modern Principles of Physical Education. New York: A. S. Barnes and Company, Inc., 1937.

23. Simpson, George Gaylord. "What Is Man?" (A review of The Naked Ape by D. Morris), The New York Times Book Review, February 11, 1968.

24. Staley, Seward C. Sports Education. New York: A. S. Barnes and Company, 1939.

25. Wayman, Agnes R. *A Modern Philosophy of Physical Education*. Philadelphia: W. B. Saunders Company, 1938.

26. Williams, Jesse F. *The Principles of Physical Education*. Philadelphia: W. B. Saunders Company, 1927.

27. _____ and Hughes, W. L. *Athletics in Education*. Philadelphia: W. B. Saunders Company, 1930.

28. Wood, Thomas D. and Cassidy, Rosalind. *The New Physical Education*. New York: The Macmillan Company, 1927.

29. Zeigler, Earle F., "History of Physical Education and Sports." *FIEP-Bulletin*, 3-4, 41-45, 1967.

30. _____ and McCristal, K. J., "A History of the Big Ten Body-of-Knowledge Project in Physical Education." *Quest*, IX, 79-84, December, 1967.

31. _____ and VanderZwaag. *Physical Education: Reconstructionism or Essentialism*. Champaign, Illinois: Stipes Publishing Company, 1966.

APPENDIX A

THE HISTORICAL ROLE OF SPORT IN SELECTED SOCIETIES: AN APPROACH TO DESCRIPTION, EXPLANATION, AND EVALUATION

Earle F. Zeigler
The University of Western Ontario, London

Introduction*

The description, explanation, and evaluation of the historical role of sport in selected societies could readily consume a lifetime of endeavor for a considerable number of qualified scholars. It is for this reason that the writer wishes to quickly dispel any thought that he may be unwarrantedly presumptupus in implying that this preliminary paper will be definitive in regard to fingings and conclusions. Its aim is to show some progress, and also to alert fellow historians about some possible opportunities for enlightenment through cooperation with scholars in related disciplines – and, of course, through the employment of some of their research techniques and/or findings.

This paper is, therefore, a follow-up of a proposal made at the International Relations Meeting of the National College Physical Education Association for Men Meeting at Portland, Oregon, December 28, 1970. The plan was for the establishment of a long-term comparative analysis of educational values in selected countries with their implications for sport and physical education. [31] The basic assumption is that the need is most urgent to make our earth sort of a "global village" in which the level of personal communication among people of all countries will be increased tremendously. The achievement of such status would be more than a mere "opportunity to promote international relations and goodwill"; it would, rather, be mandatory if civilization as we know it is to survive. As Asimov has predicted, mankind is fast reaching the point where "signs of breakdown are everywhere, for the problems introduced by our contemporary level of technology seem insuperable." His dire prediction is that we are as a result faced with a race "between the coming of the true fourth revolution [in man's ability to communicate with his fellow man everywhere!] and the death of civilization that will inevitably occur through growth past the limits of the third." The message here is simply that all men on earth must learn to communicate more efficiently and effectively very soon![1]

---

* A paper presented at the Second World Symposium on the History of Sport and Physical Education, Banff, Alberta, Canada, June 1, 1971.

Why, therefore, should anyone be concerned with the historical role of sport in society? The answer would appear to be obvious and straightforward - "history is actually a bridge connecting the past with with the present, and pointing - the road to the future." History, thus conceived, is "a lantern carried by the side of man, moving forward with every step taken. . ."[24] And we simply cannot forget the importance of the rays from the lantern that shine to the rear, to our side, and on the road ahead!

How may such a comparative analysis and interpretation of the historical role of sport in society be made in the best possible way? What knowledge is needed before any assessment can be made even tentatively? The remainder of this paper will consist of certain steps recommended by one fallible person who has been working at the subject. It will soon be obvious that much assistance and collaboration is indicated. To approach the task at hand, the following topics will be considered: (1) the disciplines through which men have gained knowledge about the individual and group values held by past societies; (2) the research methods and techniques available for investigation, and which have special relevance for this problem; (3) the chronology of civilizations considered in this delimited paper; (4) the discipline of history, and the persistent problems approach adopted by this investigator; (5) the discipline of sociology, and the relevance of one broad theory to historical investigation; (6) the discipline of anthropology, and how some of the theories of cultural anthropology shed light on the topic at hand; (7) the discipline of psychology, and how social psychology may explain how man has made certain emotional and social adaptation to his environment through sport and physical activity; (8) the discipline of philosophy, and how a type of language analysis may assist with the understanding of the meaning of sport terms both in the past and present; (9) the theories of sport and play propounded by scholars from a variety of disciplines; (10) a persistent historical problems approach based on the analysis of the social institutions of a society and the influence of values and norms on education, including sport and physical education; and (11) and a brief summary including some tentative findings and conclusions based on the relatively limited perspective of this preliminary analysis and interpretation.

Related Disciplines

Men have employed a variety of psychological or learning processes to gain knowledge about the present and the past, notably (1) thinking (rationalism), (2) feeling (intuitionism), (3) sensing (empiricism), and (4) believing (authoritarianism).[28] As the discipline has become more scientific, and has, therefore, placed increased emphasis on research techniques involving a more empirical approach, there has been a marked tendency to turn to a variety of related disciplines for assistance. The late Allan Nevins, writing in

1968, reaffirmed the idea that the discipline of history was employing "many powerful new forces . . . and few men understand half of them."[25] He was referring to such aspects as new studies from archeology; advancements in epigraphy; development of the carbon-dating process; comparative ancient literature, etc.[25] With the present topic, however, the need is to turn to those disciplines through which men have gained knowledge about the individual and group values held by past societies. Thus, in addition to history, brief reference will be made to direction and knowledge that may be gained from sociology, cultural anthropology, social psychology, and philosophy.

Research Methods and Techniques

There have been many types of historical investigation embodying both critical and constructive intellectual processes. Basically, the historian is confronted initially with a mass of data which he must organize, analyze, interpret, evaluate, and synthesize in such a way that his efforts enable him to write history that reflects man's past as accurately as possible. As Kahler tells us, "there is no history without meaning."[16] And if the meaning is "teased out" of the data, there is no doubt but that the question of values will arise.

Historians are now confronted with a need to understand the research methods and techniques of the related disciplines described above. The other two broad methods are typically designated as descriptive and experimental group method, each offering a multitude of techniques and variations for the eager researcher to employ in his effort to investigate his problem in the most adequate fashion. "Philosophical method" has often been considered a fourth broad method of research, but it is difficult to claim that much of the earlier philosophical endeavor produced new knowledge in a scientific sense; yet much of present philosophical investigation is highly scientific in nature and approach. This brings the discussion full circle back to the employment of descriptive techniques, mathematical logic, or experimental investigations in which a control group is employed.[11]

History - Chronology of Selected Societies

It is to history that the investigator turns for the main subdivisions of this preliminary analysis. The analysis and interpretation will be limited to: (1) Primitive and Early Societies; (2) Greece and Rome; (3) The Middle Ages; (4) The Enlightenment and Nineteenth Century Europe; and (5) North America.[32] It is granted immediately that such a presentation is definitely provincial (Western world) when it arrives at the modern period especially. This deficiency must be remedied just as soon as possible by the combined efforts of many of us, and there is no doubt but that this will be done soon. As we work together for further understanding, the maxim - "neither a borrower nor a lender be" - most certainly should <u>not</u> apply to the matter at hand.

It is literally frightening today if one reflects deeply in the area of historical interpretation, and the investigator must keep in mind further that historical theories of interpretation are almost inescapably attached to the needs that people have and the values that they hold at the time that the history of any era is being written.[37] For example, the writer does not subscribe to the cyclical rise and fall of civilizations, nor does he believe that there are certain systematic rules or principles which describe historical change in a way applicable to all societies. Nor is he convinced that history is ever completely objective <u>or</u> subjective. He <u>is</u> pragmatic and pluralistic in his approach, and accepts always the idea of multiplicity of causation. An <u>ad hoc</u> theory may well offer a very sound reason for a particular historical development. Thus, because it is not possible to repeat historical events, historians will probably never be able to attain complete objectivity. They should remain open-minded in a world characterized by evolutionary humanistic change.[12]

As this topic is approached, it will be possible to obtain considerable help from the earlier work of Marvin H. Eyler entitled "Origins of Some Modern Sports."[8] From a methodological standpoint, the writer has, over a period of several decades, been identifying and collecting data about some fifteen persistent historical problems that have had a relation to sport and physical education.[39] The first six of these so-called problems have been identified as <u>social forces</u> which have influenced sport and physical education significantly in the societies being considered. These forces or influences are: (1) values and norms; (2) type of political state; (3) nationalism; (4) economics; (5) religion; and most recently (6) ecology, or man's use of his environment. The remaining <u>nine</u> of these problems may be considered as <u>professional problems</u> for the person who practices in the field of physical education and sport, although most certainly each one of these problems is of somewhat greater or lesser concern to the general public in all of our societies. These "persistent problems" are: (1) professional preparation, including curriculum; (2) methods of instruction; (3) the role of administration; (4) the concept of health; (5) the use of leisure; (6) amateurism, semi-professionalism, and professionalism in sport; (7) dance in physical education and recreation; (8) physical education and sport for women; and (9) the concept of progress.[32] The investigator has adapted an approach to educational problems which is employed also by John S. Brubacher in his historical and philosophical investigations.[4,5] (Professor Brubacher was recently selected as one of eleven leaders in American education in the twentieth century.)[23]

Sociology - Parsons' Theory of Action

The discipline of sociology can be extremely helpful to the sport and physical education historian, and especially so when the concern is for an analysis and interpretation of the values and norms of various social systems. Parsons' theory of action, a structural-functional theory, has been described by Johnson as "a type of empirical system."[14] Four levels of social structure are postulated as (1) values; (2) norms; (3) the structure of collectivities; and (4) the structure of roles. These proceed from highest to lowest, with the higher levels being more general than the lower ones. Values, for example, are categorized, and values in sport would, of necessity, reinforce the important societal values and shared sanctioned norms of a particular social system.

To get at the historical role of sport in a society, there would appear to be a prior need to achieve an acceptable synthesis of the history of the social system being considered. The functional interchanges between and among the subsystems of the social system should be understood (e.g., how its economy serves as an effective adaptive subsystem), as should the means whereby a social system maintains its equilibrium (e.g., the social processes whereby a society maintains a given structure or changes it).[15] If, as is typically postulated, sport, games, and physical activity exert significant social force within a society (and vice versa), a knowledge of these factors will offer increased "explanatory power." Just recently, Lüschen has reported that there is a "strong relationship" between sport and society, and he cited for evidence analyses of American football, the running races of Hopi Indians, three Illinois frontier subcultures, and the log races of the Timbira tribe in Brazil.[20] It can only be hoped that in the future an increasingly greater number of sociologists will concern themselves with sport as an important social institution. Thus, the function it fulfills in the total system of social integration would be gradually much better understood.

Anthropology - a "Giant" of a Discipline

The fields of anthropology include the study of the physical, cultural, and social development and the behavior of men and women since they appeared in the evolutionary development of the planet that has been designated as Earth. For this reason anthropology can readily be called a "giant" of a discipline! The human animal has a culture or a social heritage, and this subdivision of the total field has been named cultural or social anthropology. As man's various social units are traced, the interrelationship of cultural values and human behavior is a perennial concern for the members of a particular society.

Cultural anthropology has only recently been recognized as a science, and anthropological theories about sport and games as dynamic processes of social life have not been given the attention that perhaps ought to have been the case. Of course, the work of the cultural anthropologist would often not even be sufficiently exact to warrant the employment of complex statistical procedures – and may never be when one is studying the processes that occasion the development or change of cultural patterns. This is not to say, however, that games and sporting patterns of early cultures cannot or should not be described with care or that ad hoc theories may not be applied to them wherever possible. It seems reasonable to assume that certain types of games and sports will appear as identifiable cultural elements in the culture complex of a society (e.g., the idea of sportsmanship and fair play in the games of a democratic society).[13]

An example of a recent effort to relate game theory to cultural complexes is an investigation completed by Glassford in 1970. He traced sporadic attempts to prove that an interrelationship exists between a culture and its game forms. He postulated that the nature of sport and games would undergo changes depending upon the possible changes in values and norms of a culture undergoing transition. Based on a theory of games and economic behavior outlined by Von Neumann and Morgenstern[30], Glassford developed a game classification model which he then tested on a culture (Eskimo) which was undergoing a marked transition. Basically, he hypothesized that "the orientation of the traditional generation toward the values of reciprocity and sharing would be reflected in their game preferences," and that "the new era generation would express a stronger preference for competitive games." The findings enabled Glassford to verify his postulations (at least tentatively), and also confirmed the hypotheses that the traditional generation seems to prefer self-testing games more, and also preferred a game strategy which afforded "tolerable satisfactions" with minimum risk.[10]

Social Psychology – Emotional and Social Adaptation to Environment

There is no doubt but that the historian will need to keep the investigation of social psychologists increasingly in mind in the future as he hypothesizes about the historical role of sport and games in various civilizations. Fundamentally, the present concern is with "the development of the social phases of personality, attitudes, and values by means of" these activities.[6] The challenge of explaining how personality is developed and maintained in a culture is such that fully adequate explanations may not be available for some time to come. The many variables involved complicate the possibility of investigation greatly. And yet society readily accepts the hypothesis that physical activity in competitive sport situations does lead to social development. It seems true further that social behavior and personality growth can be influenced positively or negatively according to a society's values and depending upon the quality of the leadership and the opportunities for participation afforded. Thus, the profession of sport and physical education has a responsibility to provide practitioners exhibiting the finest type of leadership consonant with the highest values of the social system.

An inventory of findings about human behavior is now available[3], which serves as a foundation "layer" of knowledge for investigators in sport and physical education. The 1960 project of the Research Council of the American Association for Health, Physical Education, and Recreation, entitled The Contributions of Physical Activity to Human Well-Being, includes the late Charles Cowell's "The Contributions of Physical Activity to Social Development." This particular section is to be up-dated as soon as possible. One cannot help but feel, however, that this highly important aspect of the disciplinary approach to sport and physical education is not receiving sufficient support and encouragement from the many people who have made such strong but unsupported claims for the social values of sport and games in the past. (Can it be that they fear the results of such investigations because they suspect that current leadership is of such a calibre that positive benefits may be at a low level?) At any rate, the classification of games based on socio-psychological phenomena should go on (e.g., 27 and 18), as should the "people experiments" discussed by Martens[21] and broadened in his plea for "a social psychology of physical activity."[22]

Philosophy - Definitions and Value Theories

The field of philosophy offers a storehouse of data to the sport and physical education historian; the difficulty is how and on what basis the historian can or should approach all of this information. Philosophy has traditionally been subdivided into four subdivisions with axiology (system of values) as the end result of philosophical endeavor. Thus, fundamental beliefs about values - whether in life generally, or in education, or in sport - would tend to be as consistent as possible with a person's beliefs in regard to the other three subdivisions of the total discipline or subject matter. Metaphysics (questions about the nature of reality) is combined with axiology to form what has been called speculative philosophy. Epistemology (acquisition of knowledge) and logic (exact relating of ideas) are designated typically as critical philosophy.

How a particular historian employs philosophy to serve his purposes as a historian depends almost completely on his background and experience within the culture in which he is living. Pragmatists would tend to be concerned about learning theory prior to questions about the nature of reality. Another philosopher might wish to study the many histories of philosophy in which certain theories about the various branches would be presented chronologically. (Some of these treatments might be in the form of biographies of great philosophers of the past.) A third approach might be to read progressively from the actual works of the philosophers themselves (often through the location of the best translations available). Another method would be useful - the determination of the major recurring issues or problems with which philosophers have concerned themselves over the centuries. It was this approach that Brubacher used with the departmental philosophy of education, and was also employed by this investigator because of its seemingly effective application to sport and physical education[33] through the application of a structural analysis research technique.[9]

Strangely enough, just at the time that people all over the world seem to have become more "value conscious," so to speak, the professional field of philosophy - in the English speaking world at least - seems to have "cast the common man adrift in waters that are anything but calm and peaceful." The main reason why many philosophers seem to be devoting less time to the "service" aspects of the general education of students is undoubtedly that they have taken more of a "disciplinary approach" by the adoption of research techniques which are more effective in the achievement of the goals of the philosophical analysis movement. As Kaplan has indicated in describing this twentieth-century movement, "philosophy is a kind of logico-linguistic analysis, not a set of super-scientific truths about man and nature, nor a sustained exhortation to live one's life in a particular way."[17] He clarifies this explanation further by intimating that the professional activity of the philosopher is a type of "linguistic therapy" directed toward restoring both ordinary language and scientific propositions to a state of "semantic well-being" through a "rational reconstruction of the language of science." For example, the philosopher would be asking, "what makes sense, and what is nonsense?" He does not determine whether a theoretical proposition is true or false - that is the scientist's realm - but he does try to see to it that they are expressed clearly, precisely, and logically.

Returning to the task of the historian, it is possible to conclude with some confidence that a philosopher may approach his work speculatively, normatively, or analytically - or through some combination of these approaches with the employment of several techniques. The historian may, therefore, look to the language analyst for a more careful delineation of the terms "sport," "play," and "athletics," for example, or he may be guided by the normative philosophizing of some outstanding person who evolves a systematic, coherent plan of a society and explains how sport and the culture displayed greater or lesser interdependence.[40]

One last suggestion may be made in the delineation of possible approaches to the task accepted for this present paper. It is a type of normative and analytic philosophizing applied to comparative and international education, which may be adapted to the social institution of sport. Lauwerys recommends that an investigator should make an effort to understand the dominant philosophy and philosophy of education in a culture undergoing study. The assumption is that such an assessment will provide true insight concerning the reasons why a definitive pattern of education is carried out by those responsible for policy formulation and execution in the educational system of a culture.[19]

Theories of Play, Sport, Athletics - from Various Disciplines

As soon as one attempts a reasonably careful analysis of the literature on play theory, he realizes that there are in existence of plethora of theories emanating from a variety of disciplines. In the past most people have tended to use the words "play," "sport," and "athletics" with the blithe assurance that they would not be seriously challenged. Because this statement could typically applied to scholars as well as laymen, the situation is now such that an unabridged dictionary includes the word "sport" thirteen different ways as a noun, two ways as an adjective, six as an intransitive verb, and five ways as a transitive verb. "Play" is employed in 74 different ways, and the terms "game" and "athletics" are used in 23 and three ways, respectively.[26] For the purpose of this paper, the appropriate definition of sport can be "an athletic activity requiring skill or physical prowess, usually of a competitive nature" (e.g., wrestling, racing, tennis, rugby, etc.). But does this definition apply to the past?

Most recently, Ellis at Illinois' Motor Performance and Play Research Laboratory has accomplished some fine analytical and integrative theorizing about play theory.[7] After a precise recapitulation of the so-called "classical" theories of play, he continues with an analysis, interpretation, and evaluation of the more recent theories that have been presented since the end of World War II - theories typically postulating homeostatic behavior patterns. Accepting the basic premise that man is the most neophilic (novelty-liking) of all animals, Ellis takes a stand that man's non-utilitarian behavior (play) is largely arousal-seeking in nature. Thus, he is saying that man plays competitive sport because he as an individual (and probably as a social animal) has a need "to generate interactions with the environment or self that elevate arousal towards the optimal for the individual."

It seems obvious to this investigator that the historian needs to keep the above-mentioned definitions of terms in mind as he approaches his work. Further, he should have as comprehensive an understanding of play theory as is needed to help him comprehend as best possible the true role of sport in the society which he is analyzing.*

Persistent Historical Problems Approach – Comparison and Interpretation

The persistent or perennial historical problems approach employed by this investigator has been explained earlier in this paper and, as was indicated, values in sport and physical education has been selected as first in a list of some fifteen problem areas. Further, the matter of amateurism, semi-professionalism, and professionalism in sport was considered important enough to warrant inclusion in this tabulation of historical problems. (It is admitted readily, of course, that this organization of problems is contemporary, and that it must necessarily have an "American bias" to a degree.)[33]

The following, then, is a recommended step-by-step approach for the description, explanation, and evaluation of the historical role of sport in selected societies. It is an approach that is multi-disciplinary in nature and which also rests upon findings that are available – and which will become increasingly available – from all research methods and techniques known to man.

1. Review the best evidence available concerning the social foundations of the society, culture, or social system being considered (e.g., values, norms, type of political structure, economic system, leading religions, etc.).

2. Assess the available evidence in regard to the educational foundations of the society (e.g., educational values in some hierarchical order; the curriculum and the process of education; and the relationship among the school, society and the individual).

3. Describe, interpret, and assess tentatively – based on tentative hypotheses – the sport and physical education practices of the society available through historical sources of both a primary and secondary nature. Categorize according to (1) aims and objectives, (2) methods of instruction, and (3) possible strengths and weaknesses.

4. Based on the literature of sociology, and available sociological analyses of the society being investigated, attempt to discover whether the functionally necessary processes of the social system

---

* Because of space limitations, economics as a pivotal social institution with highly significant implications for sport and physical education was not included, nor was the developing sub-discipline of comparative education.

(e.g., according to Parsons' theory of action) are operating in such a fashion that a hierarchy of control and conditioning is present that enables functional interchanges to take place in order to maintain equilibrium or to promote change. (The aim here, of course, is to learn whether an acceptable synthesis of the social system under investigation has been determined; whether there has been a realization to at least a certain extent of the society's value system; and the extent to which the social institution of sport and physical education has facilitated the achievement of the society's values.)[15]

5. Based on the literature of anthropology, and available anthropological theories of the culture being examined, attempt to discover to what extent games and sporting patterns have been assessed as dynamic processes within that specific culture. If careful ethnographical descriptions have been carried out, it is possible that an ad hoc theory such as Glassford's[10] may be applied, and at least compared with the evidence from sociological analysis available.

6. Based on the literature of social psychology and closely related aspects of the other behavioral sciences, attempt to learn if currently tenable theories about social behavior and personality growth may have been applicable in the social system being investigated. And, further, is it possible that such behavior and growth were influenced markedly by the society's value system as leaders sought to employ sport and physical activity to develop the desired individual and social values?

7. Based on the literature of the history of philosophy, it should be possible for the historian to correlate still further his earlier findings relative to the values considered important in the social system involved, and to relate the concerns ("persistent problems!") of the philosophers of a particular society to "value determinations" that have been postulated in the findings from other disciplines. In this way a type of "normative philosophizing" might be carried out in which the dominant philosophy and philosophy of education could be postulated and substantiated (perhaps) through "verification" by means of knowledge available from the related disciplines. Further, philosophical language analysis techniques may be providing means of determining inadequacies in the language of the people within the system.

8. At this point – and there is no doubt but that further evidence will become available from sub-disciplines not yet "invented" – the sport historian and philosopher should be able to "proclaim the 'validity and reliability'" of his earlier tentative hypotheses about the historical role of sport in a particular social system at a much higher "level of confidence" than previously.

9. At least one more possibility is available for <u>cross-cultural comparison</u> of the role of sport and physical education in society. This is the <u>comparative method</u> as developed by Bereday as a type of descriptive investigation.[2] Here the stages or steps are (1) <u>description</u>, in which descriptive data will be obtained about the plan of sport and physical education in each of the countries being studied; (2) <u>explanation</u>, in which an attempt will be made to explain the theory and practice in sport and physical education based upon the prevailing educational philosophy in each of the countries; (3) <u>juxtaposition</u>, in which the patterns of sport and physical education in the countries being compared cross-culturally will be <u>related</u> on the basis of the implications for sport and physical activity from the hierarchy of educational values existing in each of the countries; and (4) <u>comparison</u>, in which the findings and some reasonable conclusions will be presented based on the similarities and differences – with the final comparison taking into consideration the economic and educational status of the countries being considered.

Conclusions and a Final Word

In essence the writer hopes that the reader will conclude that it has now become possible for the sport historian to become ever so much more sophisticated in his work. The historian is being urged to become increasingly aware of the literature and evidence that is being provided steadily by sociology, cultural anthropology, social psychology, philosophy, and comparative education. Still further, the sport historian should consider the advisability of adopting at least certain of the research techniques available through the other disciplines. Much sport history has been written on the basis of common sense and simple description, which are, of course, necessary steps in the early development of a discipline. The time has come, however, for the sport historian to make apparent his underlying theory of history. He may wish further to apply his own <u>ad hoc</u> theory to his evaluation of the history of sport. It is only in this way that the field can look forward to the future development of "theories of the middle range" and ultimately far more complex theories about sport in the history of man.[39]

Lastly, it seems important at this particular moment to mention that scholars have been identifying "recurrent elements in the various world philosophies."[17] Kaplan asserts that there are four themes displaying a strong "family resemblance" in the living philosophies of the world today. The first is a theme of <u>rationality</u> displaying either casual or historical systematic unity. Secondly, there is a theme of <u>activism</u> which implies that understanding is a guide to positive action. Thirdly, he has detected a theme of <u>humanism</u>, a pervading belief that there is a continuity of man and nature in both the East and the West. Lastly, there is a preoccupation with <u>values</u> – a view that the life of man should be strongly related to values, and that his highest aspiration is to fulfill moral and spiritual values in his life.[38]

The sport historian, by identifying the historical role of sport in all societies and cultures, can help to make internationalism in sport and physical education one of the highest professional goals.

Footnotes and References

1. Asimov, Isaac., "The Fourth Revolution." Saturday Review (October 24, 1970), pp. 17-20.

2. Bereday, G. Z. F. Comparative Method in Education. New York: Holt, Rinehart, and Winston, 1964, p. 19 et ff.

3. Berelson, Bernard and Steiner, G. A. Human Behavior: An Inventory of Scientific Findings. New York: Harcourt, Brace & World, Inc., 1964.

4. Brubacher, John S. A History of the Problems of Education. New York: McGraw-Hill Book Company. Second edition, 1966.

5. _____. Modern Philosophies of Education. New York: McGraw-Hill Book Company. Fourth edition, 1969.

6. Cowell, Charles C., "The Contributions of Physical Activity to Social Development," in Research Quarterly, Vol. 31, No. 2:286-306 (Part II), May, 1960.

7. Ellis, M. J., "Play and Its Theories Re-examined," in America's Leisure, Yearbook of the National Recreation and Park Association, 1971.

8. Eyler, Marvin H. "Origins of Some Modern Sports." Unpublished Ph.D. thesis, University of Illinois, Urbana, 1956.

9. Fraleigh, Warren P., "Theory and Design of Philosophic Research," in Proceedings of the 74th Annual Meeting of the National College Physical Education Association for Men, Portland, Oregon, December 27, 1970.

10. Glassford, R. G. "Application of a Theory of Games to the Transitional Eskimo Culture." Unpublished Ph.D. thesis, University of Illinois, Urbana, 1970.

11. Good, Carter V. and Scates, D. E. Methods of Research. New York: Appleton-Century-Crofts, Inc., 1954.

12. Harvard Guide to American History (Written by Oscard Handlin, et. al.). New York: Atheneum, 1967, pp. 15-21.

13. Hershkovits, M. J. Cultural Anthropology. New York: Alfred Knopf, 1955, pp. 33-85.

14. Johnson, Harry M., "The Relevance of the Theory of Action to Historians." Social Science Quarterly, June, 1969, pp. 46-58.

15. _____. Sociology: A Systematic Introduction. New York: Harcourt, Brace & World, Inc., 1960.

16. Kahler, Erich. The Meaning of History. New York: George Braziller, 1964.

17. Kaplan, Abraham. The New World of Philosophy. New York: Random House, 1961, pp. 3-12.

18. Kenyon, Gerald S., "A Conceptual Model for Characterizing Physical Activity," in Research Quarterly, Vol. 39, No. 1:97-105, March, 1968.

19. Lauwerys, Joseph A., "The Philosophical Approach to Comparative Education." International Review of Education, Vol. V, 1959, pp. 283-290.

20. Lüschen, Günther., "The Interdependence of Sport and Culture." International Review of Sport Sociology (Poland), 2:127-141, 1967.

21. Martens, Rainer., "Demand Characteristics and Experimenter Bias." A paper presented at the Research Methodology Symposium, Research Council, AAHPER Convention, Detroit, April 5, 1971.

22. _____., "A Social Psychology of Physical Activity." Quest, 14:8-17, June, 1970.

23. National Society for the Study of Education (Seventieth Yearbook). Leaders in American Education (editor, R. J. Havighurst). Chicago: The University of Chicago Press, 1971, pp. 17-64.

24. Nevins, Allan., "The Explosive Excitement of History." Saturday Review, April 6, 1968.

25. _____. The Gateway to History. New York: Doubleday & Co., Inc., 1962, p. 14.

26. Random House Dictionary of the English Language, The. New York: Random House, 1967.

27. Roberts, J. M. and Sutton-Smith, B., "Child Training and Game Involvement." Ethnology, Vol. I, 1962. (The reader might wish to review also "Games in Culture," which appeared in 1959 in American Anthropologist (Vol. 61) by Roberts, Arth, and Bush.)

28. Royce, J. R., "Paths to Knowledge," in The Encapsulated Man. Princeton, N. J.: Van Nostrand, 1964.

29. Toffler, Alvin. Future Shock. New York: Random House, Inc., Inc., 1970.

30. Von Neumann, Jr. and Morgenstern, O. The Theory of Games and Economic Behavior. Princeton, M. J.: Princeton University Press. Second edition, 1947.

31. Zeigler, Earle F., "Amateurism, Semi-professionalism, and Professionalism in Sport - a Persistent Educational Problem," in Arnold W. Flath's A History of Relations between the National Collegiate Athletic Association and the Amateur Athletic Union of the United States, 1905-1963. Champaign, Illinois: Stipes Publishing Co., 1964.

32. _____, "A Comparative Analysis of Educational Values in Selected Countries: Their Implications for Physical Education and Sport," in Proceedings of the 74th Annual Meeting of the National College Physical Education Association for Men, Portland, Oregon, December 27, 1970.

33. _____, "Foreword," in Physical Education Around the World (editor, William Johnson). Indianapolis, Indiana: Phi Epsilon Kappa Fraternity, Monograph #4, 1970.

34. _____, A History of Physical Education and Sport to 1900. Champaign, Illinois: Stipes Publishing Company, 1973.

35. _____, "Persistent Historical Problems of Physical Education and Sport," in Proceedings of the First International Seminar on the History of Physical Education and Sport, Wingate Institute for Physical Education, Netanya, Israel, April 9-11, 1968, pp. 1-13. (Published in March, 1969 by the Institute, Editor, Uriel Simri).

36. _____. Philosophical Foundations for Physical, Health, and Recreation Education. Englewood Cliffs, N. J.: Prentice-Hall, Inc., 1964.

37. _____. Problems in the History and Philosophy of Physical Education and Sport. Englewood Cliffs, N. J.: Prentice-Hall, Inc., 1968.

38. _____, "Putting the Greek Ideal in Perspective." A paper presented to the History of Sport Section, AAHPER Convention, Detroit, April 5, 1971.

39. _____, Howell, M. L. and Trekell, Marianna. Research in the History, Philosophy, and International Aspects of Physical Education and Sport. Champaign, Illinois: Stipes Publishing Company, 1971, 350 p.

40. _____ and VanderZwaag, H. J. Physical Education: Progressivism or Essentialism? Champaign, Illinois: Stipes Publishing Co., 1968.

APPENDIX B

AN ANALYSIS OF MASTER'S AND DOCTORAL STUDIES RELATED TO THE HISTORY OF PHYSICAL EDUCATION COMPLETED IN THE UNITED STATES, 1930-1967*

Thomas D. Abernathy
University of Illinois, Urbana

The question of the meaning of history has been dealt with by many authors in many places. In general, the relationship of the events of the past with the status of the present and the hope of the future has been emphasized by the historian as the role of history. Carr has defined history as "a continuous process of interaction between the historian and facts, an unending dialogue between the past and the present" (1961, p. 35). Nevins stated that "history enables bewildered bodies of human beings to grasp their relationship with their past, and helps them chart on general lines their forward course" (1963, p. 21). "The relative significance of historical materials," as proposed by Barnes, "is to be determined, in part, by the nature of the period in which they fell, and in part by their bearing on contemporary life..." (1963, p. 379). These reflections display the viewpoint that the meaning of history is related to how the historian views history. With this in mind, a common understanding on the meaning of history has not been possible.

History is a special type of discipline, which has its utility measured in other ways than that of science, economics, or even art. No other subject, except possibly philosophy, embraces the whole story of man. The historian must confine his special research to a restricted area, but he must at all times look at the whole of life. He should be able to specialize to the extent of studying a subject in depth and, at the same time, he cannot neglect the breadth of any particular subject. The relationship of one activity area to another is part of the job of the historian. For example, the history of politics may be related to the history of culture, or the story of the growth of religion may have affected the history of economics. The historian

---

*Master's thesis completed at the University of Illinois, Urbana, in 1969. A complete bibliographic listing of 166 theses (and also thirty-seven more of a biographical nature by Dr. Marianna Trekell) appears in Research in the History, Philosophy, and International Aspects of Physical Education and Sport: Bibliographies and Techniques (edited by E. F. Zeigler, M. L. Howell and M. Trekell). Champaign, Illinois: Stipes Publishing Company, 10 Chester Street, 1971. See pages 118-130 and 162-168.

cannot be narrow-minded in his view of the past. If the historian becomes too narrow in his outlook, thus a specialist, he misses some of the values of his profession. A delicate balance between depth and breadth should prevail.

The role of the historian of physical education is to develop a meaningful interpretation of the events in the past for the purpose of making present-day physical educators aware of the background of their field. A knowledge of the background of physical education will assist the physical educator in understanding the present status of the field. The historian of physical education presents his view of the past in order to clarify the subject with which he is dealing. As well as clarifying his subject, he also brings up the data for consideration and so widens the field of investigation. As the knowledge of a subject increases, the possibilities of further research also increase. From this point of view, the meaningful interpretation of the past developed by physical education historians is not completed only for the purpose of determining a final conclusion or answer, but may also serve as a suggestive stimulus for further research.

Some of the research conducted in the history of physical education has been the result of the writing of master's theses and doctoral dissertations. A number of master's and doctoral studies in physical education, which used the historical method, has been written. In general, the quality of this work has not been high, but most of the studies have made a contribution to our historical knowledge of the development of the field of physical education. A central guide or index of these graduate studies has not been compiled; therefore, an analysis could not be made until a collection of these theses were made. Through an extensive search of sources, a number of historical theses in physical education were located. Studies, which were included in this collection, were required to use a form of the historical method. As dates of reference, studies completed between 1930 and 1967 were used. Finally, only theses completed in the United States were considered. With these delimiting factors, an analysis of the master's and doctoral studies related to the history of physical education completed in the United States between 1930 and 1967 was developed.

In developing the collection of studies related to the history of physical education, the aim was to include the total scope of studies completed in the area. Even though an extensive search of sources was made, it was possible that some studies were not included. This may be the result of being overlooked by the researcher or due to the fact that some studies may have never been reported to indexes, guides, or bibliographies of theses. Another factor, which affected the inclusion of all of the studies, was the matter of a study including some or all of the allied fields in its scope. In order for a thesis to be included its main emphasis should have been on physical education, but the inclusion of health, recreation, intramurals, safety, or athletics in the title or scope did not always exclude it from consideration. Within these limitations, a total of 203 studies were located which were related to the history of physical education.

The studies were classified into twelve topical categories in order to assist in making the analysis. The twelve categories were as follows:

1. General Histories of Physical Education in Colleges and Universities

2. Histories of Physical Education in Individual Colleges or Universities

3. Histories of Professional Preparation in Physical Education

4. Histories of Elementary School Physical Education

5. Histories of Secondary School Physical Education

6. Histories of Physical Education in City or County School Systems

7. Histories of State Physical Education

8. Histories of Associations, Organizations, and Projects Related to Physical Education

9. Histories of Trends, Objectives, and Attitudes Related to Physical Education

10. Histories of Physical Education in Foreign Countries

11. Biographies

12. General Histories Related to Physical Education.

Some of the studies could have been placed in more than one category, but were placed only in the category which seemed most appropriate.

The analysis of the studies, which were discovered to be related to the history of physical education, was based on the categories into which the studies were divided. The analysis was made in order to detect certain trends and generalizations about studies related to the history of physical education. The present status of graduate research in the history of physical education was the goal for determining these trends. The general aim of the analysis was to discuss the nature, value, scope, and frequency of the studies within their categories.

1. General Histories of Physical Education in Colleges and Universities

The purpose of this category was to determine the scope of the histories of physical education concerned with the broad perspective of higher education. There were only five studies classified under this category. None of the studies attempted to include the entire field of physical education throughout the whole range of higher education. All were delimited in some form. The two approaches used in this type of study were: (1) to view a particular aspect of physical education over a large range of institutions; and (2) to view a large number of factors in a smaller number of institutions. The value of these studies is that from them certain generalizations and conclusions can be reached about the status of physical education in institutions of higher education (more than if just one school was used.)

(For the specific titles under this category, the reader is referred to the work of the following authors: Ainsworth, Martin, Nash, Salls, Williams, S. A.)

2. Histories of Physical Education in Individual Colleges or Universities

This classification is one of the two largest in which studies related to the history of physical education were located. The histories of physical education in individual colleges or universities was, and is, popular for three reasons: (1) the sources for material are readily available in college and university files and archives; (2) the writing of these types of histories is relatively simple because of the possibility of forming clear, chronological narratives; and (3) the demand for such studies by administrators is usually due to their desire for a knowledge of the background of their departments or divisions. Within this classification, there were six doctoral dissertations and thirty-eight master's theses identified.

(For the specific titles under this category, the reader is referred to the work of the following authors: Averette, Bahr, Best, Bippus, Boycheff, Bridgewater, Degen, Detrick, Flannigan, Gordon, Graham, B., Hess, Jackson, Jacobs, Jenkins, Johns, Johnson, J. E., Kassen, Keeler, Kinsey, Kinzig, Latzke, Malizola, Mariner, Matthews, Mayne, Mintz, Neill, Oakes, Olsen, Raines, Rezac, Rosen, Sage, Schwarberg, Seidler, B. M., Simmons, Sisco, Smallwood, Summers, Tidwell, Wray, Wright, Zimmerli.)

3. Histories of Professional Preparation in Physical Education

The purpose of this classification was to identify those histories of physical education dealing with professional preparation in physical education. The attempt of most of these studies has been to assist physical educators to obtain a historical view of the teacher training programs in physical education. The nine doctoral dissertations related to the history of professional preparation were all completed in the last twenty years. The concern for professional preparation before this time may have been somewhat meager. The eight master's theses involved in the history of professional preparation in physical education were limited in scope in comparison to the doctoral studies. For the large part, the master's studies looked at the teacher training at one institution and were, in general, quite curriculum oriented. The professional preparation program has followed some traditional patterns and concepts which these studies have been able to point out. A thorough search of the past plans of study in teacher training should help the field of physical education to evaluate and upgrade its program of professional preparation.

(For the specific titles under this category, the reader is referred to the work of the following authors: Agnew, Coffey, Foss, Gilcoyne, Graham, Hall, Hulce, Johnson, Kennedy, LaPoint, Pierro, Runquist, Seidler, Taylor, Wacker, Weber, Zeigler.)

4. Histories of Elementary School Physical Education

The topic of elementary school physical education has not, apparently, been reviewed very completely by graduate students in the area of history. Only one study was located which was designed specifically for the study of this topic. This area would seem to deserve more consideration than it has been given.

(For the specific title under this category, the reader is referred to the work of Abernathy which gives the bibliographical reference for the thesis of Cieniawski; see footnote on page 379 above.)

5. Histories of Secondary School Physical Education

The secondary school has been the traditional place for teachers of physical education to start their professional careers. The studies which related to this classification were quite adequate in scope. There were four doctoral dissertations and five master's theses which described the history of physical education in secondary schools. The doctoral dissertations were informative because the trends noted in the studies were substantiated by primary source material. The emphasis of the master's theses, involved with this classification, was placed on certain aspects within the limitations of a locality, such as county, city, or state.

(For the specific titles under this category, the reader is referred to the work of the following authors: Dohr, Driscoll, Markgraff, Pesavento, Perry, Pickett, Stafford, Stoddart, Street.)

6. Histories of Physical Education in City and County School Systems

Within this category, three doctoral dissertations and eleven master's theses were completed. The scope of these studies should include both the history of elementary school physical education and the history of secondary school physical education, as well as general factors affecting both of these areas. The historical approach of these studies was somewhat limited, because the writers generally failed to use the technique of internal criticism in evaluating the sources. Nevertheless, the theses were valuable in relating the development of physical education in these school systems, and in relating the factors affecting the local programs in physical education.

(For the specific titles under this category, the reader is referred to the work of the following authors: Anderson, Brancato, Brimhall, Burke, Copp, Gallagher, Gill, Junkin, Riordan, Shetterly, Swanson, Thompson, Tierney, Wilson.)

7. Histories of State Physical Education

The histories of state physical education were, in general, very extensive in scope. They have tended to include public school physical education, college and university physical education, the role of the state government in physical education, and the role of the allied fields in physical education. There were five doctoral dissertations and four master's theses placed in this classification.

(For the specific titles under this category, the reader is referred to the work of the following authors: Anderson, DeGroot, Garber, Grant, King, E. L., Kiracofe, Mitchell, Newland, Sinclair.)

8. Histories of Associations, Organizations, and Projects Related to Physical Education

The field of physical education has been greatly affected by professional organizations and associations which have helped to form the principles and objectives of the field. Histories involved with these organizations and associations have traditionally attempted to elucidate and evaluate their contributions along this line. There were six doctoral dissertations and eight master's theses identified with this classification. The studies relating to this category were varied in nature and scope.

(For the specific titles under this category, the reader is referred to the work of the following authors: Beasley, Bellino, Bennett,

Berridge, Bevington, Bray, Breiner, Cleland, Daves, Dunbar, Johnson, Smith, Valentine, Washke.)

9. Histories of Trends, Objectives, and Attitudes Related to Physical Education

Throughout the history of physical education, the objectives and aims of the field have been discussed and written about in many different situations. The studies of the history of physical education involved in these aspects reflect such of the past concern for these important factors. In general, there were two different approaches to this type of study. One approach was to examine certain key physical educators and to present or compare their views of physical education. The second approach involved studying the objectives in a more general nature, which was unrelated to individual physical education leaders. In this classification, there were eight doctoral dissertations and seven master's theses identified.

(For the specific titles under this category, the reader is referred to the work of the following authors: Burnstine, Caldwell, Ervin, Felshin, Gamage, Gerber, Hess, King, Lynn, McPherson, Means, Meyer, Palm, Schutte, Sherman.)

10. Histories of Physical Education in Foreign Countries

This classification was devised due to the number of master's theses related to the history of physical education in foreign countries. There were eleven master's theses and no doctoral dissertations in this category. Some of the studies in this category were probably written by foreign students describing their homeland.

(For the specific titles under this category, the reader is referred to the work of the following authors: Anderson, Diamantides, Harsky, Hunt, Meshizuka, Olivar, Osborne, Powell, Wertz, Wu, Yu.)

11. Biographies

A large number of studies dealing with the history of physical education have been biographical in nature. The emphasis on the leading physical educators is definitely a trend which is easily seen by the fact that there were twenty-two doctoral dissertations and fifteen master's theses identified as biographical in nature. The biography, when carried out with imagination and originality, can contribute much to the preservation of the writings, ideas, accomplishments, and contributions of the physical education leaders. In all of these studies, the intent of the author was usually more to present the contributions of these leaders in physical education, rather than just recording the events which occurred in their lives. Most of the master's studies centered on local physical education leaders, rather than national ones (which were used more for doctoral dissertations).

(The specific titles under this category are not included in the back of this volume; the reader should, however, examine Professor Trekell's listing for a complete recording of biographical studies - 1971.)

12. General Histories Related to Physical Education

This classification served the purpose of a miscellaneous category. The quality of the theses in this group was the same as in other categories. But due to the nature of these studies, they did not relate to any of the other categories. There were eight doctoral dissertations and nineteen master's theses in this classification.

(For the specific titles under this category, the reader is referred to the work of the following authors: Backus, Barton, Beck, Bishop, Bryson, Burgam, Bynum, Carolan, Cassell, Drew, Foster, Freehill, Ghilardi, Greene, Gunther, Hilby, Jenson, McDonald, Meek, Miller, Petroskey, Sneddon, Studer, Todd, Trone, Williams, Wysocki.)

As a result of the analysis of the master's and doctoral studies related to the history of physical education, the following conclusions seem appropriate:

1. The frequency of graduate studies relating to history of physical education has been somewhat low in relation to the total number of theses completed in all areas.

2. The subject of a large number of the studies relating to the history of physical education was either about an individual college or university physical education program or the biography of a physical educator.

3. There has been a small number of studies in the areas of (1) the history of elementary school physical education; (2) the history of physical education in higher education; and (3) the history of physical cal education in foreign countries.

4. The quality of a large number of master's theses involved in the history of physical education is seemingly not high.

5. In general, the purposes of the studies related to the history of physical education have been clearly defined in the studies.

6. The methodology, used by a large number of graduate theses in the area of the history of physical education, was limited to a mere presentation of the facts (as they could be located).

7. Studies, which were identified as relating to the history of physical education, used, for the most part, primary sources in developing their presentations.

8. Indications of the use of critical thinking were shown in the use of sources in most of these studies.

9. The presentation of the results of a large number of theses in the history of physical education was made in a rather uninteresting manner, and followed strictly chronological order typically.

10. A lack of significant conclusions or generalizations can be found in a number of graduate studied involved in the history of physical education.

As a consequence of the present analysis, the following recommendations were developed to improve the status of graduate study related to the history of physical education:

1. Graduate thesis advisors should encourage more graduate students to develop topics of an historical nature for research.

2. More historical research should be encouraged in the follow following topics:

    a) elementary school physical education,
    b) physical education in foreign countries,
    c) physical education in higher education.

3. Graduate students writing their theses in the area of history should be trained in historiography to assure the best possible results in their study.

4. A certain degree of latitude should be afforded the graduate student in developing the historical study, so that the study may exhibit some originality and imagination.

5. In order to develop generalizations and conclusions, which contribute to the knowledge of the history of physical education, a high degree of critical thinking must be encouraged and required.

6. Studies, such as the present investigation, should be carried out periodically.

7. In-depth studies, involving more critical analysis of the "history of history" within physical education, are needed.

General Bibliography

Barnes, Harry Elmer. _A History of Historical Writing_. New York: Dover Publications, 1963.

Carr, Edward Hallett. _What Is History?_ New York: Random House, 1961.

Nevins, Allan. _The Gateway to History_. Chicago: Quadrangle Books, 1963.

APPENDIX C

AN ANALYSIS OF MASTER'S AND DOCTORAL STUDIES RELATED TO THE HISTORY OF SPORT AND ATHLETICS COMPLETED IN THE UNITED STATES, 1931-1967[1]

Melvin Adelman
University of Illinois, Urbana

It was the major purpose of this investigation to compile, classify, and assess selected graduate theses in the area of sports history completed in the United States from 1931-1967. The studies selected were those doctoral dissertations written by individuals doing their work in colleges or departments of physical education. In addition, it was decided to compile and classify Master's theses and doctoral dissertations (by individuals doing their work outside of colleges or departments of physical education) written in the area of sports history during this period.

In order to assess the work of sport historians, it was felt some criteria must be established. The criteria can be based upon a concept of the role of the sport historian. By establishing this role, this investigator maintained that he would have an adequate basis for judging the various doctoral dissertations.

Gottschalk's spectrum was used to identify the six different approaches to the philosophy of history along with their corresponding views of the historian's role (Gottschalk, 1963, p. 113). With this as a focal point, this investigator tried to ascertain which school of philosophical thought would be the most productive in the development of a body-of-knowledge in sports history (Adelman, 1969, pp. 61-65).

From this investigation it was concluded that the role of the sport historian is to discover and interpret the mark the past has left on the present situation, in order that the institution of sport may have a deeper awareness of the forces now affecting it.

Assessment of Graduate Work in Sports History

All the studies found were classified under ten headings, thirty-one sub-headings, and fifty-one sub-sub-headings. The major headings were: (1) studies relating to the history of the administration of

---

[1] This work was drawn from a Master's thesis completed at the University of Illinois entitled "An Assessment of Sports History Theses in the United States, 1931-1967." (See note on page 402.)

intercollegiate athletics; (2) studies relating to various athletic associations, organizations and leagues; (3) studies relating to bibliographical history; (4) studies relating to sports in foreign cultures; (5) studies relating to games and contests; (6) studies relating to intercollegiate athletics; (7) studies relating to interscholastic athletics; (8) studies relating to the origin and development of sports and games; (9) studies relating to sports and athletics; and (10) studies relating to women and sports.

This investigator, although admittedly he has not read the Master's theses, feels that a discussion of the various categories can be attempted. This discussion will be based upon the number of studies completed in each area, as well as the themes of the studies as reflected by their titles. In addition, the summaries will include statements relevant to doctoral works in these areas.

Studies Relating to the Administration of Intercollegiate Athletics

This category comprised only a minor area in sports history (2.4%). With respect to the Master's theses, all were basically related to the history of administration of intercollegiate athletics at a particular university, with the exception of Woerlin's thesis, whose study had a much broader outlook.

This category produced two doctoral dissertations or 3.3% of the doctoral works. The dissertations of Voltmer and Powell treated the administration of intercollegiate athletics in the "Big Ten." These studies were strongly factual in nature, and this reviewer would have liked to have seen "an interpretive form of history" employed. With this recommended approach, it is possible to establish greater historical perspective.

In general more work can be done in this area, especially on the doctoral level, although it must be admitted that much work in the area of "studies relating to history of athletics at a particular university" overlapped with the investigations completed here.

Studies Relating to Associations, Organizations and Leagues

This category comprised 12.3% of the studies in sports history. The Master's theses usually consisted of: (1) the history of a particular college conference (mainly the lesser known ones); (2) the history of the various interscholastic associations, leagues, and conference; and (3) the history of interscholastic coaching associations. In the last two cases, Master's students contributed all the work completed on these themes. In addition, they wrote the only studies on professional sport organizations.

This category included eight doctoral dissertations or 7.5% of the doctoral work. These dissertations done on a much broader scope, consisted of several investigations into the large sport associations. The dissertations of Korsgaard, Stagg, Forbes, and Flath made "meaningful" contributions to the body-of-knowledge in sports history. Their analysis of the A.A.U., or the N.C.A.A., or the relationship between these giant sport bodies presents a clear picture of the growth, development, and impact that these organizations had on sports. The works of Hoover, Fleischer, Pierce and Hoffman had their good points, but in general did not seem to be as comprehensive and detailed.

In concluding, it can be stated that the major associations have been largely, as should be the case, left to doctoral students, while the Master's theses have dealt mainly with the smaller intercollegiate conferences, and also with associations related to interscholastic activities. A greater amount of work is needed in areas not related to intercollegiate or interscholastic activities.

Studies Relating to Biographical History

This category comprised only 3.0% of the studies in sports history. All but two of the studies were done at the Master's level. These theses consisted largely of men connected with some phase of intercollegiate or interscholastic athletics. The two doctoral dissertations were good examples of contrasting studies. Lucas revealed the direct effect his subject, de Coubertin, had on a specific movement, whereas Dewar tended towards a much broader outlook of his subject (Naismith).

The dearth of work in this area must be supplemented by more work on both levels of study. However, it is felt that on the doctoral level the orientation should be to relate man to some movement within the field.

Studies Relating to Foreign Cultures

This category also comprised 3.0% of the studies in sports history. Almost evenly divided between Master's and doctoral theses, this area covered a wide scope. The two doctoral dissertations done by physical educators reveals the difference between the narrative and interpretive forms of history. While Davidson's narrative history of Canadian sport does point out several trends, Abdou's investigation into sport and games in Ancient Egypt indicated the meaning of these activities. Consequently, the latter study probably makes a greater contribution to the body-of-knowledge.

The 1930's produced two dissertations outside our field. Both dealt with the classical civilization of either Greece or Rome. More work in this comparative area is definitely required.

Studies Relating to Games and Contests

This category comprised only 2.4% of the studies done in the area of sports history. The Master's theses consisted of a variety of themes, although the Olympic Games and various football bowl games were the dominant ones.

Three doctoral dissertations or 5% of the doctoral work, were completed in this area. The studies of Lucas and Fouss each made a thorough examination of some facet on the Olympic Games, and thereby contributed to the body-of-knowledge. Emery's dissertations, which used a narrative form largely, did not observe the "interpretive criterion" laid down by this investigator.

The lack of work in this area requires further investigation not only on the Olympic Games, but in all phases of both international and national contests and events.

Studies Relating to Intercollegiate Athletics

This category comprised by far the largest single area of investigation. The large amount of work in this area stems probably from the fact that: (1) sources are readily available; (2) a close personal involvement with the subject is possible; and (3) the writing of these types of histories are relatively less complex because of the possibility of forming clear chronological narratives.

In addition, this area produced the largest number of studies in specific sub-headings; namely, intercollegiate athletics at a particular institution (27), football at a particular institution (16), and track and field at a particular institution (12).

A large proportion of the Master's theses were related to the history of athletics at a particular university (whether it be with the entire program or with a particular sport). On the doctoral level, this category included nineteen or 31.7% of the doctoral work. This area of investigation naturally tended to be broader in scope, and probably the material was treated in greater depth. As in the case of the Master's theses, the majority of the dissertations were involved with the history of intercollegiate athletics at a particular university (7), or the history of an intercollegiate sport (7).

The works of Dean, Kovacic, Scott, Shults, and Ziegenfuss read quite similarly in their content. Dealing basically with the question of control and administration of intercollegiate athletics at a particular university, they reveal that most colleges and universities underwent similar problems. Although these studies had particular good points, they did not depend heavily on the interpretive form of history criterion recommended by this investigator.

The studies of Wolf, Runkle, Ilowit, Torney, Baptista, and Bowen related to the growth and development of a particular intercollegiate sport, respectively. Largely dependent upon a narrative form, these investigations as a combined group present some picture of the growth of intercollegiate athletics. However, only Torney's study of rowing which depended more on an interpretive process, really captures adequately the "meaning" that an intercollegiate sport had on American life.

On the other hand, Lewis' investigation, treating actually only a part of the history of intercollegiate football, set an outstanding example of good historical endeavor in this investigator's opinion. In delimiting the problem, Lewis was able to treat the problem more intensively. As a result, he provided definite historical perspective to current problems.

The three investigations of McConnell, Green and Thomas into rules changes in basketball, football and wrestling, respectively, combined the unique and narrative forms of history. These studies were thus very factually oriented. This investigator would have preferred greater interpretation given to the data. With this recommended approach, greater insight into the causes of rules changes and their impact on the game may be gained. It is felt that studies dealing with the compilation and classification of rules changes can be done effectively on the Master's level, and would lead the way towards greater interpretation into the meaning of these rules changes on the doctoral level. "Joined" studies on both levels might be more successful in producing "meaningful" work in this area.

Finally, the works on related themes of intercollegiate athletics dealt with interesting and important areas of investigation. Scott's interpretive study on "the sports page," and its relation to intercollegiate athletics, showed the impact that the press had on the intercollegiate game; however, Rowan's thesis on gambling, although having various interesting comments, did not satisfy the interpretive criterion. More work in the related phases of intercollegiate sport is necessary.

Studies Relating to Interscholastic Sports

This area produced 9.5% of the investigations. All but two of these studies were on the Master's level, and they dealt with a wide variety of themes. The two doctoral dissertations by Montgomery and Stone related to the broad history of the interscholastic movement.

Whereas Montgomery's disssrtation was concerned mainly with the
trends in interscholastic athletics, Stone went a step further by interpreting the trends of this movement. Nevertheless, both studies
made a "meaningful" contribution to the body-of-knowledge. Greater
in-depth historical analysis of themes related to high school sports is
required.

Studies Relating to the Origin and Development of Sports and Games

This category, the smallest area of investigation, consisted
only of five studies, or 1.5% of the work done. However, three of
these studies were completed on the doctoral level. Consequently,
this small area included 5% of the total number of studies on the
doctoral level.

The combined studies of Eyler and Moore investigated the
origins of 128 modern sports. It was felt that in-depth work in this
area of history, if done well, can provide the basis for late interpretive investigations. Eyler's more detailed assessment seemingly
makes a greater contribution to the body-of-knowledge then Moore's
more limited investigation. Nevertheless, both of these studies provide insight into the area under investigation.

Simri's dissertation was an outstanding study into the origins of
ball games. This very astute and critical assessment into the
religious and magical function of ball games makes a significant contribution to the body-of-knowledge. The dearth of material in this
area indicates a need for further investigation at an early date.

Studies Relating to Sports and Games

This area consisted of 24.9% of the work completed. This area
which could almost have been called "Miscellaneous" since it includes
a wide variety of subjects. Although generalizations are difficult to
make in this category, we do find numerous Master's theses revolving
around the history of a particular sport. Likewise, several theses on
the master's level related to the history of sports journalism.

On the doctoral level, twelve dissertations, or 20% of the
doctoral work were completed in this area. Investigation at this level
tended to be more specific. Holliman and Hill examined the origin of
American sport and, although each reached different conclusions,
both made a significant contribution to the body-of-knowledge. Dauer
and Fall presented an interesting analyses of the amateur code and its
related problems. Hart wrote a "meaningful" investigation into the
nature of sports as reflected in selected sports magazines, while
Watson's study of private athletic clubs relied too heavily on narrative
history. Conroy, Hendrix and Davenport assessed various aspects

related to tennis. Whereas Conroy's narrative investigation did not satisfy the criteria established in this investigation, Davenport and Hendrix's interpretive histories contributed the historical perspective necessary to develop the body-of-knowledge in sports history.

This category also produced studies completed outside of physical education. It is interesting to note that the doctoral dissertations of Seymour and Voigt, completed in departments of history, concerned themselves with the professional sport of baseball. This investigator has looked at Seymour's thesis and Voigt's book, which was an outcome of his thesis. These works indicated a high level of preparation for the work of the historian. It would probably be helpful for physical educators who are writing sports history to examine the work done outside of our field.

Studies Relating to Women and Sports

The studies relating to the history of the women's role in sport comprised 5.5% of the work done. All but one of the 18 studies completed in this area were done by women. The Master's theses consisted of a variety of themes, although the historical development of a particular sport for women was the predominant one. This area included five doctoral dissertations (or 2.0% of the work). As in the case of the Master's theses, the investigation in this area was varied in nature.

Watts' investigation into the changing attitude of women towards sport from 1880 to 1960, and Peterson's cultural analysis of Olympic skiing for women, made meaningful contributions to the body-of-knowledge. However, it was felt that Price's study into the role of women in the Olympics and Cheatum's investigation into the development of the Ladies Professional Golf Association concentrated too heavily on the narrative form. The use of the recommended approach might have allowed for greater insight into these movements. As in the case of almost all the other areas, greater work in this area is necessary.

Direction of Sports History

It is the purpose of this section to express the investigator's opinion on the direction of graduate work in sports history, and to make suggestions concerning the reorientation of this area of investigation.

Eyler notes that the literature on the history of physical education and sport is "extremely diverse, and, in many instances generally unknown" (Eyler, 1960, p. 647). After completion of this intensified investigation into only one phase of the literature of sports history, this investigator heartily concurs. This investigator in reading the numerous doctoral dissertations, was surprised by the unfamiliarity on the part of the doctoral students with the available literature. However, not only the graduate students are to blame, since there are very few textbooks relating to sports history with extensive bibliographies. Many of the sources found in this investigation, at least on the basis of their titles, appear to be interesting areas of study. They would, if done well, contribute much to the body of knowledge. Thus, a lack of recognition for much of the literature is unfortunate.

This dilemma is especially true in the case of many Master's theses, but is also found with respect to several doctoral dissertations. An excellent example of this criticism can be found in the case of Fall's dissertation. This investigator believes that Fall's study on the amateur code was a powerful one--a study that makes an immense contribution to the body-of-knowledge; yet, it is relatively unknown.

The unfamiliarity with the literature, while not only stifling the body-of-knowledge, causes another problem for graduate students; namely, the use of identical material as secondary sources. The consequence of such action is that the introductions to many dissertations read quite similarly. In conjunction with this problem, another dilemma will be discussed in reference to the background material provided by physical educators writing sports history. The following criticism by Tollas concerning historians is also applicable to us.

> Personally, I am bored stiff when, reading biographies of Jefferson's contemporaries, I come repeatedly upon the same half designated "background" material on say, the Louisiana Purchase--the same tired quotations (We must marry outside to the British fleet and nation), the same overworked incidents (Napoleon in his bath silencing Joseph's objections by splashing him with water). I feel like Lord Asquith, who once irritably asked: What is really necessary for every biographer of the late-Victorian statesmen is to tell the whole story of the fight for Irish Home Rule and to tell it in the same way? (Tollas, 1966, p. 75)

Similarly, it is boring to find the same background material written by physical educators in connection with sports history. Is it necessary for graduate students to recount quickly the entire history of sport or to repeat the same material that appears in the texts concerning the history of American sport in their dissertations? Concerning background and secondary material Tollas' statement relevant to the writing of biographical history is also applicable to our field. He maintains that:

background material in a biography should be kept down, I think, to the barest minimum necessary to set the stage and place the central figure in context. Contemporary events, no matter how stirring or how important, must never crowd the main actor into the wings. (Tollas, 1966, p. 75)

Sport historians should heed these words.

The quantity of material found in this investigation surprised this investigator. Despite the discovery of this abundant literature, this investigator believes that there must be more studies--not found largely because they were overlooked by this researcher, or due to the fact that some studies may have never been reported to indexes, guides, or bibliographies of theses.

Although this bibliography of theses (see note at article's end), may appear somewhat large, this investigator maintains that sports historians have barely begun to make an impression on the total study of sports history. One has to think only of the vast historical work on one theme, the American Civil War, to truly comprehend the dearth of work done in sports history. As a result, this investigator disagrees to a degree with Eyler, who maintained that sport history appears "to have some of the characteristics of the fledgling and awakening period only." (Eyler, 1965, p. 57) Eyler views the awakening period, the second stage of development in sports history, as being characterized by the "developing body-of-knowledge in sports history supplementing recognized historical texts covering the major periods presently studied in institutions of higher learning." (Eyler, 1965, p. 57) Whereas, the fledgling period, the first stage of development is characterized by the following type of research done.

For the most part, it will be narrative history. Only a few good studies are available. Very few involve what both Teggart and Cohen have called causation. Little or no attention has been given to the identification and the study of "theories of why." (Eyler, 1965, p. 58)

After extensive investigation into doctoral dissertations, along with knowledge of other forms of sports history, this investigator is convinced that our work is definitely characteristic of the fledgling stage.

This contention is based upon the fact that most our doctoral dissertations were of a narrative form. The works consisted largely of narrating the data in chronological order--providing the highlights and events of their subject only. Only a few attempts were made at interpreting the meaning of events. As a result of this work in our field, this investigator feels that in general the quality of much of the work completed on the doctoral level cannot be asserted as "high."

Few of the studies made a "meaningful" contribution necessary to provide the historical perspective necessary to comprehend the forces now affecting the institution of sport. (This statement is based upon the criterion accepted for this study.)

It must be speculated further that, if problems exist on the doctoral level, these same problems are undoubtedly more serious on the Master's level.

It is now appropriate to ask what must be done in order for the field of sports history to develop. It is obvious to this investigator that one of the major steps is to shift the orientation of the role of the sport historian from its present condition of being a narrator to that of an interpreter. In addition, it was felt that the orientation of the sport historian should be shifted from the past to the present. In other words, he should indicate the mark that the past has left on the present. Combining these two beliefs, it was felt that the role of the sport historian is to discover and interpret the mark the past has left on the present situation. This is needed so that institution of sport may have a "deeper awareness" of the forces now affecting it.

Given this premise, how would it affect the graduate work in sports history? To better comprehend how this might occur, it seems necessary to distinguish between the history of sport and sports history. Although these terms are often used interchangeably, maybe a distinction between them can be made. Howell contended that the terms "are not precisely the same, and may perhaps be differentiated." (Howell, 1969, p. 77) In differentiating between these terms, Howell felt that "any isolated study is one in sport history, whereas the accumulation of the body-of-knowledge, the subdivision, is the history of sport." (Howell, 1969, p. 77) Drawing his concept of history from the work of F. M. Fling, Howell saw the history of sport

> concerned with the unique evolution of sports and games in culture. It deals with the past and all that has happened in the past and is cognizant of movement and change. It deals with the evolution of sports and games as well as their role in culture. (Howell, 1969, p. 78)

This investigator does not totally agree with Howell's contention, in that he believes that such a differentiation seems to be somewhat superficial. It implies that American history is a part of the history of America, or that political history is part of the history of politics. This investigator feels that the terms "sports history" and "history of sport" may emphasize different yet interrelated historical questions. The latter term, history of sport, deals with the development of the particular sports, their rules, organization, and techniques. This aspect would correlate with what Howell described as "the evolution of sport." On the other hand, the former term, sports history, would discuss the development of the institution of sport within our larger social system. This would correspond to Howell's "role of sport in culture." This investigator prefers to use the term "relationship" rather than "role" in describing the interaction between sports and other social institutions.

Before ascertaining the ramifications of the above differentiations for the writing of sports history on the graduate level, one more speculation must be examined. This is the question of whether sports history as described by this investigator above is the same as what Lewis called the cultural approach to the writing of sports history. (Lewis, 1965, pp. 48-50) It must be admitted that the cultural approach would probably be used most frequently in the writing of sports history. At the same time, we should be cognizant of the fact that the cultural approach has been the most productive one found in this investigation in the writing of sports history. Nevertheless, this investigator is not ready at this time to accept the fact that sports history is merely the employment of a cultural approach to the writing of history in our field. The reason for this stems from the fact that good sport history can also be written by, for example, the persistent problems approach as presented by Zeigler (1968, pp. 8-15).

From this investigation it can be observed that our emphasis in graduate work has been on writing the history of sport rather than sports history. Consequently, if the field is to grow and truly develop a body-of-knowledge, a redress of the balance of power between the writing of sports history and the history of sport must be made.

How can this best be accomplished? It would seem that work on the doctoral level should concern itself with the writing of sports history, since it is felt by this investigator that this type of history results in greater historical awareness. By the use of such a procedure, graduate students could make a greater contribution to the body-of-knowledge. However, it must be noted, that this recommendation should not be followed dogmatically. Studies on the history of sports, such as done by Eyler, can be productive if done with similar intensity and insight.

Work on the Master's level appears to mitigate against the writing of sports history for three reasons: first, for some students, the thesis is written to satisfy a personal interest, and a desire to foster a body-of-knowledge might only be secondary; second, insufficient time makes the writing of sports history difficult; and, finally, the general unpreparedness of many Master's students to write a deeper analysis. Consequently, the Master's thesis should probably be a place for the writing of the history of sport. Such a procedure would hopefully serve a twofold purpose; namely, the provision of insightful investigations into the history of sport, while helping lay the foundations for further sport histories.

Conclusion

As a result of this investigation into graduate work concerning sports history, the following final statements seem appropriate.

1. The frequency of graduate studies relating to sports history has been somewhat low in relation to the total number of theses completed in all areas of the field of physical education.

2. The greatest amount of work in sports history on the graduate level has been in three areas: (1) studies relating to intercollegiate athletics, (2) studies relating to sports and games, and (3) studies relating to associations, organizations, and leagues.

3. There has been a relatively little amount of investigation into studies relating to origin and development of sports and games; studies relating to the history of games and contest; studies relating to the history of administration of intercollegiate athletics; studies relating to biographical history; and studies relating to foreign cultures.

4. The historical methodology employed in a large number of doctoral dissertations in sports history was narrative in nature largely.

5. The presentation of the data in most of the dissertations on sports history was made in a rather uninteresting manner, and followed strictly chronological order.

6. Little work concerning sports history (as defined herein) has been done on the master's or the doctoral level.

In addition the following conclusions can be inferred from this investigation:

7. The quality of doctoral dissertations in sports history needs some improvement, although it is true that the more recent studies do indicate a trend towards a higher quality of work.

8. For the most part doctoral dissertations concerning intercollegiate or interscholastic athletics demonstrate an effort on the part of the authors to establish these athletic programs on sounder educational principles.

9. A greater amount of work in all facets of this historical area should be encouraged.

10. A reorientation of the work in this field from narrative-descriptive history to critical-interpretive history should be made.

11. Graduate students, especially on the doctoral level should be encouraged to take a course in historiography and other social science techniques to assure the best possible results.

12. Annotated bibliographies or bibliographical commentaries should be used in all historical investigations. Such a procedure would allow for not only a clearer insight into the sources that were productive in the study, but would provide a building block for future researchers.

13. There was an overemphasis on the part of doctoral students to use their studies as a means of glancing at, pointing towards, or predicting the future. The overemphasis stemmed from the fact that many students, especially in certain categories of investigation, brought the historical narrative up to the year in which the study was written. Consequently, they felt compelled to look in to the future. Invariably this aspect of these dissertations was weak.

Recommendations for Further Study

1. Continuation of bibliographical work in sports history should be continued.

2. An investigation into the professional careers of those graduate students who wrote theses and dissertations of sports history should be made.

General Bibliography

Adelman, Melvin L., "The Role of the Sport Historian." Quest, XII (May, 1969), pp. 61-65.

Eyler, Marvin H., "The Nature and Status of Historical Research Pertaining to Sports and Physical Education," in Warren R. Johnson (editor) Science and Medicine and Sports. New York: Harper & Brothers Publishers, 1960, pp. 647-662.

Eyler, Marvin H., "Sport Historians." 68th Annual Proceedings of National College Physical Education Association for Men. Washington: A.A.H.P.E.R., 1965, pp. 57-60.

Gottschalk, Louis., "Categories of Historical Generalizations," in Louis Gottschalk (editor), Generalizations in the Writing of History. Chicago: University of Chicago Press, 1963.

Howell, Maxwell L., "Toward A History of Sport," <u>JOHPER</u>, XL (March, 1969), pp. 77-79.

Lewis, Guy M., "The Cultural Approach to Writing Sports History." 68th Annual <u>Proceedings of National College Physical Education Association for Men</u>. Washington: A.A.H.P.E.R., 1965, pp. 48-50.

Tollas, Frederick B., "The Biographer's Draft," in A. S. Eisenstadt, <u>The Craft of American History</u>, Vol. 2. New York: Harper & Row Publishers, 1966, pp. 71-83.

Zeigler, Earle F., "Persistent Historical Problems of Physical Education & Sport." (<u>Proceedings</u> of the First International Seminar on the History of Physical Education and Sport, Wingate Institute, Israel, April 9-11, 1968, pp. 1-1 to 1-13.

<u>Note</u>: A complete bibliographic listing of the theses and dissertations, included in this study appears in <u>Research in the History, Philosophy, and International Aspects of Physical Education and Sport: Bibliographies and Techniques</u> (edited by E. F. Zeigler, M. L. Howell, and M. Trekell). Champaign, Illinois: Stipes Publishing Company, 10 Chester Street, 1971.

APPENDIX D

AN ANNOTATED BIBLIOGRAPHY OF LITERATURE RELATING TO INTERSCHOLASTIC AND INTERCOLLEGIATE ATHLETICS IN THE UNITED STATES, 1875-1969

Ronald A. Smith
Pennsylvania State University, University Park

1. Adams, Charles K., "Moral Aspect of College Life," Forum, VIII (Feb. 1890), 665-675.

    Two years prior to becoming president of the University of Wisconsin, Adams states that athletics and gymnastics morally benefits colleges by providing an outlet for excessive physical energy. Improved order in colleges is in part due to the introduction of athletics in the previous 25 years.

2. American Association for Health, Physical Education, and Recreation. Athletics in Education. Washington, D. C.: A.A.H.P.E.R., 1963.

    This pamphlet represents a statement of the Division of Men's Athletics. The statement proposes that athletics should meet educational goals, and that physical, mental, emotional, social, and moral growth of the participants should be fostered.

3. Armstrong, J. E. and others, "The Question of School and College Athletics," School Review, X (Jan. 1902), 4-8.

    A conference of academies and high schools working with the University of Chicago favors faculty control in both high schools and colleges. It set guidelines for high school athletic association rules.

4. Bates, Arlo, "The Negative Side of Modern Athletics," Forum, XXXI (1901), 287-297.

    Bates, from [Massachusetts?] Institute of Technology, believes that an emphasis on athletics would lead to intellectual stagnation, while thinking that moderately emphasized athletics would be advantageous to college morals.

5.　Betts, John R.　"Organized Sport in Industrial America."
　　　Ph.D. dissertation, Columbia University, 1951.

　　　The best single source concerning organized sport in America.
　　　Much of his material concerns the growth of intercollegiate
　　　athletics.　Factual material as well as interpretations cover
　　　all areas of sport.　The bibliography is useful.

6.　_____, "The Technological Revolution and the Rise of
　　　Sport, 1850-1900," Mississippi Valley Historical Review,
　　　XL (1953), 231-256.

　　　Betts emphasizes the impact that inventions which grew out of
　　　the Industrial Revolution have had on the rise of sport.　Of the
　　　new technical advances none was more important to the rise
　　　of sport than the railroad which allowed intercity games and
　　　increased spectators.

7.　Bingham, W. J., "Athletics in School and College," School
　　　and Society, XX (11 Oct. 1924), 454-460.

　　　As a member of Harvard's committee on athletics, Bingham
　　　states that among other benefits of athletics "a boy soon
　　　realizes that his social position or his wealth count for very
　　　little" on the athletic field.　He believes that abuses in college
　　　athletics are minor in relation to the benefits.

8.　Bisher, Furman.　"A Scholarship for Jackie," in Al Silverman
　　　(editor), The World of Sport.　New York:　Holt, Rinehart and
　　　Winston, 1962, pp. 69-80.

　　　This is the case history of a high school basketball player who
　　　was victim of the recruiting pressure carried on by major
　　　American colleges.

9.　Blaikie, William,　"The Risks of Athletic Work," Harper's
　　　Magazine, LVIII (1899), 923-939.

　　　The author of How to Grow Strong and How to Stay So sees
　　　college and school athletics becoming more popular, and be-
　　　lieves that athletics are not risky to the health of the partici-
　　　pants if a sound training period is provided.

10. Bowen, W. P., "Evolution of Athletic Evils," American Phy-
     sical Education Review, XIV (Mar. 1909), 151-156.

     Intercollegiate athletics have become commercial rather than
     educational. The few benefit at the expense of the many.
     Athletics for revenue has replaced athletics for health and
     discipline.

11. Boyle, Robert H. Sport-Mirror of American Life. Boston:
     Little, Brown and Co., 1963.

     The chief concern of this volume is to show the impact of sport
     on American life and the relationship between the two.
     Chapters I and V deal with college athletics more than others.
     A useful bibliography is included.

12. Brickman, W. W., "Professionalized Sports and Higher Edu-
     cation," School and Society, LXXXVI (1 Mar. 1958), 114-115.

     A noted educator recognizes the persistent evils of college
     athletics. He claims college athletics are hypocritically ama-
     teur and sees a need for a new Carnegie Report on Athletics
     such as the 1929 report.

13. Briggs, L. B. R., "Intercollegiate Athletics and the War."
     Atlantic Monthly, CXXII (Sept. 1918), 304-309.

     An athletic idealist from Harvard believes that intercollegiate
     athletics are a definite good, but laments commercialization
     and win-at-all cost philosophy. He thinks that during World
     War I with athletics at low tide it would be the ideal time to
     reform athletics.

14. Brill, A. A., "The Why of the Fun," North American Review,
     CCXXVIII (Oct. 1929), 429-434.

     An M.D. believes that sport is a substitute for fighting, that
     man has combative instincts. Vicarious, spectator sport
     meets a real need.

15. Brogan, Denis W. The American Character. New York:
     A. A. Knopf, 1944.

     One English expert on American history sees intercollegiate
     sport as a democratizing agent and a unifying factor in Ameri-
     can society, as well as a unifying factor within the college it-
     self (see pp. 141-144).

16. Brown, Rollo W. "An Idealist in Athletics," in his Dean Briggs. New York: Harper, 1926, pp. 168-207.

Harvard's Dean Briggs questions the practice of alumni pressure in athletics as well as the granting of athletic scholarships.

17. Burns, N., "Recommended Changes in Athletic Policies," School Review, LX (Dec. 1952), 509-518.

The 1951 scandals in basketball and football stirred educational organizations to action in an attempt to control intercollegiate athletics. The American Council on Education and the North Central Association of Colleges and Secondary Schools suggest certain reforms to make athletics less commercial. Keep athletics amateur and make them responsible to educational objectives.

18. Camp, Walter, "Football in America," Frank Leslie's Popular Monthly, XLVII (Nov. 1898), 56-65.

One of football's early enthusiasts provides an account of early football equipment from the canvas jacket to the nose guard.

19. _____, "The Yale Side of the Athletic Question," Harper's Weekly, XXXVII (8 Apr. 1893), 339.

Camp explains Yale's new 1893 eligibility rules which allow participation only to undergraduates and prohibits transfer of students to play.

20. Chase, Stuart. "Play," in Charles A. Beard (editor), Whither Mankind? New York: 1928, pp. 332-353.

Puritan opposition to games and play was copied throughout America and died a slow death. College athletics were commercialized by the 1920's. There is an interesting account of the rise of Red Grange.

21. Christenson, Ade. The Verdict of the Scoreboard: A Study of the Value and Practices Underlying College Athletics Today. New York: The American Press, 1958.

A long-time coach gives his moralistic views of college sport. Athletic scholarships symbolize confusion in amateur sport, he says.

22.   Cleland, J. S., "Mid-West Collegiate Athletic Conference,"
      School and Society, LXXII (28 Oct. 1950), 275-276.

      A representative of Monmouth College notes that colleges of
      the Mid-West Conference were drawn together first because
      of athletics, but that now common educational problems are
      discussed because of the bonds brought about by athletics.

23.   Coffin, R. P. T., "Cavalier and Puritan Athletes," Outlook,
      CXXXVII (18 June 1924), 276-277.

      Coffin sees the effect of Puritanism on the American attitude
      to take everything seriously including intercollegiate sports.
      He opposes coaches, pre-season practice, secret practices,
      rigid training, and overemphasis on winning found in Ameri-
      can schools.

24.   Cohane, Tim, "Inside the West Coast Football Scandal,"
      Look, XX (7 Aug. 1956), 72-80.

      A sports editor sees the strict Pacific Coast Conference
      athletic code leading to cheating and hypocrisy.

25.   Cole, Arthur C., "Our Sporting Grandfathers," Atlantic
      Monthly, CL (July 1932), 88-96.

      This is an interesting and authoritative account of nineteenth
      century sport including some aspects of intercollegiate athle-
      tics. Cole, an historian, sees two obstacles to the rise of
      organized sport: the demand of the frontier and the Puritan
      heritage.

26.   Coleman, James S., "Athletics in High School," in the Annals
      of the American Academy of Political and Social Science,
      CCCXXXVIII (Nov. 1961), 33-43.

      Coleman argues that athletics as practiced are not contributing
      to education. He proposes substituting activities other than
      athletics, such as debate, music, and drama to achieve the
      esprit de corps which all schools need.

27. Commager, Henry Steele, "Give the Games Back to the Students," <u>New York Times Magazine</u> (16 Apr. 1961), 27, 120-121.

An eminent historian believes that athletics in the college do not contribute to education. His solution calls for getting rid of paid coaches and allowing the players to control the games. As for the spectators he says: "Let the people find their emotional safety valve elsewhere."

28. "Commercialism in College Athletics," <u>School and Society</u>, XV (24 June 1922), 681-686; and XVI (1 July 1922), 7-11.

An anonymous small college faculty athletic advisor calls for an end to commercialism in college athletics, and for a greater amount of intramural activity.

29. Conant, James B., "Athletics, the Poison Ivy in Our Schools," <u>Look</u>, XXV (17 Jan. 1961), 56-60.

"Like poison ivy, athletics are difficult to control." Conant, former President of Harvard, reaches the previous conclusion after a study of high schools in America. Because of the Cold War he claims that an emphasis upon athletics at the expense of academic excellence is placing the country in jeopardy. Yet, he advocates a greater amount of time spent in physical education.

30. Cozens, Frederick W. and Stumpf, Florence. <u>Sports in American Life</u>. Chicago: University of Chicago Press, 1953.

They believe that sport and recreation form an integral part of culture everywhere. Chapter VI discusses the role of the school in sport.

31. Crockett, Davis S., "Sports and Recreational Practices of Union and Confederate Soldiers," <u>Research Quarterly</u>, XXXII (Oct. 1961), 335-347.

Much material has been gleaned from Civil War diaries concerning sports played at that time. Crockett, however, has done no synthesizing or interpreting of the material. One might hypothesize that the Civil War helped to Americanize sport, and may have been one of the causes of the rise of intercollegiate sport after the War.

32.   Curti, Merle and Carstensen, Vernon R. The University of Wisconsin; A History, 1848-1925. 2 volumes. Madison: University of Wisconsin Press, 1949.

This is an excellent example of an institutional history which contains material on the social life of the University, a large part of which is devoted to intercollegiate athletics.

33.   Danzig, Allison. History of American Football. Englewood Cliffs, N. J.: Prentice-Hall, Inc., 1956.

A sportswriter for over 30 years takes a look at the development of football in America.

34.   Dashiell, Alfred, "The National Religion of Football," Forum, LXXVI (Nov. 1926), 680-689.

Dashiell denounces commercialized athletics, especially that found in intercollegiate football. He chides the colleges to make the courses of study furnish some of the excitement.

35.   Davis, Andrew M. F., "College Athletics," Atlantic Monthly, LI (1883), 677-684.

Davis comments on student-run intercollegiate athletics before commercialization and finds them favorable additions to college life. He favors them because they take the student outdoors, gives him a diversion from study, and are healthful as well as enjoyable.

36.   Davis, Parke H. Football: The American Intercollegiate Game. New York: Charles Scribner's Sons, 1911.

A former player and coach traces the history of football from its origin to the rule changes of 1906 and 1910. A number of pictures of early games and formations add to the value of this volume.

37.   Dawkins, Pete, "We Play to Win, They Play for Fun," New York Times Magazine (24 Apr. 1960), 34, 36.

A Heisman Trophy winner at West Point participates in Rugby at Cambridge University as a Rhode's Scholar. He notes the difference between the British stress on participation by all and enjoyment in playing the games, and the American stress upon winning and dedication.

38.   Deming, Clarence, "Money Power in College Athletics,"
        Outlook, LXXX (July 1905), 569-572.

        A muckraking article calls the commercial aspect of college
        athletics, "bacillus athleticus." The 1903-04 Yale athletic
        receipts are shown to be over 1/8 of the total gross income of
        Yale University.

39.   Duer, A. O., "Basic Issues of Intercollegiate Athletics,"
        Journal of Health, Physical Education and Recreation, XXXI
        (Jan. 1960), 22-24.

        The executive secretary of the N.A.I.A. believes that the
        pressure to win has resulted in: 1) extensive recruitment;
        2) open and hidden subsidies; and 3) selection of coaches for
        victorious records. He calls for college presidential
        responsibility for athletics.

40.   Dulles, Foster Rhea. A History of Recreation: America
        Learns to Play. Second edition. New York: Appleton-
        Century-Crofts, 1965.

        This is an excellent book. The two most valuable chapters
        dealing with intercollegiate athletics are Chapter XI, "The
        Rise of Sports," and Chapter XX, "Sports for All." This so-
        cial history of recreation is the best in the field.

41.   Dwight, Benjamin W., "Intercollegiate College Regattas,
        Hurdle-Races, and Prize Contests," New Englander, XXXV
        (April 1876), 251-279.

        An early anti-intercollegiate athletic article emphasizes the
        following harmful effects of athletics: 1) possible physical
        harm; 2) false values; 3) excessive costs; 4) student-athletes
        challenge college authorities; 5) waste of study time; and
        6) the interest generated among the common classes in muscu-
        lar activity.

42.   Ehler, George W., "The Regulation of Intercollegiate Sports,"
        American Physical Education Review, XIX (Apr. 1904), 284-
        291.

        A physical educator at the University of Wisconsin believes
        that athletics should be part of physical education, and that
        coaches should be chosen as other faculty members are.

43. Eliot, Charles W., "President Eliot's Report, Athletics,"
    Harvard Graduates' Magazine, II (Mar. 1894), 376-383.

    The Harvard president sees the advantage of college athletics
    in the past 25 years in reduced dissipation, respect for body
    excellence, and in building manly qualities. The disadvan-
    tages center around overemphasis which tends to hurt intel-
    lectual pursuits. (See also, Ibid. III (Mar. 1895), 366-379,
    for another Eliot report.)

44. _____, "The Value of Athletics," Mind and Body,
    VII (1900), 141-142.

    Although he did not always speak as favorable, in this article
    he states that "nobody appreciates more highly than I do the
    value of athletics in a university." He claims that in general
    the better the athlete, the better is his scholastic standing.

45. Emmons, Robert W. II, "Needed Football Reforms,"
    Harvard Graduates' Magazine, III (Mar. 1895), 318-322.

    A Harvard graduate asks: Do college games exist for the col-
    lege or for the public? He calls for reform to do away with
    excessive injuries, brutality, excessive time spent on foot-
    ball and professionalism.

46. Epernay, Mark, "Allston Wheat's Crusade," Harper's Maga-
    zine, CCXXVI (May 1963), 53-57.

    This well-written parody and satire on the thinking of the
    radical right, or strict individualism, is applied to team
    sports. According to Allston Wheat's philosophy team sports
    or collectivized sports are the training ground for socialism
    and collectivism in the United States. A very interesting arti-
    cle for discussion.

47. Eyler, Marvin H., "Origins of Contemporary Sports," Re-
    search Quarterly, XXXII (Dec. 1961), 480-489.

    Eyler attempts to trace the origin of 95 sports, dating their
    origin to their becoming primarily sporting activities rather
    than utilitarian in nature. It is based upon his Ph.D. disserta-
    tion.

48. Farrand, Wilson, "Scholarships for Athletics; Position of the Association of Colleges and Secondary Schools of the Middle States," School and Society, XL (7 July 1934), 6-7.

The Association opposes any athletic scholarship or payment for jobs above the service rendered.

49. Faunce, William H. P., "Character in Athletics," National Education Association Proceedings, XLIII (1904), 558-564.

The president of Brown University traces the previous 30 years of the history of college sport and classifies it into three periods: 1) genuine recreation; 2) expansion and publicity; and 3) systematic prevarication. He emphasizes what he considers evils, most of which exist six decades later.

50. Flath, Arnold W. A History of Relations Between the N.C.A.A. and the A.A.U. of the United States, 1905-1963. Champaign, Illinois: Stipes Publishing Company, 1964.

The long-time feud between the N.C.A.A. and the A.A.U. centers around track and field and the Olympics. The feud was strongest in the 1920's and 1960's.

51. "Football Reform by Abolition," Nation, LXXXI (30 Nov. 1905), 437-438.

An editorial criticizes football for brutality, professionalism, and demoralization of the student body. It calls for abolition or a remaking of the game.

52. Foster, William T., "An Indictment of Intercollegiate Athletics," Atlantic Monthly, CXVI (Nov. 1915), 577-588.

The president of Reed College favors athletics for education, not for winning games, making money, or getting advertised. He calls for the abolition of intercollegiate athletics, believing in intramurals.

53. Giddens, Paul H., "Scramble for College Athletics; Increasing Professionalism," Atlantic Monthly, CCXVI (Dec. 1965), 49-52.

The president of Hamline University states well what he believes are the abuses of intercollegiate athletics in the 1960's. He lists many of the evils, from recruiting to red-shirting. He fears that overcommercialization, which is spreading to smaller colleges, may financially jeopardize all intercollegiate sports.

54.   Godkin, E. L., "Athletic Craze," Nation, LVII (7 Dec. 1893), 422-423.

Editor Godkin could see that the professionalism of intercollegiate athletics was beginning to reach down into the preparatory schools. Moderation and decency in athletics is his theme, believing that colleges do not exist for athletics.

55.   _____, "Athletics and Health," Nation, LIX (20 Dec. 1894), 457-458.

Football, to Godkin, is an extravagant exercise which makes students believe that bodily vigor is of little use unless one is going to participate in a game.

56.   _____, "The Future of Football," Nation, LI (20 Nov. 1890), 395.

A perceptive editor saw that football would soon be an established national sport, that professional football would attract thousands, and that if the gentleman's code of ethics was lost the game of football might be prohibited by law.

57.   Green, George W., "Athletics in Colleges," New Englander, XXXV (July 1876), 548-560.

Green sees the possible beneficial aspects of college sports on both physique and intellect. He fears the possible newspaper glorification of athletics and athletes.

58.   Gulick, Luther H., "Athletics From the Biologic Viewpoint," American Physical Education Review, XI (1906), 157-160.

A noted physical educator argues that competitive athletics are appropriate for men but not for women. He builds the argument on evolutionary theory, that men through the ages have used running, striking, and throwing and have built up a lo e of these exercises. "Athletic events are thus, to some extent...a measure of manhood."

59.   _____, "Team Games and Civic Loyalty," School Review, XIV (Nov. 1906), 676-678.

The belief that athletics can be beneficial both socially and morally is furthered by Gulick. Even if only a small portion of the student body participates he believes that the spirit of the games influences all.

60.   Haas, John A. W., "Migration of Athletes from One Institu-
       tion to Another," School and Society, III (13 May 1916), 712-
       714.

       The one-year migrant student rule is seen as a deterrent to
       the win-at-all-cost philosophy and hypocrisy in college sports.

61.   Harden, Edgar L., "Time Out for Responsibility," Vital
       Speeches, XXV (15 Sept. 1959), 728-730.

       The president of Northern Michigan College attempts to define
       the role of athletics on the college campus. Athletics are a
       vital part of college life, but the evils such as over-zealous
       recruiting, lavish subsidies, and lowered academic standards
       for the athlete must not exist. He desires to do away with the
       faculty representative system, and make athletic directors
       directly responsible to the president.

62.   Hart, Albert Bushnell, "The Documents on the Football
       Question," Harvard Graduates' Magazine, III (June 1895),
       519-527.

       A noted Harvard historian summarizes the history of the
       Harvard Athletic Committee, and the suspending of intercol-
       legiate athletics at Harvard in 1885. Differing points of view
       of intercollegiate athletics as practiced in eastern colleges
       are presented.

63.   _____, "Evils of Organized Athletics in
       American Colleges," Current History, XXXI (Dec. 1929),
       558-561.

       After the publication of the 1929 Carnegie Report on athletics,
       Hart wrote this interesting account of present-day evils in
       intercollegiate athletics. Hart believes that "organized athle-
       tics are as old as the world and much older than history.
       The Greeks made it a cult; the English a spectacle; the Ameri-
       cans have made it a business." Yet, he claims that colleges
       are better for having sports.

64.   _____, "Status of Athletic Sports in American
       Colleges," Atlantic Monthly, LXVI (July 1890), 63-71.

       To Hart, "the Civil War gave a singular impetus to field sports
       of all kinds." This informative article discusses the pros and
       cons of intercollegiate athletics. Hart claims that college
       athletics have done away with the caricature of the college stu-
       dent who is the "stoop-shouldered, long-haired grind."

65. Hartwell, Edward M. "President's Address--The Condition
and Prospect of Physical Education in the United States,"
American Association for the Advancement of Physical Education Proceedings, VII (1892), 13-40.

Although this is basically a history of physical education,
Hartwell shows that the athletic movement has had a much
greater force than has physical education since 1860. He also
notes that athletics have had "little to do with urging or promoting the educational side of physical training." A worthy
article.

66. Henderson, Edwin B. The Negro in Sports. Revised edition.
Washington, D. C.: Associated Publishers, 1949.

This name-oriented volume attempts to show some of the
firsts in athletics for blacks. There are no footnotes or
bibliography, but an appendix has some records of black
athletes.

67. Henderson, W. J., "College Football Twenty-five Years Ago,"
Outing, XXXVII (Oct. 1900), 15-18.

An 1875 Princeton football player recalls the pre-Rugby-type
of football, which consisted of catching, kicking, and batting
the ball to advance it. Twenty men were on a side.

68. Henry, Ralph L. The Midwest Collegeiate Athletic Conference. n.p.: Published by the Midwest Conference, 1964.

One of the conference faculty representatives traces the history of a small liberal arts college conference to the 1920's.

69. Hetherington, Clark W., "Analysis of Problems in College
Athletics," American Physical Education Review, XII (June
1907), 154-181.

To Hetherington, "athletics are play activities with rivalry
added." He believes that athletics should be under educational
control, and should be made available to all students regardless of their abilities.

70. _____. "Organization and Administration of Athletics," National Education Association Proceedings, (1907), 330-340.

Hetherington believes that the elimination "of all athletic evils and the realization of educational athletics, are simply questions of proper administrative policies and adequate organization."

71. Hitchcock, Edward, "Athletics in American Colleges," Journal of Social Science, XX (June 1885), 27-44.

The best known American physical educator at the time believes that "gymnastics and athletic sports are a part, and an essential part, of college education...." Athletics, in need of control, are not as beneficial as are gymnastics for symmetrical development of students.

72. Hollis, Ira H., "Intecollegiate Athletics," Atlantic Monthly, XC (1902), 534-544.

The intense desire to win in intercollegiate athletics, says Hollis, is part of the environment which pervades America. His seven years of experience as head of Harvard's athletic committee gives him insight into problems as well as favorable aspects of college sports.

73. Hoover, Francis L. "A History of the National Association of Intercollegiate Athletics." P.E.D. dissertation, Indiana University, 1958.

A pedestrian account of the N.A.I.A. is given from its 1930's beginnings as a basketball tournament.

74. Hughes, William L., "The Place of Athletics in the School Physical Education Program," Journal of Health, Physical Education and Recreation, (Dec. 1950), 23-37.

An attempt is made to show beneficial aspects of interscholastic athletics, which to Hughes include physiological efficiency, leisure values, appreciation of skills, character building, relief of tensions, and appreciation of the value of fitness.

75. Hutchinson, R. C., "Football: Symbol of College Unity," *Christian Century*, LXIX (16 Apr. 1952), 461-463.

Football, like the flag for the country, is the emotional integrating force in colleges. The college cannot claim that athletics are contributing to the physical education program, to character building, or to money-making.

76. Jackson, Allen, "Too Much Football," *Atlantic Monthly*, CLXXXVIII (Oct. 1951), 27-33.

A star guard on the University of Michigan championship football teams of the late 1940's and early 1950's criticizes professionalized college athletics in a well-stated article.

77. Jones, Oliver S., "Morality in College Athletics," *The North American Review*, CLX (May 1895), 638-640.

While praising physical exercise he questions the excessive time and money spent on athletics at American universities.

78. Jordan, Edward S., "Buying Football Victories," *Collier's* XXXVI (11 Nov. 1905), 19-20, 23; (18 Nov. 1905), 22-23; (25 Nov. 1905), 21-22, 24; (2 Dec. 1905), 19-20, 23.

A muckraking article on commericalized intercollegiate athletics at Minnesota, Wisconsin, Michigan, Chicago, Northwestern, and Illinois.

79. Keating, James W., "Sportsmanship as a Moral Category," *Ethics*, LXXV (Oct. 1964), 25-35.

Athletics and sport differ as to their goals. Thus, sportsmanship applied to both may differ; the athlete because of the nature of the game has more difficulty being a sportsman.

80. Kennedy, Charles W. *College Athletics*. Princeton: Princeton University Press, 1925.

The Princeton athletic faculty representative believes that the chief value of athletics is the development of sportsmanship.

81. Keppel, Frederick P., "Athletic Sports," in his *Columbia*. New York: Oxford University Press, American Branch, 1914.

Although football had been abolished at Columbia in 1905, Keppel believes that football is a powerful factor in awakening the loyalty and enthusiasm of the alumni.

82. Knight, Edgar W., "Athletics," in his What College Presidents Say. Chapel Hill: University of North Carolina Press, 1940, pp. 162-203.

Knight has collected statements of college presidents on athletics from 1827 to 1940. This is a good source for the pros and cons of intercollegiate athletics.

83. Krout, John A. Annals of American Sport. Volume XV of Pageant of America. New Haven, Conn.: Yale University Press, 1929.

Krout's well-documented history of sport in America is made more valuable by the hundreds of pictures illustrating sporting conditions since Jamestown.

84. _____, "Some Reflections on the Rise of American Sport." Association of History Teachers of the Middle States and Maryland: Proceedings, XXVI (1929), 84-93.

Krout sees sport as arising out of the industrialization and urbanization, and becoming nationalized as a result of the Civil War. He sees Americans becoming, unfortunately, a nation of spectators rather than participants.

85. Lewis, Guy M., "Adoption of the Sports Program, 1906-29: The Role of Accommodation in the Transformation of Physical Education," Quest, XII (May 1969), 34-46.

Sport historian Lewis views the early 1900's reconstruction of physical education, which began to emphasize sports and athletics, as a means to accommodate and serve the interests of intercollegiate athletics.

86. _____. "The American Intercollegiate Football Spectacle, 1869-1917." Ph.D. dissertation, University of Maryland, 1965.

College football's early years is the theme of Lewis' Ph.D. dissertation. Problems which occurred in the development of the game are emphasized. It is more valuable for source material than for its interpretation of the development of sport in America.

87.   _____, "America's First Intercollegiate Sport: The Regattas From 1852 to 1875," Research Quarterly, XXXVIII (Dec. 1967), 637-647.

The early years of intercollegiate boating and regattas is presented in a well-documented article. Crew as an early dominating sport in eastern colleges is emphasized.

88   Littleton, Edward., "Athletics in Schools," Popular Science Monthly, XVI (Mar. 1880), 677-684.

An Englishman reveals that a serious evil of athleticism is that it tends to become a power in the school, rivaling consti- tuted authorities. He suggests making the school subjects furnish some of the interest in schools, a point later raised in American schools.

89.   Lowman, Guy S., "The Regulation and Control of Sport in Secondary Schools of the United States," American Physical Education Review, XII (Dec. 1907), 307-323.

The findings of a survey of private and public school athletic regulations are reported. Lowman favors faculty control of athletics with considerable amount of student initiative.

90.   MacCracken, H. M., "Speech Before the Third Annual Con- vention of the Intercollegiate Athletic Association of the United States," National College Athletic Association Proceedings, III (1909), 6.

The chancellor of New York University recalls the progress since the inception of his idea to reform football and athletics during the 1905-06 crisis in college football.

91.   McKenzie, R. Tait, "The Regulation of Athletic Sports in Colleges," National Education Association: Proceedings, (1839), 636-641.

McKenzie was, at the time, a rising physical educator influ- enced by Herbert Spencer. He believed that play-type activi- ties (athletics) were the "safety-valve" to let off excess physi- cal energy.

92. McPherson, Frances A. "Development of Ideas in Physical Education in the Secondary Schools in the United States Between 1889-1920." Ph.D. dissertation, University of Wisconsin, 1965.

While this is basically a history of physical education, the study does discuss some aspects of early interscholastic sport.

93. Martin, John F., "Walter Camp and His Gridiron Game," American Heritage, XII (Oct. 1961), 50-55, 77-81.

Martin has shown that Camp was the guiding hand in the development of American-style football.

94. Mathews, Joseph J., "First Harvard-Oxford Boat Race," New England Quarterly, XXXIII (Mar. 1960), 74-82.

The first international intercollegiate athletic contest was won by the Oxford crew before an estimated 1,000,000 spectators in 1869.

95. Meiklejohn, Alexander, "What Are College Games For?" in Atlantic Monthly, CXXX (1922), 663-671.

Colleges should rid commercialism from athletic games, as well as the hiring of players. Coaches are charged with taking independence away from the players.

96. Meylan, George L., "Athletics," American Physical Education Review, X (June 1905), 157-163.

A Columbia University physical educator discusses the advantages and disadvantages of college athletics, and offers five means to rid the unfavorable aspects.

97. Moore, John H., "Football's Ugly Decades, 1893-1913," Smithsonian Journal of History, II (Fall 1967), 49-68.

An historican concludes that brutality and questionable administration of athletics in the late nineteenth and early twentieth centuries nearly caused its abolishment. Rule changes and the effective use of the forward pass changed the nature of the game helped to save it. A good article, well-documented and illustrated.

98. Naismith, James, "Basketball," American Physical Education Review, XIX (1914), 339-351.

The founder of the game in 1891 discusses the necessary requisites for a new indoor game which had to eliminate certain aspects of football to be successful.

99. Needham, Henry B., "The College Athlete," McClures' Magazine, XXV (June, July 1905), 115-128; 260-273.

The attack of college athletics by Needham is centered on professionalism in the hiring of players and in the conduct of summer baseball programs. Good examples of these occurrences are detailed for Columbia, Yale and the University of Pennsylvania.

100. New York Times, The, "Ivy League Agreement Against Abuses in College Sports," by Allison Danzig, (22-24 Mar. 1954).

A long-time New York Times sports writer shows that the colleges that gave shape to the American game of football are trying to save it with more stringent rules.

101. Olsen, Jack. The Black Athlete. New York: Time-Life Books, 1968.

A journalist, in a non-objective way, presents a picture of the exploitation of the black athlete in America. College football coaches, especially, come under attack.

102. Paxson, Frederic L., "The Rise of Sport," Mississippi Valley Historical Review, IV (1917), 143-168.

The Turner frontier thesis has a strong impact on Paxson's thesis that sport was the "safety-valve" of a frontier-less society. Athletics were an outgrowth of wealth and leisure and the sedentary life resulting from urban life.

103. Pittman, Marvin S., "Football, Sport or Spoils?" in School and Society, XLVIII (13 Aug. 1938), 213-217.

A questionnaire was sent to presidents of all teachers colleges in the United States concerning subsidization of football players. The south was found to be most liberal in granting athletic scholarships.

104. Raycroft, J. E., "Educational Value of Athletics in Schools and Colleges," School and Society, III (26 Feb. 1916), 295-300.

A Princeton University official opposes semi-professional baseball playing, side-line coaching, and the win-at-all cost athletic philosophy.

105. "Recruiting High-School Athletes; Code of the Committee of Sixty," School and Society, XXV (11 June 1927), 687.

A committee of the Western College Conference opposes all scholarships based upon athletic skills.

106. Reed, William R., "Big-Time Athletics' Commitment to Education," Journal of Health, Physical Education and Recreation, XXXIV (Sept. 1963), 29-30, 64-65.

The commissioner of the Big Ten believes that big-time athletics are educationally justified. He defines an amateur as one who is not a professional.

107. Richards, Eugene L., "College Athletics," Popular Science Monthly, XXIV (1884), 456-453; 587-597.

A Yale mathematics professor sees the value of college athletics. He discusses athletic evils, but sees the decreasing number of campus disorders as a positive influence of sports.

108. _____, "The Football Situation," Popular Science Monthly, XLV (Oct. 1894), 721-733.

Richards defends football as a superior sport creating school esprit de corps, denying that it is a brutal game.

109. Riesman, David and Denney, Reuel, "Football in America: A Study in Cultural Diffusion," American Quarterly, III (1951), 309-325.

Two sociologists see an ethnic significance in the development of American football, as well as an American cultural influence on the distinct American form of football.

110. Roberts, Howard. The Big Nine, Story of Football in the Western Conference. New York: G. P. Putnam's Sons, 1948.

The story of the Big Ten is told in a light manner with emphasis on winning teams and outstanding players and coaches.

111.   Rogers, Frederick R. The Future of Interscholastic Athle-
       tics. New York: Bureau of Publications, Columbia Univer-
       sity, 1929.

       Rogers was one of many critics of athletic policies in the
       1920's. His attack upon interscholastic athletics as practiced
       is based upon overemphasis of athletics. Among other sug-
       gestions he favors abolishment of all athletic championships.

112.   Roosevelt, Theodore, "Value of an Athletic Training,"
       Harper's Weekly, XXXVII (23 Dec. 1893), 1236.

       A future president believes that manly sports, including foot-
       ball, are needed in a sedentary society. Virile qualities of
       sports should be emphasized.

113.   Root, Robert K., "Sport Versus Athletics," Forum, LXXII
       (Nov. 1924), 657-664.

       Intercollegiate athletics have ceased to be amateur, especially
       football, for they are run as organized, commercial specta-
       cles.

114.   Roper, William, "The Value of Football," Forum, LXXVI
       (Nov. 1926), 690-695.

       Comparing American football to Greek athletics, Roper finds
       football benefitting players both mentally and physically and a
       positive influence in college morals.

115.   Rousseau, Edward L., "Great American Ritual: Watching
       Games," Nation, CLXXXVII (4 Oct. 1958), 188-191.

       Spectator sport as entertainment depends upon a ritual identi-
       fication of spectators with the triumph of good. Rousseau be-
       lieves that spectator sport began when the idea of the self-
       made man began to decay.

116.   Rudolph, Frederick. "The Rise of Football," in his The
       American College and University. New York: Alfred A.
       Knopf, Inc., 1962, pp. 373-393.

       An educational historian traces the rise of intercollegiate foot-
       ball believing that it was likely responsible for reducing rebel-
       lion, rioting, and hazing. Football was also consciously used
       as an agency for student recruitment and raising finances for
       colleges. At the same time it served democracy on campus
       and off.

117.   Ryan, W. Carson. "The Literature of American School and College Athletics." Bulletin Number Twenty-four of the Carnegie Foundation for the Advancement of Teaching. Boston: The Merrymount Press, 1929.

This is a monumental review of the literature of athletics to 1929. It is another of the Carnegie Foundation's study of athletics in the schools and colleges.

118.   Sargent, Dudley A., "Athletics in Secondary Schools," American Physical Education Review, VIII (June 1903), 57-69.

The value of interscholastic athletics is questioned by Sargent, while athletics for the many are considered valuable. He is opposed to advertising the school through athletics.

119.   _____, "History of the Administration of Inter-collegiate Athletics in the United States," American Physical Education Review, XV (1910), 252-261.

Sargent traces the early history of control over intercollegiate athletics pointing out the roles played by eastern colleges and the Big Ten.

120.   _____, A Physical Instructor's Suggestions for Improvement," Review of Reviews, (Jan. 1906), 74-75.

An eminent physical educator, who believes in the value of athletics, desires to improve football. He suggests that football incorporate the best points of basketball and football with limited tackling.

121.   Seaver, J. M., "Inter-School Athletics," Education, XXII (Mar. 1902), 420-425.

Athletics and play activities are vital to expend excess energies of school students. Teacher control over athletics is necessary.

122.   Savage, Howard J. "American College Athletics." Bulletin Number Twenty-three of the Carnegie Foundation for the Advancement of Teaching. Boston: The Merrymount Press, 1929.

A thorough study of the problems of intercollegiate athletics is presented with an emphasis upon football. Criticism of professionalism and commercialization is found throughout the report.

123.   Savage, Howard J. and others. "Current Developments in American College Sport." Bulletin Number Twenty-six of the Carnegie Foundation for the Advancement of Teaching. Boston: The Merrymount Press, 1931.

A follow-up study of the problems of intercollegiate athletics of the 1929 Report believes that the deflation of American football has begun. It still emphasizes that the athletic scholarship has no place in American colleges.

124.   Schlesinger, Arthur M. and Fox, Dixon Ryan (editors). A History of American Life. 13 volumes. New York: The Macmillan Co., 1927-1948.

This 13 volume social and cultural history of the American people contains reference to athletics, sports, games, and amusements of the people throughout American history. Extensive bibliographies are an aid to the sport historian.

125.   Scott, Harry A., "New Directions in Intercollegiate Athletics," Teachers College Record, LVIII (Oct.-May 1957), 29-37.

Athletics cannot be justified because of their entertainment, commercial, or advertising values, but must be defended on their contribution to the education of all students. Scott suggests reforms that college presidents are advised to consider.

126.   Shaler, N. S., "The Athletic Problem in Education," Atlantic Monthly, LXIII (1889), 79-88.

Twenty years of Harvard cause Shaler to believe that athletics are beneficial to higher learning. He is concerned that the win-at-all costs philosophy may become dominant.

127.   "Shall Intercollegiate Football Be Abolished?" Literary Digest, LXXXVII (10 Oct. 1925), 68-76.

Yes, states the article, football should be abolished in favor of intramural sport. College athletics have no place for professionalism, fake scholarships, bribery, scouting, and "kidnapping" of players.

128.   Smith, Judson, "College Intercollegiate Contests." New Englander, XXXIV (July 1875), 518-529.

An early critic of intercollegiate athletics, Smith believes that crew races especially are disadvantageous to the college welfare.

129. Smith, Ronald A. "From Normal School to State University: A History of the Wisconsin State University Conference." Ph.D. dissertation, University of Wisconsin, 1969.

The history of a small midwestern athletic conference is seen from an internal as well as extended viewpoint. The influence of college presidents and faculty representatives upon the problems and development of athletics is emphasized.

130. Stagg, Amos A. and Stout, Wesley W. Touchdown! New York: Longmans, Green and Co., 1927.

A star Yale player and noted football coach at the University of Chicago recalls football from its early days to the 1920's.

131. Star, Jack and Mollenhoff, Clark, "Football Scandal Hits the Big Ten," Look, XX (21 Aug. 1956), 19-25.

Look writers view the Big Ten, especially Ohio State, with sympathy, as big-time athletic schools with strict scholarship rules to obey.

132. Stearns, Alfred E., "Athletics and the School," Atlantic Monthly, CXIII (Feb. 1914), 148-152.

Stearns believes that the values of interscholastic sports--development of character, self-control, courage, quick thinking, and self-restraint--permeate the whole school. Coaches are to blame for undesirable aspects of athletics.

133. Stewart, C. A., "Athletics and the College," Atlantic Monthly, CXIII (Feb. 1914), 153-160.

Unethical athletics, according to Stewart, affect the whole college. He compares the "get away with it" attitude with that of big business.

134. Stoke, Harold W., "College Athletics: Education or Show Business," Atlantic Monthly, CXCIII (Mar. 1954), 46-50.

A college administrator believes that the colleges should accept athletics as entertainment to prevent hypocrisy; accept athletics as business and make rules accordingly.

135.   Thwing, Charles F., "Football: Is the Game Worth Saving?"
        Independent, LIV (15 May 1902), 1167-1174.

        The president of Western Reserve backs football despite
        numerous evils. Thwing reports the comments of a survey of
        college presidents who generally favored the game of football.

136.   Tunis, John R. The American Way in Sport. New York:
        Duell, Sloan and Pearce, 1958.

        A long-time writer of sport in America gives his idealistic
        views on what athletics should be and what they have been.

137.   _____, "The Great God Football," Harper's Maga-
        zine, CLVII (1928), 742-752.

        College football is a great game, but it should not be deified.
        "Someday football may cease to be a religion...and become
        merely a sport."

138.   _____, "More Pay for College Football Stars," The
        American Mercury, XXXIX (Nov. 1936), 267-272.

        Tunis classifies 100 colleges into amateur, semi-pros, or
        professionals according to their emphasis on athletics. He
        claims that colleges should end their hypocritical attitude
        about amateur athletics and pay the players openly.

139.   Underwood, Arthur W. (Secretary). "The Right and Wrong of
        Athletics," The Sunset Club Yearbook, 1893-1894. Chicago:
        Privately printed, 1895, pp. 213-232.

        A Chicago professional and businessmen's club discusses the
        values of athletics as they exist in the early 1890's.

140.   Voltmer, Carl D. A Brief History of the Intercollegiate
        Conference of Faculty Representatives with Special Consider-
        ation of Athletic Problems. Menosha, Wisconsin: George
        Bantar Publishing Co., 1935.

        Voltmer traces the problems and rule changes which occurred
        in the Big Ten Conference until the mid-thirties.

141. Walker, Francis A. "College Athletics," Harvard Graduates'
      Magazine, II (1893), 1-18.

      According to the president of M.I T., a reaction to the con-
      tempt in which physical activity was held in pre-Civil War
      society has resulted in a stress on athleticism. This is an
      enlightening oration delivered to a Phi Beta Kappa gathering
      at Harvard College.

142. Weyand, Alexander M. The Saga of American Football. New
      York: The Macmillan Co., 1955.

      Like many others, Weyand traces American football to the
      Rutgers-Princeton game of 1869. The volume lacks foot-
      notes, but offers many facts on winning teams, coaches, out-
      standing players, and all-American teams.

143. "What Football Players Are Earning this Fall," Literary
      Digest, CVII (15 Nov. 1930), 28, 33.

      Payments of up to $75 per month to athletes are discussed as
      Kansas is ousted from the Big Six in 1930, only a year after
      Iowa was suspended from the Big Ten for a "slush fund."

144. Whitney, Caspar W. (editor), "Is Football Worthwhile?"
      Collier's, XLV (18 Dec. 1909), 13, 24-25.

      The views of various college presidents are recorded during a
      crucial period in the development of football.

145. Whiton, James M., "The First Harvard-Yale Regatta (1852),"
      Outlook, LXVIII (1901), 286-289.

      The Yale crew member most responsible for the first inter-
      collegiate contest in the United States recalls the first
      Harvard-Yale boat race on Lake Winnipesaukee, New
      Hampshire in 1852.

146. Wingert, H. Shindle and others, "Report of the Committee on
      the Encouragement of Intra-Collegiate and Recreative Sports,"
      American Physical Education Review, XIX (Apr. 1914), 352-
      369.

      A survey of 150 colleges reveals the amount spent and the
      number of students involved in inter- and intra-collegiate sport
      in the United States. Conclusion: more should be done for
      intra-collegiate sport.

147. Wriston, Henry M., "The Responsibility of a College President in a Changing Physical Education Program," Research Quarterly, III (May 1932), 5-18.

More aptly titled "a sane approach to intercollegiate athletics" Wriston, President of Lawrence College, sees the value of college athletics in terms of educational and recreative objectives rather than exploitation of the individual by the college.

148. Young, C. A., "College Athletic Sports," Forum, II (Oct. 1886), 142-152.

This is a revealing article on the effect that athletics have made on the colleges since the 1860's. Young notes the excesses of athletics as of the mid-eighties, but claims that the benefits far exceed the evils. Athletics serve the purpose of play, to provide a "safety-valve" for "superabundant physical effervescence."

149. Young, C. V. P., "Intercollegiate Athletics and the Professional Coach," American Physical Education Review, XIX (May 1914), 331-338.

A Cornell University professor believes that a permanent coaching staff, selected like other teaching staff members, should replace the graduate coach who has little experience in training athletes.

150. Youngert, Eugene, "College Athletics, Their Pressure on the High School," Atlantic Monthly, CCII (Oct. 1958), 35-38.

As a Chicago area high school superintendent, Youngert worked with Conant's study of American high schools. He blames commercialized college athletics for placing great pressure on high schools in the form of recruiting and scholarships. The pressures affect the sense of values of high school boys.

APPENDIX E

AN INTRODUCTION TO SPORT AND PHYSICAL EDUCATION
IN CANADA

Editor's Note: The reader should understand that these four
selected historical papers on the history of sport and physical education in Canada in no way represent a definitive treatment of the subject from the standpoint of comprehensive coverage. There is a scar-
city of material currently available, however, and it was felt that
making these fine papers available would be helpful to those who are
teaching in this subject-matter both in the United States and in Canada.

THE HISTORICAL BACKGROUND AND PRESENT STATUS OF CANADIAN PHYSICAL EDUCATION

Garth A. Paton
University of Western Ontario, London

Canada, a Western and Northern country, resembles a distorted parallelogram; the location is such that it lies at the crossroads of contact with some of the principal powers and most populous areas of the world.* Bordered on the south by the United States, with the southern peninsula of the province of Ontario probing into the heartland of the United States, the people of Canada are strongly influenced by their neighbour to the south. Frequently overlooked are the remaining three borders which provide the closest North American contact with Russia, England and France, and the Far East. Canada's far north brings her into geographical proximity to Russia. The land mass of Newfoundland jutting into the North Atlantic provides the shortest distance between North America and England and France, while the province of British Columbia and the Yukon territory are the closest North American points to the Far East.

In terms of geographical area, Canada is the second largest country in the world. The 3,851,809 square miles exceeds that of the United States by some 230,000 square miles; yet Canada is less than one-half the area of Russia. There are five distinct geographical regions: The Eastern Maritimes including the four provinces of Newfoundland, Nova Scotia, Prince Edward Island and New Brunswick; the Great Lakes - St. Lawrence River Basin is constituted by the provinces of Ontario and Quebec; the Prairies composed of Manitoba, Saskatchewan and portions of Alberta; the Rocky Mountains and the Pacific Coast Region encompasses the western portion of Alberta and the Province of British Columbia and the Far North region includes the Yukon and Northwest Territories.

The population of Canada is sparse and unevenly distributed; only within the last decade has the population figure attained the twenty-million mark. Canada has only two cities with populations in excess of one million, but the population is distributed such that ninety per cent of the people live on ten per cent of the land. The greatest

---

* This article appeared originally in Monograph #1 of Physical Education Around The World (William Johnson, editor) Phi Epsilon Kappa Fraternity, 6919 E. 10th, Suite E4, Indianapolis, Ind. 46218. It is published with the kind permission of Dr. R. R. Schreiber, National Executive Secretary, and Professor William Johnson (editor) University of Illinois, Urbana. It was revised in 1974.

concentration of population is in the Great Lakes - St. Lawrence Valley region, thus leaving vast areas of thinly populated or unpopulated regions.[4]

The vastness of the country presents problems, but this immensity is also one of its most attractive aspects. The coalescence of the best natural scenery of Switzerland, Norway, France, Scotland, Russia and Rumania provides unmatched geographical variation; yet, the great extent of these areas have been one of the influences impeding Canadian nationalism. An example is the relatively recent completion of Canada's first coast-to-coast highway. Individual provinces have long had excellent roads, but it was 1962 before the Trans-Canada Highway was completed.

The typical Canadian character is non-existent. As the geography of Canada exhibits infinite variety, similarly does the character of Canadians. The Canadian travelling in Europe is frequently looked upon as an American; yet, the Canadian has basic differences. The most striking difference is the contrasting views of themselves. The American has usually looked inward, strong in the belief of what America means and stands for; the melting pot has forged and tempered the conviction of self-determination. Contrastingly, the Canadian has tended to look outward. The European heritage of Britain and France runs deep; geography has reinforced regional differences. The splendid isolation of Newfoundland has developed a determination and camaraderie in a people forced to wrest a living from the bleak Atlantic and a ruggedly beautiful landscape, with little arable soil. The intense regional loyalty of the citizens of the Eastern Maritimes has developed a reserved, conservative group of Canadians - this in a region that is most logically a geographical extension of New England (United States). The "joie de vie" of the French Canadian "habitant" molded with the fine intellectual background of the "collèges classiques" and the strong bond of religion, has maintained North America's most unique culture. The tradition of the more than fifty thousand United Empire Loyalists, who left the Thirteen Colonies and settled in Ontario, parts of Quebec and New Brunswick, perpetuates the British heritage and the British Crown. The Prairie Provinces of Manitoba, Saskatchewan and Alberta, wheat-growing and oil-wealthy entities, imprisoned by the Rocky Mountains on one side and vast distance and the Great Lakes on the other, tend to look to the south, and constitute a distinctiveness and openness of their own. The Province of British Columbia, isolated by the Rocky Mountains, and thriving on tremendous natural resources, more closely approximates the American belief in self-determination than possibly any other region of Canada.[6,16]

Historical Background of Physical Education[12]

In 1967 Canada celebrated her one hundredth birthday, by most standards a young country. Typical of evolving countries, organized physical education was virtually non-existent until there was sufficient urbanization. Early settlers had more than they could do in coping with the problems of survival. Yet, even in the pioneer years, there are traces of recreational activity, growing out of the heritage and environment. Games and dances were transported from England and France, and lacrosse, an Indian originated game, later developed into Canada's National Game. Prior to Confederation in 1867, there were evidences of sports clubs influenced strongly by European culture (e.g. The Halifax Curling Club; The Halifax Yacht Club and the Wanderers Athletic Club of Halifax, established in 1824, 1836 and 1861 respectively) that reflect the tradition and interests of the people. The latter group were engaged in lacrosse, soccer, rugby, cricket, lawn bowling, and track and field. Several athletic clubs were also established in the Montreal area around the mid-nineteenth century, and in 1881 several of these clubs amalgamated to form the Montreal Amateur Athletic Association.

Egerton Ryerson, an early and influential Ontario educator, promulgated the cause of physical education in the schools. Impelled by his plea, a curriculum of exercises was published in 1852. Within a decade, a normal school was equipped with a gymnasium in order to train teachers.

One of the most illustrious and well-recognized figures in physical education in Canada and the United States, R. Tait McKenzie, assumed the post as Director of Physical Education for Men at McGill University until 1903 when he moved to the University of Pennsylvania where he remained until his death in 1938. He is best remembered for his outstanding sculpture and is commemorated annually by both the American and Canadian Association for Health, Physical Education and Recreation through the R. Tait McKenzie Memorial Lectures. A lesser known, but equally impressive artistic contribution of Dr. McKenzie's, is the stone plaque that remains in the Houses of Parliament, Ottawa. This plaque was presented to the Government of Canada by former Canadians, who had moved to the United States, as a tribute to their homeland. A national shrine, The Mill of Kintail, stands to his memory at his former home and studio in Almonte, Ontario.

Miss Ethel M. Cartwright exercised a long and influential force on women's physical education. She served as Director of Physical Education for Women at McGill University from 1906 to 1927 and previously taught at Halifax Ladies College. In 1929 she joined the faculty of the University of Saskatchewan and was instrumental in establishing physical education at each of these institutions.

A unique fund that shaped physical education in the country was established in 1909 by Lord Strathcona. This fund provided provincial grants to establish school curricula for physical training. Instructors from the military were utilized because of a deficiency of civilian teachers. Since the fund also encouraged cadet training, the result was a continuing relationship between cadet corps and physical education instructors in Canada, until after World War II.

As history has so frequently shown, interest in physical fitness increases during a time of war. Canada was no exception after World War I. The depression had its effects on facilities as well as on leisure time. An attempt to utilize leisure time profitably was made by the Federal Government in 1939 through the enactment of a Youth Training Act.

The outbreak of World War II again exposed the unfitness of Canadian youth. The federal government stepped into the breach again and passed the National Physical Fitness Act of 1943. The act aimed specifically at improvement of the physical fitness of Canadians by encouraging extended physical education programs in the schools as well as better facilities. This act improved training as well as recreation development in numerous provinces.

Kindergarten-Elementary Physical Education

Strong influences in recent years, such as urbanization, improved transportation and communication, and increased population, have thrust education toward the centralization of elementary schools. These same trends exerted their influences on physical education at the elementary school level. In earlier years, the one-room rural districts were common. One teacher, grappling with the responsibilities of teaching the fundamentals of reading, writing, and arithmetic to students spanning the grades one through eight, found little time for teaching physical education. Recess periods were regularly scheduled, but physical activity was deemed a diversion and release, not a phase of education. As districts amalgamated and schools consolidated, transformations in physical education occurred. Gymnasia and indoor facilities are essential because of the winter's length and severity and the need is gradually being filled. Several provinces report a staggering increase in new gymnasia in the last few years. In urban centers where elementary schools are large, gymnasia are common.[16]

Most provinces have been reticent to press for improved physical education programs in elementary schools because of inadequate staff. Across the country the typical elementary school teacher has only a general professional training, with little physical education, and the overwhelming proportion of teachers at the elementary level are women. The heavy emphasis has been upon upgrading the secondary program. Elementary programs generally stress fundamental skills of movement, some sport skills, a varying emphasis on physical fitness and teachers frequently allude to the development of attitudes and social skills.

Elementary physical education has been caught in a circular cycle that recently has shown signs of being interrupted. At the bottom of the circle has been a lack of professionally qualified personnel. This lack of professional leadership is responsible for the failure to sell physical education to the public; in turn, lack of public support has strangled program and facility development. Thus, the unappealing prospect of poor facilities and program discourages personnel from entering the field, and the cycle regenerates itself. Even though the profession has long recognized the importance of elementary physical education, it is just beginning to come to grips with the problem. Recently, school boards have begun to appoint coordinators with the direct responsibility for developing the elementary school program.

Secondary School Physical Education

Secondary school physical education has improved steadily in the past twenty-five years, with progress due largely to the professional leadership and preparation offered by teacher education programs. Women's professional preparation programs antedate programs for men; the first undergraduate major for men in Canada was conceived at the University of Toronto as late as 1940.[19] In the secondary program both male and female programs in physical education are expected to contribute towards the goals of general education. Detailed description of all aspects of the programs are beyond the scope of this brief report, especially since education is a provincial concern. Some generalization is possible and will be attempted; exceptions and unique aspects will be pointed out when possible.

Among the girls, an emphasis on "movement" has been strong. Frequently referred to as "fundamental movement" or "movement education" the aim is to teach correct and proper use of the body. This inclusive term ranges from the basic locomotor movements through to creative dance. Gymnastics also forms an integral part of the program and basic tumbling provides the foundation that progresses to stunts and apparatus work. Folk and ballroom dancing, as well as the team games of basketball, volleyball, softball, field hockey, and track and field, are popular. Where possible, swimming is included in the program; however, schools with swimming facilities are the exception.

Along with the core curriculum in physical education, the girls' program usually includes provision for competitive athletics at both the intramural and interschool level. The scope of the program varies, but in theory and practice the intramural program is much more extensive. Again location and population are factors; urban centers naturally provide the means for competition that is frequently not available in sparsely settled areas. Student bus transportation creates problems in rural areas as well.[3]

Six of the ten provinces have divisions of the Department of Education devoted exclusively to physical education: Prince Edward Island, Nova Scotia, New Brunswick, Quebec, Ontario and Manitoba. The remaining four provinces have agencies at the provincial level that aid school physical education. Initially, the development of these latter departments has been in recreation, but frequently these agencies now offer aid to physical education.[16]

The time allotment for physical education in the secondary curriculum likewise is a provincial policy. Different provinces recommend minimum number of hours on a per-week basis, but this is not always indicative of what actually exists. Local conditions, such as lack of physical education teachers, lack of facilities, overcrowded schools, or administrators unwilling to overcome these difficulties, frequently result in a situation where the actual opportunities for physical education fall below the provincial recommendations. The larger centers of population adhere most closely to the recommendations, whereas the smaller schools tend to deviate. The allotment of time recommended by the provinces for physical education ranges from three activity periods and one health period per week in Ontario to the Province of Newfoundland, where there is no physical education required. Generally, the requirements approximate three periods per week. In all fairness to Newfoundland, it should be pointed out that there are physical education programs in many schools; recent changes by the Government there, bode well for the future of physical education in that province.

The goals of physical education, as well as the means of attaining these goals, show considerable similarity through the country. Concern is shown for proper growth and development; implicit with this concern is the need for some level of physical fitness. A goal of establishing certain basic skills in sports and games has wide agreement. Through the attainment of skills, the assumption is made that sports participation will follow; this, in turn, leads to situations where the emotional and social characteristics of the student may be developed. The expression of these goals varies widely, but the four goals: physical growth, acquisition of skills, emotional development and social development, form a core that is common throughout the country.

The bases of the activity programs are sports and games. The sports found in the programs are very similar to those found in the schools of the United States such as football, basketball, volleyball, track and field, cross-country, tumbling, gymnastics, wrestling, soccer, softball and swimming. Where facilities, equipment and personnel permit, emphasis is also placed on individual sports such as tennis, golf, badminton and archery. Increased emphasis on the problems of leisure has increased the emphasis on carry-over activities.

Sports and games such as skiing, curling, lacrosse and rugby add uniqueness to the program. Skiing competition between schools, often on a province-wide basis, is growing in popularity. The climate and geography of Quebec, Ontario, Alberta and British Columbia specifically, are ideally suited to the rigorous winter sports. As well as competitive skiing, some programs institute curricular instruction in skiing, school ski clubs, and opportunities for school-sponsored recreational skiing.

The sport that sparks the greatest national enthusiasm and interest is ice hockey. Canadians take a great deal of pride in the fact that the National Hockey League and the more recently established World Hockey League are mostly composed of Canadian players. The hockey program outside the schools is profuse. Age group hockey exists in almost all towns. Secondary schools are extending the broad base upon which hockey operates, and increasing numbers of schools are including the sport in their programs.

Curling is another winter sport that is enthusiastically supported by thousands of Canadians. Originally played outdoors, and in earlier years by older adults only, it is now played in thousands of arenas across the breadth of the land on both artificial and natural ice surfaces. From coast to coast, it is a rare town or village that does not have a curling rink. The secondary schools very frequently include curling in their program. Curling is presently the only high school sport in which a national school boy championship is held annually.

Lacrosse was originally an Indian game. Down through the years it has maintained a modicum of popularity. The vigorous nature of the game, and the skill involved in controlling a hard rubber ball with a lacrosse stick, provide a challenge to many youths. Equipment is negligible, and the similarity between lacrosse and hockey sparks its popularity in many areas of Canada.

Rugby, with its British tradition, minimal equipment, considerable running and body contact has appeal to students in some programs. It is not played as extensively as many other sports presently, but in specific areas its popularity is increasing.

The general philosophy in Canadian school programs emphasizes sports for the masses. Thus, the curriculum program is of paramount importance, followed by the intramural athletic program, and finally by the interscholastic program. The intramural programs are typically coordinated with the curricular program. The extent of intramural athletics is contingent on facilities and student interest. The coordination with the instructional program is based upon an assumption of skill carry-over. Intramural athletics are variously organized, but basically the aim is to provide competitive opportunities for the maximum number of students. Intramurals are frequently conducted prior to school hours or after school. An activity period scheduled into the school day often provides opportunity for bus students to enjoy the same advantage as local students.

Interscholastic athletics provide for those who excel in specific sports, and are often employed as a medium for developing esprit de corps in a school. The program base is broadened by organizing two or three teams that represent the school in a particular sport; age is the most common criterion used in determining classification.

The team sports common to interscholastic competition are hockey, football, basketball, cross-country, track and field, wrestling, volleyball and soccer. In urban areas, as well as in selected leagues formed by adjacent small towns, individual sports such as badminton and golf are popular. When schools have the necessary facilities, swimming competition is organized.[16]

The governing of interscholastic athletics shows some differences from province to province. In Newfoundland the St. John's area provides competition in a local league in soccer, basketball and hockey. The provinces of Quebec, Alberta and British Columbia leave the administration of athletics to local or regional authorities. The remaining provinces have provisional associations that coordinate leagues and provide for championship play in ten or more sports.

The outstanding feature across the country is the close surveillance exercised by educators over athletics. Principals and headmasters influence policy; coaches are selected according to their teaching qualifications and coaches are paid as teachers, rarely receiving remuneration for coaching. Athletics function in and as a part of total physical education program; the entire program is directed toward the goals of education.

College-University Physical Education

Basic instruction, or physical education service programs, in colleges and universities are limited in Canada. Three rather important issues directly affect these programs. The first is the traditional, essentialistic philosophy of higher education found in Canada; the second is the increased pressure of enrollment in higher education with a concomitant shortage of staff and the third has been the lack of graduate programs in physical education and the resulting absence of teaching assistants. The _fundamental issue_ is the philosophical concept of higher education and it may well affect the other issues.

The essentialistic tradition of Canadian education has had many ramifications for physical education. This trend, if not completely propagating a mind–body dichotomy, had certainly left physical education as a second–class citizen in many universities.

Although basic skills courses are rarely available to the general university student, in many universities the physical recreation and intramural programs provide basic instruction in sports on a non-credit basis. In addition, there has been an increase in the offering of a disciplinary–oriented introductory courses which attempt to wed physical education theory with some practical laboratory experiences. Often this type of course may be available on a university–wide basis.

Intercollegiate athletics were conceived in Canada as far back as 1881. In 1906 the original Canadian Intercollegiate Athletic Union was formed. The schools represented were all in Ontario. In 1910 the Maritime Intercollegiate Athletic Union was founded and the year 1920 marked the beginnings of the Western Canada Intercollegiate Athletic Union. However, it wasn't until 1961 that all intercollegiate associations in the country were united into one body. The original name, Canadian Intercollegiate Athletic Union, was retained. This organization is now the governing body for competitive sports in Canadian universities. However, regional differences and the geographical size of Canada has presented enormous problems for the effective operation of the C.I.A.U.

The shortness of the university academic year in Canada (from the latter part of September through early May) restricts competition; however, football, hockey, basketball, wrestling and swimming, in addition to individual sports such as squash, badminton, tennis and golf, comprise many college programs. The early termination of school restricts baseball, and to some extent track and field, although some institutions sponsor track and field and cross–country competition in the fall.

There are visible efforts to keep athletics within the framework of the educational structure; athletic scholarships, or grants–in–aid scholarships, are infrequent in Canada. There are few full–time coaches, and those who may be classified as such have multiple coaching tasks. Generally, coaching goes hand–in–hand with additional teaching or administrative responsibilities.

The "low pressure" athletic programs seemingly result from two factors: (1) the dominant philosophy of "education for the intellect", and (2) the absence of extensive professional athletics in Canada. Professional football and professional hockey and recently the Montreal Expos in the National League in baseball, are the sole professional leagues of any consequence. In the case of football, Canadian teams import a significant percentage of their players from the United States, thus limiting opportunities for Canadians; furthermore, the universities have not been prime suppliers of hockey talent.

Intramural athletics exist in most universities. Facilities are often limited, since intercollegiate athletics have tended to take precedence in the time schedule. The variety of activities parallels those of the intercollegiate programs, and in many universities a very high percentage of the student body participates in the intramural program. The newer universities, such as York University, Toronto, Ontario; Trent University in Peterborough, Ontario; and Simon Fraser, University in Burnaby, British Columbia, tend to place a heavy emphasis upon the development of the intramural athletic program. There have been increased student demands and a willingness to back the development of facilities primarily for physical recreation in some universities. The University of Western Ontario, London, has recently erected a community centre and a winter sports building with substantial percentages of the costs contributed directly by the students.

Teacher Education in Physical Education

Teacher education in Canada evolved through gradual government control of the educational system. Initially, schools were operated privately or by churches. Then, as the need for education grew, it became the domain of the provinces. In 1867, the British North America Act established Canada as a self-governing nation, and this act clearly placed education in the control of the individual provinces. Similarities exist among provinces, but there are differences too numerous to discuss.

The earliest institutions for training teachers were the normal schools, with the first being established in 1847. Within a decade normal schools were established in each of the five eastern provinces. There was evident concern for physical training in the normal schools by 1852. The Strathcona Trust Fund (mentioned earlier) was established in 1909. It influenced the development of physical education in the curriculum of the normal schools.

Teacher certification for the elementary school usually requires one year of study at a provincial certified teachers college after completion of high school, but some provinces require a two-year period of training. In the Western provinces teacher education is placed within the university in an education faculty. In the Eastern provinces professional preparation for elementary school teaching takes place in an institution independent from a university.

Where elementary teacher education is obtained through the university, there is an emphasis on basic arts and science courses, as well as on the general and specialized education courses. In the normal schools, or now more appropriately the teachers colleges or faculties of education, as they are contemporarily named, the emphasis is placed on teaching methods, and on psychology, philosophy, and school law. Practice teaching is required in both the teachers colleges and universities.

Two basic approaches are taken to teacher certification for secondary schools, both of which emphasize a broad liberal arts and science background with specialization in a subject-matter area, as well as in professional education course work. The Province of Ontario typifies the one concept; the Provinces of Alberta, Saskatchewan and British Columbia the other. Ontario secondary school teachers complete their undergraduate degree program prior to entrance to a school or faculty. In Ontario universities there are essentially two types of bachelor degrees granted: (1) the honours degree, granted after four years of university work and thirteen grades of high school; and (2) the regular baccalaureate degree is granted for three years of successful study after thirteen grades of high school. The four-year honours degree involves broad liberal arts and sciences study including specialization in a particular major area. The three-year degree is essentially a liberal arts and science degree with an opportunity for limited specialiaation. Upon graduation from university, the prospective teacher attends a school of education for one year where emphasis is directed to teaching methods, history and philosophy of education, educational psychology, and practice teaching. Teacher certification is granted upon graduation from this education unit. Thus, there is a vertical separation and a consecutive as opposed to a concurrent approach to professional preparation.

The second method, typical of the Western Provinces and some universities in the east, centers teacher preparation in professional education units of the universities. Under this system a concurrent approach is utilized, combining liberal education, special emphasis on teaching subject matter, and teacher education into one curriculum. This approach is analagous to the teacher education programs in the United States

Undergraduate degree courses in physical education in the universities of Canada have a short history. The first program was established at the University of Toronto in Ontario in 1940.[19] In this decade six other institutions instituted programs and by 1964 there were seventeen institutions offering various degrees in physical education. By 1974 there were more than thirty programs in Canada.

The types of degrees and structures of the various curricula show wide variation. Only three institutions offer a Bachelor of Arts degree in physical education. The remaining universities offer a variety of degrees such as Bachelor of Physical and Health Education, or some combination thereof. One can only speculate upon the reasons for this variation.

The structure of the curricula in all universities emphasizes liberal education. In some cases the Bachelor of Arts degree is earned first; in a second approach, the professional phase and the liberal education phase are offered in a parallel manner. A third method is to offer the professional degree first and this is followed by the Bachelor of Arts degree in a succeeding year. The pros and cons of each approach could be debated endlessly.

The curricula context emphasizes arts and science courses, as well as professional theory and activity courses. Depending on the teacher education system in vogue in the particular province, practice teaching and professional education courses may be included.

Graduate programs in physical education have not exhibitied the same rapid growth as the undergraduate programs. The only institutions offering work at the master's level are British Columbia, Simon Fraser, Alberta, Saskatchewan, Western Ontario, Windsor, Waterloo, Ottawa, New Brunswick and Dalhousie University in Nova Scotia. At the doctoral level only the University of Alberta offers a program. However, institutions in Ontario, the University of Western Ontario, the University of Windsor and the University of Waterloo, are close to initiating programs. Many Canadians undertaking graduate work in physical education attend universities in the United States. Unless one expects to teach at the college or university level, little pressure exists, and, therefore, relatively little incentive, for the individual to pursue graduate work in physical education. The educational attainment of most university faculties of physical education has risen sharply over the past decade; yet, there is still room for considerable improvement. Increased availability of graduate programs, as well as increased financial aid for graduate study bodes well for the future. Indeed, the future of graduate education in Canada looks very promising. The insistence on pursuing programs appropriate to the Canadian situation may mean that graduate work in Canada will have an unique orientation that is neither American nor European.

Special Characteristics

Canadian Association for Health, Physical Education and Recreation, Inc.[2] Dr. A. S. Lamb and Miss Ethel Cartwright were instrumental in initiating action to form the national association of Canada. Primarily, through the efforts of these individuals, the Canadian Association was established in 1933. The early years were characterized by a small, but hard-working membership. By the early 1940's the Association had a firmer foundation and began influencing developments in physical education. Some credit must go to the Association for early developments in professional preparation programs and CAHPER also helped develop Canada's National Physical Fitness Act of 1943. In 1946 the name was changed to the present one - The Canadian Association for Health, Physical Education and Recreation, Inc.

The Canadian Association had some difficulty earlier in putting a regular publication on a sound footing. Prior to 1950, a bulletin had been published; this was discontinued in 1951. In 1952 another attempt was made to publish a journal, and in 1957 the first printed journal became an entity and has been published regularly since then.

A Research Committee was established in 1961, and it has served as a central group through which researchers in the field could identify. This Committee has undertaken some specific projects, with the most noteworthy probably being the C.A.H.P.E.R. Fitness-Performance Test. The results of this Canadian testing project is being used to establish national norms for children between the ages of seven and seventeen.

The Association was instrumental in developing and has cooperated further in the development of the R. Tait McKenzie Memorial at Almonte, Ontario. Lastly, the role played by the C.A.H.P.E.R. in developing the Fitness and Amateur Sport Act of 1961 was a vital one.

The Fitness and Amateur Sport Act (Bill C-131). It is doubtful if any one incident has been more stimulating to the field of physical education than the passage of Bill C-131 in 1961. The objectives of the bill were: (1) to assist the development of international and national sport; (2) to aid in training coaches; (3) to provide bursaries for training of personnel; (4) to aid research in fitness and amateur sport; (5) to arrange conferences in this area of concern; (6) to provide for recognition of achievements; (7) to distribute information; and (8) to coordinate interested agencies in the area of fitness and amateur sport. The work was to be coordinated in a national office established in Ottawa.

Since the inception of the Act, many bursaries have been granted to physical educators enabling them to pursue advanced studies in
their field. Financial assistance has been provided for many amateur
organizations supporting developments in sport, or in underwriting
the costs of national teams. The results of the Act have been spectacular, and the benefits accruing to the field of physical education
will continue to multiply.

Sport Canada - Recreation Canada

In an effort to assist the various sport associations in Canada,
as well as to encourage mass participation, the federal government
has built upon the Fitness and Amateur Sport Act. John Munro, then
Minister of National Health and Welfare, outlined the government
plan in a speech presented in 1970.[13] The approach was to provide
substantial assistance through a national office to help amateur sport,
financially and administratively. A parallel unit would function in the
same fashion to assist in the recreation sphere.

Since 1970 several re-organizations have taken place and the
amount of money has been increased. One of the major tasks of the
national office will be the coordination of the Canadian efforts for the
1976 Olympics in Montreal.

Physical Education Research in Canada[7]

Since 1958 when graduate study in physical education began,
considerable advances in research facilities, as well as in the quality
and quantity of research personnel have been made. The number of
research units in physical education has paralleled the rapid growth
of professional preparation programs in Canada. With government
assistance three fitness research institutes were established in the
mid-1960's.[15] Since that time many universities have slowly but
surely increased their efforts in physical education and sport research. Indeed, in a submission to the Commission to study The Na-
tionalization of University Research in 1971, the Faculty of Physical
Education at the University of Western Ontario spoke of sixteen different areas of interest. As the submission phrased it:

> Physical education and sport will be successful as a profession
> only to the extent that the field is able to assimilate this knowl-
> edge and the resultant ordered generalizations that have mean-
> ing for physical education practitioners. It will then be neces-
> sary for researchers and scholars in this field to set up tenta-
> tive hypotheses increasingly - hypotheses based on the findings
> of scientists in related fields and our own, and to apply all
> known methods and accompanying techniques of research care-
> fully and painstakingly to problems which belong to physical
> education and sport (defined above). This task belongs to us

alone, and we must accomplish this goal primarily through our own efforts if we hope to survive and to serve our fellow men! No other discipline will do this for us, except in a secondary way and belatedly.[18]

The Province of Quebec,[1,8] Deserving of special mention is the Province of Quebec and its uniquely constituted system of education. There are two distinct school systems in the Province: the first encompasses about seven-eighths of the population and is Roman Catholic; the remainder, non-Roman Catholic, is predominantly Protestant. The Roman Catholic system is patterned after the French system of Education. The elementary grades stress the basic tools of learning; the secondary level includes a general section and a scientific section, and in some schools a special 12th-year course, a commercial course, and a classical section. The private schools in the province offer equivalent courses, except at the secondary level there are the classical colleges. These classical colleges offer preparation for entrance to the Roman Catholic universities, and most offer an eight-year classical course through to the Bachelor of Arts degree.

It was through the "Colleges Classiques" that sports programs were initiated in Franch Canada. The physical education programs and facilities in the public schools were slow to develop. Abortive attempts under the 1939 "Loi Instituant le Conseil Provincial des Sports," and through a publication in 1943 by the Department of Public Instruction based on the 1933 British physical education training syllabus, did not stimulate the development of physical education in the schools significantly. The progress of intramural and interscholastic athletes in the classical colleges led the way. Private organizations in the Province have given considerable impetus to sports programs in various localities. Physical education and sports programs have now reached the stage where they are considered an essential phase of education in the schools of the province.

The administrative structure of education in Quebec has just recently been revised. Established in 1961, a royal commission has investigated problems inherent in education in Quebec, and a reorganization within the Province has been effected. Although the effects of the reorganization have not been fully felt in physical education, there are several recommendations arising out of this report that bode well for physical education in the schools. Some of these recommendations are: (1) at least two hours of physical education per week; (2) summer programs for present elementary school teachers; (3) physical education specialists to direct programs in school regions and to teach in secondary schools; (4) the employment of a director of physical education to prepare curricula and supervise their implementation; and (5) that new schools and existing schools be properly equipped for physical education.

Construction of physical education facilities has been increased in recent years. Greater availability of qualified personnel, as well as of facilities and equipment, will have a great impact on physical education in Quebec in the immediate future.

Conclusion

The intent of these few brief pages has been to draw some generalizations on physical education in Canada. Geographical size, variance of population and provincial autonomy in the field of education limit the similarities. The force that transcends this uniqueness is the role of physical education in the educational setting. Hence, even though the means may differ, there is considerable agreement on the ends to be achieved. This core of agreement has vitalized the field in recent years, and serves as the basis for optimism about the future.

General Bibliography
(as it appeared in original article)

1. Association d'Éducation Physique et Recreation de Quebec, Le Rapport Parent et L'Éducation Physique. (A report prepared by the Association d'Éducation Physique et Recreation de Quebec, Sillery, Quebec.)

2. Blackstock, C. R. "The Canadian Association for Health, Physical Education and Recreation," in Physical Education in Canada. Edited by M. L. Van Vliet. Scarborough, Ontario: Prentice-Hall of Canada, 1965.

3. Bryans, Helen. "Secondary School Curriculum for Girls," in Physical Education in Canada. Edited by M. L. Van Vliet. Scarborough, Ontario: Prentice-Hall of Canada, 1965.

4. Canada, Bureau of Statistics. Canada Yearbook, 1965. Ottawa: Queen's Printer and Controller of Stationery, 1965.

5. Carson, Audry M. and Leiper, Jean M. "Elementary School Curriculum," in Physical Education in Canada. Edited by M. L. Van Vliet. Scarborough, Ontario: Prentice-Hall of Canada, 1965.

6. Conway, John, "What is Canada?" The Atlantic Monthly. Vol 214, No. 5, (Nov. 1964), pp. 100-105.

7. Howell, Maxwell L. "Physical Education Research in Canada," in Physical Education in Canada. Edited by M. L. Van Vliet. Scarborough, Ontario: Prentice-Hall of Canada, 1965.

8. Landry, Fernand and Montpetit, The Reverend M. "Physical Education in French Canada," in Physical Education in Canada. Edited by M. L. Van Vliet. Scarborough, Ontario: Prentice-Hall of Canada, 1965.

9. L'Heureux, Willard J., "Sport in Canadian Culture," Journal of the Canadian Association for Health, Physical Education and Recreation, XXIX, 4, (April-May, 1963), pp. 7-10.

10. Loosemore, J. P., "Intercollegiate Athletics in Canada: Its Organization and Development," Journal of the Canadian Association for Health, Physical Education and Recreation, XXVIII, 2, (December, 1961 - January, 1962), 9.

11. Meagher, John W. "Professional Preparation," in Physical Education in Canada. Edited by M. L. Van Vliet. Scarborough: Ontario: Prentice-Hall of Canada, 1965.

12. Munro, Iveagh. "The Early Years," in Physical Education in Canada. Edited by M. L. Van Vliet. Scarborough, Ontario: Prentice-Hall of Canada, 1965.

13. Munro, John. "A Proposed Sports Policy for Canadians." Speech presented March 20, 1970. Department of National Health and Welfare, Ottawa, Canada.

14. Passmore, John H. "Teacher Education," in Physical Education in Canada. Edited by M. L. Van Vliet. Scarborough, Ontario: Prentice-Hall of Canada, 1965.

15. Shepard, R. J., "Progress and Activities of the Fitness Research Unit, Toronto," Journal of the Canadian Association for Health, Physical Education and Recreation, XXXII, 3 (February-March, 1966), 12.

16. Spicer, Stanley T. "The Provinces Today," in Physical Education in Canada. Edited by M. L. Van Vliet. Scarborough, Ontario: Prentice-Hall of Canada, 1965.

17. Stock, Brian, "Why Young Men Leave," The Atlantic Monthly Vol. 214, No. 5, (November, 1965), 113-114.

18. University of Western Ontario, Faculty of Physical Education. "A Submission Concerning Research in Physical Education." Presented to the Commission to Study the Rationalization of University Research. London, Canada, December 14, 1971, pp. 1-2. (Edited by E. F. Zeigler).

19. Wipper, Kirk, "Silver Anniversary - University of Toronto's School of Physical and Health Education," <u>Journal of the Canadian Association for Health, Physical Education and Recreation</u>, XXXII, 3, (February-March, 1966), 11-12.

A HISTORY OF SPORTS AND GAMES IN EASTERN CANADA PRIOR TO WORLD WAR I

Stewart A. Davidson
University of Ottawa, Canada

The Social, Political and Economic Milieu

Early history of Eastern Canada is a story of exploration, Indian fighting, and individual heroism. The first settlers in Quebec were ex-soldiers from France, and they gave rise to two character-istic groups in this new land--the habitants and the coureurs-des-bois. Acadia was also founded by French settlers, but they were from a different part of France. Since they were cut off from Quebec by impenetrable wilderness, they remained, in effect, quite isolated from their Canadian fellow-subjects.

The English settlers were composed of British soldiers, United Empire Loyalists, Scotch and Irish immigrants--all of whom settled alongside the French colonists without much attempt to alter the economic or social organization of the country.

With the English element simply settling alongside with no evi-dence of assimilation, the situation deteriorated until it reached the stage of political deadlock, and the general stagnation which ensued stimulated a heavy Canadian exodus to the United States. A small minority of leaders, however, inspired by wide political division, actuated by economic interest, and stimulated by dangers of foreign aggression initiated efforts which culminated in Confederation in 1867. Sir John A. Macdonald was the first Prime Minister of the new feder-al government, which comprised three divisions--Ontario, Quebec, and the Maritime Provinces of Nova Scotia and New Brunswick.

Canada is essentially a country of natural resources, and agri-culture was the chief pursuit in the early days, adhering to the tradi-tion of the French Canadian, who was a country man in touch with nature and attached to the soil. Although immigration was heavy about the middle of the nineteenth century, the industrial development of the east was too slow to absorb this addition to the population. The stream of settlers was gradually diverted to the west, and the Cana-dian frontier was extended northward as well. Large groups of desir-able immigrants deserted Canada to go to the United States, which was passing through a period of phenomenal development during this period.

Conditions improved tremendously under the Liberal government of Laurier at the turn of the twentieth century, and the expansion of railroads, an increase in industrial capacity, and a vigorous immigration policy resulted in Canada sustaining a rapid rise to a position of relative world prominence at the outbreak of World War I in 1914.

Sports and Games of this Period in Canadian History

Basketball. Although this game originated in Springfield, Massachusetts in 1890, it was a McGill graduate, Dr. James A. Naismith, who is recognized as the inventor. The influence and spread of interest in basketball with the men who graduated from Springfield after 1892 showed itself in the Maritime Provinces, Montreal, and Toronto. At first it was a nine-man game. Then the number of players was reduced to seven, and finally to five players.[1]

Bicycling. Montreal was one of the first communities in North America to organize a club to promote the popular sport of bicycling. The first bicycle club was founded in Boston, Massachusetts in February, 1878, and the second in Bangor, Maine. The organization of the Montreal Club was completed on December 3, 1878, and when the Bangor Club ceased to exist, Montreal was left as the second oldest club on the American continent. The Boston Bicycle Club also passed into a moribund state for some time. Montreal was the only one of the original clubs which kept in continuous operation (as shown by the minute books of the club).

Canoeing. Little is recorded in historical documents concerning canoeing as an organized activity. Although canoes were utilized by the early settlers as a means of transportation, the formation of clubs to promote canoeing as a sport does not appear to have occurred before the organization of the Point St. Charles Club of Montreal in 1875. In the same year, the Grand Trunk Boating Club (also of Montreal) came into being, but it was not granted its charter by the Council of the City of Montreal until May 21, 1888.

The Canadian Canoe Association was formed in 1900, and one of the pillars on which the organization was built was the determination to foster and promote canoeing in Canada, to protect it from professionalism, and to establish canoe championships for singles, tandems, fours, and war canoes in the Dominion.

Curling. There is every indication that the oldest organized outdoor sporting club on the North American continent is the Montreal

---

[1] See Appendix A of this paper for a description of the early game of basketball.

Curling Club founded in 1807. The Montreal Curling Club has the distinction also of being the oldest of the colonial and foreign clubs in affiliation with the Royal Caledonia Curling Club of Scotland (1841).

Football. The chief difficulty encountered in any attempt to trace the origin of Canadian football is to distinguish between that sport and its sister-game, soccer. Sports historians generally agree that English rugby was the original game, and that Canadian football and soccer are offshoots or derivatives of it. (Soccer derived its name from the term, "Association football," which was shortened to "assoc.", and eventually to "soccer".)

The Montreal Football Club has the honour of being the pioneer club in Canada, having been founded in 1868, and in the early years many exciting matches were played with the officers of Her Majesty's regiment quartered in Montreal. In an attempt to encourage support of the game, the Montreal Football Club offered a Challenge Cup for competition in 1873. This trophy was for years the emblem of supremacy on the football field. At present it rests in the Trophy Room of the Montreal Amateur Athletic Association, and bears approximately thirty shields upon which are inscribed the names of the winners with the dates of the matches.

The game was played at McGill University under English Rugby Rules as early as 1873, when Arts defeated Science by a score of one touchdown to nil. The first representative team was formed in 1874, and was captained by David Rodger, Jr. This was the team which introduced rugby football to the United States, playing a match against Harvard in 1874. This inaugurated what is probably the oldest international intercollegiate rivalry in the world.

Golf. It is written in the records that golf was played by certain Scots on the Priests' Farm (located near the outskirts of Montreal) on December 25, 1824, and on January 1, 1825. This was evidently more incidental playing, because no golf club was formed until fifty years later.

The first golf club founded in America was the Montreal Golf Club. A Mr. Sidey was instrumental in forming the club on November 4, 1873, and the course was laid out on the Fletcher's Field side of Mount Royal. A club house was erected and, in 1884, the Marquess of Lansdowne, then Governor-General, obtained permission from Her Majesty, Queen Victoria, to use the word "Royal" in the name of the club. Interest in the game spread rapidly, and the Royal Canadian

Golf Association was formed in 1895 with a membership of thirty clubs.[2]

Hockey. In an effort to settle the much-disputed question of the origin of ice hockey, the Amateur Hockey Association of Canada appointed a committee in 1941 to investigate and report. This committee, comprised of W. A. Hewitt, George H. Slater, and James T. Sutherland, reported that it was their opinion that the first hockey was played by the Royal Canadian Rifles, an Imperial unit, stationed in Halifax and Kingston in 1855. On the recommendation of this committee, Kingston was favoured as the site of the first game of ice hockey. Thus, the Hockey Hall of Fame has been erected in that city. Although the date of origin of ice hockey may be indefinite, there is no uncertainty concerning the remarkable growth of the game. Montreal, Quebec City, and Halifax have all contributed in some measure to this development.

When the game was first played, it was evidently a modified form of "shinny." There were definite rules for this new game, and they appear to have been fashioned after the rules of field hockey. The "Halifax Rules," as they were known, were followed in early matches in Montreal. One of the features of the "Halifax Rules" was the forward pass, and one of the oddities was that the goal posts were parallel to the sides of the rink instead of being at right angles as they are today. It was thus possible to score from either side or, in fact, from behind the goal tender.

An article which appeared in the Montreal Gazette (March 4, 1875) reported that the ball generally used in the game of hockey had been replaced by a flat, circular block of wood which would slide along the ice without rising. The change was made to guard against any accident occurring in which spectators might be injured by the bounding ball. This was evidently the first step in an evolutionary development to the rubber disc used in the game of hockey today and now known as the "puck."

In the McGill University Trophy Room may be seen a hockey stick, flat on both sides, which was used by Lewis Skaife in the years 1878-81. On it is inscribed: "Hockey stick used by Lewis Skaife at McGill University, 1878-81." There is also a cup at McGill University which was awarded for the ice hockey championship of a Montreal Winter Carnival in 1885. That the same type of stick was used at this time is indicated by the three models of them used as supporting legs for the cup. The object used in play was a cube, approximately two

---

[2] Letter from W. D. Taylor, Secretary-Treasurer, Royal Canadian Golf Association, to Dr. A. S. Lamb, McGill University, February 18, 1946.

inches to a side, a model of this puck forming part of the base of the trophy, which is believed to be the oldest hockey trophy in the world.

Lacrosse. This is a sport which is certainly indigenous to Canada. It originated with the Indians, and many different types of games existed, the number of players varying from practically un-limited participation to five-player teams. In some instances there was no defined ground area, whereas other fields were restricted by natural landmarks or by the position of the tribal medicine men. The medicine man's tent often represented the goal or boundary, and he would often shift his location a distance of miles in order to avoid defeat.

Various reasons are given for participation in the game. Some writers claim that it was a preparation for war--the idea of training in close combat and the crippling of opponents. Others say that the game was of a religious nature, and was preceded by elaborate cere-monies, pow-wow, feasting, and dancing. Others assert that the impelling motive was simply the joy of contest.

Baggataway was the most common name given to the game by the Indians. The French Canadians, however, were impressed with the resemblance of the "stick" to a bishop's crosier, and called it "La Crosse." W. G. Beers recalls the historical event of July 4, 1763, when two Ojibway teams played a game of lacrosse near Fort Michilimackinac with an intent which seemed more warlike than athle-tic. (Beers, 1869)

Early in 1860, the first rules and laws of the game were com-piled and published by Dr. Beers, who was then the Honorary Presi-dent of the Montreal Club. His active efforts in promoting lacrosse as Canada's national sport fully entitled him to the appellation of "the father of lacrosse."

1867 saw the birth of Canadian nationality, and Canadian youth --strongly backed by the press of the country--adopted lacrosse as the national game. To celebrate it, the Montreal Club played a championship match with the Caughnawaga Indians on the first Domin-ion Day, July 1, 1867.

Rowing. Watermanship is something which a Canadian youth learns early in his outdoor life and never forgets. Even when the ability to participate actively is lost, interest in the feats of others is continued through strong club associations, where tradition is the cornerstone.

McGeachey reported on the story of the "Paris Crew," which is one of the oldest existing records of a sporting event in New Brunswick. (McGeachey, 1948) This epic occurred in 1846 at what is now Renforth:

On a summer day, 1846, the famed Tyne crew of England went down to defeat. The "Paris Crew" was composed of hardworking fishermen from St. John. It was such a strenuous race that the captain of the Tyne crew, a Mr. Renforth, collapsed and died. It was after this gallant sportsman that the village of Renforth was named.

The four-man Paris Crew retained their world title for three years before finally going down to defeat.

Canada long has been the land of remarkable oarsmen. Her stars competed in the American Regatta at Peekskill, New York as far back as 1848. Of these great oarsmen, Edward Hanlan is generally recognized as Canada's most amazing sculler. He compiled a record of 338 wins in 350 contests against the greatest oarsmen in the world.

Another great oarsmen was Joseph Wright, Sr., known as the "Dean of Canadian Rowing". He was a champion who won more rowing titles than any man of any time.

The Lachine Rowing Club is generally recognized to be the oldest rowing club in North America, being founded in the summer of 1863, and its colours still fly at Canadian regattas. In the early years, the original clubhouse was a floating structure moored near the Lachine wharf, and afterwards connected to the mainland. The Longueuil Boating Club, which is still in existence also, was organized in 1867.

Skating. Skating was evidently introduced into Canada by the early settlers, though little was heard about it as a pastime until the 1840's. Quinpool reported in 1860 that:

The first record of skates in America is DeMont's expedition to Acadia in 1604. At St. Croix during the winter, some of the young men went hunting in spite of the cold weather and brought down rabbits with snowballs. They went skating on the ponds. The temporary St. Croix settlement was transferred to Annapolis (Port) Royal in 1605, where the first permanent skating in Canada must have taken place.

The officers of the British Regiments in Canada were especially fond of the sport, and they strongly advocated covered rinks and figure skating. Quebec was the first to erect a covered rink, and Montreal followed suit in 1859 with the formation of the Montreal Skating Club and the erection of a rink on Upper St. Urbain Street. John Quinpool reported that the first covered ice rink in the Maritimes was erected at the Horticultural Gardens in Halifax, and was formally opened with a fashionable skating function in 1863.

The old Victoria Rink in St. John, New Brunswick was the scene of the first organized speed skating competitions. Hugh McCormick, of the Willows on the Kennebacasis River, started on his road to world recognition in this same rink on the night of April 5, 1863. He was a farm boy with country clothing, and his skates were long blades mounted on wood and fashioned by the blacksmith of the Willows. Although his appearance evoked laughter from the spectators, his performance demonstrated that here was a great skater. He went from St. John to New York and then to Minneapolis, where he smashed all the speed records of his day. He defeated Alex Paulsen of Norway, who was the international champion, and reputed to be the fastest thing on steel. McCormick skated a mile in two minutes and forty-eight seconds, and he also skated five miles in sixteen minutes, five and one-half seconds. He remained world champion until 1893, when he was defeated by Fred Breen who, strangely enough, was born and bred near the Kennebacasis within a half-hour's skate of his opponent.

Skiing. A copy of the Canadian Illustrated News, 1879 had an illustration of a man walking on what we now call "skis." Under the caption, "From Montreal to Quebec on Norwegian Snowshoes", appeared the following:

A snowshoe trip to Quebec--Mr. A. Birch, a Norwegian gentleman of Montreal, has a pair of patent Norwegian snowshoes upon which he has taken a trip to Quebec, starting on Friday last. The snowshoes are about nine feet long, six inches broad, and have a footboard and toe strap. He walks with the aid of a pole, and crosses ice not strong enough to bear a good-sized dog, so buoyant are these shoes in their action.

Although it may be accepted that skis were used at this early date, the new sport was not generally popular until the twentieth century. There are records which show that skis were introduced to Eastern Canada in the 1880's, but nothing was done to promote the new sport until the formation of the Montreal Ski Club in 1904. A meeting was held at the Windsor Hotel in Montreal on the evening of February 11, 1904. A report was read, describing skiing and its fascinations, and it was decided to call the new organization the "Montreal Ski Club."

From its inception the new club exercised a strong influence over Canadian skiing, and for years held its place as the premier ski

club in the Dominion. Among the early members were quite a few
Norwegians, and the club profited from their instruction. The aim of
the Montreal Ski Club was similar to that of the ski clubs in Europe,
England, and the United States--to support a ski jump. At the beginning this was the only competition in skiing. A jumping hill was built
on Fletcher's Field in Montreal, and there the first competition was
held on February 13, 1904. Also in 1904, the club introduced the
Mount Royal Cross Country Race, which is the oldest racing fixture
of its type on this continent.

Techniques at this period were quite elementary. According to
Mr. N. P. Douglas, Past President of the Canadian Amateur Ski
Association, "Hard experience was our principal teacher. When we
wanted to stop, we just sat down. When we finally learned the tele-
mark to the left and a sort of christie to the right, we were pretty
well pleased with ourselves." In an attempt to overcome this difficulty and to improve the style of its members, the Montreal Ski Club
instituted efficiency tests, and badges were awarded in the different
classes. This provided for keen competition, and the badges were
highly prized. Special jumping and racing competitions were held for
school boys and juniors, and from this source a continual flow of new
talent was developed.

Snowshoeing. The Montreal Snowshoe Club contends that it is
one of the oldest athletic clubs on this continent. Its members date
its history and formation back to 1840. Representing a pastime
indigenous to Canada, it is essentially a Canadian sport. It has perhaps flourished more in Montreal than in other portions of the Dominion, owing somewhat to the prevalence there of a more abundant
supply of snow than is enjoyed by many of the other athletic cities and
towns of Canada. The snowshoe was originally devised by the Indian
centuries ago to aid him in travelling over the snow in pursuit of
game. Despite the ingenuity of the white man, it has today essentially the same principle of construction, slightly altered in weight and
style to suit the present conditions of use. Snowshoeing, like skating
or tobogganing, is more of a pastime or outdoor exercise than a sport
or game, but as a healthy, invigorating exercise it cannot be excelled.

It was in 1843 that the first snowshoe races were inaugurated,
and the annual races of the club (with a dinner in the evening) were
continued for over half a century. The popularity of this sport continued to grow throughout the latter part of the nineteenth century,
and many new clubs being formed to compete with the Montreal Snowshow Club.

In 1869, the Montreal Snowshoe Club adopted a blue tuque with a
red tassel as the official headgear of the club, and the title the "Old
Tuque Bleue" became the accustomed cognomen of the club. One of
the most beautiful sights in the history of the club was witnessed in

1873, when the first torchlight procession across Mount Royal was held in honour of Earl Dufferin, Governor-General of Canada. The Governor-General was greatly impressed by the scene and honoured the Club by accepting a life membership.

Another colourful ceremony was that of attacking the Ice Palaces, which were erected on Dominion Square in Montreal during the winters of 1883, '84, '85, '87 and '89. At night, the members of the snowshow clubs would divide into two groups--one to defend the "Fort" or ice palace and the other to attack it. The offensive group would meet on Mount Royal and, carrying torches, would tramp through the city on snowshoes to attack the "Fort." A mock battle would then ensue, making a most impressive and colourful spectacle.

Swimming. The history of swimming in Eastern Canada is in reality a history of the Montreal Swimming Club. This organization was formed in August, 1876, and is the oldest swimming club in North America. The first available official report of the Montreal Swimming Club is under the date of June 11, 1878.

At this meeting it was decided that a swimming master be engaged, and that he be paid $4.50 a week. Jack Williams, a swimmer from Malta, had made a reputation for himself in 1880 by defeating Captain Webb, of world reputation, in a race of 1,000 yards in the Lachine Canal. The Montreal Swimming Club secured his services as swimming master, allowing him the privilege of giving lessons members at the price of a dozen for $1.00.

As the interest in swimming gained impetus, it was decided that an association to govern the activity was needed. To this end, a meeting of those individuals who were interested was held in 1909. The minutes of the meeting indicated that the response was good. The Montreal Amateur Athletic Association, the Montreal Swimming Club, the Young Men's Christian Association, the Grand Trunk Boating Club, the Club Nautique, and McGill University were represented.[3] At a later meeting of this group, it was unanimously decided to organize the Canadian Amateur Swimming Association to govern amateur swimming, diving, and water polo throughout the Dominion of Canada.

Tobogganing. There are conflicting dates given for the formation of Canada's pioneer toboggan club; the Montreal Toboggan Club, with 1879 and 1881, receives the greatest support typically. It is generally agreed, however, that tobogganing was participated in by

---

[3] The business transacted and the names of the officials representing these various Associations are found in the Minute Book of the Canadian Amateur Swimming Association dated April 22, 1909.

devotees of the sport for many years before any club was organized, with Esdaille's Hill, Brebaut's Hill, and Fletcher's Field in Montreal, as well as the slopes of Peel and McTavish Streets, used as slides.

The Winter Carnivals in Montreal in 1883 and succeeding years gave such impetus to the sport that a slide was built by the Tuque Bleue Club, on the old lacrosse grounds on Sherbrooke Street, and was available on November 20, 1883. A week earlier, the Park Toboggan Club was formed, and they later erected a slide on Mount Royal. The latter club is the only one still in active existence in Montreal.

Track and Field. This activity has had a long and varied history in Eastern Canada. The Olympic Club of Montreal, which was the forerunner of the Montreal Lacrosse Club, was formed for "foot-running and summer outdoor sports" in 1843. It is probably the oldest athletic club in the British Empire, since it was organized eight years before the Exeter Club in England, which claims to be the oldest one in that country.

Early newspaper accounts of track and field events are interesting to the sports historian, since they report the results of events in which our athletes still participate today. (Montreal Weekly Gazette, September 5, 1857.) For some events, the nomenclature was different, with the running high jump known as the "running high leap." The "running long leap" was the descriptive title given to the running broad jump,[4] with a distance of seventeen feet six inches being recorded in 1857. "Vaulting" was also engaged in, with heights of seven feet two inches reported in the same year. This was probably the equivalent of the pole-vault. The weight events consisted of throwing the hammer and putting the stone. The heavy stone weighed twenty-one pounds and the light stone sixteen pounds. Events which we now consider novelty events, such as the sack race or wheelbarrow race, had a definite place in "The Games" in those early days. The account of a meet in Halifax in 1860 lists such events as climbing a greased pole, throwing the sledge, wheelbarrow blindfold, greased pig race, and rolls and treacle. No explanation of the procedure to be followed in these events is available, but the emphasis appears to have been placed on the amusement of spectators and participants rather than on the athletic ability of the competitors.

One of the most important athletic events of the early twentieth century was a track and field meet held in Montreal on September 14, 1901. This was a meet which brought together the finest English

---

[4] This event is now commonly known by its International and Olympic title of "running long jump."

athletes from Oxford and Cambridge Universities in competition with a team representing Toronto and McGill Universities.

The results of the meet, as they were published in the Montreal Gazette (September 16, 1901), indicated that the English collegians won eight out of the nine events, the only Canadian win being registered by J. D. Morrow of McGill, in the 440-yard run. Although it was expected that several new records would be established, there was no change in the existing Canadian standards--a fact from which the Canadians drew some small satisfaction.

In 1905 the undergraduates of McGill University presented a handsome bronze trophy for intercollegiate competition. It was a replica of "The Sprinter," a beautiful figure designed and executed in 1900 by Dr. R. Tait McKenzie, a member of the McGill staff.

Impetus wss given to distance running in Canada when William Sherring of Hamilton, Ontario won the marathon race at Athens in 1906. Following Sherring, there came Longboat and many other outstanding runners. With the crest of the marathon-running era came the golden age of track and field sports between 1907 and the beginning of the Great War, with audiences of twenty thousand not uncommon for an afternoon of sport. A twelve-man team was sent to England for the Olympic Games of 1908, with Robert Kerr and George Goulding contributing excellent performances.

Water Polo. Mr. Chris H. Goulden, whose name is synonymous with swimming in Canada, also helped to organize the Montreal Swimming Club Aquatic Polo team in 1905. He was president of this club for eight years, and during this time the renowned "Sea Lions" held undisputed possession of the Goulden Challenge Cup, emblematic of the Canadian Championship, winning fifty-one games without a single defeat. At the Canadian Olympic trials in 1908, this same team was victorious. It did not go to the Olympic Games at London, however, since the Olympic Committee did not have sufficient funds available. Another factor was the difference between Olympic and Canadian rules.

In 1909 the recognition by the Canadian Intercollegiate Athletic Union of swimming as an intercollegiate activity resulted in the formation of a Water Polo League. McGill University and the University of Toronto were the first members.

Conclusion

Other sports and games in which Canadians participated during this period of history in Eastern Canada were baseball, cricket, rackets, soccer, and tennis. Unfortunately space does not permit the inclusion of these activities in this chapter. Interested readers will find them described in the author's unpublished doctoral thesis submitted to Teachers College, Columbia University, 1951.

A more exhaustive examination of the sports and games described in this chapter will also be found in the above-mentioned thesis along with excerpts from the original documents which served as primary sources for the author.

Appendix A

Description of the early game of basketball, with accompanying illustrations, reproduced from an untitled original document dated 1890.

"The game can be readily played in almost the smallest gymnasium. As the sizes of exercising rooms vary, the game played by each team is slightly different. All the match games are played under regular rules, however, and the peculiar disadvantage which a gym may have for the visiting team is remedied so far as possible. The game can be played out of doors on a large field quite as well as in a small gymnasium.

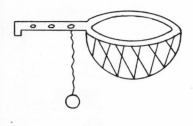 

The goals pictured in this column are used--the upright one for the field, on which it can be placed at any point, and the other for indoor play. The latter is attached to the gallery or the wall of the room. The string is used to turn the goal so that the ball may readily be regained. These goals are the improved article. The first goals, from which the game got its name, were only peach baskets nailed to the wall or running track.

Positions of Players

Goal

X

Home

Left Forward		Right Forward
X		X
Left Centre	Centre	Right Centre
X	X	X
Left Back	Goal Keeper	Right Back
X	X	X
	Goal	

The game can be played by a number of men at once. In a small gymnasium, however, five a side is the most convenient number. In large rooms, nine men can play on a side. This is consisered the regular number, and they are placed as shown in the accompanying illustration. The game itself is strictly one of passing the ball from man to man. It can neither be kicked nor batted with the fist. The object is to get the ball into the basket or goal. To get an uncovered position is of the utmost importance, as the player can thus easily get the ball and as easily pass it to one of his side near the goal. It requires a great deal of practice to put the ball in the goal, which is placed at some distance above the players' heads. Not alone must a player be skillful, he must also be very lively. A player must throw the ball from the spot where he catches it, but he can turn around to throw it. No interference is allowed and tackling and pushing are strictly prohibited. A player may only obstruct the passage of the ball after it is thrown.

When the game is played on a field, the player may run with the ball if he continually throws it above his head and catches it again. The ball may also be dribbled along the ground with the hand.

Team play counts for everything in basketball. The two forwards and the home man should always work together, to get the ball into the goal. The backs guard the goal and the centre men are supposed to get the ball and pass it forward toward the home man.

The game is usually played in two halves of fifteen minutes each, with a slight intermission. When a goal is made the game goes right on. It is perhaps the "fastest" game played today and is played with a snap which football players in lining up may well envy.

The game is being slowly introduced into women's gymnasiums and is played by the fair gymnasts without any injurious effects.

General Bibliography

Primary Sources

Amateur Athletic Association of Canada. Minutes of First Annual Report, September 27, 1884.

Canadian Amateur Swimming Association. Minutes of meeting, April 22, 1909.

Canadian Amateur Swimming Association. "The Swimmer," article by Chris W. Goulden, July, 1931.

Canadian Illustrated News, February 8, 1879.

McGill University Football Club. Constitution and By-laws, 1876.

Montreal Gazette, March 4, 1875.

Montreal Gazette, September 16, 1901.

Montreal Gazette. Article written by H. P. Douglas, January 14, 1944.

Montreal Herald, September 11, 1901.

Montreal Swimming Club. Minutes of meeting, June 11, 1878.

Whyte, William H. and Baylis, Samuel M. Our City and Our Sports, Souvenir and Official Programme of the Twelfth Annual Meet of the Canadian Wheelmen's Association, 1894.

Secondary Sources

Beers, William G. Lacrosse - The National Game of Canada. Montreal: Dawson Brothers, 1860.

Canadian Amateur Hockey Association. Report on the Origin of Hockey in Canada. Submitted by W. A. Hewitt, George M. Skater, and James T. Sutherland, 1941.

McGeachey, Duncan. A History of Physical Education in New Brunswick. Paper written for McGill School of Physical Education, December, 1948.

Menke, Frank. Encyclopedia of Sports. New York: A. S. Barnes and Co., 1947.

Quinpool, John (J. W. Regan). First Things in Acadia. Halifax, Nova Scotia: First Things Publishers, 1936.

The Telegraph-Journal. "New Brunswick Parade," by Ian Sclanders, November 15, 1948.

3.

SPORTS AND GAMES IN CANADIAN LIFE PRIOR TO CONFEDERATION

Nancy Flint Howell, San Diego, California
and
Maxwell L. Howell, California State University at San Diego

There are innumerable social, economic and cultural factors that influenced the growth of sport and games in Canadian life prior to 1867, the year of Confederation.[1] In such a short paper it is not possible to develop all of these factors, or indeed to develop them adequately.[2]

It was not until the seventeenth century that attempts at settlement of this vast new country met with any degree of success. The pages of Canada's history in these first years are replete with the stories of explorers, missionaries, fur-traders, and Indian fighters. The diaries that remain rarely mention relaxation or amusements, as relatively extreme hardship was experienced by all.

The settlements of New France and Acadia began to take on more permanent shape near the end of the seventeenth century. Towns became better established, farms more settled and successful. There were marked differences in the way of life of the various classes.

On the one hand we have the officials, the rich merchants, and seigneurs, most with large estates but residing principally in Quebec, Montreal, and Three Rivers, living a life which has been described as a "miniature of the great doings of Versailles," (Frégault, 1954, p. 13) (Careless, 1963, p. 68) taking dancing lessons and delighting in the visits of influential people.

The habitants lived a very pleasant life, their concerns being primarily their family, their farms, and the church. Visits with

---

[1] This paper was presented originally at the First International Seminar on the History of Physical Education and Sport, Wingate Institute, Israel, April, 1969.

[2] A more detailed analysis, including 1867 to the present, is in a book by the authors, Sports and Games in Canadian Life: 1700 to the the Present, Macmillan & Co., Toronto, 1969; for a general history of Canada which adequately develops the background material the following is recommended: McInnis, Edgar. Canada: A Political and Social History. New York: Holt, Rinehart & Winston, 1960.

neighbors by foot, but more often by caléche in the summer and car-
riole in the winter, dining and singing and dancing with friends afforded relief from the continual pre-occupation with the soil.

The coureurs-de-bois, principally engaged in the fur trade,
contrasted markedly with the other groups. Tough and adventurous,
they provided the link with the Indian population, from whom they
borrowed many practices such as the use of the canoe, the toboggan,
the sledge, the snowshoe, and the moccasin (Creighton, 1944, p. 83).
They participated also in the gambling games in which the Indians de-
lighted, as well as in wrestling, running, and other games.

From the mid-1700's to Confederation there was intensified
immigration, which resulted in the growth of new towns and farming
areas. The Treaty of Utrecht in 1713 resulted in the French sur-
render of Acadia and acknowledgement of the English title to
Newfoundland and Hudson Bay. Later, the Treaty of Paris in 1763
ratified the victory of Wolfe over Montcalm on the Plains of Abraham,
and spelled the downfall of New France.

The ensuing years saw an influx of immigrants from the British
Isles and Europe in addition to the United Empire Loyalists who
moved to Canada from the south. Life became more sophisticated in
this period. Travel was a little easier; the economy of the country be
became more diversified; and people made time to enjoy life. The
inhabitants of the cities and towns of Lower Canada led in setting the
social pattern of life there (Bender, 1882, p. 61, p. 101). Balls,
parties, card-playing, and carrioling highlighted the lives of the affluent, as they did also in the Maritimes (Clark, 1942, p. 72).

In Upper Canada, with the growth of such towns as Kingston,
Niagara, and York, life tended to be modelled after that in contemporary English towns (Guillet, 1933, pp. 321-333), class distinctions
being rigid. The military had a considerable influence, and much of
the social life was centered around the inns and taverns. As well as
being the meeting place of groups such as the Orangemen, Masons,
Foresters, St. Patrick, St. George, St. Andrew and even the Sons of
Temperance, the inns were often political centres. Dances and
banquets were also held at the inns (Talbot, 1824, pp. 22-23). These
were also the locale for such callous "sporting" events as bull- or
bear-baiting, and dog-fighting and cock-fighting, until subsequently
they were prohibited by law.

The people on the farms in all these areas lived simply, working
particularly hard in the summer, though often lumbering or logging in
the winter as well (Clark, 1942, pp. 153-154). One of the principal
diversions was the "frolic" or "bee."

One of the most notable characteristics of pioneer life in Canada was the spirit of cooperation..., but the most notable means of aiding one another was the "bee," or gathering of neighbours to help with farm work, a form of cooperation prevalent throughout the pioneer period... All bees provided entertainment and social intercourse as well as hard work... Besides large quantities of food and drink, it was customary to provide a dance or "hoe-down" as the main amusement, while those who chose not to dance engaged in sports, games and conversation. (Guillet, 1933, p. 274)

Among the sports contests popular at the bees were gymnastic contests, various trials of strength such as lifting bales and weights, wrestling, running, jumping, putting the stone, and throwing the hammer. Canoe and rowing races were also held if lakes and rivers were nearby. Many excesses were prevalent (Guillet, 1933, p. 279) at such functions, such as the excessive drinking of alcohol.

Similar functions were held and often run as contests to clear predators, such as bears, from the land. The losers often paid for a banquet and "hoe-down" (Guillet, 1963, p. 146). Charivariing was also practised, and this also helped to relieve the monotony of rural life (Caniff, 1869, p. 631).

The growth of the town and country fair occurred in this period, and these were the scenes of ploughing matches, pigeon shooting contests, horse races, trials of strength and various other athletic events.

In the 1800's, we see the influence of technological advances, which were to have a profound effect on the sports, games, and amusements of the population. In 1809 the introduction of the steamboat by John Molson considerably reduced a previous twelve-day trip from Detroit to New York, and hence allowed for increased north-south exchanges. The continued growth of railroads brought towns closer together and allowed for the exploitation of natural attractions, an emerging phenomenon (Morrison, 1954, p. 78). Commercialized picnic grounds, lake hotels, island resorts, and sports areas all increased in number. The travelling circus was part of the way of life, a resident circus being at York by 1827. Dare-devil performances (Collard, 1963, p. 104) such as Blondin's tight-rope walk across Niagara Falls, and balloon ascensions, were widely heralded and the public thrilled at the opportunities provided by the first Maid of the Mist, built in 1846, to explore the foot of the falls.

These developments, so briefly sketched, depicting the growing establishment and affluence of the eastern and maritime communities, were in marked contrast to the still rugged, adventurous, wilderness life of the vast central and western regions of the continent. In the prairie regions, in particular, settlers followed the traders and explorers and slowly established themselves. And soon after, in these regions, one saw the gun and fishing rod, driving parties, horse races, picnic feasts, athletic competitions (Schofield, 1913, p. 176), the visiting of neighbours, the balls, the "bee," and carrioling in the winter (McWilliams, 1928, p. 79). The western coast was more high highly developed, and the garrison influence was strong, as was also the influence of such groups as the Caledonian Society with their picnics and athletic carnivals (British Colonist, June 26, 1867). One saw such varied entertainments as canoe races against the Indians (Gibbon, 1951, pp. 100-104) and dance houses for the general public (British Colonist, Oct. 28, 1865). It was against this colourful background of life in the widely separated areas of settlement in Canada that so many sports and games took root and flourished. Some of the main influences will be discussed.

The Indians themselves exerted a considerable influence on the life of the early settlers. Canoes were readily adopted by the coureur-de-bois, and the tales of the voyageurs and their exploits with this craft have become some of the legends of early Canada:

Ah! Messieurs, those were the good days in the far back time when my brothers Jean and Francois and myself were leading the canoes up the "Uttawa"... up the "Uttawa" for the great captain Macdonnell. As our jolly voyageurs struck the water with their paddles, the boats would spring faster than the jumping deer that went flying away from us on the shore as we turned a point on the pretty river. The sturgeon and the pike heard our paddles, and they fled away... "Bon voyage," resumed the storyteller, "and the boats glide up the stream, where the carsmen, as their paddles strike the water, keep time to the lively strain of 'La Claire Fontaine'. And soon we are on the lake of Two Mountains with the Indian villages. The Indians give their friendly cheer as we pass, for they are good friends of the voyageurs. The young men are strong, and the canoes fly through the water. Ah! you think your steamers are swift, and you laugh at the speed of the voyageurs, but I have seen the day when with my crew of ten men we could give the steamboat a good push." (Bryce, 1882, pp. 34-35)

The feats of the voyageurs are still part of the Canadian folklore, and the romance of the canoe was maintained by the later introduction of the Canadian canoeing as an Olympic event, by the continued world popularity of the Peterborough canoe and by the wide adoption of canoeing in North America as an outdoor pursuit. Perhaps its popularity gave rise to the rowing regattas and competitions which have been held in high regard to the present.

The toboggan, sledge and the moccasin were all readily borrowed from the Indians, but the adoption of the snowshoe was perhaps of
more significance as it had a recreational as well as utilitarian value.
Snowshoes were, of course, known in Europe, but the extent of their
use and their practicability in the Canadian climate were quickly
established. Snowshoeing was early taken up as a recreational pastime, particularly in Lower Canada.

The Montreal Snowshoe Club is one of the oldest athletic clubs
in North America, dating its formation to 1840. The name "Tuque
Bleue" was associated with this club, the blue woollen habitant's cap,
with long tassel and the Hudson Bay "blanket" coat being part of the
colourful uniform. Originally the club would meet weekly for ten- to
twelve-mile walks, terminating at a coffee house. By 1843 snowshoe
races were held, which continued for fifty years or more. Many
other clubs sprang up; cups were awarded, particularly by military
commanders, for various contests (Montreal Weekly Gazette, Feb.
26, 1859).

And, of course, the Indians gave lacrosse or baggataway to
Canada. Observed frequently by Jesuit missionaries and early
settlers, its spread among the white population received a set-back
on June 4, 1763, when the Ojibway and Ottawa tribes used a game
outside Fort Michillimackinac as a subterfuge to massacre the
English troops and capture the fort (Beers, 1869). It was not until
1842 that the Olympic Club of Montreal was formed and, to add variety to their programs, they scheduled matches between and against
Indian teams. And it was not until 1851 that a white team was victorious against the Indian teams.

In the 1850's and the 1860's numerous clubs formed such as the
Lacrosse Club of Montreal (1856), the Hochelaga Club (1858), the
Beaver Club (1859). The game of lacrosse was enhanced by the work
of Dr. W. George Beers, who codified the rules in 1860 and 1861.
He is known as the "Father of Lacrosse" (Menke, 1947, p. 671).

The various immigrant groups, particularly the English, Scotch
and French, had their particular influences on the sports and games.
The English brought with them many of the sports of their own country. This is not to say they were the only nationality participating in
such activities; in fact, the contrary is true--that is, that the English
seemed to have a major influence on the development of certain
sports. Bull- and bear-baiting, cock and dog-fighting, with their
locale mainly the various inns, were activities of contemporary
England. The English military garrisons, in particular, were instrumental in the continuance and popularization of such activities as
horse racing (Caniff, 1869, pp. 630-631), and in 1860 the first
"Queen's Plate" was run in Toronto. And even though the origin of

ice hockey remains in doubt, the Amateur Hockey Association of Canada committee reported that:

> The first hockey was played by the Royal Canadian Rifles, an Imperial unit, stationed in Halifax and Kingston in 1855; it is quite possible that English troops stationed in Kingston from 1783 to 1855 played hockey, as there is evidence in old papers, letters and legends that the men and officers located with the Imperial troops as early as the year 1783, were proficient skaters and participated in field hockey. It is more than likely that the pioneers played their field hockey in those early days on skates but it is not an established fact. (Hewitt, 1953, p. 2).

Football was another sport of the British garrisons.

> Tuesday afternoon the Champs de Mars presented a picturesque scene, a good number of artillerymen being engaged in a game of football amid the falling snow. (Montreal Gazette, Nov. 17, 1864).

Rifle matches, in particular, had a military influence (British Colonist, July 3, 1865) as did cricket (British Colonist, July 4, 1865).

And the English settlers, as well as the soldiers in the garrisons, influenced sports. Fox hunting was one of these sports.

> The Montreal Fox Hunt is one of the established institutions of the city. It was founded so long ago as 1829 and has been maintained with varying success but continuously we believe from that time to this. Thus a thoroughly English sport – the chief and foremost of the English manly sports – has been firmly established in Montreal, the only place in all America where a pack is kept, we believe, and regular hunting takes place... The riding across country here is declared by competent judges to be more difficult than in Britain, from the frequent repetition of stiff timber fences... The pack has recently been almost or altogether renewed, gathered with great care and expense from the kennels of the leading Masters of Hounds in Britain, and is believed to be the most excellent ever got together here (Montreal Gazette, Nov. 20, 1860).

Such hunts, however, were engaged in well before this time, there being one at Fort York in 1801 (Upper Canada Gazette, Feb. 14, 1801). Billiards was also influenced by the English, the first championship of Upper Canada being played in Toronto in 1864 (The Globe, Nov. 21, 1864). Then, too, exclusive fishing clubs appeared, patterned on those of England.

Among the few private clubs in Montreal is one called "The Prince of Wales' Fishing Club". It has been establsihed for some years, and is so extremely exclusive as to be limited to eight members. (Day, 1864, p. 170).

Cricket, of course, was not confined to the garrisons and was probably the most popular sport in Upper Canada particularly. Upper Canada College opened its doors in 1830, and cricket was played there from at least 1834, the same year that the Toronto Cricket Club was formed (Lindsey, 1893, p. 263). Very detailed accounts of cricket games were featured in the early newspapers throughout the country, from Upper and Lower Canada to Fort Garry, Manitoba (Lucas, 1923, p. 163), and to Victoria, British Columbia (British Colonist, June 1, 1859).

Sailing and yachting were other "social" sports, and in 1837 Canada's first yacht club was formed in Halifax and with the granting of a royal charter it became known as the Royal Nova Scotia Yacht Squadron. (Roxborough, 1967, p. 54). The Canadian Yacht Club of Toronto, formed in 1852, became the Royal Canadian Yacht Club in 1854. The Prince of Wales, on his visit in 1860, presented silver trophies to both these clubs for competition.

The influence of the Scotch people was mainly felt in curling, track and field athletics, and golf. It is believed that the first curling in Canada took place in Nova Scotia and eastern Quebec in the latter part of the eighteenth century. The first organized club of curlers was formed in 1807 as the Montreal Curling Club. Other settlers did not originally approach the game with the same enthusiasm as the Scots.

French Canadians did not know what to think of these activities of the Scotchmen upon the ice. One of them, a farmer near Quebec who had just seen the game for the first time, related excitedly to his neighbours: "Today I saw a band of Scotchmen, who were throwing large balls of iron like tea-kettles on the ice, after which they cried 'Soop! Soop! and then laughed like fools. I really believe they ARE fools!" (Guillet, 1933, pp. 362-363).

A reviewer of golf's early history in Canada reports that:

A group of Scots who were identified chiefly with the fur trade desired to introduce to Montreal two favorite games of their native land, curling and golf (The Montreal Star, Jan. 13, 1934).

It is known that these gentlemen formed the Montreal Curling Club in 1807, but the records do not reveal anything further about golf until the 1820's. No golf club was formed at the time, but it was reported that certain Scotchmen played golf on the Priests' Farm on Christmas Day, 1824, and on New Year's Day, 1825.

Track and field athletics was probably equally influenced by all the main immigrant groups, but the Annual Gatherings of the Caledonian Society in the various geographical centres were significant events at the time. In 1857, for example, over 4,000 people watched such a gathering in Montreal where the events were throwing the heavy hammer, throwing the light hammer, vaulting, the short race, tossing the caber, the running high leap, the standing high leap, putting the heavy stone, putting the light stone, the running long leap, the standing leap, the standing hop and leap, the sack race, and the barrow race (Montreal Weekly Gazette, Sept. 5, 1851).

The French influence appeared to be predominant in the early growth of such sports as snowshoeing, lacrosse, racquets, and canoeing. Snowshoeing, lacrosse, and canoeing have already been mentioned, in that they were inspired by the Indian population, but it is probably equally true that the French adopted and adapted these native sports originally and popularized them. They appeared to be more able to assimilate such activities from the native population rather than continue their own cultural heritage as the English and the Scotch were more inclined to do.

The game of racquets evidently came to Canada from France, and the first court was built in Montreal in 1836. The Montreal Racquet Club was formed in 1840, and the champion of the time was E. H. Lamontagne (The Montreal Gazette, Jan. 21, 1933).

It must again be re-emphasized that the foregoing classifications are inevitably generalizations. Horse racing was enjoyed by the French as well as the English, as were such sports as ice-skating and ice hockey. All groups, for example, were ardent hunters, and the tradition and freedom to hunt were held in high esteem by the habitants.

Sir - It appears that in the Bill lately brought forward before the Legislature "For the Protection of Wild Fowl", a clause has been introduced, the purpose of which is to prevent persons from shooting on Sunday. Admitting the propriety of a due observance of the Sabbath, I think the end proposed to be obviated by this clause scarcely bears sufficient weight with it to have necessitated the interference of our legislators, for nine-tenths of those who will fall under the ban of such a law, would be the habitants, who, from time immemorial have been accustomed to take a stroll into the fields with their gun, after having performed the duty of attending mass... It savours rather of persecution to attempt to persuade these men that their favorite

source of pastime must now be looked upon as a crime...
(Montreal Gazette, Feb. 27, 1845).

Likewise, we see the McCullochs, the McCords, the
MacFarlanes and the McDougalls as well as the Stanleys (Montreal
Weekly Gazette, Feb. 26, 1859) competing in the early snowshoe
races for prizes donated by such as General Eyre, General Sir
Frederick Williams and General Lord Paulet. The law-maker of
lacrosse was not of French lineage, but was Dr. George Beers. In
this sport we once again see teams consisting of the McLennans and
McCullochs as well as Brown and Taylor, and Duclos and Bruneau
(Montreal Gazette, Oct. 4, 1860). We see Chanlebois and Guilbeault
and Duchesbeau and L'Esperance playing in probably the first ice
hockey game on record, as well as Hogan and McClune and Knox
(Montreal Gazette, Jan. 1, 1861).

We see "barbarian" curling teams comprised of non-Scots, and
so on. Sport does not recognize national distinctions, and participants who desire physical activity search for such experience with
little regard to nationality. One cannot be dogmatic about certain
nationalities being responsible for the growth of certain sports in
Canadian life. Though a certain national group may have had a primary influence, many sports were soon adopted by all of the citizens.

Other sports activities seemed to have a much more universal
appeal, almost from the outset, and it is difficult to ascertain any national group having even a primary influence on their development.
Sleighing is one of these which we see practised in every town by all
groups (Gale, 1915, p. 270), as are hunting and fishing (Day, 1864,
p. 60) and boxing and wrestling. As Talbot reflected (1824, pp. 51-
60):

When the race was over, wrestling commenced; which was soon
succeeded by boxing in the modern style of rough and tumble.
This detestable practice is very general in Canada, and nothing
can be more abhorrent to good sense and feeling. Instead of
fighting, like men whose passions have gained momentary
ascendency over their reason, - which would to all intents be
bad enough, - they attack each other with the ferociousness of
bull-dogs, and seem in earnest only to disfigure each other's
faces, and to glut their eyes with the sight of blood... The
principal object of the combatants appears to be the calculation
of eclipses, or in other words, their whole aim is bent on tear-
ing out each other's eyes, in doing which they make the fore-
finger of the right hand fast in their antagonist's hair, and with
the thumb - as they term it - gouge out the day-lights. If they
fail in this attempt, they depend entirely on their teeth for conquest, and a fraction of a nose, half an ear, or a piece of lip,
is generally the trophy of the victor.

Swimming (La Gazette de Québec, Aug. 10, 1769) knew no national boundaries either, and was practised by all. The same may be
said for track and field (Davidson, 1931, p. 48), though, as already
mentioned, the Caledonian Society had a considerable influence. But
there were other societies such as the St. George's Society and the
Irish Protestant Benevolent Society which held similar athletic meets,
and often athletic events were held at that early Canadian institution,
the "bee." And almost every Canadian town, at its annual celebration, or in celebration of events such as the King's birthday, included
various races and athletic competitions in the festivities, as well as
more "exotic" contests such as climbing the greased pole, rolls and
treacle, greased pig races, and blindfold races.

The climate, of course, was of major importance in providing
Canada's sports with unique direction. The long, harsh winters
allowed for the growth of snowshoeing as a sport, as well as sleighing, skating, curling, ice fishing, tobogganing and ice hockey. Ice
hockey, in particular, was to be a major contribution to sports life
internationally, and fundamental rules were established and contests
were engaged in prior to Confederation. The first covered rinks for
skating in the world appeared in Canada, (Brown, 1959, p. 83) mainly because participation was halted so often because of snow on the
outdoor rinks. The first of these enclosed facilities was built in 1859
in Montreal (Montreal Gazette, Nov. 29, 1860); another followed in
the same city in 1862, and yet another in 1864 (Montreal Gazette,
Dec. 15, 1864). The Maritimes followed suit, one opening at Halifax
in 1863, and another at St. John in 1864. The latter was an exciting
piece of architecture and attracted visitors from all over the world
(The Telegraph-Journal, Nov. 15, 1848):

> The main structure is of circular form, 160 feet in diameter,
> and covers an area of 20,000 superficial feet. It is an immense
> dome resting on a perpendicular wall 20 feet high and pierced
> with 39 windows, and is surmounted by a principal cupola or
> lantern, the height of which is 80 feet from the ground.

And Canadians developed a further innovation that influenced
skating and ice hockey. Until the middle of the nineteenth century,
the only style of skate available was a wooden-frame skate which
screwed into the heel of a boot and was strapped on with leather
fasteners. All-metal skates evolved in the mid-nineteenth century,
but these were also cumbersome and unwieldy, albeit indeed an improvement over the old wooden-frame. In the 1860's the Maritime
Provinces were the proud birthplace of the first spring ice-skates in
the world (Quinpool, 1936). Their keynote was simplicity, since no
screws or straps were required. These skates were widely heralded.

Ice trotting became very popular also, since the citizens were
inventing sports that could be adapted to the climate. This perhaps

reached its peak around 1845 when the Canadian horse, <u>Corbeau</u>, beat the fastest horse in British North America, <u>Dread</u> (<u>Montreal Gazette</u>, March 20, 1845).

Sleighing on the ice was a popular recreational activity, as well as a sporting pursuit (Gale, 1915, p. 270), and novel techniques developed for the rescue of the horses (Gray, 1809, pp. 276-278):

> When the horses fall through the ice, the struggles and exertions they make, serve only to injure and sink them; for, that they should get out of themselves is, from the nature of the thing, impossible. When horses go on the lake, they always have, round their necks, rope with a running noose... The moment the ice breaks, and the horses sink into the water, the driver, and those in the sleigh, get out, and catching hold of the ropes, pull them with all their force, which in a very few seconds, strangles the horses, and no sooner does this happen than they rise in the water, float on one side, and drawn out on strong ice, the noose of the rope is loosened, and respiration recommences; in a few minutes the horses are on their feet, as much alive as ever... They tell you that horses which are often on the lake, get <u>so accustomed to being hanged, that they think nothing of it at all</u>.

The early settlers became fishing enthusiasts did not allow the climate to interfere with their interests. The grand sport of ice fishing evidently became a flourishing enterprise (Gray, 1809, pp. 276-278):

> The manner of catching these fish is to cut holes in the ice, and put down either nets or lines... A hole is dug in the ice, and a temporary house is built over it, large enough to hold half a dozen people, and a stove to keep them warm. Those who cannot afford to purchase deals to make a house, substitute large pieces of ice, with which they form a kind of defence from the weather. The middle of the night is the best time for fishing. They place a strong light near the hole, which attracts the attention of the fish, and brings them round, in large quantities; so that they are caught as fast as they can be pulled in.

Geographical factors also had an effect on the development of sports and games. One-third of the inland water in the world is in Canada, and the vast number of lakes and rivers as well as the extensive coastlines encouraged the development of such activities as sailing and yachting (Roxborough, 1961, p. 54). These sports, along with canoeing (Wrong, 1908, pp. 234-5), attained a new peak in popularity. Rowing (Buckingham, 1843, p. 41), in which Canada has performed so well over the years, also began as a competitive and recreational sport during this period, and during the 1840's and 1850's rowing regattas were popularized. The Lachine Rowing Club, founded in 1863, is believed to be the oldest rowing club in North America. The Toronto Rowing Club and the Windsor Rowing Club appeared in 1865 (Morrison, 1954, pp. 75-76), as did the Vancouver Rowing Club (British Colonist, Sept. 30, 1865). Swimming also prospered in such an environment and, as early as 1769 (La Gazette de Québec, Aug. 10, 1769), public concern was expressed over drownings and the lack of safety precautions. Baths opened in Toronto in 1864 (The Toronto Globe, Nov. 21, 1864). The natural geographic features, of course, assisted the growth of such sports as skating, ice hockey, curling, and sleighing.

The development of sport and games prior to 1867 was, of course, quite variable, but there was a distinct move from family participation per se to local, to town, to inter-town, to provincial, to inter-provincial, and finally to international participation. Some sports exhibited all these developments, which others did not go beyond the local community or town.

There was a phenomenal growth of clubs for all sports. The Quebec Turf Club was formed in 1789; the Montreal Club (for fox hunting) in 1829; the Quebec Tandem Club (sleighing) in 1830; the Montreal Snowshoe Club in 1840; the Montreal Olympic Athletic Club (mainly for lacrosse) in 1842; the Montreal Curling Club in 1808; the Toronto Cricket Club in 1834; the Halifax Yacht Club in 1837; the Olympic Club of Montreal (track and field) in 1842; and so on. That Montreal was the scene of the first club in so many sports is evident. What is also evident is that in many sports, such as lacrosse, cricket, snowshoes, curling, and yachting, in particular, the formation of one club appeared to act as a stimulus to the formation of others. Or perhaps it is simply that a certain level of community development provides the stimulus for such a growth.

By 1846 such sports as horse racing (Dodds, 1909, p. 112) included thoroughbreds that came from as far off as Vienna to compete against Canadian horses (as well as some from America, of course) (Montreal Gazette, March 20, 1845). Canada participated in curling against the U.S.A. in 1866 (The Globe, Feb. 10, 1866). By 1835 a U.S. cricket team had played in Montreal, and by 1859 an English cricket team had visited Canada. Other sports, such as fox hunting, swimming, and golf remained local in nature. Provincial championships were held in billiards in 1864 (The Toronto Globe, Nov. 21, 1864).

Sport was subjected to a north and south influence prior to 1867. but it had not become truly Canadian in character. There was no east and west participation at this point. Developments such as these must also be viewed with an understanding of the problems and cost of transportation in Canada prior to 1867. Technological improvements, such as improved methods of transportation, did much to change sporting restrictions of the time. Town could now play town and other country districts more easily, as rail transit was improved. In 1845 the journey from the United States to Montreal to play cricket was mainly by stagecoach. The development and expansion of the railroads, as well as steamboats on the lakes, made travel easier, improved opportunities for competition, and, at the same time, made larger picnic areas and holiday resorts more accessible to the public. The citizen began looking from the town to inter-town competition, and in some cases to provincial and international competition. The stagecoach and the horse-drawn bob-sleigh lost some of their romance as Confederation approached.

Excursions to Niagara Falls provided a very popular summer holiday. A typical one occurred on the week of Friday, August 30, 1861. The train left Windsor at 5:45 Friday morning – Return train left Suspension Bridge at 6 a.m., Monday, September 2. Those who wished a shorter stay might return by the night express Friday. Tickets for the round trip were $3, though the regular fare from Windsor to Suspension Bridge and return was $14... (Morrison, 1954, p. 78).

This was a far cry from the journeys of, say, the early curlers, who likewise pursued their recreation and extended their vision to inter-club matches. In 1835, when Montreal met Quebec in probably the first inter-club curling match on record in Canada, the two clubs met halfway on "neutral" ice at Three Rivers. This was a formidable journey through deep snow, but the pleasures were there, nevertheless (Guillet, 1933, p. 359):

At Three Rivers there was difficulty in finding ice, and the curlers had to make use of a very uneven piece at the mouth of the Black River. Two rinks a side engaged in the match, and when it was over the score stood: Quebec 31, Montreal 23. At the grand dinner afterward there was no haggis, nor was there 'good nor even tolerable whiskey to be had at Three Rivers', but these deficiencies were in some degree made up by nine roast turkeys, and excellent champagne, though the latter appeared to some to be very much out-of-place at a Scotchman's dinner. The Montrealers, who had been defeated, paid Ł 3.2.0 d. each for the dinner and about the same amount for transportation, so it was no wonder that victory in these matches was so desirable.

That curling institution, the "bonspiel," was assisted by the improvement of transportation. The Grand Trunk Railway from Montreal to Toronto was completed in 1856, and the building of the Great Western Railway in the Lake Erie region at the same time allowed curlers to attend the bonspiels from widely separated towns

(Guillet, 1933, pp. 365-6). By 1860 curling, as one example, held the annual meeting of the Canadian Branch of the Royal Caledonian Curling Club of Scotland and nearly all the clubs of Upper and Lower Canada were represented. Inter-town schedules were established for each year at that time (Montreal Gazette, Nov. 1, 1860).

The establishment of approved connections with famous clubs and institutions aided considerably in improving the status of sport in Canada. The beginning of the Queen's Plate for horse racing in 1869; the original connection of curling, in 1841, with the Royal Caledonian Society; the Royal Charter granted, in 1837, to the Royal Nova Scotia Yacht Squadron; and the visit of the Prince of Wales in 1860, when he gave trophies to and visited many sports events, all assisted the expansion and development of respectability of sport on the Canadian scene.

The U.S. influence was also strong, particularly when transportation such as the rail and the steamboat connections improved. As mentioned previously, sporting influences, at the time, were north and south rather than east and west because of the geographical factors involved; consequently, Canadian and U.S. teams exchanged visits in many sports. The professional-amateur problem was beginning to be debated prior to Confederation. It perhaps reached its peak, strangely, in the game of cricket, the social sport of the time, and because of the international matches against the United States (Montreal Gazette, Aug. 4, 1860):

> There is one prominent feature of difference between the two
> Elevens that merits particular notice, namely, that while all
> the Canada Eleven are amateurs, gentlemen who play cricket
> only as an amusement, in the intervals of business pursuits; a
> very large proportion, say even seven out of the Eleven, of the
> States side are professional cricketers, who play the game for
> a livelihood, pursuing it as a regular occupation just the same
> as a gardener or mason follows his trade. Amateurs are sel-
> dom successful in contending against professionals in anything,
> and although if it be true that exceptions have sometimes occur-
> red, especially in Cricket, yet we cannot help thinking that the
> Canada Eleven of 1860 is destined to bring back from New York
> the emblem of victory which the States carried off from Canada
> in 1857.

Many factors, then, influenced the growth of sports and games in Canada. Climate and geographical factors played their part and influenced some unique developments; the military, and national groups, likewise played vital roles in promoting certain sports; and technological developments, such as the railroad and the steamboat, opened up new vistas for sport on the vast continent of Canada.

Participation in sports and games gave relief to monotony and an outlet for the desire for pleasure. Games and sports were a means to an end rather than an end in themselves in this period. The physical pleasures of participation were generally accompanied by the social pleasures of meeting with friends and the enjoyment of feasts and dances which were arranged in conjunction with sports meetings.

By the year of Confederation, Canadians young and old were avid participators in such activities as horse-racing, fox-hunting, boxing, wrestling, pigeon shooting, rifle matches, racquets, golf, sleighing, tobogganing, curling, ice-skating, snowshoeing, lacrosse, fishing, hunting, ice-fishing, ice hockey, football cricket, rowing, canoeing, yachting, sailing, gymnastics, fencing, weight lifting, swimming, track and field, and quoiting.

General Bibliography

Books and Periodicals

Beers, William G. Lacrosse - The National Game of Canada. Montreal: Dawson Bros., 1869.

Begg, Alexander. History of the Northwest. Volume I. Toronto: Hunter, Rose & Co., 1894.

Bender, P. Old and New Canada, 1753-1844. Montreal: Dawson Bros., 1882.

Brown, Nigel. Ice-Skating, a History. London: Nicholas Kay, 1959.

Bryce, Rev. Professor. Manitoba: Its Infancy, Growth and Present Condition. London: Sampson, Low, Marston, Searle & Rivington, 1882.

Buckingham, James S. Canada. London: Fisher & Sons, 1945.

Canniff, Wm. History of the Settlement of Upper Canada. Toronto: Dudley & Burns, 1869.

Careless, J. M. S. Canada, a Story of Challenge. Toronto: Macmillan, 1963.

Clark, S. D. The Social Development of Canada. Toronto: University of Toronto Press, 1942.

Collard, Edgar Andrew. Canadian Yesterdays. Toronto: Longmans, Green & Co., 1955.

Collard, Edgar Andrew. Montreal Yesterdays. Toronto: Longmans, Green & Co., 1963.

Coues, Elliott. New Light on the Early History of the Greater Northwest. The Manuscript Journals of Alexander Henry and David Thompson, 1799-1814. New York: Harper, 1897.

Craig, Gerald M. (editor). Early Travellers in the Canadas, 1791-1867. Toronto: Macmillan, 1955.

Creighton, Donald Grant. Dominion of the North. A History of Canada. Boston: Houghton-Mifflin, 1944.

Davidson, Stewart Alexander. "A History of Sports and Games in Eastern Canada prior to World War I." Unpublished doctoral thesis, Teachers' College, Columbia University, 1951.

Day, Samuel Philips. English America. Volume I. London: T. Coutley and Newby, 1864.

Dickson, George & Adam, G. Mercer (editors). A History of Upper Canada College, 1829-1892. Toronto: Rowsell & Hutchison, 1893.

Dodds, E. King. Canadian Turf Recollections. Toronto, 1909.

Fregault, Guy. Canadian Society in the French Regime. Canadian Hist. Soc., Hist. Booklets, No. 3, Public Archives. Ottawa, Montreal: Quality Press, 1954.

Gale, George. Quebec 'Twixt Old and New. Quebec: The Telegraph Printing Co., 1915.

Gibbon, John Murray. The Romance of the Canadian Canoe. Toronto: Ryerson Press, 1951.

Gray, Hugh. Letters from Canada Written During a Residence There in the Years, 1806, 1807 and 1808. London: Longman, Hurst, et. al., 1809.

Guillet, Edwin C. Early Life in Upper Canada. Toronto: The Ontario Publishing Co., 1933.

_____. The Pioneer Farmer and Backwoodsman. Volume I. Toronto: The Ontario Publishing Co., 1963.

_____. Pioneer Inns and Taverns. Volume III. Toronto: The Ontario Publishing Co., 1958.

Harvey, Charles (editor). <u>Sport International. Companion to the Encyclopedia of Sports</u>. London: Low and Marston, 1960.

Hewitt, Foster, <u>Hockey Night in Canada</u>. Toronto: Ryerson Press, 1953.

Jenness, Diamond. <u>The Indians of Canada</u>. Department of Mines, National Museum of Canada, Bulletin 65, Ottawa: F. A. Acland, 1932.

Lamb, W. Kaye (editor). <u>The Letters and Journals of Simon Fraser, 1806-1808</u>. Toronto: Macmillan (Pioneer Books), 1960.

Lighthall, W. D. <u>Montreal After 250 Years</u>. Montreal: F. E. Grafton & Sons, 1892.

Lucas, Fred C. <u>An Historical Souvenir Diary of the City of Winnipeg, Canada</u>. Winnipeg: Cartwright & Lucas, 1923.

Mackenzie, Alexander. <u>Voyages from Montreal</u>. Volume II. Toronto: Courier Press, 1911.

Mackenzie, W. L. <u>New Almanack for the Canadian True Blues</u>. 1834.

Marshall, Charles. <u>The Canadian Dominion</u>. London: Longmans, Green & Co., 1871.

McDougall, John. <u>Saddle, Sled & Snowshoe: Pioneering on the Saskatchewan in the Sixties</u>. Toronto: William Briggs, 1896.

McWilliams, Margaret. <u>Manitoba Milestones</u>. Toronto: J. M. Dent, 1928.

Menke, Frank G. <u>The New Encyclopedia of Sports</u>. New York: A. S. Barnes, 1947.

Montreal Herald. <u>This Was Montreal in 1814, 1815, 1816, and 1817</u>. Compiled by Lawrence M. Wilson. Privately printed for the Chateau de Ramezey, 1960.

Morrison, Neil F. <u>Garden Gateway to Canada. One Hundred Years of Windsor and Essex Counties, 1854-1954.</u> Toronto: Ryerson Press, 1954.

Morse, Eric W. <u>Canoe Routes of the Voyageurs</u>. Quetico Foundation of Ontario, 1962.

Morton, W. L. The Canadian Identity. Madison: University of Wisconsin Press, and Toronto: University of Toronto Press, 1962.

Nute, Grace Lee. The Voyaguer. New York: D. Appleton, 1931.

Quinpool, John (J. W. Regan). First Things in Acadia. Halifax: First Things Publishers, 1936.

Reed, T. A. The Blue and White. Toronto: University of Toronto Press, 1944.

Reed, T. A. (editor) A History of the University of Trinity College, Toronto, 1852-1952. Toronto: University of Toronto Press, 1952.

Schofield, F. H. The Story of Manitoba. Volume I. Winnipeg: S. J. Clarke, 1913.

Stanwick, Ted. Lacrosse. New York: A. S. Barnes, 1940.

Talbot, Edward Allen. Five Years' Residence in the Canadas. Volume II. London: Longman, Hurst, et. al., 1824.

U. S. Bureau of American Ethnology. 24th Annual Report, 1902-1903. Washington: Government Printing Office, 1907.

Westropp, Edward. Canada, Land of Opportunity. London: Oldbourne, 1959.

Wrong, George M. A Canadian Manor and Its Seigneurs, 1761-1861. Toronto: Macmillan, 1908.

Newspapers and Magazines

The British Colonist. Victoria, years 1858-1866.

The Colonist & Chronicle. Victoria, October 1866.

La Gazette de Québec. Years 1764-1866.

Montreal Gazette. From August 25, 1785 to June, 1867.

Montreal Gazette. January 21, 1933.

Montreal Gazette. Article by Harold McNamara (quoting John P. Knox), January 1, 1941.

Montreal Star, January, 1934.

Montreal Weekly Gazette.   September 5, 1857.

The Telegraph-Journal.   "New Brunswick Parade" by Ian Sclanders, Nov. 15, 1948.

The Toronto Globe.   Years 1860-1866.

Upper Canada Gazette.   The year 1801.

A CANADIAN PHYSICAL EDUCATOR -
JOHN HOWARD CROCKER, LL.D.

Mary E. Keyes
McMaster University, Hamilton, Ontario

The athlete is worshipped in our society; every boy from the bustling city to the lonely mountain cabin knows his face and life story. Few people, however, know the name of the physical educators through the years who have given their lives for the betterment of sport. Ideals have helped to keep sport at a relatively high level in Canada. Dr. John Howard Crocker was a man of high ideals--an amateur athlete, an educator, and a philatelist. The world is a better place because he lived so fully. As McAree wrote, "Tall Pines of Crocker variety are not common in any woods - and they are, after all, the landmarks of today and tomorrow and all time to come."

Youth

The first born of an old United Empire Loyalist family, John Howard Crocker was born 19th April, 1870 in St. Stephens, New Brunswick. As a lad of sixteen he found himself an employee in a lumber camp to earn money to help support his mother and four younger children. From this experience he gained a lifelong appreciation of nature, not to mention an "education" based upon life in its most rugged form. His teachers were the oftimes rough, crude, powerful lumbermen. This adventure into manhood was cut short by a bout of rheumatic fever which left him an invalid for two years. He wrote later of his youth, "I used to think my life was hard as a kid, getting up to light fires, carrying water, cutting wood, etc. Now I realize that it put some guts and backbone into me."

Following his recovery he apprenticed himself to the local "smithy" as a blacksmith and machinist, and in his leisure hours "worked out" at the local YMCA to "rebuild" his body.

Crocker was able to talk some influential St. Stephen's residents into sponsoring an annual track and field meet at the local horse racing track. He became instigator, organizer, promoter, competitor, and often winner of one of the most popular track and field meets in the Maritime Provinces.

Basketball also proved to be one of the most useful devices at Crocker's disposal in forwarding his work. The sport was first introduced into Canada at the YMCA in Montreal by Wm. Ball in 1892

(Cross, p. 175). Crocker introduced the game into Nova Scotia at the YMCA in Amherst in 1894. (Leonard, 1947, p. 404). Basketball was thought to develop self-control, competitive instincts, and self-reliance, all traits which were felt to be so necessary in the building-up of character.

Crocker soon took a leading part in the wider aspects of the development of the game. He became the Canadian representative on the Joint Rules Committee of the United States and Canada from its formation in 1905 until he was succeeded in 1947 by Alex Dewar.

Crocker worked part-time in the Y's in Amherst and Halifax, Nova Scotia, and accepted a permanent position as Physical Director at the Central YMCA in Toronto, Canada. This latter decision was taken after he was forced to withdraw from medical school due to eye strain. "J. H." proved to be a successful Physical Director at the Central YMCA. He initiated medicals for all participants; he formed a Leaders Club of eighteen members; and developed a "powerful" basketball team, enthusiastic track and field athletes, and outstanding swimmers. In 1901, Crocker was asked to conduct a school in physical training for other physical directors in Toronto. The idea of a combination school and camp was born, and in 1907 a permanent site was chosen 80 miles from Toronto on Lake Couchiching by C. M. Copeland (Provincial Secretary for Ontario and Quebec) and J. H. Crocker. Geneva Park has since become one of the most widely known centres in Canada for conferences, not only for the YMCA but other groups as well.

Crocker moved from Toronto in 1908 to become General Secretary of the Brantford YMCA. Membership was about one hundred when he arrived, but before he left it had increased to eight hundred, and planning for a new building was in its final stages.

In 1911 an invitation arrived from the International YMCA inviting Crocker to promote their physical work by serving on the National Committee in China. While in China, Crocker served as Manager of the 1915 Chinese team to the Far Eastern Athletic Association games held in Shanghai, China (Fu, 1931, p. 10). Never before in the history of this nation had men from the North, East, South, and West stood stood together to cheer for their native land, as they did at this time in competition with 350 representative athletes from China, Japan and the Philippine Islands. Although support for sport was great, he reported in this same year that there were only eight men in China trained for physical work and that of these six were with the YMCA (Latourette, 1957, p. 267). C. H. McCloy and Crocker lectured to students in the cities, and then in the summer months they toured the more remote parts of China conducting short-term training courses.

The Chinese people had a profound influence on Crocker during his six years in this country. He grew to respect their gentleness and their loyalty in spite of personal danger. He left China with regret in 1917 despite the fact that a challenging rebuilding job awaited him as Western Director of Physical Education for the National Council of YMCA's in Canada.

The post-war was a time of crisis for the Canadian YMCA. Criticism had spread rapidly in 1918. It was varied, but it seemed to revolve around two contentions: (1) the YMCA is building up a tremendous financial surplus; and (2) if the YMCA wants to help privates, why were their men not wearing privates' uniforms (Ross, 1951, p. 291).

Crocker was not active with the Canadian forces during the World War I, although he had been commissioned a Lieutenant in the Shanghai Volunteer Corps in 1916. Thus, he was not personally able to refute both of the rumours which were damaging the YMCA work. He had to be well organized, and able to account for every move made. Further he felt it necessary to trust his physical directors to such an extent that the very existence of the YMCA depended on their good work.

In 1921, Crocker moved back to Toronto as National Director of Physical Education. His duties were once again supervision on a large scale, and it was his responsibility to see the national standards for physical education. He served as liaison with other organizations interested in similar work, such as the Amateur Athletic Union of Canada and its affiliated bodies, the Royal Life Saving Society, as well as with school and university physical education organization. Within the YMCA organization Crocker represented Canada in the North American Physical Education Society. In 1924 he was made a Fellow in Physical Education of the YMCA of both the United States and Canada, and in 1928 he served as the first Canadian President of the Society.

Crocker was also a guiding light in the Physical Directors' Society of the YMCA of Canada (Ontario). This society was organized in 1921 to unite the YMCA Physical Directors of Ontario in a province-wide programme of physical education in all its phases, in accordance with the general spirit and methods of the YMCA of Canada. Secondly, it was the interchange of ideas and the development of friendship and rapport among its members.

In 1930 his active days with the YMCA were terminated by retirement because he had reached the age of sixty. He continued to serve in an advisory capacity until his death. Friends in the YMCA's across Canada presented him with a new Pontiac automobile, and "J. H." was truly overwhelmed with such a retirement gift. In 1951, he was one of twenty-three men who were presented with life membership awards at Toronto, when the YMCA launched a celebration of the 100th Anniversary of its organization in North America.

Crocker was too young at sixty to retire to a rocking chair. There was still much for him to do with his talents, and so he gladly accepted the offer of the University of Western Ontario to become Director of Physical Education. Thus, the realm of higher education offered yet another challenge although he had been "educating" youth for forty years.

The Royal Life Saving Society

Since childhood days spent along the St. Croix River, Crocker had loved to swim. In 1898 he took lessons and obtained his Bronze Medallion. This was the beginning of a sixty-one year association with the R.L.S.S.

The first meeting of the Ontario Branch of the Royal Life Saving Society was held December 10th, 1908. Charter members were Messrs. A. L. Cochrane, Arnold Morphy, E. A. Chapman, J. H. Crocker, S. J. Hardy, P. G. Might, H. A. Sherrard, C. A. Norris, and C. Johnson. In 1909, Crocker was appointed Honorary Secretary-Treasurer of the Society; then he was elected Vice-President in 1910 and 1911.

He resumed his affiliation and interest in the Society upon his return to Canada in 1917, serving as Vice-President again from 1922 to 1933.

In 1930, the Royal Life Saving Society in London, England bestowed the Distinguished Service Medal on him for outstanding services to the Ontario Branch. From 1934-1937, Crocker served as President of the Society. In 1938, he was made a Life Governor by the Central Council in England. In 1950, he received the Bronze Star to the Distinguished Service Medal and, in 1953, the Silver Star awarded by the Central Council in England.

The Amateur Athletic Union of Canada

The Amateur Athletic Association of Canada was formed on September 27, 1884. In 1898, this body changed its name to the Canadian Amateur Athletic Union, and outlined its objectives as follows:

1. The encouragement of systematic physical exercise and education in Canada.

2.   The advancement and improvement of athletic sports among amateurs.

3.   The establishment and maintenance throughout Canada of a uniform test of amateur standing and uniform rules for the government of all athletic sports within its jurisdiction.

4.   The institution, regulation, and awarding of the Amateur Athletic Championships of Canada.

5.   The protection of the mutual interest of its members.

The YMCA Athletic League became affiliated with the A.A.U. of C. in 1905, and in 1908, J. H. Crocker became its representative. He had probably first become associated through the Maritime Province Amateur Athletic Association in St. Stephen, when he was organizing the track and field meet there the 24th of May of each year.

He was a competing athlete for several years. In 1896 and 1897 he won the pentathlon, which consisted of the 100-yard dash, one mile run, running high jump, pole vault, and hammer throw. He was also the 1895 and 1897 Pole Vault Champion, vaulting 6 ft. $6\frac{1}{2}$ in. and 9 ft. $6\frac{1}{2}$ in., respectively. This achievement could be easily underrated when one considers that the present day champion pole vaulter has cleared over 17 ft. But Crocker's achievement was quite remarkable, when one considers the conditions under which the event was conducted at the time. He had made his own pole, and it was heavy and cumbersome to handle. One end had two prongs protruding which dug into the ground as the vault was being made. In addition, the pole vaulter of the 1890's landed on the hard ground.

"J. H." was top man in the field events. In 1897 he placed first in both the 12 lb. and 16 lb. hammer throws, with distances of 99 ft. and $64\frac{1}{2}$ ft., respectively.

In 1908, Canada sent an official team of athletes to Olympic competition, and J. H. Crocker attended as Manager of the team; W. J. Sherring was the Coach.

The Battle of Shepherd's Bush (Roxborough, 1963, p. 45), the name given to the IV Olympiad in London, England, provided events for concern to the Canadian Manager. One such incident concerned Tom Longboat, an Onondaga Indian. He had been accused of being a professional athlete; however, he was allowed to enter the marathon race and was considered the favourite. But he collapsed and never finished. Crocker believed Longboat had been drugged. In his official report Crocker wrote a lengthy interpretation of the incident, and exonerated both Longboat and his manager. He realized the ramifications of this unfortunate incident, but on the other hand was

proud of Canada's first official team which returned with 1 Gold,
1 Silver, and 6 Bronze Medals. The London Times wrote of the team:

> The Canadian Olympic Athletes furnished a good example
> of the combination of physical excellence with other qualifica-
> tions which make athletics a higher thing than they may some-
> times appear to be on the surface. The bearers of the red
> Maple Leaf have shown throughout these games a dogged pluck
> and a cheerfulness in the face of disappointment which the re-
> presentatives of none of the other nations have surpassed
> (J. H. C., 1908, p. 4).

Much of Crocker's work in the A.A.U. was concerned with the
question of amateurism. He fought diligently to uphold the amateur
ideal ("a true amateur who competes for the joy he receives and to
whom a small token in the form of a medal or ribbon is given for perhaps years of preparation"). Crocker served with A. S. Lamb on the
1932 special Amateur-Professional Committee, which emphatically
restated the amateur ideal of the Union and stressed its role in the
wise guidance of the youth of the country in wholesome play pursuits.

In 1922, an Olympic Committee for Canada was formed following a motion of J. H. Crocker and seconded by Dr. Lamb. This had
been an organizational goal of theirs since the Olympics of 1908.
Crocker accepted the position of Honourary Secretary of the Executive Committee (a position he held for 26 years). In 1925, Crocker
was honoured by the Olympic Committee for his untiring efforts in the
cause of sportsmanship. He was presented with a tea service.

Although worldwide Olympic competition was perhaps the most
important single athletic competition available for aspiring amateur
athletes, many prominent sportsmen from the British Commonwealth
were of the opinion that a more intimate competition would provide
the competitive stimulus of the Olympics, but would perhaps eliminate
the keen rivalry.

Although the idea was not new, in 1928, Mr. M. M. Robinson
proposed a Commonwealth athletic competition. He stated at the
A.A.U. Annual Meetings: "The germ of the idea of the British Empire Games in Canada was dropped to me in the Spring of this year
by Mr. Crocker,......"

The A.A.U. backed Mr. Robinson's plan to organize the
British Empire Games, with the first meet to be held in Hamilton,
Ontario, August 16-23rd, 1930. These first games in Hamilton,
Canada are regarded as the true starting point of the present series
of games.

Crocker served on the Canadian British Empire Games Committee from its formation in 1930. At the time of his death in 1959, he was Honourary Vice-President of the British Empire and Commonwealth Games Association of Canada, and a member of the Association's Advisory Board. He had served the Association thirty-one years.

In Halifax, Nova Scotia, John Howard Crocker was elected a member of the Hall of Fame of the Amateur Athletic Union of Canada (its highest award). Amateur sport has received a great deal of criticism in recent years because of a double standard often practised. While much of the criticism may be warranted, it unfortunately hides a great deal of the good work of the A.A.U. of C., and of men as dedicated to sport as Crocker had been.

The University of Western Ontario

In 1930, Howard Crocker, aged sixty, was invited to join the faculty of the University of Western Ontario as Director of Physical Education. His responsibilities included the tasks of arranging intercollegiate trips, planning accommodation, travel, tournaments, and overseeing the coaching of the intercollegiate sports; the organizing and operating the intramural programme of sports and games for the student body; and the administration of the Athletic Department of the University.

He wrote to the students in their yearbook the "Oxy" (Occidentalia, 1931, p. 113):

Physical Education sensitizes the nervous system; brings the body under more direct control of the mind thus ensuring a better mastery of the environment.

The great educational law "learn by doing" is the method of teaching in this field of training.......

Crocker was determined to make "sportsmanship" more than just a word used by athletic coaches to justify their existence on a university campus. He realized the pitfalls to be avoided in university athletics--too much reliance on gate receipts, "glory," and pressure from students, alumni, the public, and the press were not enough to dissuade him from his belief that a winning football team did not constitute a successful physical education programme. He believed that his responsibilities at the University included more than athletic administration. He took a great interest in the problems of individual students.

Crocker was at Western Ontario during two periods of financial crisis--the Depression and World War II. He made a policy with his secretary, "Mr. Crocker told me to leave his office door open so that any student would feel welcome to chat with him. It was also very important to learn the name of every student that entered the office" (Kay Jenkins, 1963). He became concerned when so many students were so worried about their money problems that they could not concentrate on their studies. As a result of voicing this concern, he was elected to two University committees--the Bursary Committee and the the Finance Committee.

In the area of physical education, Crocker realized two requirements to provide better programmes. The first was the necessity of a fieldhouse on campus to house intercollegiate, intramural, and recreational athletics. O. Roy Moore & Company, Architects drew up the plans for a fieldhouse and estimated the cost at $400,000. Crock Crocker carried the plans in his car for several years, and showed them to anyone and everyone who would listen to him in his appeal funds. The building was officially opened in October of 1949 by Viscount Alexander at the Fall Convocation. After twenty years of persistent planning and dreaming, "athletics for all" became a reality on the University campus.

Crocker's idea of a degree course in physical education was the second phase of his developmental plans for Western. He envisioned a course in physical education and another in recreation to prepare leaders in the field for teaching careers in the high schools or as directors of recreation in the communities, respectively.

At the age of seventy-six Crocker realized the necessity of choosing as associate as a possible successor upon his second retirement. This man was W. A. Dewar and together they outlined a course which was advanced for its time. It was proposed as a four-year Honours Bachelor of Arts program. This course commenced in the fall of 1947, and produced three physical education graduates in 1950.

On June 30th, 1947, J. Howard Crocker formally retired from the University of Western Ontario as Director of Physical Education. While at Western, Crocker gave to the students a high standard of excellence in athletics and a philosophy which will be timeless:

> Honour the game thou playest.
> For he that playeth the game hard and fair,
> Wins even when he loses.

Another of his Western projects was as Curator of the A. O. Jeffery Stamp Collection, the most elaborate stamp collection in the possession of a Canadian educational institution. This Work kept him actively associated with the University for several more years. Crocker had become seriously interested in stamp collecting while in China. He became an enthusiastic philatelist, collecting Canadian and British Commonwealth stamps as well as world Olympic stamps. In November 1951, he was elected to the Royal Philatelic Society. Membership in this society is for life, and one is elected to it for prominence in collectors' circles as a specialist and for leadership.

The University of Western Ontario, recognizing J. Howard Crocker's contribution to the University for eighteen years as Director of Physical Education and his outstanding work in organizing the A. O. Jeffery Stamp Collection, conferred the degree of Doctor of Laws, honoris causa, on him March 7th, 1950.

Retirement

Thus, at the age of seventy-seven, Crocker retired permanently from the University of Western Ontario. His health and eyesight were failing, and his letters reveal that he was finding it difficult to adjust to retirement after all his busy years. From his permanent home in Brantford, Ontario, he travelled frequently to London or to Toronto to attend meetings of interest. Each summer, as had been his practice for many years, he returned to his real home, his cottage "Sous Bois" at Whitefish Falls, Ontario.

In the fall of 1953 he became gravely ill. In September he had been intensively X-rayed in the Brantford General Hospital. The doctors were fearful of bone cancer. In December, having been unable to secure a bed for him in any chronic care hospital, his daughter asked if he could be flown to Sidney, British Columbia to convalesce in the warmer climate. Mrs. Cumming described meeting the plane: "I was to meet him in Sidney. I phoned the airport and was told there was a stretcher case on board, so then I was sure Dad had collapsed. The plane door opened and out stepped J. Howard, jaunty and waving..... That night after dinner, he said he had done a lot of thinking during the long flight and had come to the conclusion that if you are going to live, you have to work at it."

His eyesight became progressively worse after his illness in 1953. He suffered from glaucoma and cataracts. In November 8th, 1959 he entered the Royal Jubilee Hospital in Victoria. The operation for removal of the cataract on his left eye was most successful, but just before he was to return home he suffered a mild stroke and died November 29th, 1959.

The work of John Howard Crocker was not only of long duration, but it was also of the highest quality. What makes a man of such a character? In studying the life of J. H. Crocker there seems to be two important components, which, though greatly simplified, had probably influenced his philosophy of life. The one was the influence of Thomas Henry Huxley's essay "A Liberal Education: And Where To Find It." The other was Christian love.

Crocker believed fully in Huxley's unified concept of man. He believed that a man should develop and train all his faculties--his mind through reading and study, his body through exercise, and his spirit through the worship of God. A sound mind in a sound body expressed his concept of man--his objective in life for himself as well as for all the young men with whom he worked.

Crocker's Christian Love could be demonstrated over and over with his wife, sons or daughter, his friends, students, and athletes. He put the welfare of others before himself - not only when he was sure to gain from such a maneuvre, but often at the expense of his personal comfort and happiness.

The honours bestowed upon him during his lifetime indicate the opinion of his fellow workers, and acknowleged their appreciation for his untiring dedication toward the service of youth through the medium of sports and games. He was made a Life Member of the Young Men's Christian Association of Canada. Springfield College granted him an honorary M.P.E. degree for his work with the YMCA in China and his contribution in the formation of the Far Eastern Olympic Games Association. The Central Council of the R.L.S.S. (in England) made him a life governor and awarded him the Distinguished Service Medal for the outstanding service rendered the Ontario Branch of the Society. He was elected to the Hall of Fame of the A.A.U. of C. He received a Doctor of Laws degree, honoris causa, from the University of Western Ontario. In the summer of 1959 he received the following letter which made him extremely happy:

Dr. J. H. Crocker,
Glen Sitka,
Land's End Road,
R. R. #1,
SIDNEY, British Columbia   July 14th, 1959

Dear Dr. Crocker:

It was with a great deal of satisfaction that I asked Mr.
W. J. L'Heureux, Director of Physical Education at the University of
Western Ontario, to put the resolution that you be named Honorary
President for the Canadian Association for Health, Physical Educa-
tion and Recreation. This was duly seconded by C. R. Blackstock,
and unanimously approved by the Representative Assembly.

I would like you to know how pleased all of us are in the Association, and, more particularly, the pleasure it gives those of us who
know personally of your great devotion and accomplishments to the
field over a span of so many years. Thank you for accepting our
invitation.

Wishing you the best of health and happiness, I remain.

Very truly yours,

Maury,
M. L. Van Vliet,
Past President.

General Bibliography

Books

Cross, Harold C. One Hundred Years Service with Youth. Montreal: Southam Press, 1951.

Edwards, C. A. M. Taylor Statten. Toronto: Ryerson Press, 1960.

Huxley, Thomas Henry. Autobiography and Essays. New York: The Gregg Publishing Co., 1919.

Inter-Allied Games, 1919. The Inter-Allied Games, Paris, 22nd June to 6th July, 1919. Published by the Games Committee. (Paris: Printed by the Société Anonyme de Publications Periodiques, 1919).

Latourette, Kenneth Scott. World Service. New York: Association Press, 1957.

Leonard, F. E. and Affleck, G. B. A Guide to the History of Physical Education. Philadelphia: Lea & Febiger, 1947.

Occidentalia. London: The University of Western Ontario, 1930-1947.

Ross, Murray G. The Y.M.C.A. in Canada. Toronto: Ryerson Press, 1951.

Roxborough, Henry. Canada at the Olympics. Toronto: Ryerson Press, 1963.

Royal Life Saving Society Handbook of Instruction, The. London, England: Spottiswoode, Ballantyne & Co., Ltd., 1954.

Talman, J. J. and Talman, R. D. "Western", 1878-1953. London, Canada: The University of Western Ontario, 1953.

University of Western Ontario, The Golden Jubilee Endowment Fund Campaign. London, Canada: The University of Western Ontario, 1928.

Reports

Amateur Athletic Union of Canada. Annual Report, 1884-1963.

Crocker, John Howard. Report of the First Canadian Olympic Athletic Team, 1908.

Fu, Daniel C. <u>The 1930 Special Study Report of the Young Men's Christian Associations of China</u>. Shanghai: National Committee of YMCA of China, 1931.

Royal Life Saving Society of Canada. <u>Annual Report</u>, 1909-1964.

University of Western Ontario, London. <u>Report of the President to Board of Governors</u>, 1929-1948.

Young Men's Christian Association of Canada. <u>Annual Report of Physical Directors' Society</u>, 1921-1930.

Unpublished Material

Crocker, J. H. "Amateurism!'" (Typewritten).

_____. "Amateur Sports and Games in Canada," written by for 75th Anniversary of A.A.U. of Canada. (Typewritten).

_____. "History of Athletic League of the YMCA of Canada." (Typewritten).

Canada (continued):
history prior to Confederation:
seventeenth century:
coureurs-de-bois
(voyageurs), 468
habitants, 467, 468
Indian influence on
games and equip-
ment, 468
Quebec, 467
eighteenth century:
"bee" or "frolic",
468, 469
fairs, town and
county, 469
immigration, 468
lower Canada, 468
maritimes, 468
sports contests, 469
upper Canada, 468
nineteenth century:
British influence on
sports, 471, 472,
473
climate, influence of,
476
development, eastern
vs. western, 469,
470
French influence on
sports, 474
geographical influ-
ences, 477, 478
immigrant influence
on sports, 471
Indian influences on
sports, 471
Scottish influences on
sports, 473, 474
transportation de-
velopment, 469,
478, 479, 480
United States influ-
ence on sports,
480
National Physical Fitness
Act, 435

Canada (continued);
population, 432, 433, 447
provincial autonomy, 447
Youth Training Act, 435
Canada, physical education,
historical background (see
physical education, Canada,
historical background)
Canadian Association for
Health, Physical Education
and Recreation:
development, 444
Fitness and Amateur
Sport Act, 444, 445
R. Tait McKenzie
commemoration, 434
Canoeing, 468, 469, 470, 477,
481
Canada, eastern, 452
Canadian Canoe Associ-
ation, 452
Canoe Racing, 33, 64
Canoe Slalom, 46, 53
Capitalism, 19, 106, 226
Carnegie Steel Corporation,
96
Cartwright, Ethel, 434, 444
Cassidy, Rosalind, 170
Castle, Vernon and Irene, 188
Certification of teachers, 15,
25, 131, 229
Chalif, Louis, 187
Channing, Walter, 132
Chariot Driving, 141
Chicago Tribune, 194
Chicago, University of, 21,
24, 238
China, 488, 489
physical activity, girls,
140
sport origin, 36
Chivalry, 4
Christians, early:
asceticism, 3
attitudes toward the physi-
cal, 2
monasteries, 3

Gymnasiums, 74, 75, 97, 103,
116, 117, 121, 122, 143,
226, 227, 230, 255, 259,
260, 262, 263, 264, 265,
266, 267, 296, 297
    Canada, 434, 435
Gymnastic drills, 333
Gymnastics, 32, 70, 71, 73,
75, 76, 83, 84, 87, 102,
108, 114, 116, 117, 118,
130, 157, 158, 162, 169,
170, 171, 176, 211, 213,
226, 227, 228, 229, 230,
233, 236, 255, 256, 257,
258, 263, 264, 265, 333,
357, 436, 438, 469, 481
    Denmark, 172
    Germany, 69, 94, 103,
        104, 105, 106, 107,
        112, 113, 134, 145,
        168, 231, 232
    Swedish, 104, 105, 106,
        131, 132, 134, 145,
        146, 168, 231, 232
    women, 307
    Y.M.C.A., 298

Hadley, Arthur, 202
Hall, G. Stanley, 20, 23, 88,
170, 322
Hall, Samuel R., 16
Hall, Winfield S., 299
Halle, University of,
(Germany), 273
Hammer throw, 302, 469, 474,
491
Hampton Institute, 256, 257,
258, 262
Handball, 33, 232
Hanlan, Edwards, 455
Hanna, Delphine, 130, 230
Harness racing, 32
Harper, William Rainey, 21
Harris, William T., 21, 87,
88, 231
Harrison, William Henry, 84,
85, 86, 87

Hartwell, Edward Mussey,
83, 88, 104, 108, 118,
123, 132, 229, 231
Harvard, 6, 13, 17, 74, 96,
104, 112, 122, 129, 130,
131, 132, 133, 134, 136,
187, 194, 196, 197, 198,
199, 200, 201, 202, 203,
218, 226, 227, 230, 231,
255, 256, 257, 274, 453
    Business school, 164
    school of education, 132
Hayford, E. L., 299
Hazelton, Helen, 175
H'Doubler, Margaret, 176,
177, 187, 188
Health, 95, 97, 114, 121,
122, 123, 130, 131, 141,
142, 143, 144, 146, 147,
158, 162, 165, 168, 182,
227, 228, 238, 239, 242,
245, 257, 258, 259, 261,
263, 277, 298, 324, 325,
340, 381
    American Public Health
        Association, 227
    education, 295, 353,
        357, 358
    faddists, 70
    instruction, 226
    Journal of Health, 69
Health Education (see health)
Healthy body, importance of,
346
Hearst, William Randolph, 95
Hecker, Friedrich, 112, 113
Hemenway, Mrs. August,
168, 231
Hemenway Gymnasium, 96,
104, 129, 133, 136, 230,
231
Hetherington, Clark, 170,
171, 233, 279, 333, 335
Hewlitt, Abram, 255
Higginson, Thomas
Wentworth, 94
High jump, 302
High schools, junior, 22, 23

Ice skating, 32, 145, 156, 157, 474, 476, 478, 481
    Canada, eastern:
        British Regiments, 456
        Demont's expedition to Acadia, 456
        McCormick, Hugh, 457
        Montreal Skating Club, 457
        Quebec, 456
        St. John, New Brunswick, 457
Ice trotting, 476, 477
Illinois, University of, 283, 287, 288, 290, 291, 293, 299
    Chicago Circle, 290
    Motor Performance and Play Research Laboratory, 371
India:
    physical activity, girls, 140-141
Indian clubs, 132, 134
Indian scepter exercises, 145
Indiana, University of, 288
Industrial Revolution, 14, 30, 107, 139, 156
Instruction, methods of as a persistent problem, 348
Intelligence testing, 22
Intercollegiate Athletic Association of the United States, 198, 200, 201, 202, 203, 209
Intramurals, 381
Iran:
    physical activity, women, 141
Ireland, 36
Israel:
    physical activity, women, 141
Italy, 36, 81
    Olympics - Rome, 211

Jackson, Andrew, 69, 72, 76
Jackson, William Tecumseh Sherman, 256
Jahn, Friedrich Ludwig, 5, 111, 112, 113
Jai Alai, 34
James, William, 20
Japan, 81, 123, 124, 211
Javelin throwing, 141
Jefferson, Thomas, 14, 69, 83, 84
Jeu de Paume, 30
Johns Hopkins University, 274
Johnson, G. B., 279
Johnson, William, 291
Judo, 34
Juggling, 142
Juilliard School of Music, 188
Jumping, 74, 162, 334
Junior College Movement, 237

Kallenberg, Henry, 297, 299, 303
Kennedy, John F., 212, 240, 320, 321
Kennedy, Robert, 211
Keynes, John Maynard, 319
Kilpatrick, William H., 25, 170
Kindergartens, 25
Kite flying, 31
Knox Plan, 83, 84, 85
Kraus-Hirschland Muscular Fitness Report, 310
Kraus-Weber, 336

Laban method, 172
Labor, organized, 19
    American Federation of Labor, 95, 96, 97, 98, 99
    Brotherhood of Electrical Workers, 99
    Committee for Industrial Organizations, 97, 98, 99

Physical education, persistent
problems (continued):
  psychology, social, 373
  sport historian, 374
Physical education, philosophy,
professional:
  ideal, healthy man:
    McCloy and Nash, 324
  man, instinctive drives:
    McCloy, Nash, and
      Williams, 323,
      324
  man, organic unity of:
    McCloy, Nash, and
      Williams, 322
  methodology, teaching,
    333, 334, 336
  physical education, defi-
    nitions, 325
  physical education, ob-
    jectives, 326, 327,
    328, 329, 335
  program concepts, 331-
    333, 336
Physical education, professional preparation, 225-
249, 276
  accreditation, 248
  certification require-
    ments, 239
  cooperative study in
    teacher education,
    245, 246
  curriculum, 234, 235
  degrees, master's, 245
  Department of School
    Health and Physical
    Education:
      national standards,
      244
  faculty, 235
  Negro colleges and uni-
    versities, 255
      budgets, 267, 268
      colleges, white,
      257
      facilities, 262,
      263, 267

Physical education, professional preparation
(continued):
      Hampton Institute,
      256, 257
      Howard Univer-
      sity, 257
      Lincoln Univer-
      sity, 260, 265
      Morehouse Col-
      lege, 260, 265
      Morgan College,
      266
      Southern Univer-
      sity, 264, 265
      standards, 267,
      268
      teacher certifi-
      cation, 261,
      267
      teacher training
      programs, 256
      Tuskegee Insti-
      tute, 258, 259,
      263, 264
      Virginia State
      College, 264
      Wilberforce Uni-
      versity, 259,
      260
Physical education, professional preparation as a
persistent problem, 348
Physical education, summer
schools:
      American Gymnastics
      Union, 229, 230,
      231, 233
      Cambridge, Massachu-
      setts School of Phy-
      sical Training, 298
      Chautauqua summer
      school of Physical
      education, 135, 136,
      229, 236
      dance, 188
      Harvard, 129-136, 187,
      229, 236, 257, 261

- 524 -

Races, blindfold, 476
Races, greased pig, 476
Racquets, 32, 461, 474, 481
Rarick, Lawrence, 288
Realists, 143
Rebound tumbling (trampolin-
    ing), 49
Reconstruction, 17
Recreation, 94, 95, 107, 144,
    146, 147, 304, 328, 329,
    333, 340, 353, 357, 358,
    381
        buildings, 163
        Canada, 434, 494
        city systems, 164
        curriculum, 245
        dance, 182, 186
        fitness oriented, 165
        industrial, 96, 97, 98
        interest in, 226
        Israel, early Hebrew
            civilization, 141
        municipal, 98
        Municipal Directors,
            233
        Outdoor Recreation
            Commission, 99
        program for students,
            134
        separation from physi-
            cal education, 277
        specialization, 170
        summer school courses,
            132
        women, recreation, 156,
            157, 158, 159
Recreation, Canada, 445
Reformation, 4, 112, 143
Reid, William, 199, 200, 201,
    202
Religion, influence of, 346
Renaissance, 4, 5, 143, 348,
    350
Reuther, Walter, 99
Rice, Emmett A., 220
Riding, 70, 71, 75, 84, 141,
    145
Rifle matches, 472, 481

Rifle shooting, target, 31
Rinks, ice, indoor, 476
Rivero, Manuel, 260
Roberts, Amelia, 259
Roberts, R. J., 230, 296,
    297, 298
Robinson, M. M., 492
Rockefeller, Lawrence, 99
Rodeo, 34
Rogers, F. R., 315
Roller derby, 50
Roller skating, 33, 157
Rolls and treacle, 476
Rome, 349, 350
Rome, ancient:
    Campus Martius, 85
    Circus Maximus, 2
    decadence, 85
    military training, 2
    women, status of, 142
        physical activity, 142,
            143
Roosevelt, Franklin Delano,
    163
Roosevelt, Theodore, 89,
    193, 194, 196, 197, 199,
    200, 201, 202, 203, 209
Root, Elihu, 89
Rope spinning, 34
Roque, 34
R.O.T.C., 259
Round Hill School,
    Northampton, 112, 226
Rousseau, Jean Jacques, 5
Rowing, 32, 69, 75, 76, 469,
    470, 477, 478, 481
Rowing, Canada, eastern:
    American Regatta,
        Peekskill, New York,
        455
    Lachine Rowing Club, 456
    Longueuil Boating Club,
        456
    "Paris Crew", 455
Royal Life Saving Society,
    490
Rudolph, Wilma, 164
Rugby, 33, 438

Running, 63, 69, 74, 76, 83,
141, 159, 162, 334, 468,
469, 474
Running, obstacle courses,
306
Rush, Benjamin, 69, 83
Ryerson, Egerton, 434

Sack race, 474
Safety education, 277, 353,
358, 381
Sailboat racing, model, 33
Sailing, 75, 76, 159, 473,
477, 481
Salassa, Maurice C., 303
Salwak, Stanley, 289, 290,
293
Sand yachting, 50, 53
San Francisco Club (athletic),
208
Sargent, D. A., 6, 89, 96,
104, 106, 123, 129, 130,
131, 132, 133, 134, 135,
136, 146, 168, 229, 230,
231, 236, 256, 298, 311
Savage, Watson L., 123, 230,
256
Saxman, Ethel J., 279
Schools, city and county, physical education:
history bibliography,
master's and doc-
toral studies, U.S.,
1930-1967, 384
Schools, common, 72
Schools, elementary, 12, 13,
15, 16, 20, 22, 25, 26,
147, 226, 229, 232
Schools, elementary, Canada
(see physical education,
Canada, elementary
schools)
Schools, elementary, physical
education:
history bibliography,
master's and doctoral
studies, U.S., 1930-
1967, 383

Schools, normal, 15, 16, 18,
21, 23, 118, 130, 132,
135, 160, 227, 228, 229,
230, 231, 232, 234, 236,
348
Canada:
certification, 441
Strathcona Trust
Fund, 441
teacher training, 441,
442
Schools, public:
attendance, compulsory,
225
growth, elementary
schools, 226
growth, high schools, 227,
229
Kansas City, 230
sports, 227
system, public school, 225
teacher training, 227, 228
Schools, secondary, 12, 13,
15, 17, 19, 20, 22, 25, 26,
27, 82, 164, 217, 218,
219, 220, 221, 222, 227,
229, 232, 236, 237
sports, interscholastic,
studies, 393-394
Schools, secondary, Canada
(see physical education,
Canada, secondary schools)
Schools, secondary, girls,
167
Emma Willard, 167
Mary Lyon, 167
Catherine Beecher, 167
Schools, secondary, physical
education:
history bibliography,
master's and doctor-
al studies, U.S.,
1930-1967, 383
Schrader, Carl, 132
Schroeder, Louis C., 304
Schwert Physical Education
Bill, 91
Scotland, 36
Scott, Gladys, 171

Scott, Harry A., 244, 282
Scuba diving, 50
Sculling, 32, 75
Searcy, Paulajean, 173, 174
Sears, Eleanora, 160, 161
Seaver, Jay, 135, 230
Seerley, Frank, 300
Selective Training and Service
    Act, 1940, 316
Seven Years' War, 13
Shaw, John W., 299
Sheldon, Edward, 17
Sherman, Atara, 321
Sherring, William, 461, 491
Shooting, 64, 161
Shot, indoor, 297
Shuffleboard, 31
Simri, Uriel, 394
Sims, Harry J., 303
Skaife, Lewis, 454
Skates, ice:
    development of, 476
Skating, ice (see ice skating)
Skeet, 50
Skiing, 33, 335, 438
    Canada, eastern:
        Canadian Amateur Ski
            Association, 458
        Montreal Ski Club,
            457, 458
        Mont Royal Cross
            Country Race, 458
        Norwegian snowshoes,
            457
Skin diving, 35
Skipping, 74
Skish, 35
Sky diving, 51
Slalom, 51
Sledding, 71
Sleighing, 475, 476, 478,
    481
        ice, 477
Smith College, 158, 167
Smith-Hughes Act, 22
Smith, J. Gardner, 299
Smith, Leon, 290
Smith-Lever Act, 22

Snowshoeing, 468, 470, 474,
    475, 476, 478, 481
    Canada, eastern:
        development,
            Indians, 458
        Montreal Snowshoe
            Club, 458, 459
        "Old Tuque Bleue",
            458
Soapbox racing, 35
Soaring, 35
Soccer, 33, 160, 169, 173,
    264, 438, 439, 461
Society for College Gym-
    nasium Directors, 124
Sociology:
    analyses of society, influ-
        ence of sport and physi-
        cal education, 373
    of education, 170
    Parson's theory of action,
        367
    of physical education, 356
    of sport education, 290
Softball, 35, 73, 98, 164,
    305, 436, 438
Somers, Florence A., 173,
    175
Southern University (Baton
    Rouge), 264
Spain, 36
Spalding Basketball Guide for
    Women, 160
Sparta, 349
Speedball, 35
Spiess, Adolf, 6, 113
Sport and athletics, history:
    conclusions, 400-401
    directions, criticism, 395,
        396, 397, 398
    history, analysis master's
        and doctoral studies,
        U.S., 1931-1967:
        administration,
            intercollegiate
            athletics, 390
        associations, orga-
            nizations and
            leagues, 390

- 528 -

Sweden, 6, 310
Swedish gymnastics, 7
Swett, John, 115, 117
Swimming, 33, 70, 83, 131,
    140, 141, 145, 160-162,
    164, 169, 173, 176, 228,
    303, 438, 439, 440, 476,
    478, 481, 488
        Canada, eastern history:
        Canadian Amateur
            Swimming Associ-
            ation, 459
        Montreal Swimming
            Club, 459
        survival, 306
Swimming pools, 163, 165,
    264, 265, 297, 299
Switzerland, 36
Sylvis, William H., 95

Table tennis, 34
Teacher education, Canada
    (see professional prepar-
    ation, Canada)
Teachers:
    dance, 176, 189
    gymnastic, 113, 118
    physical education degrees,
        169, 170
    policy making, 25
    requirements, 147
    salaries, 25
    Sargent, D. A., 129, 136
    women, 25
Teacher training, 15, 16, 18,
    21, 23, 129, 130, 131,
    158, 168, 226, 227, 228,
    229, 230, 231, 232, 234,
    235, 236, 239, 241, 242,
    244, 245, 246-249, 256,
    257, 258, 259, 260, 261,
    262, 264, 266, 267, 276,
    348
Tennis, 30, 31, 132, 157,
    158, 161, 163, 164, 168,
    169, 232, 264, 265, 335,
    438, 440, 461
        paddle tennis, 34

Thomas, R. J., 98
Thorndike, Edward, 20, 23,
    322
Throwing games, 63, 162
Tnemevom, 357
Toboganning, 34, 468, 470,
    476, 481
        Canada, eastern
            history:
            Montreal Tobog-
                gan Club, 459
            Montreal Winter
                Carnivals, 460
            Park Toboggan
                Club, 460
            Tuque Bleue Club,
                460
Tolan, Eddie, 256
Toronto, University of, 436,
    442, 460, 461
Tournaments, national, 1,
    175
Townball, 219
Track and field, 31, 131,
    169, 173, 209, 212, 213,
    258, 265, 331, 436, 438,
    439, 440, 473, 474, 476,
    481, 487, 488
        Canada, eastern
            history:
            English vs.
                Canada, 460
            Montreal Lacrosse
                Club, 460
            nomenclature, 460
            Olympic Club of
                Montreal, 460
            Olympic Games,
                1908, 461
            "The Sprinter",
                461
Track, indoor, 297
Transylvania University, 70
Trapeze work, 296
Trap shooting, 33, 161
Tremont gymnasium, 296
Truman, Harry S., 316
Tumbling, 132, 436, 438

Western Ontario, University
of, 490, 493
    physical education de-
      gree course, 494
West Point, 84
Wey, 6
Wigman, Mary, 177, 188
Wilberforce University, 259,
263
Willard, Emma, 167
Williams College, 72, 226
Williams, George, 295
Williams, Jack, 459
Williams, Jesse Feiring,
170
    health, use of, 325
    influence, 334, 335
    man, instinctive drives,
      323
    man, organic unity of,
      322
    methodology, teaching,
      333, 334
    physical education,
      definitions of, 325,
      327, 328, 330, 335
    physical education ob-
      jectives, 327
        character de-
          velopment, 328
        historical, 330
        recreation, 328
    program concepts:
      natural activities,
      333
      personality develop-
      ment, 333
    writings, 320
Wills, Helen, 163
Winship, George Barker, 6,
145
Wisconsin, University of, 24,
176, 188, 233, 235
Women in sport and physical
education, 63, 69, 70, 71,
73, 74, 75, 76, 88, 117,
130, 131, 133, 134
    aims of, 147, 148

Women in sport and physical
education (continued):
    AAHPER:
      dance division, 189
      National Section on
        Women's Athletics,
        174
      women's sport con-
        sultant, 175
    athletics, inter-
      collegiate, 173, 175
    ballet, 186
    Civil War, post period,
      145, 146
    classical civilization:
      Athens, 142, 184
      Rome, 142, 143,
        184
      Sparta, 141, 184
    dance major, 176
    dance, "natural" and
      modern, 176, 187,
      188
    dance in physical edu-
      cation, or theater or
      art, 177, 188
    degree programs, 280
    eighteenth century
      Europe, 144, 185
    equalitarianism, 139
    Hampton Institute, 258
    Harvard annex, "sana-
      tory gymnasium",
      230
        Radcliffe College,
          230
    historical background,
      early:
        China, 140, 183
        Crete, 141, 183
        Egypt, 140, 182
        India, 140, 183
        Iran, 141
        Israel, 141, 183
    Howard University, 257
    Lewis, Dio, 145
    Middle Ages, 143, 185
    modern, early, 143-
      144, 185

Women in sport and physical
  education (continued):
    movement education,
      147
    nationalism, nineteenth
      century, 144, 145
    Nebraska, University
      of, 235
    Negro physical educa-
      tion teachers, 257
    Olympics, 161, 162, 174
    physical education in
      women's colleges,
      167-170
    professional prepar-
      ation, 243
    program changes, 171,
      172
    Renaissance:
      dance, 185
    Seventeenth Century:
      dance, 185
    teachers, 237
    tournaments, national,
      175
    Turners, 145
    Tuskegee Institute, 258,
      259, 260, 263
    Twentieth Century,
      early:
        athletics, inter-
          scholastic, 146
        intramural sports,
          146
        "natural" move-
          ment, 146
    Twentieth Century, 1930-
      1960's:
        American Physical
          Education
          Association,
          Division of
          Girls' and
          Women's Sports,
          147, 243
    United States, early, 145
    Virginia State College,
      264

Women in sport and physical
  education (continued):
    Women's rights move-
      ments, 155-165
    World War II, 147, 175
    Y.M.C.A., 306
Women in sport and physical
  education, Canada:
    athletics, competitive,
      437
    basketball, early, 464
    Cartwright, Ethel
      (McGill University),
      434
    curriculum, 437
    Montreal Amateur
      Athletic Federation:
        Women's Division,
          162, 173, 174
    movement education,
      436
    professional prepar-
      ation, 436
Women in sport and physical
  education, persistent problem, 349
Women's Christian Temper-
  ance Union, 88
Women's colleges and physical activities:
    Colleges:
      Barnard, 169, 171,
        177
      Bennington, 188
      Bryn Mawr, 169, 171
      Connecticut College
        for Women, 188
      Elmira, 167, 169
      Goucher, 169
      Mount Holyoke, 169,
        172
      Radcliffe, 169, 172
      Smith, 167, 168, 169,
        172, 177
      Vassar, 167, 168,
        169, 177

Y.M.C.A., physical educa-
tion (continued):
basketball, invention,
300
rules, 301
world spread, 301
Boston Association, 296,
297
facilities, 297
George Williams Col-
lege, 299
Gulick, L. H., contri-
butions, 298
gymnasiums, 296, 297
health, 300
Leaders' Corps training
program, 299
leadership, 297
Montreal Association,
299
National Physical Educa-
tion Committee, 304
National Wartime Physi-
cal Fitness Program,
306
New York Association
Building, 296
pentathlon, 302
physical director, first,
296
Physical Directors
Society, 302

Y.M.C.A., physical educa-
tion (continued):
physical education,
training in, 297
physical fitness, 306,
307
professionalism in
sport, 301
sports bodies, inter-
national cooperation,
307
Springfield College, 298,
305
Springfield Training
School, 300, 301
summer schools, 303,
305
swimming pools, first,
299
volleyball, origin, 301
red triangle, official
badge, 301
world spread, 301
women and girls, ad-
mission, 306
World War I:
games, inter-allied,
304
recreation and athletics,
304
Zeigler, Earle F., 288, 290,
399
Zoölogy, 245

GV211 .Z454x   c.1
Zeigler, Earle F., 1
A history of physical educatio   100105 000

3 9310 00032159 4
GOSHEN COLLEGE-GOOD LIBRARY

WITHDRAWN